Handbook of Motivation and Cognition

VOLUME 3

HANDBOOK OF
MOTIVATION AND
COGNITION

VOLUME 3

The Interpersonal Context

Edited by

Richard M. Sorrentino
University of Western Ontario

E. Tory Higgins
Columbia University

THE GUILFORD PRESS
New York • London

© 1996 The Guilford Press
A Division of Guilford Publications, Inc.
72 Spring Street, New York, NY 10012

Last digit is print number: 9 8 7 6 5 4 3 2 1

Library of Congress Cataloging-in-Publication Data

(Revised for volume 3)

Handbook of motivation and cognition.

  Includes bibliographies and indexes.
1. Motivation (Psychology)   2. Cognition.   3. Inter-
personal relations.   I. Sorrentino, Richard M.
II. Higgins, E. Tory (Edward Tory), 1946–
BF503.H36   1996   153.8   85-24916
ISBN 0-89862-667-6 (v. 1)
ISBN 0-89862-432-0 (v. 2)
ISBN 1-57230-052-3 (v. 3)

Contributors

Susan M. Andersen, PhD, Department of Psychology, New York University, New York, New York

Laura M. Bogart, PhD, Learning Research and Development Center, University of Pittsburgh, Pittsburgh, Pennsylvania

Marilynn B. Brewer, PhD, Department of Psychology, Ohio State University, Columbus, Ohio

Thomas W. Britt, PhD, Department of Psychology, University of Florida, Gainesville, Florida

Mary Carrillo, MA, Department of Psychology, University of California, Los Angeles, Los Angeles, California

Patricia G. Devine, PhD, Department of Psychology, University of Wisconsin–Madison, Madison, Wisconsin

John A. Edwards, PhD, Department of Psychology, Ohio State University, Columbus, Ohio

Victoria M. Esses, PhD, Department of Psychology, University of Western Ontario, London, Ontario, Canada

Sophia R. Evett, PhD, Department of Psychology, University of Wisconsin–Madison, Madison, Wisconsin

Susan T. Fiske, PhD, Department of Psychology, University of Massachusetts at Amherst, Amherst, Massachusetts

Noah S. Glassman, PhD, Department of Psychology, New York University, New York, New York

Carolyn L. Hafer, PhD, Department of Psychology, Brock University, St. Catharines, Ontario, Canada

David L. Hamilton, PhD, Department of Psychology, University of California, Santa Barbara, Santa Barbara, California

Amy S. Harasty, MA, Department of Psychology, Ohio State University, Columbus, Ohio

Curtis D. Hardin, PhD, Department of Psychology, University of California, Los Angeles, Los Angeles, California

S. Alexander Haslam, PhD, Department of Psychology, The Australian National University, Canberra, Australian Capital Territory, Australia

E. Tory Higgins, PhD, Department of Psychology, Columbia University, New York, New York

John G. Holmes, PhD, Department of Psychology, University of Waterloo, Waterloo, Ontario, Canada

Günter L. Huber, PhD, Department of Educational Psychology, Universität Tübingen, Tübingen, Germany

Arie W. Kruglanski, PhD, Department of Psychology, University of Maryland–College Park, College Park, Maryland

John M. Levine, PhD, Learning Research and Development Center, University of Pittsburgh, Pittsburgh, Pennsylvania

Diane M. Mackie, PhD, Department of Psychology, University of California, Santa Barbara, Santa Barbara, California

Craig McGarty, PhD, Department of Psychology, The Australian National University, Canberra, Australian Capital Territory, Australia

Beth Morling, PhD, Department of Psychology, University of Massachusetts at Amherst, Amherst, Massachusetts

Steven L. Neuberg, PhD, Department of Psychology, Arizona State University, Tempe, Arizona

Penelope J. Oakes, PhD, Department of Psychology, The Australian National University, Canberra, Australian Capital Territory, Australia

James M. Olson, PhD, Department of Psychology, University of Western Ontario, London, Ontario, Canada

John Pennington, PhD, Department of Psychology, University of Florida, Gainesville, Florida

Sarah Queller, PhD, Department of Psychology, University of California, Santa Barbara, Santa Barbara, California

Barry R. Schlenker, PhD, Department of Psychology, University of Florida, Gainesville, Florida

Clive Seligman, PhD, Department of Psychology, University of Western Ontario, London, Ontario, Canada

Andrew F. Simon, MS, Department of Psychology, Rutgers–The State University of New Jersey, New Brunswick, New Jersey

Richard M. Sorrentino, PhD, Department of Psychology, University of Western Ontario, London, Ontario, Canada

Steven J. Stroessner, PhD, Department of Psychology, Barnard College, New York, New York

Shelley E. Taylor, PhD, Department of Psychology, University of California, Los Angeles, Los Angeles, California

Megan M. Thompson, PhD, Defence and Civil Institute of Environmental Medicine, Toronto, Ontario, Canada

John C. Turner, PhD, Department of Psychology, The Australian National University, Canberra, Australian Capital Territory, Australia

Kristin A. Vasquez-Suson, PhD, Department of Psychology, University of Wisconsin–Madison, Madison, Wisconsin

Heidi A. Wayment, PhD, Department of Psychology, University of California, Los Angeles, Los Angeles, California

Gifford Weary, PhD, Department of Psychology, Ohio State University, Columbus, Ohio

David A. Wilder, PhD, Department of Psychology, Rutgers—The State University of New Jersey, New Brunswick, New Jersey

Bozena Zdaniuk, PhD, Learning Research and Development Center, University of Pittsburgh, Pittsburgh, Pennsylvania

Preface

This is the third volume of the *Handbook of Motivation and Cognition*. The general purpose of all three volumes has been to elicit original chapters specifically for the *Handbook* that present theory and research on the interface of motivation and cognition. When we began this pursuit, cognition and social cognition were the *Zeitgeist;* motivation and social motivation were only of historical interest. Since our first volume emphasizing the synergism of motivation and cognition (the "Warm Look"), the marriage of motivation and cognition has become popular again. Now there are numerous books and articles reflecting this approach. In this volume, we have turned our concerns from looking within the individual to examining his or her focus on others. The subtitle of Volume 3 reflects this emphasis, as it has changed from *Foundations of Social Behavior* to *The Interpersonal Context*. Rather than looking at the self, affect, and goals as primarily intrapersonal variables, as in the first two volumes, we turn our attention to the role of motivation and cognition in interpersonal and intergroup behavior. Although this focus represents a rather natural progression from what has been presented in our two previous volumes, it is also a timely endeavor. Ever since Kurt Lewin's inspiring demonstration that we can take the lab to the real world, social psychology has been at the forefront of relating the science of psychology to events in the real world. One of the biggest social problems to be carried into the 21st century is social relations. With free trade, common markets in Europe and North America, transmigration, and the dissolution of the megalopoly formerly known as the Soviet Union, prejudice, intragroup conflict, and intergroup strife have all raised their ugly heads once more. This book brings together some of the very best researchers and theorists who have contributed and will contribute much to our understanding of social relations. As the reader will see, however, such attention is never far removed from the self, affect, and goals, as these issues continue to pervade outward behavior. Hence, as the century turns, so does our attention to the realm of the interpersonal perspective.

CHAPTER SUMMARIES

The 18 chapters in this book are grouped into three parts. The first deals with how we use others to further evaluate the self; the second, with how the self affects our judgments of others; and the third, with how all of this gets transferred to our evaluations and interactions with our ingroups and our outgroups. Most of this preface is an attempt to provide the reader with a brief description of the issues, proposals, and perspectives found in each chapter. These summaries emphasize the authors' proposals and perspectives rather than research findings. Throughout, it is evident that the "Warm Look" is no less important to the interpersonal perspective than it has been to the intrapersonal one.

Part I, "Self-Evaluation: The Looking-Glass Self," begins with two new approaches to social comparison. In Chapter 1, Taylor, Wayment, and Carrillo point out that social comparison satisfies various personal needs and is guided by several distinct motivational processes. They suggest that in contrast to the fairly simple picture painted by laboratory research, social comparison processes have a number of important moderators, such as threat, self-esteem, time frame, the mutability and controllability of the attribute being compared, and the motives comparisons are assumed to serve. The authors cite recent research that has elucidated the dynamics of upward, downward, and lateral comparisons, in ways that broaden their implications for self-regulation. This research has examined how people make social comparisons and what their effects are in real-world circumstances over the long term, rather than solely in laboratory settings involving short-term reactions. Moreover, this viewpoint has clarified how social comparisons may serve multiple self-evaluative motives, including self-assessment, self-enhancement, self-improvement, and the need for affiliation. Individual differences related to these processes are also identified. For example, individuals high in self-esteem can construe downward social comparisons in ways advantageous to themselves; they do the same with upward social comparisons, seeing them as inspirational rather than as threatening. Individuals low in self-esteem, however, seem to be susceptible to the potential adverse emotional implications of both downward and upward social comparisons. Taylor et al. conclude by stating that our understanding of social comparison processes in the past has failed to take both motivational and temporal complexity into consideration. Acknowledging the multiple motivational bases for upward, downward, and lateral social comparisons reveals a wide range of potential emotional and performance consequences with various implications for behavior, depending upon the salient motive. Expanding the time frame within which the impact of upward and downward comparisons is observed illustrates how the immediate motivational dynamics and consequences of such comparisons may be diminished or even reversed as time goes by. These dynamics are further influenced by such factors as immediacy of threat, self-esteem, qualities of the target attribute, characteristics of the target, and whether the comparison to another is based on real contact with another individual or simply on assumptions about a hypothetical other.

Hardin and Higgins take social comparison to new boundaries in Chapter 2. They suggest that in the absence of social verification, experience is transitory, random, and ephemeral. Once acknowledged by others and shared in a continuing process of social verification termed "shared reality," experience is no longer mere capricious subjectivity, but instead achieves the phenomenological status of objective reality. In other words, experience is established as valid and reliable to the extent that it is shared with others. In developing the hypothesis of shared reality, the authors examine classic social-psychological research and theory as well as more recent research, especially that pertaining to the role of communication processes in social cognition. Several literatures corroborate the hypothesis that shared reality creates reality for the individual by delineating the form and function of the external world. Hardin and Higgins suggest several implications of the hypothesis for such topics as stereotyping, self, language, attitudes, and persuasion. Weighing all the evidence presented, the authors suggest that (1) the individual creates and maintains the experience of reality or meaning by sharing it with others in a process of social verification; (2) social interaction depends upon and is regulated by the achievement of shared reality; and (3) the shared reality that is established in social interaction in turn functions to regulate the self, closing the dialogical circle. The authors close by situating the hypothesis in the broader context of social-psychological theory, arguing that the process of sharing reality provides a crucial integration of the self–society dialectic.

In Chapter 3, Olson and Hafer discuss the cognitive, affective, and motivational components of the concept of "relative deprivation"; research on the preconditions to such deprivation; and research on its consequences. With regard to the concept, the authors address many inconsistencies. Although most researchers agree that relative deprivation involves both (1) the perception of deprivation compared to some standard and (2) discontent, their operationalizations often focus on either perceived discrepancies or emotions. It is the relative emphasis on either the cognitive or the affective component that has led to inconsistencies or confusion in the literature. Researchers need to be clear about how they conceptualize relative deprivation in their work: Is it affective, cognitive, or both? Olson and Hafer believe that although the four types of relative deprivation (affective and cognitive, personal and group) may be distinguishable in some situations, a synergistic perspective is best. In keeping with the "Warm Look," they argue that relative deprivation occurs when a discrepancy is perceived between what is deserved and what is obtained, and when that discrepancy results in resentment or anger. They also demonstrate that particular topics within the relative-deprivation literature would benefit from a synergistic perspective. For example, the personal–group distinction (in which individuals generally perceive that they are better off than their reference group) results from both cognitive and motivational processes. Also, work on the preconditions to feelings of relative deprivation needs to be more explicit about which preconditions are cognitive and which are affective/motivational. In addition, the authors propose that the role of self-presentation motives needs to be explored further. Self-presentation is a clear example of a motivational force that can influence reports of resentment. Finally, with regard to consequences of relative deprivation, the authors again emphasize the importance of synergism. For example, consequences of relative deprivation may differ according to whether strong affect is associated with the deprivation. Various other psychological and sociological variables may moderate the relation between relative deprivation and various behavioral consequences. Moderators, which themselves can be classified as "hot" or "cold" processes (e.g., whether victims blame themselves or society, level of personal control, availability of opportunities for various types of assertive action), will also affect specific responses to relative deprivation. Hence a synergistic approach to the study of relative deprivation would appear to be essential for future research.

In Chapter 4, Schlenker, Britt, and Pennington propose that impression regulation and management are fundamental features of social behavior. "Impression management" is defined as a goal-directed activity of controlling information about some person, object, idea, or event. The authors state:

> To ask the question, "When are people engaging in impression regulation?" is akin to asking, "When are people engaging in cognition?" It is always occurring, although it can vary on dimensions such as whether it is in or out of awareness, effortful or effortless, automatic or controlled, motivated by purer or baser motives, and effective or ineffective in accomplishing its tasks (just as cognition can vary on these dimensions). In short, it is a fundamental characteristic of interpersonal experience, just as cognition is a fundamental characteristic of private experience. (p. 118)

It is also misleading to think of impression management as superficial, deceptive, an afterthought, a simple bias of socially desirable responding, or immoral. Rather, it plays a crucial role for self-identification. People try to regulate and control—sometimes consciously and sometimes not—the information they present to audiences. Three themes contribute to current conceptions of impression management: people as agents, communication as purposive, and audiences as an integral component of self-regulation. People actively construct their own social environments; communication influences the ideas, feelings, and behaviors of audiences in ways that can have important effects on an actor's own outcomes and relationships; and the interplay between actors and their audiences shapes and reshapes how the actors view themselves and how they are viewed by others. In emphasizing the point that no one is oblivious to an audience, Schlenker et al. present research demonstrating that persons high in private self-consciousness are just as desirous of creating their self-images, in their own minds and for others, as are those high in public self-consciousness. The remainder of the chapter focuses on impression management involving the self-presentation. For Schlenker et al., defining and expressing one's identity are ubiquitous features of social life; they serve important intrapersonal and interpersonal functions, and can affect an actor's self-esteem, reputation, and social outcomes. Self-identification, then, is a goal-directed activity reflecting a transaction between an actor and an audience who are interacting in a particular social setting. This includes numerous self-presentational goals (e.g., gaining respect, creating fear), and people want to construct and protect desirable identities that are personally beneficial and believable. Self-identification always occurs in the context of one or more audiences (real or imagined) whose members serve as recipients and evaluators for the performance. People may also use themselves as an audience, and they use relationship scripts and schemas (which include information about self and other people or audiences) to interpret events, to store information in memory, and to guide conduct. Moreover, self-identification emphasizes the role of accounting in interpersonal relations. People shape and negotiate realities through their interpretations of events, as they attempt to explain possible discrepancies between their actions and valued prescriptions for conduct. Self-identification may be in the foreground or background of an actor's attention, depending upon importance, familiarity, routineness, and self-identification expectancies. All of these behaviors, which initially may have been intended to create a particular impression on others, may ultimately come to influence the actor's own view of self. Schlenker et al. conclude by noting that a number of psychological disorders (e.g., shyness, social anxiety, depression) seem to be produced or maintained by self-presentational problems. Impression regulation and management then, are vital and omnipresent components of social conduct and shape people's conceptions of themselves and their social worlds.

In Chapter 5, Weary and Edwards present a model of motivation that builds upon the notion of "causal uncertainty," or the failure to understand the fairly stable underlying causes of events. The model argues that some people in some situations are chronically more motivated than others to resolve causal uncertainty. Such chronic individual differences, the authors propose, have fundamental consequences for adoption of social information-processing goals and for the manner in which information is encoded, interpreted, and stored. The model of the motivation to reduce causal uncertainty differs in an important way from the model of uncertainty orientation: Uncertainty-oriented persons are positively motivated by uncertainty (i.e., they like to find out new things about the self or environment), and certainty-oriented persons are positively motivated by certainty (i.e., they adhere to predictable and familiar situations), whereas the motive to reduce causal uncertainty is reactive and negative. Its aim is extrinsic to the form of the activity. There is no real interest in finding out something new; uncertainty is simply a negative state to be removed. Feelings of uncertainty are presumed to arise from a metacognitive monitoring of the extent to which one understands something. They provide a cue to the individual that his or her knowledge is inadequate to cope with some situation or achieve some goal. In response to such feelings, actions to rectify the state of affairs are undertaken. This model builds on previous research by the authors on the effects of depression on social information processing. Here, mildly and moderately depressed individuals are hypothesized to increase their systematic, effortful processing of social information in order to restore their subjective sense that they understand the world. The causal-uncertainty model employs as a central part of uncertainty resolution the idea of a negative feedback loop, the purpose of which is to reduce discrepancies between some actual state and some desired comparison state. The motive to resolve causal uncertainty is conceived of as a structure with several components: "goal representation," or a mental picture of a desired state that when achieved permits a better feeling; a "comparator," which compares current and desired states of causal knowledge (yielding negative affect if a discrepancy exists); "action plans," which are designed to bring the current and desired states of causal knowledge closer; and an "outcome expectancy assessor," which assesses the outcome expectancy of any action. The second major structure of the Weary and Edwards model consists of causal-uncertainty beliefs about one's uncertain or inadequate understanding or detection of causal relations in the social world, as well as cognitive feelings of uncertainty. The model stipulates that causal-uncertainty beliefs are available for all people, but that they are chronically accessible for some. Weary and Edwards also present their Causal Uncertainty Scale, which measures these differences, as well as various validity indices. Research supporting the predictive validity of their measure is likewise presented.

The final chapter in Part I is Chapter 6, by Haslam, Oakes, Turner, and McGarty. The chapter stresses the importance of the interaction of motivation and cognition for social identity, self-categorization, and the perceived homogeneity of ingroups and outgroups. The goal of the chapter is to make sense of the seeming contradiction between the phenomenon of relative outgroup homogeneity and the need (and demonstrated capacity) for people to perceive their ingroup to be at least as homogeneous as outgroups. Haslam et al.'s analysis focuses on the manner in which perceived group homogeneity is related to "consciousness of self," and especially, on the way in which it is mediated by the salience (i.e., the psychological activation) of a perceiver's social identity. The authors seek to emphasize the special psychological role played by group memberships and intergroup relations in social perception. The chapter begins by examining the metatheoretical and empirical origins of the influential cognitive approach to group homogeneity. This approach generally depicts perceived homogeneity as a distorting error of simplification inherent in the categorization process. The distortion is at work less in a person's perception of those with whom he or she is familiar (ingroups) than in the person's perception of those whom he or she knows less well (outgroups). The authors then go on to discuss the role of identity-related, group-based motivations in such perceptions. They note how homogeneous representations of outgroups may be a vehicle for intergroup discrimination, and they show how perceived ingroup homogeneity may be just as important to the advancement of a group's aims, by creating a positive social identity for its members. These latter considerations lead to an interactionist analysis derived from self-categorization theory. This is an integration of features of cognitive and social-motivational approaches, and it seeks to provide a resolution to the seemingly paradoxical evidence of both symmetry and asymmetry in perceived ingroup–outgroup homogeneity by pointing to the way in which the cognitive process of categorization is sensitive to and changes with variations in social context (e.g., whether categorizations are being made at the personal, group, or societal level). Haslam et al. cite research indicating that there is no inherent dualism between cognition and motivation, and that their contributions to perceptions of homogeneity are not merely additive. The chapter concludes that a full understanding of this feature of stereotyping cannot be gained without a grasp of the dynamic interplay between cognition and motivation.

Part II, "Evaluation of Others: Perceiving through Role-Colored Lenses," begins with Neuberg's scrutiny in Chapter 7 of social motives and expectancy-tinged social interactions. His primary argument is that an understanding of expectancy influences is incomplete until such processes are considered within the social-motivational context. Neuberg proposes that because certain classes of common social motivations regulate the behavioral and cognitive underpinnings of the expectancy confirmation process, these motives should moderate the influence of preinteraction expectancies on postinteraction impressions. If we know the motivational context of any expectancy-tinged social encounter, this permits us to predict with considerable precision the nature (if any) of expectancy influences. The factors moderating the expectancy confirmation process must be those that influence the ability of perceiver expectancies to affect one or more of four mediating mechanisms: (1) perceiver information-gathering behaviors; (2) perceiver expressive behaviors; (3) a target's decisions regarding accommodation of a perceiver's behavioral script; and (4) perceiver attention to and interpretation of target behaviors. Neuberg proposes that two general classes of perceiver social motives (impression formation goals and self-presentation goals) and one general class of target motives (self-presentational goals) do have such a regulatory influence, and thus are especially likely to moderate expectancy influences. One must also consider the availability of cognitive and/or behavioral resources required to implement any goal. These resources are often quite limited, with the result that the ability of social goals to moderate the expectancy confirmation process will be diminished. Hence, participants revert to relatively effortless default strategies in the resource-neglected domains (domains neglected by the participants). The expectancy-tinged interaction is conceptualized as a dynamic cycle of interpersonal behavior and thought, with each participant potentially influencing the other at each turn. The social goals of both perceiver and target are accorded central status, as such goals are proposed to have major influences on key mediators in the expectancy confirmation process. In the remainder of the chapter, Neuberg reviews the literature in light of his model and discusses related frameworks. This model is seen to have important practical implications, as nearly all social interactions are at least somewhat susceptible to expectancy influences, and expectancies are too often inaccurate. In the area of stereotypes and prejudice, the author suggests that rather than focusing on changing the nature of the expectancies themselves, we should design social interventions that (by focusing explicitly on altering participants' acute motivational states and on making requisite cognitive and behavioral resources available) attempt to reduce the impact of such stereotypes and prejudices on individual targets within the context of each particular interaction.

One expectancy-based form of interaction is that of transference, as proposed in Chapter 8 by Anderson and Glassman. Devoid of Freudian content, "transference" as these authors define it refers to the activation and application of a mental representation of a significant other to a new person. Anderson and Glassman present their information-processing model of transference in everyday social perception and discuss findings in the literature that support the model. They then describe the basic structures and processes in memory, social judgment, and self-judgment that provide the theoretical and empirical context for their work; they consider these literatures in light of informing our understanding of some of the complex processes that are likely to transpire in transference. They then return to their transference paradigm and describe it in detail, as they believe the central innovation of this work is its combining of idiographic and nomothetic research methods and procedures. Next, new lines of research are considered, such as studies concerned with basic activation mechanisms, links between affect and motivation, and the impact of interpersonal roles in transference. This research demonstrates that notable interpersonal and intrapersonal experiences are evoked in transference—namely, those that are inferential, evaluative, affective, and motivational. Among some of the broader implications of this work is that the use of a category consisting of multiple persons (e.g., "people like my mom") is not necessary for transference to occur, since an individual-person exemplar (e.g., "my mom") can represent a significant other and produce transference. Formulating a clear model of the differential implications for transference of individual-person exemplar representations and representations designating types of people (such as stereotypes) would thus advance the literature. The authors conclude by stating that the experimental demonstration of transference is important in conceptualizing not only social-cognitive processes in interpersonal relations, but also the clinical phenomenon of transference. The process of transference is a basic one, not a process limited to the psychotherapy setting between patient and therapist.

Fiske and Morling focus in Chapter 9 on two phenomena exemplifying the tension between accuracy as a means of gaining control and constraints on mental capacity that prevent accuracy. First, social structures, such as people's positions in power hierarchies, can affect the tension between people's need for prediction and control and their limitations of attention and memory. The tradeoff between these two situationally influenced variables affects how people form impressions of others. Fiske and Morling then address how personal motivations (particularly anxiety) can influence impression formation through the same two variables. Power relationships and personal anxiety, although importantly distinct, share the metatheoretical perspective that impression formation often entails a compromise between needs for accuracy and available resources. The authors point out that social-cognitive research has greatly neglected the study both of power and of the larger social context that might confer power. Various predictions are made in terms of power relations between the powerful and the powerless. For example, powerful perceivers will tend to stereotype others because their outcomes are not so contingent on those subordinate others, their capacities are limited by overburdened, and they can be personally motivated by a dominance orientation. However, powerless perceivers are control-deprived, so they may be more motivated to form accurate impressions of the powerful. With regard to anxiety, the basic idea proposed is that people who are anxious experience a loss of mental control and may compensate by trying to control others. It is suggested that anxiety simultaneously generates a capacity decrement and heightened control motivation, which both result from intrusive thoughts. Fiske and Morling believe that their analysis of anxiety is unique, in that it examines personal motivations in impression formation in terms of capacity and mental control variables. In general, personal motives are only beginning to be reconsidered as a source of influence in person perception. Although the dynamics of interpersonal power and personal anxiety are seen to differ in some respects, the authors state that they do share a metatheoretical perspective of an orientation toward social control, hampered by capacity limits. Power raises issues of socially sanctioned social control and capacity decrements that result from hierarchical social structure. Anxiety raises issues of personally motivated social control and capacity decrements that result from uncontrollable intrusive thoughts. Addressing power and anxiety together elicits interesting theoretical and practical notions.

In Chapter 10, Brewer and Harasty accept Donald Campbell's challenge to develop objective criteria by which social aggregates can be legitimately described as "entities." Drawing upon gestalt psychology, Campbell proposed that the basic principles of organization—proximity, similarity, common fate, and pattern—can be made applicable to the assessment of group boundaries and internal coherence. He created the term "entitativity" to refer to the extent to which a group has the nature of an entity. Social aggregates may be more or less "entitative," depending upon such factors as clarity of boundaries, correlated movement of members in time and space, and intragroup similarity. By posing the issue of group entitativity in terms of the structure of cognitive representations, Brewer and Harasty call attention to the relationship between this concept and other recent lines of research and theory on group perception (i.e., prototype- versus exemplar-based models of social categories; research on perceived group variability and the outgroup homogeneity effect; social identity theory's distinction between interpersonal and intergroup orientations; and social categorization theories of intergroup relations). The authors demonstrate that the concept of entitativity links these otherwise disparate lines of research. They then consider potential implications of the concept for research on stereotyping, person memory, intergroup behavior, and perceptions of social justice. The authors point out that objective indices of entitativity have been difficult to codify, possibly because the relevant features are necessarily subjectively defined. They suggest that a more fruitful approach to understanding the determinants of perceived entitativity may be to look for perceiver variables that mediate group perceptions, such as individual differences in such traits as cognitive complexity and uncertainty orientation. Situational factors, such as processing goals, expectancies, mood, and motivation, can also be examined. In the remainder of the chapter, Brewer and Harasty describe several experiments illustrating how perceiver expectancies, goals, and motives related to group entitativity determine how behaviors of individual group members are encoded and organized in memory.

In Chapter 11, Mackie, Queller, Stroessner, and Hamilton challenge the idea that enjoyable interaction between members of different groups can improve the groups' relations. They state that their cause for concern is an unlikely one—the mildly pleasant emotional state that is generally thought to accompany enjoyable interaction. The authors deal specifically with the effects of happy mood on group perception and with the conditions under which such effects may facilitate or hinder the aims of pleasant contact between groups. They first describe a series of studies indicating that a happy mood may be more likely to increase perceptions of homogeneity and stereotypicality than to promote more diverse or nonstereotypic views of other groups. In attempting to discern why this may be, they report that it may result at least in part from happy subjects' tendency to engage in reduced processing of information, particularly of the kind that may convey distinctiveness. Thus, such subjects may tend to maintain rather than reduce their stereotypes. With more time or encouragement to process information more thoroughly, subjects do increase their perceptions of group variability, but only to levels shown by subjects in neutral moods. In considering when positive mood may actually have an advantage, Mackie et al. suggest that when processing of distinctive information is necessary for stereotypic judgments, then happy subjects should be less likely than neutral-mood subjects to form such judgments. Their research has supported this assumption. However, the authors report that their findings are not especially encouraging:

> In general, the presence of positive mood increased perceptions of group homogeneity; it heightened the extent to which behavior was seen as consistent with expectations; it enhanced the perception of individual group members as being typical of the group; and it increased the likelihood that expectancy-based stereotypic judgments about groups would be made. Thus, especially for negatively valued groups, positive mood seems to have predominantly detrimental effects. (p. 387)

The authors suggest caution in recommending interventions until further investigation has increased the theoretical understanding of intergroup perception, as well as the ability to improve the outcomes of contact between groups in practice.

In Chapter 12, on a similar note, Wilder and Simon examine incidental and integral affect as triggers for stereotyping. Following a review of the literature, they propose a model to explain the findings and to suggest avenues for further exploration. With regard to the literature, the authors conclude that the pattern of results is difficult to summarize. Overall, evidence suggests that positive affect enhances reliance on stereotypes, but this is limited to negative traits. A simple conclusion for negative affect is even more difficult. Anger and anxiety/fear facilitate greater reliance on stereotypes, but findings for sadness have been most inconsistent. In addition, the authors note methodological concerns with these data, such as manipulations of affect that are independent of the target group about which stereotypic judgments are later made, and assessments of affect manipulations that occur following affect inducement and before presentation of the target group to subjects. With regard to their model of affect and stereotyping, Wilder and Simon have two versions: one for "incidental affect," or affect created apart from the target group, and one for "integral affect," or affect whose source is attributed directly to the target group. Research indicates that incidental affect is likely to distract the perceiver, and thus to increase reliance on heuristics such as social stereotypes. Integral affect focuses attention on the outgroup and should tap stereotypes associated with that group. A match between those expectations and the affect linked with the outgroup should reinforce stereotypes. A mismatch will provoke a more careful, specific examination of the outgroup's behavior. This in turn may lead to a bolstering of outgroup stereotypes or to a change in these, depending on the outcome of the attributions generated by the affect–expectations mismatch. However, to the extent that affect generates arousal, this arousal can create distraction, regardless of whether the affect is integral or incidental. Any such distraction can foster peripheral processing of information about the outgroup, leading to a dependence on outgroup stereotypes. Wilder and Simon believe that integral and incidental affect can help explain the failure of contact to reduce prejudice in an apparently pleasant context. Manipulations of pleasant contact often involve incidental affect. To the extent that participants see the affect as incidental, then it may function as a distraction, so that earlier attitudes and beliefs about the outgroup remain unchallenged. If the outgroup is perceived as responsible for the enjoyable setting (integral affect), however, then the positive mood created may very well decrease hostility toward the outgroup and make it possible to change negative stereotypes.

Part III, "Group Dynamics: Getting to Know You," begins with Chapter 13 by Devine, Evett, and Vasquez-Suson. It is an exploration of the different sources and forms of intergroup tension, in order to clarify their potential effects on interpersonal intergroup interactions. Although the authors believe that some of the work done by social scientists in this area is impressive, they feel that the field has generally not examined people's goals and concerns in intergroup situations, or their subsequent influence on the interpersonal dynamics of intergroup contact. A central tenet of their analysis is that a major barrier to positive intergroup relations is the potential for miscommunication between majority and minority group members, arising from the expectations and concerns brought by each interactant to an encounter. Both the majority and the minority participants enter an interaction with a set of motivations (e.g., the impression they want to create, the kind of interaction they wish to have) and cognitions (e.g., expectations about the other group and about their own likely responses). These motivations and cognitions control the nature of the dynamics of the interaction by influencing the behaviors, emotional responses, and perceptions of both interactants. The authors present a still-evolving theoretical framework aimed at determining how individuals from majority and minority groups think about and approach intergroup contact situations. Their motivations and cognitions will probably affect majority and minority group members' thoughts and feelings about themselves, their interaction partners, and interactions in general. Preliminary data concerning the way in which majority and minority group members perceive intergroup contact situations are presented, and a promising research agenda is described. Only by understanding majority and minority group members' specific motivations and cognitions about intergroup contacts can researchers explore the reciprocal dynamics of such interactions. And only by understanding the dynamic nature of actual intergroup encounters can researchers develop strategies to promote more positive intergroup relations at the interpersonal level.

Kruglanski, in Chapter 14 describes theory and research about the "need for cognitive closure." This term refers to an individual's desire for a firm answer to a question and aversion to ambiguity. The chapter focuses on the individual's need for *nonspecific* closure, or the desire for an answer (*any* answer) on a given subject. This need may be an individual-difference variable, or it may be situationally induced. Diverse situational or individual differences should be functionally equivalent regarding phenomena affected by the need for closure. These include early "seizing" and "freezing" upon accessible cues and insensitivity to subsequent relevant information. The author documents these mechanisms in research on impression formation, stereotyping, and anchoring or attributional correspondence bias. He points out, however, that the need for closure is not limited to intra personal aspects of social perception. Instead, the mechanisms documented are seen to extend to various interpersonal and group phenomena of major significance. For example, need for closure may play an important role in interpersonal communication—specifically, with regard to the accuracy of interpersonal impressions and communication. On the group level of analysis, Kruglanski suggests that heightened need for closure may prompt the emergence of a conservative group culture characterized by a hierarchical power and decision-making structure, resistance to normative change, and ingroup favoritism. Although the author points out that many of the hypotheses concerning the interpersonal and group-level consequences of the need for closure are currently speculative and remain to be investigated empirically, they do indicate the potential of a motivated social cognition approach as a new general paradigm in social psychology.

In Chapter 15, Thompson and Holmes discuss the psychological dynamics of ambivalence in close relationships, with a focus on the interface of motivation and cognition. This focus is based on the fact that feelings of ambivalence may require a particular configuration of an individual's cognitive representations of his or her partner. Even conflicting positive and negative partner perceptions that are denied or carefully kept separate can result in great discomfort as conflicts among the cognitions emerge. The authors propose that the experience of an unstable interchange between positive and negative evaluations can, itself motivate individuals to resolve the internal conflict, either by leaving their relationships or by coming to terms with the ambivalence through cognitive and affective means. Thus, ambivalence can create a motivational state that help bring about change in relationships. In addition, Thompson and Holmes explore how people reconcile their wishes about the future of their relationships with their beliefs about their partners, which may include various amounts of ambivalence. Specifically, they demonstrate that individuals' commitment to their relationships has a strong effect on their experience of ambivalence. Results of research concerning the nature and long-term impact of ambivalence in dating relationships are presented. The authors conclude by exploring possible sources of ambivalence, including the conflicts that arise when individuals' romantic ideals diverge from the reality. Ambivalence may be considered an "early-warning system," as it predicts the breakup of dating relationships better than interpersonal conflict does. Just as importantly, however, these findings emphasize the powerful moderating effects of a strong commitment on the full force of ambivalence about a romantic partner. Ambivalence, then, may be an important early-warning system, but it does not invariably signify doom for relationships.

Levine, Bogart, and Zdaniuk, in Chapter 16, examine the impact of anticipated group membership on cognition. They point out that although students of cognition have tended to focus on how individuals perceive, interpret, and manipulate information, there are several reasons for viewing cognition as a socially imbedded activity. This has been demonstrated in work on the mere presence of others, research on the way people construe their social situations, studies of mental representations of others, work on the relationship between social interaction and cognitive change, and studies of cognition as an emergent product of social interaction. Surprisingly little attention, however, has been given to the cognitive consequences of anticipated group membership. In this chapter, the authors discuss several ways in which the expectation of group membership can influence the cognitions of both prospective members and current members. First, they focus on the cognitive processes occuring during the investigation phase of group membership. They then discuss two ways in which impending group membership can affect the cognitions of prospective and current members: (1) changes in the prospective and current members' understanding of the group culture, including task and social knowledge; and (2) changes in prospective and current members' cognitions about people, including themselves, other members of their present or future group, and members of other groups related to this group. In the final section, Levine et al. consider the case in which prospective members expect to form a new group that has not been in existence before. Here, they discuss how prospective members' cognitions are altered by the belief that after they enter such a group, they will encounter dissent from other members and will have to defend their views. The authors conclude by calling for investigators to consider carefully the motivational and cognitive consequences of anticipated group membership.

In Chapter 17, Esses and Seligman question the assumption that when programs intended to assist a particular group are successful at changing perceptions of specific individuals or of the group as a whole, both will benefit. For example, if such a program improves perceptions of a sample of blacks, it is assumed that perceptions of blacks as a group will also improve. The authors discuss social-psychological theories that describe the relation between perceptions of groups and of individual group members. These theories suggest that perceptions of groups and their individual members will sometimes be similar and at other times will not. Esses and Seligman then propose a framework for examining the efficacy of strategies designed to improve intergroup relations. Their model incorporates the individual–group distinction by distinguishing between outcomes for specific individuals and those for a group as a whole. It also differentiates outcomes according to their source: Do they originate from members of other groups or from members of the intended target group (i.e., the intended beneficiaries)? The value of the model is demonstrated by applying it to affirmative action programs. The model is seen as valuable not only for classifying the outcomes of strategies to reduce prejudice and discrimination, but for highlighting one reason why affirmative action and similar programs result in much controversy. That is, public debates of the costs and benefits of such programs are often unproductive because the discussants are failing to distinguish between individual and group outcomes and between the sources of these outcomes. Finally, implications of the model for the successful implementation and evaluation of prejudice-reducing strategies are considered.

Chapter 18, the final chapter of the book, is by Huber and Sorrentino. Citing various problems with reducing prejudice and intergroup conflict in European classrooms, these authors consider the importance of a chronic individual difference in information seeking (i.e., uncertainty orientation) in terms of its possible role in interpersonal and intergroup relations. The authors elaborate on how interpersonal communication and intergroup relations have been approached primarily from an uncertainty-oriented point of view. Some models in the communication area assume that a major component of communication is the reduction of uncertainty, both in the nature of the communication and in the relations between the communicators. Similarly, many models of improving intergroup relations assume that contact in some form (e.g., cooperative intergroup interaction, positive interdependence, prepared contact, informed contact, personalization of self in contact with others) will reduce intergroup conflict. The authors believe that these suggestions for intervening in intergroup relations focus on uncertainty-oriented persons' preferences and habits in social situations, and that certainty-oriented persons will not benefit from these approaches. In some cases, they argue, such attempts can in fact boomerang. Huber and Sorrentino introduce the dimension of uncertainty versus certainty orientation and discuss the consequences of individual differences on this dimension for methods of coping with uncertain situations. This distinction sheds light on the aforementioned uncertainty bias in the fields of interpersonal communication and intercultural relations, and on recommendations for educational interventions in these fields. Research on the interpersonal level suggests that adapting learning situations to the learners' personal characteristics can be effective for both uncertainty-oriented and certainty-oriented students.

However, the strategy of minimizing the situational uncertainty for certainty-oriented learners has thus far been tested only in group situations arranged to promote interpersonal skills. At the intergroup level, there has been no empirical research on differing effects of interventions on uncertainty-oriented and certainty-oriented members of groups in conflict. However, the authors report considerable data in support of an individual-difference approach regarding uncertainty for intergroup and interpersonal relations. Research in this field is needed to clarify the uncertainty bias of suggestions for promoting intergroup relations, and especially to develop nonbiased approaches to intercultural education. The authors conclude by pointing out that uncertainty has colored the 20th century, and that concerns with uncertainty can be expected to increase well into the next century. And, although uncertainty may be an intriguing concept for some, it is a terrifying concept for others. This must be taken into account if attempts to promote and produce harmony in interpersonal and intergroup relations are to succeed.

ACKNOWLEDGMENTS

Our sincere appreciation goes first to the contributors of this volume of the *Handbook*. It is clear that they were as excited about extending their research to the motivation–cognition interface as we were. The timely nature of their work from a motivation–cognition perspective will no doubt lead to major theoretical and practical advances in the years to come. Our deepest thanks again go to Seymour Weingarten and The Guilford Press in standing by us in this, our third volume. Thanks also to our wives and children, Judy, Robin, Eric, and Kayla, for enriching our lives and contributing to all three volumes in no small way.

Contents

PART I

Self-Evaluation: The Looking-Glass Self

CHAPTER 1

Social Comparison, Self-Regulation, and Motivation

SHELLEY E. TAYLOR
HEIDI A. WAYMENT
MARY CARRILLO
University of California, Los Angeles

For over 40 years, social comparison theory as formulated by Leon Festinger (1954) has provided the theoretical underpinnings for hundreds of social-psychological investigations. As a result, our understanding of how people choose targets with whom to compare themselves and how they respond to the results of those comparisons has been greatly increased. In recent years, the study of social comparisons has moved heavily into the field, investigating these processes in the context of coping with a variety of threatening experiences (see Taylor, Buunk, & Aspinwall, 1990, for a review). The expansion of the settings and frameworks within which social comparison processes have been investigated has made it evident that such processes are more complex than laboratory investigations have suggested. In particular, social comparison processes are now known to satisfy a variety of personal needs and to be guided by a number of distinct motivational processes.

In this chapter, we address the motivational origins and consequences of social comparison processes. We suggest that social comparison processes, their likelihood, their purposes, and their consequences are best understood from the standpoint of a more general model of self-regulation. We first characterize four motivational processes argued to be fundamental to self-regulation, and we relate them to social comparison processes. In the remainder of the chapter, we examine the propensity to make different kinds of social comparisons, and also examine the outcomes of these comparisons with respect to the different underlying motivational processes. We suggest that in contrast to the relatively simple portrait painted by laboratory research, social comparison processes are importantly moderated by such factors as threat, self-esteem, time frame, the mutability and controllability of the attribute in question, and the motives social comparisons are assumed to serve.

MOTIVATION AND SOCIAL COMPARISON

Traditionally, social comparison processes have been understood in terms of a need for self-assessment. As originally articulated, social comparison theory maintained that people need to have stable, accurate appraisals of themselves. According to Festinger (1954), people prefer to evaluate themselves using objective and nonsocial standards, but if such information is unavailable to them, they will evaluate themselves using social information, namely, other people. In particular, comparisons to similar others ("lateral social comparisons") are thought to be especially useful for self-assessment. This formulation implies that social comparisons are the outcome of a motivational process. When information about themselves falls below a certain level and uncertainty results, people have a motivation to self-assess—to stabilize their sense of self through self-evaluation (cf. Thibaut & Kelley, 1959). Accurate information, which is diagnostic concerning one's abilities and other attributes, is thought to be essential to self-knowledge (Festinger, 1954; Trope, 1975, 1979, 1980). In theory, accurate self-knowledge enables people to select activities that are appropriate for their level of skill, and it provides a foundation on which to grow or change.

A second motivational process argued to be fundamental to self-regulation is self-enhancement, or the need to maintain a positive sense of self (e.g., Taylor & Brown, 1988; Tesser, 1988). Although some have suggested that the need for a positive sense of self is a pre-eminent, ubiquitous concern (e.g., Taylor & Brown, 1988), others have maintained that the need for self-enhancement is particularly acute following failure, threat, or negative feedback (e.g., Steele, 1988; Tesser, 1988). Both positions may be correct. The potential importance of social comparison processes to self-enhancement needs has been especially noted by Wills (1981). Comparisons with those whose outcomes are worse than one's own ("downward comparisons") are thought to be self-enhancing, because they demonstrate that one is better off than others on the dimension under evaluation. Such downward comparisons are assumed to be affectively rewarding and, as such, they may satisfy self-enhancement needs.

A third line of work has emphasized the importance of self-improvement to self-knowledge and self-evaluation (e.g., Markus & Nurius, 1986; Taylor & Lobel, 1989; Wood, 1989; cf. Atkinson, 1957; Atkinson & Birch, 1978). Many life tasks, including education, most work situations, and many leisure activities (e.g., athletics), have as their goal the improvement of specific skills. Recent work (Taylor & Lobel, 1989; Wood, 1989; Wood & Taylor, 1991) has emphasized the potential importance of "upward comparisons" (i.e., comparisons with those performing better or doing better than the self) for meeting self-improvement needs. Upward comparisons are thought to be especially helpful when people desire to improve themselves, both because these comparisons provide concrete information about what a superior performance looks like, and because they may provide hope and inspiration and instill motivation.

A fourth line of work has emphasized the importance of social comparison processes to affiliative needs. Schachter (1959) argued that under conditions of threat, people seek to affiliate with others similar to themselves (lateral comparisons) for the purpose of comparing and evaluating their emotional state. More recent extensions of this analysis (see Taylor et al., 1990, for a review) have argued for the importance of social comparison processes to social support. People may compare themselves with others sharing a similar fate not only to evaluate their own emotional experiences, but also to create the experience of social bonding and comfort that may arise from the observation of a shared fate (e.g., Ybema & Buunk, 1995; Helgeson & Taylor, 1993). Taylor and Lobel (1989) have argued for the importance of distinguishing between self-evaluation and affiliative choice in the measurement of social comparison, maintaining that the psychological dynamics and outcomes of these two sets of processes may be distinct.

To all appearances, the theoretical integration of social comparison processes provided by the original theory (Festinger, 1954; Schachter, 1959) and recent theoretical extensions (e.g., Taylor & Lobel, 1989; Wills, 1991; Wood, 1989) would seem to resolve the question of how social comparison processes are related to motivational processes.[1] Downward comparisons serve self-enhancement needs; upward comparisons serve self-improvement needs; and lateral comparisons serve self-assessment needs and needs for affiliation. However, as we illustrate in the next sections, social comparison processes are more complex than this portrait suggests: They are importantly moderated by the motive that is salient, individual differences, attribute-specific qualities, and situational factors that qualify or even reverse these general patterns.

DOWNWARD COMPARISON PROCESSES

As noted earlier, downward comparisons are comparisons of oneself with an individual whose atttributes, outcomes, or emotional states are worse than one's own; that is, the comparison target is more disadvantaged, more inadequate, or more distressed than oneself. Furthermore, the motivational underpinnings of downward comparisons are generally argued to be the need to feel good about oneself—in other words, self-enhancement (Wills, 1981, 1991). According to this viewpoint, self-enhancement provides the motivational impetus for downward comparisons, and downward comparisons in turn have the motivational consequences of satisfying self-enhancement needs.

Yet a number of variables may represent boundary conditions that modify downward comparison processes. Taken together, they suggest that self-enhancement needs and the ability of downward comparisons to satisfy them may occur primarily in response to short-term threats. Over time, other motives that are not well served by downward comparisons (e.g., self-improvement or needs for affiliation) may assume precedence, with the result that downward comparisons are less likely to be made and/or lose their capacity to be self-enhancing. We develop this line of argument with reference to the moderating conditions of threat, self-esteem, temporal frame of reference, the mutability and/or controllability of the attribute in question, whether a downward comparison occurs in response to an actual individual or is cognitively manufactured, and the motive driving the downward comparison processes.

Threat

Downward social comparisons are thought to be especially important for restoring self-esteem under conditions of threat, because threat makes self-enhancement needs salient. Threats such as failure or personal tragedy may increase distress and uncertainty about one's standing in a domain or one's ability to progress (e.g., Molleman, Pruyn, & van Knippenberg, 1986). These states in turn may generate greater responsiveness to social comparison information generally, and especially to information that is self-enhancing (Wills, 1981). Hakmiller (1966) conducted the first known empirical study of this point. He provided subjects who had taken the Minnesota Multiphasic Personality Inventory (MMPI) with theatening feedback, suggesting that they harbored a high level of hostility toward their parents—a trait that was described as quite negative. Subjects who were threatened in this way commonly responded by comparing themselves with a target who was depicted as the most hostile person in a group of six, whereas subjects exposed to little threat compared themselves with someone who was closer to them in hostility. The findings were interpreted to mean that under conditions of threat, people make downward comparisons for the purpose of restoring self-esteem.

Wills (1981) formalized these observations into a theory of downward comparison processes. He reviewed a large amount of literature suggesting that under conditions of threat, people make downward comparisons (see also Gibbons & Gerrard, 1991; Wills, 1987). He reviewed laboratory studies replicating Hakmiller's initial findings with a variety of other threats (Pyszczynski, Greenberg, & LaPrelle, 1985; Sherman, Presson, & Chassin, 1984), as well as conceptually related bodies of literature, such as the literature demonstrating that negative evaluations about groups are made by threatened individuals. His observations that downward comparisons are made in response to threat have been confirmed in a variety of field investigations of how individuals cope with naturally occurring stressors or victimizing events, conditions that may arguably produce a chronic experience of threat. For example, Wood, Taylor, and Lichtman (1985) analyzed the spontaneous social comparisons made by cancer patients during interviews, and found that 63% of those made about coping ability and 95% made for physical situation were in a downward direction. Similar findings have been reported by other investigators studying individuals coping with a variety of other stressors, including rheumatoid arthritis patients (Affleck, Tennen, Pfeiffer, Fifield, & Rowe, 1987), the mentally retarded (Gibbons, 1985), patients with spinal cord injuries (Schulz & Decker, 1985), heart disease patients (Helgeson & Taylor, 1993), and bulimics (Gerrard, Gibbons, & Sharp, 1985).

Is threat a necessary condition for the self-enhancement benefits of downward social comparisons? Some research suggests that it may be. Recent studies that have asked subjects to report on their social comparison processes suggest that a substantial majority report making such comparisons rarely, if ever, and that a substantial minority report never making social comparisons at all (e.g., Foddy & Crundall, 1993; Helgeson & Taylor, 1993; Schulz & Decker, 1985; Taylor, Aspinwall, Giuliano, Dakof, & Reardon, 1993; Taylor, Wayment, Neter, & Woo, 1994; see also Sorrentino & Short, 1986; Roney & Sorrentino, in press). Of the three subtypes of social comparison—namely, upward, lateral, and downward comparisons—downward comparisons have been found to be least commonly reported (Taylor, Wayment, et al., 1993). Although social desirability concerns may explain this effect, inasmuch as people may feel that it is inappropriate or "not nice" to benefit psychologically from comparisons with unfortunate others (Brickman & Bulman, 1977), studies that have assessed social desirability in conjunction with downward comparisons find that the absence of downward comparisons is not explained by such concerns (Wayment & Taylor, in press). A possible inference, then, is that downward social comparisons are made only when conditions of threat obtain and not otherwise.

More direct evidence for these assertions comes from experimental investigations exposing subjects to threat (or not), making downward social comparison information available, and assessing subjects' responses (Gibbons & Boney-McCoy, 1991; Aspinwall & Taylor, 1993). These studies found that low-self-esteem subjects experiencing threat reported more favorable self-evaluations and higher expectations of future success following exposure to downward comparison information. Under conditions of no threat, exposure to upward or downward social comparison information had no differential effects; nor were psychological benefits of downward social comparisons observed among those high in self-esteem under conditions of threat.

Two implications of these findings are important. First, the downward comparison phenomenon may be more circumscribed than originally assumed. Specifically, downward comparisons may be self-enhancing primarily under conditions of threat, and then only for those initially low in self-esteem. A second implication is that self-esteem may importantly moderate social comparison processes—an issue to which we now turn.

Self-Esteem

Self-esteem appears to moderate reactions to downward social comparison information, especially affective reactions. In the past, the assumption on which the downward comparison/self-enhancement relationship has been predicated is that downward comparisons are driven by self-enhancement needs: People feel better after they witness someone who is worse off than themselves. Research suggests that this is often not the case. Buunk, Collins, Taylor, Van YPeren, and Dakof (1990) predicted and found that downward comparisons could have either of two types of affective consequences: They could provide a sense of relief or gratitude that one was not as poorly off as the target, or they could produce a sense of dejection and despair resulting from the observation of an unfortunate other or from the fact that things could be or could become so much worse.

What factors moderate the tendency to derive positive versus negative affect from downward comparisons? In their first study, Buunk et al. (1990) found that cancer patients high in self-esteem were generally able to construe downward comparisons in self-enhancing terms; that is, they reported feeling better in comparison to someone who was worse off. Those low in self-esteem, however, were vulnerable to the negative affective conseqences of downward comparisons and felt worse. In their second study, Buunk et al. (1990) found that married people high in marital satisfaction and high in certainty about their marriages were able to construe benefits from downward comparisons to those whose marriages were worse than their own; conversely, those who experienced low satisfaction or little certainty about the state of their marriages were more likely to experience negative affective consequences of downward comparisons to marriages worse than their own. Thus, the general observation that downward comparisons may be affectively rewarding appears to be true for only some of the people some of the time. Those high in self-esteem or high in satisfaction with their outcomes may be more able to derive positive affect from downward comparisons to others worse off than themselves; by contrast, individuals low in self-esteem or low in satisfaction concerning their attributes or outcomes may be less able to do this.

The Buunk et al. (1990) results and those uncovered by Gibbons and Boney-McCoy (1991) and Taylor and Aspinwall (1993) appear contradictory. On the one hand, research finds that low-self-esteem individuals experience affective gains in response to downward social comparisons under conditions of threat, whereas low-self-esteem individuals are also found to experience more negative affect in response to downward comparisons. The resolution may hinge on the the fact that low-self-esteem individuals may have the greatest needs for self-enhancement, but the fewest or least developed skills with which to make self-enhancing comparisons. In highly structured and short-term situations, such as those in the laboratory with an available downward comparison target, low-self-esteem individuals may profit emotionally from downward comparisons. However, in the real world there is more opportunity to mull over the implications of downward comparisons, and there is a wider range of downward comparison targets from which to choose. In these cases, the low-self-esteem individual's tendency to construe all feedback in self-denigrating terms may take over, leading to fears that his or her own circumstances may decline, or leading to dejection or depression over observing the unfortunate state of another. Because the high-self-esteem individual is more skilled at construing information in a self-enhancing manner (Taylor & Brown, 1988; Wayment & Taylor, in press), he or she may be more able to avoid the negative implications of downward comparison information. Moreover, by virtue of being high in self-esteem, these individuals may have less initial need for downward social comparisons for feeling better.

Time Frame

The likelihood and consequences of making downward social comparisons may vary over time, as our previous comments have suggested. When people are faced with a stressful event, downward comparisons may have their affective benefits early, when self-enhancement needs are at their peak. On the short term, the realization that things could be worse may improve mood, bolster self-evaluations, and make people feel better about their circumstances. Over the long term, however, the risks embodied in downward comparisons may become more evident. Individuals may come to realize that their circumstances may indeed grow worse, and the fact that downward comparisons provide little information useful for improvement may take its toll (Crocker & Major, 1989). Thus, when the immediate impact of a threat has subsided and the need for self-enhancement is no longer preeminent, interest in downward comparisons may decline (Gibbons & Gerrard, 1991; Gibbons, Gerrard, Lando, & McGovern, 1991). In fact, cross-sectional investigations of coping with injuries or illnesses over the long term reveal that individuals who have been exposed to threatening events over a long period of time often show little interest in downward social comparisons (e.g., Schulz & Decker, 1985; Taylor, Aspinwall, et al., 1993).

Mutability and Controllability

Researchers have suggested that the implications of downward social comparison processes will differ, depending upon whether an attribute or outcome is seen as mutable (i.e., it is viewed as changeable over time) and/or controllable (i.e., any change in an attribute is regarded as being under personal control) (Testa & Major, 1990). Little research has directly addressed the relation of attribute mutability or controllability to the motivational impetus for making downward comparisons, to the propensity to make downward social comparisons, or to the consequences of downward comparisons, but there are good bases for generating predictions. (See Major, Testa, & Bylsma, 1991, for a discussion of the impact of perceived control on responses to social comparisons.)

Under conditions when a personal quality is seen as neither mutable nor controllable, the tendency to make downward comparisons may be muted; however, if such comparisons are made, their affective consequences should be in the service of self-enhancement needs and should be largely positive. Specifically, if one's standing on an attribute is unlikely to change, there may be little impetus for making social comparisons in any direction. But if a downward comparison is made, the affective consequences of fear and anxiety that can arise in response to the perception that one's circumstances can change in a negative direction should be offset by the perception that one's standing on the attribute is stable. The positive aspect of downward comparisons—namely, the comfort that comes from the recognition that one is better off than others—may remain intact. The benefits gained from downward comparisons under these conditions may also lead to an increase in the importance of the comparison dimension, thus also meeting self-enhancement needs (Major et al., 1991).

If one experiences threat in a domain in which the attribute or outcome is seen as immutable and uncontrollable, downward comparisons may be especially likely to occur, since threat makes self-enhancement needs especially salient. There may be relatively few alternative ways to manage threat effectively in an area in which one cannot expect to improve. Moreover, downward comparisons should involve little risk, because the perception that one's own situation is immutable and uncontrollable should reduce the potential negative emotional consequences of downward comparisons.

When an attribute or outcome is seen as mutable but low in controllability, the potential adverse affective consequences of downward social comparisons should be especially threatening. That is, when one perceives that one's situation may change and that one has little control over this change, the prospect of getting worse may be especially salient, thus enhancing the negative affective consequences of downward social comparisons. For example, in their study of cancer patients, Buunk et al. (1990) found that cancer patients who perceived themselves as having little control over their symptoms typically felt worse following downward comparisons.

Major et al. (1991) have proposed that when an attribute is seen as both mutable and controllable, downward comparisons enhance positive affect because one feels equipped to maintain one's preferred position on the comparison dimension. Whether or not such a conclusion is reached, however, may be moderated by self-esteem. Because high-self-esteem individuals generally see themselves as able to bring about favorable outcomes for themselves, they may be able to avoid the negative implications of downward social comparisons while maintaining the affective benefits derived from those comparisons. For high-self-esteem individuals, self-improvement needs may take precedence over self-enhancement needs, inasmuch as they see themselves as able to bring about change for the better. A different pattern may be true for low-self-esteem individuals: Their perception of themselves as generally inefficacious may lead them to fear the worst, thus bringing about the adverse emotional consequences of downward social comparisons (cf. Buunk et al., 1990).

Thus, in summary, the mutability or controllability of the personal quality on which one is making comparisons should importantly moderate the salience of different motivational needs, the corresponding tendency to make downward comparisons, the affective consequences that are likely to follow from downward comparisons when they are made, and the degree to which self-esteem differences are in evidence.

Are Downward Comparisons Real?

Considerable recent research suggests that much of what has previously been interpreted as downward social comparison activity may actually represent a false-consensus effect. That is, when individuals experiencing a threatening event, such as cancer, rheumatoid arthritis, or another victimizing circumstance, report that they are doing better physically or coping better than others like themselves, they may not be basing their self-inferences on any real downward comparison targets, but instead may be reporting general impressions of themselves as better off or others as worse off. Taylor, Wood, and Lichtman (1983), for example, found that cancer patients and their spouses often evaluated themselves against "manufactured others"—hypothetical individuals who were thought to be coping worse than themselves.

Carrying this argument one step further, Taylor and Lobel (1989) suggested that people may compare themselves to others less fortunate than themselves, whether real or hypothetical, but may avoid contact with such individuals. That is, when affiliative needs are salient, or when actual affiliation is likely, individuals may desire to protect themselves emotionally; affiliation may make salient the potential negative affective consequences of downward social comparisons that may arise from fear or anxiety about becoming like the downward comparison target, or the sympathy and sadness that may arise in response to the downward comparison target's fate. In fact, there is ample evidence that people avoid direct contact with those less fortunate than themselves (see Taylor & Lobel, 1989, for a review). Thus, the downward comparison effect alluded to by Wills (1981) may be a general esteem-maintaining self-perception of being better off than others, and not usually a process that results from actual contact with or an explicit comparison of the self with someone who is worse off.[2] Other motives, such as affiliative needs, may engender quite different comparison processes. We now turn directly to these other motives and their implications with respect to downward comparison processes.

Other Motives

There are multiple needs that drive self-regulation, including self-assessment, self-improvement, and the need to affiliate. How do downward social comparisons relate to these self-evaluative needs? On the face of it, downward social comparison would appear to be a poor method of self-assessment. Because the downward comparison target is chosen precisely for being inferior, the view of the self that results—namely, that one is better off—is a foregone conclusion. Moreover, downward targets provide little useful information about one's own outcomes, performance, or attributes, because one cannot calibrate one's own attributes or outcomes against an uninformative target.

For self-improvement, downward social comparisons may actually be deleterious. A longitudinal investigation (Wayment, Taylor, & Carrillo, 1994) alludes to the potential adverse long-term consequences of downward comparisons. Incoming freshmen at a large Western university were asked to complete a questionnaire detailing how they evaluated their academic and social qualities. Among the questions were ones assessing how frequently they used downward comparisons as a source of information for self-evaluation. Specifically, subjects were asked to indicate the frequency with which they compared themselves to others worse off than themselves separately for both their social and their academic qualities. Standardized measures of adjustment were also completed, and were completed a second time approximately 4 months later. The results indicated that in both the social and the academic domains, students who reported frequently comparing themselves with others worse off than themselves showed better psychological adjustment in the short term. However, 4 months later, these findings had actually reversed: Those who had reported initially that they reacted to the threat of college by making downward comparisons in the academic and social domains were more poorly adjusted at the second point in time (see also Taylor, Wayment, et al., 1993).

An experimental study (Wayment et al., 1994) revealed similar findings. Subjects performed an anagrams task either alone or in the company of a partner who either substantially outperformed them (upward social comparison condition) or substantially underperformed them (downward social comparison condition). In the downward social comparison condition, subjects solved somewhat fewer anagrams but felt good about their performance, in comparison to the upward comparison condition, where they solved more anagrams but felt worse about their performance. Thus, downward comparisons may be self-enhancing in the short term, but appear to provide little incentive for improvement or information that is helpful for improvement. Spontaneous comments made by the participants in the first study supported this line of analysis. As one student put it, "Comparing myself with someone doing more poorly makes me glad that I'm adjusting better, and I sort of relax about improving myself." These results imply that, although downward comparisons may temporarily assuage self-enhancement needs, they may be counterproductive for meeting other needs—specifically, self-improvement and self-assessment.

What are the implications of downward comparisons for affiliative needs? The previous research has, for the most part, examined the affective consequences of downward social comparisons from the standpoint of self-interested emotions. Individuals are argued to feel better in response to downward social comparisons, because such comparisons are self-enhancing (Wills, 1981). The potential negative affective consequences of downward social comparisons have also been looked at largely from the standpoint of self-interest. Downward comparisons are said to be potentially fear-arousing and threatening, because they imply that one's own circumstances could become worse and suggest that one could, in effect, become like the target (cf. Buunk et al., 1990).

But there are also potential empathetic and interpersonal affective consequences of downward social comparisons that have collectivist rather than individualistic implications. Observations of others whose situation is worse than one's own can engender sadness and sympathy. The experience of perceiving oneself to be similar to others less fortunate than oneself can lead to an experience of interpersonal bonding, producing a range of potential responses, including anger or indignation over the disadvantaged state of one's social group (Pettigrew, 1967; Davis, 1959), or distress over the likelihood that another person's situation may deteriorate further. A full consideration of the affective consequences of downward comparison, then, must take into account not only self-interested emotional outcomes, but also those that may result from empathy or the experience of bonding, as may arise when needs for affiliation drive social comparison processes.

Summary

To summarize, research since the early 1980s has elucidated the complex dynamics of downward social comparison processes and has importantly qualified the guiding theoretical framework offered by Wills (1981). Although there is substantial evidence that people see themselves as better off than others, under both threatening and nonthreatening circumstances, there is little evidence that actual downward social comparison processes are responsible for these effects. Rather, such favorable ratings of the self in comparison to others may be part of a more general pattern of self-enhancement that paints the self as especially talented, successful, and effective (Greenwald, 1981; Taylor & Brown, 1988). There is also evidence that the predicted affective consequences of downward social comparisons—namely, that people will feel better in response—are by no means inevitable. When self-enhancement needs are pre-eminent, the affective consequences of downward social comparisons are positive; however, when other motives such as self-assessment, self-improvement, and affiliation are salient, the affective consequences of downward social comparisons may be negative. There is evidence that low-self-esteem individuals under threat make and/or use downward social comparisons for the purposes stated by Wills (1981)—namely to feel better about themselves—but even these results are subject to important qualifications. Low-self-esteem individuals' responses to downward social comparison information can be adverse, with such comparisons creating feelings of dejection, despair, fear, or anxiety (Buunk et al., 1990). Thus, recent research on downward comparison processes suggests that their ability to satisfy self-enhancement needs may be confined to situations of short-term threats to self-esteem. When other motives are salient, such as self-assessment, self-improvement, or the need for affiliation, the likelihood of making downward comparisons may decrease, and their ability to be self-enhancing may give way to the fear that one may become like the downward comparison target or to concern and distress over the unfortunate plight of others.

UPWARD COMPARISON PROCESSES

Until recently, upward social comparison processes were assumed to be useful for self-improvement because they are informative, but esteem-reducing because they show that one is not performing as capably as another. As has been the case for downward comparison processes, however, our understanding of upward comparison processes has expanded and grown more complex in recent years. Specifically, the effects of upward comparisons depend upon what motive is salient, the time frame of upward comparisons, whether they are imposed or self-selected, and individual differences among self-evaluators. Taken together, the literature suggests that adverse emotional responses to upward social comparisons may be primarily short-term, and that the ability of upward social comparison processes to satisfy needs for self-improvement and affiliative needs may mute and even reverse the hypothesized negative affective consequences.

Affective and Performance Consequences

Generally speaking, the early literature on social comparison concluded that upward social comparisons, though informative, are made at the expense of positive affect. Because they imply that an individual is not as successful or talented as the comparison target, they reduce feelings of self-worth. Morse and Gergen (1970), for example, found that subjects exposed to a well-groomed and self-confident "Mr. Clean" on a competitive job interview felt significantly worse about themselves, compared with those exposed to a downward comparison target ("Mr. Dirty") or to no target. Cash, Cash, and Butters (1983) found that women exposed to upward comparisons through photographs of attractive women perceived themselves to be less attractive than women who were exposed to photographs of unattractive women. Salovey and Rodin (1984) found that subjects exposed to a student who had performed better than themselves on a self-relevant dimension reported more envy, jealousy, depression, and anxiety than subjects exposed to others performing more poorly or better on non-self-relevant dimensions.

Despite their adverse emotional effects, upward comparisons can exert beneficial effects on performance (cf. Atkinson, 1957; Atkinson & Birch, 1978). Seta (1982) had each subject perform a pattern recognition task in the presence of another student whose performance was inferior to, identical to, or slightly superior to the subject's. Those who participated with the slightly superior other showed superior performance relative to subjects who worked with an identical or inferior other. In a second study, each subject participated in the task alone or with another student whose performance was inferior to, identical to, slightly better than, moderately better than, or much better than the subject's. Those who participated with a better-performing other exhibited superior performance to subjects performing alone or with an inferior other, with the best performance emerging in the condition where subjects completed the task with a moderately superior other. We (Wayment et al., 1994) found that subjects exposed to a confederate who outperformed them on a task performed better than those exposed to no target or to a confederate who underperformed them, but that they felt worse about their performance. Thus, benefits in performance resulting from upward comparisons may occur in conjunction with a decline in self-evaluation and/or mood.

Time Frame

Generally speaking, the studies that have uncovered increases in performance coupled with declines in self-evaluations or affect have used a very circumscribed time frame. The studies have typically been conducted in the laboratory under conditions of short-term exposure to imposed upward comparisons and immediate assessments of self-evaluations and performance. We (Wayment et al., 1994) reasoned that declines in affect in response to upward social comparisons may be only short-term. Specifically, if upward social comparisons provide information that is useful for bettering one's circumstances, the process of making progress and improving should itself be self-enhancing, leading in the long term, to improved mood and self-evaluations (cf. Boninger, Gleicher, & Strathman, 1994). In a longitudinal investigation of these dynamics, we (Wayment et al., 1994) found that college freshmen who reported evaluating their academic performance and social lives in comparison to those doing better than themselves felt worse in the short term. However, over the long term, as predicted, this relationship was reversed: Initial reports of frequent upward comparison predicted better adjustment 4 months later. Although this study does not assess or quantify the dynamics associated with the relation of upward social comparisons to long-term improvement in psychological adjustment, it implies that information about successful others may indeed be useful for improving one's self-evaluations in the long term.

Self-Esteem

Self-esteem is an important moderator of the dynamics of upward social comparisons. Specifically, the affective consequences of upward social comparisons do not appear to be inevitably negative; rather, they depend in part upon self-esteem. Like downward comparisons, upward social comparisons may have negative or positive affective implications: Although upward comparisons alert a person to the fact that he or she is not doing as well as another individual, they may also be inspiring and motivating, or may enable an individual to take pleasure in another's achievements. The Buunk et al. (1990) study described earlier found that cancer patients who were high in self-esteem reported feeling better in response to comparisons to cancer patients doing physically better than themselves or coping better than themselves. As one cancer patient commented:

When I was going through the worst period, you know, the acute time of therapy and stuff, it was gratifying to see people recovering, having their hair grow back, getting their strength, and so on. Yeah, that was very positive and very helpful. (quoted in Buunk et al., 1990, p. 1242)

Those low in self-esteem reported feeling worse in response to these upward comparisons. Thus, negative emotional responses to upward social comparisons may occur primarily among those who have chronic self-enhancement needs (i.e., those low in self-esteem), but not to the same degree in individuals who have less need for self-enhancement (i.e., those high in self-esteem); these people may be more oriented toward other needs, such as self-improvement.

Mutability and Controllability

The implications of upward social comparison processes should differ, depending on whether or not an attribute or outcome is seen as mutable and/or controllable (Testa & Major, 1990; see also Major et al., 1991). Parallelling the predictions for downward social comparisons, when a personal quality is seen as neither mutable nor controllable, the tendency to make social comparisons should be muted, and the affective consequences of upward comparisons should be largely negative. Specifically, if one's standing on an attribute is unlikely to change, there may be little impetus for making any social comparisons, but the recognition that others are doing better than oneself may produce discouragement or depression.

When an attribute or outcome is mutable but low in controllability, upward comparisons may also be muted; it seems likely that one would attend disproportionately to the possibility of getting worse (Taylor, 1991). If upward comparisons are made under these conditions, the sense that one cannot improve one's circumstances may result in lowered self-esteem, depressed affect, and decreased striving in the domain (Major et al., 1991).

When an attribute or outcome is seen as both mutable and controllable, the implications of upward social comparisons may be construed as positive. Ybema and Buunk (1995) found that disabled individuals experienced positive affect following upward social comparisons when perceived controllability over the possibility of improving was high. Major et al. (1991) suggest that when one feels able to control changes in one's circumstances, upward comparisons should result in increased self-efficacy and efforts at self-improvement. However, self-esteem differences in the impact of upward social comparison information should be especially potentiated under these conditions. Because high-self-esteem individuals see themselves as able to bring about favorable outcomes, they should be more able to avoid the negative implications of upward social comparisons, instead seeing them as useful and inspirational. Low-self-esteem individuals, in contrast, may see themselves as less likely to control their outcomes, and thus the positive implications of upward social comparisons may not be so evident to them.

Other Motives

Upward social comparisons have generally been construed in terms of their cognitive implications for self-improvement (e.g., Taylor & Lobel, 1989; Wood, 1989) and their affective implications for self-enhancement. But they may also have implications for other motives associated with self-regulation, including self-assessment and affiliative needs. Social comparison research on the self-assessment motive has generally focused on the value of comparisons to similar others for assessing oneself; these have been construed to be lateral social comparisons. Although it is undoubtedly the case that lateral social comparisons are often useful for self assessment (Festinger, 1954; Trope, 1979), upward social comparisons may have valuable self-assessment functions as well.[3] From someone performing at exactly the same level as oneself, it may sometimes be difficult to extract information useful for assessing exactly how one performs well or badly. Consider, for example, the information that a mediocre tennis player can obtain from self-evaluation in comparison to another mediocre tennis player: Neither may have a very good forehand, backhand, or serve, and this may minimize the degree to which each can learn about the self from the other. However, both can learn about their own weaknesses from someone performing better.

Empirical evidence for the idea that upward social comparisons may lead to useful self-assessment is provided by Wayment and Taylor (in press). Specifically, they found that individuals rated upward social comparisons and lateral social comparisons as equally useful for self-assessment of social competence, and upward social comparisons as more useful than lateral social comparisons for self-assessment in the academic domain. Comparison of the self against someone doing slightly better may provide more precise information concerning the tasks on which one is doing well or badly. As this analysis implies, the self-assessment functions of upward social comparisons may be especially in evidence when self-improvement is possible (i.e., when one has the possibility of getting better at something). Self-assessment via upward social comparison may be muted if few possibilities for improvement exist.

In terms of self-enhancement, upward social comparisons are generally regarded as maladaptive, because, as noted, individuals are assumed to feel worse when they perform more poorly than others. Such an analysis ignores several possible ways in which the usual threat to a positive sense of self engendered by upward comparisons may be muted or eliminated. As already implied, the emotional consequences of upward social comparisons need not be solely self-centered, but may result from at least four other features of upward social comparisons that have intrinsic emotional benefits.

The first quality, already mentioned, is the capacity of upward social comparisons to be motivating and inspiring. For example, individuals often select mentors or role models on whom to pattern their self-improvement efforts, and may derive substantial inspirational benefits from these upward comparison targets (see Taylor & Lobel, 1989). Thus, when one compares the self against someone doing better than the self, it may engender no negative affect, because the comparison is used to derive a plan for patterning self-improvement efforts. Moreover, because the target selected is dissimilar to the self, (e.g. the target is older or more advanced on the dimension for comparison), many of the customary negative qualities of upward social comparisons, such as jealousy or discouragement, should not be felt.

Second, it is possible that information useful to self-improvement can actually reduce or eliminate the negative affect that might normally be associated with an upward social comparison. Thus, for example, failing to perform as well as a fellow athlete may lead to some despondency, but focusing on how one could learn from the experience to perform better in the future may mute that negative affect (cf. Boninger et al., 1994).

Third, there appear to be empathetic emotional benefits to upward social comparisons that have been largely ignored in the literature. Under certain circumstances, one feels good when one witnesses others succeeding. Tesser and his associates (Tesser, 1988, 1991) have found that, when someone close to an individual, such as a close friend or a relative, succeeds on a non-self-relevant task or quality, one can take pleasure in that accomplishment without suffering adverse emotional consequences.

Fourth, upward social comparisons may satisfy affiliative needs, by enabling an individual to identify with, become like, and bond with an upward comparison target; such affiliative activities should produce positive affect (cf. Thornton & Arrowood, 1966). Ybema and Buunk (1995) found that disabled individuals who perceived their ability to change their situation as high made upward comparisons and identified with those upward targets; furthermore, the positive affective consequences of upward comparisons were largely mediated by this identification. Thus, upward social comparisons may serve a social bonding function that serves self-enhancement needs. We comment further on this pattern of affective responses in a later section.

Choice of Target

As the preceding analysis implies, type of upward comparison target may be a moderating factor in determining whether the emotional benefits of upward social comparisons will be predominantly positive or negative. When individuals select a role model on whom to pattern their own efforts to succeed, they often choose someone who is older, wiser, or more advanced concerning the target attribute than they are. This may occur not only because such individuals are more informative, but also because by selecting an individual dissimilar on these qualities, one may avoid adverse emotional consequences of the upward comparison. Tesser and his associates (Tesser, 1988) have found that when someone close to or similar to the self, such as a good friend, outperforms the self on a self-relevant attribute, the emotional consequences of upward social comparisons are negative, leading individuals to withdraw from the friend or to devalue the attribute. Thus, one may resolve the affective implications of upward social comparisons, in part, by suggesting that when the target person is highly similar or close to the self, upward social comparisons are more likely to have adverse emotional effects, whereas when the target is perceived to be dissimilar to the self or when an attribute is not directly self-relevant, then upward social comparisons may have more emotional benefits.

Summary

To summarize, then, the traditional view of upward social comparisons as informative but ego-deflating requires substantial amendment. Such findings may be especially in evidence in laboratory studies in which comparison targets are highly similar to the self, performance is competitive, and the performance context is short-term. However, in the real world, the implications of upward social comparisons are importantly moderated by self-esteem, time frame, selection of a target, and the motivational impetus for making upward comparisons. Specifically, high-self-esteem individuals appear to be especially able to construe upward social comparison information in positive terms; role models who are dissimilar on the dimension under evaluation may produce inspiration and motivation rather than envy; the possibility of improving or learning by virtue of upward social comparisons may mute their potential negative implications; over time, upward social comparisons may lay the groundwork for geniuine self-improvement, providing the basis for long-term positive affective consequences and improved performance; and upward social comparisons may be in the service of affiliative needs rather than self-enhancement needs, leading to positive rather than negative affective consequences.

LATERAL COMPARISONS: A NOTE

Lateral social comparisons are comparisons of the self with someone whose personal qualities, attributes, or outcomes are roughly the same as one's own. Traditionally, lateral social comparisons have been viewed as the most common and the most useful to an individual, because similar others are construed as being most informative for self-evaluation (Festinger, 1954). A large experimental literature reveals support for the idea that lateral social comparisons are useful for self-assessment (see Wood, 1989, for a review).

However, lateral social comparisons are more easily operationalized in the laboratory than in the real world, and as a result there is little real-world support for the importance of lateral social comparisons. Specifically, in the laboratory it is possible to create a phantom other or expose a college student subject to a confederate, and to manipulate information about the other's attributes and/or manipulate the other's performance in such a way as to create lateral social comparisons. In the real world, however, what constitutes a lateral social comparison is more difficult to define. Typically, others do a little better than the self on some dimensions and a little worse than the self on others, leading to upward or downward comparisons respectively. What are often studied as lateral social comparisons in the real world are actually simply similarities.

Lateral comparisons are also difficult to examine in real-world contexts because, as Wood (1989) points out, comparisons are rarely made along a single specific dimension. People make informative comparisons by considering several dimensions related to the dimension under evaluation (Suls & Miller, 1977; Zanna, Goethals, & Hill, 1975). Thus, although these related attributes (Goethals & Darley, 1977) may be defined in a lateral direction, the outcome of the comparisons may not be constrained to be lateral (see Wood, 1989, for an extended discussion of the role of similarity in social comparisons). Indeed, the outcome itself may be upward or downward, suggesting that a lateral comparison to a similar other provides the basis for comparisons that have directional (upward or downward) outcomes. Thus, lateral social comparisons may be manifested in the selection of attributes related to the dimension under evaluation or other dimensions important to the self (e.g., gender, etc.), rather than the outcome of the comparison itself.

Despite these reservations, some evidence regarding the role of lateral social comparisons in self-regulation can be gleaned from research that asks individuals to rate their reactions to others similar to themselves and/or at about the same level on the target dimension. In a study of heart disease patients, Helgeson and Taylor (1993) found that affiliation with similar others made heart patients feel comfortable, happy, and inspired. Why should contact with others who are similar elevate one's spirits? As noted, a potentially important and previously largely ignored motive for social comparison processes is affiliation, the need to create or experience a common bond with another person (see also Helgeson & Mickelson, in press). Sharing common bonds can provide sympathy and support, facilitate the sharing of experiences, and alleviate feelings of isolation. Indeed, the heart patients' questionnaire responses to their feelings about contact with others who were similar suggested that the experience of sharing a common bond was an important source of comfort (Helgeson & Taylor, 1993).

We have already commented briefly on the potential role of lateral social comparisons in self-improvement. To reiterate, both theory and research (Wood, 1989; Taylor & Lobel, 1989) suggest that self-improvement may be better served by upward social comparisons than by lateral social comparisons. Someone whose performance, outcomes, or personal qualities are at the same level as those of the self can be relatively uninformative for improving one's own qualities. When self-improvement is the guiding motive, a target comparison person who paints a picture of where one is headed may be especially useful.

CONCLUSIONS AND GENERAL ISSUES

Recent research has elucidated the dynamics of upward, downward, and lateral comparisons in ways that broaden their implications for self-regulation. This increase in knowledge has come in large part from the fact that many recent studies of social comparisons have examined how people make social comparisons and what their effects are in real-world circumstances over the long term, rather than solely in laboratory studies that assess short-term reactions to social comparison information in self-relevant domains under explicitly or implicitly competitive circumstances. Examining the dynamics of social comparison processes in the real world and over time has helped to clarify their manifold implications for motivation, affect, and performance, and has also clarified their relation to other psychological processes. In particular, it is evident that social comparison processes may be usefully considered within a more general framework of self-regulation. Such a viewpoint has also clarified how social comparisons may serve multiple self-evaluative motives, including self-assessment, self-enhancement, self-improvement, and the need for affiliation.

Among the findings contributing to this insight are those from recent research on affective responses to social comparison processes. The view of affective consequences of social comparisons has traditionally been narrow, characterizing the expected affect from social comparison processes in individualistic emotional terms (cf. Markus & Kitayama, 1991). Downward comparisons are thought to make people feel better because they look good relative to others, and upward social comparisons are supposed to make people feel worse because they look bad relative to others. Such an analysis ignores important interpersonal affective consequences of social comparison activities—what may be thought of as interdependent emotions (Markus & Kitayama, 1991).

Empathetic reactions to downward social comparisons are negative, prompting sadness and depression at the unhappy circumstances of others. Empathetic responses to upward social comparisons are positive, taking pleasure in the accomplishments of others, without considering implications for the self. The affective consequences of downward social comparisons that come from bonding with others more poorly off than oneself may be negative; they may include anger, outrage, or indignation over the way in which one's disadvantaged group is treated by others (cf. Pettigrew, 1967; Davis, 1959), or distress and fear over the likelihood that the disadvantaged situation of those one feels close to may deteriorate further. The interpersonal bonding consequences of upward social comparisons are largely positive, resulting from a feeling of being similar to an individual one wishes to emulate or part of a group that one admires. Upward social comparisons may lead one to feel similar to and bond with others who are better off, and bonding with those worse off may contribute to a collective sense of social responsibility and the need to work together to enhance or restore collective outcomes.

Indeed, the general finding that individuals avoid contact with those less fortunate than themselves, instead affiliating with those better off than themselves (Taylor & Lobel, 1989), can only be meaningfully understood within the context of interpersonal emotional experiences; otherwise, avoidance of downward comparisons would rob individuals of affective benefits, and affiliation with better-off others would produce chronic self-dissatisfaction. Thus, our understanding of the motivational causes and consequences of social comparison may profit from a reconceptualization and extension of the basic self-regulatory processes that social comparison is intended to serve. Rather than focusing primarily on self-evaluation and its concomitant needs of self-assessment, self-improvement, and self-enhancement, social comparison researchers also need to consider affiliative functions relating to empathy, bonding, and other interdependent social and emotional states.

A perspective on social comparisons that emphasizes their potentially important role in satisfying affiliative needs provides a basis for linking social comparison processes to social support (Taylor et al., 1990). Social comparison processes may be integrally involved in socially supportive interactions during times of stress. Social support is known to produce a wide range of psychological and physical benefits, including less emotional distress in response to trauma, and faster recovery from surgery and illness (see Taylor, 1994, for a review). Thus, the affiliative functions of social comparisons may both enhance psychological well-being and actually promote physical health. Moreover, different patterns of social comparisons may be importantly related to different aspects of social support. Taxonomies of social support typically distinguish among emotional support (e.g., empathy, concern), appraisal support (e.g., feedback about a stressful event), and informational support (Winnubst, Buunk, & Marcelissen, 1988; House, 1981). Upward comparisons may supply informational support by providing individuals with information valuable for effective coping, and may supply emotional support by offering them hope and motivation. In addition, the bonding aspects of upward social comparisons may provide both appraisal support and emotional comfort. Paradoxical findings in the social comparison literature showing that people sometimes prefer to affiliate with authority figures over peers (e.g., Helmreich & Collins, 1967; Marcelissen, Winnubst, Buunk, & de Wolff, 1985) may be understood from the standpoint of upward comparisons as well. There may be a desire for information from experts, as well as a desire to bond with and be comforted by an upward comparison target. Further links between the literature on social support and that on social comparison processes may yet emerge.

Acknowledging the complex affective dynamics of upward and downward social comparisons has also helped identify individual-difference moderators of the likelihood and outcomes of these processes. In particular, self-esteem has been uncovered as an important moderator of social comparison activity. High-self-esteem individuals are able to construe downward social comparisons in ways that are advantageous to themselves; they do the same with respect to upward social comparisons, seeing them as inspirational and motivating, rather than as threatening. Low-self-esteem individuals, in contrast, appear to be vulnerable to the potential adverse affective implications of both downward and upward social comparisons. Such findings underscore the importance of a perspective on self-esteem that emphasizes the skills and deficits of high- and low-self-esteem individuals, respectively, in their abilities to make use of feedback from the social environment in ways that are constructive or maladaptive for the self (cf. Wheeler & Miyake, 1992).

Previous analyses have paid insufficient attention to the time frame of social comparison processes, examining their affective and performance consequences at a fixed point in time. But upward social comparisons, though temporarily ego-deflating, can be inspirational in the long term, and the capacity to think in the long-term perspective may mute the adverse implications for the self in the present (cf. Boninger et al., 1994). Similarly, exposure to downward social comparisons from a future-oriented perspective may be frightening, alerting a person to how his or her circumstances may change, and thus any immediate emotional benefits of feeling better than the target other may be muted in anticipation of future change.

In conclusion, our understanding of social comparison processes in the past has been relatively static, both motivationally and temporally. Acknowledging the multiple motivational bases for upward, downward, and lateral social comparisons reveals a wide range of potential affective and performance consequences with differential implications for behavior, depending upon the motive that is salient. Expanding the time frame for observation of the impact of upward and downward comparisons illustrates how the immediate motivational dynamics and consequences of upward or downward comparisons may be muted or even reversed over time. As the previous sections attest, these dynamics are further moderated by such factors as immediacy of threat, self-esteem, qualities of the target attribute (e.g., its mutability and/or controllability), characteristics of the target (e.g., similarity or dissimilarity on related attributes), and whether the comparison to another is based on real contact with that individual or merely assumptions about a hypothetical other. With continued research on these and other moderators, we may see social comparison processes fully integrated into our understanding of motivation and self-regulation.

Acknowledgments

Preparation of this chapter was supported by a National Institute of Mental Health grant (No. MH 42152) to Shelley E. Taylor. Heidi A. Wayment was supported by a National Institute of Mental Health Postdoctoral AIDS Training Grant (No. MH 19200). Mary Carrillo was supported by a predoctoral fellowship from the National Science Foundation. We thank Lisa Aspinwall for her comments on an earlier draft of this chapter.

Notes

1. Self-verification is a fifth self-evaluative motive that has received considerable attention (Swann, 1984). Self-verification involves the active confirmation and solidification of important personal attributes that are held with certainty. Social comparisons are unlikely to be made under such circumstances (Festinger, 1954). Thus, self-verification needs would seem to be, virtually by definition, largely unrelated to social comparison processes.

2. It may be that low-self-esteem individuals actually do pick real downward social comparison targets for self-evaluation under conditions of threat, hoping to achieve self-enhancement; instead, however, they may leave themselves vulnerable to the negative affective consequences of downward comparisons, precisely because they seek out such contacts.

3. It is important to reiterate that not all people have pronounced self-assessment needs and that not all people employ social comparison in response to needs for self-assessment. For example, whereas self-assessment may be important to people high in needs for certainty, this is not the case for people low in such needs (see, e.g., Sorrentino & Hewitt, 1984). Thus, the likelihood that such individuals will use either lateral or upward social comparisons for assessing their personal qualities is low (see also Roney & Sorrentino, in press).

References

Affleck, G., Tennen, H., Pfeiffer, C., Fifield, J., & Rowe, J. (1987). Downward comparison and coping with serious medical problems. *American Journal of Orthopsychiatry, 57,* 570–578.

Aspinwall, L. G., & Taylor, S. E. (1993). The effects of social comparison direction, threat, and self-esteem on affect, self-evaluation, and expected success. *Journal of Personality and Social Psychology, 64,* 708–722.

Atkinson, J. W. (1957). Motivational determinants of risk-taking behavior. *Psychological Review, 64,* 359–372.

Atkinson, J. W., & Birch, D. (1978). *Introduction to motivation* (2nd ed.). New York: Van Nostrand.

Boninger, D. S., Gleicher, F., & Strathman, A. (1994). Counterfactual thinking: From what might have been to what may be. *Journal of Personality and Social Psychology, 67,* 297–307.

Brickman, P., & Bulman, R. J. (1977). Pleasure and pain in social comparison. In J. M. Suls & R. L. Miller (Eds.), *Social comparison processes: Theoretical and empirical perspectives* (pp. 149–186). Washington, DC: Hemisphere.

Buunk, B. P., Collins, R. L., Taylor, S. E., Van YPeren, N., & Dakof, G. (1990). The affective consequences of social comparison: Either direction has its ups and downs. *Journal of Personality and Social Psychology, 59,* 1238–1249.

Cash, T. F., Cash, D. W., & Butters, J. W. (1983). "Mirror, mirror, on the wall . . . . ?": Contrast effects and self-evaluations of physical attractiveness. *Personality and Social Psychology Bulletin, 9,* 351–358.

Crocker, J., & Major, B. (1989). Social stigma and self-esteem: The self-protective properties of stigma. *Psychological Review, 96,* 608–630.

Davis, J. A. (1959). A formal interpretation of the theory of relative deprivation. *Sociometry, 22,* 280–296.

Festinger, L. (1954). A theory of social comparison processes. *Human Relations, 7,* 117–140.

Foddy, M., & Crundall, I. (1993). A field study of social comparison processes in ability evaluation. *British Journal of Social Psychology, 32,* 287–305.

Gerrard, M., Gibbons, F. X., & Sharp, J. (1985, August). *Social comparison in a self-help group for bulimics.* Paper presented at the annual meeting of the American Psychological Association, Los Angeles, CA.

Gibbons, F. X. (1985). Social stigma perception: Social comparison among mentally retarded persons. *American Journal of Mental Deficiency, 90,* 98–106.

Gibbons, F. X., & Boney-McCoy, S. (1991). Self-esteem, similarity, and reactions to active versus passive downward comparisons. *Journal of Personality and Social Psychology, 60,* 414-424.

Gibbons, F. X., & Gerrard, M. (1991). Downward comparison and coping with threat. In J. Suls & T. A. Wills (Eds.), *Social comparison: Contemporary theory and research* (pp. 317-345). Hillsdale, NJ: Erlbaum.

Gibbons, F. X., Gerrard, M., Lando, H. A., & McGovern, P. G. (1991). Social comparison and smoking cessation: The role of the "typical smoker." *Journal of Experimental Social Psychology, 27,* 239-258.

Goethals, G. R., & Darley, J. M. (1977). Social comparison theory: An attributional approach. In J. M. Suls & R. L. Miller (Eds.), *Social comparison processes: Theoretical and empirical perspectives* (pp. 259-278). Washington, DC: Hemisphere.

Greenwald, A. G. (1981). Self and memory. In G. H. Bower (Ed.), *The psychology of learning and motivation* (pp. 201-236). New York: Academic Press.

Hakmiller, K. L. (1966). Threat as a determinant of downward comparison. *Journal of Experimental Social Psychology, 2* (Suppl. 1), 32-39.

Helgeson, V. S., & Mickelson, K. (in press). Motives for social comparison. *Personality and Social Psychology Bulletin.*

Helgeson, V. S., & Taylor, S. E. (1993). Social comparisons and adjustment among cardiac patients. *Journal of Applied Social Psychology, 23,* 1171-1195.

Helmreich, R. L., & Collins, B. E. (1967). Situational determinants of affiliative preference under stress. *Journal of Personality and Social Psychology, 6,* 79-85.

House, J. A. (1981). *Work stress and social support.* Reading, MA: Addison-Wesley.

Major, B., Testa, M., & Bylsma, W. H. (1991). Responses to upward and downward social comparisons: The impact of esteem-relevance and perceived control. In J. Suls & T. A. Wills (Eds.), *Social comparison: Contemporary theory and research* (pp. 237-260). Hillsdale, NJ: Erlbaum.

Marcelissen, F. H. G., Winnubst, J. A. M., Buunk, B. P., & de Wolff, C. J. (1988). Social support and occupational stress: A causal analysis. *Social Science and Medicine, 26,* 365-373.

Markus, H., & Kitayama, S. (1991). Culture and the self: Implications for cognition, emotion, and motivation. *Psychological Review, 98,* 224-253.

Markus, H., & Nurius, P. (1986). Possible selves. *American Psychologist, 41,* 954-969.

Morse, H., & Gergen, K. J. (1970). Social comparison, self-consistency, and the concept of the self. *Journal of Personality and Social Psychology, 36,* 148-156.

Molleman, E., Pruyn, J., & van Knippenberg, A. (1986). Social comparison processes among cancer patients. *British Journal of Social Psychology, 25,* 1-13.

Pettigrew, T. F. (1967). Social evaluation theory: Convergences and applications. In D. Levine (Ed.), *Nebraska Symposium on Motivation* (pp. 241-318). Lincoln: University of Nebraska Press.

Pyszczynski, T. A., Greenberg, J., & LaPrelle, J. (1985). Social comparison after success and failure: Biased search for information consistent with a self-serving conclusion. *Journal of Experimental Social Psychology, 21,* 195-211.

Roney, C. J. R., & Sorrentino, R. M. (in press). Self-evaluation motives and uncertainty orientation: Asking the "who" question. *Personality and Social Psychology Bulletin.*

Salovey, P., & Rodin, J. (1984). Some antecedents and consequences of social comparison jealousy. *Journal of Personality and Social Psychology, 47,* 780-792.

Schachter, S. (1959). *The psychology of affiliation.* Stanford, CA: Stanford University Press.

Schulz, R., & Decker, S. (1985). Long-term adjustment to physical disability: The role of social support, perceived control, and self-blame. *Journal of Personality and Social Psychology, 48,* 1162-1172.

Seta, J. (1982). The impact of comparison processes on coactors' task performance. *Journal of Personality and Social Psychology, 42,* 281-291.

Sherman, S. J., Presson, C. C., & Chassin, L. (1984). Mechanisms underlying the false consensus effect: The special role of threats to the self. *Personality and Social Psychology Bulletin, 10,* 127–138.

Sorrentino, R. M., & Hewitt, E. C. (1984). Uncertainty-reducing properties revisited. *Journal of Personality and Social Psychology, 46,* 884–903.

Sorrentino, R. M., & Short, J. C. (1986). Uncertainty orientation, motivation, and cognition. In R. M. Sorrentino & E. T. Higgins (Eds.), *Handbook of motivation and cognition: Foundations of social behavior* (Vol. 1, pp. 379–403). New York: Guilford Press.

Steele, C. M. (1988). The psychology of self-affirmation: Sustaining the integrity of the self. In L. Berkowitz (Ed.), *Advances in experimental social psychology* (Vol. 21, pp. 251–302). New York: Academic Press.

Suls, J. M., & Miller, R. L. (Eds.). (1977). *Social comparison processes: Theoretical and empirical perspectives.* Washington, DC: Hemisphere.

Swann, W. B., Jr. (1984). Quest for accuracy in person perception: A matter of pragmatics. *Psychological Review, 91,* 457–477.

Taylor, S. E. (1991). The asymmetrical impact of positive and negative events: The mobilization–minimization hypothesis. *Psychological Bulletin, 110,* 67–85.

Taylor, S. E. (1994). *Health psychology* (3rd ed.) New York: McGraw-Hill.

Taylor, S. E., & Aspinwall, L. G. (1993). Coping with chronic illness. In L. Goldberger & S. Breznitz (Eds.), *Handbook on stress* (pp. 511–531). New York: Free Press.

Taylor, S. E., Aspinwall, L. G., Giuliano, T., Dakof, G. A., & Reardon, K. (1993). Storytelling, social comparison and coping. *Journal of Applied and Social Psychology, 9,* 703–733.

Taylor, S. E., Buunk, B. P., & Aspinwall, L. G. (1990). Social comparison, stress, and coping. *Personality and Social Psychology Bulletin, 16,* 74–89.

Taylor, S. E., & Brown, J. D. (1988). Illusion and well-being: A social psychological perspective on mental health. *Psychological Bulletin, 103,* 193–210.

Taylor, S. E., & Lobel, M. (1989). Social comparison activity under threat: Downward evaluation and upward contacts. *Psychological Review, 96,* 569–575.

Taylor, S. E., Wayment, H. A., Neter, E., & Woo, G. M. (1994). The self in transition. In P. Bertelson, P. Eelen, & G. d'Ydewalle (Eds.), *Current advances in psychological science: Ongoing research* (Vol. 7, pp. 181–195). London: Erlbaum.

Taylor, S. E., Wood, J. V., & Lichtman, R. R. (1983). It could be worse: Selective evaluation as a response to victimization. *Journal of Social Issues, 39,* 19–40.

Tesser, A. (1988). Toward a self-evaluation maintenance model of social behavior. In L. Berkowitz (Ed.), *Advances in experimental social psychology* (Vol. 21, pp. 181–227). New York: Academic Press.

Tesser, A. (1991). Emotion in social comparison and reflection processes. In J. Suls & T. A. Wills (Eds.), *Social comparison: Contemporary theory and research* (pp. 117–148). Hillsdale, NJ: Erlbaum.

Testa, M., & Major, B. (1990). The impact of social comparisons after failure: The moderating effects of perceived control. *Basic and Applied Social Psychology, 11,* 205–218.

Thibaut, J. W., & Kelley, H. H. (1959). *The social psychology of groups.* New York: Wiley.

Thornton, D., & Arrowood, A. J. (1966). Self-evaluation, self-enhancement, and the locus of social comparison. *Journal of Experimental Social Psychology, 2* (Suppl. 1), 40–48.

Trope, Y. (1975). Seeking information about one's own ability as a determinant of choice among tasks. *Journal of Personality and Social Psychology, 32,* 1004–1013.

Trope, Y. (1979). Uncertainty-reducing properties of achievement tasks. *Journal of Personality and Social Psychology, 37,* 1505–1518.

Trope, Y. (1980). Self-assessment, self-enhancement, and taste preference. *Journal of Experimental Social Psychology, 16,* 116–129.

Wayment, H. A., & Taylor, S. E. (in press). Self-evaluation processes: Motives, information use, and self-esteem. *Journal of Personality.*

Wayment, H. A., Taylor, S. E., & Carrillo, M. A. (1994). *The motivational and performance implications of upward and downward comparisons.* Manuscript in preparation.

Wheeler, L., & Miyake, K. (1992). Social comparison in everyday life. *Journal of Personality and Social Psychology, 62,* 760-773.

Wills, T. A. (1981). Downward comparison principles in social psychology. *Psychological Bulletin, 90,* 245-271.

Wills, T. A. (1987). Downward comparison as a coping mechanism. In C. R. Snyder & C. Ford (Eds.), *Coping with negative life events: Clinical and social-psychological perspectives.* (pp. 243-268). New York: Plenum Press.

Wills, T. A. (1991). Similarity and self-esteem in downward comparison. In J. Suls & T. A. Wills (Eds.), *Social comparison: Contemporary theory and research* (pp. 51-78). Hillsdale, NJ: Erlbaum.

Winnubst, J. A. M., Buunk, B. P., & Marcelissen, F. G. H. (1988). Social support and stress: Perspectives and processes . In S. Fisher & J. Reason (Eds.), *Handbook of life stress, cognition and health* (pp. 511-528). New York: Wiley.

Wood, J. V. (1989). Theory and research concerning social comparisons of personal attributes. *Psychological Bulletin, 106,* 231-248.

Wood, J. V., & Taylor, K. L. (1991). Serving self-relevant goals through social comparison. In J. Suls & T. A. Wills (Eds.), *Social comparison: Contemporary theory and research* (pp. 23-50). Hillsdale, NJ: Erlbaum.

Wood, J. V., Taylor, S. E., & Lichtman, R. R. (1985). Social comparison in adjustment to breast cancer. *Journal of Personality and Social Psychology, 49,* 1169-1183.

Ybema, J. F., & Buunk, B. P. (1995). The effects of social comparison direction and social comparison dimension upon affect and identification among disabled individuals. *British Journal of Social Psychology, 34,* 279-292.

Zanna, M. P., Goethals, G. R., & Hill, J. F. (1975). Evaluating a sex-related ability: Social comparison with similar others and standard setters. *Journal of Experimental Social Psychology, 11,* 86-93.

CHAPTER 2

Shared Reality
How Social Verification
Makes the Subjective Objective

CURTIS D. HARDIN
University of California, Los Angeles

E. TORY HIGGINS
Columbia University

> You accept my verification of one thing, I yours of another. We trade on each other's truths.
>
> —*W. James (1907/1992)*

> Once a value is standardized and becomes the common property of a group . . . it acquires objective reality.
>
> —*M. Sherif (1936)*

Human consciousness is not an inchoate flux of colors, sounds, tastes, and odors. Instead, people experience the world as a palpable whole, real and organized, despite all its kaleidoscopic complexity. This fact has puzzled many a student of the human condition—and there are nearly as many explanations for it as there have been theorists to consider it (James, 1890). Although contemporary psychological theory focuses most on individually held and maintained cognitive structures to account for the individual's grasp of reality, we offer a hypothesis congruent with social psychology's renewed emphasis on the social bases of cognition (e.g., Brewer, 1988; Higgins, 1981a, 1992a; Levine, Resnick, & Higgins, 1993; Oakes, Haslam, & Turner, 1994; Ostrom, 1984; Resnick, Levine, & Teasley, 1991; Schwarz, 1994). It is informed by insights of the North American pragmatic tradition, classic social-psychological theory, and empirical findings suggesting that even basic cognitive processes are defined by the social activities in which they are manifested. In particular, we suggest that in the absence of social verification, experience is transitory, random, and ephemeral, like the flicker of a firefly. But once recognized by others and shared in an ongoing, dynamic process of social verification we term "shared reality," experience is no longer subjective; instead, it achieves the phenomenological status of objective reality. That is, experience is established as valid and reliable to the extent that it is shared with others.

The notion that social verification is crucially involved in the construction of individual experience is hardly new, for the social-psychological tradition is replete with theoretical statements and empirical demonstrations that are directly derivative of the assumption (e.g., Asch, 1952; Cooley, 1902; Dewey, 1922/1930; Durkheim, 1897/1951; Festinger, 1950; Heider, 1958; Kelley, 1967; Kelman, 1958; Lewin, 1931; Marx & Engels, 1846/1970; Mead, 1956; Rommetveit, 1974; Schachter, 1959; Sherif, 1936; Weber, 1971). However, despite the distinguished tradition, the idea has maintained an almost ghostly presence, subsisting in the background of the workaday theories that have dominated social psychology, seemingly everywhere and nowhere at the same time.

It is our goal to draw on this tradition and extend it by formulating the hypothesis of shared reality in such a way that it may be meaningfully used to empirically engage significant issues in social psychology. In so doing, it is necessary first to contrast our formulation of shared reality with its most important precursor, the theory of social comparison (Festinger, 1950, 1954). In it, Festinger described the conditions in which people are most dependent upon others for their own understanding. Social comparison theory rests on the assumptions that (1) social comparison processes are initiated when external reality is ambiguous and difficult to grasp; (2) a dualism between physical and social realities exists; and (3) physical reality takes precedence over social reality. As Festinger (1950) summarized, "where the dependence upon physical reality is low, the dependence upon social reality is correspondingly high" (p. 272).

The hypothesis of shared reality represents a crucial extension. Following the pragmatic tradition, shared reality assumes no distinction between "physical" and "social" realities (Dewey, 1929/1958; Mead, 1936; see also Moscovici, 1976; Tajfel, 1972). Instead, we postulate that any experience—ranging from the immediate tactile sensation of a stone to the abstract understanding of a philosophical concept—survives as a reliable, valid, and predictable state of the world to the extent that it is socially verified. Furthermore, although social comparison theory has since been developed most in terms of its self-assessment functions (see Taylor, Buunk, & Aspinwall, 1990), we argue that shared reality's functions extend well beyond self-understanding, and are orthogonal to issues of ego protection. Indeed, we offer evidence that in some circumstances shared reality can function at the expense of self-regard.

In another relevant formulation, Rommetveit (1974) has argued that the goal of even the most common social interaction is to establish a mutually shared social reality or "intersubjectivity" (cf. Schutz, 1962). However, his emphasis is on the great difficulty of calibrating discrepant individual subjectivities. In contrast, we propose that any sustainable individual understanding is itself predicated on shared reality. We suggest throughout the chapter ways in which the hypothesis of shared reality may be employed to understand the dynamics of individual understanding, including its maintenance in the face of newly posed conflicting or otherwise discrepant alternatives.

In sum, we argue that the hypothesis of shared reality can function as a generative hypothesis that engages a broad array of social-psychological issues—

by complementing existing theory, as well as by generating unique and competing empirical predictions. We develop the hypothesis of shared reality by examining classic research and theory in social psychology as well as more recent research, especially that which has been motivated by an appreciation for the role of communication processes in social cognition. We review several extant literatures which lend support to the hypothesis that shared reality creates meaning for the individual by delineating the form and function of the external world, and suggest several implications of the hypothesis for a variety of topics, including stereotyping, the self, language, attitudes, and persuasion. In addition, we present new evidence from our own experiments that elucidates the role of shared reality in social judgment as well as the experience and regulation of the self. Our review suggests that (1) experience of reality or meaning is created and maintained for the individual when it is mutually shared with others; (2) social interaction is predicated upon and regulated by the establishment of shared reality; and (3) the shared reality that is achieved in social interaction in turn functions to regulate the self, closing the self–society circle.

FUNCTIONS OF SHARED REALITY

> It is individuals with this particular capacity to turn toward one another who in concrete action validate and consolidate in each a *mutually shared field,* one that includes both the surroundings and one another's psychological properties as the objective sphere of action.
>
> —*S. Asch (1952)*

> An opinion, a belief, an attitude is "correct," "valid," and "proper" to the extent that it is anchored in a group of people with similar beliefs, opinions, and attitudes.
>
> —*L. Festinger (1954)*

In a discussion of hermits, castaways, and other social isolates, Cooley (1902) concluded that the individual completely divorced from social contact quickly loses its human grasp of the world, understanding no more than an "intelligent animal," with the capacity to respond to little but immediate situational contingencies. Skinner (1957) punctuated a similar discussion by relating this anecdote: "An experiment appears to have been tried by Frederick the Great in which children were reared in isolation with the object of discovering whether they would naturally speak Hebrew. The experiment failed when all the subjects died" (p. 462).

We share the belief that social verification processes are crucial—perhaps even necessary—to establish and maintain individual understanding, and illustrations of shared reality in everyday life are numerous and familiar. Children's development is dominated by the establishment of consensus about the ways, whats, and whys of the world, as any parent can testify. The achievement of the basic vocabulary through naming is a ubiquitous example, in which parents and children collaboratively establish agreement about "how a thing shall be called" (Brown, 1958). The process is hardly one-way, for serendipitous utterances by children (e.g., "nana" for "nanny" or "munchkey" for "monkey") are often selected and subsequently used by parents and friends, and hence become meaningful realities for the group. The process of shared reality also may be seen in children's interactions with one another. For example, one of us recently observed his young daughter participate in a lengthy discussion with her friend about whether a toy animal was a porcupine or a skunk. Although each began the interaction with a different opinion about the name of the animal, they were unwilling to proceed with their play until they reached consensus about what they were playing with. Instructively, their negotiation appeared to have little to do with persuasion on the basis of accuracy, truth, or power; rather, it was dominated by heartfelt entreaties for consensus, apparently for its own sake. As one said to the other, "Agree with me, *please!*"

Shared reality is also illustrated by "consciousness raising," which suggests that even the experience of one's own oppression is qualitatively changed when it is shared with others. For example, until the experience is socially recognized and shared, women understand their own discomfort with sexual harassment, including rape, as a subjective quirk about themselves rather than as a problem that exists with objective reality for themselves and others. As MacKinnon (1989) summarized, the consciousness-raising process

> redefines women's feelings of discontent as indigenous to their situation rather than to themselves as crazy, maladjusted, hormonally imbalanced, bitchy, or ungrateful. . . . Consciousness raising, through socializing women's knowing, transforms it, creating a shared reality that "clears a space in the world" within which women can begin to move. (pp. 100–101)

Consciousness raising not only functions within tightly knit groups of people, but can also take place with remarkable rapidity and coherence at the cultural level, as illustrated by the recent establishment of "sexual harassment" in the national consciousness in the widely discussed confirmation hearings of U.S. Supreme Court Justice Clarence Thomas. For many who previously "just didn't get it," the discourse newly established sexual harassment as a set of particular behaviors that had once been unknown, unacknowledged, or (for many) understood in terms of a quite different reality—that is, an inherent and acceptable part of romantic courtship.

Interestingly, the very etiology of the words "subjective" and "objective" reflects a long-standing appreciation for the role of social verification in the status of experience. According to the *Oxford English Dictionary* (1971), both words are rooted in late Latin and have come to signify an elementary distinction between kinds of knowledge. Whereas "subjective" refers to solipsistic experience known only to the individual mind, "objective" refers to 'things' or 'realities' that are known to exist independently of the individual and can be observed by others.

More recently, in the history of science, objective is used to refer to phenomena that can be verified by other scientists. Hence, even the common English lexicon reflects the recognition of the distinction between experience that is shared and unshared.

A Classic Experimental Demonstration of Shared Reality

We believe that one of the best examples of the role of shared reality in the creation and maintenance of individual experience is found in Sherif's classic autokinetic experiments (reviewed in Sherif, 1936). In them, a fixed point of light exposed to subjects in a completely darkened room appears to move with an erratic quality, often attributed to saccadic eye movement (Gregory, 1966). In the basic paradigm, subjects are told by the experimenter that the light may appear to move, and that their task is to judge the direction and magnitude of the movement.

Sherif initially compared the autokinetic effect as it manifested for subjects "alone" versus those in groups of other subjects. Results indicated that the judgments of each subject who worked only with the experimenter clustered around a central tendency, and that there were individual differences across subjects. However, when subjects subsequently performed the task with others, their individual judgments converged to form a group norm. When subjects began the task in a group, convergence was even greater, and the number of trials necessary for the norm to be established was smaller. Follow-up studies have demonstrated that the shared reality created by the groups survives across generations of subjects, indicating that once a shared reality is achieved, it can be maintained with stability long after the originators of the norm have gone (Jacobs & Campbell, 1961; Weick & Gilfillan, 1971). Importantly, significant variation among group norms is typically observed, suggesting that the subjective becomes objective through whatever consensus happens to develop. In this case, the shared reality established by the groups has a relatively arbitrary relation to the external physical stimulus, just as the word "dog" no better represents a slobbering four-legged creature with tail awag than the word "chien"—suggesting that functions of shared reality are not limited to issues of accuracy or "truth" (cf. Festinger, 1950, 1954). Nevertheless, social consensus about "what it is," "how it functions," and "what it is called" are vital predicates for social interaction and the individual's own hold on reality.

Several additional aspects of the Sherif findings are germane to the hypothesis of shared reality. First, the subjects did not understand their experience in terms of conformity, but rather described their judgments as reflecting their actual perception of reality. Subjects denied that they were merely going along with their colleagues, but instead insisted that they were expressing their true experience (Sherif, 1936). Indeed, one of us participated in an autokinetic experiment as an undergraduate and can provide further testimony to the felt reality of the experience.

Most importantly, all evidence suggests that the experience was modulated by being shared with others. The creation and maintenance of the group norms are the most celebrated aspects of these experiments, and they clearly demonstrate how individual experience is constructed through public communication and social verification. Equally persuasive evidence is found by considering the experience of subjects who participated "alone." Of course, subjects did not perform the task in solitude, but in full collaboration with the experimenter. Hence, the situation involved a mutual understanding of the experimental 'theatre' and its concomitant roles, perspectives, and tasks (e.g., Goffman, 1959; Higgins, 1992b; Schwarz, 1994). In particular, the experimenter expressly implied that subjects would see the light move, and each subject's public expression of his or her experience was duly accepted by the experimenter (cf. Grice, 1971; Schwarz, 1994).

Even the identification of conditions in which there was no convergence to group norms suggests the operation of shared reality. For example, Sperling (1946) found that no convergence toward a confederate was observed for 60% of the subjects who were told that there was no objective movement but instead that whatever movement, they saw was entirely subjective. In this case, subjects may be said to have achieved shared reality with the experimenter, who was the legitimate authority in the situation. Not only was it the shared reality that subjects might differ from the confederate, but implicit in the instruction was that their judgments should differ. Further, even when subjects were told that there was no objective movement, they were still required to tell what the stimulus looked like to them, hence establishing a shared reality that afforded disagreement about the particulars of the movement but still suggested that movement would be observed. Finally, it is important to point out that the remaining 40% of the subjects did exhibit the usual convergence effect. Their explanation? They did not believe the experimenter. Consistent with the assumption that shared reality is necessary to maintain belief in the veracity of experience is the possibility that these subjects brought with them knowledge previously shared with other students (or perhaps their psychology instructor) that experimenters tend to lie (cf. Kassin, 1979).

This latter finding illustrates two additional points. First, many experiences and beliefs have a history of being shared with significant others, and thus may be relatively resistant to challenge by new information. Indeed, we review evidence suggesting that once shared reality has been achieved, participants act in ways that protect and maintain it. The second and related point is that there are many situations in which previously or currently shared realities may be in conflict. For example, one may grow up sharing the reality with a religious authority that alcohol is uniformly unhealthy, but later in life may come to share the conflicting reality with a medical authority that a glass of wine a day is beneficial to the circulatory system. This possibility raises interesting questions about how multiple competing shared realities are managed in the regulation of social interaction and individual experience. A full description of the conditions in which one shared reality versus another will be adopted and maintained as veridical for oneself awaits direct research at present, but in much that follows we offer speculations based on existing evidence concerning how conflicting shared realities may be managed in the course of social interaction.

Shared Reality in the Genesis of Experience

We believe that the social construction of experience demonstrated in the Sherif (1936) experiments epitomizes the more general claim of shared reality. As such, the hypothesis of shared reality adopts the pragmatic assumption that all human experience is defined in the dialectical relation between the human organism and its environment—in particular, as mediated by social conventions including (but not limited to) language (e.g., Dewey, 1922/1930, 1929/1958; James, 1909; Mead, 1932, 1934, 1936, 1982). As Dewey (1929/1958) wrote:

> Without language, the qualities of organic action that are feelings are pains, pleasures, odors, colors, noises, tones, only potentially and proleptically. With language they are discriminated and identified. They are then "objectified"; they are immediate traits of things. This "objectification" is not a miraculous ejection from the organism or soul into external things, nor an illusory attribution of psychical entities to physical things. The qualities were never "in" the organism; they always were qualities of interactions in which both extra-organic things and organisms partake. (pp. 258–259)

The hypothesis of shared reality is consistent with the common assumption that the functional properties of the world, such as values, beliefs, attitudes, and self-conceptions, are constructed through the individual's interactions with society (e.g., Triandis, 1989; Markus & Kitayama, 1991; Moscovici, 1993; Shweder & LeVine, 1984). For example, Berger and Luckmann (1966) have argued that the individual's understanding of the world emerges both through the internalization of its culture's world view as well as role-specific knowledge and vocabularies. Social currencies, including language, religion, values, vocation, economic status, and roles, act in concert to provide the reasons for being and doing. In addition, new contents of socialized knowledge come to be experienced as immediate reality by linking new roles and identifications to the known language of culture through ongoing social interaction (e.g., Mead, 1934, 1982; Schutz, 1967).

In addition to its role in defining the functional properties of the world (i.e., why something matters or what its utility is), we believe that shared reality also plays a definitive role in the experience of the stable properties of reality, both through social transmission and through the social construction of direct perceptions.[1] The establishment of reality through social transmission is non-controversial, and merely describes the fact that much of our knowledge is based not upon our own direct experience with a given phenomenon, but instead comes to be known only through social communication. For example, no one is left alive who witnessed the French Revolution in person, yet virtually every educated person is quite sure that it occurred. Further, individual understandings that are at odds with prevailing knowledge (e.g., denials of the existence of the Nazi-perpetrated Holocaust) are themselves established and maintained through elaborate social networks, which often include books, newsletters, and other group activities.

In addition to social transmission, the stronger claim of shared reality includes the social construction of even direct perceptions, as in the Sherif (1936) study. That is, for one to know that even immediate sensation corresponds to objective reality, it too requires social validation. Many illustrations of how social consensus creates direct experience may be found in the common lexicon, which is itself built of social consensus. For example, it is through social convention that a sofa and a chair are experienced and immediately known as distinctive pieces of furniture. As Helen Keller (1903) wrote in her autobiography, "Everything had a name, and each name gave birth to a new thought." From the perspective of shared reality, Keller's individual experience was qualitatively changed and objectified when her grasp of language catapulted her into a new, socially shared world of tables, chairs, candles, and cakes.

Although such anecdotal examples are striking, it is important to note that the shared reality afforded by linguistic practice has measurable effects on broader populations, both in the laboratory and in everyday circumstances (reviewed in Hardin & Banaji, 1993). Even the temporary instantiation of shared reality through simple labels or linguistic descriptions is implicated in color perception and memory (e.g., Kay & Kempton, 1984; Lucy & Shweder, 1988; Schooler & Engstler-Schooler, 1990), memory for pictures (e.g., Carmichael, Hogan, & Walter, 1932; Daniel, 1972; Santa & Baker, 1975; Schooler & Engstler-Schooler, 1990), problem solving (e.g., Higgins & Chaires, 1980; Schooler, Ohlsson, & Brooks, 1993), social perception (e.g., Hoffman, Lau, & Johnson, 1986), and the perception of speech-related sounds (e.g., Nusbaum & Goodman, 1994). Indeed, in a remarkable series of experiments, Moscovici and colleagues have reported findings suggesting that group consensus to call a blue stimulus "green" systematically changes individual perceptions of the afterimage (Doms & Van Avermaet, 1980; Moscovici & Doms, 1981, cited in Moscovici, 1985; Moscovici & Personnaz, 1980; Personnaz, 1981; see also Moscovici, 1985; Sorrentino, King, & Leo, 1980).

A Metaphor for the Functions of Shared Reality

To summarize the functions of consensual social verification in the establishment and maintenance of individual experience, we adopt a statistical metaphor. When an experience is recognized and shared with others in the process of social interaction, it achieves reliability, validity, generality, and predictability. Further, we suggest that an important corollary implied by the statistical metaphor is that shared reality will assume a prominent place in social regulation.

Reliability

Shared reality functions to establish the reliability of an experience, just as repeated observation of a phenomenon gives it statistical reliability. When an experience is shared, its reliability is demonstrated by its repeated recognition by members of the community who share the perception or belief. As one's experience is recognized by others, one learns that it is reproducible in others, and therefore not random or capricious. As in statistics, the reliability of an experience established through shared reality does not guarantee its "truth" or validity, although validity is predicated on reliability.

Validity

As in the scientific experiment, a basic function of shared reality is to establish that a given phenomenon is valid—that is, corresponds to some objectively real aspect of the world. Reliably shared experience is validated experience. Hence, through social verification, individual experience is transformed from a subjective ephemerality into an objective actuality. Of course, the validity of an experience as established within a given social group does not necessarily mean that this shared reality will correspond to the "facts" that may be known from a different perspective as established by another group. We simply propose that such a shared reality is sufficient to ground the individual's *experience* as veridical of the external world.

Generality

A goal of any scientific theory is to establish some level of generality, for a theory is not a theory if it merely redescribes the specific phenomenon to which it is supposed to apply. Generality is established to the degree that understanding is broader than a particular datum. Likewise, the process of sharing one's experience with others demonstrates directly that the experience is not one of a kind or unique, but that it has a reality that is broader and more general than the immediate moment. It exists across people, time, and particular situations. The generality of an experience, like the generality of a scientific theory, is established to the extent that it is verified by people other than the self (cf. Kelley, 1967).

Predictability

As it does for good scientific theories and statistical analyses, predictability follows from the reliability, validity, and generality that is achieved through shared reality. Hence, shared reality serves the fundamental epistemic function of facilitating the prediction and control of oneself and one's environment.

Although we have adopted a statistical analogy to help elucidate the functions of shared reality, research on memory suggests that these functions may be more literal than metaphorical. For example, several studies have demonstrated that collaborative recall is more accurate than individual recall (for a review, see Hartwick, Sheppard, & Davis, 1982). Importantly, these findings are not limited to cases involving a division of labor, such as when different memories are distributed among members of a dyad or group (e.g., Wegner, 1987). Even under conditions in which the identical stimulus material is learned, groups outperform individuals on a variety of retrieval tasks, including free recall, recognition, hits, false alarms, and discriminability, as well as confidence in accurate versus inaccurate memories (e.g., Hinsz, 1990; Stephenson, Clark, & Wade, 1986; Vollrath, Sheppard, Hinsz, & Davis, 1989). Further, this research indicates that superior collective memory is achieved through several consensus-based processes. Although groups do generate a larger sample of potential memories, the larger sample in itself does not require that memory will be more accurate, for it could just as well lead to more false alarms (see Green & Swets, 1966; Lockhart & Murdock, 1970). Instead, it appears that consensus about accurate memories is established in groups, whereas little or no consensus is developed about inaccurate memories. Hence, consistent with the functions of shared reality, memories are established as reliable and valid to the extent that social consensus about them is achieved. In contrast, individuals have no comparable basis upon which to discriminate the validity of correct versus incorrect subjectivities. Consistent with the general utility of shared reality, it is not surprising that subjects are more confident about the accuracy of their memories when they have been achieved collectively than individually.

Although this research suggests that individuals operate on the principle that shared reality is accurate reality, this generally adaptive tendency may not yield "truth" in every instance. For example, Luus and Wells (1994) found that witnesses' confidence in the accuracy of their identification of a suspect from a police lineup varied twofold, depending on whether they thought another witness had corroborated their identification. Although the relationship between corroboration and confidence is consistent with the general adaptive properties of shared reality, it did not serve witnesses well in this particular case, for the variation in confidence was completely independent of their objective accuracy.

Social Regulation

A corollary of the statistical metaphor is that shared reality will be regularly realized in ongoing social regulation. Just as statistical models (or scientific theories) regulate the hypotheses addressed, tested, and pursued, the basic functions of shared reality suggest that its achievement should be a dominant regulatory goal of social interaction. That is, to the extent that shared reality is required for establishing the reliability, validity, predictability, and generality of experience, efforts to establish shared reality should be in ubiquitous evidence in social interaction, and not limited to special circumstances involving highly ambiguous stimuli. In particular, efforts to establish shared reality should dominate social interaction, guiding its course and consequences (see Asch, 1952; Higgins, 1981a; Reiss, 1981; Rommetveit, 1974; Ruesch & Bateson, 1968; Watzlawick, Beavin, & Jackson, 1967).

Communication and Shared Reality

The hypothesis that the individual's grasp of reality is determined by the extent to which it is socially shared implies that communication plays an essential role in human cognition, and, indeed, that it will be impossible to understand individual cognition fully outside the context of ongoing communicative activity (see Fiedler & Semin, 1993; Higgins, 1981a; Krauss & Fussell, in press; Schwarz, 1994). In particular, it suggests that the cognitive system is not just the organ of communication, but instead that social activity and cognition are mutually defined in dialectical relation (e.g., Ostrom, 1984).

In an earlier discussion of the importance of shared reality, the "communication game" approach described the irreducibly social character of communication (Higgins, 1981a, 1992b; Higgins & McCann, 1984). In particular, communication is known (1) to involve shared, rule-governed conventions concerning social roles and behavior (cf. Austin, 1962; Cushman & Whiting, 1972; Gumperz & Hymes, 1972; Peirce, 1940; Rommetveit, 1974; Ruesch & Bateson, 1968; Searle, 1969; Watzlawick et al., 1967); (2) to require cooperative coorientation and mutual perspective taking (cf. Cushman & Whiting, 1972; Grice, 1971; Mead, 1934; Merleau-Ponty, 1962; Rommetveit, 1974); (3) to function not only to transmit information, but also to create and define social relationships, with the content and relationship being interdependent (cf. Blumer, 1962; Bolinger, 1975; Garfinkel, 1967; Gumperz & Hymes, 1972; Hawes, 1973; Watzlawick et al., 1967); and (4) to be a socially interdependent process in which the purpose and very meaning of the interchange are collaboratively determined (cf. Blumer, 1962; Burke, 1962; Garfinkel, 1967; Goffman, 1959; Krauss & Fussell, in press; Hawes, 1973; Merleau-Ponty, 1962; Rommetveit, 1974; Watzlawick et al., 1967). Our current position on shared reality takes this approach one crucial step further by postulating that these factors not only characterize communication, but determine the individual's grasp of reality as well. That is, a hold on reality requires cooperative social activity; in particular, consensually validated social roles and relationships are required for the mutual creation, monitoring, and maintenance of the individual experience of reality.

Despite the conspicuous absence of communication as a dominant emphasis in social psychology, increasing numbers of theorists are attempting to integrate the study of communication and social cognition (e.g., Fiedler & Semin, 1993; Higgins, 1981a, 1992a; Schwarz, 1994). Contemporary models of communication focus on processes directly related to shared reality, in their emphases on perspective taking as well as on the joint construction of meaning (for a review, see Krauss & Fussell, in press). Shared knowledge is constructed in part through a process of reciprocal perspective taking, in which communicators must "take the role or attitude of the other" (Mead, 1934). That is, for communication to proceed effectively, each communicator must experience the situation as it is experienced by the other. In addition, meaning is understood to emerge out of the joint process in which individual contributions are understood within the interaction situation as a whole, arising as speakers and addressees come to agree that a mutually consistent understanding has been achieved (Clark & Brennan, 1991; Clark & Schaefer, 1989; Clark & Wilkes-Gibbs, 1986; Isaacs & Clark, 1987). Hence, much of the research to which we now turn involves the direct examination of communicative interaction.

EMPIRICAL EVIDENCE OF SHARED REALITY

In the experience of conversation, a common ground constitutes itself between the other one and myself, my thought and his make up a single tissue, my words and his are called out by the phase of the discussion, they insert themselves in a common operation of which neither one of us is the sole creator . . . we coexist within the same world.

—*M. Merleau-Ponty (1945)*

The paramount fact about social interaction is that the participants stand on common ground, that they turn *toward one another,* that their acts interpenetrate and therefore regulate each other.

—*S. Asch (1952)*

The achievement of shared reality requires collaboration—in particular, the mutual recognition and verification of experience in ongoing social activity. Evidence suggests that shared reality occurs not only through processes involved in message formulation, but also through the active role recipients play in the selection of particular meanings to achieve shared reality. Perhaps most importantly, evidence suggests that these social verification processes create meaning for the participants, as indicated by effects on perception, judgment, and memory.[2]

In broad outline, this section is organized heliotropically, in a way we think reflects to some degree the iterative, dialectical relationship between self and society. We begin at the broadest level of social regulation by reviewing evidence that efforts to establish shared reality play a prominent role in communicative activity, as implied by the statistical metaphor. We then discuss evidence that these efforts are met with success. Not only do participants in communicative activity reach consensus, but the shared reality they establish has important consequences for both the recipients and the formulators of messages, implicating shared reality in the creation of meaning for the individual. We then discuss evidence suggesting that shared reality is further implicated in social regulation, particularly in who shares which realities with whom. The heliotrope circles round again with a discussion of how realities shared both temporarily and chronically in social relationships create and maintain the self-concept. Finally, we present evidence from our own laboratory suggesting that self-concepts with a strong basis in shared reality, in turn, modulate new opportunities for social interaction.

Efforts to Achieve Shared Reality in Ongoing Communication

It has long been observed that social interaction requires taking others into account (e.g., James, 1890; Lewin, 1931; Mead, 1934; Weber, 1967), and moreover, that perspective taking is an essential attribute of communication and emergent meaning (e.g., Bakhtin, 1986; Brown, 1965; Clark & Brennan, 1991; Clark & Carlson, 1982; Higgins, 1981a; Krauss & Fussell, 1991b; Mead, 1956; Rommetveit, 1974; Volosinov, 1986). The symbolic–interactionist movement is probably most closely associated with emphasizing the role of perspective taking in social interaction (e.g., Stryker & Statham, 1985), but theorists of communication have increasingly emphasized the essential role of perspective taking in their models as well (e.g., Clark & Wilkes-Gibbs, 1986; Sperber & Wilson, 1986). In particular, this literature suggests that communicators take into account both relatively stable aspects of one another's perspectives, such as background knowledge and attitudes, as well as more immediate situational factors, such as momentary vantage point and states of current comprehension (Krauss & Fussell, 1988, 1991a)—evidence consistent with the hypothesis that the experience of reality may be shared chronically, through long-standing social and cultural practices and relationships, as well as situationally, through the immediate verification of experiences and attitudes in ongoing social interaction.

Efforts to achieve shared reality are reflected by a variety of linguistic strategies regularly utilized in everyday conversation. Communicators modulate their utterances to elicit specific feedback from their partners that the utterance is mutually understood (see Clark & Wilkes-Gibbs, 1986; Sacks & Schegloff, 1979; for a review, see Krauss & Fussell, in press). For example, "try-markers" (uttering declarative statements as questions) and "installment phrases" (presenting new information in incremental segments) function to elicit confirmation that mutual understanding is accruing (e.g., "The Tarantino film . . . we saw together . . . over Thanksgiving . . ."). Explicit preliminary queries called "presequences" also function to establish that a given body of knowledge is mutually known (e.g., "You know the film about the botched bank robbery?"). Verification that communication is understood is accomplished by various factors, including tone of voice, facial expression, and motor mimicry (e.g., Bavelas, Black, Chovil, Lemery, & Mullet, 1988; Bavelas, Black, Lemery, & Mullet, 1986; Brunner, 1979; Chovil, 1991; Goodwin, 1981), as well as vocal and nonvocal "back-channel" responses like "uh-huh" or head nods (e.g., Duncan & Fiske, 1977; Kendon, 1967; Schegloff, 1982). These strategies not only establish a shared reality that can be assumed and utilized in subsequent interaction, but are employed in ways that suggest that the ongoing achievement of shared reality is required for communication to proceed at all. Anyone can readily observe this by simply withholding such feedback in conversation. Without feedback, communicators suspend the communication of new information and immediately initiate attempts to rectify the apparent breakdown in shared reality.

Perhaps the most rudimentary way in which shared reality is achieved through perspective taking is when knowledge directly available about another is utilized in communication, such as when communicators modify messages to suit the immediate informational needs of their partners (e.g., Clark & Schaefer, 1987). Although children are not initially adept at such perspective taking, the ability develops rapidly as they mature (e.g., Glucksberg, Krauss, & Higgins, 1975; Higgins, 1977). Even young children will vary their messages to suit the immediate needs of their communication partners. For example, children's messages about identical stimuli are different depending upon whether they are addressed to (1) adults versus children their own age (Sachs & Devin, 1976; Shatz & Gelman, 1973), (2) someone blindfolded versus someone not blindfolded (Maratsos, 1973), and (3) people they know have information in common with them versus those they know do not (Higgins, 1977). Piaget and Inhelder (1956) argued that the ability to appreciate differences between one's own and others' perspectives is a crucial early developmental achievement, and described children's perspective taking in the context of, physically different vantage points. More recent research shows that adult communicators require more time to create messages to the degree that their perspective is different from another's, and that a speaker's descriptions of the relative location of an object are more likely to take the addressee's perspective as the difference in their vantage points increases (e.g., Schober, 1993).

Physical vantage point is not the only directly available information communicators use in perspective taking. For example, Hupet, Seron, and Chantraine (1991) had subject pairs communicate about sets of nonsense figures that varied in terms of their discriminability. Although communicators typically used simple descriptive labels alone when the figures were easily discriminable, they provided supplemental information in addition to the label when the figures were difficult to discriminate. Fussell and Krauss (1989a) found that communicators' descriptions of nonsense figures were over twice as long when they were formulated for the use of other persons than when they were formulated for themselves. Descriptions for others employed commonly known features, such as the geometric elements of the stimuli, rather than idiosyncratic characterizations that would be uninterpretable to others.

Perspective taking also involves inferences about how others will respond to a particular stimulus or situation, and plenty of evidence suggests that communicative behavior reflects mutual efforts to take into account what the participants know, feel, think, and believe (e.g., Manis, Cornell, & Moore, 1974; Zimmerman & Bauer, 1956). Several classic experiments have demonstrated that people can and do adopt the perspectives of others through role taking. For example, Jones and DeCharms (1957) found that subjects' attributions concerning the personality characteristics of a former prisoner of war who had signed ene-my propaganda statements varied, depending upon whether they adopted the role of a friend, an examining psychiatrist, or a member of a military tribunal. Zukier and Pepitone (1984) found that subjects who adopted the role of "scien-tist" used more ostensibly objective base-rate information in a person judgment task than those who adopted the role of "clinical counselor," who instead employed more personality-based information. Janis and Mann (1965) demon-strated that information learned through role playing has larger effects on sub-sequent behavior than does equivalent information learned outside a perspec-tive-taking context.

Social categories are a ubiquitous basis for inferences about the perspec-tives of others. For example, a field experiment by Kingsbury (1968) suggests that communicators act on the knowledge that nonlocals may require more in-formation. Responses to requests for directions were longer and more detailed when the requester was perceived as an "out-of-towner" rather than as a "local" (cf. Higgins, 1977). Communicators proved to be quite sensitive to group mem-bership cues. Asking for directions in a nonlocal accent produced the same re-sults as did explicitly claiming to be from out of town. More controlled labora-tory studies have provided corroborating evidence of the use of social category information in the achievement of shared reality. For example, Isaacs and Clark (1987) had participants communicate about New York City landmarks, and found that communicators quickly adapted their expressions to their audience's apparent degree of familiarity with New York City. Fussell and Krauss (1992) found that communicators' prior beliefs about their recipients were correlated with speakers' referential strategies. Communicators provided more elaborate de-scriptions as the perceived probability that the listener would know the refer-ent's name declined, whether communication involved everyday objects or pub-lic figures. Furthermore, the results suggested that social categories were used initially to tailor messages and then adjusted as a function of the ongoing feed-back recipients subsequently provided.

A relatively more abstract way in which communicators collaborate in the attempt to achieve shared reality is demonstrated by experiments on "cognitive tuning," which demonstrate effects of the communicative orientation partici-pants adopt early in the communication sequence. In an early study, for exam-ple, Zajonc (1960) found that in order to produce clear, concise messages, com-municators polarize and distill stimulus information to a greater extent than do recipients, who must remain prepared for a wide range of possible information contained in the message. This effect has been replicated many times, and Zajonc's basic interpretation has been corroborated through direct manipula-tions of both the speaker's and the recipient's communication roles, as well as manipulations of both the speaker's and the recipient's expectations of receiving further information (e.g., Higgins, McCann, & Fondacaro, 1982).

In sum, evidence abounds that communicators in both natural and labora-tory conditions go to great lengths to ensure that their messages are mutually understood. However, although the ubiquity with which the achievement of shared reality is attempted provides one index of its importance in the modulation of social interaction, the hypothesis of shared reality is predicated on the actual establishment of shared reality—the issue to which we now turn.

Shared Reality Is Achieved

From the perspective of shared reality, evidence of attempts to modulate communication by taking others into account would be academic if the attempts were not successful. However, evidence suggests that perspective taking is indeed successful in the achievement of shared reality. In an early study, for example, Krauss, Vivekananthan, and Weinheimer (1968) asked subjects to describe color chips either for their own use or for someone else's, and found that the chips were more accurately identified by others when they were originally intended for another person. Mutual understanding was achieved because messages intended for another person employed conventional color terminology as well as comparisons to colors of broadly familiar objects, whereas those intended for the subject's own use were more likely to involve idiosyncratic associations. More recent experiments have also demonstrated that subjects are better able to correctly identify referents of messages intended for another's use than of those intended for personal use (e.g., Fussell & Krauss, 1989a). Further, evidence suggests that shared realities established in ongoing relationships can facilitate subsequent mutual understanding. For example, Fussell and Krauss (1989b) found that descriptions addressed to a specific friend communicated more effectively to that friend than to a randomly selected recipient. Shared reality can be achieved even under conditions that involve highly confusable stimuli. For example, Hupet et al. (1991) demonstrated that establishing efficacious communication required more time and effort when either the discriminability or codability of the stimuli was low than when it was high. By the final trial of the study, however, dyads in all conditions were equally proficient at communicating about the stimuli. The achievement of shared reality has been documented in more ecological conditions as well. For example, Sturgis (1959) found that teachers' knowledge of their students' background was associated with superior learning.

The achievement of shared reality is reflected by a variety of linguistic phenomena—including the fact that indefinite and definite articles distinguish between initial acts of reference and subsequent ones (Linde & Labov, 1975; Osgood, 1971; Sridhar, 1988). Use of the definite article implies that the noun following the article is already known rather than "new" information (e.g., *a* boat versus *the* boat). Hence, comparing the use of definite versus indefinite articles is one index of the degree to which the information conveyed in communication is assumed to be mutually known. In one study, Hupet and Chantraine (1992) manipulated whether subjects believed they were interacting with the same partner over the course of four trials in which they communicated about a set of nonsense figures. Subjects who believed that they were addressing the same individual were more likely to use definite articles on subsequent trials than those who thought they were addressing a different partner on each trial.

Given evidence that more communicative activity is required under conditions in which shared reality is difficult to achieve (as indicated by elaborate descriptions, more feedback, etc.), and that communicative behaviors such as comments and questions increase when there is a disconfirmation of expectations (Stamm, 1972) or a deviancy from consensus (Schachter, 1951), the achievement of shared reality is reflected by communicative abbreviation. In particular, several studies have established that communicators' referring messages become shorter with repeated reference to the same stimulus, and that the total number of speaking turns taken by communicators declines over subsequent encounters with the stimulus, both of which indicate when meaning of the reference is mutually understood (e.g., Clark & Wilkes-Gibbs, 1986). For example, Krauss and Weinheimer (1964, 1967) found that when pairs of communicators repeatedly referred to nonsense figures their descriptions became more succinct over successive occasions of mention. This abbreviation phenomenon has been replicated in a variety of studies using nonsense figures, (Clark & Wilkes-Gibbs, 1986; Hupet, Chantraine, & Neff, 1993; Hupet et al., 1991; Wilkes-Gibbs & Clark, 1992), as well as studies employing more everyday objects, locations, and people (Clark & Schaefer, 1987; Fussell & Krauss, 1993; Garrod & Anderson, 1987; Isaacs & Clark, 1987; Schober, 1993).

Consistent with the hypothesis of shared reality, research suggests that the maintenance of shared reality requires ongoing social verification. For example, communicators in the Clark and Wilkes-Gibbs (1986) experiment often requested clarifying information and frequently proposed additional details to ensure understanding in the early trials of the experiment. However, by the later trials, when a joint perspective had been achieved, communications were usually accepted without further verbal communication (see also Fussell & Krauss, 1992; Hupet et al., 1991; Isaacs & Clark, 1987; Schober, 1993; Wilkes-Gibbs & Clark, 1992). Krauss and colleagues have directly implicated such feedback in the achievement of shared reality by demonstrating that under conditions in which communicators' feedback is delayed or otherwise disrupted, the abbreviation effect is reduced (Krauss & Bricker, 1966; Krauss & Weinheimer, 1966).

Especially important evidence of the establishment of shared reality is the appropriateness of responses to communicative attempts, for inappropriate responses imply that there has been a misunderstanding (e.g., Grice, 1971, 1975). In one line of study, for example, Traxler and Gernsbacher (1992, 1993) demonstrated that such feedback is employed in the modification of future communication, and that this in turn facilitates the achievement of a shared perspective. Subjects were asked to write descriptions of nonsense figures that would allow another person to identify the figure in an array of distractors. Each description was given to two subjects who attempted to identify the referent correctly. Half the original writers were given feedback about whether their descriptions were understood or not, and half were not given feedback. Communicators were then allowed to modify their descriptions. When communicators received feedback, the effectiveness of their messages increased over trials, as measured by their partners' accuracy in correctly identifying the referent. Without feedback, no improvement was observed.

The utility of ongoing communicative appropriateness in establishing shared reality is also revealed by evidence suggesting that even communicative styles come to be shared. For example, Garrod and Anderson (1987) had dyads play a computerized maze game that required subjects to refer to specific locations on the maze. Results indicated that (1) subjects employed a variety of communication strategies; and (2) the relative use of particular types of strategies was highly correlated within dyads but not across dyads, suggesting that subjects had developed a joint perspective on the maze. Interestingly, subjects rarely decided upon a strategy explicitly; instead, mutual understanding was achieved implicitly over the course of the interaction. Schober (1993) found that when communicators switched roles, they tended to adopt the referential strategy that their partners had just used. Complementary evidence is found in the group literature in research demonstrating that individuals adopt the decision-making strategies used by their group later when they work individually, both on the same type of problems that their group worked on (e.g., Laughlin & Ellis, 1986), and on different but related problems (e.g., Stasson, Kameda, Parks, Zimmerman, & Davis, 1991).

Consistent with the notion that shared reality is achieved ipsatively, from situation to situation and partner to partner, evidence suggests that communicators do not assume that the joint perspective achieved with one partner can be extended to a new partner, even when the new partner was privy to the previous conversation. In a two-phase experiment, Wilkes-Gibbs and Clark (1992) found that the participatory status of subjects in one conversation was an important determinant of the collaborative strategy employed in a second conversation. Each subject first communicated about nonsense figures with one partner. In the second phase, each subject performed the same task using the identical stimuli but with a different partner. The crucial manipulation was the participatory status the second partner had adopted in the first phase of conversation. During the first conversation, the second partner had been either (1) an "omniscient" bystander, who could see the figures and hear the conversation via audiovisual link; (2) a side participant, who did not verbally participate but was physically proximal, could hear the conversation and see the figures, and could also see and be seen by the other participants; (3) a bystander, who was situated at some distance from the focal interaction and could hear the conversation but could not see the figures; or (4) a completely naive partner who was not present for the initial interaction.

Participatory status affected perceived shared reality, as indicated both by message length and by the use of definite versus indefinite articles. In the second phase, communicators with naive partners or either of the bystanders from the first phase switched immediately from using definite references (as they had been doing by the end of the first phase) to indefinite articles. Moreover, messages to naive partners and bystanders at the beginning of the second phase were over twice as long as messages had been at the end of the first phase. Messages to side participants from the first phase, although longer than they had been by the end of the first phase with the initial partner, were appreciably shorter than messages to naive participants and bystanders, including "omniscient" bystanders. This finding is striking evidence that the shared reality afforded by actual participation in communicative activity is not easily duplicated, even under conditions in which the referent-relevant information required for common ground is otherwise available. Even though omniscient bystanders were privy to all the information required to achieve common ground (i.e., which referent expressions applied to which objects), the audiovisual link did not fully afford the achievement of shared reality established by actual interaction.

This finding suggests that shared reality and common ground are not equivalent concepts (see Higgins, 1992b), and that the benefits of social interaction exceed the transmission of explicit, task-relevant information (cf. Schachter, 1959). Shared reality varied directly with the amount and quality of *actual* social interaction. Not only was the shared reality achieved by side participants more complete than that achieved by omniscient bystanders, but the shared reality achieved by full participants (by the end of the first phase) was greater than that achieved by side participants (at the beginning of the second phase). Employing a similar procedure, Schober and Clark (1989) demonstrated that subjects who merely overheard the initial interaction identified the intended referents less accurately than participants, suggesting that such differences in shared reality do in fact affect communicators' understanding.

In sum, research indicates that communicators' attempts to establish shared reality in the course of interaction are met with success. Shared knowledge is established through communicative negotiation, which facilitates further interaction. Evidence suggests that shared reality is negotiated ipsatively, as appropriate to the immediate task and with each new communicative partner, even if the new partner has been partially privy to previous similar interactions. Finally, efforts to achieve shared reality have consequences for the recipients' understanding of communicative messages. We now examine evidence that further implicates shared reality in the creation of meaning—in particular, not only for recipients of messages, but also for speakers.

Shared Reality and the Communicator: The Creation of Meaning

As we have seen, research in the communication literature has emphasized how individuals take into account their audience's knowledge of a topic (e.g., Krauss & Fussell, in press). Other research demonstrates that communicators also take others' attitudes into account (Manis et al., 1974; Newtson & Czerlinsky, 1974). From the perspective of shared reality, however, it is important to examine how taking others into account influences one's own representation of knowledge—that is, how it creates meaning for the communicator of the message.

Several studies demonstrate that perspective taking creates meaning as assessed by memory measures. For example, Anderson and Pitchert (1978) found that subjects remembered different, role-consistent aspects of a house they examined, depending upon whether they had adopted the perspective of a burglar or a home buyer (see also Bellezza & Bower, 1981; Clark & Woll, 1981; Snyder & Uranowitz, 1978). In a classic study demonstrating effects of communicative intent on representation, Zimmerman and Bauer (1956) found that subjects who expected to communicate information they received on an issue to an audience with a particular attitude on that issue remembered information that was congruent with the audience's attitude better than information that was incongruent.

In more recent studies, Higgins and colleagues have demonstrated the role of perspective taking in the creation of meaning for communicators. For example, Higgins and Rholes (1978) found not only that messages were tailored to audience attitudes, but that this perspective taking, in turn, affected the communicators' own judgment and memory. Subjects were given a target description of a person and led to believe that someone they expected to interact with either liked or disliked the target person about whom their communication centered. Descriptions were distorted positively when subjects believed that their partner liked the target, but distorted negatively when subjects believed that their partner disliked the target. Evidence that shared reality was achieved was demonstrated by effects of the descriptions on the communicators' own attitudes about the target. Under conditions in which subjects communicated with their partners, subjects' attitudes about the target were more positive when their partners' attitudes were positive, but more negative when their partners' attitudes were negative—an effect that did not obtain under conditions in which subjects did not actually communicate with their partners. Finally, results indicated that the shared reality achieved by communicating about the target had a lasting impact. Communicators' memory for the original target description became increasingly distorted over a 2-week period in the direction of their audience-tailored messages (cf. Bartlett, 1932; Ross, 1989).

In another study, Higgins et al. (1982) demonstrated that communicators varied their message description of a stimulus person, depending on whether their recipient had been exposed to the same or different information about the person, and that this variation also produced effects on the communicators' own perception and memory. Subjects were told that their partner had read the same paragraph or a different paragraph describing a stimulus target. Prior to communication, subjects were asked to reproduce the paragraph word for word. Subjects then communicated about the target person to their partner. Finally, subjects were again asked to reproduce the original stimulus paragraph. Results indicated that communicators' descriptions of the stimulus person were less distorted when they believed that their listener had different information about the stimulus person than when they believed the listener had identical information—a finding consistent with the goal of providing maximally informative information (see Grice, 1975). These differences in communication produced corresponding effects on memory. Reproductions of the stimulus paragraph became more accurate after communicating to a listener with "different" information, but became less accurate after communicating to a listener with "identical" information. Similar results have been obtained under conditions in which subjects are given the information about the message target before they receive communication instructions or learn about the audience attitude (Sedikides, 1990).

Interestingly, communicators appear to take the audience into account when creating messages, but do not take the audience into account when later using the message in reconstructive memory (see Higgins & Stangor, 1988). Hence, one reason why social action is so influential on communicators' own understanding over time is that it is very difficult to calibrate the extent to which the social circumstances, which in large part determine message meaning, change from situation to situation. For example, McCann, Higgins, and Fondacaro (1991) had male subjects interact face to face with two confederates across two experimental sessions about a target person. Communicators were led to believe that their summaries would be used to help the others decide whether or not to accept the target as a roommate. The confederate mentioned incidentally that he either "kinda liked" or "kinda disliked" the target. Results indicated that communicators tailored their messages to the first audience, despite the fact that the recipient stated that his impression was based only on a brief interaction, and that accurate information would be the most useful for his decision. Communicators also tailored their messages to a second confederate after either a brief delay (15 minutes) or a long delay (1 week). However, after a long delay, the evaluative tone of second message was determined more by the evaluative tone of the first message. This suggests that, all other things being equal, and given a difference in the shared reality achieved between communicative interactions, the first interaction will determine more what (shared) reality is utilized (see Zimmerman & Bauer, 1956).

Although all things rarely are equal under ecological conditions, these findings provide an important clue toward an eventual understanding of the relationship between competing shared realities. That is, under conditions in which one shared reality has already been established, it can survive at least for a time to influence individual judgment and experience, even under subsequent conditions in which a competing shared reality is established. Further research is necessary to establish the conditions in which a once-shared reality may survive in the face of new interactions that produce incompatible shared realities. However, findings from the construct accessibility literature offer a plausible working hypothesis (e.g., Bargh, Lombardi, & Higgins, 1988; Higgins & King, 1981; Higgins, Bargh, & Lombardi, 1985). This research demonstrates that temporarily accessible information may become "chronically accessible" if it is repeatedly employed in social judgment. Likewise, once a particular shared reality has been established and repeatedly realized over multiple social interactions, it too may become chronically accessible for the individual, even in subsequent interactions in which competing shared realities are afforded.

It is interesting to note that evidence of shared reality through audience tuning appears to fly in the face of Grice's (1975) maxim of relevance, in which communicators are said to attempt to provide one another with maximally informative information. In this case, the maxim of relevance would suggest that communicators should give a different impression of the target (at least when it is accurate) than the audience already has. However, in some cases, perhaps especially when new relationships are being established, the achievement of shared reality may supersede goals of relevance and informativeness (cf. Hilton, 1991; Schwarz, 1994; Trope, 1986). For example, Brown and Levinson (1978) demonstrated that communicators will sacrifice the maxims of "quality," "quantity," and "manner" for the sake of politeness. These kinds of results provide converging evidence that the achievement of shared reality not only may be necessary for the individual's grasp of reality, but may also be utilized to regulate social interaction.

Shared Reality in the Regulation of Social Interaction

Given the crucial functions of shared reality in the construction and maintenance of experience, as well as its regular achievement in ongoing social interaction, individuals may attempt to further regulate social interaction by exerting control over when, how, and with whom they cooperate in the achievement of shared reality. Evidence suggests that in some circumstances people do indeed wrest control over social interaction by modulating which reality is shared with whom. For example, the literature on "speech accommodation" shows that communicators will shift their speech style to converge with or diverge from the speech style of their audience, in order to associate themselves with or dissociate themselves from their audience (e.g., Giles, Mulac, Bradac, & Johnson, 1987; Giles & Smith, 1979).

Particularly interesting conditions in which shared reality functions to regulate social distance are those that involve "multiple audiences," in which communication occurs among a variety of people who share different spheres of information (e.g., Fleming & Darley, 1991). For example, in a cocktail party conversation that involves one's spouse, one's boss, and a visiting uncle, each member may be said to hold a different "participatory status," as defined by who shares which realities with whom (Clark & Carlson, 1982; Goffman, 1959). One basic problem in such a situation concerns how to formulate messages that will communicate best to all. Communicators may attempt to take into account the perspective of each individual addressee, or may attempt to generalize across the group (e.g., Volosinov, 1986).

Another multiple-audience problem involves attempts to share a particular set of information with one part of the audience but to exclude others who are nevertheless simultaneously participating in the conversation (Fleming & Darley, 1991; Fleming, Darley, Hilton, & Kojetin, 1990). That is, one may want to maintain different shared realities with different participants. For example, teenagers are notorious for employing slang that their parents do not understand, or, better, misunderstand in a benign way. Although the multiple-audience problem poses a unique set of regulatory problems that must be negotiated in communication, people nevertheless appear to be quite adept at solving them (for a review, see Fleming, 1994).

Several factors appear to mediate the degree to which communicators will attempt to achieve shared reality with another. For example, convergence of attitudes or opinions is especially likely under conditions in which communicators are attracted to or seek approval from the audience (e.g., Giles et al., 1987). Such attraction or approval seeking is defined in large part by the power relations of the communicators (e.g., Fiske, 1993; Kelman, 1958; French & Raven, 1959; Kelley, 1979). Considerable evidence exists that persons high in authoritarianism are more responsive and deferential to a higher-status partner than are persons low in authoritarianism (e.g., Adorno, Frenkel-Brunswik, Levinson, & Sanford, 1950; Berg & Vidmar, 1975; Harvey & Beverly, 1961; Thibaut & Riecken, 1955), and some evidence suggests that low authoritarians may actually respond negatively to a higher-status partner (e.g., Epstein, 1965). Higgins (1992a) has summarized these various audience-tuning effects by characterizing them as (1) "supertuning" under conditions in which the establishment of shared reality is especially likely to occur; (2) "non-tuning" under conditions in which the establishment of shared reality is not attempted or resisted; and (3) "anti-tuning" under conditions in which the establishment of shared reality is not only actively resisted, but an alternative understanding is expressly adopted.

Most importantly, such evidence illustrates that shared reality may be used by communicators to modulate social relations. That is, people may differentially attempt to share reality in order to create or maintain social distance, or otherwise to regulate social relationships (Higgins, 1992a). For example, employing the same paradigm as Higgins and Rholes (1978), Higgins and McCann (1984) found that with a higher-status partner high authoritarians converged or supertuned in order to express association, whereas low authoritarians diverged or anti-tuned to express disassociation. When communicators' and partners had equal status, normal audience tuning was found. As in previous studies, communicators own memory was distorted in the direction of the tailored messages. Providing converging evidence, McCann and Hancock (1983) compared audience tuning between persons high and low in self-monitoring (see Snyder, 1979). Because high self-monitors are said to be motivated to act in situation-appropriate ways but low self-monitors are motivated to maintain consistency with "internal" values and beliefs, high self-monitors tailored their messages to the audience but low self-monitors did not. Congruent memory distortions were obtained for high but not low self-monitors.

Results suggesting that people modulate social relations through the regulation of shared reality may be interpreted as evidence that shared reality is not obligatory in social interaction, or that there are circumstances in which communicators' knowledge has a basis other than shared reality. However, we think that these findings are better understood in terms of competing shared realities. In particular, we believe that they are consistent with the assumption that newly alternative shared realities may be resisted, and older beliefs maintained and defended, to the extent that the older beliefs have a strong basis in being regularly shared with others. Consistent with models of information processing that delineate how new instantiations of information use may become chronically accessible if they have been applied frequently over a long period of time (e.g., Higgins, in press), we believe that experiences may be objectified temporarily within particular situations as a function of immediate social verification, as well as shared chronically with others over time. Further, it is likely that under conditions in which competing alternative shared realities are plausible alternatives, the shared reality that is adopted will be determined by the recency and frequency with which that reality has been shared in the past in combination with what realities are currently being shared.

Hence, even the studies demonstrating the differential extents to which communicators will adopt high-status partners' attitudes may be understood from the perspective of shared reality. It is likely, for example, that low authoritarians have a history of sharing with significant others the reality that demanding authorities, or those who press for compliance, should be actively resisted. On the other hand, high authoritarians have probably shared with significant others the alternative reality that the attitudes of authorities require special consideration. Unless these particular realities cease to be socially supported, or until alternative shared realities are achieved and regularly realized, they should be expected to regulate social interaction in circumstances in which obvious power discrepancies exist. The corollary of this hypothesis is that in the absence of regular social verification, even chronically shared realities may not be maintained for long under conditions in which a sustained attack is posed through the selection and verification of an alternative, competing reality. For example, Schein (1956) found that even very basic beliefs in capitalism held by most U.S. prisoners of war during the Korean conflict were changed when the prisoners came to share the reality of their communist captors in Chinese prison camps. Although the prisoners initially resisted their re-education, most were isolated from the social support of like-minded others, and hence eventually came to share the view of their captors by adopting a previously unimagined appreciation for communism. Equally important is Schein's finding that the same process occurred in reverse when the prisoners returned to the United States. Although upon return most espoused pro-communist beliefs, these beliefs typically changed as their new social conditions not only afforded well-orchestrated attacks on their newer communist beliefs, but also reinstantiated social support for their older capitalist ideology (see also Newcomb, 1943; Newcomb, Koenig, Flacks, & Warwick, 1967).

In sum, why might shared reality achieved through social tuning be an especially powerful force in creating meaning? Social tuning not only involves taking others into account, but also involves achieving a common understanding of the world that in turn facilitates social interaction. Hence, the establishment of shared reality is basic to social regulation. Socialization involves people's learning how other respond to the world, including how others respond to them, and using this knowledge in self-regulation. As a basic feature of the self-regulatory system, then, social tuning is charged with motivational significance, including serving the basic needs of nurturance and security, which are essential to the establishment and maintenance of the self (see Higgins, 1989b, 1996).

Shared Reality in the Regulation of Self

We have seen that processes of shared reality are involved in the creation of meaning for the individual. Achieving shared reality in social interaction also affects the representation of information, which is strong evidence that shared reality creates meaning for the participants. Given that the lineage of the hypothesis of shared reality may be traced through the writings of the social behaviorists to the symbolic-interactionist theories of sociology, it should be no surprise that we would expect to find similar evidence of shared reality in the development, maintenance, and regulation of the self (cf. Cooley, 1902; Mead, 1934; Stryker & Statham, 1985). As Mead (1934) argued, even self-awareness is established through social interaction:

> The individual experiences himself as such, not directly, but only indirectly, from the particular standpoints of other individual members of the same social group, or from the generalized standpoint of the social group as a whole . . . and he becomes an object to himself only by taking the attitudes of the other individuals toward himself within a social environment or context of experience and behavior in which both he and they are involved. (p. 138)

We turn now to evidence suggesting that, once established, the shared realities achieved and utilized in social interaction function for self-regulation, closing the dialogical circle of self and society (cf. Mead, 1934, 1956; Piaget, 1976; Vygotsky, 1962, 1978).

Shared Reality in Development

Today, it is safe to say that the most fundamental assumption shared by theories of socio-emotional development is that children learn to regulate themselves in relation to the desires and demands of the significant others in their lives (e.g., Case, 1985, 1988; Damon & Hart, 1986; Fischer, 1980; Selman, 1980). Indeed, some have suggested that the only means by which a child can establish an understanding of the outside world is as it is objectified through social interaction (e.g., Berger & Luckmann, 1966; Mead, 1982; Vygotsky, 1962, 1978). Very early in development, children exhibit the capacity to associate events (e.g., Case, 1988; Kagan, 1984), which affords communication with others. Not only does emerging communicative activity qualitatively change the course of social and cognitive development, it is the mechanism by which self and society are integrated. By the end of the second year, a dramatic shift in children's representation of the world has occurred, which is usually associated with the emergence of symbolic representation (Bruner, 1964; Case, 1985; Fischer, 1980; Huttenlocher & Higgins, 1978; Piaget, 1951; Werner & Kaplan, 1963). Because children can now consider the bidirectional relationship between themselves and another person, children are capable of role taking—the ability to anticipate the responses of others to their actions and the personal consequences of these social responses (e.g., Bertenthal & Fischer, 1978; Harter, 1983; Lewis & Brooks-Gunn, 1979). These self–other contingencies link a child to the larger society by providing the social meanings of the child's attributes, affording new forms of self-regulation such as social identification. Shortly thereafter, children shift from "egocentric" to "nonegocentric" thought (Case, 1985; Feffer, 1970; Fischer, 1980; Flavell, Botkin, Fry, Wright, & Jarvis, 1968; Piaget, 1965; Selman & Byrne, 1974; Werner, 1957), which indicates the emergence of full-fledged perspective taking (Higgins, 1981b; Shantz, 1983). Children infer expectations, values, and preferences that others have about them. Hence, they can self-regulate in reference to another person's standpoint on them, giving them both the ability and the motivation to acquire internalized standards or "self-guides" (Gesell & Ilg, 1946; Fischer & Watson, 1981; Higgins, 1990; Higgins, Loeb, & Moretti, in press).

Hence, the early developmental sequence engenders the incorporation of others' knowledge, expectations, and desires in social regulation and ultimately in self-regulation. Children soon learn the complex of social attitudes that will guide their own self-understanding and behavioral regulation, including others' beliefs about their duties and obligations as well as others' hopes and aspirations for them (e.g., Higgins, 1989a; Higgins et al., in press). That is, shared reality appears to be implicated in the most basic processes of self-regulation, including the establishment and maintenance of security and nurturance, which are the very bases of survival (see Bowlby, 1969, 1973; Damon, 1977; Higgins, 1996).

Chronic and Temporary Shared Realities about the Self

Increasingly, research on the self has focused upon motivation, including ego protection (e.g., Greenwald, 1980), future achievement (e.g., Markus & Nurius, 1986), as well as goals and standards concerning who one "ought" or "ideally" would like to become (Higgins, 1989a, 1991; Rogers, 1951; Schlenker & Weigold, 1989). We believe that each aspect of self-identification and self-regulation is influenced by processes of shared reality, particularly by one's personal history of social recognition and verification. Most research in social psychology, however, has emphasized the self-concept—that is, people's view of the attributes that *actually* characterize them (e.g., Greenwald & Pratkanis, 1984; Markus & Wurf, 1986; McGuire & McGuire, 1988; Wylie, 1979). It is this literature to which we now turn to illustrate the role of shared reality in the establishment and maintenance of self-understanding.

Shared reality is implicated in the regulation of self as demonstrated by two complementary processes. On the one hand, research suggests a crucial role for ongoing, immediate social verification in the regulation of one's current experience of self. That is, much of one's experience of self is determined by what understandings about the self are being shared in the current social situation. On the other hand, research also suggests that over time, certain aspects of self that are shared regularly with significant others may become relatively resistant to change and actively defended, even in circumstances that would seem to offer more self-enhancing alternatives. Such chronically shared realities may lend a certain stability to the experience of self, even as it navigates changing circumstances and their concomitant variety of newly shared, self-relevant experiences. We consider each of these complementary processes in turn.

The shared reality achieved temporarily within a particular situation can have powerful effects on one's experience of self, even when it involves self-related values and beliefs that have been held with conviction over a long period of time. For example, current experience of self is known to be defined in part as a function of (1) salient characteristics of others (e.g., Morse & Gergen, 1970; Strack, Schwarz, Chassein, Kern, & Wagner, 1990); (2) current behavior of others (e.g., Brickman, Coates, & Janoff-Bulman, 1978; Festinger, 1954; Schachter, 1959, 1964); (3) immediate standards of comparison (e.g., Clark, Martin, & Henry, 1993; Higgins & Stangor, 1988; Manis & Armstrong, 1971); (4) current evaluations of others (e.g., Gergen, 1965; Snyder & Swann, 1978); (5) one's own strategic self-presentation (e.g., Jones, Rhodewalt, Berglas, & Skelton, 1981); (6) currently salient autobiographical information (e.g., Fazio, Effrein, & Falender, 1981; McGuire & McGuire, 1988; Salancik & Conway, 1975); and (7) currently salient social relationships (e.g., Baldwin, Carrell, & Lopez, 1990).

Such findings are typically explained in terms of individual cognitive or motivational mechanisms, which are assumed to be principally independent of interpersonal relationships. Yet virtually all such demonstrations include the real or implied presence of others, and thus allow for the possibility that processes of shared reality may be involved. In an experiment that directly implicates the operation of shared reality, Tice (1992) found that subjects internalized their own behavior (whether indicating emotional expressiveness or emotional stability) as representing their "true selves" significantly more when it was expressed to a peer than when it was expressed anonymously. Control conditions, as well as independent ratings of subjects' behavior indicated that the effect could not be attributed to subjects' behaving differently in the public versus private conditions. In a second experiment, the effect was generalized to another dimension of self and linked to subjects' subsequent behavior with a confederate. Subjects who publicly behaved in an introverted or extraverted manner internalized the behavior more than subjects who performed the identical behavior privately. Effects of public behavior on the self-concept were further reflected by subjects' behavior with the confederate, as assessed by sitting distance and the degree to which they initiated and participated in conversation with the confederate (cf. Fazio et al., 1981).

In an especially striking demonstration, Ross, Amabile, and Steinmetz (1977) found that temporary role enactments have large effects on the experience of self. In the experiment, subject pairs randomly assigned to role participated in a "quiz game," in which one partner attempted to give correct answers to general knowledge questions posed by the other. Although "contestants" were able to answer a significant proportion of the questions correctly, this performance was perceived by the contestants themselves as undistinguished. By design, "questioners" asked only questions to which they knew the answers, and hence appeared to be more knowledgeable than "contestants," despite the fact that this difference in perceived knowledge was completely defined by the roles that the participants had adopted in the quiz game. Nevertheless, the contestants themselves came to believe that the questioners had a greater command of general knowledge than they did.

Further evidence consistent with the hypothesis that current self-understanding through social interaction creates meaning for the participants is indicated by findings implicating changes in how the self is cognitively represented. Hardin (1994) demonstrated that the shared reality achieved in the quiz game situation affected not only subjects' perceptions of themselves and their partners, but memory for their own previous self-evaluations. In one experiment, after participating in a quiz game procedure adapted from Ross et al. (1977), subjects attempted to recall self-evaluations they had made several weeks previously in another situation. Results indicated that subjects' memory for their own previous self-evaluations was distorted congruently toward the current shared reality that had been established in the quiz game.

These findings are consistent with other research demonstrating that people's memory of their personal history tends to be consistent with their currently shared understanding of reality (e.g., Ross, 1989; Ross & Conway, 1986). For example, McFarland and Ross (1987) found that subjects' evaluations of themselves and their dating partners' past demeanor was highly correlated with their current understanding of the relationship, whether positive or negative. In addition, several experiments have demonstrated that attitudes currently shared with the experimenter about exercise and personal hygiene produce corresponding memory distortions about the frequency with which subjects remember exercising, brushing their teeth, and bathing in recent months (Olson & Cal, 1984; Ross, McFarland, Conway, & Zanna, 1983; Ross, McFarland, & Fletcher, 1981). Such results provide converging evidence, in concert with research on audience tuning in communication, that the shared reality achieved in ongoing social interaction has important consequences for cognitive representation. Not only does currently shared reality affect communicators' judgments of some external social target, but it even exerts influence on one's understanding of one's own history of behavior and self-evaluation.

Complementary research demonstrating the role of temporarily shared reality in the experience of self comes from literatures suggesting that aspects of self that have been socially recognized and shared over a long period of time may be able to survive temporary challenge, especially under conditions in which the currently posed alternative is weak or is proposed by an unreliable source. That is, over time, like any other information that is regularly utilized, the self-understanding achieved through a consistently shared reality may become chronically utilized (e.g., Higgins, 1990, in press).

The extent to which historically shared information is defended is illustrated by literatures documenting that people's behavior often functions to verify, protect, and maintain their extant conceptions and evaluations of themselves (e.g., Swann, 1990). Counterintuitively, such behavior can occur at the expense of ego protection, since people sometimes act in ways that maintain even very negative self-concepts (cf. Greenwald, 1980). Whether information about the self is positive or negative, subjects (1) spend more time looking at remarks of a partner they suspect will confirm rather than disconfirm their self-concept (cf. Pyszczynski & Greenberg, 1987; Swann & Read, 1981a); (2) rate information as more diagnostic if it is consistent than if it is inconsistent with the self-concept (Swann & Read, 1981b); (3) indicate more confidence in partners who confirm than is ones who disconfirm the self-concept (Swann, Griffin, Predmore, & Gaines, 1987); (4) solicit more feedback that is consistent rather than inconsistent with the self-concept, even if they think it might make them depressed (Swann & Read, 1981b; Swann, Wenzlaff, Krull, & Pelham, 1992); and (5) intensify efforts to elicit self-consistent information when they think their partner has an inaccurate conception of them (Swann & Read, 1981a; Swann & Hill, 1982). The preference for new information consistent with the self-concept occurs more on dimensions on which subjects are certain rather than uncertain (cf. Pelham, 1991; Swann & Ely, 1984; Swann, Pelham, & Chidester, 1988; Trope, 1986). Remarkably, the pattern extends to people's interaction choices. Subjects will choose to interact with those who give unfavorable evaluations of them over those who give favorable evaluations of them if the unfavorable evaluations are consistent with their self-beliefs (Swann, Pelham, & Krull, 1989; Swann, Stein-Seroussi, & Giesler, 1992). Further, Swann, Hixon, and De La Ronde (1992) found that people were more committed to their marriages when the views of their spouses matched rather than mismatched their self-concepts. Subjects with high self-concepts were more committed to partners who appraised them positively, but subjects with low self-concepts were more committed to partners who appraised them negatively.

Various motives have been proposed to account for these kinds of findings, including needs for cognitive consistency (e.g., Lecky, 1945; Secord & Backman, 1965) and for dissonance reduction (e.g., Aronson, 1968; Steele, 1988; Tesser & Cornell, 1991), as well as more epistemic motives of uncertainty reduction (Trope, 1986) and the ability to predict and control the environment through self-verification (Swann, 1990). We believe that they also can be understood from the perspective of shared reality. In particular, evidence suggests that self-conceptions are themselves achieved through processes of sharing reality with significant others (e.g., Stryker & Statham, 1985). For example, Pelham and Swann (1994) found that subjects' self-concepts were highly correlated with their own mothers' and friends' views of them on dimensions of high certainty, but that the correlations were lower on dimensions of low certainty—a pattern that did not hold for randomly paired classmates and mothers. Further, the correlations between self-views and others' views were higher when the others were subjects' own mothers rather than classmates.

Such findings are consistent with the assumption that significant others are particularly important in the selection and maintenance of one's self-understanding (e.g., Cooley, 1902; Freud, 1923/1960; James, 1890; Mead, 1934). Congruently, we propose that people's preference for information that is consistent rather than inconsistent with their extant self-understanding occurs *because* it has a history of being shared with others. This preference is not only consistent with the hypothesis that shared reality is worth defending on basic epistemic grounds, but that shared reality functions in part to maintain valued social relationships (e.g., Cameron, 1963; Freud, 1937; Hoffman & Saltzstein, 1967; Kelman, 1958; Mowrer, 1960; Rommetveit, 1974; Stryker & Statham, 1985).

Shared Realities about the Self Are Utilized in Social Regulation

The hypothesis of shared reality implies that information about the self will be preferred to the extent that it is shared with others. That is, the more a given aspect of self has been recognized in the social verification process, the more "reality" it achieves, and the more likely it is that it will be maintained and defended. The preference for shared reality should hold for both positive and negative information, because the functions of shared reality are assumed to be principally independent of evaluative valence. Hence, the hypothesis of shared reality provides a useful complement to self-verification theory (e.g., Swann, 1990) in understanding the role of self-understanding in social regulation. In addition to providing an account of how self-understanding develops, shared reality subsumes some predictions of self-verification theory and makes additional predictions about which self-enhancement and self-verification theories are silent.

We explored these hypotheses in two experiments employing a preference paradigm (Hardin, Higgins, & Schachinger, 1995). In Experiment 1, subjects indicated whom they would prefer to meet in an upcoming study on the basis of impressions their potential partners supposedly held of them. In Experiment 2, subjects indicated which aspects of themselves they would prefer to learn more about from a supposedly newly developed computer program designed to make personality assessments. In both experiments, the attributes of self on which subjects made their choices were idiographically constructed from their responses to a questionnaire administered several weeks previously in an ostensibly unrelated psychological battery. In it, subjects had listed attributes they believed were characteristic of themselves, as well as attributes they believed significant others thought were characteristic of them. In the experiments, preference judgments were made between (1) attributes that were self-descriptive versus their opposites, and (2) self-descriptive attributes that were shared with significant others versus those that were not. Hence, the design allowed a replication of the basic self-verification finding, in which subjects prefer information about themselves that is consistent rather than inconsistent with the self-concept. In addition, the design allowed a test of the prediction unique to the shared-reality hypothesis—in particular, that subjects would prefer information about themselves that was shared with significant others to unshared self-relevant information.

As part of a battery of tasks administered near the beginning of the term, each subject listed attributes characteristic of the self, as well as attributes believed about the subject by (1) the subject's mother, (2) the subject's father, (3) the subject's best friend, (4) people in general, and (5) a typical new acquaintance.[3] In addition, subjects rated the degree of certainty with which they believed each attribute they listed was truly self-descriptive. Subjects' responses were utilized in the idiographic construction of individualized attribute sets on which the preference judgments were made. A self-attribute was defined as "shared" if subjects believed at least one other thought the attribute characteristic of them, and "unshared" if the attribute was listed as self-descriptive only by the subject.[4] The shared and unshared attributes later given to subjects for their preference judgments were matched on certainty. Hence, any preferences for shared self-attributes over unshared self-attributes could not be attributed to differences in certainty. Finally, in both experiments, subjects made preference judgments on attributes that they had listed as self-descriptive, as well as attributes that another "yoked" subject had listed as self-descriptive. This procedure provided experimental control for any effects of the content of the attributes.

EXPERIMENT 1   Subjects were contacted by telephone, ostensibly to be recruited for an upcoming study concerning "how people get acquainted." Subjects were asked to choose among several potential interaction partners they would prefer to meet who had supposedly formed impressions of them on the basis of the psychology inventory they had completed earlier that term. In a two-phase procedure, subjects were asked to consider the various impressions of them held by those who had examined their responses, and to choose whom they would prefer to meet in the upcoming study. In the first decision phase, each attribute and its opposite were presented for a preference judgment. For example: "One person thought you seemed *opinionated,* but another person thought you seemed *not opinionated.* Which person would you prefer to meet?" Alternatively: "One person thought you seemed *gullible,* but another person thought you seemed *not gullible.* Which person would you prefer to meet?" Subjects were given at least three attributes and their opposites they had listed earlier as self-descriptive, as well as at least three yoked control attributes and their opposites. In the second decision phase, subjects chose between partners who held impressions that were "shared" versus "unshared." Each impression pair consisted of either positive attributes or negative attributes. For example: "One person thought you seemed *lazy,* but another person thought you seemed *depressed.* Which person would you prefer to meet?" Here too, subjects indicated their preferences on both self-descriptive attributes and yoked control attributes. In all, subjects made no more than 12 and no fewer than 8 choices across both decision phases.

From the perspective of shared reality, subjects were predicted to choose to interact with partners whose impressions were (1) consistent rather than inconsistent with their self-concepts, even if the impressions were negative; and (2) "shared" versus "unshared" attributes, whether positive or negative. As predicted by both self-verification theory and the shared-reality hypothesis, subjects chose reliably more partners who held self-consistent rather than inconsistent impressions of them. Not only was the overall relationship reliable, but it remained reliable when choices were broken down by trait valence: Subjects chose partners whose impressions were consistent rather than inconsistent, whether the impressions were positive or negative. The preference for confirming over disconfirming partners was not found on the yoked attributes.

Strong support for the unique prediction of shared reality was also found. Subjects chose reliably more partners whose confirmatory impressions of them were "shared" rather than "unshared." Again the relationship held whether the impressions were positive or negative, suggesting that shared reality is not moderated by valence. And, again, the preference for impressions that were shared versus unshared was not found for the yoked attributes.

EXPERIMENT 2   The procedure of Experiment 2 essentially replicated that of Experiment 1. Subjects were contacted by telephone, ostensibly to be recruited for an upcoming study concerning "the development of a new computer program designed to make personality assessments." Subjects were told that an initial run of the program had utilized data from the psychological inventory they had completed earlier in the term to generate a series of attributes describing them. Subjects were asked to choose the self-attributes they were most interested in learning more about in an upcoming study in which the computer program would generate a more detailed analysis. Subjects indicated their preferences in a two-phase procedure that mimicked Experiment 1. For example, "One attribute generated about you was *unfocused,* but another was *excitable.* Which would you prefer to learn more about?" In all, each subject made 12 choices across both decision phases.

Again, the hypothesis of shared reality predicted that subjects would prefer to learn more information about aspects of the self that were (1) consistent versus inconsistent with their self-concepts, and (2) "shared" versus "unshared." Replicating Experiment 1, subjects preferred reliably more information that was consistent rather than inconsistent with their self-concepts whether it was positive or negative.

Support for the unique prediction of shared reality was also found, replicating Experiment 1. Subjects preferred to learn more about reliably more self-consistent attributes that were "shared" rather than "unshared" with significant others, whether the attributes were positive or negative, suggesting that shared reality is not moderated by valence. Importantly, the preference for attributes that were shared versus unshared was not found for the yoked attributes.

In sum, research from existing literatures as well as from our own laboratory suggests that shared reality is a promising theoretical strategy with which to integrate understanding of the development and maintenance of self-understanding. Shared reality is implicated in research demonstrating the role of immediate ongoing interaction in the construction of experience of self, as well as in research demonstrating that well-established self-concepts may be defended in new situations that offer alternative understandings of the self. The analysis is corroborated by direct evidence from our own laboratory, which suggests that extant self-concepts are defended through the regulation of future social interaction to the extent that they are currently shared with significant others. Hence shared reality provides one synthesis of the decades-old debate concerning whether the self-concept is relatively fixed or fluid. In particular, self-understanding emerges from what is recognized and verified in ongoing social interaction, and this self-understanding may acquire some stability to the extent that aspects of self are grounded in a network of regular social verification. Finally, however, the perspective of shared reality implies that even highly valued, long-held beliefs about the self will not survive indefinitely if they cease to be verified by others or if competing aspects of self are newly recognized and regularly established in social interaction. The peculiarities of the degree to which self-concepts that are not supported by ongoing social verification can be maintained awaits direct research. However, current assumptions of cognitive theory suggest that the answer to this question may involve the frequency and recency with which particular existing aspects of self have been shared, in combination with what realities are newly established through social interaction.

GENERAL DISCUSSION AND CONCLUSIONS

> But the human essence is no abstraction inherent in each single individual. In its reality it is the ensemble of the social relations.
>
> —*K. Marx (1888/1970)*

> From the outset, we, the actors on the social scene, experience the world we live in as a world both of nature and of culture, not as a private but as an intersubjective one, that is, as a world common to all of us, either actually given or potentially accessible to everyone; and this involves intercommunication and language.
>
> —*A. Schutz (1962)*

> We must keep open the view that many distinctive psychological operations take form only within a social field and that the changes they produce alter individuals at their center.
>
> —*S. Asch (1952)*

The hypothesis of shared reality not only is consistent with the literatures we have already reviewed, but has several important implications for future research. Shared reality engages current empirical issues in social psychology, as well as suggesting an alternative to some prevailing metatheoretical assumptions that characterize the contemporary social psychological enterprise.

Further Empirical Implications of Shared Reality

We believe that the hypothesis of shared reality has implications for several prominent topics in social psychology, including stereotyping, attitude change, and group influences on the individual. We briefly consider each of these topics in turn.

Stereotyping and Attitudes

As traditionally defined, stereotypes are beliefs consensually held by individuals about social groups and their members (see Allport, 1954). Various functions have been attributed to stereotypes, including cognitive efficiency (e.g., Allport, 1954; Hamilton & Trolier, 1986), ego maintenance (e.g., Adorno et al., 1950; Allport, 1954; Katz & Braly, 1935), group justification (e.g., Allport, 1954; Sherif & Sherif, 1956; Tajfel, 1981; Oakes et al., 1994), and justification of the social status quo (e.g., Allport, 1954; Jost & Banaji, 1994; MacKinnon, 1989). The contemporary social-cognitive view of stereotypes has coalesced around issues of mental representation, or how information is organized and utilized in cognition (e.g., Banaji & Greenwald, 1994; Hamilton & Sherman, 1994; Stangor & Lange, 1994). Interestingly, with few exceptions, the consensual nature of stereotypes has not been emphasized in stereotyping theory. This is probably attributable in part to the fact that stereotypes are consensual by definition. It has been suggested recently, however, that existing theories of stereotyping may be distinguished in terms of consensus—that is, how they account for which stereotypes are held by whom (see Jost & Banaji, 1994).

The perspective of shared reality provides yet another alternative by implying that stereotypes exist in part *because* they are based in social consensus. Stereotypes serve social-regulatory functions by creating and maintaining social relationships, including relationships between social groups (cf. Tajfel & Turner, 1979; Oakes et al., 1994). In addition, because stereotypes are consensus-based "shared realities" about social groups, they may be maintained and defended by individuals in order to protect their own grasp of reality, even at the expense of the self. This is not to deny other functions of stereotyping, such as their role in perpetuating the status quo (e.g., Hoffman & Hurst, 1990; Jost & Banaji, 1994). Indeed, we view many of these functions as fully compatible with the perspective of shared reality.

The perspective of shared reality, however, does make empirical predictions that are not as easily derived from other stereotyping theories. For example, to the degree that stereotypes exist because they are shared, they may be relatively more fluid than alternative accounts would predict. Stereotypes should survive only so long as they benefit from social verification. Further, the use of a particular stereotype would be expected to be minimized to the extent that alternative beliefs are established and maintained in social interaction and stereotyping effects should be strongest to the degree that the stereotypes are grounded in shared reality.

Processes of shared reality may also be involved in stereotype subtyping (e.g., Crocker & Major, 1989; Judd & Park, 1988; Park, Ryan, & Judd, 1992). Common stereotypes of social groups are rarely monolithic, but instead appear to have a variety of potentially incompatible components. For example, although one stereotype of men is that they can be pious and responsible (e.g., "Father knows best"), another is that men can be irresponsible rakes (e.g., "Boys will be boys"). To the extent that each subtype represents a different consensual belief or shared reality, the perspective of shared reality suggests at least one counterintuitive implication. Inducing subjects to think about a variety of stereotypes of a particular group may actually reduce subsequent stereotyping. Why? Because the exercise demonstrates a lack of consensus about the reality of the target group, hence reducing the individual's confidence in the veracity of its understanding of the group (cf. Park et al., 1992).

Shared reality appears to be implicated in the maintenance and change of other beliefs and attitudes. For example, research suggests that the amount and type of cognitive activity are affected by the amount of social support a person expects to receive either during or outside the interaction (cf. Doms & Van Avermaet, 1985; Miller, Gross, & Holtz, 1991). Gross, Riemer, and Collins (1974) found that there was greater self-persuasion from producing a counterattitudinal essay when the communicators believed the audience considered them sincere than when they believed the audience considered them insincere. In a complementary finding, Carver and Humphries (1981) demonstrated that students who associated an opinion with a negative group showed less agreement with the position than did students who did not make the association (see also Asch, 1952).

Shared reality is also implicated by belief change that occurs in anticipation of future social interaction. For example, subjects who expect to interact with another target person remember information about that person better on a variety of measures (Devine, Sedikides, & Fuhrman, 1989; Fiske & Von Hendy, 1992; Osborne & Gilbert, 1992), and learn material better when they expect to teach it to others than when they do not (Bargh & Schul, 1980; Benware & Deci, 1984). Several hypotheses have been suggested to account for such effects, including the production of issue-relevant thought (e.g., Cialdini & Petty, 1981; McFarland, Ross, & Conway, 1984), as well as pre-emptive self-criticism, self-justification, and simply saying what others want to hear (e.g., Tetlock, 1992). We believe that many of these findings may be understood by assuming that attitude change occurs when people *expect* to share reality. If so, anticipatory attitude change should be a function of who the expected interaction partners are (e.g., a significant other, an expert, or a new acquaintance), and in particular the relevance of the anticipated interaction partner to the dimension of judgment. This hypothesis is consistent with findings demonstrating that attitude change is greater when the anticipated partner is an expert than a layperson (e.g., Fitzpatrick & Eagly, 1981).

Group Processes

The social-regulatory functions of shared reality are implicated by the extent to which social groups impose shared realities on and maintain them among their participants. For example, research indicates that (1) a group's efforts to transmit its norms are particularly strong when newcomers are involved (Levine & Moreland, 1991; Moreland & Levine, 1989); (2) groups provide newcomers with the knowledge, ability, and motivation they will need to play the role of full members (e.g., Van Maanen & Schein, 1979; Wanous, 1980); (3) newcomers are especially receptive to group influence (e.g., Van Maanen, 1977); and (4) opinion deviants receive more influence attempts by the group than others do (e.g., Festinger & Thibaut, 1951; Levine, 1989), particularly when the deviants appear to be uncertain about their position (Levine & Ranelli, 1978). Further, group members typically do not exchange all the information available to the members; instead, rather than disseminating unshared information, group discussions tend to be dominated by information that members initially share and that supports their initial preferences (e.g., Stasser, 1992).

If the establishment of shared reality creates meaning for the participants in social interaction, then the use of shared reality to modulate social regulation should influence individual understanding. In addition to research we have already discussed, support for this proposition can be found in research on the role of group membership in the formation and maintenance of individual attitudes, beliefs, and behavior (e.g., Asch, 1952; Deutsch & Gerard, 1955; Festinger, 1954; Kelman, 1958; Levine & Russo, 1987; Tajfel & Turner, 1986; Turner, Hogg, Oakes, Reicher, & Wetherall, 1987). Evidence includes well-known demonstrations of group polarization, in which participants in group discussions express increasingly extreme attitudes in the direction of the prevailing group position (e.g., Burnstein, 1982; Janis, 1982; Jellison & Arkin, 1977), as well as judgment convergence in the direction of inaccurate group norms (e.g., Asch, 1952). Importantly, research suggests not only that individuals act in ways that are consistent with the social groups to which they belong, but that this social regulation has consequences for individuals' privately held beliefs. For example, Charters and Newcomb (1952) found that increasing the salience of Roman Catholic students' religious identity by emphasizing their common religious identification caused students' opinions to shift toward more orthodox Roman Catholic beliefs (see also Gerard, 1954).

Traditionally, such group effects on the individual have been understood in terms of "informational" versus "normative" influences (cf. Deutsch & Gerard, 1955; Kelman, 1958; Moscovici, 1976). Informational influence involves the dependence of individuals on others for information, particularly when others are regarded as valid and reliable. This includes new and persuasive information, as well as social comparisons that reduce subjective uncertainty (cf. Festinger, 1954; Levine & Moreland, 1986; Suls & Miller, 1977; Trope, 1986). Normative influence or conformity involves the power of groups to regulate the behavior of individuals through demands, expectations, rewards, and punishments, including the groups' power to accept or reject individuals (cf. Deutsch & Gerard, 1955; Fenigstein, 1979; Kiesler & Kiesler, 1969; Levine & Russo, 1987; Nail, 1986). For example, group polarization effects, in which individuals over the course of discussion adopt increasingly extreme views in the direction of the prevailing group attitude, have been explained in terms of the new information afforded by the group discussion (e.g., Burnstein, 1982; Burnstein & Vinokur, 1977; Vinokur & Burnstein, 1978), as well as in terms of social desirability (e.g., Jellison & Arkin, 1977; Myers, Bruggink, Kersting, & Schlosser, 1980; Sanders & Baron, 1977).

In discussions of group influences that are not assumed to involve conformity or compliance, two mechanisms have been proposed. Under conditions in which alternative opinions are initially proposed by an individual and others, "informational influence" may occur, such that the individual is persuaded on the basis of new information provided by others who participate in the group discussion. Later, this information is used in the individual's opinion (e.g., Burnstein, 1982). On the other hand, in cases of "mediated memory" later opinion convergence occurs because individuals misremember the source of the new information by assuming that they had generated the information themselves (e.g., Bem & McConnell, 1970). Interestingly, both processes assume a fundamental distinction between information generated by the self versus that generated by others (i.e., "I" vs. "they"). The perspective of shared reality, in contrast, does not assume that opinion convergence is a memory error in which different subjectivities are mismanaged, but rather that shared reality changes the character of individual representations. For example, to adopt connectionist language (e.g., Smith, 1990), a particular thought may be characterized by a particular complex of activation states. To the extent that the thought is not shared with others, it is less likely to be reactivated. If it is shared, however, reactivation is more likely. Hence, sharing reality strengthens what is agreed upon, which in turn is more likely to be accurate (cf. Hinsz, 1990). The individual subjectivity is transformed through social consensus (i.e., "we") into an objective reality, which is experienced as an "entity" or "it" (see Kelley, 1967).

In a related vein, it is interesting to note that until relatively recently Kelman's (1958) observation that group influence can also occur because individuals identify with the group has been little studied, perhaps because the notion was difficult to operationalize. But the emergence of the social identity literature has brought issues of identification to the fore by emphasizing the individual's self-definition as a group member (Hogg & Turner, 1987a; Turner, 1982, 1985). In particular, individuals act to create or maintain positive social identities through processes of intergroup comparison. Social identity theory assumes that both normative and informational influences reflect the same underlying "self-categorization" or identification process. It proposes that group influence is maximized to the extent that individuals identify themselves as members of the group, and is minimized to the extent that individuals disidentify with the group. From this perspective, then, group polarization arises from the recognition of a shared group membership concerning the items under discussion (Mackie, 1986; Mackie & Cooper, 1984; Turner et al., 1987; Turner & Oakes, 1986; Wetherall, 1987). Research in this tradition has demonstrated that (1) individuals act in ways that distinguish their own group from other groups, particularly when group membership boundaries are salient (e.g., Abrams, 1985); (2) information is more influential when it comes from ingroup members than when it comes from other sources (e.g., Hogg & Turner, 1987b); (3) individuals endorse attitudes that increase their proximity to the stereotypical group position, even in the absence of explicit group pressure (e.g., Reicher, 1984); and (4) self-categorization processes moderate the autokinetic effect, judgment conformity, and group polarization (Abrams, Wetherall, Cochrane, Hogg, & Turner, 1990).

Although we applaud the new emphasis on the social aspects of individual behavior found in the social identity and self-categorization literatures, we believe that shared reality offers a useful alternative understanding of the role of groups in the construction and maintenance of individual perception, behavior, and attitudes. Although the perspectives of shared reality and of social identity both predict that processes of social identification should modulate group influence on the individual, they do so for different reasons. First, social identity theory assumes that social identities are managed in service of the individual's self-esteem (cf. Hogg & Abrams, 1988; Tajfel & Turner, 1979). Shared reality, in contrast, views social identification pragmatically—that is, in terms of its role in serving epistemic functions of reality construction and maintenance, as well as social regulation. Second, despite the role of social identity and self-categorization theories in renewing a proper emphasis on the social construction of individual experience (e.g., Turner et al., 1987), they remain essentially individualistic in several important ways. Social identification processes are performed by the individual to serve individual ego maintenance needs by means of individual cognitive categorization processes. Although social circumstances may moderate whether individuals view themselves in terms of their group identification or of an "individual" identification, they do so by making one or the other identity more cognitively salient. In contrast, the perspective of shared reality emphasizes the essential role of mutual, social cooperation in the regulation of self, including social identities—functions which, as we have seen, need not be gratifying to the self. We would hardly deny the role of individual cognitive representation in mediating these processes, but believe that even the most basic information processes are themselves crucially defined by the social activity in which they operate. Finally, we are uncomfortable with the distinction between social and individual identities proposed by social identity and self-categorization theories. If reified, such a terminological distinction would be unfortunate because we believe it unlikely that any identification could be described independently of some social relationship.

At the same time, the perspective of shared reality implies that social identification can proceed in a variety of ways that include but are not limited to abstract social categories. In particular, evidence suggests that shared reality is achieved in the service of valued relationships between people or valued reference groups, in which the individuals may or may not perceive themselves as members of the same social category (e.g., Siegal & Siegal, 1957). For example, although "basking in the reflected glory" of others typically occurs between those who share a currently valued relationship (e.g., Tesser, 1988), the individuals do not necessarily perceive themselves as forming a group. Further, attempts to achieve shared reality, regardless of group membership, seem to us to be a more plausible description of relatively temporary social convergence effects, such as those found in the literature on dyadic communication.

The perspective of shared reality may also be compared with Moscovici's (1976) theory of minority influence. Moscovici (1985) points out that the relationship between public acts of compliance and private acceptance or "conversion" remains theoretically problematic, but he argues that differences between majority and minority influence may be understood by comparing the respective cognitive processes of deviant individuals. Majority influence is characterized by compliance more than conversion because the individual does not ruminate on the controversial reality, presumably because the group opinion is perceived to represent current consensus. Perceiving relatively little power to influence the majority, the individual "is tempted to make concessions, being impelled by the need to reach a consensus, even if consensus is actually unjustified" (Moscovici, 1985, p. 394). Conversion is minimized because individual consideration of the majority position is superficial. Minority influence, in contrast, is characterized by conversion because members of the majority ruminate on how the minority members could possibly believe what they claim to believe. This produces a "validation process," in which the minority responses are examined with respect to the reality in question, "before seeking to negotiate an agreement and reestablishing a consensus" (Moscovici, 1985, p. 394). Conversion is maximized because in attempting to take the perspective of the minority in an effort to understand it, individuals are at least in part successful.

Interestingly, this account in both cases presupposes that individuals are motivated to achieve some social consensus—a motivation consistent with the perspective of shared reality. In addition, from the perspective of shared reality, minority conversion is minimal in the face of majority pressure because that very pressure makes the absence of shared reality salient. That is, the experience of feeling pressured undermines the experience of shared reality. Because the minority is not in a position to threaten or pressure for consensus, the lack of shared reality is less salient to majority members. This account could be tested by making the lack of shared reality salient to the majority. For example, the experimenter might say, "While you are reaching a group decision, it is important that you not feel pressured to adopt a position you do not believe." Although such an instruction would appear to reduce mere compliance, it might function implicitly to highlight the experience of feeling pressured, thereby reducing feelings of shared reality, and consequently conversion.

We should point out that the existing research regarding group influences on the individual is consistent with the perspective of shared reality. For example, even normative influence is greatest when individual behavior is open to actual (Deutsch & Gerard, 1955) or anticipated (Lewis, Langan, & Hollander, 1972) group surveillance, both of which would appear to afford or imply shared reality. Findings indicating that individuals are more influenced by groups in which they are members are also consistent with the perspective of shared reality. Such findings complement those of studies demonstrating the role of perspective taking in judgment and memory. Given the facility with which people can adopt the perspectives of others (e.g., Clark & Brennan, 1991; Stryker & Statham, 1985), even in situations that involve hypothetical perspectives or anticipated interaction (e.g., Anderson & Pitchert, 1978; Bargh & Schul, 1980; Jones & DeCharms, 1957), it is not surprising that individuals who actually participate in group activities adopt the perspective of their own group (e.g., Abrams et al., 1990; Burnstein, 1982).

Shared reality is implicated even in studies that traditionally have been understood in terms of disrupting individual self-regulation in social situations (e.g., Brown & Turner, 1981; Latané & Darley, 1970; LeBon, 1896). For example, "social loafing" studies show that the contribution of individuals in groups is less than their contribution alone, findings often understood in terms of "deindividuation" (Latané, Williams, & Harkins, 1979). However, social loafing can be reduced or eliminated by increasing the identifiability and uniqueness of members' task contributions (e.g., Harkins & Petty, 1982, 1983), ease of evaluating those contributions (e.g., Harkins & Szymanski, 1989), and members' accountability (e.g., Weldon & Gargano, 1988). Although the latter findings are typically understood in terms of reasserting individual self-regulation, each of these variables probably enhances the ability of individuals in groups to share reality, and in particular to reach a mutual understanding of task-appropriate behavior (e.g., "doing your share").

Some Metatheoretical Implications of Shared Reality

The story has now come full circle. First, we have proposed the hypothesis that the individual's grasp of reality is achieved and maintained through processes of social recognition and verification, which establish a "shared reality" that serves both epistemic and social-regulatory functions. Our review of the literature suggests not only that people attempt to achieve shared reality, but that these attempts succeed. Second, evidence suggests that the establishment of shared reality modulates the very construction and maintenance of meaning. Research reveals that shared reality facilitates social interaction and has profound representational implications, affecting both ongoing judgment and memory for past activity. Evidence suggests that shared reality plays a prominent role in the establishment and maintenance of the experience of self through two complementary processes. Shared reality established temporarily within particular situations has significant effects on individuals' experience of self, as well as on memory for their own earlier experience. In addition, evidence suggests that realities about the self shared with significant others—presumably with some regularity over a long period of time—may be defended in the face of newly posed alternatives, even at the expense of self-enhancement. Finally, we have suggested a few ways in which the perspective of shared reality engages issues concerning stereotyping, attitudes, and group influences on the individual. In sum, we believe that the perspective of shared reality offers a promising integration of individual and social contributions to the structure of individual experience, suggesting that they may be synthesized as complementary processes in a fully dialectical self-society system.

As such, the perspective of shared reality takes a clear stand in the long-running debate concerning the place of the individual in society, and more recently the privileged position of the individual in North American (social) psychology. Consistent with an emerging re-emphasis on the social foundations of individual behavior and cognition (Brewer, 1988; Fiske, 1993; Higgins, 1981a, 1992a, 1992b; Jost & Banaji, 1994; Levine et al., 1993; Markus & Kitayama, 1989; Ostrom, 1984; Resnick et al., 1991; Fiedler & Semin, 1993), the perspective of shared reality represents an empirically driven attempt to ground even the most basic aspects of cognition—including how experience is represented in memory—in terms of the individual's place in ongoing social activity.

It is worth noting that shared reality differs essentially from an important, if usually implicit, assumption in psychological theory that the individual stands somehow independent of its society. Although most theorists assume that society is one source of influence on the individual, a driving theme has been that psychological integrity is to be found in the individual (cf. Allport, 1961; Bakhtin, 1986; Cooley, 1902; Freud, 1923/1960; LeBon, 1896; Marx & Engels, 1846/1970; Mead, 1982; Moscovici, 1986; Piaget, 1976; Rogers, 1951; Skinner, 1953; Vygotsky, 1978; Weber, 1967; Wittgenstein, 1980). For example, LeBon (1896) assumed that the individual loses its normal self-regulatory ability in the crowd (cf. Reicher, 1984). Piaget (1976) assumed that social development is predicated on antecedent individual cognitive development (cf. Vygotsky, 1978). Freud (1923/1960) assumed that the fundamental conflict the individual faces is achieving the satiation of its desires against the strictures of society (cf. Dewey, 1922/1930). Both psychodynamic and behaviorist approaches assume a drive for individual need satisfaction, which provides "meaning" and "significance" (cf. Mead, 1934).

Contemporary social psychology also locates the basis of individual experience and behavior within the individual. Instead of social circumstances or processes of social interaction, theory in social psychology has focused on individually held psychological processes. For example, although individual behavior and experience are now assumed to be determined by a person–situation interaction (e.g., Higgins, 1990; Lewin, 1935; Mischel, 1968; Ross & Nisbett, 1991), theories proposed in part to explain cross-situational behavioral inconsistency have nevertheless emphasized individual processes, including individual capacities or competencies (e.g., Cantor & Kihlstrom, 1987), individual construals of self (e.g., Markus & Wurf, 1987; Swann, 1983, 1984), individual construals of situations (e.g., Cantor & Kihlstrom, 1987), individual goals and motives (e.g., Markus & Nurius, 1986), and even individually held tendencies to behave with consistency across situations (e.g., Bem & Allen, 1974; Snyder, 1979).

The perspective of shared reality, in contrast, views the individual as fully of the society in which it exists. Social influence is not the stepchild of individual choice, but is its very basis. Society's discontents do not exist in opposition to the social world. They are full participants in it. As Mead (1934, 1956, 1982) argued, the individual mind exists only among other minds that share understandings. If one's gesture evokes in oneself the functionally identical response that it does in others, it is no longer private. By being socially shared and accepted by others, it becomes objective and real. In relieving knowledge of its subjectivity, Mead broke with introspectionism, phenomenology, and, ultimately solipsism. By embracing this tradition in an empirically tractable way, we hope to pursue with others a truly social cognition.

Acknowledgments

This research was supported in part by Grant No. MH-10544 to Curtis Hardin and Grant No. MH-39429 to E. Tory Higgins from the National Institute of Mental Health. We are grateful to Miguel Brendl, Robert Krauss, Alexander Rothman, Helga Schachinger, John Skowronski, and Richard Sorrentino for thoughtful comments on a previous draft of this chapter.

Notes

1. We argue that shared reality is required for understanding what exists, as well as its function. Although these two aspects of knowledge are often distinguished, some have argued persuasively that they are mutually definitive—that is, function determines form (e.g., Dewey, 1929/1958; James, 1909; Mead, 1934; Wittgenstein, 1953, 1980).

2. It is important to point out that most, following Weber (e.g., 1967), have defined an action as a social action insofar as participants take others into account. This definitional strategy has been useful for delineating the applicable range of study for social psychology. But the perspective of shared reality makes the stronger, empirical claim that all experience—whether it be of social or seemingly nonsocial objects—is validated and objectified through social verification, which may be evidenced by perspective taking.

3. The instrument used was a modified form of the Selves Questionnaire (see Higgins, 1989a), which also asks subjects to indicate attributes that characterize who they aspire to become ("ideal self"), as well as attributes that characterize who they feel obligated to become ("ought self"). Because these data are not relevant for present purposes, they are not discussed further here.

4. Although the perspective of shared reality implies that any attribute held to be self-descriptive must have a history of being socially verified by someone, we assumed that the degree to which an attribute is shared with significant others would be reflected by this operationalization.

References

Abrams, D. (1985). Focus of attention in minimal intergroup discrimination. *British Journal of Social Psychology, 24,* 65-74.

Abrams, D., Wetherall, M., Cochrane, S., Hogg, M. A., & Turner, J. C. (1990). Knowing what to think by knowing who you are: Self-categorization and the nature of norm formation, conformity and group polarization. *British Journal of Social Psychology, 29,* 97-119.

Adorno, T. W., Frenkel-Brunswik, E., Levinson, D. J., & Sanford, R. N. (1950). *The authoritarian personality.* New York: Harper.

Allport, G. W. (1954). *The nature of prejudice.* New York: Holt.

Allport, G. W. (1961). *Pattern and growth in personality.* New York: Holt, Rinehart & Winston.

Anderson, R. C., & Pitchert, J. W. (1978). Recall of previously unrecallable information following a shift in perspective. *Journal of Verbal Learning and Verbal Behavior, 17,* 1-12.

Aronson, E. (1968). A theory of cognitive dissonance: A current perspective. In L. Berkowitz (Ed.), *Advances in experimental social psychology* (Vol. 4). New York: Academic Press.

Asch, S. E. (1952). *Social psychology.* New York: Oxford University Press.

Austin, J. L. (1962). *How to do things with words* (2nd ed.). Cambridge, MA: Harvard University Press.

Bakhtin, M. (1986). *Speech genres and other late essays* (C. Emerson & M. Holquist, Eds.; V. W. McGee, Trans.). Austin: University of Texas Press.

Baldwin, M. W., Carrell, S. E., & Lopez, D. F. (1990). Priming relationship schemas: My advisor and the Pope are watching me from the back of my mind. *Journal of Experimental Social Psychology, 26,* 435-454.

Banaji, M. R., & Greenwald, A. G. (1994). Implicit stereotyping and unconscious prejudice. In M. P. Zanna & J. M. Olson (Eds.), *The Ontario Symposium: Vol. 7. The psychology of prejudice.* Hillsdale, NJ: Erlbaum.

Bargh, J. A., Lombardi, W. J., & Higgins, E. T. (1988). Automaticity of chronically accessible constructs in person × situation effects on person perception: It's just a matter of time. *Journal of Personality and Social Psychology, 55,* 599-605.

Bargh, J. A., & Schul, Y. (1980). On the cognitive benefits of teaching. *Journal of Educational Psychology, 72,* 593-604.

Bartlett, F. C. (1932). *Remembering: A study in experimental social psychology.* Cambridge, England: Cambridge University Press.

Bavelas, J. B., Black, A., Chovil, N., Lemery, C. R., & Mullet, J. (1988). Form and function in motor mimicry: Topographic evidence that the primary function is communicative. *Human Communication Research, 14,* 275-299.

Bavelas, J. B., Black, A., Lemery, C. R., & Mullet, J. (1986). "I show how you feel": Motor mimicry as a communicative act. *Journal of Personality and Social Psychology, 50,* 322-329.

Bellezza, F. S., & Bower, G. H. (1981). Person stereotypes and memory for people. *Journal of Personality and Social Psychology, 41,* 856-865.

Bem, D. J., & Allen, A. (1974). On predicting some of the people some of the time: The search for cross-situational consistencies in behavior. *Psychological Review, 81,* 506-520.

Bem, D. J., & McConnell, H. K. (1970). Testing the self-perception explanation of dissonance phenomena: On the salience of premanipulated attitudes. *Journal of Personality and Social Psychology, 14,* 23-31.

Benware, C. A., & Deci, E. L. (1984). Quality of learning with an active versus passive motivational set. *American Education Research Journal, 21,* 755-765.

Berg, K. S., & Vidmar, N. (1975). Authoritarianism and recall of evidence about criminal behavior. *Journal of Research in Personality, 9,* 147-157.

Berger, P. L., & Luckmann, T. (1966). *The social construction of reality.* Garden City, NY: Doubleday.

Bertenthal, B. I., & Fischer, K. W. (1978). Development of self-recognition in the infant. *Developmental Psychology, 14,* 44-50.

Blumer, H. (1962). Society as symbolic interaction. In A. M. Rose (Ed.), *Human behavior and social processes.* London: Routledge & Kegan Paul.

Bolinger, D. (1975). *Aspects of language* (2nd ed.). New York: Harcourt Brace Jovanovich.

Bowlby, J. (1969). *Attachment and loss: Vol. 1. Attachment.* New York: Basic Books.

Bowlby, J. (1973). *Attachment and loss: Vol. 2. Separation: Anxiety and anger* . New York: Basic Books.

Brewer, M. B. (1988). A dual process model of impression formation. In T. K. Srull & R. S. Wyer (Eds.), *Advances in social cognition* (Vol. 1). Hillsdale, NJ: Erlbaum.

Brickman, P., Coates, D., & Janoff-Bulman, R. (1978). Lottery winners and accident victims: Is happiness relative? *Journal of Personality and Social Psychology, 36,* 917-927.

Brown, P., & Levinson, S. (1978). Universal in language use: Politeness phenomena. In E. Goody (Ed.), *Questions and politeness: Strategies in social interaction.* New York: Cambridge University Press.

Brown, R. (1958). *Words and things.* New York: Free Press.

Brown, R. (1965). *Social psychology.* New York: Free Press.

Brown, R. J., & Turner, J. C. (1981). Interpersonal and intergroup behavior. In J. C. Turner & H. Giles (Eds.), *Intergroup behavior.* Oxford: Blackwell.

Bruner, J. S. (1964). The course of cognitive growth. *American Psychologist, 19,* 1-15.

Brunner, L. J. (1979). Smiles can be backchannels. *Journal of Personality and Social Psychology, 37,* 728-734.

Burke, K. (1962). *A grammar of motives and a rhetoric of motives.* Cleveland, OH: World.

Burnstein, E. (1982). Persuasion as argument processing. In H. Brandstatter, J. H. Davis, & G. Stocker-Kreichgauer (Eds.), *Group decision making.* New York: Academic Press.

Burnstein, E., & Vinokur, A. (1977). Persuasive argumentation and social comparison as determinants of attitude polarization. *Journal of Experimental Social Psychology, 13,* 315-332.

Cameron, N. (1963). *Personality development and psychopathology.* Boston: Houghton Mifflin.

Cantor, N., & Kihlstrom, J. F. (1987). *Personality and social intelligence.* Englewood Cliffs, NJ: Prentice-Hall.

Carmichael, L., Hogan, H. P., & Walter, A. (1932). An experimental study of the effect of language on the reproduction of visually perceived forms. *Journal of Experimental Psychology, 15,* 73-86.

Carver, C. S., & Humphries, C. (1981). Havana daydreaming: A study of self-consciousness and the negative reference group among Cuban Americans. *Journal of Personality and Social Psychology, 36,* 324-332.

Case, R. (1985). *Intellectual development: Birth to adulthood.* New York: Academic Press.

Case, R. (1988). The whole child: Toward an integrated view of young children's cognitive, social, and emotional development. In A. D. Pellegrini (Ed.), *Psychological bases for early education.* Chichester, England: Wiley.

Charters, W. W., & Newcomb, T. W. (1952). Some attitudinal effects of experimentally increased salience of a membership group. In G. E. Swanson, T. M. Newcomb, & E. L. Hartley (Eds.), *Readings in social psychology* (2nd ed.). New York: Holt, Rinehart & Winston.

Chovil, N. (1991). Discourse-oriented facial displays in conversation. *Language and Social Interaction, 25,* 163-194.

Cialdini, R. B., & Petty, R. E. (1981). Anticipatory opinion effects. In R. E. Petty, T. M. Ostrom, & T. E. Brock (Eds.), *Cognitive responses in persuasion.* Hillsdale, NJ: Erlbaum.

Clark, H. H., & Brennan, S. E. (1991). Grounding in communication. In L. B. Resnick, J. M. Levine, & S. D. Teasley (Eds.), *Perspectives on socially shared cognition.* Washington, DC: American Psychological Association.

Clark, H. H., & Carlson, T. B. (1982). Hearers and speech acts. *Language, 58,* 332-373.

Clark, H. H., & Schaefer, E. F. (1987). Concealing one's meaning from overhearers. *Journal of Memory and Language, 26,* 209-225.

Clark, H. H., & Schaefer, E. F. (1989). Contributing to discourse. *Cognitive Science, 13,* 259-294.

Clark, H. H., & Wilkes-Gibbs, D. (1986). Referring as a collaborative process. *Cognition, 22,* 1-39.

Clark, L. F., Martin, L. L., & Henry, S. M. (1993). Instantiation, interference, and the change of standard effect: Context functions in reconstructive memory. *Journal of Personality and Social Psychology, 64,* 336-346.

Clark, L. F., & Woll, S. B. (1981). Stereotype biases: A reconstructive analysis of their role in reconstructive memory. *Journal of Personality and Social Psychology, 41,* 1064-1072.

Cooley, C. H. (1902). *Human nature and the social order.* New York: Scribner's.

Crocker, J., & Major, B. (1989). Social stigma and self-esteem: The self-protective properties of stigma. *Psychological Review, 96,* 608–630.

Cushman, D., & Whiting, G. C. (1972). An approach to communication theory: Toward consensus on rules. *Journal of Communication, 22,* 217–238.

Damon, W. (1977). *The social world of the child.* Washington, DC: Jossey-Bass.

Damon, W., & Hart, D. (1986). Stability and change in children's self-understanding. *Social Cognition, 4,* 102–118.

Daniel, T. C. (1972). Nature of the effect of verbal labels on recognition memory for form. *Journal of Experimental Psychology, 96,* 152–157.

Deutsch, M., & Gerard, H. B. (1955). A study of normative and informational social influences upon individual judgment. *Journal of Abnormal and Social Psychology, 51,* 629–636.

Devine, P. G., Sedikides, C., & Fuhrman, R. W. (1989). Goals in social information processing: The case of anticipated interaction. *Journal of Personality and Social Psychology, 56,* 680–690.

Dewey, J. (1930). *Human nature and conduct: An introduction to social psychology.* New York: The Modern Library. (Original work published 1922)

Dewey, J. (1958). *Experience and nature.* New York: Dover. (Original work published 1929)

Doms, M., & Van Avermaet, E. (1980). Majority influence, minority influence and conversion behavior: A replication. *Journal of Experimental Social Psychology, 16,* 283–292.

Doms, M., & Van Avermaet, E. (1985). Social support and minority influence: The innovation effect reconsidered. In S. Moscovici, G. Mugny, & E. Van Avermaet (Eds.), *Perspectives on minority influence.* Cambridge, England: Cambridge University Press.

Duncan, S., & Fiske, D. (1977). *Face-to-face interaction: Research, methods, and theory.* Hillsdale, NJ: Erlbaum.

Durkheim, E. (1951). *Suicide* (G. Simpson, Ed.; J. A. Spaulding & G. Simpson, Trans.). New York: Free Press. (Orginal work published 1897)

Epstein, R. (1965). Authoritarianism, displaced aggression, and social status of the target. *Journal of Personality and Social Psychology, 2,* 585–589.

Fazio, R. H., Effrein, E. A., & Falender, V. J. (1981). Self-perceptions following social interaction. *Journal of Personality and Social Psychology, 41,* 232–242.

Feffer, M. (1970). Developmental analysis of interpersonal behavior. *Psychological Review, 77,* 197–214.

Fenigstein, A. (1979). Self-consciousness, self-attention and social interaction. *Journal of Personality and Social Psychology, 37,* 75–86.

Festinger, L. (1950). Informal social communication. *Psychological Review, 57,* 271–282.

Festinger, L. (1954). A theory of social comparison processes. *Human Relations, 7,* 117–140.

Festinger, L., & Thibaut, J. (1951). Interpersonal communication in small groups. *Journal of Abnormal and Social Psychology, 46,* 92–99.

Fiedler, K., & Semin, G. (Eds.). (1993). *Language and social cognition.* Cambridge, England: Cambridge University Press.

Fischer, K. W. (1980). A theory of cognitive development: The control and construction of hierarchies of skills. *Psychological Review, 87,* 477–531.

Fischer, K. W., & Watson, M. W. (1981). Explaining the Oedipus conflict. In K. W. Fischer (Ed.), *New directions for child development: No. 12. Cognitive development.* San Francisco: Jossey-Bass.

Fiske, S. T. (1993). Social cognition and social perception. *Annual Review of Psychology, 44,* 155–194.

Fiske, S. T., & Von Hendy, H. M. (1992). Personality feedback and situational norms can control stereotyping processes. *Journal of Personality and Social Psychology, 62,* 577–596.

Fitzpatrick, A. R., & Eagly, A. H. (1981). Anticipatory belief polarization as a function of the expertise of a discussion partner. *Personality and Social Psychology Bulletin, 7,* 636–642.

Flavell, J. H., Botkin, P. T., Fry, C. L., Wright, J. W., & Jarvis, P. E. (1968). *The development of role-taking and communication skills in children.* New York: Wiley.

Fleming, J. H. (1994). Multiple-audience problems, tactical communication, and social interaction: A relational-regulation perspective. In M. P. Zanna (Ed.), *Advances in experimental social psychology* (Vol. 26). San Diego, CA: Academic Press.

Fleming, J. H., & Darley, J. M. (1991). Mixed messages: The multiple audience problem and strategic communication. *Social Cognition, 9,* 25-46.

Fleming, J. H., Darley, J. M., Hilton, J. L., & Kojetin, B. A. (1990). Multiple audience problem: A strategic communication perspective on social perception. *Journal of Personality and Social Psychology, 58,* 593-609.

French, J. R., & Raven, B. (1959). The bases of social power. In D. Cartwright (Ed.), *Studies in social power.* Ann Arbor, MI: Institute of Social Relations.

Freud, A. (1937). *The ego and the mechanisms of defense.* New York: International Universities Press.

Freud, S. (1960). *The ego and the id* (J. Strachey, Ed.; J. Riviere, Trans.). New York: Norton. (Original work published 1923)

Fussell, S. R., & Krauss, R. M. (1989a). The effects of intended audience on message production and comprehension: Reference in a common ground framework. *Journal of Experimental Social Psychology, 25,* 203-219.

Fussell, S. R., & Krauss, R. M. (1989b). Understanding friends and strangers: The effects of audience design on message comprehension. *European Journal of Social Psychology, 19,* 509-526.

Fussell, S. R., & Krauss, R. M. (1992). Coordination of knowledge in communication: Effects of speakers' assumptions about what others know. *Journal of Personality and Social Psychology, 62,* 378-391.

Garfinkel, H. (1967). *Studies in ethnomethodology.* Englewood Cliffs, NJ: Prentice-Hall.

Garrod, S., & Anderson, A. (1987). Saying what you mean in dialogue: A study in conceptual and semantic co-ordination. *Cognition, 27,* 181-218.

Gerard, H. B. (1954). The anchorage of opinions in face-to-face groups. *Human Relations, 7,* 313-326.

Gergen, K. J. (1965). Interaction goals and personalistic feedback as factors affecting the presentation of self. *Journal of Personality and Social Psychology, 1,* 413-424.

Gesell, A., & Ilg, F. (1946). *The child from five to ten.* New York: Harper & Row.

Giles, H., Mulac, A., Bradac, J. J., & Johnson, P. (1987). Speech accommodation theory: The first decade and beyond. In M. McLaughlin (Ed.), *Communication yearbook 10.* Newbury Park, CA: Sage.

Giles, H., & Smith, P. M. (1979). Accommodation-theory: Optimal levels of convergence. In H. Giles & R. St. Clair (Eds.), *Language and social psychology.* Oxford: Blackwell.

Glucksberg, S., Krauss, R. M., & Higgins, E. T. (1975). The development of referential communication skills. In F. Horowitz, E. Hetheringon, S. Scarr-Salapatek, & G. Seigel (Eds.), *Review of child development research* (Vol. 4). Chicago: University of Chicago Press.

Goffman, E. (1959). *The presentation of self in everyday life.* Garden City, NY: Doubleday/Anchor.

Goodwin, C. (1981). *Conversational organization: Interaction between speakers and hearers.* New York: Academic Press.

Green, D. M., & Swets, J. A. (1966). *Signal detection theory and psychophysics.* New York: Wiley.

Greenwald, A. G. (1980). The totalitarian ego: Fabrication and revision of personal history. *American Psychologist, 35,* 603-618.

Greenwald, A. G., & Pratkanis, A. R. (1984). The self. In R. S. Wyer & T. K. Srull (Eds.), *Handbook of social cognition* (Vol. 3). Hillsdale, NJ: Erlbaum.

Gregory, R. L. (1966). *Eye and brain.* London: World University Library.

Grice, H. P. (1971). Meaning. In D. D. Sternberg & L. A. Jakobovits (Eds), *Semantics: An interdisciplinary reader in philosophy, linguistics and psychology.* Cambridge, England: Cambridge University Press.

Gross, A. E., Riemer, B. X., & Collins, B. E. (1974). Audience reaction as a determinant of the speaker's self-persuasion. *Journal of Experimental Social Psychology, 9,* 246-256.

Gumperz, J. J., & Hymes, D. (Eds.). (1972). *Directions in sociolinguistics: The ethnography of communication.* New York: Holt, Rinehart & Winston.

Hamilton, D. L., & Sherman, J. W. (1994). Stereotypes. In R. S. Wyer & T. K. Srull (Eds.), *Handbook of social cognition* (2nd ed., Vol. 2). Hillsdale, NJ: Erlbaum.

Hamilton, D. L., & Trolier, T. K. (1986). Stereotypes and stereotyping: An overview of the cognitive approach. In J. F. Dovidio & S. L. Gaertner (Eds.), *Prejudice, discrimination, and racism.* Orlando, FL: Academic Press.

Hardin, C. (1994). *The influence of the immediate situation on memory for previous self-evaluations.* Unpublished doctoral dissertation, Yale University.

Hardin, C., & Banaji, M. R. (1993). The influence of language on thought. *Social Cognition, 11,* 277–308.

Hardin, C., Higgins, E. T., & Schachinger, H. E. (1995). *Shared reality: The role of social verification in self-verification.* Unpublished manuscript, Columbia University.

Harkins, S. G., & Petty, R. E. (1982). Effects of task difficulty and task uniqueness on social loafing. *Journal of Personality and Social Psychology, 43,* 1214–1229.

Harkins, S. G., & Petty, R. E. (1983). Social context effects in persuasion: The effects of multiple sources and multiple targets. In P. B. Paulus (Ed.), *Basic group processes.* New York: Springer-Verlag.

Harkins, S. G., & Szymanski, K. (1989). Social loafing and group evaluation. *Journal of Personality and Social Psychology, 56,* 934–941.

Harter, S. (1983). Developmental perspectives on the self-system. In E. M. Hetherington (Vol. Ed.), *Handbook of child psychology* (4th ed.): *Vol. 4. Socialization, personality, and social development.* New York: Wiley.

Hartwick, J., Sheppard, B. H., & Davis, J. H. (1982). Group remembering: Research and implications. In R. A. Guzzo (Ed.), *Improving group decision making in organizations.* New York: Academic Press.

Harvey, O. J., & Beverly, G. D. (1961). Some personality correlates of concept change through role playing. *Journal of Abnormal and Social Psychology, 63,* 125–130.

Hawes, L. C. (1973). Elements of a model for communication processes. *Quarterly Journal of Speech, 59,* 11–21.

Heider, F. (1958). *The psychology of interpersonal relations.* New York: Wiley.

Higgins, E. T. (1977). Communication development as related to channel, incentive, and social class. *Genetic Psychology Monographs, 96,* 75–141.

Higgins, E. T. (1981a). The "communication game": Implications for social cognition and persuasion. In E. T. Higgins, C. P. Herman, & M. P. Zanna (Eds.), *The Ontario Symposium: Vol. 1. Social cognition.* Hillsdale, NJ: Erlbaum.

Higgins, E. T. (1981b). Role-taking and social judgment: Alternative developmental perspectives and processes. In J. H. Flavell & L. Ross (Eds.), *Social cognitive development: Frontiers and possible futures.* Cambridge, England: Cambridge University Press.

Higgins, E. T. (1989a). Self-discrepancy theory: What patterns of self-beliefs cause people to suffer? In L. Berkowitz (Ed.), *Advances in experimental social psychology* (Vol. 22). New York: Academic Press.

Higgins, E. T. (1989b). Continuities and discontinuities in self-regulatory and self-evaluative processes: A developmental theory relating self and affect. *Journal of Personality, 57,* 407–444.

Higgins, E. T. (1990). Personality, social psychology, and person–situation relations: Standards and knowledge activation as a common language. In L. A. Pervin (Ed.), *Handbook of personality: Theory and research.* New York: Guilford Press.

Higgins, E. T. (1991). Development of self-regulatory and self-evaluative processes: Costs, benefits, and tradeoffs. In M. R. Gunnar & L. A. Sroufe (Eds.), *Minnesota Symposia on Child Psychology: Vol. 23. Self processes and development:* Hillsdale, NJ: Erlbaum.

Higgins, E. T. (1992a). Achieving 'shared reality' in the communication game: A social action that creates meaning. *Journal of Language and Social Psychology, 11,* 107–125.

Higgins, E. T. (1992b). Social cognition as a social science: How social action creates meaning. In D. N. Ruble, P. R. Costanzo, & M. E. Oliveri (Eds.), *The social psychology of mental health: Basic mechanisms and applications.* New York: Guilford Press.

Higgins, E. T. (1996). Ideals, oughts, and outcome focus: Affect and motivation from distinct pains and pleasures. In P. M. Gollwitzer & J. A. Bargh (Eds.), *The psychology of action: Linking Cognition and Motivation to Behavior.* New York: Guilford Press.

Higgins, E. T., Bargh, J. A., & Lombardi, W. J. (1985). The nature of priming effects on categorization. *Journal of Experimental Psychology: Learning, Memory, and Cognition, 11,* 59-69.

Higgins, E. T., & Chaires, W. M. (1980). Accessibility of interrelational constructs: Implications for stimulus encoding and creativity. *Journal of Experimental Psychology, 16,* 348-361.

Higgins, E. T., & King, G. (1981). Accessibility of social constructs: Information processing consequences of individual and contextual variability. In N. Cantor & J. Kihlstrom (Eds.), *Cognition, social interaction, and personality.* Hillsdale, NJ: Erlbaum.

Higgins, E. T., Loeb, I., & Moretti, M. (in press). Self-discrepancies and developmental shifts in vulnerability: Life transitions in the regulatory significance of others. *Rochester Symposium on Developmental Psychopathology.*

Higgins, E. T., & McCann, C. D. (1984). Social encoding and subsequent attitudes, impressions, and memory: "Context-driven" and motivational aspects of processing. *Journal of Personality and Social Psychology, 47,* 26-39.

Higgins, E. T., McCann, C. D., & Fondacaro, R. (1982). The "communication game": Goal directed encoding and cognitive consequences. *Social Cognition, 1,* 21-37.

Higgins, E. T., & Rholes, W. J. (1978). "Saying is believing": Effects of message modification on memory and liking for the person described. *Journal of Experimental Social Psychology, 14,* 363-378.

Higgins, E. T., & Stangor, C. (1988). Context-driven social judgment and memory: When "behavior engulfs the field" in reconstructive memory. In D. Bar-Tal & A. Kruglanski (Eds.), *The social psychology of knowledge.* New York: Springer-Verlag.

Hilton, D. (1991). A conversational model of causal explanation. In W. Stroebe & M. Hewstone (Eds.), *European review of social psychology* (Vol. 2). Chichester, England: Wiley.

Hinsz, V. B. (1990). Cognitive and consensus processes in group recognition memory performance. *Journal of Personality and Social Psychology, 59,* 705-718.

Hoffman, C., & Hurst, N. (1990). Gender stereotypes: Perception or rationalization? *Journal of Personality and Social Psychology, 58,* 197-208.

Hoffman, C., Lau, I., & Johnson, D. R. (1986). The linguistic relativity of person cognition: An English-Chinese comparison. *Journal of Personality and Social Psychology, 51,* 1097-1105.

Hoffman, M. L., & Saltzstein, H. D. (1967). Parental discipline and the child's moral development. *Journal of Personality and Social Psychology, 5,* 45-57.

Hogg, M. A., & Abrams, D. (1988). *Social identification: A social psychology of intergroup relations and group processes.* London: Routledge.

Hogg, M. A., & Turner, J. C. (1987a). Social identity and conformity: A theory of referent informational influence. In W. Doise & S. Moscovici (Eds.), *Current issues in European social psychology* (Vol. 2). Cambridge, England: Cambridge University Press.

Hogg, M. A., & Turner, J. C. (1987b). Intergroup behaviour, self-stereotyping and the salience of social categories. *British Journal of Social Psychology, 26,* 325-340.

Hupet, M., & Chantraine, Y. (1992). Changes in repeated references: Collaboration or repetition effects? *Journal of Psycholinguistic Research, 21,* 485-496.

Hupet, M., Chantraine, Y., & Neff, F. (1993). References in conversation between young and old normal adults. *Psychology and Aging, 8,* 339-346.

Hupet, M., Seron, X., & Chantraine, Y. (1991). The effects of the codability and discriminability of the referents on the collaborative referring procedure. *British Journal of Psychology, 82,* 449-462.

Huttenlocher, J., & Higgins, E. T. (1978). Issues in the study of symbolic development. In W. A. Collins (Ed.), *Minnesota Symposia on Child Psychology* (Vol. 2). Hillsdale, NJ: Erlbaum.

Isaacs, E., & Clark, H. H. (1987). References in conversation between experts and novices. *Journal of Experimental Psychology: General, 116,* 26-37.

Jacobs, R. C., & Campbell, D. T. (1961). The perpetuation of an arbitrary tradition through several generations of a laboratory microculture. *Journal of Abnormal and Social Psychology, 62,* 649-658.

James, W. (1890). *The principles of psychology* (2 vols.). New York: Holt.

James, W. (1909). *The meaning of truth: A sequel to 'Pragmatism.'* New York: Longmans, Green.

James, W. (1992). Pragmatism. In D. Olin (Ed.), *William James—Pragmatism in focus.* New York: Routledge. (Original work published 1907)

Janis, I. (1982). *Groupthink* (2nd ed.). Boston: Houghton Mifflin.

Janis, I., & Mann, L. (1965). Effectiveness of emotional role-playing in modifying smoking habits and attitudes. *Journal of Experimental Research in Personality, 1,* 84-90.

Jellison, J., & Arkin, R. (1977). A self-presentation approach to decision-making in groups. In J. M. Sulus & R. L. Miller (Eds.), *Social processes: Theoretical and empirical perspectives.* Washington, DC: Hemisphere.

Jones, E. E., & DeCharms, R. (1957). Changes in social perception as a function of the personal relevance of behavior. *Sociometry, 20,* 75-85.

Jones, E. E., Rhodewalt, F., Berglas, S., & Skelton, J. A. (1981). Effects of strategic self-presentation on subsequent self-esteem. *Journal of Personality and Social Psychology, 41,* 407-421.

Jost, J. T., & Banaji, M. R. (1994). The role of stereotyping in system-justification and the production of false consciousness. *British Journal of Social Psychology, 33,* 1-27.

Judd, C. M., & Park, B. (1988). Out-group homogeneity: Judgments of variability at the individual and group levels. *Journal of Personality and Social Psychology, 54,* 778-788.

Kagan, J. (1984). The idea of emotion in human developement. In C. E. Izard, J. Kagan, & R. B. Zajonc (Eds.), *Emotions, cognition, and behavior.* New York: Cambridge University Press.

Kassin, S. (1979). Consensus information, prediction, and causal attribution: A review of the literature and issues. *Journal of Personality and Social Psychology, 37,* 1966-1981.

Katz, D., & Braly, K. (1935). Racial prejudice and racial stereotypes. *Journal of Abnormal and Social Psychology, 30,* 175-193.

Kay, P., & Kempton, W. (1984). What is the Sapir-Whorf hypothesis? *American Anthropologist, 86,* 65-79.

Keller, H. (1903). *The story of my life.* Garden City, NY: Doubleday.

Kelley, H. H. (1967). Attribution theory in social psychology. In D. Levine (Ed.), *Nebraska Symposium on Motivation* (Vol. 15). Lincoln: University of Nebraska Press.

Kelley, H. H. (1979). *Personal relationships: Their structures and processes.* Hillsdale, NJ: Erlbaum.

Kelman, H. C. (1958). Compliance, identification, and internalization: Three processes of attitude change. *Journal of Conflict Resolution, 2,* 51-60.

Kendon, A. (1967). Some functions of gaze direction in social interaction. *Acta Psychologica, 32,* 1-25.

Kiesler, C. A., & Kiesler, S. B. (1969). *Conformity.* Reading, MA: Addison-Wesley.

Kingsbury, D. (1968). *Manipulating the amount of information obtained from a person giving directions.* Unpublished honors thesis, Harvard University.

Krauss, R. M., & Bricker, P. D. (1966). Effects of transmission delay and access delay on the efficiency of verbal communication. *Journal of the Acoustical Society of America, 41,* 286-292.

Krauss, R. M., & Fussell, S. R. (1988). Other-relatedness in language processing: Discussion and comments. *Journal of Language and Social Psychology, 7,* 263-279.

Krauss, R. M., & Fussell, S. R. (1991a). Perspective-taking in communication: Representations of others' knowledge in reference. *Social Cognition, 9,* 2-24.

Krauss, R. M., & Fussell, S. R. (1991b). Constructing shared communicative environments. In L. B. Resnick, J. M. Levine, & S. D. Teasley (Eds.), *Perspectives on socially shared cognition.* Washington, DC: American Psychological Association.

Krauss, R. M., & Fussell, S. R. (in press). Social psychological models of interpersonal communication. In E. T. Higgins & A. Kruglanski (Eds.), *Social psychology: Handbook of basic principles.* New York: Guilford Press.

Krauss, R. M., Vivekananthan, P. S., & Weinheimer, S. (1968). "Inner speech" and "external speech": Characteristics and communication effectiveness of socially and nonsocially encoded messages. *Journal of Personality and Social Psychology, 9,* 295-300.

Krauss, R. M., & Weinheimer, S. (1964). Changes in the length of reference phrases as a function of social interaction: A preliminary study. *Psychonomic Science, 1,* 113-114.

Krauss, R. M., & Weinheimer, S. (1966). Concurrent feedback, confirmation and the encoding of referents in verbal communication. *Journal of Personality and Social Psychology, 4,* 343-346.

Krauss, R. M., & Weinheimer, S. (1967). Effects of referent similarity and communication mode on verbal encoding. *Journal of Verbal Learning and Verbal Behavior, 6,* 359-363.

Latané, B., & Darley, J. M. (1970). *The unresponsive bystander: Why doesn't he help?* Englewood Cliffs, NJ: Prentice-Hall.

Latané, B., Williams, K. D., & Harkins, S. G. (1979). Many hands make light the work: The causes and consequences of social loafing. *Journal of Personality and Social Psychology, 37,* 822-832.

Laughlin, P. R., & Ellis, A. L. (1986). Demonstrability and social combination processes on mathematical intellective tasks. *Journal of Experimental Social Psychology, 22,* 177-189.

Le Bon, G. (1896). *The crowd.* London: T. Fisher Unwin.

Lecky, P. (1945). *Self-consistency: A theory of personality.* New York: Island Press.

Levine, J. M. (1989). Reaction to opinion deviance in small groups. In P. B. Paulus (Ed.), *Psychology of group influence.* Hillsdale, NJ: Erlbaum.

Levine, J. M., & Moreland, R. L. (1986). Outcome comparisons in group contexts: Consequences for the self and others. In R. Schwarzer (Ed.), *Self-related cognitions in anxiety and motivation.* Hillsdale, NJ: Erlbaum.

Levine, J. M., & Moreland, R. L. (1991). Culture and socialization in work groups. In L. B. Resnick, J. M. Levine, & S. D. Teasley (Eds.), *Perspectives on socially shared cognition.* Washington, DC: American Psychological Association.

Levine, J. M., Resnick, L. B., & Higgins, E. T. (1993). Social foundations of cognition. *Annual Review of Psychology, 44,* 585-612.

Levine, J. M., & Ranelli, C. J. (1978). Majority reaction to shifting and stable attitudinal deviates. *European Journal of Social Psychology, 8,* 55-70.

Levine, J. M., & Russo, E. M. (1987). Majority and minority influence. In C. Hendrick (Ed.), *Group processes: Review of personality and social psychology* (Vol. 8). Newbury Park, CA: Sage.

Lewin, K. (1931). Environmental forces in child behavior and development. In C. Murchison (Ed.), *A handbook of child psychology.* Worcester, MA: Clark University Press.

Lewin, K. (1935). *A dynamic theory of personality: Selected papers* (D. K. Adams & K. E. Zener, Trans.). New York: McGraw-Hill.

Lewis, M., & Brooks-Gunn, J. (1979). *Social cognition and the acquisition of self.* New York: Plenum Press.

Lewis, S. A., Langan, C. J., & Hollander, E. P. (1972). Expectations of future interaction and the choice of less desirable alternatives in conformity. *Sociometry, 35,* 440-447.

Linde, C., & Labov, W. (1975). Spatial networks as a site for the study of language and thought. *Language, 51,* 924-939.

Lockhart, R. S., & Murdock, B. B. (1970). Memory and the theory of signal detection. *Psychological Bulletin, 74,* 177-189.

Lucy, J. A., & Shweder, R. A. (1988). The effect of incidental conversation on memory for focal colors. *American Anthropologist, 90,* 923-931.

Luus, C. A. E., & Wells, G. L. (1994). The malleability of eyewitness confidence: Co-witness and perseverance effects. *Journal of Applied Psychology, 79,* 714-723.

Mackie, D. M. (1986). Social identification effect in group polarization. *Journal of Personality and Social Psychology, 50,* 720-728.

Mackie, D. M., & Cooper, J. (1984). Attitude polarization: The effects of group membership. *Journal of Personality and Social Psychology, 46,* 575-586.

MacKinnon, C. A. (1989). *Toward a feminist theory of the state.* Cambridge, MA: Harvard University Press.

Manis, M., & Armstrong, G. W. (1971). Contrast effects in verbal output. *Journal of Experimental Social Psychology, 7,* 381-388.

Manis, M., Cornell, S. D., & Moore, J. C. (1974). Transmission of attitude-relevant information through a communication chain. *Journal of Personality and Social Psychology, 30,* 81-94.

Maratsos, M. P. (1973). Nonegocentric communication abilities in preschool children. *Child Development, 44,* 697-700.

Markus, H., & Kitayama, S. (1991). Culture and the self: Implications for cognition, emotion, and motivation. *Psychological Review, 98,* 224-253.

Markus, H., & Nurius, P. (1986). Possible selves. *American Psychologist, 41,* 954-969.

Markus, H., & Wurf, E. (1987). The dynamic self-concept: A social psychological perspective. *Annual Review of Psychology, 38,* 299-337.

Marx, K. (1970). Theses on Feuerbach. In *The German ideology* (C. J. Arthur, Trans.). (Original work published 1888)

Marx, K., & Engels, F. (1970). *The German ideology* (C. J. Arthur, Ed.). New York: International. (Original work published 1846)

McCann, C. D., & Hancock, R. D. (1983). Self-monitoring in communicative interactions: Social-cognitive consequences of goal-directed message modification. *Journal of Experimental Social Psychology, 19,* 109-121.

McCann, C. D., Higgins, E. T., & Fondacaro, R. A. (1991). Primacy and recency in communication and self-persuasion: How successive audiences and multiple encodings influence subsequent evaluative judgments. *Social Cognition, 9,* 47-66.

McFarland, C., & Ross, M. (1987). The relation between current impressions and memories of self and dating partners. *Personality and Social Psychology Bulletin, 13,* 228-238.

McFarland, C., Ross, M., & Conway, M. (1984). Self-persuasion and self-presentation as mediators of anticipatory attitude change. *Journal of Personality and Social Psychology, 46,* 529-540.

McGuire, W. J., & McGuire, C. V. (1988). Content and process in the experience of self. In L. Berkowitz (Ed.), *Advances in experimental social psychology* (Vol. 21). New York: Academic Press.

McGuire, W. J., & McGuire, C. V. (1991). The content, structure, and operation of thought systems. In R. S. Wyer & T. K. Srull (Eds.), *Advances in social cognition* (Vol. 4). Hillsdale, NJ: Erlbaum.

Mead, G. H. (1932). *The philosophy of the present* (A. E. Murphy, Ed.). Chicago: University of Chicago Press.

Mead, G. H. (1934). *Mind, self, and society: From the standpoint of a social behaviorist* (C. W. Morris, Ed.). Chicago: University of Chicago Press.

Mead, G. H. (1936). *The philosophy of the act* (C. W. Morris, Ed.). Chicago: University of Chicago Press.

Mead, G. H. (1956). *The social psychology of George Herbert Mead* (A. Strauss, Ed.). Chicago: University of Chicago Press.

Mead, G. H. (1982). *The individual and the social self: Unpublished work of George Herbert Mead* (D. L. Miller, Ed.). Chicago: University of Chicago Press.

Merleau-Ponty, M. (1962). *Phenomenology of perception.* London: Routledge & Kegan Paul.

Miller, N., Gross, S., & Holtz, R. (1991). Social projection and attitudinal certainty. In J. M. Suls & T. A. Wills (Eds.), *Social comparison: Contemporary theory and research.* Hillsdale, NJ: Erlbaum.

Mischel, W. (1968). *Personality and assessment.* New York: Wiley.

Moreland, R. L., & Levine, J. M. (1989). Newcomers and oldtimers in small groups. In P. B. Paulus (Ed.), *Psychology of group influence.* Hillsdale, NJ: Erlbaum.

Morse, S., & Gergen, K. J. (1970). Social comparison, self-consistency, and the concept of the self. *Journal of Personality and Social Psychology, 16,* 148-156.

Moscovici, S. (1976). *Social influence and social change.* New York: Academic Press.

Moscovici, S. (1985). Social influence and conformity. In G. Lindzey & E. Aronson (Eds.), *Handbook of social psychology* (3rd ed., Vol. 2). New York: Random House.

Moscovici, S. (1993). *The invention of society: Psychological explanations for social phenomena.* Cambridge, MA: Blackwell.

Moscovici, S., & Personnaz, B. (1980). Studies in social influence: V. Minority influence and conversion behavior in a perceptual task. *Journal of Experimental Psychology, 16,* 270-282.

Mowrer, O. H. (1960). *Learning theory and behavior.* New York: John Wiley.

Myers, D. G., Bruggink, J. B., Kersting, R. C., & Schlosser, B. A. (1980). Does learning others' opinions change one's opinions? *Personality and Social Psychology Bulletin, 6,* 253-260.

Nail, P. R. (1986). Toward an integration of some models and theories of social responses. *Psychological Bulletin, 100,* 190-206.

Newcomb, T. M. (1943). *Personality and social change.* New York: Dryden.

Newcomb, T. M., Koenig, K. E., Flacks, R., & Warwick, D. P. (1967). *Persistence and change: Bennington College and its students after twenty-five years.* New York: Wiley.

Newtson, D., & Czerlinsky, T. (1974). Adjustment of attitude communications for contrasts by extreme audiences. *Journal of Personality and Social Psychology, 30,* 829-837.

Nusbaum, H. C., & Goodman, J. (1994). *Development of speech perception: The transition from recognizing speech sounds to spoken words.* Cambridge, MA: MIT Press.

Oakes, P. J., Haslam, A., & Turner, J. C. (1994). *Stereotyping and social reality.* Oxford: Blackwell.

Olson, J. M., & Cal, A. V. (1984). Source credibility, attitudes, and the recall of past behaviors. *European Journal of Social Psychology, 14,* 203-210.

Osborne, R. E., & Gilbert, D. T. (1992). The preoccupational hazards of social life. *Journal of Personality and Social Psychology, 62,* 219-228.

Osgood, C. (1971). Where do sentences come from? In D. Steinberg & L. Jacobivitz (Eds.), *Semantics: An interdisciplinary reader.* Cambridge, England: Cambridge University Press.

Ostrom, T. M. (1984). The sovereignty of social cognition. In R. S. Wyer & T. K. Srull (Eds.), *Handbook of social cognition* (Vol. 1). Hillsdale, NJ: Erlbaum.

Oxford English Dictionary (compact ed., 2 vols.). (1971). New York: Oxford University Press.

Park, B., Ryan, C. S., & Judd, C. M. (1992). The role of meaningful subgroups in explaining differences in perceived variability for in-groups and out-groups. *Journal of Personality and Social Psychology, 63,* 553-567.

Peirce, C. S. (1940). Logic as semiotic: The theory of signs. In J. Buchler (Ed.), *The philosophy of Peirce: Selected writings.* London: Routledge & Kegan Paul.

Pelham, B. W. (1991). On confidence and consequence: The certainty and importance of self-knowledge. *Journal of Personality and Social Psychology, 60,* 518-530.

Pelham, B. W., & Swann, W. B. (1994). The juncture of intrapersonal and interpersonal knowledge: Self-certainty and interpersonal congruence. *Personality and Social Psychology Bulletin, 20,* 349-357.

Personnaz, B. (1981). Researches in social influence: conversion in a perceptual task. Study with the spectrometer method. *European Journal of Social Psychology, 11,* 431-438.

Piaget, J. (1932/1965). *The moral judgment of the child.* London: Kegan Paul.

Piaget, J. (1951). *Play, dreams and imitation in childhood.* New York: Norton.

Piaget, J. (1976). *The grasp of consciousness: Action and concept in the young child.* Cambridge, MA: Harvard University Press.

Piaget, J., & Inhelder, B. (1956). *The child's conception of space.* New York: Norton.

Pyszczynski, T. A., & Greenberg, J. (1987). Self-regulatory perseveration and the depressive self-focusing style: A self-awareness theory of reactive depression. *Psychological Bulletin, 102,* 122-138.

Reicher, S. D. (1984). Social influence in the crowd: Attitudinal and behavioural effects of deindividuation in conditions of high and low group salience. *British Journal of Social Psychology, 23,* 341-350.

Reiss, D. (1981). *The family's construction of reality.* Cambridge, MA: Harvard University Press.

Resnick, L. B., Levine, J. M., & Teasley, S. D. (1991). *Perspectives on socially shared cognition.* Washington, DC: American Psychological Association.

Rogers, C. R. (1951). *Client-centered therapy: Its current practice, implication, and theory.* Boston: Houghton Mifflin.

Rommetveit, R. (1974). *On message structure: A framework for the study of language and communication.* New York: Wiley.

Ross, L. D., Amabile, T. M., & Steinmetz, J. L. (1977). Social roles, social control, and biases in social-perception processes. *Journal of Personality and Social Psychology, 35,* 485-494.

Ross, L. D., & Nisbett, R. E. (1991). *The person and the situation: Perspectives of social psychology.* Philadelphia: Temple University Press.

Ross, M. (1989). Relation of implicit theories to the construction of personal histories. *Psychological Review, 96,* 341-357.

Ross, M., & Conway, M. (1986). Remembering one's own past: The construction of personal histories. In R. M Sorrentino & E. T. Higgins (Eds.), *Handbook of motivation and cognition: Foundations of social behavior* (Vol. 1). New York: Guilford Press.

Ross, M., McFarland, C., Conway, M., & Zanna, M. P. (1983). Reciprocal relation between attitudes and behavior recall: Committing people to newly formed attitudes. *Journal of Personality and Social Psychology, 45,* 257-267.

Ross, M., McFarland, C., & Fletcher, G. J. O. (1981). The effect of attitude on the recall of personal histories. *Journal of Personality and Social Psychology, 40,* 627-634.

Ruesch, J., & Bateson, G. (1968). *Communication: The social matrix of psychiatry.* New York: Norton.

Sachs, J., & Devin, J. (1976). Young children's use of age-appropriate speech styles in social interaction and role-playing. *Journal of Child Language, 3,* 81-98.

Sacks, H., & Schegloff, E. (1979). Two preferences in the organization of reference to persons in conversation and their interaction. In G. Psathas (Ed.), *Everyday language: Studies in ethnomethodology.* New York: Irvington.

Salancik, G. R., & Conway, M. (1975). Attitude inferences from salient and relevant cognitive content about behavior. *Journal of Personality and Social Psychology, 32,* 829-840.

Sanders, G. S., & Baron, R. S. (1977). Is social comparison irrelevant for producing choice shifts? *Journal of Experimental Social Psychology, 13,* 303-314.

Santa, J. L., & Baker, L. (1975). Linguistic influences on visual memory. *Memory and Cognition, 3,* 445-450.

Schachter, S. (1951). Deviation, rejection, and communication. *Journal of Abnormal and Social Psychology, 46,* 190-207.

Schachter, S. (1959). *The psychology of affiliation: Experimental studies of the sources of gregariousness.* Stanford, CA: Stanford University Press.

Schachter, S. (1964). The interaction of cognitive and physiological determinants of emotional state. In L. Berkowitz (Ed.), *Advances in experimental social psychology* (Vol. 2). New York: Academic Press.

Schegloff, E. (1982). Discourse as an interactional achievement: Some uses of 'uh huh' and other things that come between sentences. In D. Tannen (Ed.), *Analyzing discourse: Text and talk.* Washington, DC: Georgetown University Press.

Schein, E. H. (1956). The Chinese indoctrination program for prisoners of war: A study of attempted brainwashing. *Psychiatry, 19,* 149-172.

Schlenker, B. R., & Weigold, M. F. (1989). Goals and the self-identification process. In L. A. Pervin (Ed.), *Goal concepts in personality and social psychology.* Hillsdale, NJ: Erlbaum.

Schober, M. F. (1993). Spatial perspective-taking in conversation. *Cognition, 47,* 1-24.

Schober, M. F., & Clark, H. H. (1989). Understanding by addressees and overhearers. *Cognitive Psychology, 21,* 211-232.

Schooler, J. W., & Engstler-Schooler, T. Y. (1990). Verbal overshadowing of visual memories: Some things are better left unsaid. *Cognitive Psychology, 22,* 36-71.

Schooler, J. W., Ohlsson, S., & Brooks, K. (1993). Thoughts beyond words: When language overshadows insight. *Journal of Experimental Psychology: General, 122,* 166-183.

Schutz, A. (1962). *The problem of social reality: Collected papers.* Boston: Martinus Nijhoff.

Schutz, A. (1967). *The phenomenology of the social world* (G. Walsh & F. Lehnert, Trans.). Chicago: Northwestern University Press.

Schwarz, N. (1994). Judgment in a social context: Biases, shortcomings, and the logic of conversation. In M. P. Zanna (Ed.), *Advances in experimental social psychology* (Vol. 26). San Diego, CA: Academic Press.

Searle, J. R. (1969). *Speech acts: An essay in the philosophy of language.* Cambridge, England: Cambridge University Press.

Secord, P. F., & Backman, C. W. (1965). An interpersonal approach to personality. In B. Maher (Ed.), *Progress in experimental personality research* (Vol. 2). New York: Academic Press.

Sedikides, C. (1990). Effects of fortuitously activated constructs versus activated communication goals on person impressions. *Journal of Personality and Social Psychology, 58,* 397-408.

Selman, R. L. (1980). *The growth of interpersonal understanding: Developmental and clinical analyses.* New York: Academic Press.

Selman, R. L., & Byrne, D. F. (1974). A structural-developmental analysis of levels of role-taking in middle childhood. *Child Development, 45,* 803-806.

Shantz, C. U. (1983). Social cognition. In J. H. Flavell & E. M. Markman (Eds.), *Handbook of child psychology* (4th ed.): *Vol. 3. Cognitive development.* New York: Wiley.

Shatz, M., & Gelman, R. (1973). The development of communication skills: Modifications in the speech of young children as a function of listener. *Monographs of the Society for Research in Child Development, 38* (Serial No. 152).

Sherif, M. (1936). *The psychology of social norms.* New York: Harper.

Sherif, M., & Sherif, C. W. (1956). *An outline of social psychology.* New York: Harper.

Shweder, R. A., & LeVine, R. A. (1984). *Culture theory: Essays on mind, self, and emotion.* Cambridge, England: Cambridge University Press.

Siegal, A. E., & Siegal, S. (1957). Reference groups, membership groups, and attitude change. *Journal of Abnormal and Social Psychology, 55,* 360-364.

Skinner, B. F. (1957). *Verbal behavior.* New York: Appleton-Century-Crofts.

Smith, E. R. (1990). Content and process specificity in the effects of prior experiences. In R. S. Wyer & T. K. Srull (Eds.), *Advances in social cognition* (Vol. 3). Hillsdale, NJ: Erlbaum.

Snyder, M. (1979). Self-monitoring processes. In L. Berkowitz (Ed.), *Advances in experimental social psychology* (Vol. 12). New York: Academic Press.

Snyder, M., & Swann, W. B., Jr. (1978). Hypothesis-testing processes in social interaction. *Journal of Personality and Social Psychology, 36,* 1202-1212.

Snyder, M., & Uranowitz, S. W. (1978). Reconstructing the past: Some cognitive consequences of person perception. *Journal of Personality and Social Psychology, 36,* 941-950.

Sorrentino, R. M., King, G., & Leo, G. (1986). The influence of the minority on perception: A note on a possible alternative explanation. *Journal of Experimental Social Psychology, 16,* 293-301.

Sperber, D., & Wilson, D. (1986). *Relevance: Communication and cognition.* Cambridge, MA: Harvard University Press.

Sperling, H. G. (1946). *An experimental study of some psychological factors in judgment.* Unpublished master's thesis, New School for Social Research.

Sridhar, S. N. (1988). *Cognition and sentence production: A cross-linguistic study.* New York: Springer.

Stamm, K. R. (1972). Environment and communication. In F. G. Kline & P. J. Tichenor (Eds.), *Current perspectives in mass communication research.* Beverly Hills, CA: Sage.

Stangor, C., & Lange, J. E. (1994). Mental representations of social groups: Advances in understanding stereotypes and stereotyping. In M. P. Zanna (Ed.), *Advances in experimental social psychology* (Vol. 26). San Diego, CA: Academic Press.

Stasser, G. (1992). Pooling of unshared information during group discussion. In S. Worchel, W. Wood, & J. A. Simpson (Eds.), *Group process and productivity.* Newbury Park: Sage.

Stasson, M. F., Kameda, T., Parks, C. D., Zimmerman, S. K., & Davis, J. H. (1991). Effects of assigned group consensus requirement on group problem solving and group members' learning. *Social Psychology Quarterly, 54,* 25-35.

Steele, C. (1988). The psychology of self-affirmation: Sustaining the integrity of the self. In L. Berkowitz (Ed.), *Advances in experimental social psychology* (Vol. 21). New York: Academic Press.

Stephenson, G. M., Clark, N. K., & Wade, G. S. (1986). Meetings make evidence? An experimental study of collaborative and individual recall of a simulated police interrogation. *Journal of Personality and Social Psychology, 50,* 1113-1122.

Strack, F., Schwarz, N., Chassein, B., Kern, D., & Wagner, D. (1990). Salience of comparison standards and the activation of social norms: Consequences for judgments of happiness and their communication. *British Journal of Social Psychology, 29,* 303-314.

Stryker, S., & Statham, A. (1985). Symbolic interaction and role theory. In G. Lindzey & E. Aronson (Eds.), *Handbook of social psychology* (3rd ed., Vol. 1). New York: Random House.

Sturgis, H. W. (1959). *The relationship of the teacher's knowledge of the student's background to the effectiveness of teaching: A study of the extent to which the effectiveness of teaching is related to the teacher's knowledge of the student's background.* Unpublished doctoral dissertation, New York University.

Suls, J. M., & Miller, R. L. (Eds.). (1977). *Social comparison processes: Theoretical and empirical perspectives.* Washington, DC: Hemisphere.

Swann, W. B., Jr. (1983). Self-verification: Bringing social reality into harmony with the self. In J.

Suls & A. G. Greenwald (Eds.), *Psychological perspectives on the self* (Vol. 2). Hillsdale, NJ: Erlbaum.

Swann, W. B., Jr. (1984). Quest for accuracy in person perception: A matter of pragmatics. *Psychological Review, 91*, 457-477.

Swann, W. B., Jr. (1990). To be adored or to be known? The interplay of self-enhancement and self-verification. In E. T. Higgins & R. M. Sorrentino (Eds.), *Handbook of motivation and cognition: Foundations of social behavior* (Vol. 2). New York: Guilford Press.

Swann, W. B., Jr., & Ely, R. J. (1984). A battle of wills: Self-verification versus behavioral confirmation. *Journal of Personality and Social Psychology, 46*, 1287-1302.

Swann, W. B., Jr., Griffin, J. J., Predmore, S., & Gaines, B. (1987). The cognitive–affective crossfire: When self-consistency confronts self-enhancement. *Journal of Personality and Social Psychology, 52*, 881-889.

Swann, W. B., Jr., & Hill, C. A. (1982). When our identities are mistaken: Reaffirming self-conceptions through social interaction. *Journal of Personality and Social Psychology, 43*, 59-66.

Swann, W. B., Hixon, J. G., & De La Ronde, C. (1992). Embracing the bitter "truth": Negative self-concepts and marital commitment. *Psychological Science, 3*, 118-121.

Swann, W. B., Jr., Pelham, B. W., & Chidester, T. (1988). Change through paradox: Using self-verification to alter beliefs. *Journal of Personality and Social Psychology, 54*, 268-273.

Swann, W. B., Jr., Pelham, B. W., & Krull, D. S. (1989). Agreeable fancy or disagreeable truth? Reconciling self-enhancement and self-verification. *Journal of Personality and Social Psychology, 54*, 268-273.

Swann, W. B., Jr., & Read, S. J. (1981a). Acquiring self-knowledge: The search for feedback that fits. *Journal of Personality and Social Psychology, 41*, 1119-1128.

Swann, W. B., Jr., & Read, S. J. (1981b). Self-verification processes: How we sustain our self-conceptions. *Journal of Experimental Social Psychology, 17*, 351-372.

Swann, W. B., Jr., Stein-Seroussi, A., & Giesler, R. B. (1992). Why people self-verify. *Journal of Personality and Social Psychology, 62*, 392-401.

Swann, W. B., Jr., Wenzlaff, R. M., Krull, D. S., & Pelham, B. W. (1992). Allure of negative feedback: Self-verification strivings among depressed persons. *Journal of Abnormal Psychology, 101*, 293-306.

Tajfel, H. (1972). La categorization sociale. In S. Moscovici (Ed.), *Introduction á la psychologie sociale* (Vol. 1). Paris: Larousse.

Tajfel, H. (1981). *Human groups and social categories.* Cambridge, England: Cambridge University Press.

Tajfel, H., & Turner, J. C. (1979). An integrative theory of intergroup conflict. In W. G. Austin & S. Worchel (Eds.), *The social psychology of intergroup relations.* Monterey, CA: Brooks/Cole.

Tajfel, H., & Turner, J. C. (1986). The social identity theory of intergroup behavior. In S. Worchel & W. G. Austin (Eds.), *The psychology of intergroup relations.* Chicago: Nelson-Hall.

Taylor, S. E., Buunk, B. P., & Aspinwall, L. G. (1990). Social comparison, stress, and coping. *Personality and Social Psychology Bulletin, 16*, 74-89.

Tesser, A. (1988). Toward a self-evaluation maintenance model of social behavior. In L. Berkowitz (Ed.), *Advances in experimental social psychology* (Vol. 21). New York: Academic Press.

Tesser, A., & Cornell, D. T. (1991). On the confluence of self processes. *Journal of Experimental Social Psychology, 27*, 501-526.

Tetlock, P. E. (1992). The impact of accountability on judgment and choice: Toward a social contingency model. In M. P. Zanna (Ed.), *Advances in experimental social psychology* (Vol. 25). New York: Academic Press.

Thibaut, J. W., & Riecken, H. W. (1955). Authoritarianism, status and the communication of aggression. *Human Relations, 8*, 95-120.

Tice, D. M. (1992). Self-concept change and self-presentation: The looking glass self is also a magnifying glass. *Journal of Personality and Social Psychology, 63*, 435-451.

Traxler, M. J., & Gernsbacher, M. A. (1992). Improving written communication through minimal feedback. *Language and Cognitive Processes, 7*, 1-22.

Traxler, M. J., & Gernsbacher, M. A. (1993). Improving written communication through perspective-taking. *Language and Cognitive Processes, 8,* 311-334.

Triandis, H. C. (1989). The self and social behavior in differing cultural contexts. *Psychological Review, 96,* 506-520.

Trope, Y. (1986). Self-enhancement and self-assessment in achievement behavior. In R. M. Sorrentino & E. T. Higgins (Eds.), *Handbook of motivation and cognition: Foundations of social behavior* (Vol. 1). New York: Guilford Press.

Turner, J. C. (1982). Towards a cognitive redefinition of the social group. In H. Tajfel (Ed.), *Social identity and intergroup relations.* Cambridge, England: Cambridge University Press.

Turner, J. C. (1985). Social categorization and the self-concept: A social cognitive theory of group behavior. In E. J. Lawler (Ed.), *Advances in group processes: Theory and research* (Vol. 2). Greenwich, CT: JAI Press.

Turner, J. C., Hogg, M. A., Oakes, P. J., Reicher, S. D., & Wetherall, M. (1987). *Rediscovering the social group: A self-categorization theory.* New York: Blackwell.

Turner, J. C., & Oakes, P. J. (1986). The significance of the social identity concept for social psychology with reference to individualism, interactionism and social influence. *British Journal of Social Psychology, 25,* 237-253.

Van Maanen, J. (1977). Experiencing organization: Notes on the meaning of careers and socialization. In J. Van Maanen (Ed.), *Organizational careers: Some new perspectives.* New York: Wiley.

Van Maanen, J., & Schein, E. H. (1979). Toward a theory of organizational socialization. In B. M. Staw (Ed.), *Research in organizational behavior: An annual series of analytical essays and critical reviews.* Greenwich, CT: JAI Press.

Vinokur, A., & Burnstein, E. (1978). Depolarization of attitudes in groups. *Journal of Personality and Social Psychology, 36,* 872-885.

Vollrath, D. A., Sheppard, B. H., Hinsz, V. B., & Davis, J. H. (1989). Memory performance by decision-making groups and individuals. *Organizational Behavior and Human Decision Processes, 43,* 289-300.

Volosinov, V. N. (1986). *Marxism and the philosophy of language* (L. Matejka & I. R. Titunik, Trans.). Cambridge, MA: Harvard University Press.

Vygotsky, L. S. (1962). *Thought and language* (E. Hanfmann & G. Vakar, Trans.). Cambridge, MA: MIT Press.

Vygotsky, L. S. (1978). *Mind in society: The development of higher psychological processes* (J. V. Wertsch, Ed.). Cambridge, MA: Harvard University Press.

Wanous, J. P. (1980). *Organizational entry: Recruitment, selection, and socialization of newcomers.* Reading, MA: Addison-Wesley.

Watzlawick, P., Beavin, J. H., & Jackson, D. D. (1967). *Pragmatics of human communication.* New York: Norton.

Weber, M. (1967). Subjective meaning in the social situation. In G. B. Levitas (Ed.), *Culture and consciousness: Perspectives in the social sciences.* New York: Braziller.

Weber, M. (1971). *Max Weber: The interpretation of social reality* (J. E. T. Eldridge, Ed.). New York: Scribner's.

Wegner, D. M. (1987). Transactive memory: A contemporary analysis of the group mind. In B. Mullin & G. R. Goethals (Eds.), *Theories of group behavior.* New York: Springer-Verlag.

Weick, K. E., & Gilfillan, D. P. (1971). Fate of arbitrary traditions in a laboratory microculture. *Journal of Personality and Social Psychology, 17,* 179-191.

Weldon, E., & Gargano, G. M. (1988). Cognitive loafing: The effects of accountability and shared responsibility on cognitive effort. *Personality and Social Psychology Bulletin, 14,* 159-171.

Werner, H. (1957). *Comparative psychology of mental development.* New York: International Universities Press.

Werner, H., & Kaplan, B. (1963). *Symbol formation.* New York: Wiley.

Wetherall, M. S. (1987). Social identity and group polarization. In J. C. Turner, M. A. Hogg, P. J. Oakes, S. D. Reicher, & M. S. Wetherall (Eds.), *Rediscovering the social group: A self-categorization theory.* New York: Blackwell.

Wilkes-Gibbs, D., & Clark, H. H. (1992). Coordinating beliefs in conversation. *Journal of Memory and Language, 31,* 183-194.

Wittgenstein, L. (1953). *Philosophical investigations.* New York: Macmillan.

Wittgenstein, L. (1980). *Remarks on the philosophy of psychology* (2 vols.). Chicago: University of Chicago Press.

Wylie, R. C. (1979). *The self concept: Vol. 2. Theory and research on selected topics.* Lincoln: University of Nebraska Press.

Zajonc, R. B. (1960). The process of cognitive tuning and communication. *Journal of Abnormal and Social Psychology, 61,* 159-167.

Zimmerman, C., & Bauer, R. A. (1956). The effect of an audience on what is remembered. *Public Opinion Quarterly, 20,* 238-248.

Zukier, H., & Pepitone, A. (1984). Social roles and strategies in prediction: Some determinants of the use of base-rate information. *Journal of Personality and Social Psychology, 47,* 349-360.

CHAPTER 3

Affect, Motivation, and Cognition in Relative Deprivation Research

JAMES M. OLSON
University of Western Ontario
CAROLYN L. HAFER
Brock University

In 1949, Stouffer, Suchman, DeVinney, Star, and Williams published *The American Soldier,* a study of performance and motivation in U.S. military personnel. Among other contributions, this work is noted for its introduction of the term "relative deprivation." Relative deprivation was used to explain the finding that military personnel's reported levels of satisfaction did not always coincide with their objective job characteristics (e.g., opportunities for promotion). Stouffer et al. hypothesized post hoc that satisfaction was related to how current outcomes compared to a standard, and not to the absolute value of those outcomes. Thus, objectively deprived individuals may be satisfied with their lot if they compare themselves to others in similar circumstances; conversely, individuals who are well off with regard to a desired resource may experience dissatisfaction if they compare themselves to others who are even better off than they are. Felt deprivation is relative.

Since Stouffer et al. introduced the term, a large body of research on relative deprivation has emerged in the social sciences. Researchers generally agree that relative deprivation involves a perceived negative discrepancy between one's own or one's group's position and some referent, as well as a feeling of discontent; relative deprivation is also assumed to motivate attitudes and behaviors. Thus, relative deprivation has both a "cold" (cognitive) component, the perception of deprivation, and "hot" (affective and motivational) components, the emotion of discontent and the subsequent energizing of attitudes and behaviors. Researchers differ in their emphasis on hot versus cold components in defining and operationalizing relative deprivation. Work on preconditions to and consequences of relative deprivation similarly indicates a conglomeration of hot (affective and motivational) and cold (cognitive) approaches and variables. A recent trend in relative deprivation research has been to recognize the interplay of cognitive, affective, and motivational processes.

In this chapter, we discuss (1) the cognitive, affective, and motivational components of the concept of relative deprivation itself; (2) research on the pre-conditions to relative deprivation; and (3) research on the consequences of relative deprivation. We then describe some of our own research that has investigated cognitive and motivational aspects of relative deprivation. Finally, we conclude that relative deprivation is best understood from a synergistic approach that acknowledges the importance of and relation between hot and cold processes. Such synergism is consistent with the "Warm Look" described in an earlier volume of this *Handbook* (Sorrentino & Higgins, 1986).

THE CONCEPT OF RELATIVE DEPRIVATION

The Cognitive and Affective Components of Relative Deprivation

A number of researchers have outlined inconsistencies in the conceptualization and operationalization of relative deprivation (e.g., Gurney & Tierney, 1982; Martin, 1986; Walker & Pettigrew, 1984). Many of these inconsistencies involve the extent to which the cognitive versus affective components of relative deprivation are emphasized. Although most researchers agree that relative deprivation involves the perception of deprivation compared to some standard (cognitive component) as well as discontent (affective component), their operationalizations often focus on either perceived discrepancies or emotions.

For example, relative deprivation is commonly operationalized through the use of Cantril's (1965) Self-Anchoring Striving Scale. This scale presents a "ladder" with 10 rungs, the top and bottom rungs of which are labeled with anchors such as "the best possible life in this country" (as the top anchor) and "the worst possible life in this country" (as the bottom anchor). Participants place themselves or their group and usually some referent(s) (e.g., an outgroup) on this ladder. Relative deprivation is operationalized as negative discrepancies between one's own or one's group's situation on the one hand, and either the top rung or the position of some other referent on the other (for examples of studies using Cantril's scale to operationalize relative deprivation, see Appelgryn & Nieuwoudt, 1988; Gurr, 1970; Walker & Mann, 1987). Such measures have been criticized for not assessing the emotional import of perceived discrepancies (e.g., Cook, Crosby, & Hennigan, 1977; Petta & Walker, 1992). Instead, the affective component of relative deprivation is assumed; however, discontent need not necessarily accompany a perceived discrepancy in status, as, for example, when low status is seen as legitimate or justified (Ellemers, Wilke, & van Knippenberg, 1993; Folger, 1986).

Other researchers have focused primarily on affect in their operationalization of relative deprivation, defining it as an emotion akin to dissatisfaction, anger, or resentment about one's situation or the situation of one's group; no particular referent is specified (Martin, 1986; Olson, Roese, Meen, & Robertson, in press). For example, an individual may be asked "How angry are you about your job situation?" In such a case, it is merely assumed that a negative comparison underlies these emotions. It is unclear, therefore, whether these studies are investigating *relative* deprivation as opposed to absolute deprivation. If the discontent is the result of a perceived negative discrepancy, knowledge of the specific referent would be useful. Recent research has shown, for example, that reported discontent can vary when different referents are specified (Hafer & Olson, 1993; Olson et al., in press, Study 2), and these different forms of discontent may have implications for predicting attitudes and behavior (Olson et al., in press).

These varying operationalizations reflect differences in the way the term "relative deprivation" is used. First, relative deprivation has been used to denote a set of preconditions (discussed in a subsequent section), the most central being a comparison with a better-off referent; these preconditions are assumed to lead to emotional arousal. On the other hand, relative deprivation has been used as a synonym for discontent, which is assumed to arise from a set of preconditions (one of which is a negative comparison). In the former case, the role of affect is assumed; in the latter, the role of cognition is assumed.

Recently, some authors have emphasized both the cognitive and affective components of relative deprivation (e.g., Birt & Dion, 1987; Dubé & Guimond, 1986; Petta & Walker, 1992; Walker & Pettigrew, 1984). As we shall see, the distinction between affective and cognitive relative deprivation becomes especially important when researchers are predicting attitudes and behavior (i.e., examining the motivational consequences of resentment) (Birt & Dion, 1987; Dubé & Guimond, 1986; Petta & Walker, 1992; Walker & Pettigrew, 1984).

Personal and Group Relative Deprivation

Another useful distinction in the relative deprivation literature is that between "egoistical" and "fraternal" relative deprivation, often referred to as "personal" and "group" relative deprivation. According to Runciman (1966), personal relative deprivation results from comparisons between one's own situation and some referent (most often, the situation of better-off ingroup members); group relative deprivation, on the other hand, results from comparisons between one's group's situation and that of a more advantaged outgroup.

Early theorists focused on personal relative deprivation. Gurr (1970), for example, defined relative deprivation as a discrepancy between what individuals believe they are personally entitled to (presumably based on interpersonal comparisons) and what they expect to obtain personally. Group relative deprivation was seen as merely a special case of personal relative deprivation. Crosby (1976) mentioned Runciman's classification, but chose to limit her theoretical propositions (discussed in more detail later) to personal relative deprivation. More recently, many researchers have measured both personal and group relative deprivation (e.g., Birt & Dion, 1987; Dion, 1986; Dubé & Guimond, 1986; Hafer & Olson, 1993; Olson et al., 1994; Petta & Walker, 1992). As with affective and cognitive relative deprivation, the distinction between personal and group relative deprivation has implications for predicting attitudes and behavior.

The Personal–Group Discrimination Discrepancy: Motivational and Cognitive Explanations

One interesting finding that has arisen out of research investigating both personal and group relative deprivation is that individuals usually report more group relative deprivation or discrimination, on average, than personal relative deprivation or discrimination (Crosby, 1984; Taylor, Wright, & Porter, 1994). Taylor, Wright, Moghaddam, and Lalonde (1990) have called this tendency the "personal-group discrimination discrepancy." Both motivational and cognitive explanations of the discrepancy have been proposed.[1]

At least three cognitive explanations have been suggested. Taylor et al. (1990) suggest that study participants may be using an additive strategy when asked about discrimination. That is, individuals may estimate personal discrimination by adding up the number of instances they can think of in which they were personally discriminated against; when asked about group discrimination, they may similarly add up the instances of discrimination experienced not only by themselves but also by other group members. The estimate for group discrimination therefore will necessarily be greater than the estimate for personal discrimination. Taylor et al. (1990, 1994) have provided some evidence against this interpretation, however.

Another cognitive explanation has been suggested by Zanna, Crosby, and Loewenstein (1986). In many studies showing the discrepancy, neither personal nor group relative deprivation is assessed with any specified referent (this problem has been mentioned earlier); therefore, it is unclear what spontaneous standard people are using, if any. Perhaps when individuals are asked about personal relative deprivation, they compare their outcomes to other members of their group, whereas when they are asked about group relative deprivation, intergroup comparisons come to mind. The former discrepancy will probably be smaller than the latter because of the different referent. Olson et al.'s (in press, Study 2) findings with working women, however, argue against such an explanation. Not only did these authors find the personal-group discrimination discrepancy when personal and group relative deprivation were assessed with no referent specified, but the discrepancy also occurred when participants were specifically asked to compare their personal situation and the situation of their group against that of an outgroup (working men).

A third cognitive explanation for the personal-group discrimination discrepancy proposes that a greater proportion of information available about one's group than of information available about oneself consists of examples of discrimination (Taylor et al., 1990). The greater amount of information available about one's group may be partly attributable to vivid and dramatic examples of group discrimination presented by the mass media, which are easily remembered in comparison to the relatively more subtle discrimination found in everyday life (Fiske & Taylor, 1991).

The most popular explanation for the difference between reports of personal and group discrimination is a motivational one. Individuals may be denying personal discrimination (Crosby, 1984; Crosby, Pufall, Snyder, O'Connell, & Whalen, 1989). Taylor et al. (1994) list several possible reasons for denial, such as a reluctance to point to a particular perpetrator of discrimination, as well as a desire to justify nonaction. Interestingly, Crosby (1984) suggests that a cognitive bias may be partly responsible for the denial of discrimination. According to Crosby, people may find it more difficult to infer discrimination from individual cases than from aggregate data, as many individual cases involve some perceived ambiguity. This explanation, while possibly adding to the effects of denial, might better be seen as a cognitive mechanism that decreases the probability of perceiving personal discrimination, not of denying its existence. We also propose that denying personal discrimination may serve to present a desirable image to others—for example, an image of strength ("No one takes advantage of me") or adjustment ("I am happy and have few personal problems in my life"). Our own research, presented later in this chapter, indicates that people do alter their reports of discontent, depending on the impression they want to portray to others. Crosby's (1982) study of working women gives some evidence for the denial of personal discrimination: Reports of personal discrimination were almost nonexistent, yet there was evidence of objective discrimination (e.g., when men and women were equated on job status and other job characteristics, men's salaries were $8,000 more a year than women's salaries). Taylor et al. (1994) suggest that the denial explanation is less compelling when individuals report moderate to high levels of personal discrimination, and that "denial" should perhaps be termed "minimization" of personal discrimination.

A second motivational explanation for the personal–group discrimination discrepancy is that group discrimination is exaggerated; thus, the distortion may be at the group level rather than at the personal level (Taylor et al., 1990, 1994). Various reasons for exaggeration of group discrimination have been proposed. According to Taylor et al. (1994), group discrimination may provide an external attribution for personal failure and serve to augment internal attributions for subsequent personal success. We also propose that exaggerating group deprivation may help the group obtain valued resources by presenting a particular image to those in power (see also Taylor et al., 1990). Those with control over valued resources may find it difficult to ignore the pleas of a group that has been severely discriminated against. Once again, our own research, presented later in this chapter, bears on this hypothesis.

Of course, it is extremely difficult to determine in a field study what motivation underlies reports of deprivation and discrimination. Taylor et al. (1994) suggest that a combination of motivational forces may come into play. For example, denying or minimizing personal discrimination may accompany exaggeration of group discrimination. We also believe that a combination of cognitive and motivational processes may often be at work, such as when differences in the information available about personal versus group discrimination (extreme examples of group discrimination in the mass media vs. subtle instances of personal discrimination) intensify a denial of personal discrimination.

PRECONDITIONS OF RELATIVE DEPRIVATION

One of the most important issues addressed by relative deprivation theorists has been the role of various antecedent factors in the experience of resentment about deprivation. That is, the "preconditions" of relative deprivation have been of considerable interest to researchers. Given that objective deprivation per se does not always produce resentment, what are the necessary and sufficient factors for resentment about deprivation to occur? It turns out that most of the factors identified by researchers have been cognitive rather than motivational in nature, although at least one motivational factor appears to be important.

In this section, we review the models proposed by two theorists: Crosby (Cook et al., 1977; Crosby, 1976, 1982; Crosby, Muehrer, & Loewenstein, 1986) and Folger (1986; Folger, Rosenfield, Rheaume, & Martin, 1983; Folger, Rosenfield, & Robinson, 1983). Although other theorists have also formulated models of relative deprivation (e.g., Davis, 1959; Gurr, 1970; Runciman, 1966; for reviews, see Crosby, 1976, 1982; Olson & Hazlewood, 1986), the theories of Crosby and Folger are the most elaborate ones and incorporate many of the ideas about preconditions contained in the earlier works.

Crosby's Five-Factor Model of Relative Deprivation

In 1976, Crosby proposed an elegant five-factor model of relative deprivation; her model has profoundly influenced subsequent research. On the basis of a review and integration of previous theories, Crosby proposed five necessary and sufficient preconditions for relative deprivation. In order for individuals to feel resentful about not possessing some desired object (X), they must (1) see that someone else possesses X, (2) want X, (3) feel entitled to X, (4) think it feasible to obtain X, and (5) lack a sense of personal responsibility for not having X. The first factor captures the idea of social comparison; individuals must be aware of someone else who has the object before they can feel resentful. The second factor (wanting) refers to the idea that the object must be desired in order for resentment to occur. The third factor (entitlement) makes the point that individuals must believe that they deserve the object before they will feel resentful. The fourth factor (feasibility) was intended to distinguish relative deprivation from fantasies; resentment will only occur when obtaining the object is realistic. The final factor (responsibility) refers to the idea that people will not feel resentful if they blame themselves for failing to obtain the object.

Survey studies of discontent and collective action, as well as archival studies of violence and revolution, can be seen as generally supportive of these hypothesized preconditions of relative deprivation (see Crosby, 1976, 1982). That is, measures assumed to assess dissatisfaction and discontent have generally co-varied with measures that plausibly reflected the preconditions. Unfortunately, many of these studies used measures of objective deprivation rather than subjective dissatisfaction; also, measures were often obtained at aggregate (group) levels rather than in terms of individual perceptions. Thus, many of the studies provide only indirect support. Nevertheless, the data have generally been consistent with the model.

One precondition that has generated some controversy is feasibility. As noted above, some theorists (e.g., Crosby, 1976; Runciman, 1966) have argued that resentment will occur when obtaining the object is feasible. Other theorists (e.g., Gurr, 1970), however, have argued that resentment is more likely when it is not feasible to obtain the object. In an attempt to resolve this controversy, Cook et al. (1977) distinguished between past and future estimates of feasibility. They reasoned that relative deprivation will be greatest when *past* feasibility was high but *future* feasibility is low. That is, obtaining the object was at one time feasible (thus unrealistic daydreams will not produce resentment), but it currently appears unlikely that the object will be obtained (thus pessimism intensifies resentment). This distinction between past and future feasibility means that there are six potential preconditions of relative deprivation.

Crosby (1976) suggested that the absence of one or more of the preconditions precludes the emotion of relative deprivation, but that other emotions may occur. For example, when wanting is absent, individuals may feel righteous indignation about lacking the object. When individuals accept personal responsibility for lacking a desired object, they may feel envy or jealousy. Thus, research on such emotions as righteous indignation, envy, and jealousy is indirectly relevant to the topic of relative deprivation. However, because these emotions have different preconditions (and presumably different consequences) than relative deprivation, we do not consider them in this chapter.

To our knowledge, the only experimental attempt to examine all of the hypothesized preconditions of relative deprivation was conducted by Bernstein and Crosby (1980). These researchers gave subjects vignettes describing situations of deprivation in which the six preconditions were all independently manipulated (e.g., wanting was sometimes high and sometimes low, past feasibility was sometimes high and sometimes low, etc.). Subjects indicated the degree of resentment (and other emotions) that the characters in the vignettes would experience. Results provided some evidence for the importance of each of the hypothesized preconditions of relative deprivation, in terms of either main effects or interactions with other preconditions. Furthermore, all of the preconditions affected resentment about deprivation in the anticipated direction, with the exception of personal responsibility: Relative deprivation was inexplicably found to be greater when the target person blamed himself or herself for lacking the object than when self-blame was absent. Thus, five of the six preconditions received some empirical support for their expected effects in this experiment.

How do the six hypothesized preconditions of relative deprivation relate to the theme of this chapter—namely, the distinction between cognitive and motivational factors? Five of the six preconditions seem best conceptualized as cognitive in nature because they involve perceptions of an object or state. Specifically, social comparisons, entitlement, personal responsibility, past feasibility, and future feasibility are all cognitive variables. These preconditions involve perceptions of other people, of personal circumstances, or of the likelihood of events. In contrast, the precondition of wanting seems best conceptualized as a motivational variable. The stronger the individual's desire for the object, the more he or she will feel resentful about deprivation. Thus, although most attention has been focused on cognitive preconditions of relative deprivation, one motivational precondition has received attention. Moreover, as we will see next, this motivational precondition may be the most important one of all.

Crosby's Two-Factor Model of Relative Deprivation

Crosby (1976) originally proposed that the five preconditions were necessary and sufficient for relative deprivation to occur. If all five preconditions are necessary, however, then resentment should occur only when all five are present; the absence of any one precondition should preclude resentment. Yet much of the evidence in support of the preconditions, both from survey studies and from the Bernstein and Crosby (1980) experiment, consisted of main effects for individual preconditions. Thus it seems plausible to conceptualize the preconditions as operating in an additive fashion, with each factor serving to increase resentment independently (although interactions between certain preconditions may also occur; see Bernstein & Crosby, 1980). It is possible that some minimal level of each precondition is necessary for relative deprivation to occur, but increases beyond that minimal level seem to be associated with greater reports of resentment.

Further complicating the case for the five-factor model is the fact that many of the preconditions are interrelated. That is, the preconditions themselves are not independent perceptions (see Crosby, 1976). For example, people may come to want things that they see others possess; people will not feel entitled to objects that they blame themselves for lacking; people may feel entitled to objects that were at one time feasible to obtain; and so on. Thus, some of the preconditions may affect relative deprivation via their effects on other preconditions.

Recognizing these issues, Crosby (1982) tested whether her model of relative deprivation could be simplified without losing its predictive power. From a survey study of women's dissatisfaction at home and in the workplace, Crosby concluded that a two-factor model was adequate to predict relative deprivation. Specifically, she found that the factors of wanting and deserving were the strongest predictors of relative deprivation. Thus, Crosby proposed that individuals will experience resentment about deprivation when they lack an object that they want and to which they feel entitled. Other preconditions, such as social comparisons and future feasibility, were also assumed to affect relative deprivation, but indirectly—via the more proximal factors of wanting and deserving.

Olson et al. (in press) tested the two-factor model in two field studies. A sample of single mothers receiving government assistance participated in one survey, and a sample of working women participated in the other survey. Subjects completed measures of the hypothesized preconditions of relative deprivation, as well as measures of resentment. Results generally supported the two-factor model of relative deprivation. Wanting was the strongest single predictor of resentment in both studies. Deserving also predicted resentment, even when wanting was held constant. The only other precondition to predict relative deprivation when wanting was held constant was future feasibility (hopes for the future), which emerged as a significant predictor of just one measure in one study. Thus, the two-factor model of relative deprivation received good but not perfect support in these two studies.

Of course, the two-factor model represents a balanced consideration of cognitive and motivational factors, with one precondition (entitlement) being cognitive in nature and the other precondition (wanting) being motivational in nature. Thus, in terms of integrating cognition and motivation, the two-factor model is quite attractive. Its simplicity is also a virtue. Future researchers need to test the two-factor model experimentally, using manipulations of the preconditions to investigate their impact on relative deprivation. Such research would confirm that wanting and deserving actually cause, rather than result from, resentment.

Folger's Referent Cognitions Model of Relative Deprivation

Folger (1986) has proposed a model of relative deprivation that takes an explicitly cognitive approach. This "referent cognitions" model is based on work in social cognition—including research on the simulation heuristic and counterfactual thinking (e.g., Kahneman & Tversky, 1982)—that focuses on how people imaginatively reconstruct events and circumstances. Specifically, Folger proposed that when people reflect upon present outcomes, their subjective evaluations of the outcomes will be affected by whatever alternative reconstructions of the past are most cognitively accessible.

Folger hypothesized that there are three preconditions of relative deprivation. First, individuals must be able to easily imagine how better outcomes could have occurred in the past. This precondition sets up the potential for resentment, because present outcomes are hedonically inferior to what they might have been. Second, individuals must think it is unlikely that better outcomes will be obtained in the future. This precondition makes the deprivation seem relatively permanent and therefore translates the potential deprivation into actual deprivation. Third, the processes or events that could have produced better outcomes must seem more justifiable (fairer) than the processes or events that actually occurred. This precondition introduces the element of unfairness or injustice into the deprivation.

Folger has conducted several experiments to document the effects of these preconditions on relative deprivation. For example, Folger, Rosenfield, Rheaume, and Martin (1983) gave subjects the opportunity to win a desirable prize. Subjects worked on two tasks, believing that their performance on one task (randomly chosen) would determine whether they would win the prize. Subjects first worked on the critical task and were told that their performance did not earn the prize. They were told, however, that they would later have a second chance at the task to win the prize. Some subjects were told that the criterion for winning the prize would be lower in the next round, which meant that they were likely to win the prize. Other subjects were told that the criterion would remain the same, which meant that they were likely to fail again. This manipulation was expected to determine whether or not subjects expected their deprivation to be permanent. Before the second set of trials, all subjects performed the task that did not count toward the prize. Some subjects were told that their performance on this task was such that they would have won the prize if this task had been their critical one. Other subjects were told that they would have failed to win the prize even if this task had been their critical one. This manipulation was expected to determine whether or not subjects could easily imagine how their outcomes could have been better. Prior to their second attempt at the critical task, subjects completed a questionnaire that included measures of resentment about the arrangements for awarding prizes in the experiment. As expected, subjects reported the most resentment when they could easily imagine how things could have been better (i.e., when they would have won the prize if the second task had been their critical task) *and* when they did not expect their outcomes to improve in the future (i.e., when the criterion for winning the prize would not change on the second trial).

Folger, Rosenfield, and Robinson (1983) had subjects compete against another subject for a desirable reward. A scoring rule for determining the winner was announced prior to the competition. After the competition, however, a change in the scoring rules was announced. All subjects were told that they had lost the competition on the basis of the new rule. Some subjects were told that they would have won the competition under the original rule, whereas others were told that they would have lost in either case. This manipulation was expected to determine whether or not subjects could easily imagine how their outcomes could have been better. Furthermore, some subjects were given a good explanation for the change in rules, whereas others were given a poor explanation that made the change seem arbitrary. This manipulation was expected to determine whether subjects would see the procedures that determined their outcomes as fair or unfair. Subjects then completed a questionnaire that included measures of resentment about the arrangements for assigning rewards in the experiment. As expected, subjects reported the most resentment when they could easily imagine how things could have been better (i.e., when they would have won under the original rules) *and* when the procedures that determined the outcome were unfair (i.e., when the explanation for the change was poor).

It is instructive to consider how Folger's (1986) preconditions map onto those proposed by Crosby (1976). The notion that individuals must be able to easily imagine how outcomes could have been better overlaps both with social comparisons and with wanting the object. That is, being able to imagine how things could have been better will often result from seeing someone else who possesses the object. Moreover, because individuals must be able to imagine how things could have been better, the concept of wanting the object is implicit. The second precondition—that people must think it is unlikely that things will improve in the future—overlaps quite precisely with Cook et al.'s (1977) concept of future feasibility. That is, relative deprivation is more likely when hopes for the future are poor. Finally, the third precondition—that people must consider the processes that produced the actual outcomes to be less fair than those that might have occurred—seems conceptually similar to the precondition of entitlement. That is, when deprivation is attributable to unfair procedures, individuals feel they deserve better outcomes. Thus, it is possible to interpret Folger's preconditions in terms of Crosby's preconditions of social comparisons, wanting, future feasibility, and entitlement, although the match is not always exact.

In comparison with Crosby's (1976, 1982) model, Folger's (1986) model is less explicitly motivational and more explicitly cognitive, as reflected in the name "referent cognitions theory." All of Folger's preconditions involve the cognitive perception of alternative possibilities. Yet, as noted above, the motivational variable of wanting the object is implicated in one of Folger's preconditions. Thus, although the model is predominantly cognitive, there is an implicit role of motivation as well. Perhaps future work on Folger's theory would benefit from an explicit consideration of motivation. For example, the *degree* to which alternative possible outcomes are hedonically superior to present outcomes (i.e., the degree to which the unobtained object is desired or wanted) may affect relative deprivation independently of the *ease* with which such possibilities can be imagined. Such reasoning would represent a more integrated view of motivation and cognition in the preconditions of relative deprivation.

CONSEQUENCES OF RELATIVE DEPRIVATION

Thus far, we have discussed hot and cold aspects of the concept of relative deprivation itself, as well as the preconditions to relative deprivation. The largest area of research within the relative deprivation literature is that devoted to the attitudinal and behavioral outcomes of felt deprivation. This section discusses how affect and cognition play roles in relative deprivation as motivators of attitudes and behavior.

Personal versus Group Relative Deprivation and the Prediction of Attitudes and Behavior

The popularity of relative deprivation reached a peak in the 1960s, when the concept was invoked to explain urban unrest in the United States. Whereas many of these scholarly works used the concept of relative deprivation in a post hoc fashion to explain civil disobedience (e.g., Geschwender, 1964), others set out to determine whether an empirical relation exists between relative deprivation and group-related attitudes, behavior, and behavioral intentions (e.g., Abeles, 1976; Bowen, Bowen, Gawiser, & Masotti, 1968; Caplan & Paige, 1968; Muller, 1972; Vanneman & Pettigrew, 1972).

Reviewers of this early research disagreed on the extent to which relative deprivation is an important determinant of collective behavior (cf. Crosby, 1976; McPhail, 1971; Snyder, 1978). Such disagreement continues (cf. Birt & Dion, 1987; Dubé & Guimond, 1986; Gurney & Tierney, 1982; Martin, Brickman, & Murray, 1984; Olson & Hazlewood, 1986); however, the link between relative deprivation and behavioral outcomes has been elucidated somewhat in recent years. This clarification can be attributed in part to the differentiation between personal and group relative deprivation.

Most researchers investigating the consequences of relative deprivation have been interested in predicting collective behavior, or behavior directed toward improving or protesting the status of one's group as a whole (rather than one's personal status). According to Runciman (1966), group-directed behavior should be better predicted by group-level comparisons than by personal comparisons; thus, group and not personal relative deprivation should predict collective action. However, early theorists often examined the prediction of collective action in the context of how deprived individuals felt *personally*, compared to some referent (e.g., Crosby, 1976; Gurr, 1970; Muller, 1972).

Despite studies in the 1960s and 1970s suggesting the superiority of group over personal relative deprivation as a predictor of group-directed behaviors (e.g., Abeles, 1976; Caplan & Paige, 1968; Vanneman & Pettigrew, 1972), this issue did not come to the forefront of relative deprivation research until the early 1980s (for reviews of research on the distinction between personal and group relative deprivation, see Dion, 1986; Dubé & Guimond, 1986). Since that time, data from a number of studies have demonstrated that group relative deprivation predicts group-directed action, intention, or attitudes better than does personal relative deprivation (e.g., Ellemers et al., 1993; Dubé & Guimond, 1986; Hafer & Olson, 1993; Moghaddam & Perreault, 1992; Olson et al., in press; Walker & Mann, 1987; for exceptions to this general finding, see Appelgryn & Nieuwoudt, 1988; Birt & Dion, 1987). For example, group relative deprivation has been shown to be superior to personal relative deprivation in predicting endorsement of Québec nationalism and protest behaviors among Québec Francophones (Dubé & Guimond, 1986); women's behaviors and intentions aimed at improving the status of working women (Hafer & Olson, 1993; Olson et al., in press); visible-minority immigrants' attempts to raise the status of their group through the promotion of group culture (Moghaddam & Perreault, 1992); and potential for violent protest among unemployed Australians (Walker & Mann, 1987).

Given that, in general, group relative deprivation predicts group-directed responses better than does personal relative deprivation, one might expect that personal discontent would predict self-directed responses (e.g., responses aimed at improving one's personal situation) better than would group discontent. Unfortunately, only a few studies have included measures of both personal and group relative deprivation as well as measures of self-directed behaviors. We (Hafer & Olson, 1993) and Olson et al. (in press, Study 2) found that personal relative deprivation among working women was a better predictor of self-improvement behaviors (e.g., looking for another job, obtaining extra training to improve qualifications) and of willingness to engage in such behaviors than was group relative deprivation. Walker and Mann (1987) found a relation between personal relative deprivation and stress symptoms, which the authors argued to be an individual-level outcome, but no relation between group relative deprivation and stress symptoms. However, other authors have found no relation between personal relative deprivation and individual-level outcomes (e.g., Moghaddam & Perreault, 1992; Olson et al., in press, Study 1). More research is needed in which various measures of group and personal relative deprivation and various measures of group-directed and self-directed responses are examined.

In summary, the predictive power of relative deprivation can be increased by ensuring that the level of comparison implied in the measure of discontent (i.e., personal vs. group relative deprivation) corresponds to the level of response (i.e., self-directed vs. group-directed behaviors), at least when group-directed outcomes are being predicted. Distinguishing between personal and group relative deprivation does not guarantee a strong relation with behavioral and attitudinal responses, however (Dubé & Guimond, 1986). The distinction between affective and cognitive components of relative deprivation also appears to be important.

Cognitive versus Affective Relative Deprivation and the Prediction of Attitudes and Behavior

Relative deprivation theorists have suggested that the mere perception of a discrepancy between one's own or one's group's outcomes and some standard does not predict behavioral and attitudinal outcomes as well as does resentment, anger, or a feeling of injustice (Dubé & Guimond, 1986; Cook et al., 1977; Walker & Pettigrew, 1984). Thus, affective relative deprivation is presumed to predict attitudes and behavior better than cognitive relative deprivation.

This presumption has rarely been tested directly. Most studies have used either cognitive measures of relative deprivation (see the examples cited earlier), affective measures (e.g., Olson et al., in press, Study 1), or a measure incorporating both components (e.g., Hafer & Olson, 1993; Isaac, Mutran, & Stryker, 1980; Tougas, Beaton, & Veilleux, 1991; Olson et al., in press, Study 2). There are only a few studies examining the separate effects of affective and cognitive relative deprivation.

Guimond and Dubé-Simard (1983) experimentally manipulated cognitive group relative deprivation in a sample of Francophones from the Canadian province of Québec by giving them information on the actual income discrepancy between Anglophones and Francophones in Québec (the large-inequality condition) or giving them no such information (the small-inequality condition). They also measured affective group relative deprivation and affective personal relative deprivation. The dependent variable was participants' endorsement of the Québec nationalist movement (a movement advocating more political autonomy for Québec, as well as measures to maintain and enhance French Canadian culture in the province). Positive attitudes toward this movement were predicted by the manipulation of perceived income discrepancy and by affective group relative deprivation. The relation between affective group relative deprivation and sociopolitical attitudes remained significant even when cognitive group relative deprivation was statistically controlled for; however, when affective group relative deprivation was partialed out of the equation, the relation between perceived discrepancy and attitudes disappeared. The authors suggested, therefore, that it is the emotion associated with disadvantaged status that predicts various responses, and not the mere perception of deprivation.

Tougas and Veilleux (1988) measured both affective and cognitive group relative deprivation in a sample of working women. They assessed the perceived discrepancy between men and women in the work force with regards to salaries, hiring, and promotion, as well as how satisfied the participants were with women's overall situation in the workforce compared to men's. Using causal-modeling techniques, Tougas and Veilleux tested the relations between cognitive and affective relative deprivation (among other variables) and attitudes toward affirmative action programs. Cognitive group relative deprivation predicted affective group relative deprivation, which in turn was related to positive attitudes toward affirmative action. The perception of a discrepancy was not directly related to attitudes.

Four Types of Relative Deprivation?

A few studies have measured the cognitive and affective components of both group and personal relative deprivation in studies of responses to injustice. Birt and Dion (1987), for example, examined four types of relative deprivation and their relation to militancy, among other outcomes, in a sample of gay males and lesbians. They assessed how much personal and group discrimination participants perceived relative to members of their own group and the outgroup (cognitive relative deprivation), as well as how much resentment participants felt over such discrimination (affective relative deprivation). Affective personal relative deprivation was the only one of the four relative deprivation measures that predicted militancy. Thus, although the results did not show that group relative deprivation predicted militancy better than personal relative deprivation, as expected from previous research, affect was a better predictor of militant attitudes than was cognition.

Petta and Walker (1992) looked at cognitive and affective, and personal and group, relative deprivation in relation to the ingroup identity of Italian-Australians. Hierarchical regression analyses were used to predict three measures of ethnic identity, with cognitive and affective personal relative deprivation entered in the first step, and cognitive and affective group relative deprivation entered in the second step of the equations. Cognitive group relative deprivation was the only significant predictor of ethnic identity.

Future research on the consequences of relative deprivation might concentrate on further testing the predictive utility of the four proposed types of discontent. This research should involve various samples (e.g., visible minorities, nonvisible minorities, disadvantaged majorities, etc.) in different social and political contexts. Also, a variety of dependent measures should be examined—both self-directed and group-directed responses, and both attitudes and behaviors (see Crosby, 1976, and Mark & Folger, 1984, for typologies of responses to relative deprivation). The influence of various operationalizations of the four types of relative deprivation on predicted consequences should also be investigated. For example, the link between relative deprivation and outcomes may depend on the referent specified (Martin, 1986) and on the particular emotions indicated in the measure of affective relative deprivation (see, e.g., Crosby's 1982 discussion of the importance of distinguishing between dissatisfaction and anger/resentment).

Researchers should also investigate how these proposed types of relative deprivation are related to one another. Guimond and Dubé-Simard (1983) suggest that the four types of relative deprivation are to some extent independent of one another, whereas other authors suggest that the cognitive and affective components as well as the personal and group forms of relative deprivation are necessarily intertwined (e.g., Petta & Walker, 1992). Similarly, several authors have proposed that cognitive relative deprivation precedes affective relative deprivation, and that the latter directly predicts behavioral outcomes (Dubé & Guimond, 1983; Petta & Walker, 1992; Walker & Pettigrew, 1984). This suggested causal chain has been tested with regard to group relative deprivation by Tougas and Veilleux (1988). Such causal-modeling approaches, perhaps including measures taken at various points in time, appear to be a fruitful direction for future relative deprivation research.

Finally, researchers could examine whether the type of standard underlying relative deprivation influences the emotional and behavioral consequences of resentment. Higgins (1990) has proposed a typology of social standards, including "factuals" (beliefs about the actual attributes of people), "self-guides" (valued end states for the self), and "self-possibilities" (representations of possible attributes for the self). Most relative deprivation researchers have focused on how discrepancies from factuals can produce resentment (e.g., comparisons to other people and/or to the self in the past). But it is also possible that discrepancies between one's outcomes and self-guides or self-possibilities may produce relative deprivation. For example, failure to reach an "ideal" self-standard could produce feelings of relative deprivation, as could failure to achieve normative guides ("ought" self-standards). Furthermore, researchers have documented particular patterns of emotional and behavioral consequences associated with discrepancies from different self-guides. For example, actual–ideal discrepancies seem to produce depression, whereas actual–ought discrepancies seem to produce anxiety (see Higgins, 1987). Thus, relative deprivation resulting from discrepancies with these different standards may be associated with specific emotions and behaviors.

ILLUSTRATIVE RESEARCH ON COGNITIVE AND MOTIVATIONAL DETERMINANTS OF RELATIVE DEPRIVATION

To this point, we have reviewed work on the nature, preconditions, and consequences of relative deprivation, mostly conducted by other researchers. In this section, we will describe two programs of research from our own laboratory—one focusing on a cognitive determinant and the other on a motivational determinant of relative deprivation. These programs illustrate the diversity of possible perspectives on resentment about deprivation. The cognitive factor we have investigated is that of perceived qualifications for obtaining the desired object; this factor is assumed to affect resentment by altering two of the preconditions of relative deprivation. The motivational factor we have investigated is that of self-presentational motives; this factor is assumed to affect resentment independently of the preconditions.

Perceived Qualifications and Relative Deprivation

The extent to which deprived individuals feel "qualified" for the desired object may influence their degree of resentment. We define "qualifications" as any characteristics that individuals believe make them legitimately entitled to a desired object or outcome. Normally, such characteristics will be perceived as directly relevant to obtaining the desired object; common examples include training, experience, or skill in a particular domain. Because, by definition, qualifications increase feelings of entitlement or deserving, it might be expected that they would increase resentment about deprivation. Consistent with this reasoning that qualifications or deserving increase resentment, Ross, Thibaut, and Evenbeck (1971) led children to believe that they had performed a task either well or poorly. When they were subsequently provided with low outcomes, children who believed that they had performed well manifested more expressive aggression than did children who believed that they had performed poorly (see also Stephenson & White, 1970).

But it is also possible that perceived qualifications could reduce, rather than increase, resentment about deprivation. Specifically, qualifications typically consist of characteristics that are instrumental in obtaining the desired object (e.g., training, education); individuals who possess these qualities are presumably more likely to obtain the object than are "unqualified" persons. Thus, good qualifications might increase individuals' hopes of obtaining the desired object (i.e., they might increase future feasibility). This increased optimism might reduce individuals' resentment about deprivation. Folger, Rosenfield, Rheaume, and Martin (1983) found that subjects expressed less resentment when their alleged chances of obtaining a desired object were good than when their alleged chances were poor (see also Bernstein & Crosby, 1980).

Thus, perceived qualifications can affect two preconditions of relative deprivation, which have opposite effects on resentment. On the one hand, qualifications increase entitlement, which should increase resentment. On the other hand, qualifications increase hopes (future feasibility), which should reduce resentment. Our studies have been designed to investigate the factors that determine which of these two effects of qualifications will emerge. That is, under what conditions will qualifications increase relative deprivation, and under what conditions will qualifications reduce relative deprivation? We report three of the studies from our laboratory on this issue.

When deprivation is permanent or when the opportunities for obtaining an object seem poor (e.g., the resource is scarce), qualifications are expected to increase resentment. Under these conditions, qualifications cannot increase hopes (because opportunities are poor), whereas qualifications do make salient a sense of entitlement or deserving. On the other hand, when the opportunities for obtaining an object seem good (e.g., the resource is abundant), qualifications are expected to reduce resentment. Under these conditions, qualifications should increase hopes of obtaining the object, which will make the deprivation seem temporary and therefore bearable.

In the first test of this reasoning (Olson & Ross, 1984, Experiment 1), a questionnaire was mailed to 50 unemployed nurses approximately 3 months after they graduated. At the time the study was conducted, government cutbacks in health spending had led to a serious job shortage for nurses in Canada. The first two questions in the questionnaire were designed to manipulate respondents' perceptions of (1) their qualifications compared to those of employed nurses and (2) the general opportunities for nursing jobs. Specifically, subjects were asked to list five or six similarities (or differences) between themselves and employed nurses, and to list five or six factors that should improve (or make even worse) the job situation for nurses. Olson and Ross assumed that if subjects thought about similarities between themselves and employed nurses, they would temporarily feel more "qualified" for employment than if they thought about differences between themselves and employed nurses. It was also assumed that if subjects thought about factors that should improve the job situation, they would temporarily perceive greater opportunities for obtaining jobs than if they thought about factors that should make the job situation even worse.

Subsequent questions in the questionnaire measured subjects' resentment

TABLE 3.1   Mean Resentment about Deprivation

Relation to employed nurses	Future of the job situation	
	Improve (abundant resource)	Worsen (scarce resource)
Similar (high qualifications)	11.60	14.09
Different (low qualifications)	15.73	11.90

Note. Possible scores range from 3 to 21, with higher scores reflecting more reported resentment. Adapted from Olson and Ross (1984).

about being unemployed, as well as their feelings of entitlement to a job and their hopes of obtaining a job soon. Table 3.1 presents the cell means for a composite measure of resentment. Analysis of this measure revealed only the predicted interaction between "improve-worsen" and "similar-different." Planned contrasts showed that, as predicted, qualifications reduced resentment when the resource was abundant. That is, similar subjects reported less resentment than different subjects when the job situation was expected to improve. Although the means in the "worsen" condition were in the predicted direction of good qualifications (similarity) increasing resentment, this difference was not reliable.

Thus, qualifications reduced resentment when the resource was abundant. Presumably, this effect occurred because qualifications increased hopes of obtaining a job. Indeed, analysis of a measure of hopes showed that similarity significantly increased optimism. Qualifications did not significantly increase resentment when the resource was scarce. This expected effect was based on the assumption that qualifications would increase perceived entitlement to a job. Yet analysis of a measure of entitlement revealed no effect for the similarity manipulation. Thus, perhaps the expected effect did not emerge because the manipulation of qualifications did not affect entitlement.

In a second study (Olson, 1986, Study 3), qualifications and opportunities for obtaining the desired object were measured rather than manipulated. Specifically, in the middle of the school year, 209 university students were asked whether they were taking any course in which they were *not* doing as well (in terms of marks) as they had hoped to do. Of the 209 students, 208 answered this question affirmatively. These 208 subjects then answered a number of questions about this course. First, to measure perceived qualifications, subjects were asked how they compared in terms of ability and effort to people who were getting the marks the subjects had hoped for; subjects were assigned to one of three groups according to their answers (either "better," "equal," or "worse" qualifications than students who *were* getting the target grade). Second, to measure opportunities for obtaining the desired grade, subjects were asked whether it was still possible for them to finish the course with their desired mark; subjects were

TABLE 3.2   **Mean Resentment about Deprivation**

Ability and effort comparisons to students who are getting the target grade (qualifications)	*Possibility of getting target grade*	
	Possible (abundant resource)	*Unlikely/impossible (scarce resource)*
Better	7.85	8.30
Equal	7.42	7.38
Worse	5.79	6.52

Note. Possible scores range from 2 to 14, with higher scores reflecting more reported resentment. Adapted from Olson (1986).

assigned to one of two groups according to their answers (either "possible" or "unlikely/impossible" to finish with the desired grade).

The remaining items in the questionnaire measured subjects' resentment about their current grades, as well as their perceived entitlement to the mark they had hoped for and their hopes of obtaining that target grade. Table 3.2 presents the cell means for a composite measure of resentment. Analysis of the resentment measure revealed only a main effect for qualifications, with "better" and "equal" subjects reporting more resentment than "worse" subjects, regardless of whether obtaining the desired grade was still possible (i.e., regardless of the abundance of the resource).

Thus, this second study produced a different pattern of results than the first experiment. Good qualifications were associated with more relative deprivation, both when this pattern was expected (scarce resource) and when it was not (abundant resource). Recall that qualifications were hypothesized to increase resentment because they would increase feelings of entitlement, whereas the ameliorating impact of qualifications on resentment was hypothesized to result from their effects on hopes. Given that qualifications served only to increase resentment in this second study, it is interesting that the qualifications classification was significantly associated with reported entitlement to the desired grade, but was not reliably associated with hopes of achieving the desired grade. Indeed, the results across the two studies seem interpretable when the effects of qualifications on entitlement and hopes are examined. In the first experiment, qualifications increased hopes but not entitlement, and the hypothesized ameliorating effect on resentment was obtained. In the second study, qualifications were associated with increased entitlement but not with hopes, and the hypothesized exacerbating effect on resentment was obtained. Perhaps, then, a study in which qualifications increased both entitlement and hopes would obtain both hypothesized effects of qualifications on relative deprivation under the appropriate conditions.

In a third experiment (Olson, 1990), subjects were told that their goal was to earn 100 "points" on some simple motor tasks, including a game called

SIMON (which requires the production of increasingly long sequences of flash-ing lights). They were told that if they reached this goal, they would be able to leave the experiment early (a potential reward that generated considerable enthu-siasm). Subjects completed several practice trials on SIMON. Perceived qualifi-cations were then manipulated by telling some subjects ("high qualifications") that, based on what they had done during the just-completed practice trials, they would have earned 50 unexpected bonus points toward their goal if the ex-perimenter's adviser (the experimenter was allegedly a student) had not recently changed the rules. In other words, these high-qualifications subjects were told that under the old rules, they would have earned 50 bonus points. Other sub-jects were told that they would *not* have earned the bonus points under the old system ("low qualifications"). A third group was not told anything about an old system for awarding bonus points ("ambiguous qualifications").[2] The rationale for the adviser's change of rules was not compelling; the experimenter implied that the change was arbitrary and perhaps even unfair.

All subjects were then given the opportunity to earn 50 bonus points "the new way," which involved a single test trial on SIMON. After they completed the test trial, subjects were told that they had not earned the bonus points.

The principal measure of relative deprivation in this experiment was the number of words subjects wrote in response to an open-ended request for sug-gestions for changes in the procedure; this request was taken as an indicant of dissatisfaction. Half of the subjects completed this measure *before* attempting the critical test trial on SIMON, whereas the other half of the subjects completed the measure *after* they had learned that they did not earn the bonus points on the critical trial; this constituted the manipulation of opportunities available for obtaining the desired object. Thus, half of the subjects completed the measure when there was still a chance that they would earn the bonus points, whereas the remaining subjects knew when they completed the measure that their depri-vation was permanent (i.e., they had not earned the bonus points).

Table 3.3 presents the cell means for the number-of-words measure. Analy-sis of this measure revealed only the predicted interaction between qualifications and opportunities available for obtaining the object. Planned contrasts showed that both hypothesized effects of qualifications occurred in this experiment. When it was still possible to obtain the bonus points, high-qualifications sub-

TABLE 3.3   Mean Number of Words in Suggestions for Changes

| | Time of measure | |
	Before test trial (abundant resource)	After test trial (scarce resource)
Qualifications		
High	9.6	19.6
Ambiguous	8.5	10.4
Low	18.3	12.8

Note. Data from Olson (1990).

jects wrote significantly fewer words (i.e., were less dissatisfied) than low-qualifications subjects. In contrast, when deprivation was permanent, high-qualifications subjects wrote significantly more words (i.e., were more dissatisfied) than low-qualifications subjects.

Thus, qualifications reduced relative deprivation when the resource was still obtainable, but increased relative deprivation when the resource was impossible to obtain. Moreover, analysis of items measuring subjects' feelings of entitlement to the bonus points and their pretrial hopes of earning the bonus points showed that the qualifications manipulation significantly affected both measures. Thus, support for the theoretical analysis was reasonably complete: Qualifications increased both entitlement and hopes, and either increased or decreased resentment as predicted, depending upon the opportunities available for obtaining the object.

In conclusion, perceived qualifications constitute a cognitive variable that affects relative deprivation. How deprived individuals evaluate themselves along dimensions pertinent to obtaining the desired object is an important determinant of their resentment about deprivation. Future research needs to explore the dynamics of perceived qualifications (e.g., how deprived individuals decide that they are well or poorly qualified for a resource), as well as the interactive effects of this variable in conjunction with factors other than the opportunities available for obtaining the desired object.

Self-Presentational Motives and Relative Deprivation

A second program of research in our laboratory has examined a motivational determinant of relative deprivation. Specifically, we have investigated the role of self-presentational motives in reports of resentment. "Self-presentation" refers to the use of public behavior to create certain impressions in others' eyes (Jones & Pittman, 1982). Self-presentational motives have been shown to affect many interpersonal behaviors, including aggression, altruism, conformity, attitude expression, and nonverbal behavior (see Baumeister, 1982, 1986; Leary & Kowalski, 1990; Schlenker, 1980; cf. Tetlock & Manstead, 1985). Our research has tested whether the desire to create certain impressions in others' eyes can affect the reporting of resentment about deprivation. We describe three experiments that we have recently conducted on this issue.

Jones and Pittman (1982) provided a comprehensive analysis of the strategies individuals use to achieve self-presentational goals. These authors distinguished five self-presentation strategies designed to create different impressions: (1) ingratiation, in which the person tries to be liked; (2) intimidation, in which the person tries to appear dangerous and to be feared; (3) self-promotion, in which the person tries to appear competent and to be respected; (4) exemplification, in which the person tries to appear worthy and to arouse guilt; and (5) supplication, in which the person tries to appear helpless and to arouse feelings of nurturance and obligation. Jones and Pittman proposed that these strategies will be used in situations where the desired impression will allow the self-presenter to gain the power to influence the target person.

In our first experiment, we used Jones and Pittman's (1982) taxonomy of self-presentation strategies as a framework for the research. We began with a study employing a hypothetical scenario, because this procedure allowed the easiest manipulation of self-presentational strategies. Our goal was to show that self-presentational motives, as manifested by the use of the strategies identified by Jones and Pittman, can influence the reporting of resentment. We predicted that the strategy of ingratiation would lead subjects to understate their resentment, because complaining about one's outcomes is usually considered unattractive. In contrast, the strategy of intimidation was expected to lead to exaggerated reports of resentment, because threats are more credible when backed up by anger. We did not have a priori predictions for the strategies of self-promotion, exemplification, or supplication.

Subjects read a hypothetical scenario describing a situation of deprivation[3]—namely, the case of a student who was receiving low marks:

> Students do not always get marks that are as high as they had hoped in a course. Sometimes, getting marks that are lower than one's goals can produce feelings of unfairness or resentment.
>
> Imagine that someone is taking a course where they [sic] are not doing as well, in terms of marks, as they had hoped to do. They have kept up with the work and have studied hard, but just haven't done well on the exams, which they know are marked by a teaching assistant. The course is now half over, and although it is still possible that they can obtain the grade they had hoped for, it seems unlikely.
>
> Imagine that this student attends a social event at one of the residences. Several teaching assistants also attend this event, including the teaching assistant for the course in which the student is not doing as well as hoped. The student and teaching assistant recognize one another, because the student sought help before one of the tests. The teaching assistant comes over to talk to the student, and asks, "How is the course going?"

Subjects indicated how the student would present himself or herself on several dimensions if he or she was employing a particular self-presentational strategy. For example, subjects were asked how the student would present himself or herself if he or she wanted to intimidate the teaching assistant. Each of the five self-presentational strategies identified by Jones and Pittman (1982) was described to subjects, as well as an "honest" self-presentation condition (which, for convenience, we also refer to as a "strategy"). Subjects made the ratings for each of the six strategies (thus strategies were manipulated within subjects). Subject rated how the student would present himself or herself on several dimensions, four of which are relevant to our present concern with relative deprivation: "feel angry" and "feel resentful" (which were averaged to form a resentment composite measure), and "feel unjustly deprived" and "feel unfairly treated" (which were averaged to form an unjust-deprivation composite measure).

TABLE 3.4 Mean Resentment and Unjust Deprivation

	Self-presentation strategy					
Measure	*Honesty*	*Ingratiation*	*Intimidation*	*Self-promotion*	*Exemplification*	*Supplication*
Resentment	4.18_d	1.56_a	5.94_e	2.28_b	3.91_c	2.07_b
Unjust deprivation	4.41_d	2.10_a	5.87_f	2.72_b	5.49_e	3.52_c

Note. Possible scores range from 1 to 7, with higher scores reflecting more resentment or unjust deprivation. Within rows, means not sharing a common subscript differ at $p < .05$ (Newman–Keuls comparisons).

Table 3.4 presents the cell means for the resentment and unjust-deprivation measures. The main effect for self-presentational strategies was significant on both measures, and Newman–Keuls comparisons of the means (also summarized in the table) revealed the pattern of differences. It is most instructive to examine the findings in terms of comparisons to honest self-presentation. As predicted, the strategy of ingratiation resulted in lower reports of resentment and unjust deprivation than did honest self-presentation. Also as predicted, the strategy of intimidation resulted in higher reports of resentment and unjust deprivation than did honest self-presentation. The strategy of exemplification resulted in more reported unjust deprivation but less reported resentment than did honest self-presentation. Finally, both self-promotion and supplication resulted in lower reports of resentment and unjust deprivation than did honest self-presentation.

Thus, this first experiment showed that reports of resentment could be either understated or exaggerated, depending on self-presentational strategies. Ingratiation was associated with lowered reports of relative deprivation, presumably because complaining is assumed to be unattractive. Intimidation produced heightened reports of relative deprivation, presumably because people are more likely to be feared when they are angry. Self-promotion resulted in lowered reports of relative deprivation; perhaps competence implies that people are satisfied with their lot. Exemplification resulted in exaggerated reports of being unjustly deprived, but lowered reports of resentment; presumably, the absence of anger in the face of unfair treatment is an effective way to arouse guilt. Finally, supplication resulted in lowered reports of relative deprivation; perhaps caring is more likely to be aroused when individuals do not complain about their situation.

Although the first experiment linked patterns of reported resentment with self-presentational strategies, it was limited by its hypothetical-scenario methodology. In the final two experiments to be described, we moved to an examination of self-presentational strategies on reported resentment during spontaneous interactions. This shift made it difficult to manipulate subjects' self-presentational strategies. Instead, we took advantage of the most ubiquitous strategy of individuals—ingratiation. All else being equal, people want to be liked; thus, they generally have a "default" strategy of ingratiation (see Jones & Wortman, 1973).

Researchers in the past have used several operational strategies for documenting the impact of self-presentational motives on spontaneous behavior (see Baumeister, 1982; Tetlock & Manstead, 1985). Two techniques have been particularly common. The first and most common technique to test for the occurrence of self-presentation has been to compare two situations that are identical in all respects, except that for some subjects the event is public, and for other subjects the event is private (e.g., Satow, 1975). The assumption underlying this technique is that self-presentation occurs only (or mostly) when subjects believe their behavior will be observed or their opinions will be public. If subjects' behaviors are different in public and private settings, then self-presentational motives are assumed to have been operative.

A second operational strategy for documenting the role of self-presentational motives has been to manipulate the perceived beliefs or values of the audience with whom subjects expect to interact (e.g., Borden, 1975). If subjects are trying to present themselves favorably to the audience (e.g., the default strategy of ingratiation), then their behavior should differ, depending on the audience's values and beliefs. Specifically, if subjects are engaging in self-presentation, then they should attempt to match the audience's standards. Thus, the manipulation of audience standards should influence subjects' behaviors.

In the final two experiments, we combined these two operational strategies. That is, we manipulated both the public–private nature of the behavior and the perceived standards of a target person. We reasoned that if subjects' responses were guided by self-presentational motives, then they should be affected by the standards of the audience in the public condition but not in the private condition (or less so in the private condition). That is, the known standards of the target person should exert a large effect on subjects' responses in the public condition, but should have less or no effect in the private condition.

Specifically, we asked subjects to report their resentment about an issue, and their answers were either public or private. Before measuring resentment, we also provided information about how another person felt about this issue, indicating that this person was either resentful or not resentful. We expected subjects' own expressions of resentment to be influenced by the alleged feelings of the other individual more in the public than in the private condition.

In the first of these two experiments, undergraduate students participated in pairs, but in separate rooms. The female experimenter went back and forth between the rooms to conduct the study. On the first visit to each subject's room, the experimenter asked subjects to think about whether they were currently taking any course in which they were not doing as well, in terms of marks, as they had hoped to do. The experimenter then left the room. On the next visit, subjects were asked whether there was a course where they were not doing as well as they had hoped. All subjects answered affirmatively. The experimenter then said that they would be completing a questionnaire about this course.

The manipulation of the public–private nature of responses was then introduced. Subjects in the "public" condition were told that after they completed the questionnaire, they would exchange questionnaires with their partners, and they would meet with their partners to discuss their answers. Thus, these subjects expected to meet and discuss their resentment about the course. Subjects in the "private" condition were told to complete the questionnaire anonymously and to leave it in a box in the room. They were told that they would meet with their partners to discuss tuition and residence fees. Thus, these subjects did not expect to discuss their resentment about the course.

The manipulation of partner resentment was then introduced. The experimenter remarked casually to each subject that she had seen the partner's questionnaire on her last visit to his or her room. Subjects in the "partner resentful" condition were told that their partners were "pretty angry" about their marks in the focal course. Subjects in the "partner not resentful" condition were told that their partners were "not angry" about their marks in the course.

Subjects then completed a brief questionnaire measuring their feelings about the course where they were not doing as well as they had hoped, including their resentment about their marks in the course. Table 3.5 presents the cell means on the resentment measure. Analysis of this measure revealed the predicted interaction between public–private condition and alleged partner resentment, as well as a main effect for partner resentment. Planned contrasts showed that subjects' reports of resentment were affected by their partners' alleged resentment in both the public and private conditions. However, as tested by the interaction (and as predicted), this effect was significantly stronger in the public than in the private condition.

Thus, when subjects expected to exchange questionnaires with their partners, they were more motivated to match their partners' alleged level of resentment than when they believed their answers were private. Presumably, subjects' self-presentational strategy in this experiment was ingratiation (i.e., to be seen as likeable). Agreeing with someone is a good way to be liked; similarity is a powerful determinant of attraction. Therefore, when subjects' answers were public, they were motivated to match the level of resentment allegedly expressed by their partners. Our findings are compatible with research in the area of interpersonal communications, which has shown that publicly produced messages, but not private messages, are tailored to suit the attitude of the audience and subse-

TABLE 3.5 Mean Resentment about Marks

	Partner resentment	
	Partner resentful	*Partner not resentful*
Public	4.73	2.32
Private	4.45	3.36

Note. Possible scores range from 1 to 7, with higher scores reflecting more reported resentment.

quently affect the personal attitudes of the communicator (e.g., Higgins & Rholes, 1978).

But why did partner resentment exert an effect even in the private condition? One possibility is that the private condition was not effective; subjects may not have believed that their answers were anonymous. In retrospect, it seems likely that the manipulation of partner resentment reduced the effectiveness of the private condition, because the experimenter made it known in each case that she had looked at the partner's answers and then communicated this information to the subject. Perhaps subjects in the private condition feared that their answers would be communicated back to their partners by the apparently talkative experimenter. If the private condition was not really private, then self-presentational motives would have continued to operate even in the private condition, which would be expected to produce a main effect for partner resentment (which was also significant).

In the final experiment, we again manipulated the public versus private nature of subjects' reports of resentment and the alleged views of a target person. In this case, however, the target person was the experimenter, and we manipulated experimenter resentment in a manner that would not weaken the effectiveness of the private condition. Also, we moved to an older sample and changed the focus of subjects' deprivation. Specifically, we measured subjects' resentment about the lack of day care facilities for working parents in London, Ontario. Although not everyone in the sample currently had children, we assumed that they would be concerned about this issue either for personal reasons (e.g., they planned to have children) or because they cared about the facilities available for their peers (which would constitute potential group relative deprivation). We predicted that the level of resentment expressed by the experimenter would have a significant impact on subjects' reported resentment when their answers were public, but little or no impact when their answers were private.

Subjects were employees of a variety of companies in London, including a telephone company, a utility company, a manufacturing firm, and the University of Western Ontario. Educational levels ranged from high school to university degrees. Sixty percent of the subjects currently had children. Subjects were approached individually or in small groups. The female experimenter (who was a mature student) introduced herself to subjects and asked them whether they would be willing to complete a brief questionnaire on the day care facilities in London. If subjects agreed to participate, the manipulations of experimenter resentment and public–private nature of responses were applied. First, subjects were exposed to information about the experimenter's own resentment about the day care situation. Subjects in the "experimenter resentful" condition were told: "I am a single, working parent. I'm certainly resentful and upset about the lack of day care facilities in London, and I am trying to find out how other people feel about this issue." Subjects in the "experimenter not resentful" condition were told: "I have to do my thesis in order to graduate, and my advisor suggested that I look at the day care issue in London. Personally, I have a child in the system, and I am satisfied with the day care situation." The public versus private nature of subjects' responses was then manipulated. Subjects in the "public" condition were asked to sign their questionnaires and were told that the experimenter would return to pick up the questionnaire from them. Subjects in the "private" condition were told that the questionnaire would be anonymous and were asked to leave the questionnaire in a central location to be picked up later by the experimenter.

Subjects were then given a short questionnaire on the day care situation in London, including items assessing their resentment about this issue. Table 3.6 presents the cell means on the composite resentment measure. Analysis of this measure revealed just the predicted interaction between public–private responding and experimenter resentment, although this interaction was only marginally significant ($p < .07$). Planned contrasts showed that, as predicted, subjects in the public response condition reported significantly ($p < .05$) more resentment when the experimenter said that she was resentful than when the experimenter said that she was not resentful. Subjects in the private condition did not differ in reported resentment according to whether the experimenter said that she was resentful or not resentful.

This final experiment yielded clearer support for our prediction that subjects would match a target person's alleged level of resentment in the public but not in the private condition. Specifically, when the experimenter was believed to be able to identify their answers, subjects' reports of resentment about the day care situation in London were significantly affected by the experimenter's alleged resentment. But when their answers were private, subjects showed no impact of the experimenter's alleged resentment. Thus, subjects matched the experimenter's relative deprivation in public but not in private. This pattern is exactly consistent with predictions based on self-presentational motives. If subjects were attempting to present themselves favorably to the experimenter (i.e., to ingratiate themselves), then they would be expected to publicly match the experimenter's known values. Thus, this experiment showed that self-presentational motives can affect subjects' reports of resentment.

To our knowledge, our experiments constitute the first direct investigations of self-presentational motives in reports of relative deprivation. The findings elucidate both the strategies of self-presentation identified by Jones and Pittman (1982) and the mechanisms underlying reports of resentment.

TABLE 3.6   Mean Resentment about Day Care Facilities

	Experimenter resentment	
	Experimenter resentful	*Experimenter not resentful*
Public	4.18	2.79
Private	3.42	3.36

Note. Possible scores range from 1 to 7, with higher scores reflecting more reported resentment.

Ingratiation was the strategy that was examined most thoroughly in our research. When individuals have information about the level of resentment felt by a target person, ingratiation motivates matching that level of resentment. Presumably, individuals intuitively understand that perceived similarity leads to liking; thus, they try to appear similar in resentment to the target person. On the other hand, when individuals have no information about a target person's level of resentment (as in our first study), ingratiation appears to motivate underreporting of resentment. Presumably, complaining about one's lot is generally assumed to be unattractive.

Future research could identify the types of deprivation situations in which various self-presentational strategies will be used. Such research might be able to provide a taxonomy of deprivation situations that are associated with each strategy. For example, ingratiation may be associated with positive interpersonal relationships, whereas intimidation may occur more frequently in negatively valenced relationships. Also, ingratiation may be more likely when the deprived person has less power than the source of the deprivation, whereas intimidation may be more likely under conditions of equal power (see Jones & Pittman, 1982). Furthermore, some deprivation situations seem likely to evoke multiple self-presentational strategies, which may have competing effects. For example, bargaining settings will often motivate several strategies, including ingratiation and intimidation. Yet these strategies may have different implications for reports of relative deprivation, with ingratiation typically motivating understatements of resentment, and intimidation typically motivating exaggeration of resentment. Perhaps some bargaining settings (e.g., cooperative ones) emphasize ingratiation, whereas others (e.g., competitive ones) emphasize intimidation. Knowledge of the conditions that induce specific strategies will advance our understanding of both reports of resentment and self-presentation.

We have mentioned earlier in the chapter that self-presentational motives may underlie the personal–group discrimination discrepancy. That is, individuals may want to understate their personal resentment or discrimination (or overstate the discrimination suffered by others in their group) in order to present an image of personal strength or adjustment. Although the data we have gathered on self-presentation of relative deprivation do not bear directly on the personal–group discrimination discrepancy, the findings support the plausibility of a self-presentation interpretation of this phenomenon. In the future, researchers might explore the effects of such manipulations as public versus private responding on subjects' reports of personal and group discrimination.

In conclusion, self-presentation is a motivational factor that can affect reports of relative deprivation. Individuals' motives to create certain impressions in others' eyes can introduce systematic distortions in reports of resentment about deprivation. Such distortions can involve either overstating or understating true levels of resentment. Self-presentational strategies ranging from ingratiation to intimidation have predictable effects on measures of relative deprivation.

CONCLUSIONS

Relative deprivation has both "hot" and "cold" aspects. We have described affective, motivational, and cognitive aspects of the definition of relative deprivation; the preconditions to relative deprivation; the consequences of relative deprivation; and our own research on resentment. Although many researchers (including ourselves) have tended to emphasize either affective/motivational or cognitive aspects of relative deprivation in their work, there is an increasing realization that a synergistic perspective (the "Warm Look"; Sorrentino & Higgins, 1986) would be most productive. Let us close by considering a few ways that such a perspective could be manifested in work on relative deprivation.

First, researchers need to be clear about how they conceptualize relative deprivation in their work. Is relative deprivation an affective, a cognitive, or both an affective and a cognitive concept? Although it may be possible to distinguish the "four types of relative deprivation" (affective and cognitive, personal and group) in some situations, we believe that a synergistic perspective is best. That is, relative deprivation occurs when a discrepancy is perceived between what is deserved and what is obtained, *and* when that discrepancy results in resentment or anger. Thus, relative deprivation has both a cognitive and an affective component.

Researchers also need to ensure that their measures of relative deprivation reflect their conceptualization. Too often, the conceptual and operational definitions of relative deprivation within a study do not correspond (Gurney & Tierney, 1982; Martin, 1986; Walker & Pettigrew, 1984). It would be desirable if researchers could adopt both a common terminology and a common operationalization of relative deprivation; the term is currently used in many different ways, making the comparison of results across studies difficult. Again, we believe that including both hot and cold aspects in the concept offers the most productive avenue for research.

Specific topics within the relative-deprivation literature would also benefit from a synergistic perspective. For example, as mentioned earlier, the personal–group discrimination discrepancy probably results from both cognitive and motivational processes. Further exploration of this phenomenon is warranted, including its limitations (for preliminary work on limitations, see Crosby et al., 1989; Taylor et al., 1994). Also, work on the preconditions of relative deprivation needs to be more explicit about which ones are cognitive and which are affective/motivational. As we have argued, whereas most preconditions are probably best viewed as cognitive factors, the precondition of wanting the desired object seems motivational in nature. The role of self-presentation motives in reports of relative deprivation also needs to be explored further. Self-presentation constitutes a clear example of a motivational force that can shape reports of resentment. Finally, research on the consequences of relative deprivation would also benefit from a synergistic approach. For example, the consequences of relative deprivation may differ, depending on whether strong affect is associated with the deprivation: Resentment and anger may motivate assertive action, whereas the simple perception of deprivation may not. Also, there may be moderators of the relation between relative deprivation and various behavioral consequences. For example, sociological variables such as those suggested by resource mobilization theorists (e.g., McCarthy & Zald, 1977), as well as psychological variables such as beliefs about the justice of the world (e.g., Hafer & Olson, 1993), may be important. Crosby (1976) suggests that specific responses to relative deprivation will depend on such factors as whether victims blame themselves or society, their level of personal control, and the availability of opportunities for various types of assertive action (see also the related work by Mark & Folger, 1984; Tajfel, 1981; Taylor & McKirnan, 1984). Of course, these moderating factors can themselves be classified as emphasizing either hot or cold processes.

In summary, relative deprivation is a concept that lends itself nicely to a synergistic perspective incorporating cognition and affect/motivation. We hope that future research on this important topic will move in this integrative direction.

Acknowledgments

Preparation of this chapter was supported by a research grant to James M. Olson from the Social Sciences and Humanities Research Council of Canada. We thank E. Tory Higgins and Richard M. Sorrentino for their comments on a previous version of the chapter.

Notes

1. We should note that, to our knowledge, the personal–group discrimination discrepancy has been studied exclusively within members of disadvantaged groups, such as women, blacks, immigrants, and so on. It is unclear whether the phenomenon would occur if the deprived individual were a member of an advantaged group in society. Certainly, several of the explanations proposed for the effect (see the following paragraphs) do not seem applicable to members of advantaged groups. It would be interesting for future researchers to investigate the discrepancy within members of advantaged groups. We thank E. Tory Higgins for bringing this point to our attention.

2. Note that our manipulation of qualifications was similar to procedures used by Folger (1986) to manipulate the ease with which individuals can imagine better outcomes' having occurred. This overlap between qualifications and "referent outcomes" makes sense, because good qualifications should make it easier to imagine how better things could have occurred.

3. Subjects actually read two hypothetical scenarios. These scenarios produced virtually identical results. Thus, for reasons of space, only one scenario is described.

References

Abeles, R. P. (1976). Relative deprivation, rising expectations, and black militancy. *Journal of Social Issues, 32*(2), 119–137.

Appelgryn, A. E. M., & Nieuwoudt, J. M. (1988). Relative deprivation and the ethnic attitudes of blacks and Afrikaans-speaking whites in South Africa. *Journal of Social Psychology, 128,* 311-323.

Baumeister, R. F. (1982). A self-presentational view of social phenomena. *Psychological Bulletin, 91,* 3-26.

Baumeister, R. F. (Ed.). (1986). *Public self and private self.* New York: Springer-Verlag.

Bernstein, M., & Crosby, F. (1980). An empirical examination of relative deprivation theory. *Journal of Experimental Social Psychology, 16,* 442-456.

Birt, C. M., & Dion, K. L. (1987). Relative deprivation theory and responses to discrimination in a gay male and lesbian sample. *British Journal of Social Psychology, 26,* 139-145.

Borden, R. J. (1975). Witnessed aggression: Influence of an observer's sex and values on aggressive responding. *Journal of Personality and Social Psychology, 31,* 567-573.

Bowen, D. R., Bowen, E., Gawiser, S., & Masotti, L. H. (1968). Deprivation, mobility, and orientation toward protest of the urban poor. In L. H. Masotti & D. R. Bowen (Eds.), *Civil violence in the urban community* (pp. 187-200). Beverly Hills, CA: Sage.

Cantril, H. (1965). *The pattern of human concerns.* New Brunswick, NJ: Rutgers University Press.

Caplan, N. S., & Paige, J. M. (1968). A study of ghetto rioters. *Scientific American, 219,* 15-21.

Cook, T. D., Crosby, F. J., & Hennigan, K. M. (1977). The contruct validity of relative deprivation. In J. M. Suls & R. L. Miller (Eds.), *Social comparison processes* (pp. 307-336). Washington, DC: Hemisphere.

Crosby, F. J. (1976). A model of egoistical relative deprivation. *Psychological Review, 83,* 85-113.

Crosby, F. J. (1982). *Relative deprivation and working women.* New York: Oxford University Press.

Crosby, F. J. (1984). The denial of personal discrimination. *American Behavioral Scientist, 27,* 371-386.

Crosby, F. J., Muehrer, P., & Loewenstein, G. (1986). Relative deprivation and explanation: Models and concepts. In J. M. Olson, C. P. Herman, & M. P. Zanna (Eds.), *The Ontario Symposium: Vol. 4. Relative deprivation and social comparison* (pp. 17-32). Hillsdale, NJ: Erlbaum.

Crosby, F. J., Pufall, A., Snyder, R. C., O'Connell, M., & Whalen, P. (1989). The denial of personal disadvantage among you, me, and all the other ostriches. In M. Crawford & M. Gentry (Eds.), *Gender and thought: Psychological perspectives* (pp. 79-99). New York: Springer-Verlag.

Davis, J. A. (1959). A formal interpretation of the theory of relative deprivation. *Sociometry, 22,* 280-296.

Dion, K. L. (1986). Responses to perceived discrimination and relative deprivation. In J. M. Olson, C. P. Herman, & M. P. Zanna (Eds.), *The Ontario Symposium:* Vol. 4. *Relative deprivation and social comparison* (pp. 159-179). Hillsdale, NJ: Erlbaum.

Dubé, L., & Guimond, S. (1986). Relative deprivation and social protest: The personal-group issue. In J. M. Olson, C. P. Herman, & M. P. Zanna (Eds.), *The Ontario Symposium: Vol. 4. Relative deprivation and social comparison* (pp. 201-216). Hillsdale, NJ: Erlbaum.

Ellemers, N., Wilke, H., & van Knippenberg, A. (1993). Effects of legitimacy of low group or individual status on individual and collective status-enhancement strategies. *Journal of Personality and Social Psychology, 64,* 766-778.

Fiske, S. T., & Taylor, S. E. (1991). *Social cognition* (2nd ed.). Reading, MA: Addison-Wesley.

Folger, R. (1986). A referent cognitions theory of relative deprivation. In J. M. Olson, C. P. Herman, & M. P. Zanna (Eds.), *The Ontario Symposium: Vol. 4. Relative deprivation and social comparison* (pp. 33-55). Hillsdale, NJ: Erlbaum.

Folger, R. G., Rosenfield, D., Rheaume, K., & Martin, C. (1983). Relative deprivation and referent cognitions. *Journal of Experimental Social Psychology, 19,* 172-184.

Folger, R. G., Rosenfield, D., & Robinson, T. (1983). Relative deprivation and procedural justifications. *Journal of Personality and Social Psychology, 45,* 268-273.

Geschwender, J. A. (1964). Social structure and the Negro revolt: An examination of some hypotheses. *Social Forces, 43,* 248-256.

Guimond, S., & Dubé-Simard, L. (1983). Relative deprivation theory and the Quebec nationalist movement: The cognition-motion distinction and the personal-group deprivation issue. *Journal of Personality and Social Psychology, 44,* 526-535.

Gurney, J. N., & Tierney, K. J. (1982). Relative deprivation and social movements: A critical look at twenty years of theory and research. *The Sociological Quarterly, 23,* 33-47.

Gurr, T. R. (1970). *Why men rebel.* Princeton, NJ: Princeton University Press.

Hafer, C. L., & Olson, J. M. (1993). Beliefs in a just world, discontent, and assertive actions by working women. *Personality and Social Psychology Bulletin, 19,* 30-38.

Higgins, E. T. (1987). Self-discrepancy: A theory relating self and affect. *Psychological Review, 94,* 319-340.

Higgins, E. T. (1990). Personality, social psychology, and person-situation relations: Standards and knowledge activation as a common language. In L. A. Pervin (Ed.), *Handbook of personality: Theory and research* (pp. 301-338). New York: Guilford Press.

Higgins, E. T., & Rholes, W. S. (1978). "Saying is believing": Effects of message modification on memory and liking for the person described. *Journal of Experimental Social Psychology, 14,* 363-378.

Isaac, L., Mutran, E., & Stryker, S. (1980). Political protest orientation among black and white adults. *American Sociological Review, 45,* 191-213.

Jones, E. E., & Pittman, T. S. (1982). Toward a general theory of strategic self-presentation. In J. M. Suls (Ed.), *Psychological perspectives on the self* (Vol. 1, pp. 231-262). Hillsdale, NJ: Erlbaum.

Jones, E. E., & Wortman, C. (1973). *Ingratiation: An attributional approach.* Morristown, NJ: General Learning Press.

Kahneman, D., & Tversky, A. (1982). Availability and the simulation heuristic. In D. Kahneman, P. Slovic, & A. Tversky (Eds.), *Judgment under uncertainty: Heuristics and biases* (pp. 201-208). New York: Oxford University Press.

Leary, M. R., & Kowalski, R. M. (1990). Impression management: A literature review and two-component model. *Psychological Bulletin, 107,* 34-47.

Mark, M. M., & Folger, R. (1984). Responses to relative deprivation: A conceptual framework. In P. Shaver (Ed.), *Review of personality and social psychology* (Vol. 5, pp. 192-218). Beverly Hills, CA: Sage.

Martin, J. (1986). The tolerance of injustice. In J. M. Olson, C. P. Herman, & M. P. Zanna (Eds.), *The Ontario Symposium: Vol. 4. Relative deprivation and social comparison* (pp. 217-242). Hillsdale, NJ: Erlbaum.

Martin, J., Brickman, P., & Murray, A. (1984). Moral outrage and pragmatism: Explanations for collective action. *Journal of Experimental Social Psychology, 20,* 484-496.

McCarthy, J. D., & Zald, M. N. (1977). Resource mobilization and social movement: A partial theory. *American Journal of Sociology, 82,* 1212-1241.

McPhail, C. (1971). Civil disorder participation: A critical examination of recent research. *American Sociological Review, 36,* 1058-1073.

Moghaddam, F. M., & Perreault, S. (1992). Individual and collective mobility strategies among minority group members. *Journal of Social Psychology, 132,* 343-357.

Muller, E. N. (1972). A test of a partial theory of potential for political violence. *American Poltical Science Review, 66,* 928-959.

Olson, J. M. (1986). Resentment about deprivation: Entitlement and hopefulness as mediators of the effects of qualifications. In J. M. Olson, C. P. Herman, & M. P. Zanna (Eds.), *The Ontario Symposium: Vol. 4. Relative deprivation and social comparison* (pp. 57-77). Hillsdale, NJ: Erlbaum.

Olson, J. M. (1990). *The changing impact over time of qualifications on relative deprivation.* Paper presented at the annual meeting of the American Psychological Association, Boston.

Olson, J. M., & Hazlewood, J. D. (1986). Relative deprivation and social comparison: An integrative perspective. In J. M. Olson, C. P. Herman, & M. P. Zanna (Eds.), *The Ontario Symposium: Vol. 4. Relative deprivation and social comparison* (pp. 1-15). Hillsdale, NJ: Erlbaum.

Olson, J. M., Roese, N. J., Meen, J., & Robertson, D. J. (in press). The preconditions and consequences of relative deprivation: Two field studies. *Journal of Applied Social Psychology.*

Olson, J. M., & Ross, M. (1984). Perceived qualifications, resource abundance, and resentment about deprivation. *Journal of Experimental Social Psychology, 20,* 425-444.

Petta, G., & Walker, I. (1992). Relative deprivation and ethnic identity. *British Journal of Social Psychology, 31,* 285-293.

Ross, M., Thibaut, J., & Evenbeck, S. (1971). Some determinants of the intensity of social protest. *Journal of Experimental Social Psychology, 7,* 401-418.

Runciman, W. G. (1966). *Relative deprivation and social justice: A study of attitudes to social inequality in twentieth century England.* Berkeley: University of California Press.

Satow, K. (1975). Social approval and helping. *Journal of Experimental Social Psychology, 11,* 501-509.

Schlenker, B. R. (1980). *Impression management: The self-concept, social identity, and interpersonal relations.* Monterey, CA: Brooks/Cole.

Snyder, D. (1978). Collective violence: A research agenda and some strategic considerations. *Journal of Conflict Resolution, 22,* 499--534.

Sorrentino, R. M., & Higgins, E. T. (1986). Motivation and cognition: Warming up to synergism. In R. M. Sorrentino & E. T. Higgins (Eds.), *Handbook of motivation and cognition: Foundations of social behavior* (Vol. 1, pp. 3-19). New York: Guilford Press.

Stephenson, G. M., & White, J. H. (1970). Privilege, deprivation, and children's moral behavior: An experimental clarification of the role of investments. *Journal of Experimental Social Psychology, 6,* 167-176.

Stouffer, S. A., Suchman, E. A., DeVinney, L. C., Star, S. A., & Williams, R. M. (1949). *The American soldier: Adjustment during army life* (Vol. 1). Princeton, NJ: Princeton University Press.

Tajfel, H. (1981). *Human categories and social groups.* Cambridge, England: Cambridge University Press.

Taylor, D. M., & McKirnan, D. J. (1984). A five-stage model of intergroup relations. *British Journal of Social Psychology, 23,* 291-300.

Taylor, D. M., Wright, S. C., Moghaddam, F. M., & Lalonde, R. N. (1990). The personal/group discrimination discrepancy: Perceiving my group, but not myself, to be a target for discrimination. *Personality and Social Psychology Bulletin, 16,* 254-262.

Taylor, D. M., Wright, S. C., & Porter, L. E. (1994). Dimensions of perceived discrimination: The personal/group discrimination discrepancy. In M. P. Zanna & J. M. Olson (Eds.), *The Ontario Symposium: Vol. 7. The psychology of prejudice* (pp. 233-255). Hillsdale, NJ: Erlbaum.

Tetlock, P. E., & Manstead, A. S. R. (1985). Impression management versus intrapsychic explanations in social psychology: A useful dichotomy? *Psychological Review, 92,* 59-77.

Tougas, F., Beaton, A. M., & Veilleux, F. (1991). Why women approve of affirmative action: The study of a predictive model. *International Journal of Psychology, 26,* 761-776.

Tougas, F., & Veilleux, F. (1988). The influence of identification, collective relative deprivation, and procedure of implementation on women's response to affirmative action: A causal modeling approach. *Canadian Journal of Behavioural Science, 20,* 15-28.

Vanneman, R. D., & Pettigrew, T. F. (1972). Race and relative deprivation in the urban United States. *Race, 13,* 461-486.

Walker, I., & Mann, L. (1987). Unemployment, relative deprivation, and social protest. *Personality and Social Psychology Bulletin, 13,* 275-283.

Walker, I., & Pettigrew, T. F. (1984). Relative deprivation theory: An overview and conceptual critique. *British Journal of Social Psychology, 23,* 301-310.

Zanna, M. P., Crosby, F., & Loewenstein, G. (1986). Male reference groups and discontent among female professionals. In B. A. Gutek & L. Larwood (Eds.), *Women's career development* (pp. 28-41). Newbury Park, CA: Sage.

CHAPTER 4

Impression Regulation and Management
Highlights of a Theory of Self-Identification

BARRY R. SCHLENKER
THOMAS W. BRITT
JOHN PENNINGTON
University of Florida

It is the theme of this chapter that impression regulation and management are fundamental features of social behavior. We define "impression management" as the goal-directed activity of controlling information about some person, object, idea, or event. People can try to control information about themselves, friends or associates, enemies, ideas (e.g., political ideologies), organizations (e.g., their company), and events (e.g., tasks they have performed). Impression management is not a type of behavior that occurs only under limited circumstances, such as during a job interview or on a date, or that is evidenced only by certain types of people, such as those high in self-monitoring or Machiavellianism. It is a characteristic of social conduct that permits us to relate successfully to others. It reflects a capacity for strategic activity that is an attribute of our species. To ask the question, "When are people engaging in impression regulation?" is akin to asking, "When are people engaging in cognition?" It is always occurring, although it can vary on dimensions such as whether it is in or out of awareness, effortful or effortless, automatic or controlled, motivated by purer or baser motives, and effective or ineffective in accomplishing its tasks (just as cognition can vary on these dimensions). In short, it is a fundamental characteristic of interpersonal experience, just as cognition is a fundamental characteristic of private experience.

In discussing the nature of impression management, we present the highlights of a theory of self-identification. In so doing, we also try to dispel some common misconceptions and misunderstandings. To many psychologists, the concept of impression management still evokes images of superficiality over substance and deception rather than authenticity. This is unfortunate, because such value-laden characterizations are not only misleading, they obscure the fundamental role impression management plays in social life. To many researchers, impression management is an afterthought in dealing with social behavior. To them, it is something that we all know happens, but that should be controlled or eliminated if possible. Socially desirable responding, for instance, is regarded as an annoying contaminant of the research process that obscures more fundamental processes that are our real interest. The feeling is that if we can eliminate such "biases" via subterfuges like the bogus pipeline, or if we can identify via "lie" scales those people most likely to engage in it, our research will be all the better. As Scheibe (1985) put it, impression management sometimes seems to concern the "cuticle" of social life, not its heart. We try to make the case that, although it may not be the heart, it is at the very least another vital organ.

Then, too, moral issues intrude in discussions of the concept. "Is it moral?" is a question that is often asked early in conversations about impression management. As such, some psychologists have been all too willing to leave discussions of the concept to those in business, advertising, and politics. Impression management activities certainly can be used selfishly and deceptively. However, they can also be used in the service of a variety of more noble motives. Impression management is a goal-directed activity whose motives can be virtuous or base. For example, although people act in ways that advance their own self-interests, they also seem to regulate information in order to support and protect the identities of others, to make others feel good, to help others cope, and to inspire them to seek new challenges (Britt & Schlenker, 1993; Schlenker & Weigold, 1992). An example is a father who helps his child interpret a failure in a way that preserves the child's self-confidence and promotes effective coping, even if the father is privately unsure about the real causes of the failure. In an experimental demonstration of beneficial impression management, Britt and Schlenker (1993) had subjects describe a partner who had recently completed a test of cognitive abilities. The partner was either a friend or a stranger, and was either in social need of help (by virtue of having to go through an exit interview to discuss the exam performance) or in no social need (by virtue of being able to leave the session immediately). It was found that subjects described the partner much more positively when the partner was a friend in social need than a friend with no social need or a stranger. These types of beneficial activities are goal-directed, in that they have as their objective creating a desired impression; however, they seem to be guided in large part by the potential consequences for the other person, not simply for the actor.

Impression management usually does not involve deception. In order to communicate important information accurately and without misunderstanding involves being able to gauge how an audience is responding and to package one's presentation accordingly, fitting the message to the beliefs, values, and competencies of the audience so that they will draw the "proper" conclusion. This too is impression management, because the actor wants the audience to draw a desired conclusion, and to do so must take the audience's perspective into account, monitor the audience's reactions, and adjust the presentation on the basis of audience feedback. For instance, advocates on both sides of the abortion debate are convinced they know the truth and hold the definitive moral stance. They each package their messages to convince others of the correctness of their own views and the incorrectness of the views of the opposite side. Whether a persuasive message is called "propaganda" or "education" is determined as much by the values and interests of the person making the judgment as by the behavior itself. In either case, impression management occurs.

INFORMATION REGULATION: THREE THEMES

The concept of impression management reflects the seminal idea that people try to regulate and control—sometimes consciously and sometimes without awareness—the information they present to audiences. People do not deal with information randomly or dispassionately. The "truth" people seek and express is invariably polished by their agendas. By "agendas," we refer to people's goals, both overt and covert, and their plans for goal accomplishment. People's agendas systematically influence how they interpret events and how they package information for consumption by audiences. Three themes have contributed greatly to current conceptions of impression management: people as agents, communication as purposive, and audiences as an integral component of self-regulation.

First, the older behavioristic view that characterized people as pawns of external stimuli and reinforcement contingencies has largely disappeared in psychology. In its place is a characterization of people as agents who actively construct and protect their own social environments. People try to structure and influence events so as to create more beneficial, less threatening surroundings. People try to place themselves in beneficial circumstances through their selection of friends, lovers, careers, and hobbies; they also try to rearrange the circumstances around them so as to facilitate their own goal achievement, such as through attempts to influence the attitudes and behaviors of those with whom they interact. People's ability to navigate their social worlds effectively has been viewed as an important component of intelligence (Cantor & Kihlstrom, 1987) and as critical to evolutionary adaptiveness (Hogan & Hogan, 1991). In short, impressing others in ways that facilitate goal achievement affects personal and even reproductive success. The idea that people regulate information in order to accomplish their goals follows directly from a view of human behavior as dynamic, purposeful, and replete with strategic elements.

Second, interpersonal communication does not involve just the description of events or the expression of thoughts and feelings. As the philosopher J. L. Austin (1962) put it, words "do things." They influence the ideas, feelings, and behaviors of audiences in ways that can have a substantial impact on an actor's own outcomes and relationships. Interpersonal communications, whether verbal or nonverbal, are inherently instrumental, so it becomes necessary to understand the participants' agendas in order to understand both interpersonal perception (Jones, 1990) and the communication process (Cody & McLaughlin, 1990; Fleming, Darley, Hilton, & Kojetin, 1990). Underlying these analyses is the idea that at the core of interpersonal processes is the witting or unwitting control of information about the participants, their relationships, their activities together, and the context in which these activities fit. Furthermore, the control of information does not take place only in first encounters or superficial relationships; it continues over the course of lifelong relationships. In discussing the literature on long-term relationships, Schlenker (1984) concluded that impression management processes occur in all stages of relationships. For instance, the success of a relationship seems to depend in part on how well the parties are able to support each other's desired identities. Partners who begin to take each other for granted and become indifferent to routine impression management considerations, which benefit both themselves and their partners, place a heavy strain on the relationship. Bragging out of proportion to one's own accomplishments, slighting the positive qualities of the partner, blaming the partner for problems, and complaining about features of a relationship are all associated with troubled relationships (Bradbury & Fincham, 1990; Tennen & Affleck, 1990). Bradbury and Fincham (1990) urged that attributions be viewed as "public events" that have consequences for the outcomes of long-term relationships. They noted that in a marriage, the public attributions made by each partner can support or challenge the desired identity of the other and thereby promote or undermine satisfaction with the relationship.

Third, audiences play a vital role in self-regulation. The conceptual roots of current views on impression management can be traced to early symbolic interactionists such as Charles Horton Cooley (1902) and George Herbert Mead (1934). They proposed that self-regulation is not a personal or private matter. Mead (1934) went so far as to assert that thought itself is social in character and takes the form of an inner dialogue (in which the self alternates between the roles of speaker and audience), not a monologue. Self-regulation involves taking the role of others, anticipating others' likely reactions to one's own possible actions, and selecting conduct accordingly. The ability to put oneself in the place of others and to imagine how they are likely to interpret information is the basis for effective communication. The interplay between actor and audience ultimately shapes and reshapes how the actor views himself or herself and is viewed by others. People are social animals whose survival, as individuals and as a species, has depended on their ability to coordinate their activities with those of others (Hogan & Hogan, 1991). Social behavior takes place in the context of real or imagined audiences, whose existence influences an actor's thoughts, feelings, and conduct.

Audiences affect self-regulation in at least three ways (Schlenker, 1986; Schlenker & Weigold, 1989a, 1992). First, audiences affect the opportunities available for an actor to attain desired outcomes (Baumeister, 1982; Jones & Wortman, 1973; Leary & Kowalski, 1990; Schlenker, 1980; Tedeschi & Norman, 1985). People are especially likely to tailor their self-presentations to make a desired impression when the audience is significant (i.e., powerful, attractive, expert), larger in size, and more proximal psychologically (Leary & Kowalski, 1990; Nowak, Szamrej, & Latané, 1990; Schlenker, 1986).

Second, audiences can cue or prime identity-relevant information and a set of prescriptive standards for evaluating conduct. As Schlenker and Weigold (1992, p. 156) noted, audiences can activate

> relevant self-schemata and roles (e.g., the sight of her child activates a set of self-images and roles relevant to the mother's behavior), goals that can be satisfied and scripts that can be followed (e.g, the sight of an attractive member of the opposite sex primes a romantic-quest script), and standards for evaluating one's performance (e.g., the presence of a tolerant friend with a reputation for goofing off suggests lower standards for evaluating one's term paper than does the stern visage of a demanding parent).

Research indicates that priming a particular audience influences people's judgments and self-evaluations (Baldwin & Holmes, 1987; Baldwin, Carrell, & Lopez, 1990), and even how they express emotions (Fridlund, 1991a, 1991b).

Finally, audiences serve as targets of communication, influencing how information is packaged or tailored. Effective communication demands that information be fitted to the audience's knowledge and value systems, using terms, symbols, and evidence that will be readily understood and accepted. In this sense, audiences are receptacles, each with a different pattern of knowledge and values, into which communications must be fitted if an actor wants to generate the desired reaction. Research finds that people will vary their verbal and nonverbal communications to take into account the nature of the audience (see DePaulo, 1992; Higgins, 1981, 1992; Schlenker & Weigold, 1992). For example, adults speak differently depending on whether the audience consists of children, mentally retarded people, foreigners, or other adults with backgrounds like their own (DePaulo & Coleman, 1986).

Are some people oblivious to audiences, like islands unto themselves, unaffected by the social world around them? Two contrasting styles of self-regulation have been described (Buss & Briggs, 1984; Carver & Scheier, 1985). One style, epitomized by public self-consciousness, is characterized by a concern about how one appears to others and the motivation to create a good impression. The second style, epitomized by private self-consciousness, is characterized by "tuning out" the social matrix, being oblivious to the expectations of others, and behaving in a way that simply expresses what is inside. Buss and Briggs (1984) associated the former style with pretension and strategic impression management, and the latter style with authenticity and expressiveness.

In response, Schlenker and Weigold (1990) argued that the independence and authenticity shown by privately self-conscious people may not be attributable to their obliviousness to social concerns. Instead, it could be attributed to their desire to create the image, in their own minds and in those of others, of being autonomous and self-reliant. As predicted, Schlenker and Weigold found that the self-descriptions of privately self-conscious people emphasized autonomy and personal identity, whereas the self-descriptions of publicly self-conscious people emphasized their ability to get along with others, be team players, and conform to expectations. Dispositional self-consciousness thus is not "content-free," but is associated with particular types of identities.

Schlenker and Weigold (1990) then examined whether privately self-conscious people really will express their own opinions, regardless of the impression it creates on others. They paired each subject with a discussion partner who initially seemed to regard the subject as either independent or dependent. Furthermore, expressing their actual attitudes (as assessed at an earlier session) would make the subjects appear to be either just like most college students (and therefore somewhat conforming) or different from most college students (and therefore independent). It was found that both privately and publicly self-conscious subjects were highly responsive to the likely attributions of the partner, but in different ways. Privately self-conscious subjects publicly changed their attitudes if by so doing they protected the appearance of being autonomous (i.e., they publicly misrepresented their attitudes if a partner supposedly thought they were conformists and could have misinterpreted their genuine attitudes as indications of conformity). Publicly self-conscious subjects, however, publicly changed their attitudes to conform to the expectations of the partner (i.e., they misrepresented their attitudes to appear to be independent or dependent, based on the partner's expectations). Interestingly, in conditions where they did misrepresent their actual attitudes, privately and publicly self-conscious subjects did so by comparable amounts. These findings suggest that audiences matter for everyone, although different people have different objectives when relating to others. Publicly self-conscious people look to the audience to tell them who they should be, and then "become" that type of person; in this sense, they are other-directed. Privately self-conscious people look to the audience to tell them whether they are creating the type of impression they want to create (e.g., "Am I coming across as autonomous?"); in this sense, they are inner-directed. It is not whether people's self-presentations are influenced by others that differentiates these two styles of self-regulation; it is how they are influenced by others.

SELF-IDENTIFICATION AS A GOAL-DIRECTED ACTIVITY

For the remainder of the chapter, we focus on impression management involving the presentation of self. Defining and expressing one's identity are ubiquitous features of social life. Specifying the properties of one's identity serves important intrapersonal and interpersonal functions and can affect one's self-esteem, reputation, and social outcomes (Baumeister, 1982; Cheek & Hogan, 1983; Hogan & Hogan, 1991; Schlenker, 1980, 1985; Schlenker & Weigold, 1989a, 1992; Tedeschi & Norman, 1985; Tetlock, 1985a). In discussing behaviors through which people describe or present themselves to others, we use the term "self-identification." Self-identification is the process, means, or result of showing oneself to be a particular type of person, thereby specifying one's identity (Schlenker, 1984, 1985). The term is meant to subsume both private self-reflections and public self-presentations.

By its nature, self-identification is a goal-directed activity in which information about the self is specified for some purpose to some audience. Three propositions form the basic core of self-identification theory (Schlenker, 1985; see also Schlenker, 1984, 1986; Schlenker & Weigold, 1989a):

1. Self-identification occurs in a particular social context and reflects the interaction of a person and one or more salient audiences for the activity.
2. An initial assessment and evaluation of self, audience, and situation evokes for the actor or prompts the actor to formulate (a) a set of goals, (b) a script or plan for goal accomplishment, and (c) a set of desired identity images that describe the type of person the actor believes he or she can and should be on the occasion.
3. These desired identity images mediate self-identification on the occasion, acting like subscripts or subplans embedded within the overall script or plan. These images organize and regulate self-identification, and may or may not correspond with the images that make up the self-concept or social roles.[1]

This theoretical approach assumes that people are purposive and planning; they are always thinking, always acting, and always trying to achieve valued objectives in life (for compatible views, see Carson, 1969; Harré, 1980; Hogan, 1982; McCall & Simmons, 1978; Miller, Galanter, & Pribram, 1960; Schank & Abelson, 1977). The actor's goals on the occasion can be important or mundane (e.g., getting a job or going bowling with friends), specific or vague (e.g., passing a test or becoming educated), immediate or long-term (e.g., enjoying a date or beginning a family), but in all cases they provide the objectives that the individual will work toward.

Scripts and plans are employed in the pursuit of goals. "Scripts" and "plans" are cognitive representations that describe the "operations," or steps, procedures, and rules, that are required to go from the present state to goal achievement (Abelson, 1976, 1981; Schank & Abelson, 1977). According to Schank and Abelson (1977), scripts are relatively specific, previously acquired and used, and available in memory as reasonably complete representations of the procedures required to achieve goals. Plans are constructed when existing scripts are unavailable, unclear, or unacceptable, and involve a more creative construction in which general information about how people achieve goals is integrated with specific information about the situation or audience. Scripts or plans can be conscious or unconscious (Langer, 1978; Miller et al., 1960); once they are activated, they direct the individual's thoughts and actions, much as a program directs the operations of a computer in order to accomplish some task or goal. In other words, they provide templates for interpreting events, activate sets of expectations for how interactions will evolve, and permit individuals to regulate and respond to ongoing events. As noted earlier, we use the term "agenda" to refer to the combination of a goal and its associated script or plan; like a particular software package, an agenda has a goal or task to accomplish and a set of procedures to do so.

Multiple Agendas

Multiple agendas are likely to be coordinated on any particular occasion. Some of these may be more important to the actor and in the forefront of awareness, whereas others may be less important or so routinized that they are operating behind the scenes, without awareness. An analogy can be made to a computer operator who is running several programs simultaneously. Some of these may be running in visible windows on the monitor, and thus may be in the forefront of awareness; others may be running in the background and become available only when the user reopens their windows, operating below the level of awareness until they are reopened.

According to self-identification theory, self-identifications are not always the sole or even the primary goal of social interactions. Agendas involving self-identifications are, however, present in all social interactions. In order to interact with others, people must present and maintain a coherent identity. An actor cannot "do" social interaction without taking a particular role in it, and this role is represented by a set of identity images characterizing the type of person the actor thinks he or she can and should be on this occasion. Furthermore, people are not indifferent to the impressions they create. Some identity images are far more desirable than others, in that they are associated with more personally beneficial consequences (e.g., approval, respect, material rewards), and the actor expects that they can be believably sustained. Desirable images, which represent what the actor believes he or she can and should be on the occasion, are the ones that are most likely to become part of the actor's self-identification agenda (for further discussion of desirability, see Schlenker, 1980, 1985; Schlenker & Weigold, 1989a, 1992).

Background Processes

Much of the time, the activities that are involved in constructing and protecting one's identity go on in the background, out of awareness. Most everyday interactions are familiar and routinized. People's self-identifying activities proceed without much conscious thought or assessment of the self and the contextual features (Schlenker, 1980, 1984, 1986). Examples include dealing with familiar people in familiar settings, playing frequently enacted roles, and performing routine or frequently encountered tasks. Under these conditions, the agenda for self-identification is in the background, guiding the system but not expending valuable resources in the form of conscious awareness and cognitive effort. Self-identifications then occur automatically, without thought and planning, based on goals and scripts that have been used repeatedly and successfully in similar past contexts. The behaviors consist of modulated, habit-molded patterns of activities that flow un-self-consciously and naturally. Of course, these behaviors may have once been diligently, even arduously, studied and practiced. Many children and adults rehearse upcoming performances in front of a mirror, trying out various gestures, facial expressions, body movements, and "lines" until they find ones they like. These behaviors, once deliberate and perhaps self-conscious, eventually become part of the everyday battery of self-identifying activities that reflect our personalities (see Hogan, 1982). William James (1890/1952, p. 79) referred to such self-identifying habits as "the enormous flywheel of society," which keep people on course and commit them to a continuation of the identities they have enacted for a lifetime.

In this nonreflective mode, self-identification involves some degree of automaticity. Automatic processes are characterized as being outside of consciousness, in that a person is unaware of the initiation or flow of the activity; effortless, in that the person does not expend limited cognitive resources; autonomous, in that the activities do not need to be consciously controlled once they are initiated; and involuntary, in that the activities are invariably initiated by certain cues or prompts (Bargh, 1984, 1989; Fiske & Taylor, 1991). Automatic processes can also be unintentional, in that they are independent of specific goals, or intentional. Goal-dependent automaticity occurs when an actor's goals influence the process (Bargh, 1989; Fiske & Taylor, 1991). Bargh (1989) suggests that the operations of most well-learned scripts and action sequences are guided by intended goal-dependent automaticity, and emphasizes that the individual need not be aware of the actions producing goal attainment. Nonreflective self-identification is characterized by such intended goal-dependent automaticity.

In the background mode, people's self-identifications are responsive to cues from the audience and situation, but people are unaware of the extent to which their activities are being shaped by the social context and their self-presentation agendas. Self-presentational shifts in behavior, such as the exaggeration of one's accomplishments or the nod and smile of agreement when talking to an attractive audience, are triggered automatically and are based on overlearned responses to social contingencies. Unless problems are encountered during the performance, self-identification proceeds routinely in the background. In the mind of the actor, he or she is *not* engaging in impression management in the sense of self-consciously and effortfully pursuing the goal of trying to impress others. However, the goal-directed activity of constructing and protecting a desired identity is taking place. It is just doing so in the background, with its agenda outside of awareness and its content consisting of well-learned sequences of activities previously associated with goal accomplishment. Attention is drawn to the behavior only if problems arise.

If problems develop during the performance, the self-presentation agenda immediately "pops up" and enters awareness. An analogy is a "terminate-and-stay-resident" (TSR) program running on a computer. TSR programs are loaded into memory when the computer is turned on and are "invisible" to the user until a special situation arises. For instance, many antivirus computer programs have TSR portions. These are loaded into memory at startup and constantly monitor the activity of the system, being omnipresent, active, but invisible. Working beneath the surface, they scan and check to ensure that their goal—protecting the system from the threat of a computer virus—is accomplished. If the monitoring detects a virus, the program seems to pop to the surface via a message on the screen, warns the user of the problem, and provides instructions for how to deal with the difficulty.

Analogously, self-presentation agendas are operating below the level of conscious awareness even when they are not in the foreground. These agendas are always there, producing monitoring and checking to ensure that events satisfy the criteria for projecting desired identity images. If deviations are detected, the self-presentation agenda pops to the surface, and the individual tries to deal with the difficulties so that the self-presentation goal can be accomplished. For instance, the actor may notice that the audience is not responding in the desired fashion, or the actor may commit a faux pas that suddenly fractures the otherwise routine performance. The actor must then take action to protect his or her desired identity.[2]

Can this background operation be called impression management? Of course, because it is. The individual's conduct is guided by the goal of creating a desired set of identity images that are represented in the self-identification agenda; the individual's self-identifying activities are controlled by the script for creating the desired identity; the individual monitors his or her own behavior and the reactions of the audience to ensure that the appropriate impression is being created and deviations from the script do not occur; and if problems develop, the individual takes action to correct the misimpression. Such behavior is goal-directed and involves the control of information about self based on well-worn scripts; if it were otherwise, people would not become upset if an audience seems to form the "wrong" impression. The behavior seems effortless and unself-conscious because it is, but that does not make it non-goal-directed or uncontrolled. Just as the TSR computer program is active but not usually apparent to the computer operator, so too is the self-presentation agenda active but not usually apparent to the actor.

Foreground Processes

To continue the analogy of the TSR program, most such programs also permit the computer operator to initiate activity and specify the tasks to be performed. The user can take control of the program and direct it to accomplish specific objectives. Most TSR antivirus programs, for instance, are streamlined and compact; they are designed to expend few system resources so that they can remain in the background in memory, doing their job, while other programs are operating in the foreground. More elaborate and thorough checking of a system can be accomplished by activating the main body of the antivirus program, which is distinct from the smaller, TSR portion. The computer operator, for example, may want to check several disks or directories thoroughly and completely, to ensure that all of the programs are virus-free, rather than simply running those programs and trusting that the TSR program will detect trouble in time to save the system.

So, too, do self-presentation agendas often operate in the foreground. There are many occasions when people expend considerable cognitive effort in assessing and planning their performances, such as before an important date, speech, or business meeting. On such occasions, people may gather relevant information, plan and rehearse, and remain especially alert during the performance itself—vigilantly monitoring and assessing themselves, their behavior, and the audience. The self-presentation agenda is then salient, and people become focused on the concern of creating the desired impression on the audience.[3]

When self-presentation agendas operate in the foreground, people are more conscious of the impression they are creating and of their self-presentational activities. These are the times when people seem to be most likely to report being self-aware, self-conscious, and perhaps "on stage." These occasions are the ones that many psychologists also think of when they describe the concepts of impression management or self-presentation.

ANTECEDENTS AND CONSEQUENCES
OF FOREGROUND PROCESSES

Antecedents

When do foreground processes occur? According to self-identification theory (Schlenker, 1985, 1986), foreground processes are initiated when (1) the performance is important, or (2) the actor anticipates or encounters impediments to the self-presentation agenda. Elsewhere, we (Schlenker, Britt, Pennington, Murphy, & Doherty, 1994) discuss the conditions that make a performance important or ego-involving to an actor, and list three features. First, performances are important to the extent that they bear on images that are highly valued and central to the actor's desired identity (e.g., a performance involving an intellectual task is more important to the individual who has pretensions of being an intellectual than to one who primarily wants to be seen as an athlete). Second, performances are important to the extent that they involve potentially valuable positive or negative outcomes (e.g., the performance can affect raises, promotions, dismissal, approval, or respect from an admired other). Third, performances are important to the extent that they are relevant to highly valued prescriptions for conduct (e.g., they pertain to moral codes of conduct rather than trivial shop rules in a factory). Important performances, like a first date with an extremely attractive individual or a job interview for the position one has dreamed of filling, marshal the actor's resources and make the self-presentation agenda salient.

Encountering or anticipating impediments to creating the desired impression also makes the self-presentation agenda salient. Impediments indicate that something is amiss, the background mode is not working, and effort is required to deal with the problem and continue toward goal achievement. Impediments can spring from many sources, including uncertainties, doubts, conflicts, or threats that are relevant to the performance (see Schlenker, 1985, 1987; Schlenker & Leary, 1982a). A situation may be novel or unfamiliar, causing actors puzzlement about how to behave and requiring them to construct a plan. An audience may be intimidating, causing actors to wonder how they will come across. Actors may doubt their ability to achieve their goals, causing them to worry about failure. The pursuit of profits may produce conflicts with actors' values and self-images, as in the dilemma of whether to lie for personal gain. As these examples illustrate, impediments can arise from personal, audience, or situational factors. When they occur, the self-presentation agenda pops to the surface and people become focused on ways to eliminate or circumvent the problem. Cognitive resources are then marshalled to deal with the difficulty. Thus, self-identification theory holds that a self-presentation agenda becomes salient when a performance is important and an actor anticipates or encounters impediments to constructing or protecting a desired identity.

Consequences

When they operate in the foreground, self-presentation agendas mobilize actors' efforts in the pursuit of the goal of constructing the desired identity images. As compared to background processes, foreground processes involve increased assessment, planning, and awareness and are associated with more intense and thorough cognitive and behavioral activities. The consequences of increased assessment can be grouped into four broad categories: (1) intensified cognitive processing; (2) intensified strategic activity designed to create and protect desired identity images; (3) accounting for potential problems; and (4) the generation of a salient outcome expectation, with its associated affective consequences.

Intensified Cognitive Processing

Foreground processing channels people's cognitive efforts in ways that usually increase the likelihood of goal achievement and overcome potential obstacles. The following types of intensified cognitive activities are likely to occur.

1. *Better information search.* When people confront impediments, they intensify the search for relevant information that will help in solving the problem, preferring information that supports desired identity images and minimizes threats (Frey, 1981; Pyszczynski, Greenberg, & LaPrelle, 1985). Furthermore, when a performance is important because it will be publicly evaluated, people

search more thoroughly for information that will make their decision look better (Tetlock, 1985b).

2. *More vigilant information processing.* When performances are important or self-presentation impediments arise, people are more likely to notice, to attend to, and to give greater weight to information relevant to their self-presentation agendas. Research supports the idea that the intensity of information processing is increased by impediments. For instance, people show better recall of self-threatening than of nonthreatening information, suggesting that they have processed it better in attempts to counterargue and refute it (Wyer & Frey, 1983). Moreover, people make self-descriptive judgments faster when aspects of identity are challenged by others (Swann & Hill, 1982). Being answerable or accountable to others for an important decision—a condition that should make the self-presentation agenda salient—will produce more intensive information processing, greater recall of relevant information, data-driven (as opposed to theory-driven) processing, and greater awareness of the strategies employed by the decision maker (Schlenker & Weigold, 1989b; Tetlock, 1985b, 1992).[4]

3. *Greater consideration of alternatives.* In contrast to background processing, where "satisficing" solutions involving simple cognitive heuristics seem to dominate, foreground processing seems to generate more thorough comparisons and integrations. For example, people who are accountable to others (as compared to those who are not) make more cognitively complex judgments and use more complex decision strategies, so long as they believe the audience will admire a "good" solution and does not favor one alternative over another (Tetlock, 1985b, 1992). When the self-presentation agenda occupies the foreground of attention, people may compare alternative strategies for achieving their goals and select the one they think will work best for the particular audience and situation, rather than simply implementing the first strategy that comes to mind.

4. *Greater rehearsal of upcoming performances.* If time permits, people will practice their contemplated performance, as in the case of an important speech that is rehearsed mentally, then before a mirror, and then before a supportive audience of family or friends. Such preparations increase the odds that the real performance will be successful (DePaulo, 1992).

5. *Increased salience of performance standards and behavior-standard correspondence.* Important performances and the occurrence of impediments seem to increase the salience of the standards for evaluating the performance (Bandura, 1982; Carver, 1979). It has been argued that self-monitoring and control are improved as a consequence of focusing attention on behavioral standards, and that greater behavior-standard matching results (Bandura, 1982; Carver, 1979; Duval & Wicklund, 1972). Research shows that people are more likely to act in ways that dramatize and assert desired identity images when these images are questioned by others than when no impediment occurs (Swann & Hill, 1982; Swann & Read, 1981). In these cases, the impediment seems to focus people on the type of impression they are creating and its discrepancy from how they prefer to come across, and actions are taken to correct the mismatch. It is also likely that

the expectations of the audience become more salient and therefore will influence the performance standards; the result is that the audience's preferences will have a greater potential to influence the actors' conduct.

6. *Increased responsiveness to personal information.* Foreground processing seems to make people more sensitive to information relevant to how well or poorly they are doing in meeting the standards. For instance, people who are made self-aware are more sensitive to feedback about whether they are making a good or bad impression (Fenigstein, 1979).

Intensified Strategic Activities

Schlenker (1987) reviewed evidence indicating that people who confront self-presentation impediments engage in more intensified strategic activities designed to preserve and reaffirm desired identity images (see also Steele, 1988; Wicklund & Gollwitzer, 1982). These include (1) direct counterattacks against the obstacle (e.g., attempting to change the opinion of a coworker who is constantly critical, or, if this is unsuccessful, getting oneself or the coworker transferred to a different location); (2) attempts to strengthen identity in response to current and future threats, including engaging in compensatory behavior that bolsters identity (e.g., the 98-pound weakling who either pumps iron to become Mr. America or studies hard to become a Nobel laureate); and (3) the pursuit of support from other people that reaffirms desired identity images (e.g., seeking validation from friends and family after being criticized by an employer). As Goffman (1959) described, when people are highly motivated to create the "right" impression, they dramatize their activities and do more of what they might otherwise have done to ensure that the audience draws the appropriate conclusion.

Accounting

When people encounter impediments, they construct explanations for the difficulty or problem. An "account" is an explanation that interprets an event whose meaning may be unclear, misconstrued, or disadvantageous. These accounts are usually personally beneficial, in that they try to place the event in a better light than it might otherwise appear. In his theory of impression management and self-identification, Schlenker (1980, 1982, 1987) proposed that an actor will construct an account when events (1) appear to violate prescribed standards in ways that threaten desired identity images (e.g., failures, transgressions); or (2) appear to meet or exceed prescribed standards, but ambiguity exists about whether the actor should receive the appropriate commendation (e.g., was his or her promotion in the company a result of talent or, as some coworkers are insinuating, of brown-nosing?). Both of these conditions seem to associate the actor with undesired images or dissociate the actor from desired images, respectively. As part of the self-identification agenda, the actor will try to explain the event in ways that support desired identity images and refute undesired identity images. The greater the potential threat to the actor's desired identity, the more the self-presentation agenda will come to the forefront of attention and generate a self-serving account.

Research attention has been captured by cases in which events violate prescribed standards and thereby threaten desired identity images. When such events occurs, people seem to use one or more of five general types of accounts: a defense of innocence, an excuse, a justification, an apology, or a refusal (Schlenker, 1980, 1982; Schlenker & Weigold, 1992; Schlenker, Weigold, & Doherty, 1991; Semin & Manstead, 1983; Scott & Lyman, 1960; Tedeschi & Riess, 1981). A defense of innocence asserts that the event did not occur (e.g., an accused murderer proclaims, "It was a suicide, not a murder") or that the actor was in no way involved. An excuse proclaims that the actor was not as responsible for the event as it might otherwise appear (e.g., the person claims that the consequences were unanticipated or caused by factors beyond personal control). A justification proclaims that the consequences were not as bad as they might otherwise appear, or that the consequences were actually good because the actor was working toward a valued, superordinate goal. An apology admits blameworthiness and expresses remorse, thereby splitting the misbehaving "bad" self from the current "good" self that will try to do better and does not require rehabilitative sanctions. Finally, refusals deny the audience the right to question or judge the actor (McLaughlin, Cody, & French, 1990). All of these types of accounts "work," in that when they are regarded as sincere and legitimate interpretations, audiences are more positive (less negative) toward actors and administer less punishment for violations of prescriptions (for reviews, see Schlenker & Weigold, 1992; Schlenker et al., 1991; Snyder & Higgins, 1988). Furthermore, self-serving accounts can produce psychological benefits for actors, including feelings of greater self-efficacy, higher self-esteem, and less psychological stress (Snyder & Higgins, 1988; Taylor & Brown, 1988).

Generation of Outcome Expectations

Schlenker and his colleagues (Schlenker, 1985, 1987; Schlenker & Leary, 1982a, 1985; Schlenker & Weigold, 1989a) have proposed that an actor's initial assessment of a social situation produces a self-identification outcome expectation, which is the perceived likelihood that the self-presentation agenda will be successful (i.e., the actor will be able to construct and protect the desired identity images). These self-identification outcome expectations reflect the extent to which the actor anticipates encountering and resolving potential problems, given the actor's own attributes (e.g., social skills, self-esteem) and the qualities of the audience and situation. As discussed elsewhere (Schlenker & Leary, 1982a, 1985), these outcome expectations will be lower when (1) the audience is perceived to be more demanding, critical, and judgmental; (2) the situation is more demanding, difficult, evaluative, or ambiguous (e.g., difficult tasks on which numerous past failures have occurred, novel or unfamiliar settings, tasks that are defined as "tests" rather than "games"); and (3) the actor's perceived skills and resources relevant to the performance are lower (e.g., low self-regard, poor social or communication skills), especially when the actor is highly concerned about the evaluative implications of the performance (e.g., high need for social approval, high public self-consciousness, high fear of failure).

If the outcome expectation is relatively high, indicating that the self-identification agenda is likely to be achieved, people experience positive affect and an enhanced feeling of personal control, and continue to work toward accomplishing their multiple goals. People who expect success on valued tasks (provided they are not unrealistically overconfident) have been shown to perceive greater personal control and to evidence greater determination on the task, as indicated by less procrastination, greater effort expenditure, and greater persistence in the face of obstacles (Bandura, 1977, 1982). In their review of the literature on personal control, Deci and Ryan (1987) concluded that feelings of greater personal control result in greater intrinsic motivation, greater interest in the task, more creativity, greater cognitive flexibility, better learning, less pressure and tension, more positive emotional tone, higher self-evaluations, and better psychological health in the long run. Not surprisingly, then, feelings of personal control are strongly associated with more effective problem solving (Baumgardner, Heppner, & Arkin, 1986). Although these findings have come from assessing people's activities on intellectual or physical tasks, there is every reason to anticipate similar patterns on social tasks that involve self-presentation. The pattern describes the feelings everyone has when on a "social roll," feeling confident, flexible, creative, and happy. One's mind is clear and one is in charge.

In contrast, low self-identification outcome expectations are associated with negative affect, insecurity, social anxiety, and suboptimal performance (Schlenker, 1985, 1987; Schlenker & Leary, 1982a, 1985). In their self-presentation theory of social anxiety, Schlenker and Leary (1982a, 1985) proposed that people experience social anxiety when they are motivated to create a desired impression but have doubts about whether they can do so. The increased arousal and negative affect interfere with memory, producing a mental "tunnel vision" and causing people's minds to blank, thus making effective performance difficult. Furthermore, the increased intensity of information processing, which is produced by encountering a problem, turns against an actor. The actor searches for useful information but continually returns to a self-conscious examination of personal liabilities and deficiencies (Carver, 1979; Hill, Weary, & Williams, 1986; Pyszczynski & Greenberg, 1987). Information processing declines in effectiveness; self-monitoring and control worsen as signs of insecurity and anxiety leak through the actor's weakened guard; and the actor engages in protective self-presentation designed to minimize further losses. Protective self-presentations are characterized by minimal and safe social participation, such as engaging in less communication, exhibiting social withdrawal and retreat, avoiding touchy or provocative subjects, describing oneself as average or moderate on traits rather than making extreme or committing characterizations, and engaging in innocuous but pleasant behaviors such as smiling and nodding (Schlenker &

Leary, 1985). This protective self-presentation style contrasts with a more assertive style that characterizes self-confident actors (Arkin, 1981; Tedeschi & Norman, 1985).

EFFECTIVENESS OF SELF-PRESENTATIONS

What characterizes effective social behavior? Is it better to be totally non-self-aware, seeming to be spontaneous and unrehearsed? Or is it better to assess the situation carefully, plan and practice, and monitor the reactions of audience members to ensure that they are forming the desired impression? If one does engage in careful assessment, would it produce a self-conscious awkwardness that seems unnatural and forced? Self-identification theory holds that the answers to these questions depend on a combination of the importance of the performance and the self-identification outcome expectations of the actor (Schlenker, 1987; Schlenker & Leary, 1982a; Schlenker & Weigold, 1989a, 1992).

Self-Presentation in Routine Situations

When the social situation is unimportant, familiar, or routine, and the actor has high self-identification outcome expectations, the self-presentation agenda will run in the background mode. A quick initial assessment of the situation engages a seemingly appropriate self-presentation package and runs it outside of awareness and with minimal cognitive effort. It will enter awareness only if problems develop during the subsequent performance. In this background mode, self-presentations can be effective, at least in exceeding threshold standards, but may be less than optimal. There are several reasons why the performance may be less than optimal:

1. A hasty assessment may prompt the actor to select a suboptimal script—that is, one that will not be effective in creating the desired impression on the particular audience. For instance, a careless assessment of the audience's interests and values could lead the actor to discuss a topic the audience finds uninteresting or even objectionable.

2. There may be insufficient monitoring of self and other. For instance, an insensitive or offensive comment may be made—one that, if the actor were monitoring his or her behavior better, would have been noticed, identified as problematic, and suppressed before it was made public.

3. The actor may be less sensitive to subtle changes in the audience's reactions or in the situation that otherwise might produce a shift in strategy. For instance, the actor may not notice that the audience is getting bored with the current topic of conversation.

4. The actor may not dramatize his or her behavior sufficiently to create

the desired impression. In background mode, the process of matching behavior to standards may be less precise because the standards are less salient and the monitoring is less careful (see Bandura, 1982; Carver, 1979). Larger deviations from the standard may be tolerated than when the same agenda is operating in foreground mode. As such, the behavior may not clearly create the desired impact on the audience. For instance, a husband's compliments may begin to sound routine and insincere to his wife because they lack special emphasis or enthusiasm.

5. There may be less than optimal consistency between communication modalities, so that verbal and nonverbal channels are not in perfect synchronization. DePaulo (1992) suggested that planned presentations are usually more effective than spontaneous ones in creating the desired impression on an audience, because the speaker is more attentive to coordinating verbal and nonverbal modalities.

6. Because of the lower priority of the self-presentation agenda, other agendas, running in the foreground (i.e., occupying a higher place in the priority hierarchy), may generate goal-directed activities that coincidentally undermine the self-presentation goal. In other words, the self-presentation agenda may be compromised in order to pursue other agendas that are momentarily more important or where the outcome seems to be less in doubt. For instance, watching a football game on TV may occupy a high priority in a husband's agenda system for the afternoon and prompt him to seem insensitive to his wife's interests or comments. Feeling secure in his wife's regard, he directs attention elsewhere; he may not notice a problem in the relationship until it is too late.

The background mode offers advantages that can compensate for these problems. When self-presentation agendas can be run in the background mode, it makes the job of dealing with social life much easier, more efficient, and relatively effortless. For instance, as friendships grow and self-presentation agendas recede into background mode, people feel more comfortable in each other's presence. They are relatively secure in each other's regard, and attention does not have to be directed continually toward strategically shaping and maintaining the impressions that are formed.

Nonetheless, the preceding list of problems reminds us that being comfortable often does not mean being optimally effective. Athletic coaches dread situations where their players seem to be overconfident. Overconfident players place their performance scripts in background mode and do not attend carefully to what they are doing; by the time they realize their efforts are insufficient, it may be too late to salvage the game. Or a college professor—preoccupied with other matters, overconfident of his or her expertise, and bored with teaching the class—walks into class without carefully planning what to talk about and how to organize it. The result is a poor lecture. Or a husband, comfortable in the relationship, begins to take his wife for granted. Performance standards that were once part of his impression management agenda, such as showing interest, enthusiasm, and consideration to his wife, have become less salient and only approximated in his behavior; he may not even realize how far his wife feels he is falling short of the standards.

Important Performances and Self-Confident Actors

In cases like those of the overconfident player, indifferent teacher, and overly comfortable husband, performance can be improved by running the appropriate performance agenda in the foreground, provided that the actor maintains relatively high outcome expectations. The ideal performance state occurs when attention is focused on the task—say, because the task is redefined as very important—and the actor is confident, feeling that with the proper diligence and effort, success will be achieved. Focusing attention on the self-presentation agenda permits it to be fine-tuned and improved to match the situational details better, and to occupy a foreground location where it is less likely to be compromised by other agendas. The foreground location produces more salient standards and better monitoring and control of behavior and audience reactions in the effort to match the standards. It produces dramatized behaviors that are more likely to have the desired impact. The result is a more optimal performance.

In this foreground state produced by the combination of an important performance and self-confidence, people can be described as self-aware but not self-conscious.[5] In everyday life, the term "self-consciousness" is associated with nervousness, awkwardness, stilted conduct, and feeling as if one is the center of unwanted attention. To be self-conscious is undesirable, because it implies negative affect and ineffective behavior that makes a poor impression on onlookers. As we discuss below, self-consciousness is associated with self-doubts about an important performance, not with self-confidence. In contrast, to be self-aware is to focus attention where it belongs: on the self-identification agenda of performing successfully under conditions where an actor is confident the goal can be achieved. When people expect to perform well, focusing attention on the self has been shown to improve performance. Confident people are better at deliberately conveying desired impressions to audiences through both verbal and nonverbal channels than are those who lack confidence or who are not deliberately trying to create a particular impression (DePaulo, 1992; DePaulo, LeMay, & Epstein, 1991). The improved performance appears to result from the factors described above—that is, better fine-tuning of plans, more salient standards, better monitoring and control of behavior in the effort to match standards, and greater consistency across communication channels (see DePaulo, 1992; Schlenker, 1980, 1987; Schlenker & Weigold, 1992; Scheier & Carver, 1988).

Furthermore, this improved performance from deliberate planning applies even when people are faking their presentations of their internal states or characteristics. People are surprisingly effective (at least, up to a point) at convincingly faking their emotional expressions, attitudes, and even personality characteristics. In her excellent review of the research on self-presentation through nonverbal behavior, DePaulo (1992, p. 219) noted that virtually every relevant study shows that "when people are deliberately trying to convey an impression of a state they are not really experiencing, their nonverbal behaviors convey that impression to others even more clearly and effectively than when they really are experiencing the state, but are not trying purposefully to communicate it to others." When people fake, they dramatize their conduct and do more of whatever it is they normally do when experiencing the state. For instance, when faking extraversion, subjects speak more quickly than do genuine extraverts (who speak more quickly than real introverts); and when faking introversion, people speak even more slowly than genuine introverts. Subjects are so successful at faking introversion and extraversion that interviewers are unable to differentiate between genuine and faked displays (Toris & DePaulo, 1984).

Encountering an impediment, then, can actually improve performance over what it might otherwise have been if it activates foreground processing and results in the expectation of success. Such impediments become momentary blips on the self-presentation landscape; they ultimately focus attention and sharpen the performance.

Important Performances and Self-Doubting Actors

In contrast to the poised self-awareness that characterizes the combination of an important performance and self-confidence, the combination of an important performance and self-doubts can doom an actor to failure. In their analysis of social anxiety, Schlenker and Leary (1982a, 1985) reviewed research indicating that social anxiety and decrements in task performance result when self-doubts contaminate an important performance. The combination produces poorer recall of relevant information, obsessive self-disparagement, aversive nervousness, communication difficulties, disaffiliative responses (including task or situational withdrawal), task distraction, and protective self-presentation. Consistent with this analysis, studies show that subjects who expect to perform poorly on a task for which they are publicly accountable do much worse than those who either anticipate success or are not publicly accountable (Schlenker, 1987; Schlenker et al., 1991). Furthermore, social facilitation research indicates that people who expect success on a task perform better in the presence of an evaluating audience, whereas those who expect failure perform worse (see Geen, 1991). Baumeister and his colleagues (Baumeister, 1984; Baumeister, Hamilton, & Tice, 1985) have found that "choking" occurs when public expectations are unrealistically high, subjects doubt they can fulfill expectations, and subjects become self-conscious about a publicly evaluated performance. Schlenker, Phillips, Boniecki, and Schlenker (in press) found that baseball players will "choke" and commit more errors when their team falls behind and is losing an important home game. Finally, the more motivated people are to create a desired impression and the less confident they are in their ability to do so, the easier it is for observers to detect any lies they tell (DePaulo, Kirkendo, Tang, & O'Brien, 1988; DePaulo et al.,

1991). The odds of successfully deceiving others seem to be increased by prior practice or experience in telling lies, lack of guilt about lying, greater confidence in one's ability to deceive, and greater expressive skills (DePaulo, 1992); each of these factors should reduce self-doubts. All of these lines of research indicate that self-doubts about an important performance produce inferior performance and self-consciousness in the negative sense of the term.

RETROSPECTIVE AND CONCLUSIONS

Work on self-presentation and impression management has come a long way in a relatively short period of time, exhibiting remarkable growth and increasing conceptual sophistication. The 1980s and 1990s have witnessed an explosion of conceptual analyses (e.g., Arkin & Baumgardner, 1986; Baumeister, 1982; Cody & McLaughlin, 1990; Cheek & Hogan, 1983; Jones & Pittman, 1982; Leary & Kowalski, 1990; Schlenker, 1980, 1985; Snyder, 1987; Tedeschi, 1981; Tedeschi & Norman, 1985; Tetlock & Manstead, 1985). The concept of impression management has been applied to topics as diverse as criminal conduct, depression, fairness, eating behavior, helping, aggression, and interaction patterns in kindergarten, to name but a few (see Schlenker & Weigold, 1992). Though often differing in specifics, these analyses share the common idea that people attempt to control information for one or more salient audiences in ways that attempt to facilitate goal achievement.

Early pioneering work in the area established a foundation for this growth. At the same time, some of the early views created one-sided portraits that caused impression management to seem to be an illicit, deceitful, superficial type of behavior in which appearance triumphs over substance. The vestiges of these early ideas still linger. Goffman (1959) popularized the idea of self-presentation, but because of his sociological emphasis on the social interaction as the unit of analysis, he de-emphasized both the self and the psychological dynamics that are involved. To many psychologists, Goffman's insights into the strategic character of social life revealed little about fundamental psychological processes and mechanisms. Jones's (1964; Jones & Wortman, 1973) pioneering work on ingratiation provided a psychological framework for understanding strategic activity. However, Jones initially portrayed self-presentation as a type of ingratiation and defined it as an illicit activity motivated by a single objective—to be liked in order to enhance one's power in a relationship.

The theory of self-identification that has been highlighted here has its roots in the 1970s and is driven in part by the notion that impression management is neither a subclass of behavior nor a morally objectionable activity, although it certainly can be used in a morally objectionable way. Impression management is a fundamental feature of social behavior. At the core of the theory are several key ideas. First, self-identification is a goal-directed activity that reflects a transaction between an actor and an audience who are interacting in a particular social setting (see Schlenker, 1980, 1982, 1984, 1985, 1986). This idea contrasts with positions that hold that people's self-presentations (or self-descriptions) are solely either expressions of their self-beliefs, or reactions to situational pressures. Self-identification is not merely an expression of the self-concept or a description of a self-belief, any more than a description of a memory is merely the retrieval of a perfectly stored piece of information that is accessed and described in precisely the way the event once happened. Memories are affected by the actor's goals and the social context in which the information is retrieved (Loftus, 1993). Autobiographical memory about the self is similarly shaped and influenced by the actor's goals, the audience for the activity, and the social setting.

Second, there are many possible self-presentational goals. In his book *Impression Management,* Schlenker (1980) criticized prior work for equating self-presentation with the need for approval and the desire to be liked. He described numerous self-presentational goals that are useful in achieving valued outcomes, including gaining respect by appearing very competent, moral, or powerful; creating fear, as in the cases of violent men, antisocial characters, or women claiming to be witches; and seeming to be helpless or weak in order to be excused from onerous obligations, as typified by the activities of some mental patients. Once it is acknowledged that a variety of goals can be pursued through impression management, it becomes more difficult to confine the concept to the status of a specific type of behavior caused by a specific motive. It is now widely held that multiple objectives can be pursued through self-presentation (e.g., Baumeister, 1982; Jones & Pittman, 1982; Leary & Kowalski, 1990; Tetlock & Manstead, 1985).

Third, people want to construct and protect desirable identities (Schlenker, 1980, 1982, 1984, 1985, 1986; Schlenker & Weigold, 1989a, 1992). In introducing the concept of a desirable identity image, Schlenker argued that an identity image is desirable when it has two features: (1) It is personally beneficial, in that the actor should regard it as facilitating his or her goals and values relative to alternative claims; and (2) it is believable, in that it should be regarded as a justifiable construal of the salient evidence. Desirable identity images represent self-glorifying yet reality-edited characterizations of the self; they are compromises between wishes and reality. Although people might like to see themselves as having outstanding and admirable attributes, social reality imposes constraints on what people can claim. It is better to admit to a publicly known liability than to deny it and be regarded both as having the liability and as being either deceitful or out of touch with reality. Schlenker (1975) showed that people will adjust their self-presentations to match publicly available information about them. When subjects expected to have their failures publicly revealed to others, they presented themselves in a consistent, less positive way than when their failures would be private or when they expected success. Furthermore, Schlenker and Leary (1982b) showed that audiences respond more favorably to actors who are consistent—that is, ones who match their words and deeds. People's reputations act as constraints on what they can justifiably claim about themselves. Instead of viewing people as driven by the motive to maximize their self-esteem or the motive to behave consistently with their self-beliefs, self-identification theory views people's self-presentations as integrations of information that is personally beneficial and believable (for further discussion, see Schlenker & Weigold, 1989a, 1992).

Fourth, self-identification always occurs in the context of one or more audiences who serve as recipients and evaluators for the performance. Early research on self-presentation emphasized only real audiences who were present at the time of the performance. Schlenker (1980, 1985, 1986; Schlenker & Weigold, 1989a, 1992) broadened the picture and emphasized the role of real and *imagined* audiences in the self-presentation process. Following the tradition of the symbolic interactionists, he also proposed that people can act as audiences for their own performances. More recent research has begun to explore the impact of imagined audiences on social behavior (e.g., Baldwin et al., 1990; Baldwin & Holmes, 1987; Fridlund, 1991a, 1991b), and theoretical analyses are increasingly taking into account the impact of imagined audiences and even the self-as-audience (DePaulo, 1992; Greenwald & Breckler, 1985; Hogan, 1982; Snyder, 1985; Tetlock & Manstead, 1985). Furthermore, people use relationship scripts and schemas (which include information about self and other people or audiences) to interpret events, to store information in memory, and to guide conduct (Baldwin, 1992; Berscheid, 1994).

Fifth, self-identification theory emphasizes the role of accounting in interpersonal relations (Schlenker, 1980, 1982). People construct and negotiate realities through their interpretations of events, as they attempt to explain possible incongruities between their actions and valued prescriptions for conduct. A burgeoning literature has developed on accounting, focusing on the role and effectiveness of excuses, justifications, and apologies in everyday life (e.g., Baumeister, Stillwell, & Wotman, 1990; Darby & Schlenker, 1982, 1989; Gonzales, Pederson, Manning, & Wetter, 1990; Ohbuchi, Kameda, & Agarie, 1989; Schlenker & Darby, 1981; Snyder, 1985; Snyder & Higgins, 1988; Tedeschi & Riess, 1981; Weiner, Amirkhan, Folkes, & Verette, 1987). Where once psychologists talked of rationalization and emphasized intrapsychic distortions of information designed to protect the ego, they now analyze the use of accounting strategies and emphasize the role of these strategies in protecting identity and minimizing negative sanctions in interpersonal relations.

Sixth, people's private self-conceptions are shaped in part by their public self-presentations and audiences' reactions to them (see Schlenker, 1980, 1986). A component of the self-presentation process is that actors' behavior, which initially may have been intended to create a particular impression on others, may ultimately come to influence the actors' own view of themselves. People come to internalize their self-presentations when their behavior appears to be a believable self-portrayal (Schlenker & Trudeau, 1990), particularly when the behavior is publicly committing (Schlenker, Dlugolecki, & Doherty, 1994).

Finally, various psychological disorders seem to be produced or perpetuated by self-presentation problems. Shyness and social anxiety arise from self-presentation difficulties (Schlenker & Leary, 1982a). Protective, defensive self-presentational postures seem to characterize people who are depressed (Hill et al., 1986; Schlenker et al., 1991). Schlenker et al. (1991) proposed that people's problems in dealing with accountability, in which they must answer to others and be judged and sanctioned, are at the core of many dysfunctional behaviors. Just as impression management skills play a vital role in achieving valued goals in life, impression management difficulties create and perpetuate the types of personal and interpersonal thoughts, feelings, and behaviors that are associated with psychological disorders.

As we hope these themes illustrate, impression regulation and management are not hardened, superficial cuticles on social life. They are vital and omnipresent components of social conduct. These fundamental interpersonal processes permeate our relationships with others and shape our conceptions of ourselves and our social worlds.

Notes

1. Desired identity images are influenced by the combination of salient personal (e.g., self-images, aspirations), situational (e.g., reward contingencies), and audience (e.g., audience expectations) factors (for further discussion, see Schlenker, 1986; Schlenker & Weigold, 1989a). Just as memories are constructed and shaped by the conditions that exist at the time of recall (e.g., the type and wording of the question being asked, the goals of the actor, the salient audience), desired identity images are constructed and are shaped by conditions that exist at the time of the self-identification. These images become the standards that are used to guide and evaluate behavior on the occasion. Over time, certain desired identity images (e.g., those frequently evoked) become the basis for generalizations about the self that make up more or less chronic components of the self-concept.

Higgins's (1987, 1989) self-discrepancy theory focuses on chronic self-domains and illuminates how certain types of self-standards are related to motivational and emotional experiences. Higgins distinguishes between the actual self and two self-guides or standards, the "ideal self" and the "ought self," as seen by self or significant others. Discrepancies between the actual self and a self-standard produce different emotions, depending on the type of self-standard and the standpoint (self or others) that are involved.

2. Logan and Cowan (1984), dealing mainly with well-learned action sequences of a noninterpersonal nature (e.g., typing, driving a car), also argued that sudden changes in the activated script (e.g., the ribbon on the typewriter runs out of ink, a police officer appears when one is going 20 miles over the speed limit) cause a switch to a more controlled process that leads to the mobilization of resources to deal with the disruption. Therefore, the idea that self-identification activities can take place in the background, outside of conscious awareness, yet still can be goal-directed and can detect problems that may occur during the self-identification activity, is compatible with more recent models of cognition.

3. In earlier writings, Schlenker (1980, 1985, 1986; Schlenker & Weigold, 1989a) either did not attach a specific label to the distinction or used the term "active processes" to describe what we are now calling "foreground processes" and the term "passive processes" to describe what we are now calling "background processes." The background–foreground distinction seems to capture the activity better, so we make the switch in terminology.

4. Research (e.g., Fiske & Taylor, 1991; Tetlock, 1992) supports the idea that cognitive activity usually intensifies when people confront important, challenging situations. However, Sorrentino and his colleagues (Brouwers & Sorrentino, 1993; Sorrentino, Bobocel, Gitta, Olson, & Hewitt, 1988) have found that there are individual differences in how people react

when confronting personally relevant information. People who are "uncertainty-oriented" (i.e., motivated to reduce uncertainty) respond to situations of high personal relevance by reducing their reliance on simple heuristics and increasing their systematic processing of information. However, people who are "certainty-oriented" (i.e., motivated to maintain certainty) respond in the opposite fashion when confronting situations of high personal relevance: They increase their use of simple heuristics and decrease systematic processing of information. Future research should examine the self-presentational implications of such individual differences. Sorrentino's approach suggests that people who are certainty oriented may prefer security to the extent that they avoid challenging, important performances and react to the obstacles they do encounter by becoming less open to the systematic analysis of information and more likely to employ rigid, frequently used heuristics for defusing threats to identity.

5. The term "self-consciousness" has been used to describe an individual-difference variation in self-attention (Carver & Scheier, 1985). We are now using the everyday meaning of the term, not this more circumscribed meaning.

References

Abelson, R. P. (1976). Script processing in attitude formation and decision making. In J. S. Carroll & J. W. Payne (Eds.), *Cognition and social behavior* (pp. 33–45). Hillsdale, NJ: Erlbaum.

Abelson, R. P. (1981). Psychological status of the script concept. *American Psychologist, 36,* 715–729.

Arkin, R. (1981). Self-presentation styles. In J. T. Tedeschi (Ed.), *Impression management theory and social psychological research* (pp. 311–333). New York: Academic Press.

Arkin, R. M., & Baumgardner, A. H. (1986). Self-presentation and self-evaluation: Processes of self-control and social control. In R. F. Baumeister (Ed.), *Public self and private self* (pp. 75–97). New York: Springer-Verlag.

Austin, J. L. (1962). *How to do things with words.* New York: Oxford University Press.

Baldwin, M. W. (1992). Relational schemas and the processing of social information. *Psychological Bulletin, 112,* 461–484.

Baldwin, M. W., Carrell, S. E., & Lopez, D. F. (1990). Priming relational schemas: My advisor and the Pope are watching me from the back of my mind. *Journal of Experimental Social Psychology, 26,* 435–454.

Baldwin, M. W., & Holmes, J. G. (1987). Salient private audiences and awareness of the self. *Journal of Personality and Social Psychology, 52,* 1087–1098.

Bandura, A. (1977). Self-efficacy: Toward a unifying theory of behavioral change. *Psychological Review, 84,* 191–215.

Bandura, A. (1982). The self and mechanisms of agency. In J. Suls (Ed.), *Psychological perspectives on the self* (Vol. 1, pp. 3–39). Hillsdale, NJ: Erlbaum.

Bargh, J. A. (1984). Automatic and cognitive processing of social information. In R. S. Wyer & T.K. Srull (Eds.), *Handbook of social cognition* (Vol. 3, pp. 1–43). Hillsdale, NJ: Erlbaum.

Bargh, J. A. (1989). Conditional automaticity: Varieties of automatic influence in social perception and cognition. In J. S. Uleman & J. A. Bargh (Eds.), *Unintended thought* (pp. 3–51). New York: Guilford Press.

Baumeister, R.F. (1982). A self-presentational view of social phenomena. *Psychological Bulletin, 91,* 3–26.

Baumeister, R. F. (1984). Choking under pressure: Self-consciousness and paradoxical effects of incentives on skillful performance. *Journal of Personality and Social Psychology, 46,* 610–620.

Baumeister, R. F., Hamilton, J. C., & Tice, D. M. (1985). Public versus private expectancy of success: Confidence booster or performance pressure? *Journal of Personality and Social Psychology, 48,* 1447–1457.

Baumeister, R. F., Stillwell, A., & Wotman, S. R. (1990). Victim and perpetrator accounts of interpersonal conflict: Autobiographical narratives about anger. *Journal of Personality and Social Psychology, 59,* 994-1005.

Baumgardner, A. H., Heppner, P. P., & Arkin, R. M. (1986). Role of causal attribution in personal problem solving. *Journal of Personality and Social Psychology, 50,* 636-643.

Berscheid, E. (1994). Interpersonal relationships. *Annual Review of Psychology, 45,* 79-129.

Bradbury, T. N., & Fincham, F. D. (1990). Attributions in marriage: Review and critique. *Psychological Bulletin, 107,* 3-33.

Britt, T. W., & Schlenker, B. R. (1993). *Regulating the public image of close others: Other-serving bias and beneficial impression management.* Paper presented at the annual meeting of the American Psychological Association, Toronto.

Brouwers, M. C., & Sorrentino, R. M. (1993). Uncertainty orientation and protection motivation theory: The role of individual differences in health compliance. *Journal of Personality and Social Psychology, 65,* 102-112.

Buss, A. H., & Briggs, S. R. (1984). Drama and the self in social interaction. *Journal of Personality and Social Psychology, 47,* 1310-1324.

Cantor, N., & Kihlstrom, J. (1987). *Personality and social intelligence.* Englewood Cliffs, NJ: Prentice-Hall.

Carson, R. C. (1969). *Interaction concepts of personality.* Chicago: Aldine.

Carver, C. S. (1979). A cybernetic model of self-attention processes. *Journal of Personality and Social Psychology, 37,* 1251-1281.

Carver, C. S., & Scheier, M. F. (1985). Aspects of self and the control of behavior. In B.R. Schlenker (Ed.), *The self and social life* (pp. 146-174). New York: McGraw-Hill.

Cheek, J. M., & Hogan, R. (1983). Self-concepts, self-presentations, and moral judgments. In J. Suls & A.G. Greenwald (Eds.), *Psychological perspectives on the self* (Vol. 2, pp. 249-273). Hillsdale, NJ: Erlbaum.

Cody, M. J., & McLaughlin, M. L. (Eds.). (1990). *The psychology of tactical communication.* Bristol, PA: Multilingual Matters.

Cooley, C. H. (1902). *Human nature and the social order.* New York: Scribner's.

Darby, B. W., & Schlenker, B. R. (1982). Children's reactions to apologies. *Journal of Personality and Social Psychology, 43,* 742-753.

Darby, B. W., & Schlenker, B. R. (1989). Children's reactions to transgressions: Effects of actor's apology, reputation, and remorse. *British Journal of Social Psychology, 28,* 353-364.

Deci, E. L., & Ryan, R. M. (1987). The support of autonomy and the control of behavior. *Journal of Personality and Social Psychology, 55,* 1024-1037.

DePaulo, B. M. (1992). Nonverbal behavior and self-presentation. *Psychological Bulletin, 111,* 203-243.

DePaulo, B. M., & Coleman, L. M. (1986). Talking to children, foreigners, and retarded adults. *Journal of Personality and Social Psychology, 51,* 945-959.

DePaulo, B. M., Kirkendo, S. E., Tang, J., & O'Brien, T. P. (1988). The motivational impairment effect in the communication of deception: Replications and extensions. *Journal of Nonverbal Behavior, 12,* 177-202.

DePaulo, B. M., LeMay, C. S., & Epstein, J. A. (1991). Effects of importance of success and expectations for success on effectiveness at deceiving. *Personality and Social Psychology Bulletin, 17,* 14-24.

Duval, S., & Wicklund, R. A. (1972). *A theory of objective self-awareness.* New York: Academic Press.

Fenigstein, A. (1979). Self-consciousness, self-attention, and social interaction. *Journal of Personality and Social Psychology, 37,* 75-86.

Fiske, S. T., & Taylor, S. E. (1991). *Social cognition* (2nd ed.). New York: McGraw-Hill.

Fleming, J. H., Darley, J. M., Hilton, J. L., & Kojetin, B. A. (1990). Multiple audience problem: A strategic communication perspective on social perception. *Journal of Personality and Social Psychology, 58,* 593-609.

Frey, D. (1981). Reversible and irreversible decisions: Preference for consonant information as a function of attractiveness of decision alternatives. *Personality and Social Psychology Bulletin, 7,* 621-626.

Fridlund, A. J. (1991a). The sociability of solitary smiling: Potentiation by an implicit audience. *Journal of Personality and Social Psychology, 60,* 229-240.

Fridlund, A. J. (1991b). Evolution and facial action in reflex, social motive, and paralanguage. *Biological Psychology, 32,* 3-100.

Geen, R. (1991). Social motivation. *Annual Review of Psychology, 42,* 377-399.

Goffman, E. (1959). *The presentation of self in everyday life.* Garden City, NY: Doubleday.

Gonzales, M. H., Pederson, J. H., Manning, D. J., & Wetter, D. W. (1990). Pardon my gaffe: Effects of sex, status, and consequence severity on accounts. *Journal of Personality and Social Psychology, 58,* 610-621.

Greenwald, A. G., & Breckler, S. J. (1985). To whom is the self presented? In B.R. Schlenker (Ed.), *The self and social life* (pp. 126-145). New York: McGraw-Hill.

Harré, R. (1980). *Social being: A theory for social psychology.* Totowa, NJ: Littlefield, Adams.

Higgins, E. T. (1981). The "communication game": Implications for social cognition. In E. T. Higgins, C. P. Herman, & M. P. Zanna (Eds.), *The Ontario Symposium: Vol. 1. Social cognition* (pp. 343-392). Hillsdale, NJ: Erlbaum.

Higgins, E. T. (1987). Self-discrepancy: A theory relating self to affect. *Psychological Review, 94,* 319-340.

Higgins, E. T. (1989). Self-discrepancy theory: What patterns of self-beliefs cause people to suffer? In L. Berkowitz (Ed.), *Advances in experimental social psychology* (Vol. 22, pp. 93-136). San Diego, CA: Academic Press.

Higgins, E. T. (1992). Achieving "shared reality" in the communication game: A social action that creates meaning. *Journal of Language and Social Psychology, 11,* 107-131.

Hill, M. G., Weary, G., & Williams, J. (1986). Depression: A self-presentation formulation. In R. F. Baumeister (Ed.), *Public self and private self* (pp. 213-239). New York: Springer-Verlag.

Hogan, R. (1982). A socioanalytic theory of personality. In M. Page (Ed.), *Nebraska Symposium on Motivation* (Vol. 29, pp. 55-89). Lincoln: University of Nebraska Press.

Hogan, R., & Hogan, J. (1991). Personality and status. In D. G. Gilbert & J. J. Connolly (Eds.), *Personality, social skills, and psychopathology: An individual differences approach* (pp.137-154). New York: Plenum Press.

James, W. (1890/1952). The principles of psychology. In R. M. Hutchinson (Ed.), *Great books of the western world.* Chicago: Encyclopaedia Britannica. (Original work published 1890)

Jones, E. E. (1964). *Ingratiation.* New York: Appleton-Century-Crofts.

Jones, E. E. (1990). *Interpersonal perception.* New York: W.H. Freeman.

Jones, E. E., & Pittman, T. S. (1982). Toward a general theory of strategic self-presentation. In J. Suls (Ed.), *Psychological perspectives on the self* (Vol. 1, pp. 231-262). Hillsdale, NJ: Erlbaum.

Jones, E. E., & Wortman, C. (1973). *Ingratiation: An attributional approach.* Morristown, NJ: General Learning Press.

Langer, E. J. (1978). Rethinking the role of thought in social interaction. In J. H. Harvey, W. J. Ickes, & R.F. Kidd (Eds.), *New directions in attribution research* (Vol. 2, pp. 35-58). Hillsdale, NJ: Erlbaum.

Leary, M. R., & Kowalski, R. M. (1990). Impression management: A literature review and two-component model. *Psychological Bulletin, 107,* 34-47.

Loftus, E. F. (1993). The psychology of repressed memories. *American Psychologist, 48,* 518-537.

Logan, G. D., & Cowan, W. B. (1984). On the ability to inhibit thought and action: A theory of an act of control. *Psychological Review, 91,* 295-327.

McCall, G. J., & Simmons, J. F. (1978). *Identities and interactions* (2nd ed.). New York: Free Press.

McLaughlin, M. L., Cody, M. J., & French, K. (1990). Account-giving and the attribution of responsibility: Impressions of traffic offenders. In M. J. Cody & M. L. McLaughlin

(Eds.), *The psychology of tactical communication* (pp. 244-267). Bristol, PA: Multilingual Matters.

Mead, G. H. (1934). *Mind, self, and society.* Chicago: University of Chicago Press.

Miller, G. A., Galanter, E., & Pribram, K. H. (1960). *Plans and the structure of behavior.* New York: Holt, Rinehart & Winston.

Nowak, A., Szamrej, J., & Latané, B. (1990). From private attitude to public opinion: A dynamic theory of social impact. *Psychological Review, 97,* 362-376.

Ohbuchi, K., Kameda, M., & Agarie, N. (1989). Apology as aggression control: Its role in mediating appraisal of and response to harm. *Journal of Personality and Social Psychology, 56,* 219-227.

Pyszczynski, T. A., & Greenberg, J. (1987). Depression, self-focused attention, and self-regulatory perseveration. In C. R. Snyder & C. E. Ford (Eds.), *Coping with negative life events: Clinical and social psychological perspectives* (pp. 105-129). New York: Plenum Press.

Pyszczynski, T. A., Greenberg, J., & LaPrelle, J. (1985). Social comparison after success and failure: Biased search for information consistent with a self-serving conclusion. *Journal of Experimental Social Psychology, 21,* 195-211.

Schank, R., & Abelson, R. (1977). *Scripts, plans, goals, and understanding.* Hillsdale, N. J. : Erlbaum.

Scheibe, K. E. (1985). Historical perspectives on the presented self. In B. R. Schlenker (Ed.), *The self and social life* (pp. 33-64). New York: McGraw-Hill.

Scheier, M. F., & Carver, C. S. (1988). A model of behavior self-regulation: Translating intention into action. In L. Berkowitz (Ed.), *Advances in experimental social psychology* (Vol. 21, pp. 303-346). New York: Academic Press.

Schlenker, B. R. (1975). Self-presentation: Managing the impression of consistency when reality interferes with self-enhancement. *Journal of Personality and Social Psychology, 32,* 1030-1037.

Schlenker, B. R. (1980). *Impression management: The self-concept, social identity, and interpersonal relations.* Monterey, CA: Brooks/Cole.

Schlenker, B. R. (1982). Translating actions into attitudes: An identity-analytic approach to the explanation of social conduct. In L. Berkowitz (Ed.), *Advances in experimental social psychology* (Vol. 15, pp. 193-247). New York: Academic Press.

Schlenker, B. R. (1984). Identities, identifications, and relationships. In V. Derlega (Ed.), *Communication, intimacy and close relationships* (pp. 71-104). New York: Academic Press.

Schlenker, B. R. (1985). Identity and self-identification. In B. R. Schlenker (Ed.), *The self and social life* (pp. 65-99). New York: McGraw-Hill.

Schlenker, B. R. (1986). Self-identification: Toward an integration of the private and public self. In R. Baumeister (Ed.), *Public self and private self* (pp. 21-62). New York: Springer-Verlag.

Schlenker, B. R. (1987). Threats to identity: Self-identification and social stress. In C. R. Snyder & C. E. Ford (Eds.), *Coping with negative life events: Clinical and social psychological perspectives* (pp. 273-321). New York: Plenum Press.

Schlenker, B. R., Britt, T. W., Pennington, J. W., Murphy, R., & Doherty, K. J. (1994). The triangle model of responsibility. *Psychological Review, 101,* 632-652.

Schlenker, B. R., & Darby, B. W. (1981). The use of apologies in social predicaments. *Social Psychology Quarterly, 44,* 271-278.

Schlenker, B. R., Dlugolecki, D. W., & Doherty, K. J. (1994). The impact of self-presentations on self-appraisals and behaviors: The power of public commitment. *Personality and Social Psychology Bulletin, 20,* 20-33.

Schlenker, B. R., & Leary, M. R. (1982a). Social anxiety and self-presentation: A conceptualization and model. *Psychological Bulletin, 92,* 641-669.

Schlenker, B. R., & Leary, M. R. (1982b). Audiences' reactions to self-enhancing, self-denigrating, and accurate self-presentations. *Journal of Experimental Social Psychology, 18,* 89-104.

Schlenker, B. R., & Leary, M. R. (1985). Social anxiety and communication about the self. *Journal of Language and Social Psychology, 4,* 171-193.

Schlenker, B. R., Phillips, S. T., Boniecki, K. A., & Schlenker, D. R. (1995). Championship pressures: Choking or triumphing on one's own territory? *Journal of Personality and Social Psychology, 68,* 632-643.

Schlenker, B. R., & Trudeau, J. V. (1990). The impact of self-presentations on private self-beliefs: Effects of prior self-beliefs and misattribution. *Journal of Personality and Social Psychology, 58,* 22-32.

Schlenker, B. R., & Weigold, M. F. (1989a). Goals and the self-identification process. In L. Pervin (Ed.), *Goal concepts in personality and social psychology* (pp. 243-290). Hillsdale, NJ: Erlbaum.

Schlenker, B. R., & Weigold, M. F. (1989b). Self-identification and accountability. In R. A. Giacalone & P. Rosenfeld (Eds.), *Impression management in the organization* (pp. 21-43). Hillsdale, NJ: Erlbaum.

Schlenker, B. R., & Weigold, M. F. (1990). Self-consciousness and self-presentation: Being autonomous versus appearing autonomous. *Journal of Personality and Social Psychology, 59,* 820-828.

Schlenker, B. R., & Weigold, M. F. (1992). Interpersonal processes involving impression regulation and management. *Annual Review of Psychology, 43,* 133-168.

Schlenker, B. R., Weigold, M. F., & Doherty, K. (1991). Coping with accountability: Self-identification and evaluative reckonings. In C. R. Snyder & D. R. Forsyth (Eds.), *Handbook of social and clinical psychology* (pp. 96-115). Elmsford, NY: Pergamon Press.

Scott, M. B., & Lyman, S. M. (1960). Accounts. *American Sociological Review, 33,* 46-62.

Semin, G. R., & Manstead, A. S. R. (1983). *The accountability of conduct: A social psychological analysis.* London: Academic Press.

Snyder, C. R. (1985). The excuse: An amazing grace? In B. R. Schlenker (Ed.), *The self and social life* (pp. 235-260). New York: McGraw-Hill.

Snyder, M. (1987). *Public appearances/private realities: The psychology of self-monitoring.* San Francisco: W. H. Freeman.

Snyder, C. R., & Higgins, R. L. (1988). Excuses: Their effective role in the negotiation of reality. *Psychological Bulletin, 104,* 23-25.

Sorrentino, R. M., Bobocel, D. R., Gitta, M. Z., Olson, J. M., & Hewitt, E. C. (1988). Uncertainty orientation and persuasion: Individual differences in the effects of personal relevance on social judgments. *Journal of Personality and Social Psychology, 55,* 357-371.

Steele, C. M. (1988). The psychology of self-affirmation: Sustaining the integrity of the self. In L. Berkowitz (Ed.), *Advances in experimental social psychology* (Vol. 21, pp 261-302). New York: Academic Press.

Swann, W. B., Jr., & Hill, C. A. (1982). When our identities are mistaken: Reaffirming self-conceptions through social interaction. *Journal of Personality and Social Psychology, 43,* 59-66.

Swann, W. B., & Read, S. J. (1981). Self-verification processes: How we sustain our self-conceptions. *Journal of Experimental Social Psychology, 17,* 351-372.

Taylor, S. E., & Brown, J. B. (1988). Illusions and well-being: A social psychological perspective on mental health. *Psychological Bulletin, 103,* 193-210.

Tedeschi, J. T. (Ed.). (1981). *Impression management: Theory and social psychological research.* New York: Academic Press.

Tedeschi, J. T., & Norman, N. (1985). Social power, self-presentation, and the self. In B. R. Schlenker (Ed.), *The self in social life* (pp. 293-321). New York: McGraw-Hill.

Tedeschi, J. T., & Riess, M. (1981). Predicaments and verbal tactics of impression management. In C. Antaki (Ed.), *Ordinary language explanations of social behavior* (pp. 271-309). London: Academic Press.

Tennen, H., & Affleck, G. (1990). Blaming others for threatening events. *Psychological Bulletin, 108,* 209-232.

Tetlock, P. E. (1985a). Toward an intuitive politician model of the attribution process. In B. R. Schlenker (Ed.), *The self and social life* (pp. 203-234). New York: McGraw-Hill.

Tetlock, P. E. (1985b). Accountability: The neglected social context of judgment and choice.

In B. W. Staw & L. Cummings (Eds.), *Research in organizational behavior* (Vol. 9, pp. 279–232). Greenwich, CT: JAI Press.

Tetlock, P. E. (1992). The impact of accountability on judgment and choice: Toward a social contingency model. In M. P. Zanna (Ed.), *Advances in experimental social psychology* (Vol. 25, pp. 331–376). New York: Academic Press.

Tetlock, P. E., & Manstead, A. S. R. (1985). Impression management versus intrapsychic explanations is social psychology: A useful dichotomy? *Psychological Review, 92,* 59–77.

Toris, C., & DePaulo, B. M. (1984). Effects of actual deception and suspiciousness of deception on interpersonal perceptions. *Journal of Personality and Social Psychology, 47,* 1063–1073.

Weiner, B., Amirkhan, J., Folkes, V. S., & Verette, J. A. (1987). An attributional analysis of excuse giving: Studies of a naive theory of emotion. *Journal of Personality and Social Psychology, 52,* 316–324.

Wicklund, R. A., & Gollwitzer, P. M. (1982). *Symbolic self-completion.* Hillsdale, NJ: Erlbaum.

Wyer, R. S., & Frey, D. (1983). The effects of feedback about self and others on the recall and judgments of feedback-relevant information. *Journal of Experimental Social Psychology, 19,* 540–559.

CHAPTER 5

Causal-Uncertainty Beliefs and Related Goal Structures

GIFFORD WEARY
JOHN A. EDWARDS
Ohio State University

Uncertainty resolution has long been viewed as a primary determinant of human behavior (e.g., Berlyne, 1960; Festinger, 1954; Kagan, 1972). Although several sources of or mental contents associated with uncertainty reduction motives have been identified, there is perhaps no more prototypical and fundamental source of uncertainty reduction motives than that associated with a failure to understand the relatively unchanging underlying causal conditions for events. That is, "man grasps reality and can predict and control it, [only] by referring transient and variable behavior and events to relatively unchanging conditions, the so-called dispositional properties of the world" (Heider, 1958, p. 79).

This chapter introduces a model of motivation that builds upon this notion of "causal uncertainty." The model outlined herein argues that some people in some situations are chronically more motivated than others to resolve causal uncertainty. Such chronic individual differences in uncertainty about one's understanding of social causation, it is proposed, have fundamental consequences for the social information-processing goals adopted and for the manner in which information is encoded, interpreted, and stored.

After presenting our model of causal uncertainty, we describe initial research findings with respect to the measurement of such individual differences in causal-uncertainty beliefs, as well as to the antecedents and consequences of such beliefs. Although research addressing key aspects of the model has necessarily awaited the development of a means of reliably and validly tapping such individual differences, we outline the directions that future research will need to assume.

Before introducing the model, however, we touch base briefly with historical and current treatments of uncertainty, some of which bear some similarity to our notion of causal uncertainty. Such treatments provide an important context within which to view our causal-uncertainty model.

HISTORICAL AND CONTEMPORARY TREATMENTS OF UNCERTAINTY

Uncertainty Motivation

Historically, treatments of uncertainty motivation have tended to explain the motivational properties of uncertainty in terms of an organism's relationship with its environment. In general, these perspectives posit that a certain amount of uncertainty is inherent in any organism's perception of its environment, but that organisms are motivated for survival purposes to reduce this uncertainty as much as possible. This view underlies functionalist interpretations of perception and cognition, of which Brunswik's was one of the earliest. According to Brunswik, organisms work to maximize the probability that they have correctly perceived the structure of the world. This structure, though lawful, is ambiguous for organisms, because the relationships between percepts and the objects they represent are probabilistic (Tolman & Brunswik, 1935). That is, although the environment has a lawful underlying structure that is available to be perceived, organisms can only have a partial understanding of this structure because of the limitations of their perceptual and cognitive systems.

Brunswik believed that the mental faculties of organisms have evolved in large part to achieve the goal of accurately perceiving the world. In other words, the primary function of perceptual and cognitive systems is to minimize uncertainty. This functionalist perspective is implicit in many modern notions of cognitive process and structure. For instance, the study of judgmental heuristics is based on the idea that people develop rules to help deal with uncertain judgment situations (Kahneman, Slovic, & Tversky, 1982). Similar inferential functions have been postulated for categories (e.g., Medin, 1988), attributions (e.g., Kelley, 1967), and attitudes (e.g., Pratkanis & Greenwald, 1989).

In part on the basis of such a functionalist perspective, Kagan (1972) asserted that the resolution of uncertainty is a primary human motivation. Kagan believed that uncertainty occurs when people believe one of their cognitive representations is incompatible with their experience or with other representations. Such a state may be caused by an unexpected event, an inability to predict the future, or incompatibility between ideas or between ideas and reality. As this suggests, Kagan explicitly believed that feelings of uncertainty are analogous to feelings of cognitive dissonance. However, unlike Festinger (1957), Kagan saw the motive to reduce such feelings as a proactive striving for knowledge, rather than a reactive reduction of tension. Kagan believed that uncertainty typically prompts an alerting response that then elicits processes intended to reorganize the uncertain individual's cognitive structures, thereby resolving the uncertainty.

Berlyne (1960) also discussed uncertainty in terms of incompatibility between cognitive elements. Berlyne described uncertainty in terms of "conceptual conflict," or incompatibilities between symbolic (i.e., cognitive and perceptual) processes. Such conflict is relieved, according to Berlyne, by the acquisition of knowledge. Thus, people are motivated to acquire knowledge because it helps them to avoid and resolve conceptual conflict. Of particular interest for the current formulation is Berlyne's suggestion that "explanations" ("a statement that answers a question beginning with 'why'"; Berlyne, 1960, p. 267) have a special ability to relieve conceptual conflict by connecting events with other pieces of knowledge.

The notion of uncertainty reduction is also essential to Festinger's (1954) theory of social comparison. Festinger posited that people are driven to evaluate their own abilities and opinions, because such self-knowledge helps people to survive. According to social comparison theory, when people are uncertain about their abilities or opinions, they are motivated to reduce this uncertainty, preferably through objective, nonsocial means (e.g., by attempting to complete some task that may be diagnostic of their ability level). Failing that, people will attempt to evaluate their abilities and opinions by comparing themselves with others. According to Festinger, people prefer to make these comparisons with other people who are similar to them on relevant dimensions, because such comparisons are most informative.

There is a substantial literature on uncertainty in decision-making contexts. Theorists in this tradition typically construe uncertainty as a property of decision situations, rather than as a motivational state. Researchers in this paradigm often characterize uncertainty as the inability to assign probabilities to outcomes (Luce & Raiffa, 1957). This inability could stem from uncertainty about alternative courses of action, potential outcomes, or outcome payoffs (Conrath, 1967). Although such work is not directly related to the current motivation-based model of uncertainty reduction, research on the strategies that people use to deal with uncertainty is relevant (e.g., Kahneman et al., 1982; Howell & Burnett, 1978). As we discuss later, such research suggests methods people may be using in the service of uncertainty reduction motives.

There is one other important treatment of uncertainty that bears at least some superficial similarity to the current notion of causal uncertainty. This is uncertainty orientation (Sorrentino & Short, 1986). "Uncertainty orientation" is thought to be a cognitive variable, an individual difference in information value that can interact with any source of affective value (e.g., achievement motivation). Briefly, the uncertainty-oriented person is thought to attend to and seek out situations that afford an opportunity to attain clarity about the self or the environment. He or she "will search for meaning, attempting to make sense out of his or her environment, and will seek out new or novel situations" (Sorrentino & Short, 1986, p. 382). The certainty-oriented person, on the other hand, will not seek to find out anything if doing so may require changing what is already known and clear to him or her; this person adheres to and is motivated by situations that do not involve uncertainty about the self or the environment. Because uncertainty orientation is, like our notion of causal uncertainty, a construct dealing with individual differences in uncertainty-related phenomena, we examine possible similarities and differences between these two constructs later in the chapter.

Certain themes recur in the theories summarized in this section. First, these theories emphasize the importance of knowledge about the world to people's ability to survive. Second, these theories imply that the state of uncertainty prompts people to take some action to reduce the uncertainty, either by gaining new knowledge or by relating a problematic stimulus to past pieces of knowledge. Third, some of these theories imply that people have multiple means at their disposal for reducing uncertainty, but that some of these means are preferred over others. All three of these notions are important for the current formulation. However, as will be seen, there are also differences between our model of causal-uncertainty motives and these theories.

Feelings of Uncertainty

The theories of uncertainty reduction motivation just described provide an important theoretical context for our model of causal uncertainty. Recent work on the effect of momentary feelings on social information processing and judgment provides a second important element. The feelings-as-information view of the effects of mood on judgment (Schwarz & Clore, 1983; Schwarz, 1990) holds that people sometimes look to their current mood to make certain types of judgments. That is, people sometimes use mood as a cue that tells them how they feel about a certain judgment object. Clore (1992) suggests that nonemotional feelings can be used in a similar fashion. These are feelings based in one's experience of thinking. Terms such as "surprise," "confusion," "understanding," and the like are typically used to describe such feelings. According to Clore, these metacognitive feelings are sometimes used as data for certain types of judgments. Relevant judgments concern such things as how well one understands something, whether something is familiar or not, or how interesting something is (see Clore, 1992, for a discussion of relevant research).

Uncertainty is a feeling of this type. Feelings of uncertainty are presumed to arise from a metacognitive monitoring of the extent to which a person understands something (cf. Clore & Parrott, 1990, cited in Clore, 1992). They provide a cue to the individual that his or her knowledge is inadequate to cope with some situation or achieve some goal. In response to such feelings, actions to rectify the state of affairs are undertaken.

This notion that feelings may serve an informational purpose is also a central argument in several functional theories of negative moods; these theories propose that negative moods act as cues signaling individuals that some stimulus or event requires attention and action (e.g., Broadbent, 1971; Fridja, 1988; Mayer, 1986). However, like Clore, we do not view uncertainty as a mood (although it may have affective consequences), but as a nonaffective, cognitive feeling.

The Weary et al. Model: Causal-Uncertainty Beliefs and Depression

A final conceptual source for the current model of causal uncertainty is the Weary, Marsh, Gleicher, and Edwards (1993) model of the effects of depression on social information processing. Briefly, this model postulates that mildly and moderately depressed individuals, because of their perceptions of lack of control and resultant causal uncertainty, adopt a goal of subjective accuracy (Swann, 1984) (i.e., they desire a subjective sense that they understand the world). This goal prompts depressives to effortfully seek out and process social information. Considerable evidence supports this model. For instance, depressives have been shown to seek out more diagnostic information about other people than nondepressives do (Hildebrand-Saints & Weary, 1988). Depressives also are more sensitive to potentially diagnostic information about others (i.e., counternormative behavior) than are nondepressed individuals (Weary, Jordan, & Hill, 1985). Such sensitivity effects have been shown to be attributable to systematic, effortful processing of social information by mildly and moderately depressed persons (Edwards & Weary, 1993b; Gleicher & Weary, 1991; Yost & Weary, in press). These and other studies support a view of mildly and moderately depressed individuals as engaging in a style of social information processing that may be characterized as effortful, vigilant, and complex.

The work of Weary and her colleagues was stimulated by research on the effects of experimentally induced control motivation on attributional processing (Pittman & D'Agostino, 1985; Pittman & Pittman, 1980). Because several researchers had noted a strong association between perceived lack of control and depression (e.g. Garber, Miller, & Seaman, 1979; Marsh & Weary, 1989; Warren & McEachren, 1983; Weisz, Weiss, Wasserman, & Rintoul, 1987), it seemed reasonable to conclude that depressed individuals would show effects similar to those obtained under experimental manipulations of loss of control. However, the Weary et al. (1993) model took this research a step further by postulating causal uncertainty as an important moderator of the effects of depressives' perceived lack of control on social information processing. Uncertainty was seen as critical to the model for two reasons. First, an association between uncertainty about causes and level of depressive symptomatology had been found both by Weary and her colleagues (Gleicher & Weary, 1991; Marsh & Weary, 1989) and by Weisz and his colleagues (Weisz, Sweeney, Proffitt, & Carr, 1993; Weisz et al., 1987). Second, it was thought that a strong belief in one's inability to understand and therefore control outcomes would probably lead to helplessness and a reduction of effort, rather than the increased motivation to ascertain contingencies found in the Weary et al. research. Therefore, uncertainty, in conjunction with perceived lack of control, was thought to be necessary to create the kinds of information-processing effects described by Weary and her colleagues.[1]

Although the Weary et al. (1993) model describes causal uncertainty in the context of depression, it is unlikely that such motives are limited to depressed individuals. In fact, we suspect that most people occasionally feel causally uncertain. However, the Weary et al. model forms a starting point for our thought on causal-uncertainty motives. We elaborate on this thought in the following section.

THE CAUSAL-UNCERTAINTY MODEL

As we have seen, then, the notion of individual differences in perceived causal uncertainty associated with differences in perceived loss of control has played an important role in work on the social perception consequences of depression. In addition, the topic of temporary feelings of causal uncertainty has received some recent attention in work concerned with the role of experiential emotional and nonemotional states on the construction of various social judgments.

In this section, we develop a new model of motivated social cognition—one that builds upon the notion of causal-uncertainty beliefs. In so doing, we hope to develop a model that is more general than either the model of depressive social perception processes outlined above or the feelings-as-information approach to the social-cognitive consequences of nonemotional feeling states. The new model, for example, is intended to address chronic individual differences in, as well as situational sources of, motive arousal. It is also able to account for the possible presence of dispositional motives to reduce causal uncertainty in the absence of significant depressive symptomatology. Figure 5.1 illustrates the model.

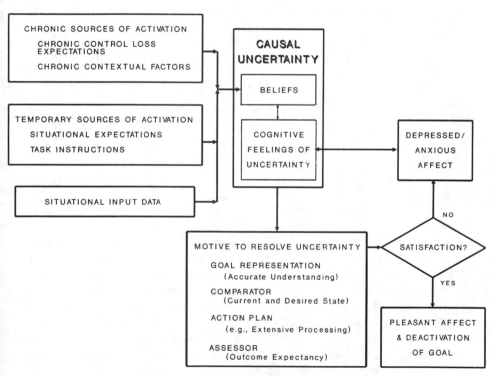

FIGURE 5.1 The full causal-uncertainty model.

Two major cognitive structures and associated processes form the core of the causal-uncertainty model: causal-uncertainty beliefs and the motive to resolve causal uncertainty. Let us begin with an examination of the components and processes that constitute the motive structure.

The Motive to Resolve Causal Uncertainty

Before describing in detail the various components of the motive to resolve causal uncertainty, we should first note that the motive to resolve causal uncertainty is viewed as a specific instance of a more general cognitive motive of uncertainty resolution. However, unlike other similar cognitive motives (e.g., Kagan, 1972; Sorrentino & Short, 1986), the motive to reduce causal uncertainty is not akin to self-actualization, mastery, or similar proactive sorts of motivations. It is reactive and negative,[2] and its aim is extrinsic to the form of the activity (i.e., the resultant goal-directed behavior serves a purely instrumental purpose; it is not engaged in for its sheer pleasure or for the satisfaction that comes with exceptional performance). We return to these important points throughout our description of the model.

We also should note that this model bears considerable similarity to several currently prominent models of motivated social cognition. In particular, it borrows heavily from cybernetic or control theory (e.g., Carver & Scheier, 1982, 1990a; Hyland, 1987; Powers, 1978), in that it employs as a central part of uncertainty resolution the concept of a "negative feedback loop"; the purpose of such a loop is to reduce discrepancies between some actual state and some desired comparison state. Such feedback systems are featured in several currently prominent theories of self-regulation (e.g., Carver & Scheier, 1990b; Higgins, 1987; Markus & Nurius, 1986).[3]

Goal Representation

As can be seen in Figure 5.1, the motive structure contains several component structures and processors. First, it contains a "goal representation"—a mental picture, so to speak, of a desired state that when achieved permits a better feeling. Whereas some other theories employing this notion of goal representation focus on more specific, lower-level goals, here the goal representation is quite abstract; it is an image or memory of possessing an accurate understanding of causal relations in the social world, of causal certainty.[4] This accuracy goal, then, refers to phenomenal or subjective accuracy (Swann, 1984)—a subjective sense that one understands the social world. We believe this goal to be universal, in that causal understanding is fundamental to adaptation; however, this is not to deny that an accurate understanding of causal relations (or a lack thereof) may be more or less important for some people under some conditions. We return to this topic shortly in our discussion of factors influencing the intensity of goal-directed behavior.

How does this goal representation develop, and how is it activated in memory? We believe that it develops through processes of social learning. That is, as people navigate their social worlds, they come to know through direct and indirect feedback from others, and through observing the degree of contingency between their own and others' responses and outcomes, whether they possess an adequate understanding of their social environments. In essence, they come to know whether or not their causal understanding generally permits adequate prediction and control (Heider, 1958; Kelley, 1967), and they learn through such effective and ineffective transactions with the environment what a subjective sense of understanding is—and, importantly, what it is not (for a similar analysis of interpersonal contingency learning and the development of self-regulatory systems, see Higgins, 1989).

Once developed, this representation of causal certainty (and causal uncertainty) can be activated directly by situational information indicating the possession of understanding. Expected outcomes are perhaps the prototypes of such information. In addition, information about the number and nature (sufficient facilitative, inhibitory) of potential causes of an outcome may activate a representation of causal certainty (or uncertainty). It can also be activated by the conscious deployment of attention. That is, individuals may consciously bring to mind stored information, including the mental structure associated with the desired (or undesired) state of causal certainty (or uncertainty). When causal certainty is used as a goal standard, or reference, we suspect that it is often activated by such conscious deployment of attention; however, in the case of frequent conscious activation, subsequent activation in response to relevant input may become automatic and represent a form of goal-dependent automaticity (Bargh, 1989).

An example of such activation by conscious deployment of attention may be useful at this point. One of us had occasion to watch an ABC-TV documentary on Jeffrey Dahmer. In this television report Lionel Dahmer, Jeffrey's father, revealed that he had spent considerable time actively thinking about the origins of his son's madness. He constantly asked himself, "Where did I go wrong?", "Did I help to create a serial killer?", and "Could I have said or done something to prevent this?" He went on to reveal that such "why" questions had become an eternal torment for him and that he felt compelled to consider all possible causal factors in an attempt to understand.

We would argue that Lionel Dahmer had stored in memory a representation of that which he desired—namely, an accurate causal understanding of his son's behavior. He had consciously brought to mind this goal and deployed his attentional resources in an attempt to attain it (cf. Klinger, 1975). Moreover, we would argue that as a result of such repeated conscious activation, the goal was automatically and involuntarily activated upon presentation of relevant information.

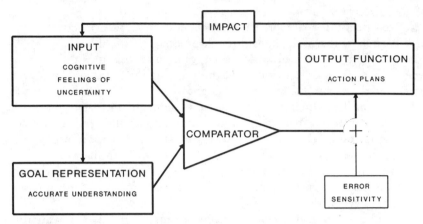

FIGURE 5.2   The causal-uncertainty model: Negative feedback loop.

Comparator and Negative Feedback Loop

In this model, as in other models of motivation, the motivational effects of the goal representation are attributed to a desire to reduce or minimize the discrepancy between the desired and some current undesired state. This is the function of the "comparator" and of the negative feedback loop referred to earlier (see Figure 5.2). If the comparison of current and desired states of causal knowledge indicates a discrepancy, negative affect in the form of depressed, anxious, frustrated feelings will result, and action plans aimed at reducing the discrepancy and negative affect may be initiated. This process of comparison will continue until the discrepancy reduction is satisfactory or until the individual disengages from the process in some other way. We have more to say about disengagement later; here, however, we stress the important point that the comparator's purpose is to detect and reduce via a negative feedback loop the discrepancy between current and desired states. Informational feedback about the presence and intensity of negative affect that results from detection of a discrepancy is used as a cue indicating the degree of goal attainment (Martin, Ward, Achee, & Wyer, 1993), but only when the goal is activated.

We must introduce one more notion related to the operation of the negative feedback loop: the notion of "error sensitivity" (Hyland, 1987). This notion refers to the amplification of a detected discrepancy between current and desired states, and helps to explain the relationship between the amount of error and the intensity of the resulting goal-directed behavior. The higher the sensitivity, the more salient will be the error, and the more intense will be the attempts to reduce it. This notion, then, suggests that for some people and for some situations, a reduction in causal uncertainty will be more important. When the motive to reduce uncertainty is active, for example, situations that create self-focused attention may result in higher levels of error sensitivity in a negative feedback loop (Carver & Scheier, 1990a). Similarly, when the likely consequences of failing to understand relevant cause–effect relationships are serious or important, then conscious attention directed toward the goal may amplify the error sensitivity.

Action Plans

"Action plans" make up the third component of the motive structure. These plans are designed to bring the current and desired states of causal knowledge closer. At a general level, these plans all involve a deliberate, intentional search for and use of social information that might reasonably render the social environment more understandable, predictable, and controllable—in short, information relevant to the unchanging underlying conditions of the social world (Heider, 1958). Such information may include explicit statements about the causes of others' outcomes; information about facilitative and inhibitory environmental (e.g., task difficulty) and personal (e.g., ability and effort) forces (Heider, 1958); information about the expected valence and hedonic relevance of an outcome (Jones & Davis, 1965; Jones & McGillis, 1976); and information about the consensus, distinctiveness, and consistency of the target's behavior (Kelley, 1973).

Some of these action plans may require the allocation of conscious attentional resources and conscious guidance to be brought to completion; such plans thus represent a form of controlled information processing. Examples of such controlled processing are the active search for information that is highly diagnostic about another's dispositions (Hildebrand-Saints & Weary, 1989), and the conscious analysis of consensus, distinctiveness, and consistency information about one's own or another's outcome. Other action plans may represent a form of goal-dependent automaticity (Bargh, 1989), requiring the specific goal of achieving causal understanding, but not attentional monitoring and not necessarily the consumption of attentional resources. Proceduralized schemas (Kelley, 1972) relevant to causal analyses are examples of such action plans.

Of course, the use of these plans may have unintended effects (Bargh, 1989). Consider, as an example, the unintended consequences of developing an accurate understanding of another's behaviors. There is now evidence suggesting that when such a goal is in place, the observed behaviors are likely to be automatically encoded in dispositional terms (Winter & Uleman, 1984). This tendency is even more pronounced if the attributor is also engaged in other concurrent cognitive or behavioral activities (Gilbert, Pelham, & Krull, 1988). Since the encoding of behaviors in dispositional terms is not in this circumstance the intention, it represents an unintended effect of an intended comprehension goal. Whether or not such dispositional encoding results in a more accurate understanding of the other is an entirely different issue and probably depends upon a host of perceiver and situational factors.

Outcome Expectancy Assessor

The final component of the motive structure is a cognitive mechanism that assesses the outcome expectancy of any action. Although the comparator may activate the goal plans if a discrepancy between current and desired states is detected, this does not mean that the plans will be undertaken. That is, there is some control over the initiation of automatic and controlled action plans. A major determinant of whether purposive cognitive or motor behavior is undertaken is the expected success of such efforts. Like others (e.g., Carver & Scheier, 1990a), we suggest that there exists a cognitive mechanism that assesses the current context and stored information about the successes of past actions in particular contexts. Moreover, this assessment of the various action plan expectancies may occur before, during, or after the initiation of any single plan. The output of this process is an expectancy of goal attainment if one or another action plan is implemented. If the expectancy of success is too low for all viable plans, given the context, then actions will not be undertaken and disengagement from the motive will be attempted.

How low is too low? This is, of course, difficult to say. However, we believe that the expectancy of success must be extremely negative before disengagement of causal-uncertainty reduction is attempted. There are two reasons behind our assertion. First, it seems reasonable to argue that the more important the goal, the more extreme the negative expectations will have to be before goal pursuit is prevented or interrupted. As we have noted earlier, we believe that a motive to understand the causal properties of the social world is a fundamental motive; satisfaction of this motive permits prediction and control of people's social worlds, and thus it is critical to adaptation. Second, it has been suggested (Carver & Scheier, 1982) that for abstract goals, goal pursuit typically unfolds over time and attainment requires many actions, whereas for more concrete goals, the time scale is typically much shorter. Because the motive to reduce causal uncertainty is such an abstract goal, attainment may require many, many attempts and considerable time. We would suggest that for this reason, negative expectations about the attainment of causal certainty must be extreme for them to be held with enough confidence to warrant disengagement.

Before leaving the topic of expectancies and disengagement, we should briefly indicate the several ways in which one can attempt to disengage from the motive to reduce causal uncertainty. One can actively attempt to suppress the goal. One can also withdraw from the situation physically, thereby avoiding information that may provide input to the comparator. One can focus attention on some other, perhaps incompatible goal. Finally, one can re-evaluate the importance of the uncertainty reduction goal, or can reduce the error sensitivity of the comparator in some other fashion. All of these strike us as very temporary and probably not very successful maneuvers. Some of these strategies are likely to produce the ironic consequence of increasing future thought about the goal (Wegner & Schneider, 1989). Others are simply likely to be ineffective because of the fundamental and general nature of the goal.

Causal-Uncertainty Beliefs and Feelings

Belief Content and Definition

Our description of the motive to resolve uncertainty employs the principles of control theory, as we have noted earlier, and so bears some similarity to other models of motivation. However, the second major structure of our model (see Figure 5.1), entailing causal-uncertainty beliefs and feelings, is unique to and constitutes the heart of the causal-uncertainty model.

Causal-uncertainty beliefs are defined as generalized self-constructs about one's uncertain or inadequate understanding or detection of causal relations in the social world. Although one may have such beliefs about the physical world, we focus our discussion on beliefs about the adequacy of one's understanding of social events—events for which oneself or others are possible causal agents. We do so for two primary reasons. First, we believe that such events are the most important and frequent events requiring causal analyses for most individuals; that is, compared to daily nonsocial events, understanding one's own and others' intentions, dispositions, and sentiments as they relate to various behavioral outcomes are tasks that on a day-to-day basis are more focal, consume more of one's cognitive resources, and supply an important and figural sense of reality. Second, and relatedly, the causal structure underlying such events is often quite ambiguous, complex, and difficult to verify. These characteristics of many social events are precisely what make them most relevant to the development of causal-uncertainty beliefs.

Indeed, we believe that causal-uncertainty beliefs—beliefs that one does not fully or adequately understand cause–effect relationships in the social world—are available for all people, because some exposure to social events of ambiguous or vague causal determination is universal. However, such constructs are likely to be more global and accessible for some people, and consequently are more likely to influence the thoughts and behavior of these people than of others.

Belief Excitation

What determines whether a particular construct will be used in the processing of social information? The probability that causal-uncertainty beliefs will be activated is viewed as a joint function of their accessibility and applicability (Higgins, 1990). Let us examine first the factors, both temporary and chronic, that increase the accessibility of causal-uncertainty beliefs; such factors should function similarly and combine additively (Bargh, Bond, Lombardi, & Tota, 1986) to influence the level of excitation.

A major assumption of the causal-uncertainty model is that generalized expectations that one's future responses and outcomes will probably be noncontingent are primary sources of activation for causal-uncertainty beliefs (see Figure 5.3). Although they may be chronic or situational, of greater concern to us here are chronic expectations of uncontrollability. Such chronic expectations,

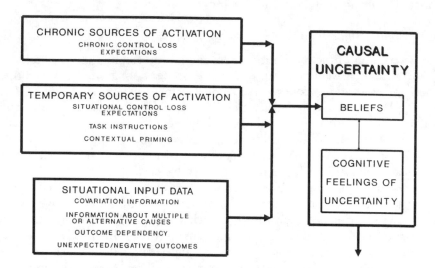

FIGURE 5.3   The causal-uncertainty model: Sources of belief activation.

we believe, are likely to result in frequent perceptions of control loss, and to activate frequently and automatically beliefs that one does not fully understand the causal structure of the social environment.

According to this logic, then, causal-uncertainty beliefs are chronically accessible self-constructs for individuals who possess chronic perceptions and expectations of control loss. For those who do not, they are available and may be activated by situational expectations of control loss; however, activation of causal-uncertainty beliefs in this instance will require a higher level of excitation from the situational input (ie., the input would have to be more detailed, elaborate, or salient), and the decay in the excitation level will be shorter than that for chronically accessible causal-uncertainty beliefs (Higgins, 1990).

In addition to situational expectations of control loss, other momentary factors can serve to activate causal uncertainty-beliefs temporarily. These include task instructions that may instantiate temporary processing goals to form an impression of another, or to comprehend the meaning of or to explain some outcome (either one's own or another person's). Such processing goals will probably lead perceivers to attend to or search for causal information, (i.e., information relevant to one's own or another's dispositions, intentions, desires, and sentiments). Contextual priming of causal-uncertainty beliefs can also, of course, temporarily activate such beliefs.

We have noted above that the activation of stored knowledge is determined by both its accessibility and its applicability. Let us turn now to the issue of applicability. "Applicability" refers to the overlap between the current situational input and the stored knowledge (Higgins, 1990). In the case of causal-uncertainty beliefs, the relevant input will be information relevant to causal analyses (e.g., number and nature of causes) and direct causal questions. In addition, informational input relevant to current perceptions of control loss will be applicable to beliefs about the causes of outcomes. Information known to result in perceptions of control loss includes information about the actual degree of noncontingency between responses, and about the timing, frequency, and valence of the outcome; decreases in actual contingency, in temporal contiguity, in frequency, and in desirability all serve to lower perceived control (Alloy, Clements, & Koenig, 1993).

Cognitive Feelings of Uncertainty

Once causal-uncertainty beliefs have been activated, cognitive feelings of uncertainty should follow automatically. These nonemotional feelings (Clore, 1992) are experienced phenomenologically as confusion, surprise, bewilderment, and so forth. Such feelings indicate to perceivers that the current state of their knowledge is not adequate; in other words, such feelings of uncertainty serve as important input to the motive structure discussed earlier. They function to activate the goal representation, and they serve as important input to the comparator regarding the current state of knowledge.

Summary

In summary, the causal-uncertainty model outlined above proposes that causal-uncertainty beliefs are available for all people, but that they are chronically accessible for some. Such individual differences in chronic accessibility have several important implications. First, chronically accessible causal-uncertainty beliefs should require less excitation from situational input to become active (see Higgins & Brendl, 1995, for empirical evidence of this general activation rule), and their activation in response to such information should be automatic. They also should be associated with a dispositional motive to reduce causal uncertainty. We believe, furthermore, that such chronically accessible self-constructs and goals should be associated with negative feedback loops that contain high error sensitivities and that direct more conscious attention toward reducing discrepancies between the current and desired states of knowledge (i.e., toward achieving the goal).

CAUSAL UNCERTAINTY: ITS MEASUREMENT, CORRELATES, ANTECEDENTS, AND CONSEQUENCES

The Causal-Uncertainty Scale

Our initial work on causal uncertainty was intended to create and validate an individual-differences measure of this construct (Weary & Edwards, 1994). This measure, the Causal-Uncertainty Scale (CUS), is a 14-item self-report inventory designed to tap the extent to which the respondent believes that he or she typically does not fully understand causal relations in the social world (see Table 5.1 for the items). The CUS was designed to be a measure of the extent to which people possess global causal-uncertainty beliefs about the social world, rather than a measure of causal-uncertainty beliefs in more specific domains.

An initial sample of 425 subjects completed this measure. Analyses revealed that the scale has good psychometric properties. In this initial investigation, the CUS had a Cronbach's alpha of .83, a mean interitem correlation of .25, and a 6-week test–retest correlation of .64. Also, scores on the scale were normally distributed, and mean scores for males and females did not differ. When the scale was administered to a second sample of subjects (Jacobson, Weary, & Edwards, 1994), similar psychometric properties were obtained (Cronbach's alpha of .86, a mean interitem correlation of .31, and a 6-week test–retest correlation of .79).

Principal-components analyses from these two samples suggested that the

TABLE 5.1   CUS Items and Factor Loadings from Exploratory Factor Analysis (Principal-Components Analysis, Oblimin Rotation)

Item	*Factor 1*	*Factor 2*
1. I do not know what it takes to get along well with others.	.55	.03
2. When I receive good grades, I usually do not understand why I did so well.	.69	.28
3. I do not understand what causes most of the problems that I have with others.	.64	.03
4. When I see something good happen to others, I often do not know why it happened.	.61	.10
5. When I receive poor grades, I usually do not understand why I did so poorly.	.51	.09
6. When someone I know receives a poor grade, I often cannot determine if they could have done anything to prevent it.	.33	.23
7. I do not understand what causes most of the good things that happen to me.	.70	.05
8. When things go right, I generally do not know what to do to keep them that way.	.69	.13
9. When bad things happen, I generally do not know why.	.42	.39
10. When there is more than one possible reason for a person's action, it is difficult to determine which one is the actual reason.	.01	.79
11. I often feel like I don't have enough information to come to a conclusion why things happen to other people.	.03	.79
12. When I see something bad happen to others, I often do not know why it happened.	.02	.80
13. I often feel like I do not have enough information to come to a conclusion about why things happen to me.	.42	.44
14. When I think about why someone does something, there are usually so many possible reasons for it that I cannot determine which one was the cause.	.02	.79

scale has a single factor. However, an inspection of the scree plots suggested that a two-factor solution might also be reasonable. These two factors corresponded to "uncertainty about the causes of one's own outcomes" and "uncertainty about the causes of others' outcomes" (see Table 5.1 for factor loadings). Confirmatory factor analysis conducted on a third sample indicated that this two-factor solution had a good fit to the data (Edwards & Weary, 1995). However, the two factors are substantially correlated ($r = .67$), and it appears that for most purposes, the use of a single score is preferable.

TABLE 5.2   Correlations of the CUS with Other Measures

Scale	n	r
Beck Depression Inventory (Sample 1)	265	.37***
(Sample 2)	320	.38***
Expanded Attributional Style Questionnaire		
Stability	98	.30***
Globality	101	.08
Internality	101	.15
Attributional Style Assessment Test–I		
Controllability	74	−.26*
Locus of Control Scale (External)	138	.23**
Desire for Control Scale	130	−.21**
Intolerance for Ambiguity Scale	122	.27**
Need for Cognition Scale	105	−.42***
Need for Closure Scale	110	.07
Preference for Order		.19*
Preference for Predictability		.07
Decisiveness		−.28**
Discomfort with Ambiguity		.24**
Closed-Mindedness		.10
State–Trait Anxiety Inventory		
State Anxiety	108	.12
Trait Anxiety	107	.41***
Rosenberg Self-Esteem Scale	129	−.40***
Marlowe–Crowne Social Desirability Scale	138	−.02
High school GPA	130	.04

*$p < .05$ (one-tailed). **$p < .01$ (one-tailed). ***$p < .001$ (one-tailed). Adapted from Weary and Edwards (1994).

Discriminant and Convergent Validity

To provide evidence of the scale's convergent and discriminant validity, we (Weary & Edwards, 1994, Study 2) examined the relationship between the CUS and measures of a number of other individual-differences variables from which it should be theoretically distinct but with which it should share some overlapping features. The obtained correlations are listed in Table 5.2.

As suggested by the work of Weary and her colleagues on depressives' social perception processes, we expected a moderate correlation between subjects' scores on the Beck Depression Inventory (Beck, 1967) and CUS scores. This prediction was supported for two samples of respondents.

For several reasons, we decided to examine the relationship between CUS scores and measures of various dimensions underlying attributional styles. One of our major reasons was the observed association of some dimensions with the level of depressive symptomatology. In addition, the stylized use of some causal dimensions would seem to be related to a belief that one does or does not understand the causes of one's own (and others') outcomes. Specifically, a positive correlation was expected between the Stability subscale of the Expanded Attributional Style Questionnaire (Whitley, 1991) and the CUS, because uncertainty about one's ability to detect causal forces in the world would seem to imply that stable causal forces exist and can be detected.[5] A negative relationship was expected between the CUS and the attributional dimension of Controllability (from the Attributional Style Assessment Test–I; Anderson, Horowitz, & French, 1983). That is, as implied by our model, high scores on the CUS should be related to a tendency to attribute events to uncontrollable causes. These predictions were supported. The CUS was predicted and found to be unrelated to the Internality or Globality subscales of this test.

The hypothesized relationship between causal uncertainty and perceived lack of control suggests that causal uncertainty should be related to expectations that one's outcomes are under the control of external forces such as luck or fate. However, a strong association was not expected, since causal-uncertainty beliefs should imply more that one does not understand the contingencies than that one understands that luck and fate are responsible. As expected, we found that the CUS was indeed correlated with a measure of external locus of control (Rotter, 1966).

Conversely, a negative relationship was expected between the CUS and a measure of the desire to have or engage in primary (i.e., active, mastery-oriented) control. Our reasoning was that successful execution of such primary control activities should require causal understanding, thus making such activities somewhat anxiety-provoking for causally uncertain individuals. Although causal uncertainty is linked to a motivation to regain control, such motivations are more similar to a desire for secondary control (i.e., understanding and interpretive control; Rothbaum, Weisz, & Snyder, 1982) than to a proactive desire for primary control. Because of this, a negative correlation was expected and found between the CUS and the Desire for Control Scale (Burger & Cooper, 1979).

A positive association between the CUS and a measure of intolerance for ambiguity (Budner, 1962) was expected, as it seemed likely that causally uncertain people should find their uncertainty aversive. However, the notion of intolerance for ambiguity contains some features that are not characteristic of causal uncertainty. For instance, people who are intolerant for ambiguity are thought to attempt to retain current conceptions of the world—a prediction we did not make for causally uncertain individuals. Therefore, we expected and found a small positive relationship between these two constructs.

Our research with depressed individuals suggests that causally uncertain people tend to put effort into thinking. Superficially, this appears to imply that there should be a positive relationship between the CUS and the Need for Cognition Scale (Cacioppo & Petty, 1982), which measures the tendency to engage in and enjoy thinking. However, we believe that the motivational bases of these two constructs are quite different. Need for cognition taps a motivation based on enjoyment of thinking and intellectual mastery, whereas causal-uncertainty motivation is more of a reactive striving to regain understanding. In fact, instead of enjoying the cognitive activity in which they are engaged, causally uncertain people probably find such activity to be anxiety-provoking. On the basis of this logic, we expected and obtained a negative relationship between the CUS and the Need for Cognition Scale.

Kruglanski's notion of "need for closure" may also bear some relationship to causal uncertainty. Need for closure is the "desire for a definite answer on some topic, *any* answer as opposed to confusion" (Webster & Kruglanski, 1994). It is hypothesized to be a latent variable manifested via several surface manifestations. Although for some of these manifestations (preferences for predictability and order, a discomfort with ambiguity, and decisiveness) we expected a weak relationship with causal uncertainty, for one (closed-mindedness) we expected no relationship. These predictions were supported, with the exception of the correlation between the CUS and a preference for predictability, which was not significant. We expected and found no relationship between the CUS and the total need-for-closure score. Although it is conceivable that need for closure may influence how people respond to causal uncertainty, it should not pertain to the existence of causal-uncertainty beliefs, or to the likelihood of their activation.

Because causal-uncertainty beliefs are by definition negative beliefs about the self, and because causal uncertainty is associated with depression, we expected and found the CUS to be related to a measure of low self-esteem (Rosenberg, 1965). We did not expect a higher association, because global low self-esteem contains components not tied directly to causal uncertainty.

We expected chronic causal uncertainty as assessed by the CUS to be related to a measure of trait anxiety (Spielberger, Gorsuch, Lushene, Vagg, & Jacobs, 1983), since frequent feelings of uncertainty should elicit anxiety. However, it is important to note that this relationship was moderate ($r = .41$), and thus does not call into question the validity of the CUS.

Finally, it seemed important to demonstrate that the CUS was unrelated to social desirability concerns and to intelligence. We found no relationship be-

TABLE 5.3 Correlations of the CUS with Additional Measures

Scale	n	r
Personal Need for Structure Scale	71	.25*
Differential Emotions Scale	71	
Merry/Gleeful/Amused		−.04
Warmhearted/Joyful/Elated		.06
Sad/Downhearted/Blue		.24*
Irritated/Angry/Mad		.25*
Fearful/Scared/Afraid		.29*
Tense/Anxious/Nervous		.40**
Disgusted/Turned-Off/Repulsed		.12
Contemptuous/Scornful/Disdainful		.22
Perceived Lack of Control Scale	320	.51**

*$p < .05$ (one-tailed). **$p < .001$ (one-tailed).

tween the CUS and the Marlowe–Crowne Social Desirability Scale (Crowne & Marlowe, 1960) or high school grade point average, which served as a crude measure of subjects' relative intelligence.

In an attempt to demonstrate further the convergent and discriminant validity of the CUS, we recently examined its relationships with several other relevant variables (see Table 5.3). In particular, we explored the relationship of CUS scores to measures of the Personal Need for Structure, of mood states, and of perceptions of control. Let us examine the relationships for each of these variables in turn.

First, we expected causal uncertainty to be positively related to Personal Need for Structure (Thompson, Naccarato, & Parker, 1992). The Personal Need for Structure Scale measures the extent to which people prefer structured situations, find lack of clarity distressing, and are motivated to cognitively structure their world (Neuberg & Newsom, 1993). We believe that causally uncertain people do find their lack of clarity regarding causal forces to be distressing. However, we do not think that causally uncertain people will necessarily resolve this distress by using simply structured views of the world, as do people high in need for structure (Neuberg & Newsom, 1993). Therefore, we expected and found a low positive correlation between the CUS and the Personal Need for Structure Scale.

We also expected causal uncertainty to be related to some types of negative moods. Specifically, we expected causal uncertainty to elicit feelings related to anxiety, fear, and sadness. However, we did not expect causal uncertainty to be related to *all* negative affects (or to many positive affects). For instance, causal uncertainty should be unrelated to feelings of disgust.

We correlated the CUS with various subscales of the Differential Emotions Scale (Cacioppo, Martzke, Petty, & Tassinary, 1988). As expected, we found moderate correlations between the CUS and feelings of sadness, fear, and anxiety, but no relationships between the CUS and feelings of merriment, warmth, or disgust. We found unexpected relationships between the CUS and feelings of anger and contempt (although the latter correlation was only marginally significant). The reasons for these latter relationships are not entirely clear. Higgins (1987, 1989) has suggested that children's failure to learn different types of interpersonal contingencies leaves them vulnerable as adults to self-discrepancies and to the affect associated with them. More specifically, uncertainty about the causes of positive outcomes can lead to problems with the ideal self-regulatory system, and thus to feelings of dejection and frustration. Uncertainty about the causes of negative outcomes can lead to problems with the ought self-regulatory system, leading to resentment and anger. It may be that our findings regarding the relationship of the CUS and feelings of anger and contempt are related to such processes.

Because of the close hypothetical relationship between causal uncertainty and perceived lack of control, it was important to consider the association between measures of the two constructs. Although our correlations between the CUS and measures of external locus of control and of controllability attributional style were suggestive, neither of the latter two scales measures perceptions of amount of perceived control per se. We correlated the CUS with a measure of perceived lack of control (Edwards & Weary, 1993a) and found the expected moderate positive relationship.

Construct Validity

Although the correlations between the CUS and various other individual-differences measures provide some evidence of the convergent and discriminant validity of the scale, it is still important to provide evidence of the scale's construct validity. One way of doing this is to show that an individual's scores on the CUS can predict uncertainty about his or her causal analyses of events. In one study, we (Weary & Edwards, 1994, Study 3) had subjects read a series of scenarios describing a person engaged in some activities. Each scenario had an outcome. Subjects were asked to generate possible causes for each outcome, and then to rate their certainty in each of the causes they listed. Subjects then completed the CUS. The results indicated that people high in causal uncertainty were more uncertain in the causes they generated, thus providing some evidence for the construct validity of the scale.

One feature of causal uncertainty that serves to distinguish it from other, similar constructs is that causal uncertainty deals specifically with the causal domain. Therefore, the CUS should be able to predict uncertainty in causal judgments but should be unrelated to uncertainty in other kinds of judgments, such as estimations or probability judgments. To test this prediction, we (Weary & Edwards, 1994, Study 4) had subjects complete the causal-judgment task described above, and then render a number of noncausal judgments (i.e., frequency estimations, estimations of typical male and female characteristics, etc.). Subjects indicated their certainty in each of the noncausal judgments. As expected, it was found that the CUS was significantly negatively correlated with certainty in causal judgments ($r = -.25$, $p < .03$), but not with certainty in noncausal judgments ($r = -.11$, $p = .23$).[6]

Further evidence of the CUS's construct validity can be obtained by examining the extent to which the CUS can predict uncertainty in causal explanations, above and beyond the ability of its major correlates to do so. We (Weary & Edwards, 1994, Study 3) examined this issue with respect to need for cognition. Subjects filled out the booklet of causal judgments, and filled out the CUS and the Need for Cognition Scale. Adding CUS scores to a regression equation already containing scores on the Need for Cognition Scale (and a variable accounting for the counterbalancing of the scenarios) resulted in a significant increment in R^2 for the CUS.

We recently collected similar data regarding the ability of the CUS to predict certainty in generated causes above and beyond the ability of other related measures to do so. For all of the data to be reported, subjects completed the CUS, the relevant other measures, the booklet of causal judgments, and the booklet of noncausal judgments. Between the two judgment booklets and the individual-difference measures, subjects completed a filler task requiring them to draw a map of Ohio and locate several cities. Several random orderings of the materials were used.

TABLE 5.4   Variance in Certainty in Causes Accounted for by the CUS, above and beyond That Accounted for by Related Variables

Scale	n	CUS increment in R^2	p	CUS β	Other scale β
Need for Cognition Scale	54	.08	.03	.33	.06
Perceived Lack of Control Scale	82	.09	.007	−.36	.17
Beck Depression Inventory	82	.06	.04	−.26	−.03
Attributional Style Assessment Test—I					
Controllability	61	.07	.04	−.28	−.01
Personal Need for Structure Scale	61	.06	.05	−.26	−.04
Differential Emotions Scale	61				
Sad/Downhearted/Blue		.08	.03	−.29	.10
Irritated/Angry/Mad		.06	.06	−.26	−.03
Fearful/Scared/Afraid		.06	.05	−.27	−.02
Tense/Anxious/Nervous		.08	.03	−.33	.12
Disgusted/Turned-Off/Repulsed		.07	.04	−.27	−.01
Contemptuous/Scornful/Disdainful		.08	.03	−.30	.11

Note. Causal judgments were coded such that higher scores indicated greater certainty, except for the study including need for cognition, where judgments were coded such that higher scores indicated greater uncertainty.

The results of these studies are summarized in Table 5.4. The increments in R^2 reported in the table were obtained by adding the CUS to an equation containing the other individual-difference measures and an order-of-materials variable. The results indicated that the CUS accounted for variance in certainty of generated causes above and beyond the measures of perceived lack of control, depression, controllability attributional style, personal need for structure, sadness, anger, fear, anxiety, disgust, and contempt.

It is also worth noting that we found the CUS to be unrelated to certainty in noncausal judgments (even when the variance attributable to the other scales was removed). However, perceived lack of control was significantly related to certainty in noncausal judgments ($r = -.19$, $p < .03$), even when parsed of the variance due to causal uncertainty ($\beta = -.32$, $p < .02$). This finding provides an important distinction between perceived lack of control and causal uncertainty, and thereby helps to differentiate the two constructs.

Antecedents of Causal Uncertainty

One of the major predictions of the causal-uncertainty model described in this chapter is that perceptions of lack of control can lead to causal uncertainty. Although the correlations between the CUS and the measures of perceived lack of control, external locus of control, and controllability attributional style provide some evidence for this hypothesis, an adequate test of this prediction requires longitudinal data. We (Edwards & Weary, 1993a) provided such a longitudinal test. In this study, subjects filled out the CUS, a measure of perceived lack of control, and the Beck Depression Inventory, and then returned 6 weeks later and filled out the same scales again.

The data were analyzed by means of structural-equations analysis. The Perceived Lack of Control Scale is composed of three correlated factors that have been previously found and discussed in the literature on control and depression. Therefore, the model that was tested looked at the relationships between these three subscales and causal uncertainty. As predicted, there was a significant path between a Fatalism subscale (beliefs that outcomes are due to chance, fate, luck, etc.) at Time 1 and Time 2 causal uncertainty ($\beta = .19$, $p < .05$), indicating that higher levels of Time 1 fatalism led to increases in causal uncertainty over time.

Also of interest was the path between Time 1 causal uncertainty and Time 2 fatalism, which indicated that higher levels of causal uncertainty led to increases in fatalism over time ($\beta = .14$, $p < .05$). Conceptually, this path makes sense, because of the critical role that understanding of causal relations plays in people's ability to control outcomes. That is, it seems likely that persons who feel uncertain about their ability to understand causal relationships may easily come to fear that they will not be able to control events in their lives. Thus, this study indicates that perceived lack of control can be both an antecedent and a consequence of causal uncertainty.

Consequences of Causal Uncertainty

The research discussed thus far has concerned the relationships between causal-uncertainty beliefs, as tapped by the CUS, and a variety of other variables. However, none of these studies pertained to the hypothesized goal structure or the associated motivation to regain causal understanding. We now turn to research bearing on these constructs.

The importance of the notion of causal uncertainty stems in part from its likely cognitive and interpersonal consequences. We believe that causal uncertainty will have important, specific effects on a variety of psychological variables. One such consequence has been described in the preceding subsection—perceptions of lack of control. However, we believe that the more interesting and important consequences of causal uncertainty will be related to the search for and processing of social information. For instance, the effortful, vigilant style of information processing exhibited by mildly depressed individuals (Weary et al., 1993) is presumably motivated by causal uncertainty. However, direct evidence of the role of causal uncertainty per se in generating such effortful information-processing effects has, of necessity, awaited development and validation of the CUS. This clearly will be a major direction of our future research efforts. However, a few studies that have already examined the effects of chronic differences in causal-uncertainty beliefs on the search for and processing of social information. One of these (Edwards, 1994) assessed the impact of causal uncertainty on dispositional inferences when the information necessary for such inferential reasoning was quite limited or ambiguous.

Edwards (1995) reasoned that when trying to ascertain another person's disposition, individuals who possess chronically accessible causal-uncertainty beliefs may, under impoverished informational conditions, be uncomfortable in performing attributional adjustments (i.e., discounting and augmentation) and may rely on their nonconscious identifications of the target's behavior (Trope, 1986). Such automatic identifications are often held with confidence, as they are viewed as things that are inherently characteristic of the stimulus, and not a product of inferential processes (Bargh, 1989). Individuals who are motivated to attain an accurate understanding, but who have less confidence in the products of their conscious cognitive activity, ought to rely on what they hold with greater confidence. In this study, then, it was predicted that causally uncertain perceivers would be more susceptible to the correspondence bias (Jones & Harris, 1967) when they had reason to suspect the products of their conscious cognitive activities.

The procedure for this study was based on research by Trope, Cohen, and Alfieri (1991). Subjects read some background information about a person named Ron, and then read an evaluation that Dan (Ron's roommate) had written about Ron. Subjects then were asked how positive or negative Dan's evaluation of Ron was (i.e., how they identified his behavior) and how harsh or lenient Dan was in general (i.e., they were asked to make a dispositional attribution about Dan). The background information about Ron served as situational information relevant to subjects' assessment of Dan's disposition. Regression analyses revealed that subjects low in causal uncertainty tended to base their attributions on both their identification of Dan's behavior and the situational information relevant to his behavior. In other words, low-causal-uncertainty subjects showed evidence of attributional adjustment. High-causal-uncertainty subjects, on the other hand, based their attributions on their identification of Dan's behavior, but showed little effect of the situational information on their attributions. They failed to adjust their impressions of Dan's disposition for other causal factors that might have affected his behavior.

On the surface, these results may seem to conflict with the notion that causally uncertain people will engage in effortful processing of social information. In fact, we believe that subjects in this study *were* putting effort into thinking through the information they were given. Indeed, data from follow-up studies suggested that there was no difference between high-and low-causal-uncertainty subjects in the number of possible causes they generated for Dan's behavior, nor in the amount of time they spent answering the attribution question. Causally uncertain subjects simply lacked confidence in most of the potential causes they generated for Dan's behavior, in part because they did not have good evidence for many potential causes, and thus did not feel comfortable basing their attributions about Dan on such uncertain hypotheses. However, they did feel comfortable in basing their attributions on their behavior identification, because they believed their identifications to be diagnostic.

Such sensitivity to perceived diagnosticity is a logical consequence of the motivation elicited by causal uncertainty (cf. Weary et al., 1985). Note that this implies that causally uncertain perceivers should show substantial discounting of dispositional causes when given diagnostic information about situational causes.

A final study has examined the motivational consequences of high- and low-causal-uncertainty beliefs. In particular, this study (Weary & Jacobson, 1995) explored the consequences of causal-uncertainty belief activation on the search for social information. In a study of "interview processes," subjects were assigned the role of interviewer and were asked to select from a list of 30 questions tapping a variety of personal and political issues those that they would like to ask another participant (a confederate) during a taped interview. For some subjects, the interviewee, who was directed to another room soon after arrival at the lab, was male; for others, the interviewee was female. In addition, half of the subjects were told that following the interview, they would be asked to discuss with the experimenter their impressions of the interviewee, the interview process, and the general experimental procedure (high-information-utility condition); the other half of the subjects were told that following the taped interview, the experimental session would be ended (low-information-utility condition).

Jacobson and Weary reasoned that activation of causal-uncertainty beliefs would be more likely with interviewer–interviewee gender mismatch than with gender match; that is, greater ambiguity about the likely reaction of dissimilar others to the interview questions (Gerard & Orive, 1987) should activate concerns about the ability to understand, predict, and control the interviewee's behaviors during the interview. As a consequence, individuals in gender mismatches should be more likely to seek highly diagnostic information from their future interaction partner than should those in gender matches. Moreover, this tendency should be most pronounced for individuals with have chronically accessible causal-uncertainty beliefs, since activation of them should require less excitation from situational input and should be associated with typically higher levels of error sensitivity. Finally, the effects of interviewee gender and CUS scores should be more pronounced under situational conditions designed to increase the salience or importance of the uncertainty reduction goal (high-information-utility condition).

The results were consistent with these predictions. Under conditions designed to increase the salience of a lack of understanding (i.e., under conditions designed to increase error sensitivity), causally uncertain subjects chose more questions designed to yield greater information (and fewer questions designed to yield less information) about their future partner when that partner was dissimilar and hence less predictable (cf. Orive, 1988).

FUTURE RESEARCH DIRECTIONS

Although the research described above is promising, it is important to recognize that the empirical investigation of the causal-uncertainty construct, as well as the model of motivation within which it is embedded, is only beginning. In this section, we outline the kinds of research questions that, in our judgment, will represent the next step in research on causal-uncertainty beliefs. This research will probably concern three general questions: (1) Do individual differences in causal-uncertainty beliefs represent individual differences in the chronic accessibility of such beliefs, as we have suggested? (2) Are they associated with relevant motivational processes? (3) Are the consequences of individual differences in causal-uncertainty beliefs attributable uniquely to these beliefs, or can they be attributed totally or in part to other variables? Let us take each of these general questions in turn.

Chronic Accessibility of Causal-Uncertainty Beliefs

Are individual differences in causal-uncertainty beliefs as measured by the CUS indicative of individual differences in the chronic accessibility of such self-constructs? Such individual differences in chronic accessibility should be associated with several features. First, chronically accessible causal-uncertainty beliefs should require less excitation from situational input to become active (Higgins & Brendl, 1995), and their activation in response to such information should be involuntary and uncontrollable (Bargh et al., 1986). Various procedures have been used to demonstrate such effects of chronic accessibility. Ease of activation, for example, has been demonstrated by means of a procedure assessing perceptual sensitivity (von Hippel, Hawkins, & Narayan, 1994). The involuntary and uncontrollable aspects of automatic construct activation have been examined with the Stroop (1935) task. Evidence from studies employing these kinds of procedures could provide converging support for the notion that scores on the CUS represent the degree to which self-beliefs about one's ability to understand cause-effect relationships in the social domain are chronically accessible constructs.

Causal-Uncertainty Beliefs and Dispositional Goals

We have also suggested that chronic individual differences in causal-uncertainty beliefs are associated with dispositional goals to reduce such uncertainty. The motivational model that we have outlined in this chapter is a complex one, and a number of hypotheses follow from it. A thorough discussion of these is beyond the scope of this chapter. However, we can suggest a few.

First, when activated, causal-uncertainty beliefs ought to be associated with an intentional and more persistent search for information that might reasonably render the social environment more understandable; this ought to be the case both for individuals with chronically accessible beliefs and for those with temporarily activated beliefs. One of the studies reviewed earlier has provided some support for this motivational consequence of activated chronically accessible beliefs. Second, causal-uncertainty beliefs ought also to be associated with a greater tendency to use piecemeal (Fiske & Neuberg, 1990) as opposed to less effortful heuristic impression formation processes. Indeed, they ought to be associated with a more systematic, thorough processing of social information when they are activated, when the information is relevant to the goal of uncertainty reduction, and when the social perceiver has adequate time and cognitive resources. Under such conditions, we might expect to find processing effects that have been found to be associated with situational inductions of accuracy goals and with other accuracy-related chronic motives; these include a reduction in assimilation of social judgments to primed constructs (Thompson, Roman, Moskowitz, Chaiken, & Bargh, 1994) and a reduction in primacy effects (Kruglanski & Freund, 1983). In short, it ought to be possible to observe differences in cognitive and overt behaviors that would follow from activation of dispositional goals to reduce causal uncertainty.

Unique Effects of Causal Uncertainty

Distinctive Effects of Causal Uncertainty and Certainty Orientation

Although research on the validity of the CUS is very promising, we need to note the need for data on the relationship between causal uncertainty and an additional individual-difference variable mentioned earlier in this chapter—uncertainty orientation (Sorrentino & Short, 1986). Recall that uncertainty-oriented people attend to and seek out situations affording an opportunity to attain greater clarity, whereas certainty-oriented persons adhere to and are motivated by situations likely to maintain clarity about the self and the environment.

Although at first blush our causal uncertainty and Sorrentino's uncertainty orientation may appear to overlap to some degree, we believe for a number of reasons that they are relatively unrelated to each other. First, uncertainty orientation is thought to be a general construct applying to all aspects of the self and to all types of uncertain outcomes; causal uncertainty applies only to beliefs about one's general level of causal understanding in social situations. Second, uncertainty orientation is described as more of a proactive form of motivation; causal uncertainty is definitely reactive. It is hard for us to imagine causally uncertain individuals seeking out new and novel causal tasks in an attempt to form a clearer sense of their causal ability; indeed, we believe that individuals who possess chronically accessible self-constructs entailing causal-uncertainty beliefs have a relatively clear sense that they do not have a fully adequate comprehension of cause–effect relationships, and consequently do not proactively seek situations where such beliefs are likely to be activated.

Finally, and most importantly, Sorrentino and his colleagues have suggested that individual differences in uncertainty orientation represent individual differences in how people respond to and handle uncertainty regarding situational outcomes; some are motivated by uncertain outcomes, whereas others are motivated by certain outcomes. Our notion of causal uncertainty does not suggest that there are differences in people's reactions to information relevant to their uncertain causal understandings. Indeed, we have argued that all people possess causal-uncertainty beliefs and that all people will be energized to reduce causal uncertainty when their beliefs are activated. Although there may be some individual differences in the action plans employed to reduce causal uncertainty, we have suggested that people differ primarily in terms of the ease of activation of causal-uncertainty beliefs.[7]

Still, we recognize that the above about arguments the relative independence of causal uncertainty and uncertainty orientation are speculative. A clear picture of the similarities and differences of these two constructs awaits future research.

Role of Affect

Finally, we believe that research on our model will, of necessity, examine further the role of affect in motivational attempts to reduce causal uncertainty. We have provided some initial discriminant and predictive validity data suggesting that the content of the CUS is not merely tapping negative affect, but rather is specific to the content of causal uncertainty. However, cognitive feelings of uncertainty are by definition unpleasant, and we have suggested that negative affect in the form of depression and anxiety are implicated in motivated uncertainty reduction processes. Specifically, we have suggested that the purpose of the negative feedback loop is to detect the existence of any discrepancy between current and desired states of knowledge; informational feedback about the presence and intensity of resultant negative affect is used as a cue indicating the degree of goal attainment.

It is important to note that we are not suggesting that negative affect will necessarily have the same motivational function when causal-uncertainty beliefs are not activated. That is, when causal-uncertainty beliefs are not activated and when there is an unambiguous cause of the negative affect, then we would not expect it to serve as any cue to goal attainment. We would not expect it to be associated with purposive attempts to reduce causal uncertainty.

Is it not possible that through some mechanism such as spreading activation, we might find activation of cognitive feelings of uncertainty—and therefore of causal-uncertainty beliefs and reduction motives—regardless of the original source of negative affect? It is possible. There is definitely some empirical evidence of spreading activation among evaluatively similar memory representations (Bargh, 1988; Clark & Isen, 1982; Greenwald, Lui, & Klinger, 1986). However, we would expect that the motivational effects of such reverberatory influences (Bargh, 1989) will be short-lived or overridden if there is little or no discrepancy between current and desired states of knowledge.

CONCLUSION

In summary, this chapter has outlined a model of a previously unexplored individual-difference construct that has its historical roots in attribution theories. A major assumption of these theories, and one supported by recent research (Pittman, 1993) is that people have a primary need to understand cause–effect relationships in interpersonal relations. The model of causal uncertainty outlined herein argues that some people in some situations are more motivated than others to resolve causal uncertainty, and that uncertainty about one's understanding of causation has fundamental consequences for the goals adopted and for the manner in which social information is encoded, interpreted, stored, and acted upon. It is our hope that the construct of causal uncertainty and the model of uncertainty reduction presented in this chapter will spark the interest of other researchers and add to the burgeoning literature on the role of individual differences in social cognition.

Acknowledgments

We would like to thank the members of our lab group, Katherine Gannon, Jill A. Jacobson, Shannon Riley, and John H. Yost, for their helpful comments on the model and on an earlier draft of this chapter. We also would like to thank members of Weary's 1994 attribution seminar, Bill von Hippel, and the editors of this volume for their insightful and provocative feedback on this chapter.

Notes

1. To be complete, we should note one additional treatment of an uncertainty construct in the depression literature. Kofta and Sedek (1989) have proposed an informational model of learned helplessness, which suggests that when people first confront an uncontrollable environment, they actively and effortfully construct a set of hypotheses that can guide their future behavior. Because the environment is uncontrollable, this cognitive effort is futile. They come to experience sustained and irreducible uncertainty about the adequacy of their hypotheses; in time, cognitive exhaustion results. This cognitive exhaustion in turn results in the motivational deficits (i.e., performance decrements) associated with learned helplessness. Although there are some general similarities between this view of the uncertainty that can result from exposure to uncontrollable events and our notion of causal uncertainty, there are also a number of differences. We (Weary et al., 1993) have addressed elsewhere the issue of performance decrements versus enhancements that follow from exposure to uncontrollable events. Let us simply note here that among other factors, there are important task differences that determine whether reactance or helplessness effects will follow from exposure to uncontrollable outcomes.

2. In describing this motive as negative, we are employing the distinction made in a number of historical treatments of motivation (e.g., Murray & Kluckhorn, 1956). The point of reference is the initiating, discomforting state, not the end state, where there is a satisfying reduction of tension. The movement of the organism in response to such motives is away from the negative situation, not toward a positive one.

3. We have adopted a control theory view of motivation with its emphasis on negative feedback loops as a general framework, primarily because of its heuristic value and its compatibility with a cognitive view of motivation. Accordingly, we use some of the terminology of control theory (e.g., "comparator," "error sensitivity"). We recognize, however, that alternative concepts employed in other theories of motivation not wedded to such a metatheoretical perspective often describe similar notions; in many instances we could have used such alternative terminology (e.g., "perception of discrepancy between initiating and end state," "goal importance") to describe the various cognitive structures and processes that we consider central to our theory.

4. We could have framed this goal representation in terms of a reduction in causal uncertainty. However, an image or memory of a reduction or lessening of a state seemed less imaginable than the possession of a positive state. Consequently, we have chosen to frame the motivation in terms of the initiating state, and the goal representation, or desired end state, in terms of its converse.

5. A belief that no stable forces exist should lead to causal certainty, at least as measured by the CUS, in that events should be seen as stemming from the arbitrary nature of the universe. That is, people who believe that no causal forces exist should disagree with the statement "I do not understand what causes most of the problems that I have with others" (item 3), because they would believe that the occurrence of such problems is simply caused by "chance" or "bad luck."

6. Because of the size of the correlation between causal and noncausal judgments ($r = .21$), and because of the small sample size in this study, the correlations of the CUS with causal and with noncausal judgments were not significantly different.

7. Astute readers may ask whether our person who possesses chronically accessible causal-uncertainty beliefs may be more similar to Sorrentino's certainty-oriented person. Both, after all, experience discomfort with ambiguity. We believe, however, that there should

be extreme differences in the responses of these two types of individuals to ambiguity. We have suggested and provided some evidence consistent with the notion that individuals whose causal-uncertainty beliefs are chronically accessible, and therefore, easily activated by ambiguous situational information should be motivated to attain a accurate understanding of the situation by, for example, engaging in causal searches. Sorrentino's certainty-oriented person should show no such inclination—unless, we would add, his or her causal uncertainty beliefs have been activated and the accompanying motivation to reduce causal uncertainty engaged. Again, we believe that the two individual-difference variables of causal uncertainty and uncertainty orientation are orthogonal and address quite different motivational systems.

References

Alloy, L. B., Clements, C. M., & Koenig, L. J. (1993). Perceptions of control: Determinants and mechanisms. In G. Weary, F. Gleicher, & K. L. Marsh (Eds.), *Control motivation and social cognition* (pp. 33-73). New York: Springer-Verlag.

Anderson, C. A., Horowitz, L. M., & French, R. (1983). Attributional style of lonely and depressed people. *Journal of Personality and Social Psychology, 45,* 127-136.

Bargh, J. A. (1989). Conditional automaticity: Varieties of automatic influence in social perception and cognition. In J. S. Uleman & J. A. Bargh (Eds.), *Unintended thought* (pp. 3-51). New York: Guilford Press.

Bargh, J. A. (1988). Automatic information processing: Implications for communication and affect. In L. Donohew, H. E. Sypher, & E. T. Higgins (Eds.), *Communication, social cognition, and affect* (pp. 9-37). Hillsdale, NJ: Erlbaum.

Bargh, J. A., Bond, R. N., Lombardi, W. J., & Tota, M. E. (1986). The additive nature of chronic and temporary sources of construct accessibility. *Journal of Personality and Social Psychology, 50,* 869-878.

Beck, A. T. (1967). *Depression: Clinical, experimental, and theoretical aspects.* New York: Hoeber.

Berlyne, D. E. (1960). *Conflict arousal and curiosity.* New York: McGraw-Hill.

Berlyne, D. E. (1962). Uncertainty and epistemic curiosity. *British Journal of Psychology, 53,* 27-34.

Broadbent, D. E. (1971). *Decision and stress.* London: Academic Press.

Budner, S. (1962). Intolerance of ambiguity as a personality variable. *Journal of Personality, 30,* 29-50.

Burger, J. M., & Cooper, H. M. (1979). The desirability of control. *Motivation and Emotion, 3,* 381-393.

Cacioppo, J. T., Martzke, J. S., Petty, R. E., & Tassinary, L. G. (1988). Specific forms of facial EMG response index emotions during an interview: From Darwin to the continuous flow hypothesis of affect-laden information processing. *Journal of Personality and Social Psychology, 54,* 592-604.

Cacioppo, J. T., & Petty, R. E. (1982). The need for cognition. *Journal of Personality and Social Psychology, 42,* 116-131.

Carver, C. S., & Scheier, M. F. (1982). Control theory: A useful conceptual framework for personality-social, clinical, and health psychology. *Psychological Bulletin, 92,* 111-135.

Carver, C. S., & Scheier, M. F. (1990a). Principles of self-regulation: Action and emotion. In E. T. Higgins & R. M. Sorrentino (Eds.), *Handbook of motivation and cognition: Foundations of social behavior.*(Vol. 2, pp. 3-52). New York: Guilford Press.

Carver, C. S., & Scheier, M. F. (1990b). Origins and functions of positive and negative affect: A control-process view. *Psychological Review, 97,* 19-35.

Clark, M. S., & Isen, A. M. (1982). Toward understanding the relationship between feeling states and social behavior. In A. H. Hastorf & A. M. Isen (Eds.), *Cognitive social behavior* (pp. 73-108). New York: Elsevier/North Holland.

Clore, G. L. (1992). Cognitive phenomenology: Feelings and the construction of judgment. In

L. L. Martin & A. Tesser (Eds.), *The construction of social judgments* (pp. 133-164). Hillsdale, NJ: Erlbaum.

Conrath, D. (1967). Organizational decision making behavior under varying conditions of uncertainty. *Management Science, 13,* 487-500.

Crowne, D. P., & Marlowe, D. (1960). A new scale of social desirability independent of psychopathology. *Journal of Consulting Psychology, 24,* 349-354.

Edwards, J. A. (1994). [The effects of chronic causal uncertainty on preferred sources of inferences]. Unpublished raw data.

Edwards, J. A., & Weary, G. (1993a, June). *The relationship between causal uncertainty, perceived lack of control, and depression.* Paper presented at the 5th annual meeting of the American Psychological Society, Chicago.

Edwards, J. A., & Weary, G. (1993b). Depression and the impression formation continuum: From piecemeal to category-based processing. *Journal of Personality and Social Psychology, 64,* 636-645.

Edwards, J. A., & Weary, G. (1995). *The factor structure of the Causal Uncertainty Scale.* Manuscript submitted for publication.

Festinger, L. (1954). A theory of social comparison processes. *Human Relations, 7,* 117-140.

Festinger, L. (1957). *A theory of cognitive dissonance.* Stanford, CA: Stanford University Press.

Fiske, S. T., & Neuberg, S. L. (1990). A continuum of impression formation, from category-based to individuating processes: Influences of information and motivation on attention and interpretation. In M. P. Zanna (Ed.), *Advances in experimental social psychology* (Vol. 23, pp. 1-74). New York: Academic Press.

Fridja, N. H. (1988). The laws of emotion. *American Psychologist, 43,* 349-358.

Garber, J., Miller, W. R., & Seaman, S. F. (1979). Learned helplessness, stress, and the depressive disorders. In R. A. Depue (Ed.), *The psychobiology of the depressive disorders: Implications for the effects of stress* (335-364). New York: Academic Press.

Gerard, H. B., & Orive, R. (1987). The dynamics of opinion formation. In L. Berkowitz (Ed.), *Advances in experimental social psychology* (Vol. 20, pp. 171-202). New York: Academic Press.

Gilbert, D. T., Pelham, B. W., & Krull, D. S. (1988). On cognitive busyness: When person perceivers meet persons perceived. *Journal of Personality and Social Psychology, 54,* 733-740.

Gleicher, F., & Weary, G. (1991). The effect of depression on the quantity and quality of social inferences. *Journal of Personality and Social Psychology, 61,* 105-114.

Greenwald, A. T., Lui, T. J., & Klinger, M. (1986). *Unconscious processing of word meaning.* Unpublished manuscript, Ohio State University.

Heider, F. (1958). *The psychology of interpersonal relations.* New York: Wiley.

Higgins, E. T. (1987). Self-discrepancy: A theory relating self and affect. *Psychological Review, 94,* 319-340.

Higgins, E. T. (1989). Continuities and discontinuities in self-regulatory and self-evaluative processes: A developmental theory relating self and affect. *Journal of Personality, 57,* 407-444.

Higgins, E. T. (1990). Personality, social psychology, and person–situation relations: Standards and knowledge activation as a common language. In L. A. Pervin (Ed.), *Handbook of personality: Theory and research* (pp. 301-338). New York: Guilford Press.

Higgins, E. T., & Brendl, M. C. (1995). Accessibility and applicability: Some "activation rules" influencing judgments. *Journal of Experimental Social Psychology, 31,* 218-243.

Hildebrand-Saints, L., & Weary, G. (1989). Depression and social information gathering. *Personality and Social Psychology Bulletin, 15,* 150-160.

Howell, W. C., & Burnett, S. A. (1978). Uncertainty measurement: A cognitive taxonomy. *Organizational Behavior and Human Performance, 22,* 45-68.

Hyland, M. (1987). Control theory interpretation of psychological mechanisms of depression: Comparison and integration of several theories. *Psychological Bulletin, 102,* 109-121.

Jacobson, J. A., Weary, G., & Edwards, J. A. (1994, May). *Causes and concomitants of depression: Causal uncertainty versus negative outcome certainty.* Paper presented at the 66th annual meeting of the Midwestern Psychological Association, Chicago, IL.

Jones, E. E., & Davis, K. E. (1965). From acts to dispositions: The attribution process in person perception. In L. Berkowitz (Ed.), *Advances in experimental social psychology* (Vol. 2, pp. 219-266). New York: Academic Press.

Jones, E. E., & Harris, V. A. (1967). The attribution of attitudes. *Journal of Experimental Psychology, 3,* 1-24.

Jones, E. E., & McGillis, D. (1976). Correspondent inferences and the attribution cube: A comparative appraisal. In J. H. Harvey, W. J. Ickes, & R. F. Kidd (Eds.), *New directions in attribution research* (Vol. 1, pp. 389-420). Hillsdale, NJ: Erlbaum.

Kagan, J. (1972). Motives and development. *Journal of Personality and Social Psychology, 22,* 51-66.

Kahneman, D., Slovic, P., & Tversky, A. (Eds.). (1982). *Judgment under uncertainty: Heuristics and biases.* Cambridge, England: Cambridge University Press.

Kelley, H. H. (1967). Attribution theory in social psychology. In D. Levine (Ed.), *Nebraska Symposium on Motivation* (Vol. 15, pp. 192-240). Lincoln: University of Nebraska Press.

Kelley, H. H. (1973). The process of causal attribution. *American Psychologist, 28,* 107-128.

Klinger, E. (1975). Consequences of commitment to and disengagement from incentives. *Psychological Review, 82,* 1-25.

Kofta, M., & Sedek, G. (1989). Learned helplessness: Affective or cognitive disturbance? In C. P. Spielberger, I. G. Sarason, & J. Strelau (Eds.), *Stress and anxiety* (Vol. 12, pp. 81-96). Washington, DC: Hemisphere.

Kruglanski, A. W., & Freund, T. (1983). The freezing and unfreezing of lay inferences: Effects on impressional primacy, ethnic stereotyping, and numerical anchoring. *Journal of Experimental Social Psychology, 19,* 448-468.

Luce, R., & Raiffa, H. (1957). *Games and decisions.* New York: Wiley.

Markus, H. R., & Nurius, P. (1986). Possible selves. *American Psychologist, 41,* 954-969.

Marsh, K. L., & Weary, G. (1989). Depression and attributional complexity. *Personality and Social Psychology Bulletin, 15,* 325-336.

Martin, L. L., Ward, D. W., Achee, J. W., & Wyer, R. S. (1993). Mood as input: People have to interpret the motivational implications of their moods. *Journal of Personality and Social Psychology, 64,* 317-326.

Mayer, J. D. (1986). How mood influences cognition. In N. E. Sharkey (Ed.), *Advances in cognitive science* (Vol. 1, pp. 290-314). New York: Halsted Press/Wiley.

Medin, D. L. (1988). Social categorization: Structures, processes and purposes. In T. K. Srull & R. S. Wyer (Eds.), *Advances in social cognition* (Vol. 1, pp. 119-126). Hillsdale, NJ: Erlbaum.

Murray, H. A., & Kluckhorn, C. (1956). Outline of a conception of personality. In C. Kluckhorn, H. A. Murray, & D. M. Schneider (Eds.), *Personality in nature, society, and culture* (2nd ed., pp. 1-35). New York: Knopf.

Neuberg, S. L., & Newsom, J. T. (1993). Personal need for structure: Individual differences in the desire for simple structure. *Journal of Personality and Social Psychology, 65,* 113-131.

Orive, R. (1988). Social projection and social comparison of opinions. *Journal of Personality and Social Psychology, 54,* 953-964.

Pittman, T. S. (1993). Control motivation and attitude change. In G. Weary, F. Gleicher, & K. L. Marsh (Eds.), *Control motivation and social cognition* (pp. 157-175). New York: Springer-Verlag.

Pittman, T. S., & D'Agostino, P. R. (1985). Motivation and attribution: The effects of control deprivation on subsequent information processing. In J. H. Harvey & G. Weary (Eds.), *Attribution: Basic and applied issues* (pp. 117-142). New York: Academic Press.

Pittman, T. S., & Pittman, N. L. (1980). Deprivation of control and the attribution process. *Journal of Personality and Social Psychology, 25,* 465-480.

Powers, W. T. (1978). Quantitative analysis of purposive systems. *Psychological Review, 85,* 417-435.

Pratkanis, A. R., & Greenwald, A. G. (1989). A sociocognitive model of attitude structure and function. In L. Berkowitz (Ed.), *Advances in experimental social psychology* (Vol. 22, pp. 245-285). New York: Academic Press.

Rosenberg, M. (1965). *Society and the adolescent self-image.* Princeton, NJ: Princeton University Press.

Rothbaum, F., Weisz, J. R., & Snyder, S. S. (1982). Changing the world and changing the self: A two-process model of perceived control. *Journal of Personality and Social Psychology, 42,* 5-37.

Rotter, J. B. (1966). Generalized expectancies for internal versus external control of reinforcement. *Psychological Monographs, 80*(1, Whole No. 609).

Schwarz, N. (1990). Feelings as information: Informational and motivational functions of affective states. In E. T. Higgins & R. M. Sorrentino (Eds.), *Handbook of motivation and cognition: Foundations of social behavior* (Vol. 2, pp. 527-562). New York: Guilford Press.

Schwarz, N., & Clore, G. L. (1983). Mood, misattribution, and judgments of well-being: Informative and directive functions of affective states. *Journal of Personality and Social Psychology, 45,* 513-523.

Sorrentino, R. M., & Short, J. C. (1986). Uncertainty orientation, motivation, and cognition. In R. M. Sorrentino & E. T. Higgins (Eds.), *Handbook of motivation and cognition: Foundations of social behavior.* (Vol. 1, pp. 379-403). New York: Guilford Press.

Spielberger, C. D., Gorsuch, R. L., Lushene, R., Vagg, P. R., & Jacobs, G. A. (1983). *Manual for the State-Trait Anxiety Inventory (Form Y).* Palo Alto, CA: Consulting Psychologists Press.

Stroop, J. R. (1938). Factors affecting speed in serial verbal reactions. *Psychological Monographs, 50,* 38-48.

Swann, W. B., Jr. (1984). Quest for accuracy in person perception: A matter of pragmatics. *Psychological Review, 91,* 457-477.

Thompson, E. P., Roman, R. J., Moskowitz, G. B., Chaiken, S., & Bargh, J. A. (1994). Accuracy motivation attenuates covert priming: The systematic reprocessing of social information. *Journal of Personality and Social Psychology, 66,* 474-489.

Thompson, M. M., Naccarato, M. E., & Parker, K. E. (1992). *Assessing cognitive need: The development of the Personal Need for Structure (PNS) and Personal Fear of Invalidity (PFI) scales.* Manuscript submitted for publication.

Tolman, E., & Brunswik, E. (1935). The organism and the causal texture of the environment. *Psychological Review, 42,* 43-77.

Trope, Y. (1986). Identification and inferential processes in dispositional attribution. *Psychological Review, 93,* 239-257.

Trope, Y., Cohen, O., & Alfieri, T. (1991). Behavior identification as a mediator of dispositional inference. *Journal of Personality and Social Psychology, 61,* 873-883.

von Hippel, W., Hawkins, C., & Narayan, S. (1994). Personality and perceptual expertise: Individual differences in perceptual identification. *Psychological Science, 5,* 401-406.

Warren, L. W., & McEachren, L. (1983). Psychosocial correlates of depressive symptomatology in adult women. *Journal of Abnormal Psychology, 92,* 151-160.

Weary, G., & Edwards, J. A. (1994). A measure of dispositional causal uncertainty. *Journal of Personality and Social Psychology, 67,* 308-318.

Weary, G., & Jacobson, J. A. (1995). *Causal uncertainty beliefs and diagnostic information seeking.* Manuscript submitted for publication.

Weary, G., Jordan, J. S., & Hill, M. G. (1985). The attributional norm of internality and depressive sensitivity to social information. *Journal of Personality and Social Psychology, 49,* 1283-1293.

Weary, G., Marsh, K. L., Gleicher, F., & Edwards, J. A. (1993). Depression, control motivation, and the processing of information about others. In G. Weary, F. Gleicher, & K. L. Marsh (Eds.), *Control motivation and social cognition* (pp. 255-287). New York: Springer-Verlag.

Webster, D. M., & Kruglanski, A. W. (1994). Individual differences in need for cognitive closure. *Journal of Personality and Social Psychology, 67,* 1049-1062.

Wegner, D. M., & Schneider, D. J. (1989). Mental control: The war of ghosts in the machine. In J. S. Uleman & J. A. Bargh (Eds.), *Unintended thought* (pp. 287-305). New York: Guilford Press.

Weisz, J. R., Sweeney, L., Proffitt, V., & Carr, T. (1993). Control-related beliefs and self-reported depressive symptoms in late childhood. *Journal of Abnormal Psychology, 102,* 411-418.

Weisz, J. R., Weiss, B., Wasserman, A. A., & Rintoul, B. (1987). Control-related beliefs and depression among clinic-referred children and adolescents. *Journal of Abnormal Psychology, 96,* 58-63.

Whitley, B. E. (1991). A short form of the Expanded Attributional Style Questionnaire. *Journal of Personality Assessment, 56,* 365-369.

Winter, L., & Uleman, J. S. (1984). When are social judgments made? Evidence for the spontaneousness of trait inferences. *Journal of Personality and Social Psychology, 47,* 237-252.

Yost, J. H., & Weary, G. (in press). Depression and the correspondent inference bias: Evidence for more effortful processing. *Personality and Social Psychology Bulletin.*

CHAPTER 6

Social Identity, Self-Categorization, and the Perceived Homogeneity of Ingroups and Outgroups
The Interaction between Social Motivation and Cognition

S. ALEXANDER HASLAM
PENELOPE J. OAKES
JOHN C. TURNER
CRAIG McGARTY
The Australian National University

> Briefly defined therefore, Black Consciousness is in essence the
> realization by the black man of the need to rally together with
> his brothers around the cause of their operation—the blackness of
> their skin—and to operate as a group in order to rid themselves of
> the shackles that bind them to perpetual servitude. It seeks to
> demonstrate the lie that black is an aberration from the "normal"
> which is white. . . . It seeks to infuse the black community with a
> new-found pride in themselves, their efforts, their value systems,
> their culture, their religion and their outlook to life.
>   The interrelationship between the consciousness of the self
> and the emancipatory programme is of paramount importance.
> —*Biko (1978/1988, p. 63)*

The above passage is taken from a document in which the black African activist Steve Biko sought to define the Black Consciousness movement for fellow members of the South African Students Organization. As this passage indicates, Biko strongly believed that in order for blacks to realize their goal of ending white minority rule in South Africa, they needed to come to define themselves *collectively* in terms of positive, *self-selected* dimensions relevant to their own culture's shared values and goals. What is more, in light of the recent political changes in South Africa—which have included formal renunciation of apartheid and the introduction of multiracial elections—it would appear that this message was fully vindicated, as these changes have in large part been made possible by the ability of black South Africans to mobilize themselves collectively as a political force. Providing a historical commentary on Biko's life, Barney Pityana thus writes:

> It is to the credit of the Black Consciousness movement that . . . it believed its primary task was to gather together every conceivable contribution that would help to bring an end to apartheid. It seemed that . . . disunity was a luxury our people could ill afford. And yet unity had to be based on clear principles. We were convinced that Black Consciousness provided a common programme, one with which the entire liberation movement could identify. (1988, p. 11)

In many respects, though, the message and palpable success of social movements like Black Consciousness appears to go against the wisdom associated with a body of latter-day social-psychological research into social stereotyping. In particular, research into perceptions of group homogeneity suggests that recognition of a group's shared features is largely restricted to the perception of outgroups, whereas a person's ingroup is much more likely to be represented in differentiated terms. Most of the research investigating this topic over the last 10 years or so has thus tended to support the original hypothesis of Quattrone and Jones (1980, p. 142):

> In general, people perceive more variability within ingroups, social categories of which they are members, than within outgroups, social categories of which they are not members. Thus the common observation that "they all look alike but we don't" may extend from the realm of physical appearance to the realm of personality attributes.[1]

This point has been confirmed in a meta-analysis of relevant empirical research (Mullen & Hu, 1989).

The generalized effects of this asymmetric bias should be to inhibit people's stereotyping of themselves in terms of attributes they share with others (i.e., "self-stereotyping"), while at the same time encouraging the stereotyping of others. However, it can be seen that if this bias were in any sense inevitable it would be quite maladaptive, especially for members of social movements who strive to recognize and act in terms of a distinctive ingroup identity. If we take Black Consciousness as an example, it can be seen that the so-called "principle of outgroup homogeneity" (Park & Rothbart, 1982, p. 1051) implies, somewhat paradoxically, both (1) that awareness of blacks' shared identity would always be stronger (or at least never any weaker) among whites than blacks, and (2) that blacks themselves would always be more aware (or at least no less aware) of shared identity among whites than among their black ingroup.

The goal of this chapter is to make sense of this apparent contradiction between the phenomenon of relative outgroup homogeneity on the one hand, and the need (and demonstrated capacity) for people to perceive their ingroup to be at least as homogeneous as outgroups on the other. In so doing, we focus on the manner in which perceived group homogeneity is related to "consciousness of self" and, in particular, on the manner in which it is mediated by the salience (i.e., the psychological activation) of a perceiver's social identity. In this, we seek to emphasize the special psychological role that group memberships and intergroup relations play in social perception.

The chapter starts by looking at the metatheoretical and empirical origins of the influential cognitive approach to group homogeneity. Broadly speaking, this considers perceived homogeneity to be a distorting error of simplification inherent in the categorization process. This distortion, some argue, is at work less in people's perception of those with whom they are familiar (i.e., ingroups) than in their perception of those they know less well (i.e., outgroups). Expanding from this base, we then go on to examine the role of identity-related, group-based motivations in such perceptions. As well as noting how a homogeneous representation of outgroups may be a vehicle for intergroup discrimination, we also examine how perceived *ingroup* homogeneity may be just as critical to the advancement of a group's objectives—in particular, by creating a positive social identity for its members.

These latter considerations lead ultimately to the presentation of an interactionist analysis derived from self-categorization theory (Turner, 1985; Oakes, Haslam, & Turner, 1994). At one level, this can be seen as an integration of features of both cognitive and social-motivational approaches: It focuses on the role of categorization in the perception of group homogeneity but also emphasizes the links between perceived homogeneity and the salience of a perceiver's own social identity. This analysis seeks to provide a resolution to the seemingly paradoxical evidence of both symmetry and asymmetry in perceived ingroup–outgroup homogeneity by pointing to the way in which the cognitive process of categorization is sensitive to, and varies with, changes in social context. This argument is supported by findings suggesting that group variability judgments are not based on preformed representations, but reflect a process of variable context-sensitive representation. We provide evidence to suggest that there is no inherent dualism between cognition and motivation, and that the contributions these make to perceptions of homogeneity are not merely additive. Accordingly, the chapter concludes that a full appreciation of this feature of stereotyping cannot be gained without an understanding of the dynamic interplay between cognition and social motivation.

OUTGROUP HOMOGENEITY AS CATEGORICAL BIAS: THE COGNITIVE APPROACH

Metatheoretical Foundations: "The Principle of Least Effort"

The first person formally to link the phenomenon of perceived homogeneity with a broader consideration of stereotyping was Walter Lippman (1922) in his seminal book *Public Opinion*. In this he was in fact developing ideas of John Dewey, who had previously remarked:

> All strangers of another race proverbially look alike to the visiting stranger. Only gross differences of size and color are perceived by an outsider in a flock of sheep,

each of which is perfectly individualized by the shepherd. A diffusive blur and indiscriminately shifting suction characterize what we do not understand. (Dewey, 1910, cited in Lippman, 1922, p. 54)

Although Lippman did not offer a detailed explanation of this phenomenon—beyond noting the role of experience in allowing people to make individuating judgments—he did couch his understanding of it within a broader metatheoretical analysis of stereotyping, which ultimately came to inform most subsequent treatments of the topic. Lippman argued that stereotyping and the perception of individual group members in homogeneous terms may be "necessary evils" insofar as they sacrifice the ideal for the pragmatic, overlooking the reality of individual differences among group members in the interests of expediency and efficiency. Having detailed the properties of stereotyping as a whole, of which the asymmetry noted above is but one, he thus remarked in a now-famous passage:

> There is economy in this. For the attempt to see things freshly and in detail, rather than as types and generalities, is exhausting, and among busy affairs practically out of the question. In a circle of friends . . . there is no shortcut through, and no substitute for, an individualized understanding. . . . But modern life is hurried and multifarious. . . . There is neither time nor opportunity for intimate acquaintance. Instead we notice a trait which marks a well known type, and fill in the rest of the picture by means of stereotypes we carry around in our heads. (1922, p. 59)

The broad thrust of this analysis was to argue that the ability to differentiate between people is a direct product of a perceiver's acquaintance with them, and thus that individuals may tend to develop less differentiated, stereotypic representations of those outside their immediate circle (i.e., outgroups) simply because practical constraints necessitate all but the most superficial interaction with them.

This view that group homogeneity is negatively correlated with personal acquaintance was subsequently reinforced by Gordon Allport (1954) in his influential book *The Nature of Prejudice.* The principal contribution of this work was to identify the role of categorization in the stereotyping process and in the etiology of attitudes toward groups. In particular, Allport noted that categorization in terms of group memberships leads people to treat individuals as psychologically equivalent. However, borrowing a term from Postman, he also suggested that some categories are more "monopolistic" than others—that some categories are inflexible and differentiated, and others are flexible and discriminated. Like Lippman before him, Allport argued that one key predictor of whether or not a category is monopolistic is a person's familiarity with the group concerned:

> Many people find, for example, that the more they know about a group the *less* likely they are to form monopolistic categories. For example, most Americans know that any fixed hypotheses about "Americans" are likely to be a poor guide to con-

duct. We know, for example, that not all Americans are dollar-worshippers, breezy, or vulgar. On the other hand, Europeans, who know us less well, often view us as one big monolithic unit having all these qualities. (p. 172)

Again, categorization was analyzed in terms of the adaptive functions it serves for the perceiver. The fact that people apply stereotypes more to outgroups than to ingroups was directly attributed by Allport to "the principle of least effort." He saw it as a consequence of the fact that "life is just too short to have differentiated concepts about everything," and so "to consider every member of a group as endowed with the same traits saves us the pains of dealing with them as individuals" (1954, p. 173).

Empirical Foundations of the Cognitive Approach

Interestingly, neither Lippman nor Allport substantiated his considerations of differences in the perceived homogeneity of ingroups and outgroups with anything other than anecdotal evidence, despite the obvious importance of these differences. Direct empirical evidence of relative outgroup homogeneity only appeared about 25 years later, and in the context of the developing social-cognitive analysis of stereotyping.

This analysis grew from the work of Henri Tajfel in the 1960s (e.g., Tajfel, 1969; see Ashmore & Del Boca, 1976; Stroebe & Insko, 1989). Tajfel, like Allport, argued that a range of stereotyping phenomena can be understood in terms of the cognitive processes of categorization common to all human perceivers. The ground-breaking studies of Tajfel and Wilkes (1963a) demonstrated that when subjects were given cues (identifying labels) that enabled them to perceive sets of lines in terms of categories (as long or short), they tended both (1) to accentuate the differences between those categories (seeing the long lines as longer and the short lines as shorter), and (2) to accentuate the similarities within those categories (tending to see less variability among both sets of lines—although this effect was nonsignificant). The crucial insight that Tajfel drew from this work was an awareness that key features of the stereotyping process (principally the accentuation of intercategory difference and intracategory similarity) can be understood as natural consequences of normal cognitive functioning. Thus, without individuals' being in any sense motivated to distort reality, distortion of the "true" properties of stimuli (in the form of intragroup homogenization and intergroup separation) can arise simply because those stimuli are perceived in categorical terms.

An important outcome of this work was that prejudice and stereotyping were no longer seen simply as products of irrational and unjustified motivations (e.g., the need to scapegoat, the need to vent frustration, the need to transfer hostility; see Adorno, Frenkel-Brunswik, Levinson, & Sanford, 1950; Dollard, Doob, Miller, Mowrer, & Sears, 1939; Williams, 1947). Instead, they could be understood in terms of a purely cognitive analysis. Tajfel thus spelled out the implications of his findings by noting that "*without the introduction of variables of a social or emotional nature* they present the essential features of social stereotypes: the subjective accentuation of differences in *relevant dimensions* between classes of stimuli, and their subjective reduction within each class" (1969, pp. 84-85; first emphasis added, second in original).

As we elaborate further below, although one necessary aspect of Tajfel's *empirical* work was the isolation of cognitive and motivational aspects of stereotyping, he was at pains to emphasize their *theoretical* interdependence (see Tajfel, 1969, 1972). It is interesting to note, too, that some of the first studies that sought to test Tajfel's analysis of the categorization process using social stimuli (i.e., groups rather than lines) actually demonstrated that not only outgroups were perceived homogeneously. These studies showed that subjects also represented members of ingroups in terms of higher-order categories. Thus Tajfel, Sheikh, and Gardner (1964) found that Canadian subjects who were asked to describe two Indians and two Canadians after listening to separate interviews with each minimized differences between the two stimulus persons in *both* racial groups on stereotype-relevant dimensions. A series of more controlled studies reported by Doise, Deschamps, and Meyer (1978) also confirmed this point. Doise et al. asked 10-year-old boys and girls to describe members of one gender group (e.g., boys), either with or without the knowledge that they would later describe members of the other group. It was found that intracategory similarity and intercategory difference were accentuated when the subjects were led to anticipate the description of both groups. Doise and his colleagues also asked Swiss subjects to describe the three linguistic groups found in Switzerland (German-, French-, and Italian-speaking) with respect to various rating scales. In alternative conditions, one of these groups was replaced with an outgroup (Germans from Germany, French from France, or Italians from Italy). In these latter conditions (where an ingroup–outgroup categorization was invoked), perceived similarity between the two Swiss sub-ingroups was accentuated.

There was, then, early evidence that contextual variation in the categorization process may be reflected in contextual variation in perceived ingroup homogeneity. However, it was not this contextual variability, but rather the apparently stable ingroup–outgroup difference in perceived homogeneity alluded to by Lippman and Allport, that drew research attention as the social-cognitive analysis of stereotyping effects gathered force in the late 1970s.

In one early study, Quattrone and Jones (1980) presented students from either Rutgers or Princeton University with decisions made by a target person who supposedly came either from their own or from the other university. Subjects then had to estimate the percentage of students at the target person's university who would make the same decision. As predicted, there was some evidence of greater perceived opinion similarity among members of the outgroup university. It is interesting to note, though, that this effect was not significant when subjects had strong preconceptions about the decisions that groups were likely to make.

Along similar lines, a series of three experiments reported by Goethals, Allison, and Frost (1979) found that subjects expected greater variation in the opinions of people who had views similar to their own (e.g., those who agreed that their college should divest itself of stock in a company doing business in South Africa) than in those of people who had different views. Specifically, a greater number of different "types" of students were seen to support the in-group rather than the outgroup position (Experiment 1), and the ingroup was directly rated as more diverse than other opinion groups (Experiments 2 and 3).

A more extensive series of studies conducted by Park and Rothbart (1982) provided more evidence of outgroup homogeneity, this time both on measures of others' perceived attitudes and on other, less direct measures seeking to detail the nature and basis of intraclass "confusability" (p. 1054). In their third experiment, members of three different college sorority groups judged intragroup similarity for each sorority. Although outgroup sororities were not always seen to be more homogeneous than ingroups, the researchers found that with every group its members were perceived to be least similar to each other by members of that ingroup. Their first two studies also revealed that males and females assigned more stereotypic traits to the gender-based outgroup than to the ingroup, the in-group in turn being assigned more counterstereotypic traits. Finally, Park and Rothbart found evidence of differential *encoding* of ingroup and outgroup behavior in a fourth experiment, where subjects had to remember details of a newspaper story describing the actions of either a man or a woman. In both free and cued recall, subjects remembered more subordinate (i.e., differentiating) attributes of members of the same-sex group than of the opposite-sex group.

An interesting feature of this last experiment was that the subjects were in fact equally familiar with the particular representatives of ingroup and outgroup categories about whom judgments were made. Accordingly, as Park and Rothbart noted, at one level these results might appear to be inconsistent with the view that lack of contact is responsible for perceived outgroup homogeneity and that subjects are more willing to perceive outgroups in terms of stereotypic attributes (as reinforced by differential encoding). However, Park and Rothbart were reluctant to abandon a familiarity-based explanation of outgroup homogeneity. They observed that the results might be interpretable as "testimony to the powerful effects of differential contact," (p. 1067) as it could be argued that earlier experience of differential contact with same- and opposite-sex groups had at some time led to the formation of qualitatively different beliefs about these categories which then served to structure the subsequent encoding of information. They thus remarked that "one direct implication of our data is that within limits the existing structures become self-perpetuating," and that learned encoding strategies could thus "perpetuate the view of the outgroup as relatively undifferentiated" (p. 1067).

However, evidence from a number of so-called "minimal-group studies" suggested that this interpretation of these results might not be entirely correct. These were modeled on experiments conducted by Tajfel, Flament, Billig, and Bundy (1971) in which subjects were assigned to groups on an essentially arbitrary basis (e.g., their supposed liking for different paintings) and then asked to assign rewards to members of those groups. These original studies (and numerous replications) indicated that even these most minimal of conditions were sufficient to encourage ingroup favoritism; that is, subjects tended to give more money to individuals who were members of their own group. Moreover, subjects tended to adopt a reward strategy that maximized the difference between groups in favor of the ingroup (i.e., choosing the option that gave relatively more to the ingroup), rather than choosing to maximize either ingroup or joint profit (i.e., simply choosing to give as much money as possible to their group or to both groups). Part of the significance of these results was that they appeared to reveal prejudicial behavior "where there was no conflict of interests nor history of hostility between the groups, no utilitarian link between intergroup discrimination and subjects' self-interest, no face-to-face interaction within or between groups and group membership was anonymous" (Turner, 1981, p. 75).

In conceptually similar studies, Wilder (1980, cited in Wilder, 1981; see also Wilder, 1984, Experiment 1) assigned subjects to minimal groups and asked them to indicate either the different positions that would be endorsed by members of their ingroup or the different positions that would be endorsed by members of the outgroup. As predicted, subjects believed that the range of ingroup members' positions would be greater than that of people in the minimal outgroup (although Wilder, 1984, also noted that perceived intra-ingroup similarity increased significantly in the presence of an outgroup). As in Tajfel's original experiments, then, it appeared that features of the stereotyping process (there, ingroup favoritism; here, outgroup homogeneity) were not simply a function of the nature of previous or ongoing social contact with the individuals being judged. Furthermore, because subjects had no prior knowledge of the particular categories of which these individuals were members—and hence no "existing structures" or "learned encoding strategies" in relation to those categories—Wilder's results can also be taken as inconsistent with an explanation in terms of experience-based information processing of the type proposed by Park and Rothbart (1982).

Cognitive Theories of Group Homogeneity

Throughout the 1980s, as studies produced more and more evidence of relative outgroup homogeneity, a number of researchers turned their attention to providing more detailed explanations of the phenomenon than were afforded by the discursive analyses of early investigators. In the spirit of the times, the most influential accounts sought to explain the effect in terms of theoretical concepts borrowed from cognitive psychology. Two competing accounts have come to dominate the landscape. The first, most closely associated with the work of Linville and her colleagues (e.g., Linville, Fischer, & Salovey, 1989; Linville, Salovey, & Fischer, 1986), has sought to develop and refine the familiarity-based analysis of earlier researchers. However, moving away from the idea that knowledge of individuals per se is the basis of outgroup homogeneity, Judd, Park, and their colleagues (e.g., Judd & Park, 1988; Park, Ryan, & Judd, 1992) have proposed a two-process model that ascribes an additional causal role to group-level knowledge (i.e., stereotypic beliefs concerning group variability).

A Familiarity-Based Analysis: The Exemplar Model

Linville's analysis of asymmetries in perceived ingroup–outgroup homogeneity developed from her earlier work suggesting that people are inclined to make relatively polarized appraisals of outgroup members (e.g., Linville, 1982; Linville & Jones, 1980). This effect was explained in terms of a tendency to have more differentiated knowledge structures, or schemas, about ingroups as a result of a "rich background of experience with the ingroup [which] generates a larger number dimensions along which individual members may be characterized" (Linville & Jones, 1980, p. 691). Consistent with this argument, and other evidence of outgroup homogeneity discussed above, Linville and Jones (1980, Experiment 3) found that when white male students were asked to sort 40 personality traits into separate groups, they created far more groups if they were asked to think about white rather than black undergraduates while performing this task.

Applying this argument directly to the explanation of outgroup homogeneity, Linville et al. (1986) subsequently claimed that perceived group homogeneity is a direct product of familiarity-based category differentiation. The model they have developed assumes that information about group members is stored in terms of knowledge of specific individuals. It argues that because people have greater familiarity with members of ingroups than with members of outgroups, they encounter and store information about more exemplars of the former (cf. Lippman, 1922; Allport, 1954). When subjects are asked to make variability judgments, this model proposes that they simply retrieve a sample of category members and report the distribution of these members on the appropriate dimension. Outgroup homogeneity is thus seen to arise from the fact that larger populations (such as ingroups) tend to be more dispersed, and so sampling leads to their being represented as more heterogeneous than smaller populations (such as outgroups).

Linville and her coworkers (1986) proposed a formal statistical measure of intracategory differentiation referred to as the "probability of differentiation" (P_d), this being "the probability that a perceiver will differentiate between two randomly chosen instances of the category in terms of the attribute in question" (1986, p. 184). Using this measure, Linville et al. (1986; 1989, Experiment 1) found further evidence of outgroup homogeneity in a task where college students, and elderly people at a retirement home were asked to imagine either 100 random people aged over 65 or 100 random college students and to distribute them across seven levels of a number of different attributes. Similar evidence was produced in a replication that involved Irish and American subjects' being asked to characterize a sample of students of their own or the other nationality (1989, Experiment 2).

Interestingly, whereas outgroup homogeneity always emerged on the P_d measure in these two studies, on a simple measure of variability (the standard deviation in subjects' responses) it was only apparent in the student–elderly experiment, and then only in the responses of the college students. The authors' own discussion of this finding suggests that it may have been attributable in part to the nature of the ingroup–outgroup comparison in question. As they point out, in certain respects ingroup–outgroup differentiation was more clearcut for the young college students, given that, unlike the elderly, they had never been members of the outgroup category. Similarly, in the second study, it seems likely that the failure to find evidence of outgroup homogeneity on the variability measure may have had something to do with the fact that in this context, what the ingroup and outgroup had in common as students was more important than the basis on which they differed.

A third experiment involving male and female college students found no evidence at all of relative outgroup homogeneity. Linville et al. (1986, 1989) argue that this finding is consistent with their model, as it can be accounted for by the fact that subjects were equally familiar with members of the same and of the opposite sex. However, as with the study of Irish and American students discussed above, the possibility remains that this failure to observe outgroup homogeneity was associated with the fact that this study's procedure (which, e.g., asked subjects to think of "male undergraduates at Yale of approximately your own age") served to draw subjects' attention to aspects of identity *shared* by these particular males and females (i.e., age and student status at the same institution). This factor would go some way to explaining the difference between these results and those reported by Park and Rothbart (1982, Experiments 1 and 2; see also Park & Judd, 1990, below).

Two further strands of research have been used to elaborate the exemplar model. The first involves evidence from computer simulations that have looked at predicted P_d and judgmental variance as a function of familiarity with differently distributed populations (i.e., normal, skewed, and bimodal; Linville et al., 1986, 1989). On the basis of these simulations, Linville and her colleagues conclude that greater familiarity leads to greater differentiation, but also that its effects are nonlinear (implying, e.g., that the first 20 exemplars of a category with which one becomes acquainted have a greater impact on differentiation than the fourth 20) and have a greater impact on the probability of differentiation than perceived variability does.

Finally (and perhaps most importantly; see Messick & Mackie, 1989, p. 56), support for the exemplar model has also been drawn from research indicating that as individuals become more familiar with a group, they develop a more differentiated representation of it. Consistent with this analysis, Linville and her colleagues (1989, Experiment 4; see also 1986, pp. 196–198) conducted a study among students in an undergraduate psychology class at Yale University, in which on three separate occasions students judged that class on a number of attributes (e.g., likeability, mood, friendliness, hours spent studying, scores in aptitude tests) by indicating its members' distribution across seven levels of each attribute. As predicted, both the variance in subjects' responses and P_d increased over time, indicating that the group came to be seen as more differentiated and variable as its members became more familiar with one another. On this basis, Linville et al. concluded that "familiarity rather than ingroup–outgroup status per se may be a critical key to differentiation" (1986, p. 198), noting later that "familiarity per se appears to be sufficient to lead to greater differentiation" (1989, p. 175).

The Dual-Process Model

Despite previously interpreting evidence of outgroup homogeneity under conditions of equal familiarity as an effect of differential contact, over time Park and her colleagues moved away from the familiarity-based approach exemplified by Linville et al.'s exemplar model. One important catalyst for this shift was additional evidence of outgroup homogeneity in a minimal-group study.

As Judd and Park (1988) pointed out, the results of Wilder's (1984) earlier experiment could still be taken as consistent with the exemplar model, given that in his minimal-group study subjects did have access to knowledge about a greater number of ingroup exemplars, because the only persons they knew anything about were themselves. In seeking to conduct a minimal-group study that would rule out this possible reinterpretation, these researchers conducted an experiment in which eight subjects were divided into two arbitrary four-person groups (supposedly on the basis of performance in a perceptual task), and subsequently had to make judgments about each person and to recall biographical information provided by each. Here it was found that an outgroup homogeneity effect emerged when subjects expected their ingroup to compete with the outgroup (i.e., that more variable judgments were made of the individuals in the same group as the subjects, and that subjects recalled more individuating information about that ingroup). Interestingly, though, this effect was fully attenuated where subjects expected intergroup cooperation. In view of the fact that in conditions of both conflict and cooperation subjects had access to the same number of exemplars (i.e., four)—and consistent with the interpretation of some of Linville's findings offered above—Judd and Park concluded that outgroup homogeneity seemed to reflect the salience of an intergroup boundary rather than availability of exemplars per se.

Although Park and Judd have never denied that familiarity *can* determine perceived homogeneity (indeed, they have stated that "it seems clear that increased familiarity [does lead] to increased perceived variability"; Park, Judd, & Ryan, 1991, p. 233), the essence of their reaction against Linville's model is therefore based on arguments (1) that differential familiarity is not the central cause of relative outgroup homogeneity, and (2) that category representation has a group-level as well as an individual-level component. Accordingly, their dual-process model (e.g., Judd & Park, 1988; Park et al., 1989, 1991; see also Rothbart, Dawes, & Park, 1984) centers on the claim that the perceived homogeneity of a given social group reflects combined knowledge of both individual group members *and* the group as a whole (in the form of stereotypes). More specifically, the model proposes that judgments of perceived variability are based on group-level representations that reflect a "running tally" of what a group is like on a number of dimensions—representations that are in certain circumstances supplemented by knowledge of particular exemplars (Park et al., 1991, pp. 220–221).

Within this framework, the phenomenon of outgroup homogeneity has been explained in terms of a general tendency for "outgroup members' representations of a group [to] embody a larger share of stereotypic than individuating information" (Rothbart et al., 1984, p. 130). More, specifically, the model asserts that asymmetries in ingroup–outgroup representation emerge (1) because during encoding more variable group-level representations are formed for ingroups, and (2) because during information retrieval supplementary exemplars are more likely to belong to the ingroup than to the outgroup. The next step has been the identification of factors responsible for these differences in encoding and retrieval. In addition to differences in familiarity, such factors include greater awareness of ingroup subgroups (Park et al., 1992) and of the individuality of ingroup members, especially oneself (Judd & Park, 1988), as well as demands to represent the ingroup more accurately (Park & Judd, 1990; Judd et al., 1991).

The contribution of subgroup information was investigated in studies showing that business and engineering students generated more subgroups when describing their ingroup rather than the outgroup, and that the difference in the number of subgroups described was the principal predictor of asymmetries in perceived ingroup–outgroup homogeneity (Park et al., 1992, Experiment 1). Measures of the latter included estimations of the positions of group members on stereotypic and counterstereotypic dimensions, estimations of the percentage of ingroup and outgroup members who would have stereotypic and counterstereotypic attributes; and, finally, ratings of the most extreme group members on those attributes. On these measures, the number of identified subgroups explained between 9% and 20% of the variance in outgroup homogeneity (defined as more stereotypic *and* less counterstereotypic representation; Park & Judd, 1990), whereas familiarity (as rated by subjects themselves) explained only between 0% and 1%, and the number of listed attributes explained only between 1% and 7%. Furthermore, the outgroup homogeneity effect was eliminated when the number of ingroup and outgroup subgroups identified by each subject was controlled for. Consistent with the thrust of Park et al.'s analysis, a second study also showed that the perceived variability of a target group was increased if subjects were instructed to identify meaningful subgroups on the basis of biographical information about its members.

The argument that demands to represent the ingroup more accurately contribute to relative outgroup homogeneity received initial support from a study (Park & Judd, 1990, Experiment 1) in which men and women judged the homogeneity of either men or women, using measures of both variability (i.e., distribution and range tasks) and stereotypicality (i.e., a percentage estimate task). In contrast to the findings of Linville et al. (1989, Experiment 3), the study produced evidence of outgroup homogeneity on both types of measures. However, there was also evidence that variability effects were better predicted by the discrepancy between subjects' self-ratings and their average ratings of other ingroup members than by the variability of retrieved ingroup and outgroup exemplars. Park and Judd (1990) interpret this as evidence against Linville et al.'s exemplar model, but as support for the idea that the outgroup homogeneity effect arises from subjects' relative sensitivity to intra-ingroup differences as a product of their greater self-involvement in those judgments. This conclusion was supported by a second study, in which business and engineering students completed both variability and stereotypicality ratings for both ingroup and outgroup, and provided think-aloud protocols as they did so. Here it was found that subjects were much more likely to talk about themselves (and to identify subgroups) but *less* likely to talk about specific exemplars when rating the ingroup than when rating the outgroup.

Further evidence for this argument comes from a study seeking to investigate the actual accuracy of ingroup and outgroup variability estimates (Judd, Ryan, & Park, 1991). This study examined business and engineering students' estimates of ingroup and outgroup homogeneity by means of variability and stereotypicality measures, and compared those estimates with the homogeneity indicated by subjects' own self-ratings. Using these self-ratings as indicators of "true" homogeneity, the authors concluded that subjects' ingroup ratings were more accurate, as the correlation between subjects' ingroup estimates and their self-ratings was generally higher than that between their outgroup estimates and others' self-ratings (although this effect was only significant on stereotypicality measures). This conclusion was also supported by evidence suggesting that subjects who were more accurate in estimating outgroup variability showed weaker overall outgroup homogeneity.

Overview

From the foregoing subsections, it can be seen that from the time that empirical evidence of the outgroup homogeneity effect was first documented, a large amount of research has been directed toward identifying its cognitive underpinnings. Although the initial focus was on the mediation of the effect by differential familiarity with group members, the work of Judd, Park, and their colleagues presents a convincing case for the view that there is much more to the effect than this. In moving away from an emphasis on the role of individual-level knowledge, their work also points to a need to see perceived group homogeneity as reflecting group-level knowledge. In terms of their model, then, asymmetries in ingroup and outgroup homogeneity are seen to reflect different *mixes* of higher- and lower-level information about each category, rather than differences in the *amount* of information per se.

However, although these advances have been significant, it would still appear that there are gaps in the explanatory scheme provided by purely cognitive theories of perceived homogeneity. Most notably, it is clear that although Park and her colleagues have succeeded in undermining the "thoroughly developed" exemplar model, their own model is "much less formally stated" (Park et al., 1991, pp. 219-220). In fact, in many respects their analysis is primarily descriptive, and a large part of their work serves simply to catalogue a host of differences in subjects' perceptions of ingroups and outgroups that are associated with differences in those groups' perceived homogeneity. Accordingly, where interesting experimental effects are observed as a function of factors other than subjects' membership or nonmembership in a judged group, the explanation of those results in terms of psychological process is often quite limited. For example, Judd and Park's (1988) finding of greater outgroup homogeneity under conditions of conflict than of cooperation is seen to be associated with the salience of an intergroup boundary (p. 786), but the *theoretical* links between this observation and the mechanisms specified under the dual-process model are unexplored. In particular, it seems unclear how such a manipulation might affect the preformed stereotypic representations upon which variability judgments are believed to be based. One of the critical questions left unanswered by their research, then, is how and why changes in social-psychological context affect the processing of different levels of information and thereby lead to variation in the outgroup homogeneity effect.

Furthermore, because both the dual-process and the exemplar models assume that representations of ingroup categories inherently contain more variability information than those of outgroup categories, both models imply that *as a general rule,* judgments of an outgroup must be more homogeneous than those of an ingroup. Yet, as we shall see, there is convincing evidence not only that the outgroup homogeneity effect can be attenuated (as observed in studies by Judd & Park, 1988, and Linville et al., 1986, 1989), but also that under certain conditions it can be reversed, so that ingroups are seen as more homogeneous than outgroups. In particular, this evidence is associated with studies pointing to the need to examine motivational as well as cognitive determinants of perceived homogeneity.

SOCIAL IDENTITY AND PERCEIVED GROUP HOMOGENEITY: A COGNITIVE–MOTIVATIONAL APPROACH

Metatheoretical Foundations: The Role of Group Values in Social Categorization

As we have noted above, although Tajfel laid the foundations for the cognitive analysis of effects associated with the accentuation of intracategory similarities, he was also at pains to stress their dependence on the motivations of the perceiver. In large part, this emphasis reflected Tajfel's early work in the area of judgment (e.g., Tajfel, 1957). Drawing heavily on the contribution of Bruner and other proponents of the "New Look" in the 1950s, this had served to emphasize the role of values and needs as important organizing principles of perception.

Evidence consistent with this position was provided by a number of studies of social judgment conducted in the 1950s (for discussions, see Eiser & Stroebe, 1972; Oakes, Haslam, & Turner, 1994, Chap. 6; Sherif & Hovland, 1961). These tended to show that when an issue was important to subjects, they were likely to accentuate the differences between classes of stimuli that were representative of contrasting categories. In one example of this research, Pettigrew, Allport, and Barnett (1958) conducted a study in which South African subjects from different racial groups (Afrikaners, English, Indians, Coloureds, and black Africans) had to assign to racial categories photographs of different group members (e.g., a black African and an Indian) that were viewed binocularly through a stereoscope and hence fused together. They found that Afrikaners were more likely (1) to see these binocular fusions either as African (i.e., black) or as European (i.e., white), and (2) to see them as African rather than European (for related findings see Secord, Bevan, & Katz, 1956; Tajfel & Wilkes, 1963b). Thus, whereas other groups assigned only about 20% of two race fusions to the black African category, Afrikaners assigned 35%. In part, it appears that this variation—reflecting a greater willingness on the part of Afrikaners to assign stimuli to an extreme "catch-all" outgroup category—can be explained in terms of an ideologically motivated desire to maintain an existing sociopolitical system of differentiation and discrimination (see Tajfel, 1972).

It is also apparent that effects of this type have some bearing upon subjects' perception of homogeneity among social stimuli. For example, Hovland and Sherif (1952) asked three groups of subjects (Negroes, pro-Negro whites, and anti-Negro whites, in the authors' terminology) to sort 114 statements reflecting a range of attitudes to Negroes into 11 categories (from most unfavorable to most favorable). As predicted, and as the data in Table 6.1 show, subjects in the first two of these groups were much more likely to assign the statements to extreme categories. Furthermore, calculations of P_d (after Linville et al., 1986) indicate that this tendency led Negroes and pro-Negro whites to represent the stim-

TABLE 6.1   Distribution of Attitudinal Statements into Categories and Associated Probabilities of Differentiation

| Subject group | Category[a] | | | | | | | | | | | P_d |
	1	2	3	4	5	6	7	8	9	10	11	
Negroes	49	11	4	3	3	4	3	4	4	7	22	.76
Pro-Negro whites	40	18	10	5	5	4	4	3	4	8	13	.81
Anti-Negro whites	20	11	9	8	7	7	6	7	8	9	22	.89

Note. The data are from Hovland and Sherif (1952, Figure 1).
[a]1, most unfavorable; 11, most favorable.

ulus set as a whole more homogeneously than did anti-Negro whites (P_d's = .76, .81, and .89, respectively).

Further evidence that perceived stimulus homogeneity varies as a function of concerns associated with specific group memberships (in interaction with features of the judgmental task; see Eiser & Stroebe, 1972) was provided in a follow-up study conducted by Sherif and Hovland (1953) with similar materials and subject groups. As well as replicating the findings above, the study indicated that when subjects could choose how many categories to use for sorting purposes, Negroes tended to use fewer categories than whites. Thus 67% of Negroes used four or fewer categories, compared to only 45% of whites (i.e., following Park et al.'s [1992], reasoning, the former subjects represented the stimuli more homogeneously). As in the data reported by Hovland and Sherif (1952), the combined effect of these sorting patterns was thus that, relative to white subjects, Negroes tended to accentuate the perceived homogeneity of *both* pro- and anti-Negro statements (categories that can be seen to represent the ingroup and outgroup, respectively). Again, then, perceived homogeneity was a function of the group memberships (and their associated world views) that subjects brought to bear upon the task, rather than simply (or even) of ingroup–outgroup status per se.

Taken as a whole, findings of this type suggested to researchers that patterns of categorization were bound up with the group-based concerns of perceivers. Negroes and whites, for example, were observed to display different patterns of categorization because the task was more relevant to the Negro group's concerns, and more consistent with its underlying values. Supportive of the latter point, an extensive program of research conducted by Eiser (e.g., 1973; see Eiser & van der Pligt, 1984) suggests that differences in the responses of pro- and anti-Negro subjects in such tasks may be accounted for by the fact that the latter subjects were "unhappy" associating statements endorsed by their group with negatively valued scale positions (i.e., those identified as anti-Negro). As with results from studies conducted by Linville (e.g., Linville et al., 1989, Experiment 3) and Park and Rothbart (1982), these patterns can be seen to point to the relevance of features of the intergroup context—specifically, the salience of a subjectively relevant and meaningful intergroup boundary—to perceived group homogeneity.

Such research also makes it clear that as Tajfel (1972) pointed out, categorization is intimately bound up with the expression and maintenance of a group's shared values (e.g., Afrikaners' desire to set themselves apart from black South Africans; Negroes' deep-seated opposition to anti-Negro racism). He thus drew attention to the fact that a distinctive feature of *social* categorization (i.e., that involving the perception of groups) is that it is necessarily affected by the values and motivations associated with a perceiver's own group as it stands in relation to others within a particular social system. "For this reason," he concluded, "predictions of differences between or within categories being magnified or minimized cannot be made without analysis of other relevant aspects of this social context of values" (1972, p. 23).

Social Identity and Self-Stereotyping

In recognition of the fact that both cognitive and social-motivational factors have an impact upon social categorization, Tajfel (1972) set himself the task of developing an integrated analysis of this process as it relates to intergroup phenomena such as stereotyping. As a starting point in this endeavor, he turned to the results of the minimal-group studies discussed above, seeking to use them to explore the links between social categorization and group behavior.

One of the points that Tajfel himself saw as most relevant to this integration was the observation that in the minimal-group studies, the act by which subjects categorized themselves as members of a group imbued their behavior with a *distinct* meaning. In particular, he argued that in these studies "social categorization required the establishment of a distinct and positively valued social identity" (Tajfel, 1972, p. 37). He defined "social identity" as "the individual's knowledge that he [or she] belongs to certain groups together with some emotional and value significance to him [or her] of the group membership" (p. 31). This was distinguished from the notion of "personal identity," which refers to self-knowledge that derives from the individual's unique attributes (e.g., concerning physical appearance, intellectual qualities, and idiosyncratic tastes; Turner, 1982).

Tajfel asserted that behavior in general can be represented in terms of a continuum ranging from interaction solely determined by the character and motivations of the individual *as an individual* (i.e., interpersonal behavior) to behavior deriving solely from his or her group membership (i.e., intergroup behavior; cf. Brewer, 1988; Fiske & Neuberg, 1990). In making this distinction, he also suggested that intergroup and interpersonal behavior are qualitatively distinct from each other and that the former is not reducible to the latter. Furthermore, in seeking to detail the material consequences of the existence of the interpersonal–intergroup continuum, he formulated the following general hypothesis:

> The nearer is a social situation to the intergroup extreme, the stronger tendency will there be for members of the ingroup to treat members of the outgroup as undifferentiated items in a unified social category, i.e., independently of the individual differences between them. This will be reflected simultaneously in a clear awareness of the ingroup–outgroup dichotomy, in the attribution to members of the outgroup of certain traits assumed to be common to the group as a whole, in value judgments pertaining to those traits, in the emotional significance associated with these evaluations, and in other forms of behavior associated with the ingroup–outgroup categorization. (1978, p. 45)

At a broad level, it can be seen that important aspects of this hypothesis are consistent with findings from studies (discussed above) suggesting that the tendency to perceive outgroups homogeneously is associated with a salient intergroup division—or at least that in the absence of any such division, the outgroup homogeneity *effect* tends to be attenuated (e.g., Linville, 1986; Judd & Park, 1988).

Having noted the distinct psychological contribution made by social identity through "creat[ing] and defin[ing] the individual's place in society," Tajfel and Turner (e.g., 1979, pp. 40-41; 1986) went on to develop a fuller explanation of the findings from the minimal-group studies, and in so doing formulated their social identity theory of intergroup behavior. This was an integrative theory that attended to both the cognitive and the motivational bases of intergroup differentiation. In essence, it suggested that subsequent to being categorized in terms of a group membership, and having defined *themselves* in terms of that social categorization (Turner, 1975), individuals are motivated to achieve positive self-esteem through an ingroup identity that is positively differentiated from outgroups on some valued dimension. In the minimal-group studies, it was argued, such differentiation was achieved through subjects' allocation of greater monetary rewards to their ingroup—an interpretation that has been supported by a considerable body of subsequent research (for reviews, see Brewer, 1979; Hogg & Abrams, 1988; Turner, 1981).

Hand in hand with research testing social identity theory, a body of work also focused on the theoretical implications of the notion of social identity itself. In particular, Turner (1982) attempted to provide a more causal analysis for individuals' movement along Tajfel's interpersonal-intergroup continuum. As a part of this development, he hypothesized (Turner, 1982; Brown & Turner, 1981) that an individual's self-concept can be defined along a continuum ranging from definition of the self in terms of personal identity to definition in terms of social identity. Moreover, he proposed that the functioning of the self-concept corresponds to, and is the cognitive mechanism underpinning, the behavioral continuum described by Tajfel (1978). It was suggested, then, that the "switching on" of social identity (or the "psychological depersonalization" of the self) allows intergroup behavior to take place. As Turner (1982) put it, "social identity is the cognitive mechanism that makes group behavior possible" (p. 21).

In essence, depersonalization may be thought of as the process of "self-stereotyping," through which the self is perceived to be interchangeable with other ingroup members. So, elaborating upon Tajfel's (1978) hypothesis that in intergroup contexts individuals should perceive outgroups as homogeneous, Turner predicted that the salience of social identity should lead to similarly homogeneous *ingroup* perception. When self-stereotyping,

> Individuals react to themselves and others not as differentiated, individual persons but as exemplars of the common characteristics of their group. It is through this process that salient or functioning social identifications help to regulate social behavior; they do so directly by causing group members to act in terms of the shared needs, goals and norms which they assign to themselves, and indirectly through the perceptual homogenization of others which elicits uniform reactions from the perceivers. (Brown & Turner, 1981, p. 39)

A fairly straightforward prediction of this analysis was that as individuals come to define themselves in terms of social rather than personal identity—becoming aware of what they share with other ingroup members, rather than of their uniqueness—perceived ingroup homogeneity should increase.

Social Identity Salience and Perceived Ingroup Homogeneity

Like Tajfel's earlier hypothesis related to the perceived homogeneity of outgroups, Turner's prediction that social identity salience (as an aspect of intergroup rather than interpersonal behavior) should lead to greater perceived ingroup homogeneity is clearly consistent with findings from a number of studies that we have already discussed. In particular, it is supported by evidence indicating that subjects believe and expect there to be more similarity among ingroup members when these judgments are made in an intergroup rather than an intragroup context (Doise et al., 1978; Tajfel et al., 1964; Wilder, 1984, Experiment 1). This effect is also apparent in more recent findings reported by Doosje, Spears, and Koomen (1992). Confirming the role of comparative context in shaping perceived homogeneity, they found that psychology students perceived much more similarity among members of their ingroup when asked to estimate variability within psychology *and* sociology students rather than psychology students alone.

Evidence that social identity salience can in fact lead to an ingroup being perceived as *more* homogeneous than the outgroup comes from other research conducted within the framework of social identity theory. Especially important in this regard is work by Simon and his colleagues, which has tested the hypothesis that an ingroup homogeneity effect is associated with demands to establish a positive and distinct social identity. This is predicted both (1) for members of minority groups and (2) for members of all groups on ingroup-defining dimensions.

The first of these hypotheses was developed and tested by Simon and Brown (1987). They reasoned that members of minority groups may be particularly motivated to act in terms of their group membership, and thereby may emphasize intra-ingroup similarities, in order to offset the threat that minority status poses to their self-esteem. They argued that such threat could be effectively counteracted both (1) by displaying greater discrimination against the majority outgroup (as observed in minimal-group settings by Gerard & Hoyt, 1974, and Sachdev & Bourhis, 1984), and (2) by accentuating intragroup solidarity through the emphasis of ingroup homogeneity.

To test the latter claim, Simon and Brown conducted an experiment in which subjects were assigned to minimal groups of different relative size, supposedly on the basis of their identification of ambiguous blue-green slides as blue or green. As predicted, they found that members of the minority identified more strongly with their group, and that these subjects reported a smaller range in the color recognition capabilities of their ingroup. The opposite pattern emerged for members of the majority. Thus members of the majority reproduced the established pattern of relative outgroup homogeneity, but members of the minority exhibited an ingroup homogeneity effect.

Of course, it could be argued that this pattern of results reflected *all* subjects' assumption that the minority would be more homogeneous than the majority simply because it contained fewer members (i.e., as would be predicted by Linville et al.'s exemplar model; see Simon, 1992, pp. 7-8). Indeed, as we discuss further below, Judd et al. (1991, pp. 366-367) and Bartsch and Judd (1993) explicitly interpret Simon and Brown's results as demonstrating an effect for the size of the target group rather than an ingroup homogeneity effect per se. Against this argument, though, is the finding that in one condition of Simon and Brown's study where *both* ingroup and outgroup were described as minorities (and thus target group size was constant), an ingroup homogeneity effect still emerged. Furthermore, in a control condition where subjects were not actually assigned to a group, subjects showed no tendency to perceive the minority group as any more homogeneous than the majority (a result that in itself poses additional problems for the exemplar model).

Further support for Simon and Brown's analysis was apparent in a follow-up study conducted by Simon and Pettigrew (1990), which afforded direct evidence of the mediating role of social identification in perceived ingroup homogeneity. Here subjects were assigned to groups supposedly on the basis of their liking for a particular painter, J. P. Wheeler. The study replicated Simon and Brown's (1987) ingroup homogeneity effect for minority group members, and also showed that its emergence was highly correlated both with the degree of subjects' liking for their ingroup (mean r = .39) and with the strength of their ingroup identification (mean r = .40) As a corollary, the study also showed that subjects only displayed relative outgroup homogeneity when they were unwilling to define themselves in group-based terms. This occurred when their social identity was poorly-defined (i.e., in conditions where subjects were not specifically identified as belonging to the Wheeler group) and when they were given no information about the percentage of people in general who were in this group.

As well as supporting predictions derived from social identity theory, in more recent investigations of the links between minority status and ingroup homogeneity, Simon and Hamilton (1994) provide direct evidence to support Turner's (1982; Brown & Turner, 1981) self-stereotyping hypothesis. In an initial minimal-group study, they found that subjects assigned to a numerical minority were more likely to define themselves in terms of ingroup attributes and to perceive themselves to be interchangeable with fellow ingroup members, as well as less likely to exhibit an outgroup homogeneity effect. Furthermore, a second experiment that orthogonally manipulated group size and group status (low vs. high) indicated that these effects interacted with group status. That is, the subjects most likely to engage in self-stereotyping and to display relative ingroup homogeneity were those assigned to a small high-status group—in other words, those subjects whose assigned group membership led them to have both a salient and a positive social identity.

Beyond evidence that relative ingroup homogeneity is associated with minority status, research in the social identity tradition also suggests that this effect emerges on specific ingroup-defining dimensions. Initial support for this view comes from an experiment reported by Kelly (1989), who asked supporters and members of the British Labour Party to judge the homogeneity of both this political ingroup and the Conservative Party outgroup. As predicted, the results indicated that party members perceived both their ingroup and the outgroup to be more homogeneous than did nonmembers. There was also evidence that the general perception of relative outgroup homogeneity was qualified by an interaction with item relevance. Specifically, outgroup homogeneity was observed on dimensions irrelevant to subjects' group membership (e.g., ratings of group members' personality); on more group-relevant dimensions, however, subjects perceived the ingroup to be more homogeneous than the outgroup. A three-way interaction also indicated that this effect was stronger for party members than for mere supporters.

On the basis of these results, Kelly argues that the perception of group homogeneity is strongly linked to the values and goals associated with a particular social identity (cf. our discussion of the responses of different racial groups in early social-judgmental studies). She suggests that the representation of the ingroup as homogeneous may reflect a functional desire (particularly marked in party members) to stress party unity and coherence, in light of the fact that disunity would be "a severe electoral handicap" (p. 248).

Similar conclusions about the dependence of perceived group homogeneity on the interrelationship between social identity salience and judgmental dimension are also endorsed by Simon (1992). He has argued that all groups (not just minorities) tend to see their ingroup as more homogeneous than the outgroup on ingroup-defining dimensions (with relative outgroup homogeneity emerging on outgroup-defining dimensions). Importantly, Simon notes that such effects may be concealed in standard experimental studies (e.g., of the type reported by Linville et al., 1989, and Park & Judd, 1990), because in these subjects typically judge the ingroup and outgroup with respect to *bipolar* dimensions.

This analysis was supported by results from a minimal-group study in which groups were based on supposed preference for paintings and subjects made separate estimates of the range of group members' liking for different paintings (Simon, 1990, cited in Simon, 1992). Here it was found that relative outgroup homogeneity was apparent in liking for outgroup paintings, but that relative ingroup homogeneity emerged in liking for ingroup paintings. If we look back on the data reported by Quattrone and Jones (1980), it is interesting to note that these also provide some evidence of relative ingroup homogeneity on dimensions where group members shared a strong ingroup stereotype (e.g., that Rutgers students liked rock music).

Overview

It is clear from the review above that just as Tajfel's interest in the cognitive aspects of social categorization ultimately fostered extensive research examining the purely cognitive aspects of perceived group homogeneity, so his interest in group-based determinants of social categorization led to significant developments in our understanding of the largely motivational role of social identity in group representations. At a metatheoretical level, the principal contribution of the latter was the demonstration that judgments of group homogeneity do not occur in a motivational vacuum, but are intimately tied to concerns associated with perceivers' group memberships. Evidence suggests that both ingroups and outgroups may be represented homogeneously primarily because the representation of those groups *as groups* is meaningful in terms of the values and beliefs associated with a particular social identity (e.g., Hovland & Sherif, 1952; Kelly, 1989). This point and its significance are underlined by Simon (1992, p. 23):

> The perception of group homogeneity is embedded in an intergroup context . . . including group(s) with which the perceiver may identify and related belief systems. Accordingly, a thorough understanding of the perception of group homogeneity . . . also requires the analysis of those determinants of perceived homogeneity which originate in the intergroup context.

At a theoretical level, the social identity approach has generated two key hypotheses. These are, first, that the perceived homogeneity of outgroups should increase as an individual's social identity becomes salient and judgments are made in the context of a salient intergroup division (Tajfel, 1978); and, second, that social identity salience should also lead to more homogeneous ingroup perception (Turner, 1982). We have seen that there is general support for these hypotheses, and also that under certain circumstances the salience of social identity leads subjects to perceive their ingroup as more homogeneous than comparison outgroups. This finding clearly challenges the view that ingroup representations are necessarily more variable than representations of outgroups because they include more known exemplars. Indeed, we would argue that above all other empirical demonstrations, this finding questions the usefulness of models that ascribe no direct causal role to social-motivational factors in perceptions of group homogeneity.

Yet it is clear that although the social identity approach has led to predictions and demonstrations that pose clear problems for cognitive theories of group homogeneity, in certain respects it fails to take these theories on in their own terms (Simon, 1993a). Thus, whereas Park et al. (1991) and Linville et al. (1989) offer integrated (if limited) analyses of social categorization (of which the explanation of outgroup homogeneity is part), the social identity analysis offers a highly circumscribed account both of the (social-)cognitive aspects of this categorization process and of the outgroup homogeneity effect (in which most cognitive researchers are interested). This shortcoming arises from the fact that although social identity salience is seen as a key determinant of perceived group homogeneity, the theory focuses largely on its motivational basis (e.g., in the need for self-esteem) and offers no rigorous examination or explanation of its determination by nonmotivational features of social context (e.g., see Triandis, 1979, p. 323).

For this reason, it appears that a satisfactory explanation of perceived group homogeneity needs to accommodate the analysis of social identity salience within a more general account of the link between the self-concept and social categorization processes. In the following section, we attempt to show how this might be achieved through an application of self-categorization theory (Turner, 1985; Turner, Hogg, Oakes, Reicher, & Wetherell, 1987).

SELF-CATEGORIZATION AND GROUP HOMOGENEITY: THE INTERACTION BETWEEN SOCIAL MOTIVATION AND COGNITION

Metatheoretical Foundations: The Interaction between Cognition and the Group

As we have seen, a key aspect of Tajfel's analysis of social categorization was the argument that a complete understanding of this process needs to examine the way in which it is affected by group values. This, he argued, is especially true in considering how categorization is implicated in stereotyping, given that social stereotypes are not idiosyncratic beliefs peculiar to different individuals, but rather are shared by members of groups (in particular, see Tajfel, 1981). This argument has been taken up by researchers seeking to extend the interactionist perspective for which Tajfel's analysis argued. In particular, this metatheory has been advanced by self-categorization theorists (Turner & Oakes, 1986; Oakes & Turner, 1990) as an alternative to the prevailing approach to social cognition.

In essence, interactionism argues against the view that psychological aspects of group-based phenomena can be understood with reference only to individuals *qua* individuals. It argues that psychological processes (which are necessarily intraindividual) serve to represent and are shaped by a social world (which is largely made up of broader-based entities, i.e., real groups). Importantly, it also contends that although individual psychology and society are interdependent, each has a distinct and irreducible reality. Thus interactionism asserts that social phenomena cannot be explained solely in terms of psychological processes, just as psychological processes cannot be interpreted simply as social (epi)phenomena. In these terms the central task of social psychology is identified by Turner and Oakes (1986) as being "*not* to provide social explanations of behavior . . . , *nor* to provide 'psychological explanations' of, i.e., 'to psychologize' social behavior but *to explain the psychological aspects of society*" (p. 239; emphasis in original).

It can be seen that this approach has distinct metatheoretical implications for the analysis of stereotyping in general and perceived group homogeneity in particular. First, it argues against the trend to identify information-processing biases that might be held responsible for the form and content of particular social stereotypes. At the same time, it also questions the strategy that has been widely adopted within the social-cognitive research community of "generaliz[ing] cognitive laws . . . without explicit regard to the *functional interaction between cognitive and social processes*" (Oakes & Turner, 1986, p. 258; emphasis in original).

Another important implication of this approach is that it explicitly rejects the prevailing metatheory of research that regards limited information-processing capacity as the *cause* of social stereotyping (Oakes & Turner, 1990; Oakes, Haslam, & Turner, 1994). Specifically, whereas other researchers see social categorization and the associated act of stereotyping very much as "second-best," self-categorization theorists argue, on the contrary, that in many contexts it is entirely appropriate. Given that groups are real, and that they have distinct psychological implications for their members (e.g., as shown by minimal-group studies), it can be argued that to perceive all group members as if they were individuals would be maladaptive. And this is *not* because individual-based perception would demand too much effort, but because it would neglect important social realities. This point was put nicely by Asch (1952, p. 238):

> Observing the distortions that follow from merging individuals with their groups, some have counselled that it is misleading to judge persons in terms of group relations and that the canons of objectivity require of us to understand persons first and foremost as individuals. . . . But it is wrong to assume that we can best achieve a correct view of a person by ignoring his [or her] group relations. . . . If there are group forces and if they exert effects, we should understand them to understand individuals.

If one asks, for example, why black South Africans often treat white South Africans as a homogeneous group, it seems likely that the answer is not because it is too hard to perceive them as individuals, but rather because whites have oppressed blacks *as a group* whose members share important properties (until recently, a right to vote, a right to political opposition, and vested interest in apartheid; and still, a higher standard of living, greater freedom of movement, and better education). Clearly, to deal with members of the outgroup as individuals in such contexts would necessarily be to deny the realities of the social system of which they are all a part. And often when black people refer to whites in undifferentiated terms, it is precisely to such realities as these that they wish to draw attention.

Self-Categorization Theory: Some Key Hypotheses

In promoting these various metatheoretical principles, self-categorization theory developed from the tradition of social identity research described above. As introduced by Turner (1987), the theory "is a set of related assumptions and hypotheses about the functioning of the social self-concept (the concept of self based on comparison with other people and relevant to social interaction)" (p. 42). In this, the theory seeks to encompass the motivational aspects of social identity theory within a more rigorous and far-reaching social-cognitive framework. Also, whereas social identity theory is oriented to the explanation of a particular type of group behavior (intergroup discrimination), self-categorization theory was originally focused on how individuals are able to act as group members in the first place (Turner, 1982) and has developed into a general analysis of the functioning of categorization processes in social perception and interaction (see Oakes, Haslam, & Turner, 1994; Turner, Oakes, Haslam, & McGarty, 1994).

The essence of the advance initially proposed by self-categorization theory was to elaborate upon "the nature of social identity as a higher order level of abstraction in the perception of self and others" (Turner, 1987, p. 42). This elaboration is formalized within a number of assumptions and related hypotheses described in detail elsewhere (e.g., Turner, 1985). Of these, the following four are most relevant to our current discussion:

1. Cognitive representations of the self take the form, *inter alia,* of "self-categorizations". That is, the self is perceived as a member of a stimulus class and as such is seen to be (a) equivalent to (and hence interchangeable with) other stimuli in that category, as well as (b) distinct from stimuli in other categories.

2. Self-categories and other categories exist at different levels of abstraction, higher levels being more inclusive (cf. Rosch's [1978], analysis of the structure of natural categories). Thus lower-level categories (e.g., "man," "woman") can become subsumed within higher ones (e.g., "human"), and indeed are necessarily defined in relation to comparisons made at that higher level. For the purposes of theoretical exposition, it is also useful to consider three important levels of the social self-concept: self-categorization (a) at the superordinate level as a human being (in contrast to other species), (b) at the intermediate level as an ingroup member (as distinct from outgroups), and (c) at the subordinate level as a unique individual (different from other relevant ingroup members). Categories formed at these various levels are referred to as, respectively, (a) human, (b) social, and (c) personal. Importantly, self-categories at all levels of abstraction are seen to be equally "real" and just as much a reflection of the "true" self. No level of self-categorization is inherently more appropriate than another, and hence none is, in Rosch's sense, any more "basic".

3. The formation and salience (i.e., cognitive activation) of any self-category or other category is determined by comparisons between stimuli at a more inclusive level of abstraction. More specifically, the formation of categories is a function of the metacontrast between interclass and intraclass differences (cf. Campbell, 1958). That is, with respect to a frame of reference consisting of salient stimuli, any given collection of stimuli will be perceived as a categorical entity to the extent that their difference from one another is seen to be less than

the difference between them and all other stimuli. So, for example, an apple and a pear are more likely to be categorized as sharing a common categorical identity (as fruit) when they are on a shopping list that also includes meat. Similarly, two black South Africans are more likely to see themselves as sharing group membership in a context that includes whites rather than blacks alone. In this manner, metacontrast contextualizes categorization by tying it to an on-the-spot judgment of relative differences.

4. The salience of a categorization at a particular level of abstraction leads to the accentuation of perceived intraclass similarities and interclass differences between people as defined by their category membership at the same level (accentuation thereby reflecting the extent of people's categorical interchangeability). So, for example, if a man's social self-category "male" becomes salient, other males will be perceived to be more similar to each other (and him) and more different from females (whose similarity to one another will also be enhanced) on dimensions that are seen to define membership of those categories (e.g., physical strength).

Self-Categorization Theory and Social Identity Salience

These statements as a whole make it clear that self-categorization theory recasts the important insights of some of the research we have already reviewed within a broader explanatory scheme. In particular, Turner's (1982) argument that the distinctive features of group behavior are attributable to a depersonalizing shift in the self-concept is here conceptualized as but one illustration (albeit the most important theoretically) of effects deriving from a change in the level of abstraction of self-categorization. The basis and consequences of such change are also understood in terms of the theoretical framework provided by Tajfel's social categorization research (e.g., Tajfel & Wilkes, 1963a).

As a development of this basic position, the principles of the theory have been formally applied to the analysis of social identity salience and ingroup–outgroup categorization by Oakes (1987). Following the work of Bruner (e.g., 1957), she hypothesizes that one crucial determinant of social category salience is "fit"—the degree to which a social categorization matches aspects of reality. "Comparative fit" is defined by the principle of metacontrast discussed above. "Normative fit" refers to the content aspect of the match between category specifications and the instances being represented. For example, in order to categorize a group of people as Australians rather than Americans, they must not only appear to differ (in attitudes, actions, etc.) from Americans more than from one another (comparative fit), but must also be perceived to do so in the right direction on specific content dimensions of comparison (Australians should, for example, support Australia rather than the United States in the America's Cup).

Evidence supporting this analysis comes from studies reported by Oakes, Turner, and Haslam (1991), which manipulated both the comparative and normative components of fit. In their second experiment, subjects watched a video of three "arts" and three "science" students discussing attitudes to university life. The content of the discussion was manipulated along comparative lines as follows: In "consensus" conditions, all the subjects agreed with one another; in "conflict" conditions, all the arts students argued for the same position while all the science students presented an opposing view; and in "deviance" conditions one arts student advanced a view opposed to that of all the other students (who all agreed with one another). The normative component of fit was manipulated across conditions where the target individual (who was the same female arts student in all cases, and the deviant in deviance conditions) took either the arts "consistent" position (i.e., stressing the importance of social activities) or the arts "inconsistent" position (i.e., arguing for the need to work hard). The most important finding was that, as predicted, the behavior of the target was most likely to be interpreted in terms of her social category membership (as an arts student) where comparative and normative fit were maximized (i.e., in the consistent/conflict condition). In other words, subjects perceived the target person in terms of her social category membership (as an arts student) only to the extent that it was fitting to do so.

One implication of the comparative-fit hypothesis, alluded to in previous examples and relevant to the analysis of a range of stereotyping effects, is that as the comparative context is extended, the salient self-category will include more others and will be defined at a higher level of abstraction. One male comparing himself with another male will tend to categorize himself in terms of personal identity and will accentuate individual differences between himself and that other person. However, as the context is extended to include different (say, female) others, so it becomes more appropriate for him to categorize both himself and the other in terms of a higher-level social identity—as "us men" who are similar to each other and different from "those women."

The theoretical basis of this analysis is elaborated in detail by Haslam and Turner (1992). Direct empirical support is also provided by a study reported by Hogg and Turner (1987), in which individuals were organized either into four-person groups consisting of two males and two females or into same-sex pairs. Subjects were more likely to define themselves in terms of gender and to accentuate their similarity with other members of the same sex when men *and* women were present rather than just another person of their own gender (i.e., in an intergroup rather than an intragroup context). Similarly, Haslam and Turner (1992, 1995) have reported a series of experiments showing that as a perceiver's frame of reference is changed through either extension of that frame or the extremitization of the perceiver, the extent to which a target person is seen to share a common categorical identity with them varies in a manner predicted by the metacontrast principle (see also Wilder & Thompson, 1988).

In these studies, the status of exemplars as representative of self- or non-self-categories—upon which the perception of similarity is based—is shown to be contingent upon context. In contrast to models that posit inherent, stable differences between representations labeled "ingroup" and "outgroup," it is apparent that the very same category (or category member) can be defined as an ingroup or an outgroup (member) in different contexts. Testimony to this point is provided, for example, in migrants' variable perceptions of their country of origin. A British migrant to Australia, for example, will define Britain as an ingroup and Australia as an outgroup in some contexts but will do the very opposite in others. Furthermore, the studies reviewed in this section make it clear that perceptions of interstimulus and intragroup similarity change with, and reflect, the context-sensitive and lawful functioning of the categorization process (for additional evidence, see Gaertner, Mann, Murrell & Dovidio, 1989).

Self-Categorization Theory and Perceived Group Homogeneity

The implications of self-categorization theory for the analysis of perceived group homogeneity follow directly from this argument that the perception of interstimulus similarity varies so as to reflect the changing categorical relations between stimuli as apprehended in different comparative and normative con-

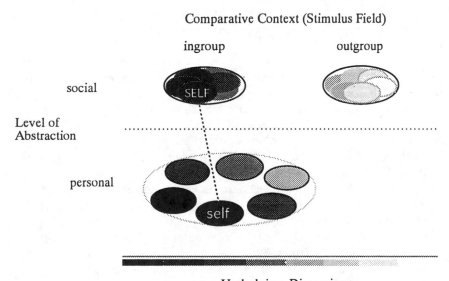

FIGURE 6.1 Variation in self-categorization as a function of comparative context. "SELF," self as group member with social identity salient; "self," self as unique individual with personal identity salient. The shift from self to SELF is produced by depersonalization (self-stereotyping). Solid lines indicate salient category boundaries. When the outgroup is present, the intergroup context makes social categories salient. Similarities within these are apparent because individuals are categorically interchangeable. When the ingroup alone is present the interindividual context makes personal categories salient. Differences between these are more apparent because individuals are not interchangeable.

texts. Indeed, following directly on from the analysis of the role of comparative fit in social category salience, the operation of metacontrast may be one very important determinant of outgroup homogeneity effects (see Haslam, Turner, Oakes, McGarty, & Hayes, 1992, p. 5; Oakes, Haslam, & Turner, 1994, Ch. 7). If, as self-categorization theory predicts, personal categories become salient in the context of intragroup comparison and social categories become salient in the context of intergroup comparison, then ingroup members should tend to be individuated more than outgroup members when judgment of those ingroup members is made in the absence of a salient intergroup division.

To clarify this point by means of an example, we can imagine three scenarios in which some men are asked (1) to make judgments of some women or (2) to make judgments of each other, or (3) to make judgments of one another in comparison to women. If we assume that scenarios 1 and 3 are both intergroup by virtue of the fact that they involve comparisons between ingroup and outgroup categories (the former implicit and the latter explicit), then self-categorization theory predicts that the social categorical properties of the judged group should be more salient in these scenarios than in the intragroup scenario (2). Accordingly, when the male ingroup is judged alone (scenario 2), it should be seen as less homogeneous than the female outgroup (scenario 1). Other things being equal, though, there should be no such asymmetry in perceived homogeneity when the ingroup is judged in comparison to the outgroup (scenario 3).

As we have seen, the first two of these scenarios are common in investigations of group homogeneity where subjects typically make ratings *either* just of the outgroup *or* just of the ingroup (e.g., Linville, 1982; Linville & Jones, 1980, Experiment 3; Linville et al., 1989; Park & Rothbart, 1982, Experiments 1 and 2; Quattrone & Jones, 1980; Wilder, 1984; see also Jones, Wood, & Quattrone, 1981; Brewer & Lui, 1984; Rothbart et al., 1984, pp. 127–129). It follows from the analysis above that when the subjects in these studies made judgments of outgroups, they should have tended to make implicit *inter*group comparisons between that group and their own ingroup, which led to the salience of social categories *within* which similarities were accentuated (as per scenario 1). Conversely, when subjects judged ingroups in the absence of a salient outgroup, they should have been more likely to make *intra*-ingroup comparisons, leading to the salience of personal categories *between* which differences were accentuated (as per scenario 2). This argument is represented schematically in Figure 6.1 (scenarios 1, 2, and 3 correspond respectively to the figure's top right, bottom left, and top left sections).

In an attempt to provide a direct test of this analysis, we conducted two studies (Haslam, Oakes, Turner & McGarty, 1995) where subjects in one set of conditions judged *both* an ingroup *and* an outgroup (both judgments thus being made in an explicitly intergroup context), while subjects in other conditions followed the common procedure of judging *either* an ingroup *or* an outgroup. Our general hypothesis was that group homogeneity judgments would vary with the categorization process, as determined by comparative context, rather than with ingroup–outgroup status. More specifically, it was predicted that on stereotypic dimensions the ingroup and outgroup would be perceived as equally homogeneous in the two-group comparative context (where both groups were salient for subjects). On the other hand, an outgroup homogeneity effect was expected where groups were judged alone, as this would represent an intergroup context for the outgroup judgment, but an intragroup context for the ingroup judgment.

In the first experiment subjects initially used a checklist to assign traits either to an ingroup (Australians) or to an outgroup (Americans)—this being a commonly used procedure for eliciting stereotype content (after Katz & Braly, 1933). As previous research led us to expect, subjects stereotyped their ingroup more positively than the outgroup (cf. Doise et al., 1972; Katz & Braly, 1933). Australians were typically described as "sportsmanlike," "pleasure-loving," and "happy-go-lucky," while Americans were generally described as "extremely nationalistic," "materialistic," and "ostentatious." Having assigned traits in this manner, subjects then either estimated the percentage of people in the stereotyped group alone who had the assigned traits or estimated the percentage of people both in this group and in the other comparison group who had the traits (i.e., in these two-group conditions, subjects estimated the percentage of Americans and Australians to whom the traits selected to describe Americans applied, or the percentage of Australians and Americans to whom the traits selected to describe Australians applied; cf. Park & Judd's [1990], stereotypicality measure). As predicted, when subjects judged the two groups alone, an outgroup homogeneity effect emerged: Stereotypic traits were seen to apply to more Americans (75%) than Australians (57%). However, when both groups were judged at the same time, this effect was eliminated: The traits selected to describe Australians were seen to apply to 74% of Australians, and the traits assigned to Americans were seen to apply to 74% of Americans.

As well as this, results from the two-group conditions provided evidence of asymmetry in the perceived applicability to the comparison group of the traits chosen to describe the stereotyped group (traits that Park & Judd, 1990, refer to as "counterstereotypic," but which we prefer to consider simply as "nonstereotypic"). Here, subjects believed the Australian traits to apply to 68% of Americans, but the American traits were seen to apply to only 48% of Australians. These results indicate that an outgroup homogeneity effect emerged on outgroup-defining dimensions, but that an ingroup homogeneity effect emerged on ingroup-defining dimensions (cf. Kelly, 1989; Simon, 1992). However, in terms of the criterion established by Park and Judd (1990), this result can also be seen to reveal an overall ingroup homogeneity effect, as the difference between the perceived applicability of stereotypic and nonstereotypic traits was greater for the ingroup than for the outgroup (26% vs. 6%).

This pattern of results clearly differs from those typically found in studies conducted by Judd and his colleagues, which have been used as evidence of the ubiquity of the outgroup homogeneity effect (e.g., Judd et al., 1991). However, one very important procedural difference between our studies and those of Judd and his colleagues is that our subjects *chose for themselves* the dimensions on which ingroup and outgroup were judged. In this experiment, then, we can be sure not only that particular traits were stereotypical of the groups involved, but also that they were explicitly recognized as such by the subjects—in other words, that the normative fit of stereotypic traits was high for both ingroup and outgroup.

Following on from this point, a further difference between these studies that may go some way toward explaining the different results obtained in each lies in the *favorableness* of the traits with respect to which ingroup and outgroup homogeneity was judged. In Judd et al.'s (1991), experiment, it is apparent that the favorableness of the traits and attitude statements used for group judgments did not differ systematically between groups. Indeed, each group was represented by one positive and one negative trait, and one positive and one negative attitude statement ("extraverted" and "impulsive" were the traits stereotypic of business majors, "analytical" and "reserved" were the traits stereotypical of engineering majors). Although this balance may have been seen as desirable for reasons of experimental control, it is apparent from content analysis of our own data (noted above) that when subjects choose traits themselves, they typically use favorable traits to characterize the ingroup and unfavorable traits to characterize the outgroup.

On the basis of this observation, it is possible to explain the relative *ingroup* homogeneity (as defined by Judd et al., 1991) observed in our study in terms of both the motivational principles articulated within social identity theory and the principles of category fit we have discussed above. It seems that although subjects were quite willing to see positive (ingroup) traits (e.g., "sportsmanlike" and "happy-go-lucky") as applicable to the outgroup, they were much more reluctant to see relatively negative (outgroup) traits (e.g., "extremely nationalistic" and "ostentatious") as applicable to the ingroup. This divergence may reflect the fact that the former tendency was much less threatening to subjects' social identity than the latter. Although such motivations would be expected to vary with context (e.g., in the face of intergroup competition), it seems reasonable to suggest that it is generally more threatening for group members to acknowledge that "we're very unpleasant" than that "they're very pleasant."

A second experiment (Haslam et al., 1995, Experiment 2) was conducted in order both to replicate the effect for comparative context obtained in the first study, and to examine this motivational account of the link between perceived variability and trait favorableness more rigorously. The design of the study was very similar to the initial experiment, although the favorableness of traits included in the checklist was introduced as an additional factor. That is, subjects characterized Australians or Americans in either a single-group or a two-group context, but did so with respect to a checklist that included either only positive traits, only negative traits, or both positive and negative traits. Predictions for the comparative-context effect were the same as those for the first experiment, and two related effects were expected to arise from subjects' reluctance to apply negative traits to the ingroup, as discussed above. First, it was predicted that the ingroup would be represented as more homogeneous when the checklist included all positive rather than all negative traits. Second, we expected the outgroup to be represented as more homogeneous than the ingroup when the checklist included only negative traits.

All these predictions were supported. A significant interaction between stereotyped group and comparative context on the stereotypical ratings replicated the effect found in the first experiment: There was outgroup homogeneity when Americans and Australians were judged alone (on average, selected traits were applied to 74% of Americans but to only 66% of Australians), but no difference in perceived homogeneity in the context of explicit intergroup comparison (here traits were applied to 76% of Americans and to 74% of Australians). Other interaction effects also provided support for both predictions relating to trait favorableness. The ingroup was seen as more homogeneous when it had to be described using all positive rather than all negative traits (traits were applied to 73% and 65% of Australians, respectively), and the outgroup was seen as more homogeneous than the ingroup when subjects could assign only negative traits (here traits were applied to 77% of Americans but to only 65% of Australians).

The effect for nonstereotypic traits obtained in Experiment 1 was also replicated here: These traits were applied to fewer Australians (58%) than Americans (66%), producing an ingroup homogeneity effect in intergroup conditions, as defined by Judd et al. (1991). The results also supported our valence-related analysis of the relative ingroup homogeneity observed in the first experiment, as subjects appeared to attribute nonstereotypic traits to the ingroup more strongly when the checklist contained only positive items, and to reject the applicability of stereotypic traits when the checklist was limited to negative items.

It seems very likely that these same normative-motivational concerns could contribute to the emergence of outgroup homogeneity effects in experimental situations where there are no differences in comparative context (i.e., where both ingroup and outgroup are judged at the same time; e.g., Park & Judd, 1990, Experiment 2). This is because in such studies both ingroup and outgroup homogeneity are typically judged on both positive and negative dimensions, and to our knowledge the dimensions are selected by the experimenters in all these experiments. Despite the fact that this procedure may appear to add symmetry and control to an experimental design (cf. Judd et al., 1991; Park et al., 1991), it may actually introduce asymmetry and systematic bias into the judgmental process, because ingroup social categories are made differentially *un*salient (leading to perceived ingroup heterogeneity) by asking subjects to define the ingroup in negative terms.

Ironically, further evidence for the importance of judgmental context in determining perceived group homogeneity is provided by a study designed to demonstrate the context-*in*dependent nature of the outgroup homogeneity effect. Bartsch and Judd (1993) sought to reinterpret ingroup homogeneity effects of the type reported by Simon (e.g., Simon & Brown, 1987) as effects for target group size. Subjects were male fraternity members and female sorority members.

On a range of dimensions, these subjects either (1) judged the homogeneity of a small or large ingroup (i.e., their own specific fraternity/sorority or all fraternities/sororities) *before* they judged the homogeneity of a small outgroup (i.e., a particular sorority/fraternity), or (2) judged the homogeneity of a small or large outgroup (i.e., a specific sorority/fraternity or all sororities/fraternities) *before* they judged the homogeneity of a small ingroup (i.e., their particular fraternity/sorority). In this manner the size of the second group was held constant, but its size relative to the first judged group and its status as ingroup or outgroup varied. The authors' objective was to see whether judgments of the relative homogeneity of the second group would be affected by both size and ingroup–outgroup status (specifically, reflecting enhanced homogeneity of ingroup minorities, as Simon would predict), or simply size (enhanced homogeneity of all small groups as Bartsch and Judd's reanalysis would suggest).

On all measures, it was found that the group judged second was perceived to be more homogeneous than the group judged first. However, a qualifying interaction indicated that this effect was very much stronger if the group judged first was an ingroup. Indeed, the outgroup was seen to be more homogeneous than the ingroup *only* when the ingroup was judged first. The authors interpret these results as evidence that "the two effects, namely outgroup homogeneity and the effects of intergroup comparison with a large versus a small group, are entirely separable and unrelated" (p. 482). Importantly, though, they draw this conclusion after "collapsing [results] across all size and order conditions" (p. 481). Yet we would argue that this conclusion is unjustified, as the interaction on which it is based may have arisen not from a tendency to see the ingroup as more heterogenous than the outgroup per se, but from the fact that when the ingroup was judged first it was judged in an intragroup rather than an intergroup context (Haslam & Oakes, 1995; Simon, 1993b). On the basis of this reanalysis, Haslam and Oakes (1995) suggest:

> Far from undermining Simon's argument that social identity salience is a critical determinant of perceived homogeneity, Bartsch and Judd's paper actually serves to reinforce such a conclusion. . . . Their data indicate not only that the outgroup homogeneity effect is context-specific and non-universal, but also that its emergence is totally dependent upon factors which dictate the relative meaningfulness of the perception of ingroup and outgroup in social categorical terms. (p. 474)

In terms of self-categorization theory, then, the process that can lead to equal levels of ingroup and outgroup homogeneity when ingroup and outgroup judgments are made in the same intergroup comparative context (as observed by Tajfel et al., 1964) can also lead to asymmetric levels of ingroup and outgroup homogeneity when those judgments are made in different comparative contexts. In this manner, both symmetry and asymmetry in ingroup–outgroup homogeneity judgments are seen as manifestations of exactly the same categorization process, rather than as orthogonal, independent effects. Accordingly, we would suggest that the results from studies that have traditionally been interpreted as evidence of stable differences in the representation of ingroup and outgroup (e.g., Linville et al., 1989; Park et al., 1991) can be reconceptualized as outcomes of a common process that leads to variable representation as a function of the contextual features of a given judgmental task.

Results from the experiments described above support this assertion that both symmetric and asymmetric patterns of group homogeneity can be produced and explained by a categorization process that responds sensitively to features of judgmental context. These studies point to two contextual features of standard experimental procedures that may contribute to the widely observed outgroup homogeneity effect: (1) the fact that outgroups are more often judged in an intergroup context (a factor that leads to greater comparative fit of outgroup categories), and (2) the fact that subjects are particularly unwilling to define the ingroup in terms of negative attributes (a factor that leads to reductions in the normative fit of ingroup categories).

Importantly, though, it is also the case that this same analysis leads us to predict an *in*group homogeneity effect under certain conditions. In particular, we would expect that this would emerge where the ingroup is judged in an intergroup context and on dimensions that are differentially ingroup-defining (i.e., where for motivational or other reasons, the normative fit of ingroup social categories is greater than that of outgroup categories). We would also expect that members of minorities may be more likely to display such an effect not only for motivational reasons (e.g., to increase self-esteem), but also because, all things being equal, they are more likely to define a given judgmental setting in intergroup terms, given that minorities should tend to make more intergroup comparisons (Haslam et al., 1992, p. 5). Clearly, these predictions are consistent with the body of evidence that has emerged from research in the tradition of social identity theory reviewed above (e.g., Kelly, 1989; Simon & Brown, 1987; Simon & Pettigrew, 1990; Simon, 1992).

Finally, a further very important and highly distinctive prediction of our approach is that increased familiarity with a group should not *necessarily* lead to its being perceived less homogeneously. As we have seen, the assumption that familiarity produces heterogeneous group representations has come to inform both theory (being central to both the exemplar and the dual-process models) and metatheory (as in Allport's "principle of least effort") to such an extent that it is now almost taken for granted. Yet our argument that perceived homogeneity reflects the appropriateness of social-categorical representation leads us to believe that when people interact with one another as members of a meaningful group, familiarity can actually *increase* perceived homogeneity.

Support for this assertion comes from a field study we conducted, which examined judgments of intragroup homogeneity among three groups of 10 people at four stages during an Outward Bound course lasting 26 days (Oakes, Haslam, Morrison, & Grace, 1995). The course involved the groups' working together in the Australian bush on collective tasks designed to develop their personal and teamwork skills. Contradicting Linville et al.'s (1986, pp. 196–197) argument that "greater category differentiation occurs with greater exposure to members of a group," and in contrast to the results of their longitudinal study with Yale students (Linville et al., 1986; 1989, Experiment 4), we found that over time individuals on this course came to regard their ingroup as significantly more homogeneous on dimensions that the group members themselves perceived to be group-defining (all p's < .001). Moreover, this pattern was confirmed on all standard measures of perceived homogeneity (P_d, rating variance, and rating range).

Although these findings are problematic for the models of variability judgment presented by Linville and by Judd and Park, they are fully consistent with self-categorization theory: They appear simply to reflect the fact that as our study progressed we were monitoring a process of group formation, which rendered homogeneous group-based representation more meaningful. On the other hand, in Linville et al.'s (1986, 1989) Yale study, it seems likely that over time the researchers were actually monitoring the *disintegration* of the class as a whole into subgroups and cliques, which led to the fragmentation of the students' shared social identity and hence to a reduction in perceived ingroup homogeneity. The results they obtained may also be attributable to the fact that the normative fit of categorization as a class group was reduced because the dimensions on which the class was rated were selected by the researchers, and some dimensions (e.g., average hours spent studying, scores in aptitude tests) may inadvertently have encouraged the subjects to make intragroup (interpersonal) comparisons. Again, then, the discrepancy between our findings and those of Linville and her colleagues supports our claim that perceived group homogeneity derives from and reflects the meaningfulness of a given social categorization (as determined, *inter alia,* by comparative and normative factors), rather than ingroup–outgroup status or the effects of familiarity per se.

GENERAL OVERVIEW AND CONCLUSIONS

In this chapter, we have attempted to show how self-categorization theory builds upon previous empirical research and the principles of social identity theory in order to provide an analysis of social categorization that incorporates the latter's motivational assumptions within a broader cognitive framework. As part of this analysis, the perception of group homogeneity is seen to arise not simply from motivational demands to counteract threats to self-esteem, but more generally to reflect the meaningfulness of group-based perception. Thus, in the most straightforward terms, we argue that both ingroups and outgroups are perceived as homogeneous when such perception is psychologically appropriate. More specifically, we have argued that perceived homogeneity reflects, among other things, the fit of a given social categorization as determined by both comparative and normative-motivational factors.

One important conclusion that we draw from this analysis is that, as Simon (1992) has shown in his treatment of relative ingroup homogeneity, outgroup homogeneity effects are not inevitable products of tendencies to represent social categories in particular ways. Rather we believe that the representation of all social categories is inherently variable; moreover, we contend that the nature of this variation serves to tie the act of categorization firmly to changes in social-psychological reality. On this basis, we have argued that comparative and normative-motivational factors may lead to outgroups being perceived as more homogeneous than ingroups, to a reversal of this pattern, or indeed to both groups being perceived as equally homogeneous. As we have seen, the last of these patterns was observed in our own studies (Haslam et al., 1995), where both groups were judged in the same intergroup comparative context and on dimensions with equally high normative fit. Furthermore, we would argue that these findings are especially significant, as they relate closely to the everyday realities of stereotyping: Ingroups are generally defined more favorably than outgroups (Allport, 1954; Tajfel, 1981), rather than both being defined with respect to dimensions of carefully balanced favorableness (cf. Park & Judd, 1990).

Importantly, though, we see *all* these various outcomes as equally valid reflections of perceivers' social-psychological reality. In contrast to the received view that the perception of homogeneity is a distortion visited largely on outgroups, we see it instead as a means of reflecting the distinct reality that accrues to *all* individuals as a function of their group memberships. As we have written elsewhere:

> In contrast to the implicit assumption of a qualitative distinction between ingroup and outgroup perceptions which underlies the almost unquestioning acceptance of outgroup homogeneity as a "principle" of person perception, our view is that *all* stereotypical homogeneity simply reflects perception operating at a distinct, collective level, and that this is appropriate for representing ingroup as well as outgroup members. Indeed, it is difficult to see how ingroups could actually exist as meaningful bases for social identification if their members did not appreciate that they *shared* beliefs, attitudes, expectations and traits—in other words, unless they were aware that the ingroup was homogeneous on relevant dimensions, in appropriate contexts. (Oakes, Haslam, & Turner, 1994, p. 173; emphasis in original)

In arguing against the claim that only individuated perception can be accurate (cf. Judd et al., 1991), we emphasize the need to acknowledge the *distinct* cognitive implications of group life and its political and ideological motivations. As a part of this analysis, we also argue against the view that motivational considerations can simply be incorporated post hoc into purely cognitive theories of perceived homogeneity. Rather than seeking to understand how social phenomena (such as prejudice) arise from fixed cognitive representations, we consider it more fruitful to show how these "pictures in our heads" are implicitly variable, and, moreover, how they vary in a manner that allows for and responds to meaningful intergroup behavior. In this sense we see the cognitive processes implicated in perceived homogeneity not as constricting social perception, but as appropriately facilitating collective action. Viewed in this light, perceived homogeneity itself is not an obstacle to valid perception, but a necessary feature of defining oneself and others that allows people to express and apprehend different social perspectives and the different political and ideological motivations associated with them.

Any defence of stereotyping as "accurate" must take into account this political dimension of stereotype validity. As participants in the political process, we are fully entitled to disagree with the views and values of those whose perspective we do not share, and hence to label their generalized representations as false (just as many white South Africans have felt it important to reject and suppress the ingroup and outgroup stereotypes that are embraced by advocates of Black Consciousness; see Biko, 1978/1988; Oakes, Haslam, & Turner, 1994, Ch. 8). However, when we reject others' stereotypes as wrong in this way, we should endeavor to recognize that their views are not manifestations of social-psychological shortcomings (e.g., a failure to make our acquaintance or a lack of concern for accuracy), but are instruments of social conflict.

In the final analysis, then, we argue that representations of groups in stereotypic terms are part of the political process through which different groups assert and communicate their competing world views. It is primarily for this reason that we propose a theory of social stereotyping that seeks to show how the cognitive aspects of this process interact with features of group life. And, ultimately, it is as reflections of this level of social-psychological reality that we affirm the accuracy, validity, and utility of perceived group homogeneity—regardless of its source and target.

Acknowledgment

This research was funded by a grant from the Australian Research Council.

Note

1. In this chapter we will refer to support for this hypothesis as "relative outgroup homogeneity" or an "outgroup homogeneity effect." The term "outgroup homogeneity" refers simply to perceived outgroup variability unrelated to perceptions of an ingroup. On a similar basis, we also differentiate between "relative ingroup homogeneity" or an "ingroup homogeneity effect" and "ingroup homogeneity."

References

Adorno, T. W., Frenkel-Brunswik, E., Levinson, D. J., & Sanford, R. N. (1950). *The authoritarian personality.* New York: Harper.
Allport, G. W. (1954). *The nature of prejudice.* Cambridge, MA: Addison-Wesley.
Asch, S. E. (1952). *Social psychology.* New York: Oxford University Press.
Ashmore, R. D., & Del Boca, F. K. (1981). Conceptual approaches to stereotypes and stereotyping. In D. L. Hamilton (Ed.), *Cognitive processes in stereotyping and intergroup behavior* (pp. 1–35). Hillsdale, NJ: Erlbaum.

Bartsch, R. A., & Judd, C. M. (1993). Majority-minority status and perceived ingroup variability revisited. *European Journal of Social Psychology, 23,* 471–485.

Biko, B. S. (1988). *I write what I like.* London: Penguin. (Original work published 1978)

Brewer, M. B. (1979). Ingroup bias in the minimal intergroup situation: A cognitive–motivational analysis. *Psychological Bulletin, 86,* 307–324.

Brewer, M. B. (1988). A dual process model of impression formation. In T. K. Srull & R. S. Wyer (Eds.), *Advances in social cognition* (Vol. 1, pp. 1–36). Hillsdale, NJ: Erlbaum.

Brewer, M. B., & Lui, L. (1984). Categorization of the elderly by the elderly: Effects of perceiver's category membership. *Personality and Social Psychology Bulletin, 10,* 585–595.

Brown, R. J., & Turner, J. C. (1981). Interpersonal and intergroup behaviour. In J. C. Turner & H. Giles (Eds.), *Intergroup behaviour* (pp. 33–65). Oxford: Blackwell.

Bruner, J. S. (1957). On perceptual readiness. *Psychological Review, 64,* 123–152.

Campbell, D. T. (1958). Common fate, similarity, and other indices of the status of aggregates of persons as social entities. *Behavioral Science, 3,* 14–25.

Doise, W., Csepeli, G., Dann, H. D., Gouge, C., Larsen, K., & Ostell, A. (1972). An experimental investigation into the formation of intergroup representations. *European Journal of Social Psychology, 2,* 202–204.

Doise, W., Deschamps, J. P., & Meyer, G. (1978). The accentuation of intra-category similarities. In H. Tajfel (Ed.), *Differentiation between social groups* (pp. 159–170). London: Academic Press.

Dollard, J., Doob, L. W., Miller, N. E., Mowrer, O. H., & Sears, R. R. (1939). *Frustration and aggression.* New Haven, CT: Yale University Press.

Doosje, B., Spears, R., & Koomen, W. (1992). *The influence of the comparative context on group judgments.* Unpublished manuscript, Universiteit van Amsterdam.

Eiser, J. R. (1973). Judgment of attitude statements as a function of judges' attitudes and the judgmental dimension. *British Journal of Social and Clinical Psychology, 12,* 231–240.

Eiser, J. R., & Stroebe, W. (1972). *Categorization and social judgment* (European Monograph in Social Psychology No. 3). London: Academic Press.

Eiser, J. R., & van der Pligt, J. (1984). Attitudes in a social context. In H. Tajfel (Ed.), *The social dimension* (Vol. 2, pp. 363–378). Cambridge, England: Cambridge University Press.

Fiske, S. T., & Neuberg, S. L. (1990). A continuum of impression formation, from category-based to individuating processes: Influences of information and motivation on attention and interpretation. In M. P. Zanna (Ed.), *Advances in experimental social psychology* (Vol. 23, pp. 1–73). New York: Academic Press.

Gaertner, S. L., Mann, J., Murrell, A., & Dovidio, J. F. (1989). Reducing intergroup bias: The benefits of recategorization. *Journal of Personality and Social Psychology, 57,* 239–249.

Gerard, H. B., & Hoyt, M. F. (1974). Distinctiveness of social categorization and attitude toward ingroup members. *Journal of Personality and Social Psychology, 29,* 836–834.

Goethals, G. R., Allison, S. J., & Frost, M. (1979). Perceptions of the magnitude and diversity of social support. *Journal of Experimental Social Psychology, 15,* 570–581

Haslam, S. A., & Oakes, P. J. (1995). How context-independent is the outgroup homogeneity effect? A response to Bartsch and Judd. *European Journal of Social Psychology, 25,* 469–475.

Haslam, S. A., Oakes, P. J., Turner, J. C., & McGarty, C. (1995). Social categorization and group homogeneity: Changes in the perceived applicability of stereotype content as a function of comparative context and trait favourableness. *British Journal of Social Psychology, 34,* 139–160.

Haslam, S. A., & Turner, J. C. (1992). Context-dependent variation in social stereotyping: 2. The relationship between frame of reference, self-categorization and accentuation. *European Journal of Social Psychology, 22,* 251–278

Haslam, S. A., & Turner, J. C. (1995). Context-dependent variation in social stereotyping: 3. Extremism as a self-categorical basis for polarized judgment. *European Journal of Social Psychology, 25,* 341–371.

Haslam, S. A., Turner, J. C., Oakes, P. J., McGarty, C., & Hayes, B. K. (1992). Context-dependent variation in social stereotyping: 1. The effects of intergroup relations as mediated by social change and frame of reference. *European Journal of Social Psychology, 22,* 3–20.

Hogg, M. A., & Abrams, D. (1988). *Social identifications: A social psychology of intergroup relations and group processes.* London: Routledge.

Hogg, M. A., & Turner, J. C. (1987). Intergroup behaviour, self-stereotyping and the salience of social categories. *British Journal of Social Psychology, 26,* 325–340.

Hovland, C. I., & Sherif, M. (1952). Judgmental phenomena and scales of attitude measurement: Item displacement in Thurstone scales. *Journal of Abnormal and Social Psychology, 47,* 822–832.

Jones, E. E., Wood, G. C., & Quattrone, G. A. (1981). Perceived variability of personal characteristics of ingroups and outgroups: The role of knowledge and evaluation. *Personality and Social Psychology Bulletin, 7,* 523–528.

Judd, C. M., & Park, B. (1988). Out-group homogeneity: Judgments of variability at the individual and group levels. *Journal of Personality and Social Psychology, 54,* 778–788.

Judd, C. M., Ryan, C. S., & Park, B. (1991). Accuracy in the judgment of in-group and out-group variability. *Journal of Personality and Social Psychology, 61,* 366–379.

Katz, D., & Braly, K. (1933). Racial stereotypes of one hundred college students. *Journal of Abnormal and Social Psychology, 28,* 280–290.

Kelly, C. (1989). Political identity and perceived intragroup homogeneity. *British Journal of Social Psychology, 28,* 239–250.

Linville, P. W. (1982). The complexity–extremity effect and age-based stereotyping. *Journal of Personality and Social Psychology, 42,* 193–211.

Linville, P. W., Fischer, G. W., & Salovey, P. (1989). Perceived distributions of the characteristics of in-group members: Empirical evidence and a computer simulation. *Journal of Personality and Social Psychology, 57,* 165–188.

Linville, P. W., & Jones, E. E. (1980). Polarized appraisals of outgroup members. *Journal of Personality and Social Psychology, 38,* 689–703.

Linville, P. W., Salovey, P., & Fischer, G. W. (1986). Stereotyping and perceived distributions of social characteristics: An application to ingroup–outgroup perception. In J. F. Dovidio & S. L. Gaertner (Eds.), *Prejudice, discrimination and racism* (pp. 165–208). Orlando, FL: Academic Press.

Lippman, W. (1922). *Public opinion.* New York: Harcourt, Brace.

Messick, D. M., & Mackie, D. M. (1989). Intergroup relations. *Annual Review of Psychology, 40,* 45–81.

Mullen, B., & Hu, L. (1989). Perceptions of ingroup and outgroup variability: A meta-analytic integration. *Basic and Applied Social Psychology, 10,* 233–252.

Oakes, P. J. (1987). The salience of social categories. In J. C. Turner, M. A. Hogg, P. J. Oakes, S. D. Reicher, & M. S. Wetherell (Eds.), *Rediscovering the social group: A self-categorization theory* (pp. 117–141). Oxford: Blackwell.

Oakes, P. J., Haslam, S. A., Morrison, B., & Grace, D. (1995). Becoming an ingroup: Re-examining the impact of familiarity on perceptions of group homogeneity. *Social Psychology Quarterly, 58,* 52–61.

Oakes, P. J., Haslam, S. A., & Turner, J. C. (1994). *Stereotyping and social reality.* Oxford: Blackwell.

Oakes, P. J., & Turner, J. C. (1986). Authors' rejoinder to Jahoda and Tetlock. *British Journal of Social Psychology, 25,* 257–258.

Oakes, P. J., & Turner, J. C. (1990). Is limited information processing capacity the cause of social stereotyping? In W. Stroebe, & M. Hewstone (Eds.), *European review of social psychology* (Vol. 1, pp. 111–135). Chichester, England: Wiley.

Oakes, P. J., Turner, J. C., & Haslam, S. A. (1991). Perceiving people as group members: The role of fit in the salience of social categorizations. *British Journal of Social Psychology, 30,* 125–144.

Park, B., & Judd, C. M. (1990). Measures and models of perceived group variability. *Journal of Personality and Social Psychology, 59,* 173–191.

Park, B., Judd, C. M., & Ryan, C. S. (1991). Social categorization and the representation of variability information. In W. Stroebe & M. Hewstone (Eds.), *European review of social psychology* (Vol. 2, pp. 211–245). Chichester, England: Wiley.

Park, B., & Rothbart, M. (1982). Perception of outgroup homogeneity and levels of social categorization: Memory for the subordinate attributes of in-group and out-group members. *Journal of Personality and Social Psychology, 42,* 1051-1068.

Park, B., Ryan, C. S., & Judd, C. M. (1992). Role of meaningful subgroups in explaining differences in perceived variability for ingroups and outgroups. *Journal of Personality and Social Psychology, 63,* 553-567.

Pettigrew, T. F., Allport, G. W., & Barnett, E. O. (1958). Binocular resolution and perception of race in South Africa. *British Journal of Psychology, 49,* 265-278.

Pityana, N. B. (1988). Introduction: Bantu Stephen Biko in perspective. In B. S. Biko, *I write what I like* (pp. 1-15). London: Penguin.

Quattrone, G. A., & Jones, E. E. (1980). The perception of variability within ingroups and outgroups: Implications for the law of small numbers. *Journal of Personality and Social Psychology, 38,* 141-152.

Rosch, E. (1978). Principles of categorization. In E. Rosch, & B. B. Lloyd (Eds.), *Cognition and Categorization* (pp. 27-48). Hillsdale, NJ: Erlbaum.

Rothbart, M., Dawes, R., & Park, B. (1984). Stereotyping and sampling biases in intergroup perception. In J. R. Eiser (Ed.), *Attitudinal judgment* (pp. 109-134). New York: Springer-Verlag.

Sachdev, I., & Bourhis, R. Y. (1984). Minimal minorities and majorities. *European Journal of Social Psychology, 14,* 35-52.

Secord, P. F., Bevan, W., & Katz, B. (1956). The Negro stereotype and perceptual accentuation. *Journal of Abnormal and Social Psychology, 53,* 78-83.

Sherif, M., & Hovland, C. I. (1953). Judgmental phenomena and scales of attitude measurement: Placement of items with individual choice of number of categories. *Journal of Abnormal and Social Psychology, 48,* 135-141.

Sherif, M., & Hovland, C. I. (1961). *Social judgment: Assimilation and contrast effects in communication and attitude change.* New Haven, CT: Yale University Press.

Simon, B. (1992). The perception of ingroup and outgroup homogeneity: Reintroducing the social context. In W. Stroebe & M. Hewstone (Eds.), *European review of social psychology* (Vol. 3, pp. 1-30). Chichester, England: Wiley.

Simon, B. (1993a). On the asymmetry in the cognitive construal of ingroup and outgroup: A model of egocentric social categorization. *European Journal of Social Psychology, 23,* 131-147.

Simon, B. (1993b). *Majority-minority status and perceived group variability revisited.* Manuscript submitted for publication.

Simon, B., & Brown, R. J. (1987). Perceived intragroup homogeneity in minority-majority contexts. *Journal of Personality and Social Psychology, 53,* 703-711.

Simon, B., & Hamilton, D. L. (1994). Self stereotyping and social context: The effects of relative size and ingroup status. *Journal of Personality and Social Psychology, 66,* 699-711.

Simon, B., & Pettigrew, T. F. (1990). Social identity and perceived group homogeneity: Evidence for the ingroup homogeneity effect. *European Journal of Social Psychology, 20,* 269-286.

Stroebe, W., & Insko, C. A. (1989). Stereotype, prejudice, and discrimination: Changing conceptions in theory and research. In D. Bar-Tal, C. F. Graumann, A. W. Kruglanski, & W. Stroebe (Eds.), *Stereotyping and prejudice: Changing conceptions* (pp. 3-34). New York: Springer-Verlag.

Tajfel, H. (1957). Value and the perceptual judgment of magnitude. *Psychological Review, 64,* 192-204.

Tajfel, H. (1969). Cognitive aspects of prejudice. *Journal of Social Issues, 25,* 79-97.

Tajfel, H. (1972). La categorization sociale. In S. Moscovici (Ed.), *Introduction à la psychologie sociale* (Vol. 1). Paris: Larousse.

Tajfel, H. (1978). The achievement of group differentiation. In H. Tajfel (Ed.), *Differentiation between social groups: Studies in the social psychology of intergroup relations.* London: Academic Press.

Tajfel, H. (1981). Social stereotypes and social groups. In J. C. Turner & H. Giles (Eds.), *Intergroup behaviour* (pp. 144-167). Oxford: Blackwell.

Tajfel, H., Flament, C., Billig, M. G., & Bundy, R. F. (1971). Social categorization and intergroup behavior. *European Journal of Social Psychology, 1,* 149-177.

Tajfel, H., Sheikh, A. A., & Gardner, R. C. (1964). Content of stereotypes and the inference of similarity between members of stereotyped groups. *Acta Psychologica, 22,* 191-201.

Tajfel, H., & Turner, J. C. (1979). An integrative theory of intergroup conflict. In W. G. Austin, & S. Worschel (Eds.), *The social psychology of intergroup relations* (pp. 33-47). Monterey, CA: Brooks/Cole.

Tajfel, H., & Turner, J. C. (1986). The social identity theory of intergroup behavior. In S. Worschel & W. G. Austin (Eds.), *Psychology of intergroup relations* (2nd ed., pp. 7-24). Chicago: Nelson-Hall.

Tajfel, H., & Wilkes, A. L. (1963a). Classification and quantitative judgment. *British Journal of Psychology, 54,* 101-114.

Tajfel, H., & Wilkes, A. L. (1963b). Salience of attributes and commitment to extreme judgments in the perception of people. *British Journal of Social and Clinical Psychology, 2,* 40-49.

Triandis, H. C. (1979). Commentary. In W. G. Austin, & S. Worschel (Eds.), *The social psychology of intergroup relations* (pp. 319-334). Monterey, CA: Brooks/Cole.

Turner, J. C. (1975). Social comparison and social identity: Some prospects for intergroup behavior. *European Journal of Social Psychology, 5,* 149-178.

Turner, J. C. (1981). The experimental social psychology of intergroup behaviour. In J. C. Turner & H. Giles (Eds.), *Intergroup behaviour* (pp. 66-101). Oxford: Blackwell.

Turner, J. C. (1982). Towards a cognitive redefinition of the social group. In H. Tajfel (Ed.), *Social identity and intergroup relations* (pp. 15-40). Cambridge, England: Cambridge University Press.

Turner, J. C. (1985). Social categorization and the self-concept: A social cognitive theory of group behavior. In E. J. Lawler (Ed.), *Advances in group processes* (Vol. 2, pp. 77-122). Greenwich, CT: JAI Press.

Turner, J. C. (1987). A self-categorization theory. In J. C. Turner, M. A. Hogg, P. J. Oakes, S. D. Reicher, & M. S. Wetherell, *Rediscovering the social group: A self-categorization theory* (pp. 42-67). Oxford: Blackwell.

Turner, J. C., Hogg, M. A., Oakes, P. J., Reicher, S. D., & Wetherell, M. S. (1987). *Rediscovering the social group: A self-categorization theory.* Oxford: Blackwell.

Turner, J. C., & Oakes, P. J. (1986). The significance of the social identity concept for social psychology with reference to individualism, interactionism, and social influence. *British Journal of Social Psychology, 25,* 237-252.

Turner, J. C., Oakes, P. J., Haslam, S. A., & McGarty, C. A. (1994). Self and collective: Cognition and social context. *Personality and Social Psychology Bulletin, 20,* 454-463.

Wilder, D. A. (1981). Perceiving persons as a group: Categorization and intergroup relations. In D. L. Hamilton (Ed.), *Cognitive processes in stereotyping and intergroup behavior* (pp. 213-257). Hillsdale, NJ: Erlbaum.

Wilder, D. A. (1984). Predictions of belief homogeneity and similarity following social categorization. *British Journal of Social Psychology, 23,* 323-333.

Wilder, D. A., & Thompson, J. E. (1988). Assimilation and contrast effects in the judgments of groups. *Journal of Personality and Social Psychology, 54,* 62-73.

Williams, R. M., Jr. (1947). The reduction of intergroup tensions: A survey of research on problems of ethnic, racial, and religious group relations. *Social Science Research Council Bulletin, 57* (whole issue).

PART II

Evaluation of Others: Perceiving through Role-Colored Lenses

CHAPTER 7

Social Motives and Expectancy-Tinged Social Interactions

STEVEN L. NEUBERG
Arizona State University

Expectancies permeate our interpersonal lives. We hold preconceptions about others' personality characteristics, physical features, abilities, preferences, and behaviors, and we use these expectancies to simplify our social encounters; they help us interpret others' ambiguous actions and choose appropriate actions of our own. Indeed, given their usefulness, we rarely if ever interact with others without the benefit of some expectancy or another.

Many expectancies are "accurate," in that they represent others well. For example, after many encounters with a friend, we may indeed come to know this friend well enough to be able to predict his or her actions with reasonable precision. Many expectancies, however, are considerably less accurate. This should come as no surprise, given their frequent sources: We derive expectancies from stereotypes and prejudices, from third-party hearsay, and from observations of others' behaviors that have been (unbeknownst to us) constrained in some manner to be atypical. Unfortunately, even inaccurate expectancies can greatly transform the nature of social interaction and impression formation. "Self-fulfilling prophecies," in which we cause others to behave in ways that objectively confirm our inaccurate expectancies, characterize some social encounters. More frequently, inaccurate expectancies lead to cognitive biases in our assessments of others' behaviors. As a consequence of such behavioral and cognitive biases, we may conclude inappropriately that the people we interact with are indeed as we had expected them to be.

When inaccurate expectancies are positive, and the social interactions unimportant, the resulting biased impressions may be of relatively little consequence. When our inaccurate expectancies are negative, however, as in the case of those generated from misguided and unflattering stereotypes, expectancy-based impressions can be quite damaging—leading to reductions in opportunity for the stigmatized targets, and even reinforcing the culprit stereotypes and prejudices.

Of course, our impressions of others are not always heavily biased by inaccurate expectancies; we clearly do not always conclude encounters with others with our expectancies confirmed and our preconceptions intact. In fact, some reviews argue that expectancy biases may occur only infrequently, and even then may generally be of little magnitude (e.g., Brophy, 1983; Brophy & Good, 1974; Cooper, 1979; Jussim, 1991; West & Anderson, 1976; but see Rosenthal & Rubin, 1978).

The purpose of the present chapter is to propose a theoretical framework that better enables us to understand and predict when preinteraction expectancies lead to expectancy-consistent impressions and when they do not. My primary argument is that an understanding of expectancy influences will be necessarily incomplete until we consider such processes within the *social-motivational context*. My proposal is straightforward: Because certain classes of everyday social motivations regulate the behavioral and cognitive underpinnings of the expectancy confirmation process, these motives should moderate the influence that preinteraction expectancies have on postinteraction impressions.

I begin by reviewing briefly the research literature on expectancy confirmation and the processes leading to it. I do not intend this review to be exhaustive, but instead illustrative and representative. In particular, I focus on the types of expectancy-tinged dyadic social encounters that people experience on an everyday basis. For this reason, the social-psychological literature provides the bulk of the presented research; areas in which domain-specific processes play an additional role (e.g., education and psychotherapy) receive less attention.

Given the relative lack of explicitly applicable empirical work on motivational influences on expectancy confirmation, data-driven conceptualizations run the risks of being both incomplete and misleading. I thus continue my presentation by arguing, on *theoretical* grounds, for a moderating role of particular types of social goals. The existing empirical evidence addressing the model's basic premises is then examined, after which I discuss several conceptual and practical implications of the proposed framework.

Before beginning, I should briefly note that I am concerned here with the *processes* through which expectancies may or may not influence postinteraction impressions. I am not concerned with the issue of whether or not the impressions formed are ultimately "accurate" (see Jussim, 1991). The nature of expectancy-tinged interpersonal and intrapersonal processes is similar, regardless of whether their outcomes would be considered accurate or not. That is, both accurate and inaccurate expectancies elicit similar processes; the difference is that the resulting impressions are likely to be accurate when the expectancies are themselves accurate, and inaccurate when the expectancies are themselves inaccurate.

Having said this, I should note that I often refer to the "biasing" influences of expectancies and expectancy-induced processes; for ease of exposition, the use of the term implies merely that an expectancy has had an influence on subsequent processes or outcomes. For example, when I write of "biased perceiver impressions," I merely mean that the impressions have been influenced toward being consistent with that perceiver's initial expectancies. Whether or not that biased impression is itself accurate is determined by the accuracy of the initial expectancy.

THE EXPECTANCY CONFIRMATION PROCESS

To possess an expectancy is to hold a belief that a particular person will be in a certain state—that is, exhibit a certain trait, behave a particular way, and so forth—at some point in the future. Much research reveals that perceivers' preinteraction expectancies can strongly influence their impressions of others, such that perceivers may form expectancy-consistent impressions even when the expectancies are inaccurate (for reviews, see Blanck, 1993; Brophy, 1983; Darley & Fazio, 1980; Fiske & Taylor, 1991; Hamilton, Sherman, & Ruvulo, 1990; Higgins & Bargh, 1987; Miller & Turnbull, 1986).[1]

One potential source of expectancy bias in postinteraction impressions springs from the nature of perceiver behaviors: Perceivers may act in ways that actually cause targets to behaviorally confirm inaccurate expectancies. In one study, for instance, experimenters manipulated men's expectancies about the physical attractiveness of women with whom they were about to have a telephone conversation (Snyder, Tanke, & Berscheid, 1977). The women expected to be highly attractive actually became more sociable and likeable (characteristics stereotypically associated with attractiveness), in this way providing "objective" evidence supporting the men's expectancies. This pattern, in which targets behaviorally confirm inaccurate perceiver expectancies, has been labeled the "self-fulfilling prophecy" (Merton, 1948; for reviews, see Blanck, 1993; Brophy, 1983; Cooper & Good, 1983; Darley & Fazio, 1980; Jones, 1986; Jussim, 1986; Miller & Turnbull, 1986; Rosenthal, 1974; Snyder, 1984). It can occur with many types of expectancies, and in domains as diverse as interview settings (e.g., Christensen & Rosenthal, 1982; Word, Zanna, & Cooper, 1974; see Dipboye, 1982), bargaining situations (e.g., Kelley & Stahelski, 1970; Snyder & Swann, 1978a), educational settings (e.g., Meichenbaum, Bowers, & Ross, 1969; Rosenthal & Jacobson, 1968), therapy interviews (e.g., Sibicky & Dovidio, 1986; Vrugt, 1990), mother–infant interactions (e.g., Stern & Hildebrandt, 1986), and casual "getting-acquainted" encounters (e.g., Ickes, Patterson, Rajecki, & Tanford, 1982).

A second source of expectancy bias in perceiver impressions is rooted in the ways that perceivers cognitively assess others' behavior. For example, in studies where target information is experimentally held constant, perceivers nonetheless often form impressions that are consistent with their inaccurate expectancies, especially when the target information is ambiguous and open to multiple interpretations (for reviews, see Fiske & Neuberg, 1990; Fiske & Taylor, 1991; Hamilton et al., 1990; Higgins & Bargh, 1987; Nisbett & Ross, 1980). For example, research on stereotyping reveals that a person's behavior is often interpreted within the context of his or her apparent group membership, and typically in ways that serve to confirm the perceiver's initial stereotype-based expectancy (e.g., Darley & Gross, 1983; Langer & Abelson, 1974; Taylor, Fiske, Etcoff, & Ruderman, 1978; for reviews see Brigham, 1971; Farina, 1982; Ruble & Ruble, 1982; Tavris & Offir, 1977). So, whereas a particular behavior may be viewed as being appropriately assertive when coming from a white child, the same behavior may be perceived as being overly aggressive when displayed by a black child (Duncan, 1976; Sagar & Schofield, 1980). In fact, under some circumstances, targets may be evaluated in an expectancy-consistent manner even when their behavior is objectively *in*consistent with perceivers' expectancies (e.g., Farina & Ring, 1965; Ickes et al., 1982; Major, Cozzarelli, Testa, & McFarlin, 1988; Swann & Snyder, 1980).

Thus, perceivers may confirm their inaccurate expectancies in two primary ways: (1) by creating self-fulfilling prophecies, in which target behavior becomes consistent with these expectancies; and (2) by exhibiting a cognitive bias, through which they inappropriately view target behavior as being expectancy-consistent.

Mechanisms Underlying Expectancy Confirmation

What enables these confirmatory processes? A review of the literature suggests several such mechanisms, four of which I address here: biased perceiver information-gathering behavior; expectancy-revealing perceiver expressive behavior; a target's decision to accommodate the behavioral script initiated by these perceiver behaviors; and biased perceiver attentional and interpretational strategies.[2]

Biased Perceiver Information-Gathering Behaviors

First, the manner in which perceivers behaviorally gather information about targets can mediate the link between perceiver expectancies and target behavior. For example, white interviewers may conduct shorter interviews with black applicants than with white applicants (Word et al., 1974). Similarly, teachers may ask more questions of students for whom they hold positive as opposed to negative expectancies (Harris & Rosenthal, 1985). Moreover, perceivers with expectancies may ask biased questions of targets that either "lead" them to provide expectancy-confirming information or do not enable them to provide expectancy-disconfirming information easily (Snyder & Gangestad, 1981; Snyder & Swann, 1978b; Snyder, Campbell, & Preston, 1982; Swann & Ely, 1984; but see Bassok & Trope, 1984; Skov & Sherman, 1986; Trope, Bassok, & Alon, 1984). It is thus clear that expectancies can influence perceiver information-gathering behaviors. Because such behaviors often steer the direction of a social interaction, and because it is often socially difficult for the recipient of such behaviors to challenge this direction once the interaction has begun (see Grice, 1975; Jones, 1986; I discuss this further below), it is not surprising that biased information-gathering behaviors can play such an important mediating role in the self-fulfilling prophecy process.

Expectancy-Revealing Perceiver Expressive Behaviors

The extent to which a perceiver's expressive behaviors reveal his or her expectancies can also mediate the link between perceiver expectancies and target behavior. For example, when perceivers hold negative expectancies for targets, their expressive behaviors may be characterized by greater interpersonal distance (Ickes et al., 1982; Word et al., 1974), fewer expressions of positive affect (Ickes et al., 1982), less warmth and general sociability (Babad, Inbar, & Rosenthal, 1982; Harris & Rosenthal, 1985; Snyder et al., 1977), more speech errors (Word et al., 1974), and so on. Given the often reciprocal nature of interpersonal behavior (Goffman, 1959), and the likelihood that targets will interpret "cold" perceiver behaviors as reflecting a perceiver's personal dislike or lack of interest, such behaviors may induce targets to respond in kind, thus fulfilling the perceiver's initial negative expectancies. Consistent with this, targets who are dispositionally better able to decode others' nonverbal communications are more likely to behaviorally confirm perceiver expectancies (Cooper & Hazelrigg, 1988). It is clear, then, that a perceiver's expressive behaviors may also mediate the self-fulfilling prophecy process, by revealing to the target the perceiver's expectancy-colored feelings toward him or her.

Target's Decision to Accommodate Perceiver's Behavioral Script

Self-fulfilling prophecies are likely to occur only if the target decides to accommodate the behavioral "script" initiated by the perceiver (see Jones, 1986). In some sense, one might view behavioral confirmation as a deference behavior, with the target deferring to the behavioral assumptions and constraints of the perceiver. Target behavioral confirmation thus occurs when the target decides to accommodate the expectancy-tinged behavioral chain introduced by the perceiver, by reciprocating the perceiver's expressive behaviors (e.g., by responding to a perceiver's coldness with coldness of his or her own) or by accepting the constraints of the perceiver's information-gathering behavior (e.g., by discussing only one's previous employment failures when specifically asked about these during a job interview). In contrast, behavioral *dis*confirmation occurs when the target decides to alter the perceiver's expectancy-tinged script, by responding "antagonistically" to the perceiver's expressive behaviors (e.g., by reacting to a perceiver's coldness with warmth and friendliness) or by challenging the constraints of a perceiver's information-gathering behaviors (e.g., by quickly moving beyond an interviewer's negative questions to discuss one's successes instead).

Note that when I speak of the target's "decision" here, I do not imply that the decision to defer is necessarily considered and strategic, although it may be at times (I discuss this below). Instead, such a decision may be founded merely on the well-socialized habit of trying to avoid an uncomfortable social scene. Indeed, the deference decision may even be made "automatically," as a result of having been made similarly many times previously (see Bargh, 1990). I also do not imply that such a decision is a simple, unitary one: When made consciously, the deference decision may require a great deal of reasonably complex, attributional thought (see Darley & Fazio, 1980). However, because I am primarily concerned with the *outcome* of this reasoning process (i.e., with the decision to defer per se), I do not explore here in any detail the underpinnings of this decision.

To my knowledge, no empirical studies have directly addressed the mediating properties of the target's deference decision for the self-fulfilling prophecy process. Nonetheless, research addressing the ability of certain other target variables to moderate the self-fulfilling prophecy provides indirect evidence for the importance of these target decisions, and I review these studies later in the chapter.

Biased Perceiver Attentional and Interpretational Strategies

Finally, recent research suggests that expectancy- or stereotype-based cognitive impression biases may be mediated by biases in perceiver attentional and interpretational strategies (e.g., Erber & Fiske, 1984; Fiske, Neuberg, Beattie, & Milberg, 1987; Kruglanski & Freund, 1983; Neuberg & Fiske, 1987; Omoto & Borgida, 1988; see Fiske & Taylor, 1991, for a more general review). In particular, people form expectancy-consistent impressions when they focus relatively few attentional resources on a target's individuating characteristics and interpret ambiguous characteristics as being expectancy-consistent; in contrast, people form unbiased impressions when perceivers increase their attention to a target's individuating characteristics and interpret these characteristics in a manner relatively unbiased by their expectancies (Fiske & Neuberg, 1990). Thus, the biased nature of both attentional and interpretive processes may also mediate the link between perceiver expectancies and ultimate impressions.

Summary

To this point, we can characterize the expectancy-confirming social interaction as follows: A perceiver enters into an interaction with a target about whom the perceiver possesses some sort of expectancy. As a result, the perceiver performs expectancy-biased information-gathering behaviors and/or exhibits expectancy-revealing expressive behaviors. The target decides to accommodate the interactional script implied by these perceiver behaviors, thus behaviorally confirming the perceiver's initial expectancies and enabling the perceiver to form an expectancy-consistent impression. Even if, for some reason, the target fails to behaviorally confirm the perceiver's expectancy, the perceiver's cognitive assessment of the target's behaviors—mediated by biased attention to and interpretation of these behaviors—will lead the perceiver to form an impression consistent with the initial expectancy.

Just because expectancies *can* have such influences, however, does not mean that they always do. Indeed, the data from many studies indicate that perceivers do not always act in ways that cause others to behaviorally confirm their inaccurate expectancies; nor do perceivers always exhibit clear cognitive confirmation biases (e.g., Andersen & Bem, 1981; Babad et al., 1982; Darley, Fleming, Hilton, & Swann, 1988; Hilton & Darley, 1985; Neuberg, 1989; Neuberg & Fiske, 1987; Neuberg, Judice, Virdin, & Carrillo, 1993; Swann & Ely, 1984; for reviews, see Brophy, 1983; Fiske & Neuberg, 1990; Higgins & Bargh, 1987; Hilton & Darley, 1991; Hilton, Darley, & Fleming, 1989; Jussim, 1986, 1991; Miller & Turnbull, 1986; Snyder, 1992). How, then, do we reconcile the apparently incompatible findings?

The purpose of the remainder of this chapter is to explicate the role of one set of potential moderating influences on expectancy confirmation—the social motivations of the interaction participants. In essence, I argue that knowing the motivational context of any expectancy-tinged social encounter enables us to predict with much greater precision the nature (if any) of expectancy influences. This chapter thus expands on several recent theoretical models in which the importance of motivational constructs is suggested, albeit not as the central feature of the respective frameworks (e.g., Darley & Fazio, 1980; Deaux & Major, 1987; Hamilton et al., 1990; Jones, 1986, 1990; Jussim, 1986, 1991; Miller & Turnbull, 1986). The present framework (see also Neuberg, 1994, 1996) has more in common with two recent models (Hilton & Darley, 1991; Snyder, 1992), both of which also assume that one must consider the motivational context to understand the dynamics and outcomes of expectancy-tinged interactions. Their differences aside, these three approaches complement one another well, sharing a common broad perspective while focusing that perspective in their own distinct fashions. I compare and contrast these conceptualizations later in the chapter. First, however, I describe the present framework.

SOCIAL GOALS AND EXPECTANCY-TINGED SOCIAL INTERACTIONS

Moderating factors work by altering the critical mediators of a process: By altering the influence of an "initiating" variable on the mediator, one changes the ability of that variable to create the focal outcome. Factors that boost the impact of the initiating variable on the mediator increase the likelihood of the focal outcome; factors that weaken the impact of the initiating variable on the mediator attenuate the likelihood of the focal outcome. According to this logic, the factors that moderate the expectancy confirmation process must be those that influence the ability of perceiver expectancies to affect one or more of the four mediating mechanisms already outlined: (1) perceiver information-gathering behaviors; (2) perceiver expressive behaviors; (3) the target's decisions regarding accommodation of the perceiver's behavioral script; and (4) perceiver attention to and interpretation of target behaviors. I propose that two general classes of perceiver social motives (impression formation goals and self-presentational goals) and one general class of target motives (self-presentational goals) do indeed have such a regulatory influence, and thus are particularly likely to moderate expectancy influences.

Perceiver Impression Formation Goals

As discussed earlier, expectancy-biased information gathering seems to mediate the impact that perceiver expectancies have on target behavior. Moreover, expectancy-biased perceiver attentional and interpretational processes mediate the impact that expectancies have on perceiver impressions. Because impression formation goals tend to regulate information-gathering, attentional, and interpretational processes—and therefore determine whether these processes are likely to be expectancy-biased or not—this class of goals should moderate the impact that perceiver expectancies have on perceiver impressions.

Impression formation goals are, simply enough, goals aimed at producing specified outcomes of the impression formation process. Sometimes the goal is to form an accurate impression; sometimes we want to confirm existing expectancies; sometimes it is to form an impression rapidly; and so on (cf. Kruglanski, 1989).[3] A particular impression formation goal may be chronically active or may be temporarily activated by the particular situational context. For example, one may be especially motivated to form accurate impressions of others when one depends on them, feels control-deprived, fears appearing obtuse or prejudiced to others, and so on. In contrast, one may be especially motivated to confirm existing expectancies when such expectancies are particularly strong and central to one's self-concept, when one is dispositionally intolerant of inconsistencies and ambiguities, or when such an impression would enable a favorable self-presentation. Similarly, the desire to form rapid impressions is likely to be activated in situations where one is aroused or in which time pressures are salient.

Such goals, when activated, call forth associated cognitive and behavioral tactics. Importantly, some of these tactics also happen to mediate the biasing influences of expectancies. Because certain impression formation goals regulate these mediational tactics, they are also able to moderate the expectancy confirmation process.

The Regulation of Information-Gathering Behaviors

To facilitate any particular impression outcome, a perceiver would be well served to gather target information compatible with the desired impression. One can thus think of information gathering as a behavior in the service of a perceiver's impression formation goal. If impression formation goals do indeed regulate information gathering, and if expectancy-biased information gathering is an important mediator of self-fulfilling prophecies, it follows that impression formation goals should moderate expectancy influences by determining whether or not the biased information gathering required for expectancy confirmation actually occurs. Hence, impression formation goals that elicit biased information gathering should encourage target behavioral confirmation, and thus expectancy-consistent perceiver impressions. In contrast, impression formation goals that elicit unbiased information gathering should inhibit such behavioral confirmation, thus leading to relatively unbiased perceiver impressions.

For example, perceivers explicitly motivated to confirm an existing expectancy may gather just enough information to confirm the expectancy, ask questions that encourage targets to provide expectancy-consistent information and discourage them from providing expectancy-inconsistent information, and so on. In a similar vein, perceivers motivated to form rapid impressions may gather only a minimal amount of information, focusing on target information that is consistent with their expectancies (on the assumption that expectancy-consistent information is easier to process cognitively than is expectancy-inconsistent information). In these cases, the goal-induced nature of information gathering (i.e., biased and limited) encourages target behavioral confirmation, and thus should increase the likelihood that the perceiver will form an expectancy-consistent impression.

In contrast, perceivers motivated to form accurate impressions may be especially likely to gather target information in a relatively unbiased and extensive manner, in order to gain a fuller understanding of the target. Because the accuracy-induced nature of information gathering discourages target behavioral confirmation, the perceiver should be less likely to form an expectancy-consistent impression.

Therefore, because of their impact on perceiver information-gathering behaviors, perceiver impression formation goals should moderate expectancy influences. Specifically, when perceivers possess the goal either of confirming their expectancies or of forming a rapid impression, the likelihood of expectancy-consistent impressions should increase; when perceivers possess instead the goal of forming an accurate impression, the likelihood of expectancy-consistent impressions should decrease.

The Regulation of Attentional and Interpretational Processes

Perceiver impression formation goals should further moderate the expectancy confirmation process by regulating perceiver attentional and interpretational processes—also important mediators of expectancy confirmation (Fiske & Neuberg, 1990).

Attention, like behavioral information gathering, serves the function of providing the perceiver with needed target information. Whereas behavioral information gathering extracts particular behaviors from the target, attentional strategies sift through these gathered behaviors for analysis. Given that different impression formation goals specify different impression outcomes, one might expect perceiver attention to serve the function of focusing on the target information that is likely to serve the active impression formation goal best. Thus, when a particular goal encourages expectancy-biased attentional processes, expectancy-consistent impressions should occur. In contrast, when a particular goal encourages unbiased attentional processes, less biased impressions should result.

For example, a perceiver motivated to confirm a particular expectancy may attend to expectancy-consistent target behaviors, to the relative exclusion of available expectancy-inconsistent behaviors. Likewise, a perceiver motivated to form a rapid impression may attend to the gathered target information only minimally, searching especially for expectancy-confirming information (again on the assumption that expectancy-consistent information is easier to process). To the extent that "true" target-based impressions are only possible if perceivers attend to an unbiased sample of target behaviors, such impression formation goals are likely to lead to expectancy-consistent impressions. In contrast, a perceiver motivated to form an accurate impression may exhibit a more comprehensive and wide-ranging attention to target behavior; such attention should increase the likelihood that perceiver impressions will be relatively unbiased by inaccurate perceiver expectancies.

Perceiver interpretive strategies serve the function of defining the *meaning* of observed target behavior. That is, the manner in which a perceiver interprets target behavior determines the extent to which the behavior "becomes" expectancy-consistent for the perceiver. Hence, one might expect perceiver interpretation to serve the function of providing the "quality" of target information likely to serve the active impression formation goal best. To the extent that a goal-induced interpretive strategy results in expectancy-compatible information, expectancy-consistent impressions should be likely; to the extent that a goal-induced interpretive strategy results in expectancy-incompatible information, expectancy confirmation becomes less likely.

Perceivers motivated to form either expectancy-consistent impressions or rapid impressions may be especially likely to interpret ambiguous target information in expectancy-consistent ways, may discount expectancy-inconsistent information (perhaps by making situational attributions for these behaviors; Crocker, Hannah, & Weber, 1983), and so on. Such biases in perceiver interpretation should induce expectancy-consistent final impressions. In contrast, perceivers motivated to form accurate impressions should be less likely to exhibit such biased interpretations, thus decreasing their likelihood of forming expectancy-consistent impressions.

Hence, it seems plausible that impression formation goals may further serve to moderate the impact of perceiver expectancies by regulating the nature and extent of perceiver attentional and interpretive processes. Considering the posited effects of impression formation goals on the behavioral and cognitive mediators addressed here, one should make the following prediction: The goals of confirming one's expectancies and of forming a rapid impression should increase the likelihood that perceivers will form expectancy-consistent impressions, whereas the goal of forming an accurate impression should decrease the likelihood that perceivers will form expectancy-consistent impressions.

Perceiver Self-Presentational Goals

Perceiver self-presentational goals—wanting to be liked, wanting to be perceived as competent or fair, wanting to be feared, and so on (cf. Jones & Pittman, 1982)—should also play an important moderating role. Like impression formation goals, perceiver self-presentational goals may have their moderating influence via information-gathering behaviors and via attentional and interpretational processes. Unlike impression formation goals, however, self-presentational goals may also moderate the expectancy confirmation process through their influence on perceiver expressive behaviors.

The Regulation of Expressive and Information-Gathering Behaviors

Self-presentational goals are those goals relevant to managing another's impression or image of oneself. In order to manage others' impressions, pereivers have at their disposal certain tactics. For many self-presentational goals, these tactics may include expressive behaviors—behaviors suggestive of a perceiver's feelings toward, and beliefs about, a target (e.g., tone of voice, body language, flattering comments, positive feedback). For example, if I want people to like me, I may smile a lot, compliment them, and so forth.

Of course, as discussed earlier, expressive behavior can mediate the self-fulfilling prophecy. Thus, a perceiver's self-presentational goal, by regulating these types of behavior, should play an important role in determining whether or not behavioral confirmation actually occurs: Self-presentational goals that elicit expectancy-biased expressive behaviors should increase the likelihood of target behavioral confirmation, and hence the likelihood that a perceiver will form expectancy-consistent impressions; self-presentational goals that discourage expectancy-biased expressive behaviors should reduce the likelihood of behavioral confirmation, thus leading to relatively unbiased perceiver impressions.

Moreover, perceiver self-presentational goals may also serve impression management aims through their influence on certain information-gathering behaviors. That is, to the extent that particular information-gathering behaviors are viewed as enabling the desired image, they are more likely to occur. If a perceiver's self-presentational goal evokes expectancy-biased information gathering, target behavioral confirmation becomes more probable, and the perceiver is likely to form expectancy-consistent impressions; if, however, the perceiver's self-presentational goal elicits unbiased information-gathering behaviors, target behavioral confirmation becomes less probable, and the perceiver is less likely to form biased impressions.

For purposes of illustration, consider the case of a racist white male interviewer who is unconcerned with self-presentation. When interviewing a black job applicant, the interviewer's prejudices may "leak," leading him to exhibit little warmth, sociability, immediacy of body language, and so on—"cold" behaviors that the applicant may in turn reciprocate, creating a self-fulfilling prophecy (Word et al., 1974). Moreover, reflecting the interviewer's negative stereotypes, his questioning may be negatively biased and the interview short—behaviors again encouraging poor applicant performance. Alternatively, if the interviewer is motivated for some reason to ingratiate himself to the black applicant (perhaps to pre-empt potential complaints about his interview style), his expressive behaviors may differ appreciably: The interviewer may strategically exhibit great warmth, positive body language, and so on—behaviors that, when reciprocated by the applicant, actually serve to disconfirm the interviewer's expectancies. Moreover, the interviewer may strategically conduct a long interview, biasing the interview with easy, positive questions—again, making a favorable performance by the applicant more likely. Because the self-presentational goal of being liked is incompatible with interpersonally distant expressions and difficult, unflattering questions, behavioral confirmation in this case becomes less likely. Thus, by regulating perceiver expressive and information-gathering behaviors, self-presentational goals may also moderate the impact of expectancies on perceiver impressions.

The Regulation of Attentional and Interpretational Processes

Finally, perceiver self-presentational goals may also influence the cognitive impression formation process, to the extent that the impression formed by a perceiver has implications for that perceiver's desired image. This is most likely to occur when the self-presentational goal implicates a related impression formation goal. For example, in a situation where the racist interviewer described above is trying to impress his boss with his aptitude at forming accurate impressions of his applicants, he may focus on utilizing unbiased attentional and interpretational processes, the result of which may be a postinteraction impression free of the influence of his negative stereotypes. In contrast, if an unbiased interviewer desires to ingratiate a racially prejudiced boss, but does not want to feel like a hypocrite for doing so (i.e., does not want to publicly articulate one impression while privately holding another), he or she may utilize biased attentional and interpretational processes in the service of forming the desired, but perhaps inaccurate, negative impression of the black applicant. Thus, in addition to moderating the expectancy confirmation process via the regulation of perceiver expressive and information-gathering behaviors, perceiver self-presentational goals may also moderate expectancy confirmation through their ability to activate particular impression formation goals, and thus the attentional and interpretational processes inherent in them.

Target Self-Presentational Goals

I have posited above that one can conceptualize target behavioral confirmation as a deference behavior, with the target accommodating the behavioral script initiated by the perceiver's information-gathering and expressive behaviors. If this is an apt representation, the self-presentational motives of the target should play a crucial moderating role, as they probably determine the deference decision.

Consider first the target who possesses no explicit self-presentational agenda, but rather is merely motivated to facilitate an amicable, noncontroversial interaction—an interaction in which no one becomes embarrassed or offended, and all participants exit the encounter no worse for the wear (e.g., Junior wants to avoid yet another argument with Dad, Mr. Smith wants to survive the dreadfully boorish annual company picnic without insulting anyone, Ms. Brown wants a peaceful night at home with her husband). As Jones (1986) has argued, to the extent that behaviorally disconfirming a perceiver's expectancies often requires the target to challenge or reject the perceiver's behavioral script, and that such rejection breaks the "face-saving" contract implicit in most social interactions (Goffman, 1959; Grice, 1975), one might expect a target motivated to encourage a smooth, easygoing interaction to actively avoid exhibiting those actions inherent to behavioral disconfirmation.

Of course, targets often possess more proactive self-presentational agendas—agendas either brought to the encounter or formed during it. How might such self-presentational goals influence the expectancy confirmation process? As addressed above, self-presentational goals carry with them specific tactics for realization—particular behaviors thought by the presenter to be effective means of creating the desired image. The target who wants to be perceived as likeable may smile a lot and feign interest in the observer; the target desiring to be perceived as competent may present past accomplishments; the target seeking to supplicate may actively yield to the perceiver's script, as may the target believing that a perceiver holds a favorable expectancy. Within the context of expectancy-tinged interactions, such behaviors have powerful implications for the likelihood of expectancy confirmation. Stated simply, to the extent that a target's goals summon behaviors compatible with a perceiver's expectancies, the perceiver should be especially likely to form expectancy-consistent impressions; to the extent that the target's goals summon behaviors incompatible with a perceiver's expectancies, the perceiver should be less likely to form expectancy-consistent impressions.

This seemingly places the target in a position of great power: To the extent that a target possesses a specific self-presentational goal incompatible with a perceiver's expectancies, one should observe no expectancy confirmation. This conclusion is misleading, however, for two reasons. First, a target's self-presentational goal may only be manifestated in the target's behavior to the extent that a perceiver provides such an opportunity. If an interviewer, for example, constantly interrupts an applicant who is attempting to present his or her more positive features, the applicant may perform poorly, regardless of the initial goal of favorable self-presentation. More important, behavioral disconfirmation is no guarantee of expectancy disconfirmation, as the perceiver's motives may allow (or even encourage) an expectancy-biased assessment of these behaviors.

Nonetheless, it is clear that targets play an active role in determining the existence and nature of expectancy confirmation. The point here is that the moderating influence of a target's deference decision originates in the target's self-presentational goals.

Social Goals and Limited Resources

In the preceding pages, I have posited that certain classes of social motives, because of their regulatory influences on the key mediators of the expectancy confirmation process, act to moderate this process. Before moving to review the evidence addressing these claims, I need to address one additional issue—that of limited resources.

To implement any goal effectively, an individual requires cognitive and/or behavioral resources. If one wishes to form an accurate impression, one needs to expend sufficient effort to gather information in a comprehensive, unbiased manner; if one wishes to appear likeable, one must monitor ongoing expressive behaviors (both one's own self and the other's) and continually make appropriate adjustments; and so forth. Unfortunately, behavioral and cognitive resources are limited: As resources are utilized in the implementation of one goal, resources available for the implementation of additional goals diminish. For example, self-presentational concerns can induce attributional biases in social inference, apparently because of a reduction in resources available for the social inference process (Baumeister, Hutton, & Tice, 1989; Gilbert, Krull, & Pelham, 1988; see also Gilbert, Pelham, & Krull, 1988). Likewise, highly salient self-presentational concerns appear to impair performance on cognitive tasks (Lord & Saenz, 1985; Saenz, 1994; Saenz & Lord, 1989), again suggesting people's limited abilities to implement multiple goals.

One would thus expect the goal influences discussed above to be dependent on the amount of cognitive and behavioral resources available to the interactants. When such resources are limited, the ability of social goals to moderate the expectancy confirmation process will be diminished. Moreover, given the usual state of limited resources and often of multiple goals, it becomes important to specify the expectancy-relevant behaviors and processes that occur in goal domains "neglected" by the participant. That is, if a perceiver's goal leads him or her to focus resources on one set of behaviors or cognitions (e.g., on the gathering of information), what kind of influence will perceiver expectancies have on other relevant, but neglected, classes of behavior or cognition (e.g., on expressive behavior)?

In short, I propose that participants revert to relatively effortless default strategies in the resource-neglected domains. In the domain of information gathering, perceivers should default toward a low-effort biased gathering of expectancy-confirming information (e.g., Snyder & Swann, 1978a), because expectancy-consistent information is relatively easy to process. In the domain of expressive behaviors, perceivers should "leak" their expectancies (cf. Ekman & Friesen, 1974), because of insufficient resources available to monitor and regulate these behaviors. In the domain of cognitive impression formation, perceivers should exhibit expectancy-confirming attention to and interpretation of the gathered target information, again because of the relative ease with which people process expectancy-consistent information. Finally, targets without resources to implement a particular self-presentational strategy should revert to deference-based behavioral confirmation, because it is typically much easier (and carries fewer potential social costs) to accommodate the behavioral script of another than it is to coax upon another a script of one's own (Goffman, 1959; Grice, 1975; Jones, 1986).[4]

To illustrate the potential implications of possessing only limited resources, let us reconsider the example of our bigoted white male interviewer who, this time, is primarily motivated to form an accurate impression of a black job applicant. According to the present conceptualization, we would expect the interviewer, in his attempt to be accurate, to ask the applicant a comprehensive series of unbiased questions—thus enabling the applicant to provide appropriately representative information, and hence avoiding one type of self-fulfilling prophecy. The interviewer's well-intentioned focus on unbiased information gathering, however, should inhibit somewhat his ability to implement the self-presentational goal of appearing likeable. As a consequence, racist prejudices may "leak" into the interviewer's tone of voice, body language, and so on, thus expressing these prejudices to the applicant—who, being offended, may reciprocate this "cold" behavior, thus creating a self-fulfilling prophecy of a second type. Thus, although the accuracy goal may enable our interviewer to avoid one type of self-fulfilling prophecy, the resulting inability to monitor and/or regulate his expressive behaviors may paradoxically allow another. Likewise, if the interviewer is particularly concerned about appearing prejudiced, and manifests this concern by concentrating his efforts on regulating his expressive behaviors, we may discover that he has, in the process, ironically increased the likelihood of relying on stereotype-confirming cognitive biases.

In sum, when one posits motivational constructs as relevant, the issue of available resources becomes critical. Goals require resources, and resources are limited. Taking these constraints under consideration, I have proposed a set of default behaviors and processes that occur when goal-directed actions are precluded by a lack of relevant resources.

These assumptions now make the motivational analysis more complete. Whereas the earlier discussion has suggested specific predictions regarding the impact of expectancies within the primary goal domains, these latter analyses suggest specific predictions concerning expectancy influences in neglected domains as well.

Summary: A Model of Expectancy-Tinged Dyadic Social Interaction

The preceding considerations suggest a revised model of expectancy-tinged social interaction—a model in which the participants' social motivations play a critical moderating role. Figure 7.1 provides a visual representation of the emerg-

ing conceptualization, integrating crucial aspects of previous empirical and theoretical work (as reviewed above; see also Darley & Fazio, 1980; Hilton & Darley,
1991; Hilton et al., 1989; Jones, 1986; Jussim, 1986; Rosenthal, 1974; Snyder,
1984, 1992) with the four guiding principles set forth here:

1. *Perceiver impression formation goals* moderate the influence of perceiver expectancies on postinteraction impressions by regulating the influence of these
expectancies on perceiver information-gathering behavior and on perceiver attentional and interpretational processes.

2. *Perceiver self-presentational goals* moderate the influence of perceiver expectancies on postinteraction impressions by regulating the influence of these
expectancies on perceiver expressive behavior, on perceiver information-gathering behavior, and on perceiver attentional and interpretational processes.

3. *Target self-presentational goals* moderate the influence of perceiver expectancies on postinteraction impressions by regulating the extent to which the
target decides to accommodate the behavioral script implicated by the perceiver's information-gathering and expressive behaviors.

4. The ability of perceiver and target goals to moderate the influence of perceiver expectancies on postinteraction impressions is constrained by *the availability of behavioral and cognitive resources.* Low-effort "default" processes will occur in those goal domains receiving insufficient resources.

The expectancy-tinged interaction is thus conceptualized as a dynamic cycle of interpersonal behavior and thought, with each participant potentially influencing the other at each turn. The social goals of both perceiver and target
are accorded central status, as such goals are proposed to have major influences
on key mediators in the expectancy confirmation process.

Having presented the theoretical framework, I move to review empirical
findings relevant to each of the model's four focal premises.

RELEVANT RESEARCH FINDINGS

Many studies demonstrate the existence of expectancy-confirmation effects, and
many other studies reveal an absence of expectancy influences. Some critics consider this a weakness of the literature. As the present framework suggests, however, to predict expectancy confirmation across all circumstances would be
rigidly myopic; instead, one should *presume* some lack of cross-situational consistency. Expectancy confirmation does not merely flow directly and automatically from the presence of a perceiver expectancy. Rather, it occurs as a function
of a host of other factors, including the nature of perceiver goals, perceiver resource availability, target goals, and target resource availability. Motivational
and resource-relevant conditions differ across situations, and such conditions
are responsible for moderating the expectancy confirmation process. Hence, one
would predict expectancy confirmation in certain circumstances but not in oth-

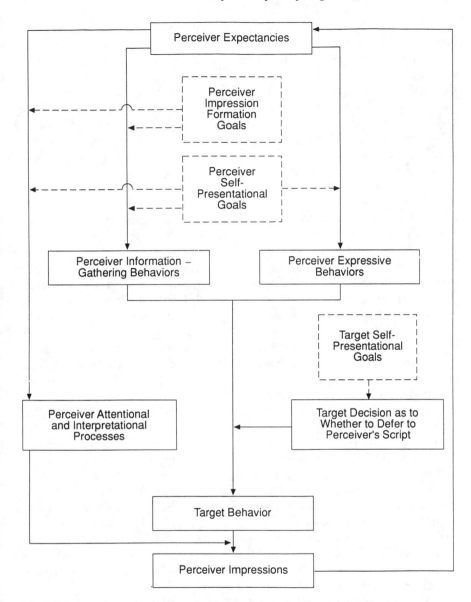

FIGURE 7.1   A framework for understanding the role of social motives in expectancy-tinged social interactions. Participant goals moderate the expectancy confirmation process by regulating perceiver information-gathering behaviors, perceiver expressive behaviors, and perceiver attentional and interpretational processes, as well as by determining the target's decision as to whether to accommodate the perceiver's behavioral script. These regulatory influences are represented by dotted arrows. The moderating abilities of participant goals are themselves constrained by the availability of behavioral and cognitive resources (not represented here for the purpose of maintaining figural clarity). From Neuberg (1994). Copyright 1994 by Lawrence Erlbaum Associates. Reprinted by permission.

ers. One test of the present framework is its ability to capture the observed data; how well does it do?

Unfortunately, most of the studies addressing issues of expectancy confirmation neither manipulate nor measure participant goals or resources; nor do the papers presenting these studies provide sufficient information to enable one to infer such states convincingly. The review that follows is thus necessarily brief, focusing exclusively on those few studies in which participant goals and resources either have been explicitly manipulated or can be straightforwardly inferred. Nonetheless, the reader will find that the existing data are quite compatible with all four of the theoretically derived premises.

Premise 1: The Moderating Role of Perceiver Impression Formation Goals

Research evidence suggests an important moderating role for perceiver impression formation goals. Within the behavioral realm, certain impression formation goals seem to determine whether or not self-fulfilling prophecies occur. For example, when perceivers are motivated to form accurate impressions—either through explicit instruction (Fein, von Hipple, & Hilton, 1989; Neuberg, 1989) or because of a lack of confidence in uncertain expectancies (Swann & Ely, 1984)—targets are less likely to behaviorally confirm their perceivers' expectancies. In contrast, when perceivers seem motivated to confirm their expectancies—in one study because of a dispositional desire to maintain a sex-typed view of the world (Andersen & Bem, 1981), and in a second study because of a more general state of dogmatism (Babad et al., 1982; see Harris & Rosenthal, 1986)—their targets become more likely to succumb to the self-fulfilling prophecy.

Importantly, research evidence increasingly suggests that this moderating influence of impression formation goals seems to operate through the regulation of information-gathering behaviors, as the first premise proposes. In three studies, perceivers motivated to be accurate—either because of a need to select a future partner for an important interaction (Darley et al., 1988; see Neuberg & Fiske, 1987), because of an experimental manipulation of control deprivation (Swann, Stephenson, & Pittman, 1981; see Pittman & D'Agostino, 1989), or because of depression (Hildebrand-Saints & Weary, 1989)—were especially likely to seek diagnostic information from their targets.

A study from my lab (Neuberg, 1989) tested this premise more directly, revealing that the moderating influence of impression formation goals can occur via the proposed information-gathering behavioral pathway. This study experimentally manipulated both perceiver expectancies and perceiver goal. The perceiver subjects interviewed target subjects for a hypothetical job. The participants' behaviors throughout the interaction were unobtrusively recorded; the perceivers' final impressions of the targets were assessed; and the data were then subjected to path analyses testing the proposed mediational pathways. Results strongly supported the hypothesis.

Perceivers in the control "no-goal" condition showed the predicted information-gathering biases against targets about whom they possessed negative expectancies: They spent proportionally less time listening to them, encouraged them less to provide additional information, and asked questions biased toward expectancy confirmation. These targets consequently succumbed to the self-fulfilling prophecy, performing poorly as judged by outside observers who were unaware of the experimental conditions. Not surprisingly, the perceivers exited these interviews with their negative expectancies intact.

In contrast, perceivers motivated to form accurate impressions created very different social interactions. Most important, they exhibited no such information-gathering biases against their negative-expectancy targets. As a consequence, there was no behavioral confirmation (in fact, these applicants performed more favorably than their no-expectancy counterparts), and the postinteraction impressions of the accuracy-motivated perceivers revealed no expectancy bias. These data directly support the premise that impression formation goals can moderate the expectancy confirmation process, and path analyses more stringently revealed that such moderation occurred via the regulation of perceiver information-gathering behaviors, as predicted. A recent study from our lab (Judice & Neuberg, 1994) has replicated these expectancy-attenuating influences of accuracy motivation.

Evidence from the cognitive domain is also supportive of Premise 1, revealing that the moderating role of impression formation goals can also occur through the regulation of perceiver attentional and interpretational processes. Indeed, the cognitive evidence is abundant and has been reviewed (Fiske & Neuberg, 1990), so I shall be brief (for more general discussions of motivational influences on cognitive processing, see Kunda, 1990; Pyszczynski & Greenberg, 1987). For example, perceivers become less biased by initial information when the goal of impression accuracy is activated—by factors such as short-term outcome dependency (i.e., the perceiver's future outcomes depend upon the target; Erber & Fiske, 1984; Neuberg & Fiske, 1987; Ruscher & Fiske, 1990), perceivers' knowledge of targets' dependence on their judgments (Freund, Kruglanski, & Shpitzajzen, 1985), the presence of ostensibly accurate standards (Tetlock & Kim, 1987), mild depression (Edwards & Weary, 1993), and explicit accuracy instructions (Neuberg & Fiske, 1987).

Moreover, such moderating influences of impression formation goals appear to be mediated by changes in the ways that perceivers attend to and interpret target information. For example, several studies indicate that perceivers become more attentive to individuating target characteristics when the perceivers' outcomes are dependent on them (Berscheid, Graziano, Monson, & Dermer, 1976; Erber & Fiske, 1984; Neuberg & Fiske, 1987; Ruscher & Fiske, 1990); in the Neuberg and Fiske (1987) studies, such attentional processes were indeed found to mediate the impact of a perceiver's negative expectancies on the perceiver's ultimate impressions. Additional evidence suggests that one's impression formation goals can also alter one's interpretations of target information (e.g., Neuberg & Fiske, 1986, cited in Fiske & Neuberg, 1990).

Thus, the empirical evidence is quite consistent with Premise 1: Perceiver impression formation goals, because of their regulatory influence on information-gathering behaviors and on attentional and interpretational processes, moderate the impact of expectancies on impression formation.

Premise 2: The Moderating Role of Perceiver Self-Presentational Goals

Perceiver self-presentational goals are proposed to moderate the expectancy confirmation process by regulating the impact that expectancies have on perceiver expressive behaviors, information-gathering behaviors, and/or the cognitive processing of target behavior.

Several studies reveal the ability of self-presentational concerns to moderate expectancy confirmation, in these cases via the cognitive mediational pathway (see Fiske & Neuberg, 1990). For example, perceivers are more apt to attend to individuating target information when they fear appearing prejudiced to others (Snyder et al., 1982). Similarly, when perceivers are concerned with having to explain their judgments to peers, and have sufficient time to consider their judgments, their impressions became less stereotypical (Kruglanski & Freund, 1983). As a last example, work by Tetlock (1983) indicates that perceivers are less likely to be unduly influenced by early information when learning that they will be accountable for their opinions to an audience with unknown opinions (thus activating accuracy concerns), but when they learn that they will be accountable to others possessing known opinions (thus activating concerns to form a particular impression), perceivers' processing seems to be biased toward generating the desired opinion.

A study by Baumeister et al. (1989) provides additional data compatible with the present view, focusing on the behavioral mediational pathway. Subjects were encouraged to present themselves to partner subjects in either a self-promoting or a modest manner. Results indicated that the partners reciprocated these behaviors: Partners of subjects motivated to be seen favorably behaved in a self-promoting fashion themselves, whereas partners of subjects motivated to be modest accordingly behaved more modestly themselves. Because these motivated subjects possessed no explicit expectancies for the "targets," this study provides no evidence for the ability of self-presentational goals to moderate the impact of expectancies on the relevant interpersonal mediators. The study does importantly illustrate, however, one component of Premise 2: the ability of self-presentational goals to influence expressive and/or information-gathering behaviors, resulting in reciprocal behaviors by others.

Finally, in an experiment similar to the Neuberg (1989) "interview" study discussed above, we investigated Premise 2 directly (Neuberg et al., 1993). As before, perceivers' expectancies and motivations were manipulated prior to their task of interviewing applicant targets for a hypothetical job. Not surprisingly, the "no-goal" perceivers created the expectancy-confirming scenario: Their negative-expectancy targets tended to perform less favorably than the no-expectancy targets, and as a consequence these perceivers formed expectancy-consistent postinteraction impressions. In contrast, perceivers with a goal of *ingratiating* themselves with their targets created very different interactions: Their negative-expectancy applicants performed objectively better than the no-expectancy applicants, thus leading the "liking-goal" interviewers to form especially favorable impressions of them. Of particular importance, the self-fulfilling prophecy failed to materialize in these latter interactions because the liking-goal interviewers acted friendlier and actively avoided asking these applicants negatively tinged and potentially embarrassing questions (the mediational properties of these behaviors were supported by path analyses). These data thus strongly support Premise 2: Perceiver self-presentational goals moderate the influence of expectancies by regulating expressive and information-gathering behaviors.

Premise 3: The Moderating Role of Target Self-Presentational Goals

I have proposed that a target's self-presentational concerns may moderate the expectancy confirmation process by influencing the target's decision to accommodate the perceiver's behavioral script. Although I am aware of no published data directly assessing the issue of the target's deference decision per se, a number of studies have assessed the role of target self-presentational concerns in a manner permitting reasonable inferences.

First, to address the issue of whether behavioral confirmation may be prudently thought of as a deference behavior, it would be profitable to assess how the relative status of the interactants may influence behavioral confirmation. That is, if behavioral confirmation is a form of deference or accommodation, expectancy confirmation should be especially likely when the target believes himself or herself to be of lower status than the perceiver, as this is when acquiescence behaviors would seem most appropriate. Indeed, a study by Copeland (1994) revealed that target behavioral confirmation was especially likely to occur when perceivers were in positions of relative power over the targets. In a similar vein, we (Virdin & Neuberg, 1990) provided data suggesting that targets believing (erroneously) that they were of relatively inferior status were somewhat more likely to create expectancy confirmation than were targets believing that they were of superior status.

Other work is also consistent with this notion. For example, a study by Christensen and Rosenthal (1982) indicated that male perceivers were especially likely to induce behavioral confirmation, while female targets were especially likely to act in a behaviorally confirming manner. To the extent that these participants were enacting socialized gender roles (i.e., men should take control and women should defer), such a finding is compatible with the present conceptualization. Moreover, targets scoring highly on the Self-Monitoring Scale and on its Self-Monitoring Other-Directed subscale are more likely to be constrained by the expectancies of others (Harris & Rosenthal, 1986). This is also consistent with the present view if one reasonably assumes that persons high in self-monitors are especially likely to be dispositionally deferent, accommodating the behavioral agendas created by others. Finally, a meta-analysis by Cooper and Hazelrigg (1988) revealed that targets who were high in "influenceability" were more likely to confirm perceiver expectancies. Thus, although direct empirical support is lacking, indirect evidence suggests that viewing behavioral confirmation as a form of interpersonal deference may be sound.

Only two studies come close to directly manipulating the target deference decision, and their results provide strong support for Premise 3. In one, targets who were encouraged to create a pleasing interaction by being responsive to the perceivers' behaviors were indeed particularly likely to behaviorally confirm their perceivers' expectancies (Snyder & Haugen, 1995). In our own lab we have recently discovered the same effect and are focusing current analyses on those cognitive and behavioral processes that bring it about (Smith, Neuberg, Judice, & Biesanz, 1995).

Numerous additional studies are compatible with Premise 3, although I should note that self-presentational goals have only been indirectly activated in these studies and that the influence of these goals specifically on the target deference decision has not been assessed. Nonetheless, their findings are revealing.

For example, Hilton and Darley (1985) provided a demonstration in which targets made aware of a perceiver's negative expectancy managed to overcome that expectancy, as compared to targets who remained unaware of the perceiver's expectancy. Such a finding fits neatly into the present conceptualization, given the assumption that an awareness of a perceiver's negative expectancy is likely to activate in a target (especially in Princeton undergraduate students) an explicit goal of positive self-presentation.

Targets who are highly certain of their self-concepts are also more likely to effectively disconfirm a perceiver's erroneous expectancies than are targets with low certainty (Swann & Ely, 1984). Again, it would appear reasonable to assume that the highly certain targets would be especially motivated to present themselves in a manner they deem as being representative of their "true" selves, whereas highly uncertain targets would perhaps be less likely to desire active pursuit of such a (potentially risky) agenda. Similarly, targets high in private self-consciousness (i.e., dispositional awareness of one's own self, values, attitudes, etc.) also seem somewhat more likely to overcome a perceiver's inaccurate expectancies (Major et al., 1988).

Third, a study by Baumeister and colleagues (Baumeister, Cooper, & Skib, 1979) provides an interesting demonstration of the potential role of target self-presentation. In their study, subjects performed below their capabilities when they were publicly expected to do so *and* when poor task performance was supposedly associated with a desirable personality characteristic. Thus, in this case the apparent motivation to be viewed favorably led targets to actively confirm expectations, even though it meant performing below personal standards.

Finally, in several intriguing studies by Zanna and his colleagues, female targets altered their self-presentations in accordance with the apparent desires of an attractive male perceiver, but did not do the same for an unattractive male. In one study, the women strategically changed their apparent sex-role traditionality (Zanna & Pack, 1975); in the other, they altered their physical appearance and nonverbal behaviors (von Baeyer, Sherk, & Zanna, 1981). The fact that this behavioral confirmation occurred only when the males were attractive implicates a role for a self-presentational motive and the decision to accommodate the preferences of these males.

In sum, the research literature suggests, consistent with Premise 3, that target behavioral confirmation may be reasonably conceptualized as a deference behavior and that target self-presentational goals play an important role in moderating the expectancy confirmation process. Clearly, however, more direct evidence—evidence in which target self-presentational goals are explicitly manipulated and their effects on the deference decision are measured—is needed.

Premise 4: The Moderating Influences of Resource Availability

The model's final premise focuses on the crucial role of cognitive and behavioral resources in the implementation of the social goals I have been discussing. Because a lack of resources generally hinders the ability to execute goal-induced strategies, it follows that such circumstances will attenuate the ability of perceiver and target goals to moderate the expectancy confirmation process.

First, because expectancy confirmation processes are generally easier (i.e., more cognitively efficient) than expectancy-disconfirmation processes, expectancy confirmation should be especially likely when resources are scarce. This indeed seems to be the case. For example, time pressure makes stereotype-based judgments likely, inhibiting the formation of individuating, target-based impressions (e.g., Bechtold, Naccarato, & Zanna, 1986; Kruglanski & Freund, 1983). Moreover, research on arousal reveals that stereotypic judgments are more likely when perceivers are highly aroused (Kim & Baron, 1988; Wilder & Shapiro, 1989). Finally, "morning people" (i.e., those who reach their peak of cognitive functioning early in the day) are especially likely to rely on their stereotypes in the evening, whereas "night people" (i.e., those who reach their peak of cognitive functioning in the evening) are especially likely to stereotype others in the morning (Bodenhausen, 1990). Given that time pressure, high arousal, and circadian "weak spots" reduce the availability of cognitive resources for complex impression formation, such findings are highly compatible with the present conceptualization. (Of course, as I mention in note 4, it may be easier to cognitively *dis*confirm an expectancy under some circumstances. In particular, when [1] the expectancy is weak and noncentral to the perceiver, and [2] the available target information is unambiguously incompatible with the expectancy, cognitive disconfirmation may be the rule rather than the exception.)

An additional implication of Premise 4 is that when perceivers are focusing their goal-driven attentions toward regulating one aspect of the interaction process, other aspects of the interaction process may lapse by default into non-regulation (Baumeister et al., 1989; Gilbert, Krull, & Pelham, 1988; Gilbert, Pelham, & Krull, 1988; Lord & Saenz, 1985; Saenz, 1994; Saenz & Lord, 1989). Although no studies have explicitly manipulated relative resource availability across potential goal domains, the findings from several studies are illustrative. For example, in the Neuberg (1989) interview study previously discussed, perceivers motivated by impression accuracy altered their information-gathering behaviors, leading their negative-expectancy applicants to avoid behavioral confirmation, and thus enabling these perceivers to form final impressions seemingly unbiased by their initial inaccurate expectancies. It is interesting to note, however, that although these accuracy-motivated perceivers were able to eliminate their expectancy biases in the domain of information gathering *behaviors*, their expectancies nonetheless negatively biased their *cognitive assessment* of the targets' behaviors. That is, their postinteraction impressions were somewhat more negative than the targets' behavior had objectively warranted, as determined by the impressions of "blind" judges who had observed the same target behaviors without the benefit of any expectations. Thus, although the perceivers' accuracy-driven efforts had eliminated the self-fulfilling prophecy, they had not reduced the expectancy-driven cognitive bias. Interestingly, these same perceivers also seemed to have had difficulties regulating the expressive domain, as their negative expectancies were especially likely to "leak" to the targets (Neuberg, 1987).

These data are highly compatible with the premise. Because the accuracy-driven perceivers had to expend so much behavioral effort and cognitive resources on unbiased information gathering, they probably possessed insufficient remaining resources for unbiased cognitive assessment of target behaviors and for the control of expressive behaviors.

A study by Babad, Bernieri, and Rosenthal (1989) is also compatible with this view. Their research revealed that although "biased" teachers were able to conceal their negative feelings in transcript accounts of their behavior (which revealed only the verbal content of their interactions), these feelings tended to "leak" into their facial expressions and body language. It appears that the teachers' attempts to control their negative feelings occurred primarily in the overt, verbal realm, as one might expect; as a consequence of these masking attempts, however, the ability to regulate such behaviors in the nonverbal expressive realm was significantly reduced.

It is thus clear that the issue of limited resources is an important one. A full understanding of social goal influences on the expectancy confirmation process must consider the fact that goals are effectively implemented only when sufficient resources are available. Expectancy influences may thus reveal themselves via biased default processes when resources are focused elsewhere. Existing data are consistent with this view, although experiments explicitly designed to test these notions would be valuable.

Summary

Although few studies have been designed to test the proposed framework directly, extant research is nonetheless compatible with its theoretically derived premises. Perceiver impression formation and self-presentational goals, as well as target self-presentational goals, indeed appear to play an important role moderating the expectancy confirmation process. Moreover, data exist supporting the posited mechanisms through which these motivations have their effect. Finally, data also support the notion that such motivational influences are constrained by the availability of behavioral and cognitive resources.

RELATED FRAMEWORKS

How does the present approach relate to similar frameworks? Although several other conceptualizations have addressed the issue of participant motivations in the expectancy confirmation process, most do so only briefly and with little attention to either the ranges of potential motivational influences or the mechanisms through which such influences are realized (e.g., Darley & Fazio, 1980; Deaux & Major, 1987; Jones, 1986, 1990; Jussim, 1986, 1991; Miller & Turnbull, 1986; Swann, 1984). Two recent approaches are particularly notable with respect to their focus on motivational issues, however, and deserve closer inspection (Hilton & Darley, 1991; Snyder, 1992).

Hilton and Darley's (1991) approach focuses on perceiver motivations, as classified into "assessment sets" and "action sets." Assessment sets represent goals having to do with forming impressions of others, and Hilton and Darley focus on the goal of forming accurate impressions, arguing that expectancy confirmation becomes less likely as perceivers become increasingly motivated to form accurate impressions. The present framework reaches the same conclusion, but also considers the implications of the impression formation goals of confirming one's expectations and of forming a rapid impression.

Action sets represent goals having to do with behaviorally managing the interaction sequence. This is a distinct feature of Hilton and Darley's approach, although small parts of what they conceptualize as action sets may overlap to some extent with the present class of self-presentational goals. Thus, the framework proposed here overlaps with Hilton and Darley's in some respects and is complementary in others. In particular, the present model also addresses issues of self-presentational motives; focuses on both the perceiver and the target; explicates the cognitive and behavioral mechanisms through which participant motives are likely to have their moderating influences; and articulates a constraining role of resource availability.

Snyder's (1992) conceptualization overlaps to a somewhat greater degree with the present framework, in that both approaches focus on a wide range of motives and on both participants as active agents of interpersonal influence.

Snyder's approach takes as its foundation a functional analysis of the behavioral confirmation process: Behavioral confirmation may serve for the perceiver a function of making the world predictive and stable, and for the target a function of facilitating social interaction; behavioral disconfirmation may serve for the target the functions of expression of personal attributes and defense of threatened identities. Thus, according to Snyder, behavioral confirmation is especially likely when perceivers are motivated by the acquisition of social knowledge and targets are motivated to facilitate social interactions. Behavioral confirmation becomes unlikely (1) when perceivers are motivated either to regulate social interactions, to express personal attributes, or to defend threatened identities, or (2) when targets are motivated either to acquire social knowledge, to express personal attributes, or to defend threatened identities.

Snyder's framework is indeed rich, placing the expectancy-tinged interaction within the broad context of individuals' motivational concerns. Under certain circumstances, however, its predictive utility is diminished somewhat by the chosen level of motivational analysis. For example, the broadly defined function of acquiring social knowledge may be served by one of several goals—to confirm one's expectancies, to form a rapid impression, to form an accurate impression—all of which have differing implications for the behavioral confirmation process.[5] Similarly, the function of expressing personal attributes may activate goals that differ significantly across individuals—different targets, for instance, may desire to express likeability, competence, submissiveness, easygoingness, and so forth—each of which again may have distinct implications for the likelihood of behavioral confirmation (e.g., targets motivated to express competence may find themselves disconfirming a perceiver's expectancies, whereas targets motivated to express submissiveness may accommodate perceiver scripts, thus confirming their expectancies). As the present framework suggests, one must make explicit assumptions regarding an interactant's *specific* goals in order to generate precise predictions about the processes and outcomes of expectancy-tinged interactions. Because Snyder's approach does not systematically specify how one moves from the level of function to specific goal, one would have difficulty using it to make clear predictions.

Hence, perhaps the greatest conceptual difference between the present framework and Snyder's is one of level of analysis. Here I address how specific goals engage the mechanisms underlying behavioral confirmation, whereas Snyder addresses the functions that may be served by such interactions. It would indeed seem profitable to link the two perspectives by generating a framework that enables one to understand how interactants move from general to more specific motivations.

In sum, although the Hilton and Darley (1991) and Snyder (1992) approaches share with the present framework the critical focus on motivational concerns and several analytic features, each approach has its unique texture. My intention here has been to focus on both behavioral and cognitive processes of expectancy confirmation; to consider both perceiver and target contributions to the interaction sequence; to assess the relevance of a wide range of everyday social motives; to explicitly link these motives to the behavioral and cognitive mechanisms underlying expectancy confirmation; and to consider the constraining function of resource availability.

IMPLICATIONS

The purpose of this chapter is to provide a framework explicating the circumstances in which expectancy confirmation does and does not occur. The main theme of this conceptualization is that expectancy-relevant processes, whether they be behavioral or cognitive, occur within the context of the participants' active motivational states, and that certain of these motivational states regulate the potential impact of these expectancies. Thus, to understand and predict the influence of interpersonal expectancies on social interactions and impression formation, one must first be cognizant of both the interactants' social goals and the resource-constrained ability of these goals to effectively regulate the behavioral and cognitive processes mediating expectancy confirmation.

Before I move on, two important caveats are in order. First, I should clearly state that the present conceptualization is proposed as a useful framework, not as any "final word." Indeed, although much research is compatible with the model's premises, empirical support for the model in its entirety is far from firm, as little work has been designed explicitly for the purpose of testing these notions. A great deal of further study is needed, particularly on the following issues:

- What other perceiver self-presentational goals moderate the expectancy confirmation process? We know that ingratiation has a predictable effect; what about the desires to intimidate, to express competence, and the like, and how may their influences interact with different kinds of perceiver expectancies?
- What target self-presentational goals in particular alter the deference decision? What is the cognitive calculus that moves one from a self-presentational goal to a decision to behave deferentially?
- In what ways do cognitive and behavioral resources constrain motivated control of the expectancy confirmation process? More generally, although existing data are compatible with the presented hypotheses, direct tests are lacking.
- Perhaps most interesting, how do the different processes discussed interact with each other? For example, if a perceiver has a strong desire to confirm his or her expectations, do target actions really make much of a difference? What happens when a perceiver creates both an unbiased information-gathering pathway and an expectancy-tinged expressive pathway? How must the present framework change as we acknowledge that each interactant is both a perceiver *and* a target? Such questions make clear the need to conceptualize expectancy-tinged social encounters in a

highly dynamic way. There probably exist layers of complex interactions among these processes—interactions that are incomprehensible in terms of simple flowchart and box-and-arrow models. Toward this end, and in conjunction with our continuing empirical work, my colleagues and I are beginning to use the modeling tools of dynamic systems to further explore the complexities of such encounters.

Second, I should remind the reader that other aspects of expectancy-tinged social encounters, beyond those addressed here, may often play crucial roles. As alluded to earlier, this may be especially likely in those domains possessing unique motivational flavors (teacher–student interactions, therapist–client relationships, etc.). The present framework is not intended to represent in their entirety the numerous influences on all expectancy-tinged encounters. Rather, my purpose here has been to address systematically one set of influences that I view as being particularly central, and to focus primarily on the types of interpersonal interactions common to everyday living.

Nevertheless, I think the framework makes important contributions, both theoretically and practically. First, it increases the precision with which one can predict the outcomes of expectancy-tinged interactions. With access to a perceiver's expectancies, perceiver and target motivations, and resource availability, one can "walk through" the implications of these factors for the critical mediators of the expectancy confirmation process, and can thus make reasonable inferences regarding the outcomes of such encounters.

The framework also potentially serves an important integrative function. As the present review has indicated, many perceiver and target variables have been proposed and investigated as potential moderators of expectancy confirmation. The present conceptualization is useful in that it suggests *why* many of these variables have their moderating effects: These variables influence the expectancy confirmation process because they elicit particular goal states in the participants. For example, perceivers who are uncertain of their expectancies (e.g., Swann & Ely, 1984) or depend in some way on their targets (e.g., Neuberg & Fiske, 1987) may be less likely to confirm their expectancies because they are motivated by accuracy concerns; perceivers who are highly invested in their expectancies (e.g., Andersen & Bem, 1981) or are under time constraints (e.g., Kruglanski & Freund, 1983) may be more likely to confirm their expectancies because they are motivated by confirmation concerns; targets who see themselves as being of low relative status (e.g., Copeland, 1994; Virdin & Neuberg, 1990) or who are dispositionally concerned with social appropriateness (e.g., Harris & Rosenthal, 1986) may be more likely to behaviorally confirm perceivers' expectancies because they are motivated to adhere to the perceivers' scripts; targets who possess a strong sense of self (e.g., Swann & Ely, 1984) should be less likely to behaviorally confirm perceivers' expectancies because they have active self-presentational agendas of their own; and so on.

The present framework may also help address the issue of the "real-world" frequency of expectancy confirmation biases. Some researchers (e.g., Brophy, 1983; Brophy & Good, 1974; Cooper, 1979; Crano & Mellon, 1978; Jussim, 1991; West & Anderson, 1976) have argued that the expectancy literature unjustifiably implies that expectancy influences are powerful and ubiquitous, whereas their own reviews reveal only small influences of inaccurate expectancies. They may indeed be correct in their conclusion that large influences of inaccurate expectancies are relatively uncommon, especially outside the laboratory. Unfortunately, it is difficult to measure bias as it occurs spontaneously in the real world, because we rarely have available all the information needed to draw such an inference. Moreover, and of special significance, the assessment of expectancies may alter the typical motivational context of the interaction, thus reducing our ability to make strong predictions about interaction outcomes. This is likely to be especially problematic, given the difficulties inherent in questioning interactants about their motives without altering these motives in some way.

In contrast, the present approach suggests an alternative but complementary approach to addressing the issue of naturalistic frequency. Specifically, it posits the psychological circumstances under which expectancy confirmation is especially likely to occur: when resources are limited, when expectancies are held with certainty, when the perceiver is minimally motivated by accuracy and favorable self-presentation to the target, when the target is motivated to accommodate the whims of the perceiver, and so on. If we are aware of the social conditions that elicit these psychological states, and are able to assess the real-world frequency of such conditions (an easier task, I would argue), we enable ourselves to draw inferences regarding the naturalistic frequency of expectancy confirmation.

My own opinion on this issue, as suggested by the model, is that expectancy confirmation is not uncommon in everyday interactions. People's expectancies are often inaccurate and held with confidence; they frequently lack the resources needed to implement unbiased behaviors and thought processes (even in the cases where they are indeed motivated to do so); social conventions often make it difficult for targets to challenge the expectancy-based assumptions of others; and so on. To the extent that the present framework represents well the processes inherent to everyday expectancy-tinged social interactions, we would be advised not to underestimate the real-world influences of inaccurate expectancies, especially given that the implications of such biases are often of great personal and societal significance.

Of course, in contexts in which the present conceptualization may play only a partial role—for example, in educational settings, where teacher goals related to the transmission of academic information may often take precedence over self-presentational and impression formation goals—we would be remiss to make strong claims about the natural occurrence of expectancy confirmation based solely on the present model. Note, however, that the type of motivational analysis performed here can also be performed for such domains. We merely need to explicate the additional mechanisms that enable expectancy confirmation in each domain (e.g., for the education domain, see Brophy, 1983; Rosenthal, 1973), and to consider the implications that naturally occurring goal states are likely to have for these mechanisms.

Finally, in addition to increasing our theoretical understanding of expectancy-related behavioral and cognitive processes, the present framework may have important practical implications as well. After all, virtually all social interactions are at least somewhat susceptible to expectancy influences. Moreover, expectancies are too often inaccurate. Previous real-world attempts to reduce expectancy influences (e.g., by prejudice researchers) have often focused on changing the nature of the expectancies themselves. As many have noted, however, this is no easy task, as stereotypes and prejudices are quite resistant to change (e.g., see Miller & Brewer, 1984). The present framework suggests an alternative strategy: Instead of attempting to change a perceiver's global stereotypes and prejudices, perhaps we should design social interventions that—by focusing explicitly on altering the participants' acute motivational states, and on making available requisite cognitive and behavioral resources—attempt to reduce the impact of such stereotypes and prejudices on the individual target within the context of each particular interaction (see Neuberg, 1994, for a more comprehensive discussion).

In closing, given the theoretical and practical significance of expectancy-tinged social encounters , it is critical that we better understand the dynamics of the interpersonal and intrapersonal processes inherent to them. The present framework, with its emphasis on the motivational moderators of expectancy-based processes, is proposed as a useful step in that direction.

Acknowledgments

The work presented here has been greatly facilitated by National Institute of Mental Health Grant No. MH45719. I would like to thank, for their helpful comments, the editors, Delia Saenz, Nicole Judice, Jason Newsom, Erika Schupak-Neuberg, and Lynn Virdin.

Notes

1. In keeping with the conventions of the expectancy confirmation literature, I use the term "perceiver" to designate the holder of an expectancy, and the term "target" to designate the person about whom the expectancy is held. Of course, in most social encounters, participants play the role of both perceiver and target. For expository purposes, however, the accepted conventions suffice.

2. I focus here on *general* classes of mechanisms—all of which are potentially relevant to most types of expectancy-tinged social encounters. Within particular contexts, however, other mechanisms can play additional roles. For example, within the educational domain, the extent to which a teacher provides a student with extra or more difficult material may mediate the impact of that teacher's expectancies on the student's academic performance (Rosenthal,

1973; for a review of education-specific mediators, see Brophy, 1983). Given the broader focus of the present chapter, however, I do not address such domain-specific mechanisms.

3. Note that my use of the term "impression formation goals" differs somewhat from its traditional use in the social-cognitive information-processing literature. In that literature, a *single* impression formation goal has been contrasted with memory goals, response goals, and the like to assess motivational influences on encoding, memory, and so on (see Srull & Wyer, 1986, for a review). In one study, for instance, people instructed to form a generalized impression of a target were found to remember more about the target than people told to remember as much about the person as possible (Hamilton & Katz, 1975). From my perspective, there exists no single impression formation goal but rather a *set* of such goals, each with the capability of orienting the perceiver somewhat differently toward his or her environment. In this chapter, I discuss three such differentiable goals: to confirm one's impressions, to form an accurate impression, and to form an impression rapidly.

4. This is not to say that these proposed defaults are ubiquitous. Under certain circumstances, it may be more efficient (i.e., may require fewer resources) to utilize other behavioral or cognitive strategies. For instance, although expectancy-biased attentional and interpretational processes may be easiest in most cases, it probably takes great efforts and cognitive resources to sustain such processes when a target's behavior is powerfully and unambiguously *in*consistent with one's expectancy, especially if the expectancy itself is weak. In this case, a more "even-handed" cognitive processing is likely to assume default status, given its lesser demands on available resources.

In addition, default processes are probably idiosyncratic to some extent. For example, the practiced insurance salesperson may easily express likeable behaviors, and the well-trained interviewer may have automatized unbiased information-gathering behaviors. These individuals should possess default strategies different from those proposed, owing to the fact that for them these particular strategies require the fewest resources. Consequently, when resources are scarce, these individuals should be better equipped to mask the impact of expectancies on their expressive and information-gathering behaviors, respectively. For most people under most circumstances, however, the posited default behaviors and cognitions are proposed to be representative.

5. Actually, Snyder's use of the term "knowledge acquisition" might be usefully replaced with "knowledge consolidation." The recent work of Stangor and Ruble (1989) suggests that when expectancies are weak or still being formed, information seeking is characterized by flexibility and accommodation in an apparent desire to be accurate. In contrast, when expectancies are either well established or accepted as legitimate, information seeking seems to be characterized by the assimilation of new information to existing knowledge. Given that Snyder's manipulation of the perceiver knowledge function consistently leads to expectancy confirmation (e.g., Snyder & Haugen, 1994)—an assimilative effect—it might be more appropriate to designate this function as knowledge *consolidation*.

References

Andersen, S. M., & Bem, S. L. (1981). Sex typing and androgeny in dyadic interaction: Individual differences in responsiveness to physical attractiveness. *Journal of Personality and Social Psychology, 41,* 74–86.

Babad, E. Y., Bernieri, F., & Rosenthal, R. (1989). Nonverbal communication and leakage in the behavior of biased and unbiased teachers. *Journal of Personality and Social Psychology, 56,* 89–94.

Babad, E. Y., Inbar, J., & Rosenthal, R. (1982). Pygmalion, Galatea, and Golem: Investigations of biased and unbiased teachers. *Journal of Educational Psychology, 74,* 459–474.

Bargh, J. A. (1990). Auto-motives: Preconscious determinants of social interaction. In E. T.

Higgins & R. M. Sorrentino (Eds.), *Handbook of motivation and cognition: Foundations of social behavior* (Vol. 2, pp. 93–130). New York: Guilford Press.

Bassok, M., & Trope, Y. (1984). People's strategies for testing hypotheses about another's personality: Confirmatory or diagnostic? *Social Cognition, 2,* 199–216.

Baumeister, R. F., Cooper, J., & Skib, B. A. (1979). Inferior performance as a selective response to expectancy: Taking a dive to make a point. *Journal of Personality and Social Psychology, 37,* 424–432.

Baumeister, R. F., Hutton, D. G., & Tice, D. M. (1989). Cognitive processes during deliberate self-presentation: How self-presenters alter and misinterpret the behavior of their interaction partners. *Journal of Experimental Social Psychology, 25,* 59–78.

Bechtold, A., Naccarato, M. E., & Zanna, M. P. (1986). *Need for structure and the prejudice-discrimination link.* Paper presented at the annual meeting of the Canadian Psychological Association, Toronto.

Berscheid, E., Graziano, W., Monson, T., & Dermer, M. (1976). Outcome dependency: Attention, attribution, and attraction. *Journal of Personality and Social Psychology, 34,* 978–989.

Blanck, P. D. (1993). *Interpersonal expectations: Theory, research, and applications.* Cambridge, England: Cambridge University Press.

Bodenhausen, G. V. (1990). Stereotypes as judgmental heuristics: Evidence of circadian variations in discrimination. *Psychological Science, 1,* 319–322.

Brigham. J. C. (1971). Ethnic stereotypes. *Psychological Bulletin, 76,* 15–38.

Brophy, J. E. (1983). Research on the self-fulfilling prophecy and teacher expectations. *Journal of Educational Psychology, 75,* 631–661.

Brophy, J. E., & Good, T. (1974). *Teacher-student relationships: Causes and consequences.* New York: Holt, Rinehart & Winston.

Christensen, D., & Rosenthal, R. (1982). Gender and nonverbal decoding skill as determinants of interpersonal expectancy effects. *Journal of Personality and Social Psychology, 42,* 75–87.

Cooper, H. (1979). Pygmalion grows up: A model for teacher expectation communication and performance influence. *Review of Educational Research, 49,* 389–410.

Cooper, H., & Good, T. (1983). *Pygmalion grows up: Studies in the expectation communication process.* New York: Longman.

Cooper, H., & Hazelrigg, P. (1988). Personality moderators of interpersonal expectancy effects: An integrative research review. *Journal of Personality and Social Psychology, 55,* 937–949.

Copeland, J. T. (1994). Prophecies of power: Motivational implications of social power for behavioral confirmation. *Journal of Personality and Social Psychology, 67,* 264–277.

Crano, W., & Mellon, P. (1978). Causal influences of teachers' expectations on children's academic performance: A cross-lagged panel analysis. *Journal of Educational Psychology, 79,* 39–49.

Crocker, J., Hannah, D. B., & Weber, R. (1983). Person memory and causal attributions. *Journal of Personality and Social Psychology, 44,* 55–66.

Darley, J. M., & Fazio, R. H. (1980). Expectancy confirmation processes arising in the social interaction sequence. *American Psychologist, 35,* 867–881.

Darley, J. M., Fleming, J. H., Hilton, J. L., & Swann, W. B., Jr. (1988). Dispelling negative expectancies: The impact of interaction goals and target characteristics on the expectancy confirmation process. *Journal of Experimental Social Psychology, 24,* 19–36.

Darley, J. M., & Gross, P. H. (1983). A hypothesis-confirming bias in labeling effects. *Journal of Personality and Social Psychology, 44,* 20–33.

Deaux, K., & Major, B. (1987). Putting gender into context: An interactive model of gender-related behavior. *Psychological Review, 94,* 369–389.

Dipboye, R. L. (1982). Self-fulfilling prophecies in the selection-recruitment interview. *Academy of Management Review, 7,* 579–586.

Duncan, S. L. (1976). Differential social perception and attribution of intergroup violence:

Testing the lower limits of stereotyping of blacks. *Journal of Personality and Social Psychology, 34,* 590–598.

Edwards, J. A., & Weary, G. (1993). Depression and the impression-formation continuum: Piecemeal processing despite the availability of category information. *Journal of Personality and Social Psychology, 64,* 636–645.

Ekman, P., & Friesen, W. F. (1974). Detecting deception from the body or face. *Journal of Personality and Social Psychology, 29,* 288–298.

Erber, R., & Fiske, S. T. (1984). Outcome dependency and attention to inconsistent information. *Journal of Personality and Social Psychology, 47,* 709–726.

Farina, A. (1982). The stigma of mental disorders. In A. G. Miller (Ed), *In the eye of the beholder: Contemporary issues in stereotyping* (pp. 305–363). New York: Praeger.

Farina, A., & Ring, K. (1965). The influence of perceived mental illness on interpersonal relations. *Journal of Applied Social Psychology, 70,* 47–51.

Fein, S., von Hipple, W., & Hilton, J. L. (1989). *The impact of interaction goals on expectancy confirmation.* Paper presented at the annual meeting of the American Psychological Association, New Orleans.

Fiske, S. T., & Neuberg, S. L. (1990). A continuum of impression formation, from category-based to individuating processes: Influences of information and motivation on attention and interpretation. In M. P. Zanna (Ed.), *Advances in experimental social psychology* (Vol. 23, pp. 1–74). New York: Academic Press.

Fiske, S. T., Neuberg, S. L., Beattie, A. E., & Milberg, S. J. (1987). Category-based and attribute-based reactions to others: Some informational conditions of stereotyping and individuating processes. *Journal of Experimental Social Psychology, 23,* 399–427.

Fiske, S. T., & Taylor, S. E. (1991). *Social cognition* (2nd ed.). New York: McGraw-Hill.

Freund, T., Kruglanski, A. W., & Shpitzajzen, A. (1985). The freezing and unfreezing of impression primacy: Effects of the need for structure and the fear of invalidity. *Personality and Social Psychology Bulletin, 11,* 479–487.

Gilbert, D. T., Krull, D. S., & Pelham, B. W. (1988). Of thoughts unspoken: Social inference and the self-regulation of behavior. *Journal of Personality and Social Psychology, 55,* 685–694.

Gilbert, D. T., Pelham, B. W., & Krull, D. S. (1988). On cognitive busyness: When person perceivers meet persons perceived. *Journal of Personality and Social Psychology, 54,* 733–740.

Goffman, E. (1959). *The presentation of self in everyday life.* Garden City, NY: Doubleday.

Grice, H. P. (1975). Logic in conversation. In P. Cole & J. L. Morgan (Eds.), *Syntax and semantics* (Vol. 3, pp. 41–58). New York: Academic Press.

Hamilton, D. L., & Katz, L. B. (1975, August). *A process-oriented approach to the study of impressions.* Paper presented at the annual meeting of the American Psychological Association, Chicago.

Hamilton, D. L., Sherman, S. J., & Ruvulo, C. M. (1990). Stereotype-based expectancies: Effects on information processing and social behavior. *Journal of Social Issues, 46,* 35–60.

Harris, M. J., & Rosenthal, R. (1985). Mediation of interpersonal expectancy effects: 31 meta-analyses. *Psychological Bulletin, 97,* 363–386.

Harris, M. J., & Rosenthal, R. (1986). Counselor and client personality as determinants of counselor expectancy effects. *Journal of Personality and Social Psychology, 50,* 362–369.

Higgins, E. T., & Bargh, J. A. (1987). Social cognition and social perception. *Annual Review of Psychology, 38,* 369–425.

Hildebrand-Saints, L., & Weary, G. (1989). Depression and social information gathering. *Personality and Social Psychology Bulletin, 15,* 150–160.

Hilton, J. L., & Darley, J. M. (1985). Constructing other persons: A limit on the effect. *Journal of Experimental Social Psychology, 21,* 1–18.

Hilton, J. L., & Darley, J. M. (1991). The effects of interaction goals on person perception. In M. P. Zanna (Ed.), *Advances in experimental social psychology* (Vol. 24, pp. 235–267). San Diego, CA: Academic Press.

Hilton, J. L., Darley, J. M., & Fleming, J. H. (1989). Self-fulfilling prophecies and self-defeating behaviors. In R. C. Curtis (Ed.), *Self-defeating behaviors: Experimental research, clinical impressions, and practical implications* (pp. 41-65). New York: Plenum Press.

Ickes, W., Patterson, M. L., Rajecki, D. W., & Tanford, S. (1982). Behavioral and cognitive consequences of reciprocal versus compensatory responses to pre-interaction expectancies. *Social Cognition, 1,* 160-190.

Jones, E. E. (1986). Interpreting interpersonal behavior: The effects of expectancies. *Science, 234,* 41-46.

Jones, E. E. (1990). *Interpersonal perception.* New York: W. H. Freeman.

Jones, E. E., & Pittman, T. S. (1982). Toward a general theory of strategic self-presentation. In J. Suls (Ed.), *Psychological perspectives on the self* (Vol. 1, pp. 231-262). Hillsdale, NJ: Erlbaum.

Judice, T. N., & Neuberg, S. L. (1994). *When perceivers desire to confirm their negative expectancies: Self-fulfilling prophecies and target misperceptions of own performance.* Unpublished manuscript, Arizona State University.

Jussim, L. (1986). Self-fulfilling prophecies: A theoretical and integrative review. *Psychological Review, 93,* 429-445.

Jussim, L. (1991). Social perception and social reality: A reflection–construction model. *Psychological Review, 98,* 54-73.

Kelley, H. H., & Stahelski, A. J. (1970). Social interaction basis of cooperators' and competitors' beliefs about others. *Journal of Personality and Social Psychology, 16,* 66-91.

Kim, H.-S, & Baron, R. S. (1988). Exercise and the illusory correlation: Does arousal heighten stereotypic processing? *Journal of Experimental Social Psychology, 24,* 366-380.

Kruglanski, A. W. (1989). *Lay epistemics and human knowledge: Cognitive and motivational bases.* New York: Plenum Press.

Kruglanski, A. W., & Freund, T. (1983). The freezing and unfreezing of lay-inferences: Effects of impressional primacy, ethnic stereotyping, and numerical anchoring. *Journal of Experimental Social Psychology, 19,* 448-468.

Kunda, Z. (1990). The case for motivated reasoning. *Psychological Bulletin, 108,* 480-498.

Langer, E. J., & Abelson, R. P. (1974). A patient by any other name . . . : Clinician group difference in labeling bias. *Journal of Consulting and Clinical Psychology, 42,* 4-9.

Lord, C. G., & Saenz, D. S. (1985). Memory deficits and memory surfeits: Differential cognitive consequences of tokenism for tokens and observers. *Journal of Personality and Social Psychology, 49,* 918-926.

Major, B., Cozzarelli, C., Testa, M., & McFarlin, D. B. (1988). Self-verification versus expectancy confirmation in social interaction: The impact of self-focus. *Personality and Social Psychology Bulletin, 14,* 346-359.

Meichenbaum, D. H., Bowers, K. S., & Ross, R. R. (1969). A behavioral analysis of teacher expectancy effects. *Journal of Personality and Social Psychology, 13,* 306-313.

Merton, R. K. (1948). The self-fulfilling prophecy. *Antioch Review, 8,* 193-210.

Miller, D. T., & Turnbull, W. (1986). Expectancies and interpersonal processes. *Annual Review of Psychology, 37,* 233-256.

Miller, N., & Brewer, M. B. (1984). *Groups in contact.* New York: Academic Press.

Neuberg, S. L. (1987). *Interpersonal expectancies and impression formation goals: Overriding the impact of negative expectancies on social interactions and impression formation.* Unpublished doctoral dissertation, Carnegie-Mellon University.

Neuberg, S. L. (1989). The goal of forming accurate impressions during social interactions: Attenuating the impact of negative expectancies. *Journal of Personality and Social Psychology, 56,* 374-386.

Neuberg, S. L. (1994). Expectancy-confirmation processes in stereotype-tinged social encounters: The moderating role of social goals. In M. P. Zanna & J. M. Olson (Eds.), *The Ontario Symposium: Vol. 7. The psychology of prejudice* (pp. 103-130). Hillsdale, NJ: Erlbaum.

Neuberg, S. L. (1996). Expectancy influences in social interaction: The moderating role of social goals. In P. M. Gollwitzer & J. A. Bargh (Eds.), *The psychology of action:. Linking motivation and cognition to behavior* (pp. 529–552). New York: Guilford Press.

Neuberg, S. L., & Fiske, S. T. (1987). Motivational influences on impression formation: Outcome dependency, accuracy-driven attention, and individuating processes. *Journal of Personality and Social Psychology, 53,* 431–444.

Neuberg, S. L., Judice, T. N., Virdin, L. M., & Carrillo, M. A. (1993). Perceiver self-presentational goals as moderators of expectancy influences: Ingratiation and the disconfirmation of negative expectancies. *Journal of Personality and Social Psychology, 64,* 409–420.

Nisbett, R. E., & Ross, L. (1980). *Human inference: Strategies and shortcomings of social judgment.* Englewood Cliffs, NJ: Prentice-Hall.

Omoto, A. M., & Borgida, E. (1988). Guess who might be coming to dinner?: Personal involvement and racial stereotypes. *Journal of Experimental Social Psychology, 24,* 571–593.

Pittman, T. S., & D'Agostino, P. R. (1989). Motivation and cognition: Control deprivation and the nature of subsequent information processing. *Journal of Experimental Social Psychology, 25,* 465–480.

Pyszczynski, T., & Greenberg, J. (1987). Toward an integration of cognitive and motivational perspectives on social inference: A biased hypothesis-testing model. In L. Berkowitz (Ed.), *Advances in experimental social psychology* (Vol. 20, pp. 297–340). New York: Academic Press.

Rosenthal, R. (1973). The mediation of Pygmalion effects: A four-factor "theory." *Papua New Guinea Journal of Education, 9,* 1–12.

Rosenthal, R. (1974). *On the social psychology of the self-fulfilling prophecy: Further evidence for Pygmalion effects and their mediating mechanisms* (Module No. 53). New York: MSS Modular.

Rosenthal, R., & Jacobson, L. F. (1968). *Pygmalion in the classroom.* New York: Holt, Rinehart & Winston.

Rosenthal, R., & Rubin, D. B. (1978). Interpersonal expectancy effects: The first 345 studies. *Behavioral and Brain Sciences, 3,* 377–386.

Ruble, D. N., & Ruble, T. L. (1982). Sex stereotypes. In A. G. Miller (Ed.), *In the eye of the beholder: Contemporary issues in stereotyping* (pp. 181–252). New York: Praeger.

Ruscher, J. B., & Fiske, S. T. (1990). Interpersonal competition can cause individuating impression formation. *Journal of Personality and Social Psychology, 58,* 832–842.

Saenz, D. S. (1994). Token status and problem-solving deficits: Detrimental effects of distinctiveness and performance monitoring. *Social Cognition, 12,* 61–74.

Saenz, D. S., & Lord, C. G. (1989). Reversing roles: A cognitive strategy for undoing memory deficits associated with token status. *Journal of Personality and Social Psychology, 56,* 698–708.

Sagar, H. A., & Schofield, J. W. (1980). Racial and behavioral cues in black and white children's perceptions of ambiguously aggressive acts. *Journal of Personality and Social Psychology, 39,* 590–598.

Sibicky, M., & Dovidio, J. F. (1986). Stigma of psychological therapy: Stereotypes, interpersonal reactions, and the self-fulfilling prophecy. *Journal of Counseling Psychology, 33,* 148–154.

Skov, R. B., & Sherman, S. J. (1986). Information-gathering processes: Diagnosticity, hypothesis confirmatory strategies, and perceived hypothesis confirmation. *Journal of Experimental Social Psychology, 22,* 93–121.

Smith, D. M., Neuberg, S. L., Judice, T. N., & Biesanz, J. C. (1995). *The role of target accommodation in the self-fulfilling prophecy.* Unpublished data, Arizona State University.

Snyder, M. (1984). When belief creates reality. In L. Berkowitz (Ed.), *Advances in experimental social psychology* (Vol. 18, pp. 248–306). New York: Academic Press.

Snyder, M. (1992). Motivational foundations of behavioral confirmation. In M. P. Zanna (Ed.), *Advances in experimental social psychology* (Vol. 25, pp. 67–114). San Diego, CA: Academic Press.

Snyder, M., Campbell, B. H., & Preston, E. (1982). Testing hypotheses about human nature: Assessing the accuracy of social stereotypes. *Social Cognition, 1,* 256–272.

Snyder, M., & Gangestad, S. (1981). Hypothesis-testing processes. In J. H. Harvey, W. Ickes, & R. F. Kidd (Eds.), *New directions in attribution research* (Vol. 3, pp. 171–196). Hillsdale, NJ: Erlbaum.

Snyder, M., & Haugen, J. A. (1994). Why does behavioral confirmation occur? A functional perspective on the role of the perceiver. *Journal of Experimental Social Psychology, 30,* 218–246.

Snyder, M., & Haugen, J. A. (1995). Why does behavioral confirmation occur? A functional perspective on the role of the target. *Personality and Social Psychology Bulletin, 21,* 965–974.

Snyder, M., & Swann, W. B., Jr. (1978a). Behavioral confirmation in social interaction: From social perception to social reality. *Journal of Experimental Social Psychology, 14,* 148–162.

Snyder, M., & Swann, W. B., Jr. (1978b). Hypothesis-testing processes in social interaction. *Journal of Personality and Social Psychology, 36,* 1202–1212.

Snyder, M., Tanke, E. D., & Berscheid, E. (1977). Social perception and interpersonal behavior: On the self-fulfilling nature of social stereotypes. *Journal of Personality and Social Psychology, 35,* 656–666.

Srull, T. K., & Wyer, R. S., Jr. (1986). The role of chronic and temporary goals in social information processing. In R. M. Sorrentino & E. T. Higgins (Eds.), *Handbook of motivation and cognition: Foundations of social behavior* (Vol. 1, pp. 503–549). New York: Guilford Press.

Stangor, C., & Ruble, D. N. (1989). Strength of expectancies and memory for social information: What we remember depends on how much we know. *Journal of Experimental Social Psychology, 25,* 18–35.

Stern, M., & Hildebrandt, K. A. (1986). Prematurity stereotyping: Effects on mother–infant interaction. *Child Development, 57,* 308–315.

Swann, W. B., Jr. (1984). Quest for accuracy in person perception: A matter of pragmatics. *Psychological Review, 91,* 457–477.

Swann, W. B., Jr., & Ely, R. J. (1984). A battle of wills: Self-verification versus behavioral confirmation. *Journal of Personality and Social Psychology, 46,* 1287–1302.

Swann, W. B., Jr., & Snyder, M. (1980). On translating beliefs into action: Theories of ability and their applications in an instructional setting. *Journal of Personality and Social Psychology, 38,* 879–888.

Swann, W. B., Jr., Stephenson, B., & Pittman, T. S. (1981). Curiosity and control: On the determinants of the search for social knowledge. *Journal of Personality and Social Psychology, 40,* 635–642.

Tavris, C., & Offir, C. (1977). *The longest war: Sex differences in perspective.* New York: Harcourt Brace Jovanovich.

Taylor, S. E., Fiske, S. T., Etcoff, N. L., & Ruderman, A. J. (1978). Categorical bases of person memory and stereotyping. *Journal of Personality and Social Psychology, 36,* 778–793.

Tetlock, P. E. (1983). Accountability and the perseverance of first impressions. *Social Psychology Quarterly, 46,* 285–292.

Tetlock, P. E., & Kim, J. I. (1987). Accountability and judgment processes in a personality prediction task. *Journal of Personality and Social Psychology, 52,* 700–709.

Trope, Y., Bassok, M., & Alon, B. (1984). The questions lay interviewers ask. *Journal of Personality, 52,* 90–106.

Virdin, L. M., & Neuberg, S. L. (1990). *Is perceived status a moderator of expectancy confirmation?* Paper presented at the annual meeting of the American Psychological Association, Boston.

von Baeyer, C. L., Sherk, D. L., & Zanna, M. P. (1981). Impression management in the job interview: When the female applicant meets the male (chauvinist) interviewer. *Personality and Social Psychology Bulletin, 7,* 45–51.

Vrugt, A. (1990). Negative attitudes, nonverbal behavior and self-fulfilling prophecy in simulated therapy interviews. *Journal of Nonverbal Behavior, 14,* 77–86.

West, C., & Anderson, T. (1976). The question of preponderant causation in teacher expectancy research. *Review of Educational Research, 46,* 613–630.

Wilder, D. A., & Shapiro, P. (1989). The role of competition-induced anxiety in limiting the beneficial impact of positive behavior by an outgroup member. *Journal of Personality and Social Psychology, 56,* 60–69.

Word, C. O., Zanna, M. P., & Cooper, J. (1974). The nonverbal mediation of self-fulfilling prophecies in inter-racial interaction. *Journal of Experimental Social Psychology, 10,* 109–120.

Zanna, M. P., & Pack, S. J. (1975). On the self-fulfilling nature of apparent sex differences in behavior. *Journal of Experimental Social Psychology, 11,* 583–591.

CHAPTER 8

Responding to Significant Others When They Are Not There
Effects on Interpersonal Inference, Motivation, and Affect

SUSAN M. ANDERSEN
NOAH S. GLASSMAN
New York University

The interpersonal context of life is widely assumed to be essential to personality, motivation, and behavior. In this view, a person's character may consist of his or her various tendencies to have particular kinds of social relationships (Sullivan, 1953). Such interpersonal patterns, learned in significant, relatively early relationships, may thus serve as models for constructing later social relations (e.g., Bowlby, 1969; Freud, 1912/1958; Greenberg & Mitchell, 1983; Guidano & Liotti, 1983; Horney, 1939; Horowitz, 1991; Kelly, 1955; Luborsky & Crits-Christoph, 1990; Rogers, 1951; Safran & Segal, 1990; Shaver & Rubenstein, 1980; Sullivan, 1953; Wachtel, 1981). Whether relationship patterns are set firmly into place very early in life, or, alternatively, evolve more gradually and continuously over time (e.g., Wachtel, 1981), it is obvious that new experiences are constructed in part on the basis of old ones, such that the past plays some role in the present. Mental representations of significant others, developed from numerous encounters with important people, may thus provide a means by which past experiences may come to bear on present interactions with new individuals. In this process, learned ways of relating to a significant other may be played out in response to a newly encountered person.

A long-standing notion in clinical theory relevant to this proposition is the concept of "transference." Although we do not endorse the complex psychosexual-conflict model proposed by Freud, we find several aspects of Freud's arguments about transference compelling. For Freud, the "patient" superimposes childhood fantasies, conflicts, and wishes about a parent onto an "analyst," and weaves "the figure of the physician into one of the 'series' already constructed in his mind" (Freud, 1912/1963, p. 107).[1] In the process, Freud argued, the patient embroils the analyst in his or her own unconscious psychosexual conflicts, and the analyst attempts to "analyze" this by making the patient aware of the displaced conflicts and their childhood origins (Ehrenreich, 1989).

A similar process, but without psychosexual content, was proposed by Sullivan (1940, 1953) in his distinctly interpersonal approach to transference, in which "parataxic illusory personal characterization" or "parataxic distortion" may occur in the course of "normal" human relations. In Sullivan's model, relationship patterns learned with important others may complicate an individual's perceptions of and reactions to various new people, including an analyst. Past experiences with significant others (encoded in the "parataxic" mode, which means both idiosyncratically and not in a fully verbal manner) are displaced onto another individual in daily life and in treatment. In this version of transference, related motivations, emotions, and patterns of action are then played out in the relationship with the new person (Andersen & Baum, 1994; Andersen & Cole, 1990). Our work concerns this basic process, conceptualized in information-processing terms.

With respect to the exact mental representations Sullivan proposed in his model of transference, he assumed that a child forms "personifications" of the self and others in memory (both good and bad aspects of each), and "dynamisms" characterizing the typical interplay between the self and the other as well (Sullivan, 1940, 1953; see also Greenberg & Mitchell, 1983; Mullahy, 1970). Although Sullivan did not postulate the existence of mental *structures* because he preferred process and energy metaphors, he did define a personification essentially as an individual mental representation that designates the self or another. Likewise, he defined a dynamism essentially as a mental representation of the relational patterns that link the self with the other. When transference occurs, the content of what is transferred reflects not only individual significant-other representations, but also the self-representation and the interpersonal dynamics between the self and the other. This model is generally consistent with our approach, although we make fewer assumptions about the specific *content* of people's mental representations of significant others and of the relation between the self and the other.[2]

In this chapter, we describe our information-processing model of transference in everyday social perception and the findings in the literature that support it. We then consider some of the basic structures and processes in memory, social judgment, and self-judgment that provide the theoretical and empirical context for this work, and consider these literatures in light of informing our understanding of some of the complex processes that are likely to transpire in transference—processes that extend beyond our present findings. Following this, we return to our transference paradigm and describe it in detail, because one central innovation of this work is its use of a combination of idiographic and nomothetic research methods (procedures that warrant specific description.) After describing the paradigm, we outline several new lines of research addressing questions at the heart of the transference phenomenon—studies concerned with basic activation mechanisms, affective-motivational links, and the impact of interpersonal roles in transference. Finally, the implications of this recent research for the transference phenomenon are considered, with an eye toward the larger theoretical and empirical issues raised at the outset.

SOCIAL INFORMATION PROCESSING AND TRANSFERENCE

We propose an information-processing model of transference, which maintains that transference occurs in everyday social judgment. (For related positions, see Singer, 1988; Wachtel, 1981; Westen, 1988.) Although some psychodynamic theorists focus on transference in the client–therapist relationship and often emphasize the importance of parental representations in particular (see Ehrenreich, 1989; Luborsky & Crits-Christoph, 1990), our model depicts a process that is widespread and common enough to occur in everyday interactions on the basis of various significant-other representations (Andersen & Baum, 1994; Andersen & Cole, 1990; Andersen, Glassman, Chen, & Cole, 1995). For example, a representation of a sibling, uncle, best friend, teacher, lover, or spouse, not only of a parent, may provide the means by which transference occurs in everyday encounters with new individuals.

Although our model of transference does not speak to the potential primordial importance of parental or other early-childhood representations, or to debates about the psychotherapeutic importance of transference or transference analysis in psychotherapy, it does speak to the basic process of transference in everyday social judgment. Indeed, our results, which have emerged in experimental research using basic social-cognitive methods, have indicated rather definitively that past experience with a significant other can be superimposed onto a new person in a way that biases inferences and memory, as well as affective responses toward the new person in everyday social perception (Andersen & Baum, 1994; Andersen & Cole, 1990; Andersen, Glassman, et al., 1995). The phenomenon is not "clinical"; the process appears to be basic. It may, however, be relevant to a widely held clinical assumption—namely, that much human suffering may result from superimposing old interpersonal patterns learned with significant others onto new individuals in one's life. Hence, well-controlled experimental research on transference in everyday social perception is of some importance.

Our basic concern has been to demonstrate the role that significant others play in subsequent social relations, with a particular focus on the use of mental representations of significant others in general social perception. To be more specific, our research has shown that mental representations of significant others, which serve as storehouses of information about particular individuals from one's life, can be triggered and applied to other individuals (Andersen & Baum, 1994; Andersen & Cole, 1990; Andersen, Glassman, et al., 1995). That is, a new person may activate a representation of a significant other, leading the perceiver to make inferences about the new person, such that this new person is misremembered as having qualities that he or she does not possess because these qualities describe the significant other. Perceivers appear to confuse what was actually *learned* about the new person at encoding with what was simply *inferred* using the significant-other representation (see also Johnson, Hastroudi, & Lindsay, 1993; Johnson & Raye, 1981). In the process, evaluations of the newly encountered person, and perhaps even "affective" responses toward him or her, become consistent with the representation as well (Andersen & Baum, 1994). Hence, schema-triggered evaluation (Fiske & Pavelchak, 1986) based on significant-other activation occurs, along with schema-triggered inference and memory. These findings provide support for the existence of a basic social information-processing mechanism underlying transference (Freud, 1912/1958) or parataxic distortion (Sullivan, 1953)—that is, the activation and application of a mental representation of a significant other to a new person.

As shown in Figure 8.1, we propose that the significant-other representation is applied to a new person when relevant stimulus cues in the target person combine with the inherent readiness of the significant-other representation to be used (Higgins & King, 1981; Higgins & Brendl, 1995; Sedikides & Skowronski, 1991). The process is conceptualized according to the principles of cognitive accessibility, including both transient and chronic sources (Higgins, 1989a; Higgins & King, 1981), and according to theories of both bottom-up (data-driven) processing and top-down (concept-driven) processing (Norman, 1969). That is, transference occurs based on the presence of triggering cues in the environment (bottom-up processing), as well as on the chronic accessibility of a given significant-other representation (top-down processing).

"Going beyond the Information Given"

Our model implies that a representation of a specific person may function in social information processing just as any other construct does, in that it may be activated and applied to a new person when relevant (Andersen & Baum, 1994; Andersen & Cole, 1990; Andersen, Glassman, et al., 1995; see also Higgins, 1989a). Indeed, the model suggests that transference is best defined in its most

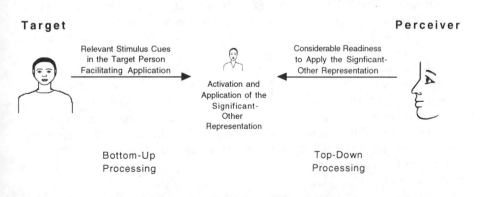

FIGURE 8.1 A depiction of the transference process conceptualized in information-processing terms: Applying the significant-other representation to a new person.

basic terms as "going beyond the information given" about the new person by inferentially filling in the blanks about him or her (Bruner, 1957). This process of filling in the blanks can be considered to be a kind of schema-triggered inference, in the sense that once the representation is activated, the target is assumed to have features of the significant other that were not learned about the target (e.g., Fiske, 1982). On this basis, the memory of what was actually learned about the target becomes biased accordingly. This is what our data have shown (Andersen & Baum, 1994; Andersen & Cole, 1990; Andersen, Glassman, et al., 1995). Representation-consistent biased memory is more likely to occur on the basis of significant-other representations than on the basis of control representations (e.g., representations of nonsignificant others, stereotypes, or traits). This kind of memory effect, of course, reflects the erroneous belief that representation-consistent information that was *not* learned about the target person *was* probably learned, in a kind of slippage in reality monitoring (Johnson & Raye, 1981). In this sense, significant-other representations have considerable inferential power to simplify what is known about a new person by enabling inferences about him or her, just as a schema or prototype does (e.g., Brewer, Dull, & Lui, 1981; Cantor & Mischel, 1977; Fiske, Neuberg, Beattie, & Milberg, 1987; Graesser, Woll, Kowalski, & Smith, 1980; Hamilton, 1979; Taylor, 1981; see also Andersen & Klatzky, 1987; Andersen, Klatzky, & Murray, 1990).

Schema-Triggered Affect

Our model of transference also predicts that the evaluative tone (and perhaps the overall affective quality) of a significant-other representation can lead a featurally relevant target person to be experienced evaluatively in a representation-consistent manner. In Fiske's model of schema-triggered affect, category-based evaluation is experienced on the basis of social categorization. That is, a category consists of various specific attributes, each its own overall evaluative tone or "affective tag" (Fiske & Pavelchak, 1986). Hence, the overall "summary" evaluation attached to the category can be attached to a new target person categorized in these terms. When an affect-laden stereotype is activated, the affective tag linked to the category is also activated, and the target person is categorized and evaluated accordingly (Fiske & Pavelchak, 1986; Pavelchak, 1989). Although there are many other cognitive models of affect (e.g., Averill, 1990; Bower, 1981; Clark & Isen, 1982; Lazarus & Averill, 1972; Ortony, Clore, & Collins, 1988), and many more models that are less focused on cognitive mediators (e.g., Berkowitz, 1993; Leventhal, 1984; Zajonc, 1980), the theory of schema-triggered affect provides a compelling explanation for how the evaluative tone of a representation can be transferred to a new person—the basic process that appears to occur in transference.

The affect in schema-triggered affect has typically been operationalized as evaluation (a positivity–negativity judgment), so that when a new target triggers a category that is positively evaluated, the new person is evaluated positively or liked, and when he or she triggers a negatively toned category, he or she is disliked. The model was constructed to characterize how stereotypes influence person perception—that is, how categories of many persons or of a "type" of person, rather than an *n*-of-one representation or an individual-person exemplar, may operate (although see Fiske, 1982). Hence, a new target person resembling a significant other ought to be liked more if the significant-other representation applied to the person is liked, and should be liked less if the significant other is disliked. This is exactly what we have found in our work—schema-triggered evaluation in transference—along with some weak effects suggesting comparable changes in transient mood (Andersen & Baum, 1994). (For more on representations of individuals, see Barsalou et al., 1993; Smith & Zarate, 1992.)

On another level, it should be noted that the distinction between "categorical" and "piecemeal" processing so central to the notion of schema-triggered affect may well be pertinent to the activation and application of significant-other representations as well (Fiske & Pavelchak, 1986; Pavelchak, 1989). That is, it is conceivable that highly complex or incongruent stimulus cues in a target person may lead to piecemeal and systematic processing of the new person rather than to representation-based processing, thus interfering with the activation and application of the significant-other representation, although this matter remains open to empirical examination.

BASIC SOCIAL-COGNITIVE STRUCTURES AND PROCESSES

In order to clarify the basic social-cognitive structures and processes involved in transference as it occurs in social perception, we consider the relevance of several literatures. First, we address the manner in which information is stored about significant others in terms of various memory systems: autobiographical and instance memory, generic memory (e.g., Tulving, 1972; see also Logan, 1988), individual-person exemplars (Smith & Zarate, 1990, 1992), declarative knowledge, and procedural knowledge. Second, we argue that significant-other representations are *n*-of-one representations rather than multiple-person categories, because they represent single individuals, and nonetheless are social constructs (Higgins & King, 1981) that operate by the parameters surrounding the activation and application of other social constructs (Higgins, 1989a). Third, we consider significant-other representations in relation to representations of self, in part in the framework of relational schemas (Baldwin, 1992), and in part also in terms of motivation (e.g., Bargh & Gollwitzer, 1994; Higgins, 1987, 1989b). Finally, we examine basic aspects of significant-other representations and self-representations in terms of information processing (Bargh & Tota, 1988; Markus, 1977), representational structure (Cantor & Kihlstrom, 1987), and content (Lord, 1980; Prentice, 1990). Throughout, we are concerned with the implications of these ideas for the manner in which transference transpires in social relations.

Memory Storage in Mental Representations of Significant Others

Fundamental to any discussion of mental representations of significant others is the manner in which such representations are stored in memory. We know that information stored about a significant other is used to fill in the gaps about what is not known about a new individual. Hence, the process of interpreting and responding to a new person depends in part on the particular memory content drawn upon involving a significant other. Although our work has not addressed the memory systems involved in transference, the way in which information and experience are encoded in memory is relevant in social cognition (see Carlston, 1992; Klein, Loftus, & Burton, 1989; Linville & Carlston, 1994; Martin & Clark, 1990; Ostrom, 1989; Wyer & Srull, 1988) and hence is likely to be relevant in transference.

Autobiographical and Generic Memory in Representing Significant Others

People clearly possess a vast store of specific autobiographical memories with specific significant others, as well as more generic, context-free knowledge about these individuals (Barsalou, 1993; Shoben, 1984; Smith & Zarate, 1992; Tulving, 1972, 1985). Autobiographical memories include concrete events and behaviors stored with spatial and temporal markers, as well as personal subjective experiences at the moment. Such memories for "scenes" or events occurring in real time are likely to include both (1) concrete information about who was present, what occurred, when and where it occurred, what feelings were evoked, what one did, what others did, and so on (Shoben, 1984; Tulving, 1993); and (2) information involving generalizations about the scene, the players, and its outcomes (Barsalou, 1993). In storing specific scenes or autobiographical memories, of course, considerable abstract knowledge is necessary to give meaning to the scene. On the basis of such autobiographical experience (plus relevant generic knowledge), "instance" memories are also formed—that is, instances of experience not linked to a context but that concern a significant other (e.g., "times I was spanked by him or her"). Without temporal and spatial markers, instances of a particular kind can accumulate over time without being temporally marked "snapshots" of the specific experiences.

From instance memory and autobiographical memory, people generalize by making abstract inferences that link various experiences together in generic knowledge. In this case, both autobiographical traces and instances may be lost while the generic, context-free information remains (Abelson, 1976; Mandler, 1984; Schank, 1982; Schank & Abelson, 1977; Shoben, 1984; see also Logan, 1988, 1989). Such abstract generic knowledge about a person may take the form "expresses great love toward everyone," "drives a Volvo," or "has red hair,"—that is, descriptive generalizations about a person, unlike autobiographical memories such as "the day I walked with him to the park on my birthday," or "when I broke my leg," or "when I saw her cry." Interestingly, research suggests that general, abstract memories are more easily recalled than specific autobiographical memories, because of greater associations in memory, greater organizing properties, and deeper levels of processing (Carlston, 1980; Craik & Lockhart, 1972; Klein & Kihlstrom, 1986; Lingle, Geva, Ostrom, Leippe, & Baumgardner, 1979; Ostrom, Lingle, Pryor, & Geva, 1980; Schneider, 1973).

We have yet to examine the role of specific autobiographical or experiential knowledge in transference, because we have focused on descriptive knowledge about significant others (Andersen & Cole, 1990; Andersen, Glassman, et al., 1995). Examining autobiographical memories along with generic significant-other representations would be of interest, however, because specific autobiographical material concerning a significant other may well be activated and applied in transference. Indeed, such memories about a significant other may have a particular readiness to be retrieved, just as does relevant generic knowledge (Andersen & Cole, 1990), in part because there is so much of it (Logan, 1988) and it is likely to be emotionally charged (Carlson, 1981; Carlson & Carlson, 1984; Tomkins, 1979). On the other hand, given that generic knowledge is easier to utilize, it may be relatively more important in transference.

It is our view that the type of memory storage used in representing significant others may be relevant not only to what is transferred in transference, but to the triggering conditions most likely to activate the particular stored memory as well. For example, to the extent that concrete, observable information is represented more commonly in instance or autobiographical memories than in generic memory, then the former may be more likely to be triggered by such concrete cues than by cues that are more abstract. By contrast, generic-cue information may be more likely to trigger generic representations. These possibilities warrant research attention. On the other hand, the links among instance, autobiographical, and generic memory about a person are likely to mean in practice that these types of memory may be activated in tandem.

Individual-Person Exemplars as the Basis of Significant-Other Representations

Although research on generic knowledge has often focused on the relative role of abstract features versus particular prototypes abstracted from specific experiences (Hayes-Roth & Hayes-Roth, 1977; Posner & Keele, 1968, 1970; Read, 1972; see also Brewer, 1988; Fiske & Neuberg, 1990; Linville & Fischer, 1993; Medin, 1989; Smith & Medin, 1981), mental representations of significant others may not map neatly onto these distinctions (Smith & Zarate, 1990, 1992).

The term "exemplar" has been used to refer to an individual-person representation that reflects the totality of knowledge about the person (Smith & Zarate, 1992), although the term has also been used to designate a particular "instance" of experience (e.g., Barsalou, 1990, 1993; Logan, 1988, 1989). The contents of an individual-person exemplar are "abstracted" from numerous experiences and exist as generic memory—that is, as descriptive knowledge (e.g., Cantor & Mischel, 1979; Higgins & Bargh, 1987; Higgins & King, 1981; Lingle, Altom, & Medin, 1983; Park & Hastie, 1987; Srull & Wyer, 1979; see also Alba & Hasher, 1983; Barsalou, 1990; Medin, Altom, & Murphy, 1984)—as well as specific autobiographical and instance memory (Barsalou, 1993; Brooks, 1987; Gilovich, 1981; Hintzman, 1976, 1986; Jacoby & Brooks, 1984; Jacoby & Kelley, 1990; Read, 1983; Smith, 1990).

Unfortunately, relatively little is known about what happens when multiple important experiences (over time) with an important person come to be stored in memory and are used in social information processing (Andersen & Cole, 1990). One thing is clear, however: The sheer number of available instances of experience with a significant other is likely to help define the individual as important (Logan, 1988). Indeed, research suggests that the more instances of experience, the more likely they are to be retrieved and used relatively automatically (Logan, 1988, 1989). Having many experiences with a single important other may be what makes the *n*-of-one person representation of a significant other influential in social information processing.

Declarative and Procedural Knowledge in Significant-Other Representations

Our work with significant others has made use of declarative memory about significant others—that is, general ideas and specific facts about the significant other (Cantor & Kihlstrom, 1987; Kihlstrom, 1987). The rules by which declarative knowledge is utilized, by contrast, constitute procedural knowledge (Cantor & Kihlstrom, 1987; Kihlstrom, 1987; Tulving, 1993; see also Smith, 1984, 1988; Smith & Branscombe, 1988; Smith & Lerner, 1986). Such procedural knowledge involves the process by which significant-other representations influence social perception, and it therefore enables a person to navigate the social environment in accordance with a significant-other representation. Although declarative and procedural knowledge may operate in parallel, they may also operate in tandem, given that particular declarative knowledge may be linked to particular procedures in memory. Representations of significant others are thus likely to contain both declarative and procedural elements, such that when a new person activates a declarative significant-other representation, the process of "filling in the blanks"(Bruner, 1957) about this new person, a procedure, transpires; the new person is misremembered accordingly (the basic transference finding). This kind of interplay between declarative and procedural knowledge may be basic and is also a hallmark of social scripts, which draw both upon declarative knowledge about a type of situation and the types of players in it, and upon procedural knowledge about *how* cognitive, affective, and behavioral responses are produced in such a situation (Cantor & Kihlstrom, 1987; Schank & Abelson, 1977; see also Baldwin, 1992).

The Activation and Application of Social Constructs as the Basis of Transference

Social constructs are most often studied as designators of a category or type of persons, such as an "adventurous" type, a "nerd," an auto mechanic, or a secretary (Higgins & King, 1981). Such classes of people, social roles, occupations, stereotypes, or trait groupings clearly operate as points of comparison in assessing others (e.g., Andersen & Klatzky, 1987; Banaji & Greenwald, 1994; Banaji & Greenwald, 1995; Brewer, 1988; Cantor & Kihlstrom, 1987; Fiske & Neuberg, 1990; Fiske & Pavelchak, 1986; Gilbert, 1989; Greenwald & Banaji, 1995; Hamilton, 1979; Higgins, 1989a; Jones, 1990; Pratto & Bargh, 1991; Schneider & Blankmeyer, 1983; Sedikides & Skowronski, 1990, 1991; Taylor, 1981; Uleman, 1989; Wyer & Martin, 1986; Wyer & Srull, 1986). "Proper" constructs, however ("proper" as in a "proper" name), also exist and operate as do other social constructs, even though they are not social categories (Higgins & King, 1981). "Proper" constructs can also be used as points of comparison for judging new individuals, just as categorical social constructs can be (Smith & Zarate, 1990; see also Andersen et al., 1995), even though this proposition has received little research attention (although see Fiske, 1982; Gilovich, 1981; Lewicki, 1985).

Hence, n-of-one representations may be activated and applied to a newly encountered person, who is then interpreted in terms of the construct—especially when there is some "match" or perceived similarity between the new stimulus and the construct (Tversky, 1977; Tversky & Gati, 1978; see also Cantor & Mischel, 1979; Nosofsky, 1986; Rosch, 1978; Schneider & Blankmeyer, 1983; Sedikides & Skowronski, 1991). That is, activation and application of a construct to a stimulus person are particularly likely when the stimulus is relevant to the construct (Higgins, 1989a, in press; Higgins & King, 1981; Higgins & Brendl, 1995; see also Kelly, 1955). In the process, a new experience with a new person may be experienced as an instance of previous experiences with a significant other or as similar to abstract descriptors of the significant other. In either case, the new stimulus may be treated as *analogous* to past instances or to a construct in memory, by being interpreted similarly in making sense of the present experience (Gilovich, 1981; Read & Cessa, 1991; Seifert, McKoon, Abelson, & Ratcliff, 1986; Spellman & Holyoak, 1992; see also Read, 1984, 1987; Gentner, 1983; Schank, 1982). This process may thus lead to inferential errors about the new stimulus (Cantor & Mischel, 1977; Higgins & King, 1981).

It is also worth noting that a newly encountered individual bearing some minimal resemblance to a significant other may "evoke" a mental representation of the significant other, even though the new person is not truly assimilated into the representation because of its n-of-one definition. For a significant-other representation, then, the process of activation and application to a new person implies only that one identifies the stimulus *with* the significant other because the stimulus seems *similar to* the significant other, and not that one identifies the stimulus *as being* the significant other (Higgins & King, 1981; see also Trope, 1986).

Chronic Accessibility of Social Constructs

Differences in the sheer *frequency* with which any construct tends to be used are important in social information processing. That is, some constructs are more "chronically accessible" than others (Higgins, 1989a, in press; Higgins & Brendl, 1995; Higgins & King, 1981; Higgins, King, & Mavin, 1982), meaning that they are readily called to mind and used. Factors contributing to the extent to which a given construct comes to mind in interpreting a social situation or person include familiarity and self-relevance (e.g., Cantor & Kihlstrom, 1987; Markus, 1977; Prentice, 1990). Because a given significant-other representation is of course highly familiar and highly important by definition, as well as frequently thought about, such representations are likely to be chronically accessible—an assumption that is supported by recent research (Andersen et al., 1995).

Transient Priming of Social Constructs

Beyond chronic accessibility, transient cuing effects in the environment play an important role in activation and application. In fact, a large and complex literature exists on the *recency* with which any given construct has been used in advance of a given judgment—a literature concerned with contextual-priming effects (e.g., Bargh, 1989; Bargh, Bond, Lombardi, & Tota, 1986; Bargh, Lombardi, & Higgins, 1988; Bargh & Thein, 1985; Fazio, Powell, & Herr, 1983; Herr, 1986; Higgins, 1989a, in press; Higgins & King, 1981; Neuberg, 1988; Schwarz & Sudman, 1991; Smith, 1990; Srull & Wyer, 1979; Wyer & Srull, 1981). The data suggest that when a construct is activated just before a stimulus person is encountered, the newly encountered target is likely to be perceived in terms of the construct in subsequent impression tasks (e.g., Higgins, Rholes, & Jones, 1977; Higgins & Brendl, 1995; Smith & Zarate, 1990, 1992; Sedikides & Skowronski, 1991; Stangor, 1988; Stangor, Lynch, Duan, & Glass, 1992; Zarate & Smith, 1990). Although such assimilation effects are not always found, in that contrast effects are also observed under certain conditions (e.g., Lombardi, Higgins, & Bargh, 1987; Higgins & Stangor, 1988; Manis & Paskewitz, 1984a, 1984b; Manis, Paskewitz, & Cotler, 1986; Martin, 1986; Martin, Seta, & Crelia, 1990; Petty & Wegener, 1993; Schwarz & Bless, 1991; Schwarz & Sudman, 1991), assimilation is nonetheless quite common (Andersen, Glassman, et al., 1995).

Although most work on priming has tended to ignore the potential for a stimulus itself to activate a given representation without priming beforehand, we argue that a target person's resemblance to a given representation may increase the likelihood of the activation and application of the representation to the new target person (Tversky, 1977). Significant-other representations are likely to have a chronic readiness to be activated, but should nonetheless be particularly likely to be applied to a stimulus when the stimulus is relevant to the representation; activated constructs are applied when they are applicable (e.g., Higgins, 1989a, in press; Higgins & Brendl, 1995; Higgins et al., 1977; see also Andersen, 1994; Bargh et al., 1986; Erdley & D'Agostino, 1988; Ford, Stangor, & Duan, 1994; Hastie, 1981).

Overall, both chronic and transient influences on accessibility appear to be important in social perception (e.g., Bargh et al., 1986; Higgins & Brendl, 1995). The cues with properties that are efficacious in triggering a representation are therefore of considerable importance. Indeed, the features that define a given representation (its "core" features), whether essential or prototypic, may constitute not only the kinds of inferences likely to be made about a new person classified in terms of the representation, but also the effective triggering cues for the representation, although defining features may not always be the best triggering cues (Smith & Medin, 1981). For our purposes, this is of interest because cuing features have yet to be operationalized independently of defining features in our research—a matter that is worthy of empirical attention (Klatzky & Andersen, 1988).

On a related note, although we assume that a significant-other representation can be activated essentially "as a whole," such that all of its defining features are applied to the new person in a manner that goes beyond what was provided in the cuing information, it is quite possible that not *all* aspects of the significant-other representation are equally likely to be applied to a given target person. The activation process itself may be more likely to set in motion some significant-other features and not others, unlike what would be expected from a more monolithic structure (see also Higgins & Bargh, 1987). That is, a particular "working" significant-other representation may be activated by contextual cues in the immediate situation, just as a particular "working" self-concept may be activated by particular contextual cues (Markus & Nurius, 1986; McGuire & McGuire, 1981). This assumption is quite consistent with recent developments in categorization in semantic memory (Barsalou, 1992, 1993) and with work in social cognition suggesting that a monolithic self-schema may not exist, except when the self is rather negatively toned (e.g., Higgins, VanHook, & Dorfman, 1988; Segal, Hood, Shaw, & Higgins, 1988; see also Linville, 1982; Linville & Carlston, 1994). In this sense, it may be that most significant-other representations are not internally organized as schemas.

The Relationship between Self-Representations and Significant-Other Representations

In conceptualizing transference, it is important to consider the potential linkages between a given representation of a significant other and one's representation of the self. We suggest that such linkages exist and include representations of the other's feelings and behaviors toward the self, along with the self's feelings and motivations toward the other, typical modes of interaction between self and other, and various outcome expectancies (see also Shrauger & Schoeneman, 1979).

Recent research has verified that linkages between self-representations and significant-other representations in memory exist. That is, the influence of mental representations of significant others on one's experience of the self has been demonstrated in terms of self-evaluative responses, presumably by means of spreading activation to the self (Baldwin, 1992; Baldwin, Carrell, & Lopez, 1990; Baldwin & Holmes, 1987). More specifically, cognitively priming subjects with a parental figure, as opposed to a friend, leads participants to report less enjoyment of sexually charged written passages and lower self-evaluations after reading such passages (Baldwin & Holmes, 1987). Similarly, exposing subjects to a visual prime of a disapproving significant-other face, outside of conscious awareness, leads to self-assessments that are significantly less positive than those obtained after similar exposure to a disapproving nonsignificant-other face (Baldwin et al., 1990). Hence, significant-other activation does appear to influence self-activation and self-evaluation (Baldwin & Holmes, 1987; Baldwin et al., 1990), suggesting that linkages between self and significant other do indeed exist in memory.

Although activating a significant-other representation activates the self-representation, studies of transference are needed that systematically examine the role of the self in the transference phenomenon (Hinkley & Andersen, 1995; see Andersen & Chen, in press). Extant data imply that the self is implicated in transference via spread of association from the significant-other representation to the self-representation. Moreover, it may also be the case that activation of the self somehow enhances or increases the likelihood of significant-other activation. Indeed, because the self is linked not only to one significant-other representation but to many, various significant-other representations may compete for use at any given time, each associated with a somewhat different aspect of self; this remains an open empirical question.

Relational Schemas

The linkages between self-representations and significant-other representations may also be fruitfully envisioned as a single representation designating the relationship between the self and the significant other. Such "relational schemas" have been proposed, in which the representations of the self and the significant other are bound up together via an interpersonal script representing typical interaction patterns (Baldwin, 1992; see also Bugental, 1992; Horowitz, 1989; Miell, 1987; Planalp, 1987; Safran, 1990). A relational schema would thus include various responses of the self toward the significant other, and various responses of the significant other toward the self. Because a relational schema mentally represents *both* the self and the other, it extends work on each representation into the arena of interpersonal relations and scripts characterizing such relations (Abelson, 1976, 1981; Graesser, Gordon, & Sawyer, 1979; Graesser et al., 1980; Schank & Abelson, 1977; see also Carlson, 1981; Tomkins, 1979). The notion also dovetails nicely with Sullivan's concept of "dynamisms" linking the self and the other.

It is worth noting, however, that the extent to which the actual relational linkages between self and significant other take the form of a relational schema also remains an open empirical question. The notion of schematicity capitalizes particularly on the presence of generic, abstract knowledge in the representation, of course, and also on strong internal linkages within the representation. But independent of whether or not relational self–other linkages are schematic in nature, their exact content, structure, and processing correlates are of considerable interest, in part because of the potential implications for transference. In these respects, in fact, the predictions emerging from the relational-schema model and from the two-representations model are not all that different. Triggering a significant-other representation in a two-representations model should ultimately trigger aspects of the self, along with various interpersonal information and response patterns, through the linkages between the representations of the significant other and the self. The consequences of activating a relational schema should thus be quite similar (Baldwin, 1992) to the consequences of activating a significant-other representation and then the relational links to the self-representation; both should result in the same inferential, affective, motivational, and behavioral processes.

Beyond the question of exactly what processes are set in motion as a consequence of activating a significant-other representation or a relational schema, there is the question of the conditions under which each type of representation is more likely to be activated. In considering this problem, it is important to keep in mind that if both representations exist, activating one will probably lead to activation of the other because of their linkages in memory. Hence, any differing activation effects as a function of which type of representation is activated first may not last long. In terms of potentially different activating conditions, however (i.e., those that are most optimal for triggering each representation), observing the actual behavior of a new person may trigger a relational schema more rapidly than triggering an individual significant-other representation. Similarly, encountering generic features similar to those of a significant other may trigger an individual significant-other representation more rapidly than triggering a relational schema.

Models of the Relationship between Significant Others and the Self

In any consideration of significant-other activation and transference, and the role of the self in the process, research on attachment theory is clearly of relevance. Attachment theory suggests that mental models of important interpersonal relations are formed in early childhood and influence subsequent behavior (Bowlby, 1980). The central assumption is that a mental model of a significant other is formed for motivational reasons; that is, such a mental model permits comfortable separation from the other and the development of autonomous behavior with respect to the other. The model is intimately related to the concept of transference, because mental models are thought to be enacted in one's later intimate relationships. Although most research on attachment has been conducted with infants and children (cf. Bowlby, 1969, 1973, 1980) and has focused on styles of attachment (e.g., Ainsworth, Blehar, Waters, & Wall, 1978), the literature on adult attachment-related behavior is rapidly growing, also with a special focus on attachment styles (e.g., Collins & Read, 1990; Feeney & Noller, 1990; Hazan & Shaver, 1987; Kobak & Hazan, 1991; Shaver & Rubenstein, 1980; Simpson, 1990; Sroufe & Fleeson, 1986). With reference to transference, activation of a mental model of a particular significant other would be expected to lead to the activation of associated attachment-related processes—a question that has yet to be examined in research on attachment-relevant processes. Moreover, it is possible that activating attachment issues may also lead, reciprocally, to the activation of a given significant-other representation, if the attachment issues with this significant other are sufficiently unique to him or her.[3] (For a related approach to interpersonal closeness, see Aron, Aron, & Smollan, 1992; Aron, Aron, Tudor, & Nelson, 1991.)

In terms of social and personality psychology, self-discrepancy theory (Higgins, 1987; Strauman & Higgins, 1987, 1988) deals explicitly with the relationship between representations of the self and the significant other, and thus may have implications for what transpires in transference. In this model, both the self and a person's parents serve as standpoints from which the person views and defines the self. The parental perspective on the self is represented in structures similar to the structures representing one's own perspective: the "actual self," the "ideal self" (the ideal the other would hope the self to be) and the "ought self" (the duties to which the other believes the self should adhere). All of these aspects of self are presumed to be linked together in memory, and the model thus implies that the knowledge of the significant other is bound up with these various aspects of self. Self-discrepancies between these aspects—that is, between the actual self and a self-guide (ideal or ought)—are linked with specific affective and motivational responses, and have both evaluative and self-regulatory consequences (e.g., Higgins, 1989b; Higgins, Klein, & Strauman, 1985; Higgins, Strauman, & Klein, 1986). Hence, within the model, it would make sense that the proposed self-relevant processes may be set in motion when a significant-other representation is activated, resulting in specific self-relevant affective responses in the context of transference.

Another model in social and personality psychology that makes explicit claims about the relationship between the self and significant others, and that may therefore have implications for transference, is the self-evaluation maintenance model, which concerns the role of affect in self-regulation (Tesser & Campbell, 1980, 1982). The basic notion is that significant others, defined particularly in terms of siblings, provide a context within which the self is defined. In order to protect self-esteem, one gravitates to areas of expertise and self-definition that are not entirely identical to areas in which siblings are accomplished (or are likely to become accomplished), so that the relationship is not compromised by competition in a self-relevant domain. The basis for this movement is that when another person close to the self succeeds in a highly self-relevant domain, the result is negative affect, whereas when this person succeeds in a non-self-relevant domain, the result is positive affect. Hence, the model speaks to processes in self-development that derive from family dynamics (Tesser, 1980) and that may be reflected in the information stored about the self and the significant other in memory. If self-relevant material of this sort is stored with a significant-other representation, this material may be activated in transference, and may thus be relevant to the affective responses elicited in transference.

On yet another level, because significant-other activation leads to self-activation, significant-other activation in transference may well lead to changes in the working self-concept specific to transference (e.g., Markus & Nurius, 1986). That is, changes in the aspects of self most active in "working" memory may well occur, in that those aspects of self most closely linked to the significant other and to the specific significant-other features may be activated in transference (Hinkley & Andersen, 1995; see Andersen & Chen, in press).

The Role of Motivation in Linkages between Self and Significant Other

In considering the role of motivation in the linkages between the self and the significant other in memory, some models of relational schemas suggest that this motivation fundamentally concerns programs for maintaining interpersonal relatedness with the significant other—that is, for maintaining attachment (Safran, 1990; see Sullivan, 1940). In such models, the motive for remaining related to significant others, particularly to those in one's early familial environment, is fundamental to human motivation. Hence, striving toward the fulfillment of this motivation, however nonconscious or "unplanned," is intimately part of the relationship between the self and the significant other (Safran, 1990; Sullivan, 1940). Thus, the typical modes of interaction between the self and other stored within the significant-other representation may be infused with motivation, including the way the self attempts (or has attempted) to maintain the self–other relationship. In this view, motivation is inherent in the linkages between representations of the self and the significant other.

In our model, motivation may be associated with significant-other representations by being experienced extensively with these others in the course of development (see also Higgins, 1989b). Such motivation may thus be susceptible to activation based on significant-other activation, in much the same manner as proposed by the theory of schema-triggered affect. In schema-triggered affect, it is assumed that there is an evaluative "tag" (positive or negative) linked to every category, and that this evaluative tag can be triggered when the category is activated (Fiske, 1982). The same basic process may characterize the activation and application of a motivational construct linked to the significant-other representation, except that the "tag" is motivational in nature. Indeed, it is worth noting that any such motivational tag would necessarily involve linkages to the self, because it is the self that evaluates the significant other and the self that experiences motivation toward the significant other.

In this sense, we assume that motivations "belong" to the self and are experienced toward others (and toward the self), and hence constitute a linkage to the self-representation stored *with* the significant-other representation. In this sense, "motivational constructs" may be constructs unto themselves that can be attached to other constructs, such as a significant-other representation (Bargh, 1990). For example, the motivation of "wanting to be close to" or "wanting to be distant from" or "or wanting to be independent from" a particular significant other may be linked to the representation of that person stored in memory. Thus, motivations are likely to be activated when the significant-other representation is activated. By the same token, when a given motivation is activated, it may be that a particular significant-other representation is also activated—if the motivation is sufficiently specific to the significant-other representation to activate it uniquely.

From our point of view, "motivation" consists of an individual's psychological needs or goals that direct his or her interpersonal behaviors in purposive ways (e.g., Lewin, 1935; see also, e.g., Carver & Scheier, 1981; Koestner & McClelland, 1990; McClelland, 1984; Miller, Galanter, & Pribram, 1960), often in the form of basic tasks the person sees himself/herself as pursuing (Cantor & Kihlstrom, 1987; Emmons, 1986; Klinger, 1977, 1987; Snyder, 1992). Our conception of motivation does not include traditional assumptions about drive reduction—for example, those concerned with physiological needs, habits, and drive–response links (e.g., Bolles, 1967; Freud, 1915/1957). Indeed, many alternative theories concerned with personality suggest that there may be a small set of "*basic*" human needs (which may often be in conflict), such as the needs for closeness and warmth, for autonomy and competence, and for safety and security (e.g., Bowlby, 1969, 1973; Deci & Ryan, 1985; Horney, 1945; Sullivan, 1940). We favor the assumption that there may be a small set of such basic interpersonally relevant motivations.

In terms of the manner in which motivations are stored in relation to significant-other representations, it is likely that the *outcomes* encountered with the significant other are stored along with the motivations themselves. This would imply that the relational patterns stored with a significant-other representation include both one's motivations toward the significant other and the significant other's response to these motivations, as well as the relevant outcomes and contingencies present in the other's behavior overall. Hence, the linkages between a given significant-other representation and the self are likely to include "if-then" contingency relations, such as "When I need/want X, he or she responds with Y, which makes me feel Z" (Higgins, 1989b). To the degree that such contingency information is part of the relational information linking the self-representation with the significant-other representation, such information is likely to be activated in transference. (See Thorne, 1989, for a related approach.)

In considering this way of thinking about motivation in relation to significant-other representations, it is instructive to note that social-cognitive models of motivational sets and goals have been extensively examined in recent years (e.g., Cohen, 1981; Ebbesen, 1980; Hoffman, Mischel, & Mazze, 1981; Wyer & Gordon, 1982; Srull, 1983; Gollwitzer, 1990; Higgins & McCann, 1984; Higgins, McCann, & Fondacaro, 1982; Kunda, 1987; Showers & Cantor, 1985; Markus &

Nurius, 1986; for relevant reviews, see Higgins & Sorrentino, 1990; Sorrentino & Higgins, 1986; Srull & Wyer, 1986; McCann & Higgins, 1988). In particular, research linking motivation with social-cognitive processes is especially relevant (Bargh, 1990; Bargh & Gollwitzer, 1994; Raynor & McFarlin, 1986; Sorrentino & Short, 1986), because it has shown that goals and motives are "represented in the mind in the same fashion as are social constructs" (Bargh, 1990, p. 100). Such motive representations appear to be linked with situations in which they are often pursued, resulting in activation when the situational cues are present (Bargh, 1990; Bargh & Barndollar, 1996; Bargh & Gollwitzer, 1994). That is, goals or motives can be activated by contextual priming, with consequences for the degree to which later behaviors consistent with primed goals are performed. Specifically, priming an achievement- or affiliation-relevant goal leads predictably to goal-related behaviors that persist over time (Bargh & Gollwitzer, 1994). Hence, goals and motivations can be defined in terms of cognitive processes (see also Cantor & Kihlstrom, 1987; Wyer & Srull, 1986), and in a manner that makes explicit the rules by which goals are set into motion on a moment-to-moment basis (Bargh, 1990).

Our conceptualization of motivation is consistent with this kind of model (Bargh, 1990), although we would argue that such motivational constructs may be linked to a particular significant-other representation, and hence that activating the significant-other representation may activate relevant motivation. From our point of view, goals and motives frequently pursued in relation to the significant other are stored *with* the significant-other representation (along with the person's attributes, specific memories of him or her, affects toward him or her, etc.), and are thus activated in transference.

Individual Mental Representations of the Self versus Significant Others

Most research has not examined the *relation* between self-representations and significant-other representations, but rather has tended to examine the two types of representations individually. This literature is relevant to transference to the extent that transference is the result of activation of representations of a significant other and of the self via spreading activation through associative relational links. Hence, information-processing and structural concerns associated with self-representations and significant-other representations are briefly considered below, along with potentially important content differences.

Information Processing

The constructive role of the self in information processing, memory, and encoding is widely known. The literature demonstrates the potency of the self-representation as a "tool" with which to process information (Jacoby & Kelley, 1987,

1990) when this information concerns the self (e.g., Bargh & Tota, 1988; Bellez-za, 1984; Bower & Gilligan, 1979; Greenwald, 1980; Greenwald & Pratkanis, 1984; Kihlstrom & Cantor, 1984; Kihlstrom et al., 1988; Markus, 1977; Markus & Nurius, 1986; Markus & Wurf, 1987; Prentice, 1990; Rogers, 1981), and also when it concerns other people. In the latter case, the self may be insinuated in social prediction (Cronbach, 1955; Dornbusch, Hastorf, Richardson, Muzzy, & Vreeland, 1965; Fong & Markus, 1982; Markus, Smith, & Moreland, 1985), in the perception of a false consensus (Ross, 1977; Ross, Greene, & House, 1977; Marks & Miller, 1987), and in projection (e.g., Bramel, 1962; Campbell, Miller, Lubetsky, & O'Connell, 1964; Edlow & Kiesler, 1966; Feshbach & Feshbach, 1963; Holmes, 1968; Lemon & Warren, 1974), such that the reach of self-repre-sentations extends well beyond information directly pertinent to the self.

In this same manner, research concerned with significant-other representa-tions has shown that these representations also serve as potent processing "tools" in information not only about the significant other himself or herself (Prentice, 1990), but also about another person (Andersen & Cole, 1990). For ex-ample, memory enhancement has been shown when information relevant to a significant other is encoded with reference to this significant other (Keenan & Baillet, 1980; Rogers, 1981; see also Bower & Gilligan, 1979; for reviews, see Greenwald & Pratkanis, 1984; Kihlstrom & Cantor, 1984), perhaps because of increased organization of the learned stimuli in memory (see Klein & Kihlstrom, 1986; Klein et al., 1989). These data suggest that significant-other representations may be quite well organized—as well organized as self-representa-tions, even though the question of internal organization in the form of schematicity among self-representations warrants continued research (see Hig-gins & Bargh, 1987; Higgins et al., 1988). In any event, related memory effects have also been obtained when the information is about a person other than the significant other. That is, biased inference and memory about a new other has been demonstrated in the context of transference (e.g., Andersen & Cole, 1990).[4]

Reference to any highly familiar concept enhances both memory (Bower & Gilligan, 1979; Keenan & Baillet, 1980; Prentice, 1990) and processing efficiency, in that people make faster decisions when referring to any familiar conceptual structure than to when referring to any unfamiliar structure (Keenan & Baillet, 1980; Prentice, 1990). Both significant-other representations and representations of self are highly familiar, of course; hence, both are easily utilized in informa-tion processing in relation to relevant information (e.g., for the self, Bargh & Tota, 1988; Markus, 1977; Prentice, 1990; for significant others, Prentice, 1990). In terms of cognitive accessibility in particular, research has shown that free-re-trieval latencies to complete sentences about a significant other are short relative to latencies to complete sentences about social categories (i.e., a stereotype label or trait label; Andersen & Cole, 1990, Studies 2 and 3). Hence, significant-other representations are cognitively accessible—both in terms of memory for a signif-icant other as an "object" about which one engages in free retrieval (Andersen & Cole, 1990), and in terms of the significant-other representation as a "tool" for making particular relevant judgments (e.g., Prentice, 1990; see Jacoby & Kelley, 1987, 1990, for more on this distinction).

Cognitive Structure

In terms of structural differences between the self and significant-other representations, the literature on cognitive reference points is informative and suggests that such differences may be few (Tversky, 1977; see also Andersen & Cole, 1990, Study 2; Andersen & Klatzky, 1987, Study 3; Hampson, John, & Goldberg, 1986; Holyoak & Gordon, 1983; Houston, Sherman, & Baker, 1987; Srull & Gaelick, 1983). Overall, this research concerns perceived similarity and shows that highly familiar others are stored in memory at a level of complexity comparable to that of the self. That is, judgmental asymmetries found in similarity ratings would appear to suggest that representations of significant others are distinctive in memory relative to those of nonsignificant others (e.g., Holyoak & Gordon, 1983; Srull & Gaelick, 1983), just as self-representations are distinctive in memory relative to representations of nonsignificant others, and that self-representations are not distinctive relative to significant-other representations (Holyoak & Gordon, 1983; Srull & Gaelick, 1983).

Significant-other representations are, moreover, distinctive in memory relative to relevant social categories (Andersen & Cole, 1990, Study 2), because the relevant ratings yield rating asymmetries typical of cognitive reference points (Tversky, 1977; see also Holyoak & Gordon, 1983; Houston et al., 1989; Srull & Gaelick, 1983). That is, the "core" features of significant-other representations are rated as less characteristic of related social constructs (stereotypes and traits) than the "core" features of these related constructs are rated as characteristic of the significant-other representations. The fact that the research made use of features idiographically generated as sentence completions makes the findings more compelling. The use of feature-to-category-label ratings, instead of the category-label-to-category-label ratings typical in the literature on cognitive reference points (see also Andersen & Klatzky, 1987), further extends the literature on rating asymmetries and similarity. As these data imply, significant-other representations are clearly associatively rich in memory (Andersen & Cole, 1990, Studies 1 and 2), in that subjects readily complete numerous sentences about a significant other relative to those completed about nonsignificant others or social categories. Both associative richness and distinctiveness in memory are structural factors that are thought to be associated with greater activation readiness (Higgins & King, 1981), and in fact they are (Andersen & Cole, 1990; see also Prentice, 1990).

Measuring a representation's distinctiveness through judgmental asymmetries involves both shared and unshared information between representations; together, these two pieces of information allow for the assessment of featural distinctiveness and hence, of the extent to which a representation "stands out" in memory (Andersen & Cole, 1990, Study 2) and thus comes to mind readily

(Higgins & King, 1981; see also Tversky, 1977). Some research has also focused more exclusively on *overlap* between representations, that is, on the amount of *shared* information. When such a measure is used, both the self and the familiar-other descriptions overlap more with unfamiliar-other descriptions than with each other, suggesting that representations of the self and the significant other are different from one another in that there is little actual overlap between them in memory. More important, perhaps, is the demonstration of less internal consistency across situations for both the self and the familiar other than for the unfamiliar other, for whom perceived uniformity across situations is high (Prentice, 1990; see also Sande, Goethals, & Radloff, 1988; Shoda & Mischel, 1993; Wright & Mischel, 1988); again, this suggests complexity in both self and significant-other representations.

Content

Because a significant other is highly familiar, the representation designating a significant other ought to contain considerable familiar content. Research concerning the types of attributes that might constitute the defining features of significant-other representations has shown that on using an open-ended general-description task, people list more privileged information about internal states to characterize both the self and a familiar other than to characterize a relatively unfamiliar person, meaning that "privileged" information about internal states and preferences is important in significant-other representations (Prentice, 1990). On the other hand, people list more privileged information to describe the self than to describe the familiar other (Prentice, 1990). That is, they describe the self largely by privileged information (32.7%) and traits (25.2%), and less so by interpersonal-relations information (9.1%), whereas they characterize familiar others primarily by interpersonal-response information (20.6%) and traits (26.5%), and somewhat by privileged information (16.7%); unfamiliar others are characterized less by privileged information (8.4%) and more by physical features (19.1%, vs. 11.1% for familiar others). These data are consistent with work suggesting that familiar-other descriptions tend to be more "abstract" than unfamiliar-other descriptions, which tend to be more "concrete" (Fiske & Cox, 1979; see also Park, 1986, on the development of descriptions of others over time).

Overall, content differences in representations of the self and of a familiar other may exist. That is, interpersonal-response patterns may be more predominant in the significant-other representation than in the self-representation, and privileged information may be more predominant for the self. Such content-based differences in self-representations and significant-other representations, if they exist, may derive from the differing perspectives from which the self and the other are viewed: One "sees" the interpersonal responses of others differently than one "sees" one's own, and one "experiences" one's own internal responses differently than one apprehends the internal states of another. The apparent implications for mental representations of self and other dovetail nicely with previous research on the role of privileged cognitive–affective information in self-inference relative to behavioral information (Andersen, 1984; Andersen & Ross, 1984). Of course, the considerable work on the role of behavior in inferences about others in the actor–observer literature is also pertinent (see also Jones, 1976; Jones & Nisbett, 1972; Nisbett & Ross, 1980; Regan & Totten, 1975; Storms, 1973; Winter & Uleman, 1984).

Consistent with this perspective, recent research has shown that privileged cognitive–affective information is more predominant in mental representations of self than is behavioral information. In freely listing sentences to describe the self, subjects list more sentences while focusing on cognitive and affective aspects of self than while focusing on behavioral aspects (Andersen, Gold, & Glassman, 1995)—a difference not evident in describing significant others or nonsignificant others. Moreover, feature-to-category-label similarity ratings concerning the self show that cognitive–affective self-aspects are distinctive in memory relative to behavioral self-aspects—a pattern that is weaker and not reliable for the significant other (but that suggests that internal states may be important in significant-other representations), and that is reliably reversed for the nonsignificant other. Finally, behavioral self-aspects show no greater cognitive accessibility than cognitive–affective self-aspects do, as indexed by free-retrieval latency, even though there is a clear accessibility advantage for behavioral aspects over cognitive–affective ones both for the significant other and for the nonsignificant other (Andersen, Gold, & Glassman, 1995). Together, these findings suggest differences in the content of self-representations and significant-other representations that may have implications for their respective structures and information-processing functions (see also Andersen & Ross, 1984; Nisbett & Ross, 1980).

Interestingly, work in the area of visual-image processing in relation to self and others similarly highlights the potential role of perspective differences in the representations that are ultimately formed of the self versus another person. Specifically, imagined visual scenes are less effective as encoding devices in relation to the self than in relation to another individual, even a significant other (Lord, 1980, 1987). This lends credence to the idea that the differing visual perspective from which the self versus another person is viewed has implications for the content of the representations of self and others stored in memory (see also Carlston, 1992).

In terms of the implications of this work for the role of self-representations and significant-other representations in social perception, privileged information is important in the inferences people make about themselves (e.g., Andersen, 1984; Harter, 1983; Rosenberg, 1979), and appears to have predominance in the mental representations formed of the self (Prentice, 1990; see also Johnson, 1987; Johnson, Struthers, & Bradlee, 1988). Hence, when the self-representation is used to make inferences about a new person, these inferences should heavily involve internal states. Because such internal-state information is also stored about a significant other, though to a lesser degree, this information should similarly lead to internal-state inferences in transference. That is, we may expect a new person to think and feel toward us as our significant other does (or did), and to behave toward us in the same way as well. The special role of behavior in representing a significant other, however, suggests that expectancies about interpersonal behavior may be more likely and internal-state inferences somewhat less likely to emerge on the basis of activation and application of the significant other (in transference) than on the basis of activation and application of the self (in projection).

On another level, these content differences may be relevant not only to the *consequences* of significant-other activation and application, but also to optimal conditions for activation. That is, encountering interpersonal-response cues or behavioral cues in a new person that resemble those offered in a significant other's behavior may trigger a significant-other representation more readily than encountering interpersonal-response cues resembling one's own behavior may trigger the self-representation. In the same vein, visual, physical, concrete cues may be more potent for significant-other representations than for self-representations, for reasons of differences in visual perspective. Nonetheless, generic personal characteristics, experiences, and acts of a significant other, presented in words and in writing, clearly trigger significant-other representations in transference, as our research has shown; this implies that visual triggering cues are far from a necessary condition in transference. Empirical examination of these matters awaits future work.

SIGNIFICANT-OTHER REPRESENTATIONS IN INTERPERSONAL PERCEPTION: BASIC PARADIGM AND FINDINGS

In our research, we have demonstrated inferential and memorial processes in transference, and we have been able to do so by using a combination of idiographic and nomothetic methods. Our basic paradigm and findings are thus described below, in preparation for considering our most recent research findings and their implications.

Examining Idiographic Meanings in a Nomothetic Experimental Design

It would be impossible to conduct research on the transference process without finding a way to incorporate into the research design the particular idiosyncratic understanding that any given individual has of any given significant other in his or her own personal life. Given that having a mental representation of a particular significant other is a necessary condition for transference in our conceptualization, in that this representation is what is applied to the new person, finding a way to measure a given significant-other representation for a given person is of the essence.

Hence, a primary methodological advance necessary in the examination of transference is the use of idiographic research methods (Allport, 1937; Kelly, 1955) in combination with a nomothetic experimental design. An individual's mental structures or constructs that are meaningfully related to his or her life cannot be examined unless there is an effective way to measure them and to monitor their functioning. A significant other will obviously be mentally represented by the individual in a highly idiosyncratic way that is unique to the individual. In our research on transference (Andersen, 1992; Andersen, Glassman, et al., 1995; Andersen & Baum, 1994; Andersen & Cole, 1990), we have utilized a set of idiographic stimulus-generation procedures, in which subjects produce idiographic descriptions of their significant others, which we can then use later as experimental stimuli in a nomothetic experimental design. That is, idiographic contents—in the form of descriptive sentences completed about a specific significant other—are used to construct the stimulus materials that are employed in a standard experimental paradigm. This combined idiographic–nomothetic methodology makes it possible to draw nomothetic conclusions about basic processes underlying transference, while at the same time using idiographic stimulus materials that index the subjects' own significant others.

Idiographic stimulus-generation procedures have been employed in various other research contexts as well. As one example, research on self-discrepancy theory (e.g., Higgins, 1987) has used such methods to demonstrate that people's idiosyncratic self-constructs are linked in theoretically meaningful ways to their emotional experiences; the degree to which discrepancies between the "ideal self" or "ought self" and the "actual self" exist is assessed by idiographic means, and yet triggering such discrepancies in a nomothetic experimental design results in predictable emotional experiences (e.g., Higgins, Bond, Klein, & Strauman, 1986).

In our research, we also use both idiographic and nomothetic methods. Subjects encounter stimulus descriptions of a new person, and some of these descriptions are ones that they themselves have produced in advance, idiographically (e.g., about a significant other). After learning about the person, subjects complete a test of recognition-memory; this permits the measurement of nomothetic processes across subjects, particularly representation-consistent biased memory. Using this method, we have demonstrated both biased memory and schema-triggered evaluation based on the activation of a significant-other representation and its application to a newly encountered person (Andersen & Baum, 1994; Andersen & Cole, 1990; Andersen, Glassman, et al., 1995). The initial studies conducted in this research program are now described.

Experimentally Demonstrating Transference in Social Perception

Our first experimental demonstration of transference (Andersen & Cole, 1990, Study 3) made use of an experimental design in which subjects learned about several target persons and then completed a recognition-memory test. In our second demonstration (Andersen & Baum, 1994), participants learned about one target person, in a between-subjects design, and completed a recognition-memory test as well as evaluation and transient-affect measures. In both paradigms, the resemblance of one target person to each subject's own significant other was manipulated.

Biased Inference and Memory

In the first study, we made use of a microcomputer program with which subjects learned about four fictional people, one of whom resembled each subject's own significant other. The three control targets resembled, respectively, a nonsignificant other from each subject's own life, a stereotype that he or she previously named and described (e.g., "redneck"), and a trait that he or she similarly described (e.g., "conservative"). All stimuli were descriptive sentences that were generated idiographically by each individual subject before the experimental session, in the first phase of the study. In the second phase, subjects participated in the learning trials and completed a recognition-memory test. All phases of the design are described in Table 8.1.

In the initial stimulus-generation phase of this study, each subject freely named the people and social categories to be studied—a significant other, a nonsignificant other, a stereotype label, or a trait label. The subject then described each by completing 14 sentences in his or her own words (limited to a six-word predicate), listing *whatever came to mind*. Afterward, each subject rank-ordered these completed sentences for descriptive importance, and also selected from a randomized list of adjectives those he or she considered "irrelevant" to the representation. This concluded the stimulus-generation phase of the research.

For our purposes, however, one of four fictional characters' names was then paired with a fixed proportion of the sentence predicates (always ranks 5 to 11) for each mental representation, along with a randomly selected set of irrelevant filler adjectives (each preceded by the verb "is"), all randomly ordered within each set or block. Then, after a brief break, subjects participated in the learning phase of the experiment by being exposed via microcomputer to learning trials about four fictional people; these were presented in randomized blocks, with the descriptors in each block randomly ordered and resembling one of the persons or categories described earlier. In the learning task, subjects were asked to try to remember what they were learning about each fictional character. As indicated, each of the fictional targets resembled one of the subject's own mental representations, with an identical degree of overlap across conditions. Moreover, each representation was important enough to the subject to come to mind, based on our instructions in the preliminary stimulus-generation phase of the research. That is, all representations were rather highly accessible.

After participating in the learning trials, subjects completed a brief distractor task, followed by a recognition-memory test, in which they rated their confidence that they had actually seen and learned each of various descriptors about each fictional target person (see Cantor & Mischel, 1977). To the extent that the

TABLE 8.1   The Experimental Demonstration of Transference: Basic Paradigm

Phase 1: Idiographic stimulus-eliciting procedures

1. Subjects name a significant other (and possibly other people or categories).
2. Subjects complete a series of sentences (usually 14) to characterize this person, and then rank-order these listed sentences in terms of how descriptive they are of the person.
3. Subjects select from a list of adjectives those that are neither descriptive nor counterdescriptive of the person (i.e., those that are essentially irrelevant to the person).

Phase 2: Learning about a new person and completing a recognition-memory test

1. Subjects participate in a learning task in which they learn about one or more new target persons.
2. In the learning task, the target person (or one of the target persons) is characterized by some of the descriptive statements subjects listed earlier to describe their significant other, as well as by some irrelevant filler statements.
3. After completing a brief distractor task to clear short-term memory, subjects rate their confidence that they actually saw and learned each of a series of descriptive statements about the target person. The descriptive statements include those that were actually learned about the target and those that were not actually learned.

Representation-consistent biased memory is indexed by relatively high confidence ratings about statements that were *not* actually presented about the target person but that *do* describe the representation. This reflects the activation and application of the representation via the tendency to "fill in the blanks" (Bruner, 1957) about the new person.

new person resembled a given representation, the representation should have been activated and applied, leading to biased inferences and memory.

As predicted, the data indicated that subjects were more likely to show representation-consistent biased memory about the fictitious target who activated their significant-other representation than about the control targets; these data are shown in Figure 8.2. Again, because each target had exactly the same overlap with the relevant representation, the data are fairly persuasive in suggesting that people may be especially likely to use representations of specific significant others from their own lives (relative to other idiographically defined social categories) in social perception.

A second study used the same basic paradigm shown in Table 8.1 to replicate and extend the findings in a between-subjects experimental design employing a "real" social context with a partner allegedly next door (Andersen & Baum, 1994). In this study, subjects learned about only one target person instead of four; this target resembled either their own significant other or someone else's significant other (i.e., the significant other of a yoked subject). Perfect yoking ensured that the stimuli encountered by subjects learning about the target resembling someone else's significant other were identical to those encountered by subjects learning about a target resembling their own significant other. The recognition-memory test employed across conditions was also identical. Moreover, the use of the features of a yoked subject's significant other provided an

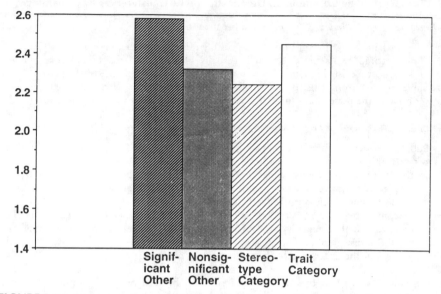

FIGURE 8.2   Representation-consistent recognition-memory ratings about a target person as a function of resemblance to a significant other versus resemblance to control representations in a within-subject design. Although the means suggest that traits may have led to more biased memory than did stereotypes or nonsignificant-other representations, post hoc tests did not support this pattern (Tukey, $p < .05$). Data from Andersen and Cole (1990, Study 3).

unequivocal control for the possibility that unusual or special features listed for any significant other, even someone else's, might account for the relative predominance of representation-consistent biased memory in this condition. As an improvement on our previous design, moreover, the session in which subjects provided their significant-other descriptors was held 2 weeks prior to the experimental session.

Again, as predicted, the findings on biased inference and memory clearly demonstrated the basic transference effect—that is, more representation-consistent memory when the target resembled the subject's own significant other rather than someone else's. These data are illustrated in Figure 8.3. Because the target also resembled either a positively toned or a negatively toned significant other (either the subject's own or a yoked subject's), the data also enabled the conclusion that the transference effect occurs independently of the overall tone of the significant-other representation. That is, it appears to occur equally for positively toned and for negatively toned significant-other representations. (Importantly, all targets were characterized by an equal number of positive and negative descriptors, independently of the tone of the representation.)

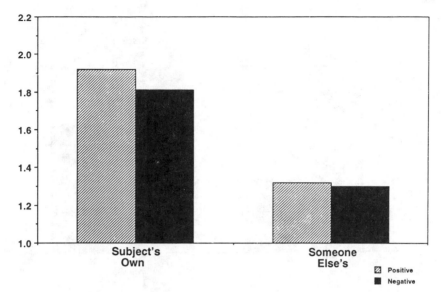

FIGURE 8.3 Representation-consistent recognition-memory ratings about a target person as a function of resemblance to the subject's own significant other (positive or negative) versus resemblance to a yoked subject's significant other (positive or negative) in a between-subjects design. Data from Andersen and Baum (1994).

Overall, when a target person activates a significant-other representation, the experiencing individual is likely to use this representation to "fill in the blanks" about the target person. The target person is thus more likely to be remembered as having extra representation-consistent characteristics that were not actually presented about the target person.

Schema-Triggered Evaluation

In this same study, we also examined subjects' evaluative responses toward the target person (Andersen & Baum, 1994). In particular, we sought to demonstrate the process of schema-triggered affect, defined in terms of the transfer of evaluation (Fiske, 1982). If significant-other representations function in this manner, any affect linked to them should be attached to a stimulus person classified in these terms (Fiske & Pavelchak, 1986), even though a significant-other representation is an *n*-of-one representation rather than a multiple-person category. This is exactly what the data showed. As shown in Figure 8.4, subjects evaluated the target who resembled their own positively toned significant other far more favorably than the target who resembled their own negatively toned significant other; when the significant other was well liked, the relevant target was better

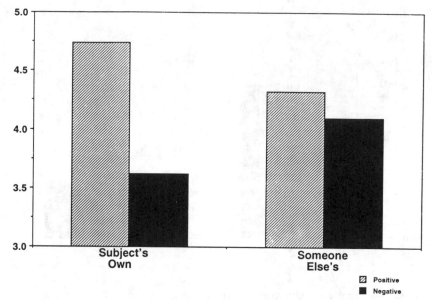

FIGURE 8.4   Evaluation of the target person as a function of resemblance to the subject's own significant other (positive or negative) versus resemblance to a yoked subject's significant other (positive or negative) in a between-subjects design. Data from Andersen and Baum (1994).

liked than when the significant other was disliked. However, subjects' evaluations of the target who resembled another subject's positively toned versus negatively toned significant other did not differ. Hence, the obtained evaluative response toward the target appears to have derived from the overall tone of the subject's own significant-other representations. These data therefore demonstrate schema-triggered evaluation (Fiske, 1982) in the context of transference.

Schema-Triggered Transient Affect

Beyond schema-triggered evaluation, this same study also examined schema-triggered transient affect, using standard self-report measures of transient mood. We tested the assumption that a significant-other representation might be so highly personal and emotionally charged that its activation might result in measurable changes in transient affect, consistent with the overall positive or negative tone of the representation. For example, if one feels unhappy and bad about oneself around a particular significant other, then one may be more likely to experience related unhappy or depressive affect when the representation of this other is activated than when a representation of a significant other around whom one feels happy and good about oneself is activated. The data concerned with self-reported transient mood essentially supported this prediction, although the effect size was much smaller than that observed for target evaluation.

The fact that transient affect did not emerge as reliably as did target evaluation as a function of our manipulations suggests that transient affect is not identical to "heated-up" evaluation. The link between a given significant-other representation and free-floating transient affect may therefore be more complex than is the link to evaluation. Induced mood effects are often rather weak and dissipate quickly over time in the laboratory (e.g., Blaney, 1986; Clark & Isen, 1982), implying that any such effect in this kind of design may be fleeting; moreover, it is possible that there simply is not one generic transient affect linked to the significant-other representation, and hence no single affective response that is always experienced when the representation is activated. For example, one can presumably dislike someone and have no particular affective response around him or her, or even feel happy around him or her. One can also love someone, and yet feel unhappy or anxious around the person, presumably for other reasons. Hence, evaluation and affect may not always covary perfectly. Moreover, multiple transient affects may presumably be linked to a significant-other representation, such that affect in transference may be evoked as a function of the particular situational and/or temporal contexts, types of interaction with the significant other, or specific autobiographical memories called to mind in the transference—in the context of the "real" situation with the target person (Andersen & Baum, 1994; see also Baldwin, 1992).[5]

TRANSFERENCE IN SOCIAL PERCEPTION: RECENT AND ONGOING RESEARCH

In our most recent research, we are examining basic social-cognitive processes underlying transference, focusing on the manner in which significant-other representations are activated and applied to a new person. More specifically, we are investigating biased inference and memory in transference—with a focus on the role of chronic accessibility and triggering stimulus cues in the phenomenon; its persistence and exacerbation over time; the elicitation of evaluation, affect, and motivation in transference; and the impact of interpersonal roles in transference.

Mechanisms Underlying Transference: Chronic Accessibility of Significant-Other Representations and Triggering Stimulus Cues

In two studies, we examined the extent to which significant-other representations are chronically accessible—that is, are readily activated and applied in social judgment, as are other chronically accessible constructs (Andersen, Glassman, et al., 1995; Glassman, Andersen, & Cole, 1994). For example, chronically accessible constructs require no priming in advance before a relevant stimulus is encountered in order to be applied to that stimulus. Moreover, effects attributable to advance priming should combine additively with the effects of chronic accessibility in terms of inferential consequences (Bargh et al., 1986).

The first study tested these propositions using a within-subject paradigm with the same idiographic stimulus-generation procedure and nomothetic experimental design used previously (Andersen & Cole, 1990). The experimental learning task concerned four fictional target persons as usual (Andersen & Cole, 1990, Study 3), but was either preceded or not preceded by a transient contextual prime. That is, before the experimental learning trials, subjects named and described a significant other and a nonsignificant other by completing 14 sentences about each. They did this either immediately before the learning trials (the priming condition), or in a session held 2 weeks earlier (the no-prime condition). Hence, in the priming condition, both the significant-other and the nonsignificant-other representations were primed in advance—just before the learning trials. (As in earlier studies, participants were led to believe that the two sessions were separate studies.) In the learning trials, the four target persons resembled, respectively, subjects' own significant other, their own nonsignificant other, a yoked subject's significant other, and a yoked subject's nonsignificant other. After learning features about all four targets, subjects completed a recognition memory test (Andersen & Cole, 1990, Study 3) from which representation-consistent biased memory was assessed in terms of subjects' confidence that they had learned particular representation-consistent features about the target person that they actually had not seen in the learning task.

As predicted, the data showed that subjects showed more representation-consistent memory about the target resembling their own significant other than about the control targets, independently of priming condition. This finding suggests that a significant-other representation can be activated and applied to a relevant target person, even if not primed in advance; it thus confirms the basic transference phenomenon and supports the chronic-accessibility argument. In addition, as predicted, the priming of subjects' own significant-other and nonsignificant-other representations in the priming condition increased representation-consistent biased memory for each of the targets resembling these representations, thus demonstrating the additivity of priming and chronicity in transference (extending Bargh et al., 1986).

Significant-other representations should also have the tendency to be applied to a new stimulus person even when there is no particular similarity-based overlap between the representation and the stimulus person, although relevant stimulus cues should, of course, increase the likelihood of application (e.g., Higgins & Brendl, 1995). To examine the application of significant-other representations in the *absence* of triggering stimuli, a second study used a comparable design in which all subjects participated in a preliminary feature-listing session 2 weeks before the learning trials. In this first session, subjects named two different significant others and completed 14 sentences about each, as well completing one sentence for each of a diverse set of people named by the experimenter (not consisting of a single representation). In the second session, subjects again learned about four fictional people. In the special no-trigger significant-other condition, the target resembled a yoked subject's significant other, and yet the recognition-memory test about this target involved the features listed for one of the subject's *own* significant others. Hence, the learned target features were *not* derived from the significant-other description, but the test features were. In the standard stimulus-triggering condition, by contrast, the target did resemble another of the subject's own significant others, and the recognition-memory test about this target involved the features of this same significant other. In the two control conditions, the target resembled either another of the yoked subject's significant others and a comparable memory test, or a set of features listed by the subject designating no single representation and a comparable memory test.

As predicted, subjects showed more representation-consistent biased memory when their significant other was triggered by the target cues than in the control conditions. Moreover, more such memory emerged concerning the significant-other representation when the target *did* resemble the significant other than when the target did not. That is, the standard significant-other condition led to greater transference than did the no-trigger condition. Hence, target relevance—or triggering stimulus cues in the target person—plays a role in activation and application of the significant-other representation in transference. On the other hand, even when not triggered by stimulus cues in the target person, the significant-other representation was still quite likely to be applied to the target person, in that more representation-consistent memory was observed in the no-trigger significant-other condition than in the control conditions. Hence, the data converge on the conclusion that very little target similarity is needed for the basic transference effect to occur.

These studies support the proposition that significant-other representations are chronically accessible. Significant-other representations have a readiness to be applied to a stimulus person without priming and even without relevant triggering cues, even though stimulus triggering clearly has an impact on significant-other activation and application. These findings locate the transference phenomenon firmly within the domain of theory and research in social cognition, by speaking to chronic and transient sources of activation in transference.

Persistence and Exacerbation over Time in the Effects of Significant-Other Activation

Although the data concerning chronic accessibility and stimulus triggering in transference speak to the basic processes underlying the transference phenomenon, they do not touch on how robust the phenomenon is in terms of its persistence over time. That is, it is of interest to determine the degree to which transference (i.e., the effect of significant-other activation and application) is long-lasting or relatively transient. In this set of studies, we explored the prediction that biased memory based on significant-other activation and application should persist over time (e.g., over a 2-week period), and may even be exacerbated over time (Andersen & Glassman, 1995; Glassman et al., 1994). That is, because significant-other representations, as chronically accessible constructs, should tend to remain active longer than other representations (Bargh et al., 1988) and have a readiness to be used, they should also have a strong likelihood of being activated over a postencoding delay period of a few weeks. During such postencoding activation, various featural pathways within the representation are traversed via spreading activation (Collins & Loftus, 1975), thereby strengthening these pathways—both between features actually learned in relation to the target person and between those not learned, each of which describes the significant-other representation. In this way, significant-other representations may lead to greater false-positive memory over a postencoding delay period, as retrieval of an item learned about the target becomes more likely to lead to retrieval of an unlearned item. Even the consequences of transient priming may increase over time (Higgins et al., 1977), and this should be true of chronic influences on activation as well.

In the first study, subjects again participated in a feature-listing session held 2 weeks before the learning trials. Later, each subject then learned about four fictional people resembling, respectively, the subject's own significant other, the subject's own nonsignificant other, the no-single-representation set of features self-generated by the subject, and a yoked subject's significant other. These learning trials were followed by a recognition-memory test, which was administered on *two* occasions: once immediately after the learning trials, as usual, and again 2 weeks afterward. The order of the items on each recognition memory test was individually randomized for each subject. Administering the memory test twice permitted the assessment of the persistence of the biased-memory effect over time, and more particularly its exacerbation over time. The results clearly showed both persistence and exacerbation over time. That is, the effect occurred at both Times 1 and 2, and the representation-consistent-memory effect favoring the significant-other representation increased over time.

A second study was designed to rule out an alternative explanation for the findings of Study 1, in which subjects' performance on the second memory test could have been the result of their performance on the first. In Study 2, subjects once again learned about four target persons, but did *not* complete the memory test immediately after the trials; memory was assessed by administering the memory test only during a follow-up session held 2 weeks later. This study manipulated target resemblance exactly as in the previous study, except that one of the targets resembled a social stereotype each subject named and described in the preliminary session, replacing the nonsignificant-other condition of Study 1. The results showed that subjects showed more representation-consistent memory bias about the target resembling their own significant other than about the control targets, as assessed in the 2-week follow-up session. These data support the finding that biased inference and memory in the basic transference effect persist over time. They also support the finding of exacerbation over time in

Study 1, by ruling out the idea that the responses on the delayed test of recognition memory in Study 1 were entirely an artifact of having taken the first test.

Triggering Evaluation, Motivation, and Facial Affect in Transference

The next line of research extends the consequences of significant-other activation in transference beyond biased memory and schema-triggered evaluation (Andersen & Baum, 1994) into the domain of schema-triggered facial affect (Andersen, Manzella, & Reznik, 1995; Manzella, Andersen, & Reznik, 1994). In this design, each subject learned about one target person who was allegedly seated next door, who resembled either one of the subject's own positively toned or negatively toned significant others or a yoked subject's positively or negatively toned significant other. (Targets in both the positive and negative conditions were characterized by an equal number of positive and negative features). While the subject was learning about the target in the experiment, his or her facial expressions were covertly videotaped so that we could assess facial affect at encoding. By focusing on nonverbal facial affect at the exact moment that the subject learned each target feature about the target person, we were able to assess transient affect in transference more directly—via a nonverbal, non-self-report measure. Two trained judges then reliably rated subjects' facial expressions for pleasantness (i.e., for positive vs. negative feeling). These judges were unaware of subjects' conditions.

We also extended our previous work by examining interpersonal-intimacy motivation as a kind of schema-triggered motivation, using self-report. Specifically, we assessed each subject's motivation to emotionally approach or to be emotionally distant from the target person, after having determined that subjects' positively toned significant other was one they felt close to and wanted to be closer to and that their negatively toned significant other was one they did not feel close to and wanted to b even more distant from. In addition, we also assessed expectancies that the target person would like the subject, as schema-triggered expectancies about the other. As in our previous work, schema-triggered evaluation and representation-consistent memory were also assessed.

Overall, we predicted that subjects would show more representation-consistent facial affect, evaluation, motivation, expectancy, and memory when the target resembled their own significant other rather than someone else's. The results for facial affect were exactly as predicted. Subjects responded with more pleasant facial affect when learning about the target who resembled their own positively toned significant other than about the target resembling their own negatively toned significant other. This pattern did not emerge when the target resembled a yoked subject's positively versus negatively toned significant other—verifying the proposition that transient facial affect is elicited in the context of significant-other activation, and importantly extending previous findings concerned with affect in transference. The data generated by this virtually instantaneous measure of transient affect indicate that learning about the target person induces representation-consistent transient affect in the form of fleeting facial expressions, presumably by means of the basic process of schema-triggered affect.

Indeed, these findings also showed that subjects expressed the most positive facial affect when the target features presented were actually *negative* ones that were also descriptive of the subjects' own positively toned significant other. This provocative finding can be understood in terms of the lay theories or narratives people construct about highly valued others *in order to* remain close with them, narratives that minimize the negative qualities that these others possess (e.g., Murray & Holmes, 1994). Hence, when a negative aspect of a positively toned significant other is encountered in a new person such that transference results, the well-rehearsed positive (minimizing) response emerges as well. These data highlight the utility of our facial-affect measure in capturing subtle affective responses in the transference paradigm. On the other hand, because even the relatively weak effects for self-reported transient mood obtained in earlier work (Andersen & Baum, 1994) were not replicated in this study, the data also suggest that effects of significant-other activation on transient affect may indeed be *very* fleeting.

In addition, our previous findings concerning subjects' evaluative responses to the target were clearly replicated, demonstrating once again the phenomenon of schema-triggered evaluation in transference. Subjects' evaluation of the target emerged exactly as predicted (see also Andersen & Baum, 1994), in that subjects reported liking the target far more when the target resembled the subjects' own positively toned versus negatively toned significant other—a pattern not found when the target resembled a yoked subject's significant other.

In terms of subjects' motivation toward the target person, the data once again confirmed our basic hypothesis. That is, subjects were more motivated to emotionally approach (and not to emotionally distance themselves from) the target person resembling their own positively toned significant other than the target resembling their own negatively toned significant other—a pattern that did not hold when the target resembled a yoked subject's significant other. Hence, emotionally relevant motivations pertaining to intimacy and connectedness between the self and the significant other appear to be activated along with the significant-other representation and applied to the new target. These data demonstrate the experimental elicitation of motivational processes in transference. Moreover, they support our conceptualization of motivation as linked to significant-other representations in the same way as is "affect" in the theory of schema-triggered affect (Fiske, 1982).

In terms of subjects' expectancies about how positively or negatively the target would be likely to evaluate them, if we assume a reciprocal evaluative relation between the self and the significant other, expectancies for reciprocal evaluation would be expected to emerge on the basis of significant-other activation. Subjects perceiving themselves as being loved by the significant other ought to expect to be more loved by the target person resembling this significant other than by the target resembling a significant other by whom they do not feel loved. The results confirmed this prediction, supporting the notion of schema-triggered expectancies. Subjects expected the target resembling their positively toned significant other to like them more than the target resembling their own negatively toned significant other—a pattern not found when the target resembled a yoked subject's significant other.

Finally, the biased-memory effect of previous research was replicated in this work, verifying once again the basic process of transference.

Eliciting Transient Mood in Transference: The Congruence or Incongruence of the Target's Interpersonal Role

A final study was designed to replicate and extend previous findings concerning the elicitation of evaluative responses and transient affect in transference by examining the effect of relational roles on transference—that is, the effect of both the situational role of the target and the chronic role of the significant other (Andersen, 1993; Baum, 1993; Baum & Andersen, 1995). The aim of this research was thus to demonstrate that nomothetic role constructs (e.g., Berscheid, 1994; Haslam & Fiske, 1992; Mills & Clark, 1993) are linked in memory to idiographic significant-other representations in a manner that has implications for transference. The study focused on self-reported evaluation and self-reported transient affect, as in prior work (Andersen & Baum, 1994), and manipulated the particular situational role of the target person to be congruent or incongruent with the chronic relational role of the significant other. It was predicted that role fit would facilitate representation-consistent transient mood states (i.e., positive affect) and that lack of role fit would interfere with it, by virtue of constituting congruent or incongruent information concerning the subject's likely relationship with target person relative to the relationship with the significant other.

The research made use of the same between-subjects experimental design just described, except that for practical reasons we focused only on significant-other representations that were positively toned, a procedure sufficient for testing our basic question about representation-consistent mood states. In the preliminary stimulus-generation session held 2 weeks prior to the experiment, we asked each subject to consider a significant other who was not only positively toned, but also in an authority position in relation to the subject, such as a parent or a teacher (as in the "expert"–"novice" relation noted elsewhere; e.g., Baldwin, 1992). Subjects were asked to characterize this person, using both positive and negative descriptive sentences.

In the experiment, subjects learned about a target person resembling either their own or a yoked subject's significant other (characterized by an equal number of positive and negative features) and anticipated interacting with the target in the role of either "expert" or "beginner" in an experimental task. Hence, resemblance to the subject's own versus to another subject's significant other was manipulated and crossed with the manipulated congruence of the target's situational role with respect to the representation. That is, the target's situational interpersonal role was either very similar to the chronic role relationship with the significant other or virtually antithetical to it. The hypothesis was that representation-consistent transient affect (i.e., positive affect) would be more likely when the target resembling the significant other was in a role similar (vs. dissimilar) to that of the significant other.

In terms of memory, subjects again showed more representation-consistent memory about the target resembling their own significant other rather than a yoked subject's, replicating other work; there was no interaction with situational role (Andersen & Baum, 1994; Andersen & Cole, 1990). Moreover, as in previous work, schema-triggered target evaluation clearly emerged (Andersen & Baum, 1994), again as an effect independent of situational role. Hence the data clearly demonstrate that the transference effect did occur, as usual, when the target resembled the subject's own significant other.

With respect to self-reported transient mood, on the other hand, a very different pattern emerged. That is, a significant interaction between resemblance and situational role showed that the relational role occupied by the target did indeed influence self-reported transient mood states when the target resembled the subject's own significant other. Subjects experienced more representation-consistent mood, meaning that they felt better, when considering the target resembling their own positive significant other in an interpersonal role *congruent* with the role of the significant other; this was not the case when the target resembled a yoked subject's positive significant other. When the target resembling the subjects' own positive significant other was in a role *incongruent* with that typically occupied by the significant other, subjects felt particularly badly, showing far less representation-consistent affect.

Hence, even though the significant-other representation was positively toned in each case, *negative* mood was observed when the role of the target who resembled the significant other was incongruent with the significant other's. Positive and representation-consistent mood was reported when the target similar to the significant other was in a role-congruent situation. Apparently, a change in role alters how one feels with the significant other, and thus alters how one feels toward the target in transference. These effects did not occur when the target resembled a yoked subject's significant other, suggesting that the effect is specific to conditions in which the perceiver's own significant-other representation is activated.

Although the lack of role fit may have produced negative affect in transference because of the unfamiliarity of not being in one's standard role with the significant other when with someone who activates this role, creating a need to think more carefully about how to respond (i.e., to engage in piecemeal or systematic processing), representation-consistent memory and target evaluation were produced with or without the congruency. Moreover, the extent of negative mood is unlikely to be attributable purely to engaging in systematic processing. Alternatively, it is likely that the lack of a familiar role implies that desired outcomes usually obtained in one's typical role with the positively toned significant other will *not* be obtained, which disrupts the goal of achieving these outcomes (see Oatley & Bolton, 1985).

In any event, relational roles appear to be relevant to the emotional concomitants of transference. Self-reported transient mood states are predicted by taking the congruence of the interpersonal role occupied by the new target person into account with respect to the relational role typically occupied by the significant other. These data extend our research on transference into the arena of interpersonal role relationships, both chronic and situational, and into the immediate social context in which the target is encountered. They also suggest that nomothetic role constructs (see also Berscheid, 1994; Mills & Clark, 1993; Haslam & Fiske, 1992) may be linked to significant-other representations.

THE EXPERIMENTAL EXAMINATION OF TRANSFERENCE: IMPLICATIONS FOR FUTURE RESEARCH

Implications of Recent Research Findings

What are the implications of our most recent findings for conceptualizing transference and for considering future research directions?

Processes of Activation and Application

These recent data speak both to the mechanisms and to the consequences of transference. That is, they support the assumption that significant-other representations are chronically accessible, in that they operate in social information-processing as any chronically accessible social construct would be expected to operate (Higgins, 1989a). Moreover, triggering stimulus cues in a target person, or applicability (Higgins, 1989, in press), make the use of a significant-other representation more likely (see also Higgins & Brendl, 1995). These data further demystify transference in everyday social perception, and link it both to chronicity and to transient contextual cues as these are involved in significant-other activation and application.

When cuing and activation are considered, the question also arises of what kinds of stimulus cues are most powerful in triggering a significant-other representation and hence in triggering transference. In particular, it would seem important to examine the extent to which visual stimulus cues (e.g., facial cues, physical appearance cues, overt behavioral cues) have particular cue diagnosticity in providing the activating conditions for significant-other representations. Especially, in contrast to self-representations, for which visual stimulus cues should be relatively less evocative (because we only rarely "see" ourselves visually in this way), significant-other representations may be readily triggered by visual cues. Research thus far, on the other hand, has relied on linguistic cues provided by the subject and therefore does not provide an ideal analogue for how transference may often transpire in ecologically valid contexts.

Also in terms of cuing and activation, another question that remains open in the transference arena is how the *degree* of similarity-based overlap between a stimulus person and a significant-other representation is related to significant-other activation (Andersen & Chen, in press). In our research, we have operationalized stimulus triggering in terms of similarity-based overlap, and yet, according to theory-based models of categorization (Medin, 1989; Medin, Goldstone, & Gentner, 1993; Murphy & Medin, 1985), the extent to which a stimulus shares features with a representation may be less predictive of its use (or of categorization) than the manner in which the various attributes within the representation are related to one another in theory-driven or explanatory ways. Together with the importance of implicit personality theory (Schneider, 1973) and personality prototypes (Cantor & Mischel, 1979) in social cognition, such a theory-based approach to significant-other activation clearly warrants investigation (Andersen & Chen, in press; see also Murray & Holmes, 1994).

Yet another empirical question that remains open with respect to transference concerns the potential automaticity with which it occurs. If significant-other representations can be utilized efficiently in social judgment, (i.e., without mental effort or strategic processing, as in efficiency-based automaticity, see Bargh, 1989, 1994) then the transference process—which depends upon significant-other representations—may also occur relatively automatically. In a related vein, it remains to be determined whether or not people are able, under the right circumstances, to short-circuit the tendency to engage in transference, even if the transference process does transpire relatively automatically (for a parallel in stereotyping, see Devine, 1989). Future research along these lines in the transference domain could thus have important implications not only for automaticity per se, but also for transference, especially to the degree that findings suggest that transference can be short-circuited by means of strategic or piecemeal processing—as a means of self-regulation.

In this respect, it is worth noting that there are individual-difference variables that may influence the likelihood that the transference process can be short-circuited. Certainty-oriented individuals, for example, appear to be more likely to rely on automatic, heuristic processing with increasing personal relevance in a set of stimuli (as in transference-relevant stimuli), whereas uncertainty-oriented individuals are more likely to engage in effortful, systematic processing with increasing personal relevance (e.g., Brouwers & Sorrentino, 1993; Sorrentino, Bobocel, Gitta, Olson, & Hewitt, 1988; Sorrentino & Short, 1986). Hence, uncertainty-oriented individuals may be more likely to short-circuit transference through systematic processing, whereas certainty-oriented individuals may be more likely to engage in transference without strategic interference. Similarly, individuals with a high need for cognitive closure (Kruglanski, 1989) may be more likely to engage in transference, because of a greater willingness to generalize from past experience relative to individuals with a preference to avoid cognitive closure (Sanbonmatsu, Harpster, Akimoto, & Moulin, 1994; see Kruglanski & Freund, 1983), who may wish to be accurate and consistent and hence may disrupt transference in an effort to avoid error. In a similar vein, individuals low in the need for cognition (Cacioppo & Petty, 1982) appear to have less motivation to engage in systematic thought about their activities than do individuals high in need for cognition, implying that the latter individuals may also be more likely to disrupt transference. Finally, the construct of self-monitoring may be relevant to transference, in that persons low in self-monitoring (e.g., Snyder, 1974; Snyder & Cantor, 1980; Snyder & Gangestad, 1986) may attempt to act in accordance with their stored knowledge and hence may be more susceptible to transference, whereas those high in self-monitoring, who are especially responsive to social cues about people in the present environment, may be less susceptible. Each of these individual-difference variables may be relevant to transference by highlighting relevant processing goals and motivations—an issue that warrants research attention.

Evaluation, Motivation, and Transient Affect

Schema-triggered evaluation in transference is now a well-replicated phenomenon. The evaluative tone of the significant-other representation is transferred to the new person, so that one feels toward the new person as one feels (or felt) toward the significant other (see also Andersen & Baum, 1994). That is, the data show that the evaluation of a significant other is transferred to a relevant target person who activates this representation; the effect has been replicated in two new studies (in addition to Andersen & Baum, 1994). Hence, schema-triggered evaluation may be a basic aspect of transference.

Extending these evaluation findings, our new data demonstrate essentially the same basic process in the area of motivation—specifically, motivation for interpersonal closeness or intimacy. That is, the data suggest that schema-triggered intimacy motivation also occurs when the target person resembles a significant other. The desire to be more emotionally open with the target resembling a positively toned significant other than with the target resembling a negatively toned significant other suggests schema-triggered motivation, a research advance in the transference arena. The data show that interpersonal-intimacy motivations are activated in transference when the significant-other representation is activated, and support the basic assumption that motivational material may be linked to significant-other representations in much the same way as is evaluation. That is, schema-triggered motivation appears to exist along with schema-triggered evaluation. The data imply in particular that interpersonal-relatedness motivations may be stored with significant-other representations, as suggested elsewhere (e.g., Sullivan, 1940), and that motivations linked to trust or mistrust are thus activated in transference (see also Bowlby, 1969). These findings pave the way for a systematic examination of motivations linked to significant-other representations (e.g., Deci & Ryan, 1985) and of the specific role of goal-related constructs (e.g., Bargh & Gollwitzer, 1994) in transference. Research on such processes is clearly needed.

On a related note, our data suggest that significant-other activation leads to specific ways of anticipating a new person's responses. That is, when a significant-other representation is activated, knowledge stored about how the significant other typically responds to and feels toward the subject forms the basis of comparable expectancies about how well the target will like the subject. People expect a new person to like them (or dislike them) in the way the significant other does, in the context of transference—a finding that extends the transference phenomenon into the realm of schema-triggered evaluative expectancies. Because these anticipations or expectancies concern the target's (and hence the significant other's) interpersonal responses, they may be linked to actual interpersonal behaviors toward the new target person as well, as other kinds of expectancies often are (Neuberg, 1994; Olson, Roese, & Zanna, in press). Indeed, the examination of transference as it plays out in interpersonal behavior is extremely important, and to the degree that expectancies are linked to behavior, these new data on reciprocal evaluative expectancies may be of considerable relevance.

It is worth noting explicitly, in addition, that to the extent that transference occurs in meaningful ways in everyday social relations, it should play itself out in terms of measurable behaviors in interpersonal contexts. Moving beyond subjects' responses *prior* to meeting a relevant target person into subjects' *actual interpersonal behaviors* in an interaction is of importance. Our understanding of transference should obviously be extended by being able to track the transference process as it unfolds in an actual interaction between two people (Andersen & Bem, 1981; Snyder, 1984, 1992; Snyder, Tanke, & Berscheid, 1977; Swann & Ely, 1984).

In terms of our recent work on affect in transference, it is also worth noting that this kind of work is of the essence, because moving from "cold" cognition to "warm" or "hot" experience in transference—by harnessing in the laboratory the affective and motivational concomitants of transference—is so deeply relevant to the dynamic underpinnings of the transference concept. Specifically, although our previous rather weak findings concerned with self-reported transient mood states (Andersen & Baum, 1994) were not replicated in one of our two most recent studies, both recent studies importantly extend these initial data. In one study, the activation of transient affect in transference was demonstrated in subjects' momentary facial expressions upon learning about the target person. That is, subjects showed more representation-consistent facial affect upon learning about the target resembling their own significant other as opposed to a yoked subject's, supporting schema-triggered affect in transference, even if only fleetingly. Hence, schema-triggered transient affect occurs in subjects' fleeting facial expressions when they are learning about the target person (at encoding). This is of particular significance, given that the extensive data on facial expressions of emotions make it conceivable that future work using measures of facial affect to test more subtly differentiated predictions about the emotions elicited in transference may now be possible.

Finally, our research on relational roles showed that in the context of transference, the congruence of the target person's role with the significant other's role has affective consequences. Hence, contextualized, role-based influences on transient mood states clearly occur in transference. That is, the role relationship between the target person and the perceiver influences self-reported transient mood in transference, in that role congruence induces more representation-consistent affect and role incongruence more representation-inconsistent affect when the target resembles the subject's own significant other, but not otherwise. These data indicate that affect in transference is linked to the immediate social role context; the similarity of the target's situational role and the relational role of the significant other in transference increases representation-based mood. Further examination of the impact of role relations (and other factors in the immediate context) on transient affect in transference is thus warranted.

The Idiographic–Nomothetic Distinction

Given the long-standing concern with transference processes in clinical theory, and the fact that this psychodynamic concept has so long eluded empirical examination (especially in experimental research), experimentally demonstrating transference in terms of basic cognitive processes is quite meaningful. The lines of research described here show that basic methods in social cognition can be modified so as to employ both idiographic and nomothetic procedures in a way that permits the investigation of transference in everyday relations. This combination of methods—idiographic stimulus definition and a nomothetic experimental design—enables generalizations about shared cognitive processes to be made. It seems likely that such procedures will continue to prove useful in research on transference, and perhaps in other research domains as well.

Broader Theoretical Implications

Overall, the data from these recent studies demonstrate that notable interpersonal (and intrapersonal) experiences are evoked in transference—namely, those that are inferential, evaluative, affective, and motivational. The demonstration of these effects in transference shows the range of applicability of the transference phenomenon as it has been examined to date, and points to further potential implications.

Knowledge Structures and Significant-Other Representations

When transference is considered in light of the broader theoretical issues concerning memory structures and systems raised at the outset, it is obvious that all of our work has examined only generic knowledge, indexed by descriptive sentences, and not autobiographical knowledge. The statement "loves to watch soap operas" may be related to observed behaviors, but it is also a generalization. Hence, little is known about the degree to which autobiographical memory versus generic memory is activated when significant-other representations are activated (see Strauman, 1990). This is relevant, in part, because the kinds of triggering conditions most likely to activate a generic significant-other representation in contrast to a specific autobiographical memory pertaining to the significant other may well differ, and this is worthy of research attention.

In terms of the exact nature of any given significant-other representation, the notion of an individual-person exemplar seems to capture adequately how a significant other is represented in memory; this implies that the use of a category made up of multiple persons, the main example of which is the significant other (e.g., "people like my mom"), is not necessary for transference to occur. Models of categorization involve multiple-*n* categories as opposed to an *n*-of-one representation, and culturally shared constructs rather than idiographic ones. Formulating a clear model of the differential implications of individual-person exemplar representations and representations designating types of people (such as stereotypes) in transference would thus advance the literature (see Brewer, 1988; Fiske & Neuberg, 1990). Work comparing the operation of a stereotype (or another multiple-person representation) derived from a particular significant-other representation with the single significant-other exemplar itself, or with a stereotype not derived from the significant-other representation, might also be helpful in increasing our understanding of the role of social categories and of significant-other representations in social judgment.

Relations among Self and Significant Others

As indicated, a mental structure that may be relevant to the examination of transference in an actual encounter is the notion of a relational schema. In our work, we have focused on a single representation of a significant other that is independent, at least in some respects, of the self-representation; it is *defined* independently. When such a significant-other representation is activated, the activation spreads to the self-representation (Baldwin & Holmes, 1987; Baldwin et al., 1990). Whether or not this implies two individual representations that are linked together in memory by various complex relational linkages or a single relationship schema is an open question, and the implications warrant attention. Indeed, depending on one's precise definition of a relational schema and of the nature of the individual linkages between the self and the other in memory as individual representations, the models may not differ particularly in terms of the predicted consequences of activation. On the other hand, as indicated, there may well be some differences between these representations and in the conditions of activation that are most optimal in triggering each. That is, it may be that ongoing behavioral interaction may be particularly likely to trigger "scripted" actions and hence a relationship schema with the significant other, so that if both significant-other representations and relationship schemas exist, the relationship schema may be triggered first on the basis of such cues before the relevant significant-other representation is activated. Further consideration of these issues would be of value.

In terms of the exact linkages between representations of the self and significant others, it is also worth examining more precisely whether or not significant-other activation in transference results in the activation of a particular "working" self-concept (Markus & Wurf, 1986) for the individual (Hinkley & Andersen, 1995; Andersen & Chen, in press). Given that the self can be activated on the basis of significant-other activation (Baldwin et al., 1990), such a "working" self-concept may well be elicited in transference. Such data would address the possibility that particular aspects of the self are particularly bound up with the significant-other representation in memory (Baldwin, 1992). Similarly, as alluded to earlier, it is conceivable that particular triggering cues may tend to activate only a particular "working" significant-other representation, rather than triggering all aspects of the significant-other representation equally (see Barsalou, 1992; Higgins & Bargh, 1987); this too may be related to the elicitation of a particular working self-concept in transference.

On a slightly different note with respect to the self, it is also likely that still other mental representations related to the self may be activated when the significant-other representation is activated in transference. For example, the standards that the particular significant other holds for the self, and their affective and motivational meaning for the person (Higgins, 1987; Higgins, Strauman, & Klein, 1986),and contingencies experienced with the significant other (Higgins, 1989b), may well be activated in transference. This would constitute yet another way in which the self might play a role in the affects and motivations experienced in transference—that is, by altering the accessibility of particular standards and/or contingencies linked to the significant other.

Finally, measured behavior in transference ought to reflect the particular kind of interpersonal behavior that typically plays out between the self and the significant other. That is, the way the interaction unfolds in transference should reflect the nature of the relational pattern or interpersonal script with the significant other, abstracted from repeated instances of particular encounters. Examining transference as it unfolds in real interpersonal interactions remains a future empirical challenge.

CONCLUDING REMARKS

Significant-other representations are important in social perception because, when triggered by a relevant target person, they lead to the assumption that the new person has characteristics of the significant other that he or she does not have, and to the memory that these features were encountered about the target person. This phenomenon has been replicated repeatedly. Significant-other representations also lead to a representation-consistent evaluation of a new person, to a similar interpersonal-intimacy (or closeness) motivation toward this person, to similar expectancies for reciprocal liking from the new person, and to similar transient affect as well. The data thus suggest that transference based on the activation of a significant-other representation exists on a number of different levels in interpersonal perception and response, and that the phenomenon may therefore be ubiquitous in social relations. In this sense, the experimental demonstration of transference is important not only in conceptualizing social-cognitive processes in interpersonal relations, but also in conceptualizing the clinical phenomenon of transference. The data suggest that the process of transference is a basic one; it is not limited to the psychotherapy setting between "patient" and "therapist." Only rarely has a basic process in psychodynamic thinking been examined and demonstrated in well-controlled experimental research, implying, in the present case, that this may eventually afford us the opportunity to speak with increased precision about the operation of the transference phenomenon. So little is known thus far about transference in interpersonal relations that applying ever more precise methods should appreciably enhance our understanding of its parameters and consequences.

Acknowledgments

Preparation of this chapter was supported by a grant from the National Institute of Mental Health (R01-MH48789) to Susan Andersen. We would like to thank Larry Barsalou, Susan Fiske, Tory Higgins, Debbie Prentice, Eliot Smith, and Dick Sorrentino for their insightful comments.

Notes

1. In a different translation (from the *Standard Edition* vs. the Macmillan paperback), this same quote reads: " . . . the cathexis will introduce the doctor into one of the physical 'series' which the patient has already formed" (Freud, 1912/1958, p. 100).
2. In our model, it is the mere *existence* of representations of significant others (as linked to the self) in memory that is essential in transference. By contrast, Sullivan explicitly defines the pathway between the self and the significant other in terms of its *content*, which assumes this content to be motivational. Various struggles and dynamics between the self and the significant other are infused with motivation in his model and constitute the link between the self with the significant other. Hence, the content transferred in the transference process importantly involves motivation in Sullivan's model. These motivational dynamics tend to concern primary strivings of the individual, such as the need to experience relatedness and warmth (integration), the need to be autonomous and develop personal competencies, and the need to be safe and secure (see also Adler, 1927/1957; Deci & Ryan, 1985; Greenberg & Mitchell, 1983; Horney, 1939, 1945; McAdams, 1985, 1989; Mullahy, 1970; Rogers, 1951; Safran, 1990; Sullivan, 1940, 1953). Because these multiple strivings may set the stage for conflictful interactions with a significant other, they may color interpersonal relations in this way with new others as well. Conflictual material in "personifications" and "dynamisms" involving long-standing motivations is thus played out in parataxic distortion (transference). Although we do not make strong claims about the content of the linkages between representations of the self and the significant other, the notion that affect and motivation *are part of* this linkage and are thus transferred in transference is essential in our model.
3. Research on attachment theory, of course, makes use of a trait-based assumptive framework in which particular styles of attachment can be nomothetically defined, have their source in infancy, persist over time, and exist across a broad spectrum of people. Beyond these assumptions, however, attachment theory also characterizes motivational processes at

play in separation and attachment in infancy and adulthood that may influence the nature of one's self-representations and significant-other representations, and hence the basic processes in transference. These motivational processes are of great relevance to the transference phenomenon.

4. It is also worth mentioning here that in psychodynamic terms, applying one's own self-representation to interpreting a new person is "projection," whereas applying a significant-other representation to a new person is "displacement" (as in transference). In information-processing terms, the basic processes may well be the same, but because they involve different representational contents, activating and applying one of these representations (vs. the other) to a new person should result in different consequences.

5. It may also be that the links between particular significant others and the self need to be taken into account if affective responses based on significant-other activation are to be meaningfully predicted (e.g., Higgins, 1987; Strauman & Higgins, 1987). In addition, it is possible that people may make more diverse, context-specific inferences about those they know well (Prentice, 1990; Sande et al., 1988; Wright & Mischel, 1988), meaning that situations may need to be taken into account more precisely in attempts to predict affective responses. If situational inferences (Cantor, Mischel, & Schwartz, 1982; see also Gilbert, 1989) are stored along with the trait inferences (e.g., Cantor & Mischel, 1977, 1979), perhaps as "if-then" context rules about how a significant other behaves (see Shoda & Mischel, 1993), there may well be considerable memorial complexity in people's significant-other representations (see also Higgins & Bargh, 1987). Hence, the situation in which the other is encountered may have implications for transient affect in transference (for related conceptualizations, see Baldwin, 1992; Carlson, 1981; Carlson & Carlson, 1984; Tomkins, 1979).

References

Abelson, R. P. (1976). Script processing in attitude formation and decision making. In J. Carroll & T. Payne (Eds.), *Cognition and social behavior* (pp. 33–45). Hillsdale, NJ: Erlbaum.

Abelson, R. P. (1981). The psychological status of the script concept. *American Psychologist, 36,* 715–729.

Adler, A. (1957). *Understanding human nature.* New York: Fawcett. (Original work published 1927)

Ainsworth, M., Blehar, M., Waters, E., & Wall, S. (1978). *Patterns of attachment.* Hillsdale, NJ: Erlbaum.

Alba, J., & Hasher, L. (1983). Is memory schematic? *Psychological Bulletin, 93,* 203–231.

Allport, G. (1937). *Personality: A psychological interpretation.* New York: Holt, Rinehart & Winston.

Andersen, S. M. (1984). Self-knowledge and social inference: II. The diagnosticity of cognitive/affective and behavioral data. *Journal of Personality and Social Psychology, 46,* 294–307.

Andersen, S. M. (1993). *The experimental demonstration of transference in everyday social relations.* Paper presented at the conference, "Cognitive Science and Psychodynamics," at the National Institute of Mental Health, Washington, DC.

Andersen, S. M., & Baum, A. (1994). Transference in interpersonal relations: Inferences and affect based on significant-other representations. *Journal of Personality, 62,* 459–498.

Andersen, S. M., & Bem, S. L. (1981). Sex typing and androgyny in dyadic interaction: Individual differences in responsiveness to physical attractiveness. *Journal of Personality and Social Psychology, 41,* 74–86.

Andersen, S. M., & Chen, S. (in press). Measuring transference in everyday social relations: Theory and evidence using an experimental social-cognitive paradigm. In H. S. Kurtzman (Ed.), *Cognition and psychodynamics.* New York: Oxford University Press.

, Andersen, S. M., & Cole, S. W. (1990). "Do I know you?": The role of significant others in general social perception. *Journal of Personality and Social Psychology, 59,* 384–399.

Andersen, S. M., & Glassman, N. S. (1995). *Effects of significant-other activation: Persistence and exacerbation over time.* Unpublished manuscript, New York University.

, Andersen, S. M., Glassman, N. S., Chen, S., & Cole, S. W. (1995). Transference in social perception: The role of chronic accessibility in significant-other representations. *Journal of Personality and Social Psychology, 69,* 41–57.

Andersen, S. M., Gold, D., & Glassman, N. S. (1995). *Mental representations of self and other: Structure and processing of cognitive/affective and behavioral aspects.* Unpublished manuscript, New York University.

Andersen, S. M., & Klatzky, R. L. (1987). Traits and social stereotypes: Levels of categorization in person perception. *Journal of Personality and Social Psychology, 53,* 235–246.

Andersen, S. M., Klatzky, R. L., & Murray, J. (1990). Traits and social stereotypes: Efficiency differences in social information processing. *Journal of Personality and Social Psychology, 59,* 192–201.

Andersen, S. M., Manzella, L. M., & Reznik, I. (1995). *Eliciting transient affect, motivations, and expectancies in transference: Significant-other representations and the self in social relations.* Unpublished manuscript, New York University.

Andersen, S. M., & Ross, L. (1984). Self-knowledge and social inference: I. The impact of cognitive/affective and behavioral data. *Journal of Personality and Social Psychology, 46,* 280–293.

Andersen, S. M., Spielman, L. A., & Bargh, J. A. (1992). Future-event schemas and certainty about the future: Automaticity in depressives' future-event predictions. *Journal of Personality and Social Psychology, 63,* 711–723.

Aron, A., Aron, E. N., & Smollan, D. (1992). Inclusion of other in the self scale and the structure of interpersonal closeness. *Journal of Personality and Social Psychology, 63,* 596–612.

Aron, A., Aron, E. N., Tudor, M., & Nelson, G. (1991). Close relationships as including other in the self. *Journal of Personality and Social Psychology, 60,* 241–253.

Averill, J. R. (1990). Emotions as episodic dispositions, cognitive schemas, and transitory social roles: Steps toward an integrated theory of emotion. In D. J. Ozer, J. M. Healy, Jr., & A. J. Stewart (Eds.), *Perspectives in personality: Vol. 3a. Self and emotion* (pp. 137–165). Greenwich, CT: JAI Press.

Baldwin, M. W. (1992). Relational schemas and the processing of information. *Psychological Bulletin, 112,* 461–484.

Baldwin, M. W., Carrell, S. E., & Lopez, D. F. (1990). Priming relationship schemas: My advisor and the Pope are watching me from the back of my mind. *Journal of Experimental Social Psychology, 26,* 435–454.

Baldwin, M. W., & Holmes, J. G. (1987). Salient private audiences and awareness of the self. *Journal of Personality and Social Psychology, 52,* 1087–1098.

Banaji, M. R., & Greenwald, A. G. (1994). Implicit stereotyping and unconscious prejudice. In M. P. Zanna & J. M. Olson (Eds.), *The Ontario Symposium: Vol. 7. The psychology of prejudice* (pp. 55–76). Hillsdale, NJ: Erlbaum.

Banaji, M. R., & Greenwald, A. G. (1995). Implicit gender stereotyping in judgments of fame. *Journal of Personality and Social Psychology, 68,* 181–198.

Bargh, J. A. (1989). Conditional automaticity: Varieties of automatic influence in social perception and cognition. In J. S. Uleman & J. A. Bargh (Eds.), *Unintended thought* (pp. 3–51). New York: Guilford Press.

Bargh, J. A. (1990). Auto-motives: Preconscious determinants of social interaction. In E. T. Higgins & R. M. Sorrentino (Eds.) *Handbook of motivation and cognition: Foundations of social behavior* (Vol. 2, pp. 93–130). New York: Guilford Press.

Bargh, J. A. (1994). The four horsemen of automaticity: Awareness, intention, efficiency, and control in social cognition. In R. S. Wyer & T. K. Srull (Eds.), *Handbook of social cognition* (2nd ed., pp. 1–40). Hillsdale, NJ: Erlbaum.

Bargh, J. A., & Barndollar, K. (1996). Automaticity in action: The unconscious as repository of chronic goals and motives. In P. M. Gollwitzer & J. A. Bargh (Eds.), *The psychology of action* (pp. 457–481). New York: Guilford Press.

Bargh, J. A., Bond, R. N., Lombardi, W. L., & Tota, M. E. (1986). The additive nature of chronic and temporary sources of construct accessibility. *Journal of Personality and Social Psychology, 50,* 869–878.

Bargh, J. A., & Gollwitzer, P. M. (1994). Environmental control of goal- directed action: Automatic and strategic contingencies between situations and behavior. In W. D. Spaulding (Ed.), *Nebraska Symposium on Motivation* (Vol. 41, pp. 71–124). Lincoln: University of Nebraska Press.

Bargh, J. A., Lombardi, W. L., & Higgins, E. T. (1988). Automaticity of chronically accessible constructs in person × situation effects on person perception: It's just a matter of time. *Journal of Personality and Social Psychology, 55,* 599–605.

Bargh, J. A., & Thein, R. D. (1985). Individual construct accessibility, person memory, and the recall–judgment link: The case of information overload. *Journal of Personality and Social Psychology, 49,* 1129–1146.

Bargh, J. A., & Tota, M. E. (1988). Context-dependent automatic processing in depression: Accessibility of negative constructs with regard to self but not others. *Journal of Personality and Social Psychology, 54,* 925–939.

Barsalou, L. W. (1990). On the distinguishability of exemplar memory and abstraction in category representation. In T. K. Srull & R. S. Wyer (Eds.), *Advances in social cognition: Vol. 3. Content and process specificity in the effects of prior experiences* (pp. 61–88). Hillsdale, NJ: Erlbaum.

Barsalou, L. W. (1992). Frames, concepts, and conceptual fields. In A. Lehrer & E. F. Kittay (Eds.), *Frames, fields, and contrasts: New essays in semantic lexical organization* (pp. 21–74). Hillsdale, NJ: Erlbaum.

Barsalou, L. W. (1993). Flexibility, structure, and linguistic vagary in concepts: Manifestations of a compositional system of perceptual symbols. In A. F. Collins, S. E. Gathercol, M. A. Conway, & P. E. Morris (Eds.), *Theories of memory* (pp. 29–101). Hillsdale, NJ: Erlbaum.

Barsalou, L. W., Wenchi, Y., Luka, B. J., Olseth, K. L., Mix, K. S., & Wu, L. (1993). Concepts and Meaning. In K. Beals, E. Cooke, D. Kalthman, S. Kita, K. McCullough, & D. Testen (Eds.), *What we think, what we mean, and how we say it* (pp. 23–61). Chicago: Chicago Linguistic Society.

Baum, A. (1993). *Role congruence and incongruence in transference: The impact of significant-other activation and role relations on interpersonal affect.* Unpublished doctoral dissertation, New York University.

Baum, A., & Andersen, S. M. (1995). *Role congruence and transference: The impact of significant-other activation and situational role relations on interpersonal affect.* Unpublished manuscript, New York University.

Bellezza, F. S. (1984). The self as a mnemonic device: The role of internal cues. *Journal of Personality and Social Psychology, 47,* 506–516.

Berkowitz, L. (1993). Towards a general theory of anger and emotional aggression: Implications of the cognitive-neoassociationistic perspective for the analysis of anger and other emotions. In R. S. Wyer, Jr., & T. K. Srull (Eds.), *Advances in social cognition* (Vol. 6, pp. 1–46). Hillsdale, NJ: Erlbaum.

Berscheid, E. (1994). Interpersonal relationships. *Annual Review of Psychology, 45,* 79–129.

Blaney, P. H. (1986). Affect and memory: A review. *Psychological Bulletin, 99,* 229–246.

Bolles, R. C. (1967). *Theory of motivation.* New York: Harper & Row.

Bower, G. H. (1981). Mood and memory. *American Psychologist, 36,* 129–148.

Bower, G. H., & Gilligan, S. G. (1979). Remembering information related to one's self. *Journal of Research in Personality, 13,* 420–432.

Bowlby, J. (1969). *Attachment and loss: Vol. 1. Attachment.* New York: Basic Books.

Bowlby, J. (1973). *Attachment and loss: Vol. 2. Separation: Anxiety and anger.* New York: Basic Books.

Bowlby, J. (1980). *Attachment and loss: Vol. 3. Loss: Sadness and depression.* New York: Basic Books.

Bramel, D. A. (1962). A dissonance theory approach to defensive projection. *Journal of Abnormal and Social Psychology, 64,* 121–129.

Brewer, M. B. (1988). A dual process of impression formation. In T. Srull & R. Wyer (Eds.), *Advances in social cognition* (Vol. 1, pp. 1–35). Hillsdale, NJ: Erlbaum.

Brewer, M. B., Dull, V., & Lui, L. (1981). Perceptions of the elderly: Stereotypes as prototypes. *Journal of Personality and Social Psychology, 41,* 656–670.

Brooks, L. R. (1987). Decentralized control of categorization: The role of prior processing episodes. In U. Neisser (Ed.), *Categories reconsidered: The ecological and intellectual bases of categories* (pp. 141–174). Cambridge, England: Cambridge University Press.

Brouwers, M. C., & Sorrentino, R. M. (1993). Uncertainty orientation and protection motivation theory: The role of individual differences in health compliance. *Journal of Personality and Social Psychology, 65,* 102–112.

Bruner, J. S. (1957). Going beyond the information given. In H. E. Gruber, K. R. Hammond, & R. Jessor, (Eds.), *Contemporary approaches to cognition* (pp. 41–69). Cambridge, MA: Harvard University Press.

Bugental, D. (1992). Affective and cognitive processes within threat-oriented family systems. In I.E. Sigel, A. McGillicuddy-De Lisi, & J. Goodnow (Eds.), *Parental belief systems: The psychological consequences for children* (pp. 219–248). Hillsdale, NJ: Erlbaum.

Cacioppo, J. T., & Petty, R. E. (1982). The need for cognition. *Journal of Personality and Social Psychology, 42,* 116–131.

Campbell, D. T., Miller, N., Lubetsky, J., & O'Connell, E. J. (1964). Varieties of projection in trait attribution. *Psychological Monographs: General and Applied, 78* (Whole No. 592), 1–33.

Cantor, N., & Kihlstrom, J. F. (1987). *Personality and social intelligence.* Englewood Cliffs, NJ: Prentice-Hall.

Cantor, N., & Mischel, W. (1977). Traits as prototypes: Effects on recognition memory. *Journal of Personality and Social Psychology, 35,* 38–48.

Cantor, N., & Mischel, W. (1979). Prototypes in person perception. In L. Berkowitz (Ed.), *Advances in experimental social psychology* (Vol. 12, pp. 3–52). New York: Academic Press.

Cantor, N., Mischel, W., & Schwartz, J. C. (1982). A prototype analysis of psychological situations. *Cognitive Psychology, 14,* 45–77.

Carlson, L., & Carlson, R. (1984). Affect and psychological magnification: Derivations from Tomkins' script theory. *Journal of Personality, 52,* 36–45.

Carlson, R. (1981). Studies in script theory: I. Adult analogues of a childhood nuclear scene. *Journal of Personality and Social Psychology, 40,* 501–510.

Carlston, D. E. (1980). The recall and use of traits and events in social inference processes. *Journal of Experimental Social Psychology, 16,* 303–328.

Carlston, D. E. (1992). Impression formation and the modular mind: The associated systems theory. In L. Martin & A. Tesser (Eds.), *The construction of social judgments* (pp. 301–341). Hillsdale, NJ: Erlbaum.

Carver, C. S., & Scheier, M. F. (1981). *Attention and self-regulation: A control-theory approach to human behavior.* New York: Springer-Verlag.

Clark, M. S., & Isen, A. M. (1982). Toward understanding the relationship between feeling states and social behavior. In A. Hastorf & A. Isen (Eds.), *Cognitive social psychology* (pp. 73–108). New York: Elsevier/North-Holland.

Cohen, C. E. (1981). Goals and schemas in person perception: Making sense out of the stream of behavior. In N. Cantor & J. Kihlstrom (Eds.), *Personality, cognition, and social behavior* (pp. 45–68). Hillsdale, NJ: Erlbaum.

Collins, A. M., & Loftus, E. (1975). A spreading activation theory of semantic processing. *Psychological Review, 82,* 407–428.

Collins, N. L., & Read, S. J. (1990). Adult attachment, working models, and relationship quality in dating couples. *Journal of Personality and Social Psychology, 58,* 644–663.

Craik, F. I. M., & Lockhart, R. S. (1972). Levels of processing: A framework for memory research. *Journal of Verbal Learning and Verbal Behavior, 11,* 671–676.

Cronbach, L. J. (1955). Processes affecting scores on "understanding others" and "assumed similarity." *Psychological Bulletin, 52,* 177–194.

Deci, E. L., & Ryan, R. M. (1985). *Intrinsic motivation and self-determination in human behavior.* New York: Plenum Press.

Devine, P. G. (1989). Stereotypes and prejudice: Their automatic and controlled components. *Journal of Personality and Social Psychology, 56,* 5–18.

Dornbusch, S. M., Hastorf, A. H., Richardson, S. A., Muzzy, R. E., & Vreeland, S. A. (1965). The perceiver and the perceived: Their relative influence on the categories of interpersonal cognition. *Journal of Personality and Social Psychology, 1,* 434–440.

Ebbesen, E. B. (1980). Cognitive processes in understanding ongoing behavior. In R. Hastie, T. M. Ostrom, E. B. Ebbesen, R. S. Wyer, Jr., D. L. Hamilton, & D. E. Carlston (Eds.), *Person memory: The cognitive basis of social perception* (pp. 179–226). Hillsdale, NJ: Erlbaum.

Edlow, D., & Kiesler, C. (1966). Ease of denial and defensive projection. *Journal of Experimental Social Psychology, 2,* 56–69.

Ehrenreich, J. H. (1989). Transference: One concept or many? *Psychoanalytic Review, 76,* 37–65.

Emmons, R. A. (1986). Personal strivings: An approach to personality and subjective well-being. *Journal of Personality and Social Psychology, 51,* 1058–1968.

Erdley, C. A., & D'Agostino, P. R. (1988). Cognitive and affective components of automatic priming effects. *Journal of Personality and Social Psychology, 54,* 741–747.

Fazio, R. H., Powell, M. C., & Herr, P. M. (1983). Toward a process model of the attitude–behavior relation: Accessing one's attitude upon mere observation of the attitude object. *Journal of Personality and Social Psychology, 44,* 723–735.

Feeney, J. A., & Noller, P. (1990). Attachment style as a predictor of adult romantic relationships. *Journal of Personality and Social Psychology, 58,* 281–291.

Feshbach, S., & Feshbach, N. D. (1963). The influence of the stimulus object upon the complementary and supplementary projection of fear. *Journal of Abnormal and Social Psychology, 66,* 498–502.

Fiske, S. T. (1982). Schema-triggered affect: Applications to social perception. In M. S. Clark & S. T. Fiske (Eds.), *Affect and cognition: The 17th annual Carnegie Symposium on Cognition* (pp. 55–78). Hillsdale, NJ: Erlbaum.

Fiske, S. T., & Cox, M. G. (1979). Person concepts: The effect of target familiarity and descriptive purpose on the process of describing others. *Journal of Personality, 47,* 136–161.

Fiske, S. T., & Neuberg, S. L. (1990). A continuum model of impression formation from category-based to individuating processes: Influences of information and motivation on attention and interpretation. In M. P. Zanna (Ed.), *Advances in experimental social psychology* (Vol. 23, pp. 1–74). New York: Academic Press.

Fiske, S. T., Neuberg, S. L., Beattie, A. E., & Milberg, S. J. (1987). Category-based and attribute-based reactions to others: Some informational conditions of stereotyping and individuating processes. *Journal of Experimental Social Psychology, 23,* 399–427.

Fiske, S. T., & Pavelchak, M. (1986). Category-based versus piecemeal-based affective responses: Developments in schema-triggered affect. In R. M. Sorrentino & E. T. Higgins (Eds.), *Handbook of motivation and cognition: Foundations of social behavior* (Vol. 1, pp. 167–203). New York: Guilford Press.

Fiske, S. T., & Taylor, S. E. (1991). *Social cognition* (2nd ed.). New York: McGraw-Hill.

Fong, G. T., & Markus, H. (1982). Self-schemas and judgments about others. *Social Cognition, 1,* 191–205.

Ford, T. E., Stangor, C., & Duan, C. (1994). Influence of social category accessibility and category-associated trait accessibility on judgments of individuals. *Social Cognition, 12,* 149–168.

Freud, S. (1957). Instincts and their vicissitudes. In J. Strachey (Ed. and Trans.), *The standard edition of the complete psychological works of Sigmund Freud* (Vol. 14, pp. 109–140). London: Hogarth Press. (Original work published 1915)

Freud, S. (1958). The dynamics of transference. In J. Strachey (Ed. and Trans.), *The standard edition of the complete psychological works of Sigmund Freud* (Vol. 12, pp. 97–108). London: Hogarth Press. (Original work published 1912)

Freud, S. (1963). The dynamics of transference. In P. Rieff (Ed.), *Therapy and technique* (pp. 105–115). New York: Macmillan. (Original work published 1912)

Gentner, D. (1983). Structure-mapping: A theoretical framework for analogy. *Cognitive Science, 7,* 155–170.

Gilbert, D. T. (1989). Thinking lightly about others: Automatic components of the social inference process. In J. S. Uleman & J. A. Bargh (Eds.), *Unintended thought* (pp. 189–211). New York: Guilford Press.

Gilovich, T. (1981). Seeing the past in the present: The effect of associations to familiar events on judgments and decisions. *Journal of Personality and Social Psychology, 40,* 797–808.

Glassman, N. S., Andersen, S. M., & Cole, S. W. (1994). *Transference derived from the chronic accessibility of significant-other representations.* Paper presented at the annual meeting of the American Psychological Association, Los Angeles.

Gollwitzer, P. M. (1990). Action phases and mind-sets. In E. T. Higgins & R. M. Sorrentino (Eds.), *Handbook of motivation and cognition: Foundations of social behavior* (Vol. 2, pp. 53–92). New York: Guilford Press.

Graesser, A. C., Gordon, S. E., & Sawyer, J. D. (1979). Recognition memory for typical and atypical actions in scripted activities: Tests of a script pointer + tag hypothesis. *Journal of Verbal Learning and Verbal Behavior, 18,* 319–332.

Graesser, A. C., Woll, S. B., Kowalski, D. J., & Smith, D. A. (1980). Memory for typical and atypical actions in scripted activities. *Journal of Experimental Psychology: Human Learning and Memory, 6,* 503–515.

Greenberg, J. R., & Mitchell, S. A. (1983). *Object relations in psychoanalytic theory.* Cambridge, MA: Harvard University Press.

Greenwald, A. G. (1980). The totalitarian ego. *American Psychologist, 35,* 603–618.

Greenwald, A. G., & Banaji, M. R. (1995). Implicit social cognition: Attitudes, self-esteem, and stereotypes. *Psychological Review, 102,* 4–27.

Greenwald, A. G., & Pratkanis, A. R. (1984). The self. In R. S. Wyer, Jr., & T. K. Srull (Eds.), *Handbook of social cognition* (Vol. 3, pp. 129–178). Hillsdale, NJ: Erlbaum.

Guidano, V. F., & Liotti, G. (1983). *Cognitive processes and emotional disorders: A structural approach to psychotherapy.* New York: Guilford Press.

Hamilton, D. L. (1979). A cognitive-attributional analysis of stereotyping. In L. Berkowitz (Ed.), *Advances in experimental social psychology* (Vol. 12, pp. 53–84). New York: Academic Press.

Hampson, S. E., John, O. P., & Goldberg, L. R. (1986). Category breadth and hierarchical structure in personality: Studies of asymmetries in judgments of trait implications. *Journal of Personality and Social Psychology, 51,* 37–54.

Harter, S. (1983). Developmental perspectives on the self-system. In E. M. Hetherington (Vol. Ed.), *Handbook of child psychology* (4th ed.): *Vol. 4. Socialization, personality, and social development* (pp. 275–385). New York: Wiley.

Haslam, N., & Fiske, A. P. (1992). Implicit relationship prototypes: Investigating five theories of the elementary cognitive forms of relationships. *Journal of Experimental Social Psychology, 28,* 441–474.

Hastie, R. (1981). Schematic principles in human memory. In E. T. Higgins, C. P. Herman, & M. P. Zanna (Eds.), *The Ontario Symposium: Vol. 1. Social cognition* (pp. 39–88). Hillsdale, NJ: Erlbaum.

Hayes-Roth, B., & Hayes-Roth, F. (1977). Concept learning and the recognition and classification of exemplars. *Journal of Verbal Learning and Verbal Behavior, 16,* 321–338.

Hazan, C., & Shaver, P. (1987). Romantic love conceptualized as an attachment process. *Journal of Personality and Social Psychology, 52,* 511–524.

Herr, P. M. (1986). Consequences of priming: Judgment and behavior. *Journal of Personality and Social Psychology, 51,* 1106–1115.

Higgins, E. T. (1987). Self-discrepancy: A theory relating self and affect. *Psychological Review*, *94*, 319–340.

Higgins, E. T. (1989a). Knowledge accessibility and activation: Subjectivity and suffering from unconscious sources. In J. S. Uleman & J. A. Bargh (Eds.), *Unintended thought* (pp. 75–123). New York: Guilford Press.

Higgins, E. T. (1989b). Continuities and discontinuities in self-regulatory and self-evaluative processes: A developmental theory relating self and affect. *Journal of Personality*, *57*, 407–444.

Higgins, E. T. (in press). Knowledge activation: Accessibility, applicability, and salience. In E. T. Higgins & A. W. Kruglanski (Eds.), *Social psychology: Handbook of basic principles*. New York: Guilford Press.

Higgins, E. T., & Bargh, J. A. (1987). Social cognition and social perception. *Annual Review of Psychology 38*, 369–425.

Higgins, E. T., Bond, R. N., Klein, R., & Strauman, T. (1986). Self-discrepancies and emotional vulnerability: How magnitude, accessibility, and type of discrepancy influence affect. *Journal of Personality and Social Psychology*, *51*, 5–15.

Higgins, E. T., & Brendl, C. M. (1995). Accessibility and applicability: Some "activation rules" influencing judgment. *Journal of Experimental Social Psychology*, *31*, 218–243.

Higgins, E. T., & King, G. A. (1981). Accessibility of social constructs: Information processing consequences of individual and contextual variability. In N. Cantor & J. F. Kihlstrom (Eds.), *Personality, cognition and social interaction* (pp. 69–121). Hillsdale, NJ: Erlbaum.

Higgins, E. T., King, G. A., & Mavin, G. H. (1982). Individual construct accessibility and subjective impressions and recall. *Journal of Personality and Social Psychology*, *43*, 35–47.

Higgins, E. T., Klein, R., & Strauman, T. (1985). Self-concept discrepancy theory: A psychological model for distinguishing among different aspects of depression and anxiety. *Social Cognition*, *3*, 51–76.

Higgins, E. T., & McCann, C. D. (1984). Social encoding and subsequent attitudes, impressions, and memory: "Context-driven" and motivational aspects of processing. *Journal of Personality and Social Psychology*, *47*, 26–39.

Higgins, E. T., McCann, C. D., & Fondacaro, R. (1982). The "communication game": Goal-directed encoding and cognitive consequences. *Social Cognition*, *1*, 21–37.

Higgins, E. T., Rholes, W. S., & Jones, C. R. (1977). Category accessibility and impression formation. *Journal of Experimental Social Psychology*, *13*, 141–154.

Higgins, E. T., Strauman, T., & Klein, R. (1986). Standards and the process of self-evaluation: Multiple effects from multiple stages. In R. M. Sorrentino & E. T. Higgins (Eds.), *Handbook of motivation and cognition: Foundations of social behavior* (Vol. 1, pp. 23–63). New York: Guilford Press.

Higgins, E. T., & Sorrentino, R. M. (Eds.). (1990). *Handbook of motivation and cognition: Foundations of social behavior* (Vol. 2). New York: Guiford Press.

Higgins, E. T., & Stangor, C. (1988). The change of standard effect in person memory. *Journal of Personality and Social Psychology*, *54*, 181–192.

Higgins, E. T., VanHook, E., & Dorfman, D. (1988). Do self-attributes form a cognitive structure? *Social Cognition*, *6*, 177–207.

Hinkley, K., & Andersen, S. M. (1995). *The working self-concept in transference: Significant-other activation and self change*. Unpublished manuscript, New York University.

Hintzman, D. L. (1976). Repetition and memory. In G. H. Bower (Ed.), *The psychology of learning and motivation* (pp. 47–91). New York: Academic Press.

Hintzman, D. L. (1986). "Schema abstraction" in a multiple-trace memory model. *Psychological Review*, *93*, 411–428.

Holmes, D. S. (1968). Projection as a defense mechanism. *Psychological Bulletin*, *69*, 248–268.

Hoffman, C., Mischel, W., & Mazze, K. (1981). The role of purpose in the organization of information about behavior: Trait-based vs. goal-based categories in person cognition. *Journal of Personality and Social Psychology*, *40*, 211–225.

Holyoak, K. J., & Gordon, P. C. (1983). Social reference points. *Journal of Personality and Social Psychology, 44*, 881-887.

Horney, K. (1939). *New ways in psychoanalysis.* New York: Norton.

Horney, K. (1945). *Our inner conflicts.* New York: Norton.

Horowitz, M. J. (1989). Relationship schema formulation: Role-relationship models and intrapsychic conflict. *Psychiatry, 52,* 260-274.

Horowitz, M. J. (Ed.). (1991). *Person schemas and maladaptive interpersonal patterns.* Chicago: University of Chicago Press.

Houston, D. A., Sherman, S. J., & Baker, S. M. (1989). The influence of unique features and direction of comparison preferences. *Journal of Experimental Social Psychology, 25,* 121-141.

Jacoby, L. L., & Brooks, L. R. (1984). Nonanalytic cognition: Memory, perception, and concept learning. In G. H. Bower (Ed.), *The psychology of learning and motivation: Advances in research and theory* (Vol. 18, pp. 1-47). New York: Academic Press.

Jacoby, L. L., & Kelley, C. M. (1987). Unconscious influences of memory for a prior event. *Personality and Social Psychology Bulletin, 13,* 314-336.

Jacoby, L. L., & Kelley, C. M. (1990). An episodic view of motivation: Unconscious influences of memory. In E. T. Higgins & R. M. Sorrentino (Eds.), *Handbook of motivation and cognition: Foundations of social behavior* (Vol. 2, pp. 451-481). New York: Guilford Press.

Johnson, J. T. (1987). The heart on the sleeve and the secret self: Estimations of hidden emotion in self and acquaintances. *Journal of Personality, 55,* 563-582.

Johnson, J. T., Struthers, N. J., & Bradlee, P. (1988). Social knowledge and the "secret self": The mediating effect of data base size on judgments of emotionality in the self and others. *Social Cognition, 6,* 319-344.

Johnson, M. K., Hastroudi, S., & Lindsay, D. S. (1993). Source monitoring. *Psychological Bulletin, 114,* 3-28.

Johnson, M. K., & Raye, C. L. (1981). Reality monitoring. *Psychological Review, 88,* 67-85.

Jones, E. E. (1976). How do people perceive the causes of behavior? *American Scientist, 64,* 300-305.

Jones, E. E. (1990). *Interpersonal perception.* New York: W. H. Freeman.

Jones, E. E., & Nisbett, R. E. (1972). The actor and the observer: Divergent perceptions of the causes of behavior. In E. E. Jones, D. E. Kanouse, H. H. Kelley, R. E. Nisbett, S. Valins, & B. Weiner (Eds.), *Attribution: Perceiving the causes of behavior* (pp. 79-94). Morristown, NJ: General Learning Press.

Keenan, J. M., & Baillet, S. D. (1980). Memory for personally and socially significant events. In R.S. Nickerson (Ed.), *Attention and performance* (Vol. 8, pp. 651-669). Hillsdale, NJ: Erlbaum.

Kelly, G. A. (1955). *The psychology of personal constructs.* New York: Norton.

Kihlstrom, J. F. (1987). The cognitive unconscious. *Science, 237,* 1445-1452.

Kihlstrom, J. F., & Cantor, N. (1984). Mental representations of the self. In L. Berkowitz (Ed.), *Advances in experimental social psychology* (Vol. 17, pp. 1-47). New York: Academic Press.

Kihlstrom, J. F., Cantor, N., Albright, J. S., Chew, B. R., Klein, S. B., & Niedenthal, P. M. (1988). Information processing and the study of the self. In L. Berkowitz (Ed.), *Advances in experimental social psychology* (Vol. 21, pp. 145-180). New York: Academic Press.

Klatzky, R. L., & Andersen, S. M. (1988). Category specificity effects in social typing and personalization. In T. K. Srull & R. S. Wyer (Eds.), *Advances in social cognition* (Vol. 1, pp. 91-101). Hillsdale, NJ: Erlbaum.

Klein, S. B., & Kihlstrom, J. F. (1986). Elaboration, organization, and the self-reference effect in memory. *Journal of Experimental Psychology: General, 115,* 26-38.

Klein, S. B., Loftus, J., & Burton, H. A. (1989). Two self-reference effects: The importance of distinguishing between self-descriptiveness judgments and autobiographical retrieval in self-referent encoding. *Journal of Personality and Social Psychology, 56,* 853-865.

Klinger, E. (1977). *Meaning and void.* Minneapolis: University of Minnesota Press.

Klinger, E. (1987). Current concerns and disengagement from incentives. In F. Halisch & J. Kuhl (Eds.), *Motivation, intention, and volition* (pp. 337–347). Berlin: Springer-Verlag.

Kobak, R. R., & Hazan, C. (1991). Attachment in marriage: Effects of security and accuracy of working models. *Journal of Personality and Social Psychology, 60,* 861–869.

Koestner, R., & McClelland, D.C. (1990). Perspectives on competence motivation. In L. A. Pervin (Ed.), *Handbook of personality: Theory and research* (pp. 527–548). New York: Guilford Press.

Kruglanski, A. W. (1989). *Lay epistemics and human knowledge: Cognitive and motivational bases.* New York: Plenum Press.

Kruglanski, A. W., & Freund, T. (1983). The freezing and unfreezing of lay-inferences: Effects of impressional primacy, ethnic stereotyping, and numerical anchoring. *Journal of Experimental Social Psychology, 19,* 448–468.

Kunda, Z. (1987). Motivated inference: Self-serving generation and evaluation of causal theories. *Journal of Personality and Social Psychology, 53,* 636–647.

Lazarus, R. S., & Averill, J. R. (1972). Emotion and cognition with special reference to anxiety. In C. D. Spielberger (Ed.), *Anxiety: Current trends in theory and research* (Vol. 2, pp. 242–283). New York: Academic Press.

Lemon, N., & Warren, N. (1974). Salience, centrality and self-relevance of traits in construing others. *British Journal of Social and Clinical Psychology, 13,* 119–124.

Leventhal, H. (1984). A perceptual-motor theory of emotion. In L. Berkowitz (Ed.), *Advances in experimental social psychology* (Vol. 17, pp. 118–182). New York: Academic Press.

Lewicki, P. (1985). Nonconscious biasing effects of single instances on subsequent judgments. *Journal of Personality and Social Psychology, 48,* 563–574.

Lewin, K. (1935). *A dynamic theory of personality: Selected papers.* New York: McGraw-Hill.

Lingle, J. H., Altom, M. W., & Medin, D. L. (1983). Of cabbages and kings: Assessing the extendability of natural object concept models to social things. In R. S. Wyer, T. K. Srull, & J. Hartwick (Eds.), *Handbook of social cognition* (Vol. 1, pp. 71–117). Hillsdale, NJ: Erlbaum.

Lingle, J. H., Geva, N., Ostrom, T. M., Leippe, M. R., & Baumgardner, M. H. (1979). Thematic effects of person judgments on impression organization. *Journal of Personality and Social Psychology, 37,* 674–687.

Linville, P. W. (1982). Affective consequences of complexity regarding the self and others. In M. S. Clark & S. T. Fiske (Eds.), *Affect and cognition: The 17th annual Carnegie Symposium on Cognition* (pp. 79–109). Hillsdale, NJ: Erlbaum.

Linville, P. W., & Carlston, D. E. (1994). Social cognition of the self. In P. G. Devine, D. C. Hamilton, & T. M. Ostrom (Eds.), *Social cognition: Impact on social psychology* (pp. 143–193). New York: Academic Press.

Linville, P. W., & Fischer, G. W. (1993). Exemplar and abstraction models of perceived group variability and stereotypicality. *Social Cognition, 11,* 95–125.

Logan, G. D. (1988). Toward an instance theory of automatization. *Psychological Review, 95,* 492–527.

Logan, G. D. (1989). Automaticity and cognitive control. In J. S. Uleman & J. A. Bargh (Eds.), *Unintended thought* (pp. 52–74). New York: Guilford Press.

Lombardi, W. J., Higgins, E. T., & Bargh, J. A. (1987). The role of consciousness in priming effects on categorization. *Personality and Social Psychology Bulletin, 13,* 411–429.

Lord, C. G. (1980). Schemas and images as memory aids: Two modes of processing social information. *Journal of Personality and Social Psychology, 38,* 257–269.

Lord, C. G. (1987). Imagining self and others: Reply to Brown, Keenan, and Potts. *Journal of Personality and Social Psychology, 53,* 445–450.

Luborsky, L., & Crits-Christoph, P. (1990). *Understanding transference: The CCRT method.* New York: Basic Books.

Mandler, J. M. (1984). *Stories, scripts, and scenes: Aspects of schema theory.* Hillsdale, NJ: Erlbaum.

Manis, M., & Paskewitz, J. (1984a). Specificity and contrast effects: Judgments of psychopathology. *Journal of Experimental Social Psychology, 20,* 217–230.

Manis, M., & Paskewitz, J. (1984b). Judging psychopathology: Expectation and contrast. *Journal of Experimental Social Psychology, 20,* 363–381.

Manis, M., Paskewitz, J., & Cotler, S. (1986). Stereotypes and social judgment. *Journal of Personality and Social Psychology, 50,* 461–473.

Manzella, L. M., Andersen, S. M., & Reznik, I. (1994). *Triggering evaluation, motivation, and mood by activation of significant-other representations.* Paper presented at the annual meeting of the American Psychological Association, Los Angeles.

Marks, G., & Miller, N. (1987). Ten years of research on the false-consensus effect: An empirical and theoretical review. *Psychological Bulletin, 102,* 72–90.

Markus, H. (1977). Self-schemata and processing information about the self. *Journal of Personality and Social Psychology, 35,* 63–78.

Markus, H., & Nurius, P. (1986). Possible selves. *American Psychologist, 41,* 954–969.

Markus, H., Smith, J., & Moreland, R. L. (1985). Role of the self-concept in the social perception of others. *Journal of Personality and Social Psychology, 49,* 1494–1512.

Markus, H., & Wurf, E. (1987). The dynamic self-concept: A social psychological perspective. *Annual Review of Psychology, 38,* 299–337.

Martin, L. L. (1986). Set/reset: Use and disuse of concepts in impression formation. *Journal of Personality and Social Psychology, 51,* 493–504.

Martin, L. L., & Clark, L. F. (1990). Social cognition: Exploring the mental processes involved in human social interaction. In M. W. Eysenck (Ed.), *Cognitive psychology: An international review* (Vol. 1, pp. 266–310). Chichester, England: Wiley.

Martin, L. L., Seta, J. J., & Crelia, R. A. (1990). Assimilation and contrast as a function of people's willingness and ability to expend effort in forming an impression. *Journal of Personality and Social Psychology, 59,* 27–37.

McAdams, D. P. (1988). *Power, intimacy, and the life story: Personological inquiries into identity.* New York: Guilford Press.

McAdams, D. P. (1989). *Intimacy: The need to be close.* New York: Doubleday.

McCann, C. D., & Higgins, E. T. (1988). Motivation and affect in interpersonal relations: The role of personal orientations and discrepancies. In L. Donohew, H. E. Sypher, & E. T. Higgins (Eds.), *Communication, social cognition, and affect* (pp. 53–79). Hillsdale, NJ: Erlbaum.

McClelland, D. C. (1984). *Human motivation.* Glenview, IL: Scott, Foresman.

McGuire, W. J., & McGuire, C. V. (1981). The spontaneous self-concept as affected by personal distinctiveness. In M. D. Lynch, A. A. Norem-Habeisen, & K. Gergen (Eds.), *Self-concept: Advances in theory and research* (pp. 147–171). Cambridge, MA: Ballinger.

Medin, D. L. (1989). Concepts and conceptual structure. *American Psychologist, 44,* 1469–1481.

Medin, D. L., Altom, M. W., & Murphy, T. D. (1984). Given versus induced category representations: Use of prototype and exemplar information in classification. *Journal of Experimental Psychology: Learning, Memory, and Cognition, 10,* 333–352.

Medin, D. L., Goldstone, R. I., & Gentner, D. (1993). Respects for similarity. *Psychological Review, 100,* 254–278.

Miell, D. (1987). Remembering relationship development: Constructing a context for interactions. In R. Burnett, P. McGhee, & D. D. Clarke (Eds.), *Accounting for relationships* (pp. 60–73). London: Methuen.

Miller, G. A., Galanter, E., & Pribram, K. H. (1960). *Plans and the structure of behavior.* New York: Holt, Rinehart & Winston.

Mills, J., & Clark, M. S. (1993). Communal and exchange relationships: New research and old controversies. In R. Gilmour & R. Erber (Eds.), *Theoretical approaches to new relationships* (pp. 29–42). Hillsdale, NJ: Erlbaum.

Mullahy, P. (1970). *Psychoanalysis and interpersonal psychiatry: The contributions of Harry Stack Sullivan.* New York: Science House.

Murphy, G. L., & Medin, D. L. (1985). The role of theories in conceptual coherence. *Psychological Review, 92,* 289–316.

Murray, S. L., & Holmes, J. G. (1994). Storytelling in close relationships: The construction of confidence. *Personality and Social Psychology Bulletin, 20,* 707–722.

Neuberg, S. L. (1988). Behavioral implications of information presented outside of conscious awareness: The effect of subliminal presentation of trait information on behavior in the Prisoner's Dilemma Game. *Social Cognition, 6,* 207–230.

Neuberg, S. L. (1994). Expectancy-confirmation processes in stereotype-tinged social encounters: The moderating role of social goals. In M. P. Zanna & J. M. Olson (Eds.), *The psychology of prejudice* (pp. 103–130). Hillsdale, NJ: Erlbaum.

Nisbett, R. E., & Ross, L. (1980). *Human inference: Strategies and shortcomings of social judgment.* Englewood Cliffs, NJ: Prentice-Hall.

Norman, D. A. (1969). *Memory and attention.* New York: Wiley.

Nosofsky, R. M. (1986). Attention, similarity, and the identification–categorization relationship. *Journal of Experimental Psychology: General, 115,* 39–57.

Oatley, K., & Bolton, W. (1985). A social-cognitive theory of depression in reaction to life events. *Psychological Review, 92,* 372–388.

Olson, J. M., Roese, N. J., & Zanna, M. P. (in press). Expectancies. In E. T. Higgins & A. W. Kruglanski (Eds.), *Social psychology: Handbook of basic principles.* New York: Guilford Press.

Ortony, A., Clore, G. L., & Collins, A. (1988). *The cognitive structure of emotions.* New York: Cambridge University Press.

Ostrom, T. M. (1989). Three catechisms for social memory. In P. R. Solomon, G. R. Goethals, C. M. Kelley, & B. R. Stephens (Eds.), *Memory: Interdisciplinary approaches* (pp. 201–220). New York: Springer-Verlag.

Ostrom, T. M., Lingle, J. H., Pryor, J. B., & Geva, N. (1980). Cognitive organization of person impressions. In R. Hastie, T. M. Ostrom, E. B. Ebbesen, R. S. Wyer, Jr., D. Hamilton, & D. E. Carlston (Eds.), *Person memory: The cognitive basis of social perception* (pp. 55–88). Hillsdale, NJ: Erlbaum.

Park, B. (1986). A method for studying the development of impressions of real people. *Journal of Personality and Social Psychology, 51,* 907–917.

Park, B., & Hastie, R. (1987). Perception of variability in category development: Instance- versus abstraction-based stereotypes. *Journal of Personality and Social Psychology, 53,* 621–635.

Pavelchak, M. (1989). Piecemeal and category-based evaluation: An idiographic analysis. *Journal of Personality and Social Psychology, 56,* 354–363.

Petty, R. E., & Wegener, D. T. (1993). Flexible correction processes in social judgment: Correcting for context-induced contrast. *Journal of Experimental Social Psychology, 29,* 137–165.

Planalp, S. (1987). Interplay between relational knowledge and events. In R. Burnett, P. McGhee, & D. D. Clarke (Eds.), *Accounting for relationships* (pp. 175–191). London: Methuen.

Posner, M. I., & Keele, S. W. (1968). On the genesis of abstract ideas. *Journal of Experimental Psychology, 77,* 353–363.

Posner, M. I., & Keele, S. W. (1970). Retention of abstract ideas. *Journal of Experimental Psychology, 83,* 304–308.

Pratto, F., & Bargh, J. A. (1991). Stereotyping based on apparently individuating information: Trait and global components of sex stereotypes under attention overload. *Journal of Experimental Social Psychology, 27,* 26–47.

Prentice, D. (1990). Familiarity and differences in self- and other-representations. *Journal of Personality and Social Psychology, 59,* 369–383.

Raynor, J. O., & McFarlin, D. B. (1986). Motivation and the self-system. In R. M. Sorrentino & E. T. Higgins (Eds.) *Handbook of motivation and cognition: Foundations of social behavior* (Vol. 1, pp. 315–349). New York: Guilford Press.

Read, S. (1983). Once is enough: Causal reasoning from a single instance. *Journal of Personality and Social Psychology, 45,* 323–334.

Read, S. (1984). Analogical reasoning in social judgment: The importance of causal theories. *Journal of Personality and Social Psychology, 46,* 14–25.

Read, S. (1987). Similarity and causality in the use of social analogies. *Journal of Experimental Social Psychology, 23,* 189–207.

Read, S. J., & Cessa, I. L. (1991). This reminds me of the time when . . . : Expectation failures in reminding and explaining. *Journal of Experimental Social Psychology, 27,* 1–25.

Read, S. K. (1972). Pattern recognition and categorization. *Cognitive Psychology, 3,* 382–407.

Regan, D. T., & Totten, J. (1975). Empathy and attribution: Turning observers into actors. *Journal of Personality and Social Psychology, 59,* 369–383.

Rogers, C. (1951). *Client-centered therapy.* Boston: Houghton Mifflin.

Rogers, T. B. (1981). A model of the self as an aspect of the human information processing system. In N. Cantor & J. F. Kihlstrom (Eds.), *Personality, cognition, and social interaction* (pp. 193–214). Hillsdale, NJ: Erlbaum.

Rosch, E. (1978). Principles of categorization. In E. Rosch & B. B. Lloyd (Eds.), *Cognition and categorization* (pp. 27–48). Hillsdale, NJ: Erlbaum.

Rosenberg, M. (1979). *Conceiving of the self.* New York: Basic Books.

Ross, L. (1977). The intuitive psychologist and his shortcomings: Distortions in the attribution process. In L. Berkowitz (Ed.), *Advances in experimental social psychology* (Vol. 10, pp. 174–121). New York: Academic Press.

Ross, L., Greene, D., & House, P. (1977). The "false-consensus effect": An egocentric bias in social perception and attribution processes. *Journal of Experimental Social Psychology, 13,* 279–301.

Safran, J. D. (1990). Towards a refinement of cognitive therapy in light of interpersonal theory: I. Theory. *Clinical Psychology Review, 10,* 87–105.

Safran, J. D., & Segal, Z. V. (1990). *Interpersonal processes in cognitive therapy.* New York: Basic Books.

Sanbonmatsu, D. M., Harpster, L. L., Akimoto, S. A., & Moulin, J. B. (1994). Selectivity in generalizations about self and others from performance. *Personality and Social Psychology Bulletin, 20,* 358–366.

Sande, G. N., Goethals, G. R., & Radloff, C. E. (1988). Perceiving one's own traits and others': The multifaceted self. *Journal of Personality and Social Psychology, 54,* 13–20.

Schank, R. C. (1982). *Dynamic memory: A theory of reminding and learning in computers and people.* New York: Cambridge University Press.

Schank, R. C., & Abelson, R. P. (1977). *Scripts, plans, goals, and understanding: An inquiry into human knowledge structures.* Hillsdale, NJ: Erlbaum.

Schneider, D. J. (1973). Implicit personality theory: A review. *Psychological Bulletin, 79,* 294–309.

Schneider, D. J., & Blankmeyer, B. L. (1983). Prototype salience and implicit personality theories. *Journal of Personality and Social Psychology, 44,* 712–722.

Schrauger, J. S., & Schoeneman, T. J. (1979). Symbolic interactionist view of self-concept: Through the looking glass darkly. *Psychological Bulletin, 86,* 549–573.

Schwarz, N., & Bless, H. (1991). *Constructing reality and its alternatives: An inclusion/exclusion model of assimilation and contrast effects in social judgment.* Unpublished manuscript, ZUMA, Mannheim, Germany.

Schwarz, N., & Sudman, S. (Eds.). (1991). *Context effects in social and psychological research.* New York: Springer-Verlag.

Sedikides, C., & Skowronski, J. J. (1990). Toward reconciling personality and social psychology: A construct accessibility approach. *Journal of Social Behavior and Personality, 5,* 531–546.

Sedikides, C., & Skowronski, J. J. (1991). The law of cognitive structure activation. *Psychological Inquiry, 2,* 169–184.

Segal, Z. V., Hood, J. E., Shaw, B. F., & Higgins, E. T. (1988). A structural analysis of the self-schema construct in major depression. *Cognitive Therapy and Research, 12,* 471–485.

Seifert, C. M., McKoon, G., Abelson, R. P., & Ratcliff, R. (1986). Memory connections between thematically similar episodes. *Journal of Experimental Psychology: Learning, Memory, and Cognition, 12,* 220-231.

Shaver, P., & Rubenstein, C. (1980). Childhood attachment experience and adult loneliness. In L. Wheeler (Ed.), *Review of personality and social psychology* (Vol. 1, pp. 42-73). Beverly Hills, CA: Sage.

Shoben, E. J. (1984). Semantic and episodic memory. In R. S. Wyer, Jr., & T. K. Srull (Eds.), *Handbook of social cognition* (Vol. 2, pp. 213-231). Hillsdale, NJ: Erlbaum.

Shoda, Y., & Mischel, W. (1993). *Cognitive-social approach to dispositional inferences: What if the perceiver is a cognitive-social theorist?* Unpublished manuscript, Columbia University.

Showers, C., & Cantor, N. (1985). Social cognition: A look at motivated strategies. *Annual Review of Psychology, 36,* 275-305.

Shrauger, J. S., & Schoeneman, T. J. (1979). Symbolic interactionist view of self-concept: Through the looking glass darkly. *Psychological Bulletin, 86,* 549-573.

Simpson, J. A. (1990). Influence of attachment styles on romantic relationships. *Journal of Personality and Social Psychology, 59,* 971-980.

Singer, J. L. (1988). Reinterpreting the transference. In D. C. Turk & P. Salovey (Eds), *Reasoning, inference, and judgment in clinical psychology* (pp. 182-205). New York: Free Press.

Smith, E. E., & Medin, D. L. (1981). *Categories and concepts.* Cambridge, MA: Harvard University Press.

Smith, E. R. (1984). Model of social inference processes. *Psychological Review, 91,* 393-413.

Smith, E. R. (1988). Category accessibility effects in a simulated exemplar-based memory. *Journal of Experimental Social Psychology, 24,* 448-463.

Smith, E. R. (1990). Content and process specificity in the effects of prior experiences. In T. K. Srull & R. S. Wyer (Eds.), *Advances in social cognition* (Vol. 3, pp. 1-59). Hillsdale, NJ: Erlbaum.

Smith, E. R., & Branscombe, N. R. (1988). Category accessibility as implicit memory. *Journal of Experimental Social Psychology, 24,* 490-504.

Smith, E. R., & Lerner, M. (1986). Development of automatism of social judgments. *Journal of Personality and Social Psychology, 50,* 246-259.

Smith, E. R., & Zarate, M. A. (1990). Exemplar and prototype use in social categorization. *Social Cognition, 8,* 243-262.

Smith, E. R., & Zarate, M. A. (1992). Exemplar-based model of social judgment. *Psychological Review, 99,* 3-21.

Snyder, M. (1974). The self-monitoring of expressive behavior. *Journal of Personality and Social Psychology, 30,* 526-537.

Snyder, M. (1984). When belief creates reality. In L. Berkowitz (Ed.), *Advances in experimental social psychology* (Vol. 18, pp. 248-305). New York: Academic Press.

Snyder, M. (1992). Motivational foundations of behavioral confirmation. In M. P. Zanna (Ed.), *Advances in experimental social psychology* (Vol. 25, pp. 67-114). San Diego, CA: Academic Press.

Snyder, M., & Cantor, N. (1980). Thinking about ourselves and others: Self-monitoring and social knowledge. *Journal of Personality and Social Psychology, 39,* 222-234.

Snyder, M., & Gangestad, S. (1986). On the nature of self-monitoring: Matters of assessment, matters of validity. *Journal of Personality and Social Psychology, 51,* 125-139.

Snyder, M., Tanke, E. D., & Berscheid, E. (1977). Social perception and interpersonal behavior: On the self-fulfilling nature of social stereotypes. *Journal of Personality and Social Psychology, 35,* 656-666.

Sorrentino, R. M., Bobocel, D. R., Gitta, M. Z., Olson, J. M., & Hewitt, E. L. (1988). Uncertainty orientation and persuasion: Individual differences in the effects of personal relevance on social judgments. *Journal of Personality and Social Psychology, 55,* 357-371.

Sorrentino, R. M., & Higgins, E. T. (Eds.). (1986). *Handbook of motivation and cognition: Foundations of social behavior* (Vol. 1). New York: Guilford Press.

Sorrentino, R. M., & Short, J. C. (1986). Uncertainty orientation, motivation, and cognition. In R. M. Sorrentino & E. T. Higgins (Eds.), *Handbook of motivation and cognition: Foundations of social behavior* (Vol. 1, pp. 379–403). New York: Guilford Press.

Spellman, B. A., & Holyoak, B. A. (1992). If Saddam is Hitler then who is George Bush? Analogical mapping between systems of social roles. *Journal of Personality and Social Psychology, 62,* 913–933.

Sroufe, L. A., & Fleeson, J. (1986). Attachment and the construction of relationships. In W. W. Hartup & Z. Rubin (Eds.), *Relationships and development* (pp. 51–71). Hillsdale, NJ: Erlbaum.

Srull, T. K. (1983). Organizational and retrieval processes in person memory: An examination of processing objectives, presentation format, and the possible role of self-generated retrieval cues. *Journal of Personality and Social Psychology, 44,* 1157–1170.

Srull, T. K., & Gaelick, L. (1983). General principles and individual differences in the self as a habitual reference point: An examination of self-other judgments of similarity. *Social Cognition, 2,* 108–121.

Srull, T. K., & Wyer, R. S., Jr. (1979). The role of category accessibility in the interpretation of information about persons: Some determinants and implications. *Journal of Personality and Social Psychology, 37,* 1660–1672.

Srull, T. K., & Wyer, R. S., Jr. (1986). The role of chronic and temporary goals in social information processing. In R. M. Sorrentino & E. T. Higgins (Eds.), *Handbook of motivation and cognition: Foundations of social behavior* (Vol. 1, pp. 503–549). New York: Guilford Press.

Stangor, C. (1988). Stereotype accessibility and information processing. *Personality and Social Psychology Bulletin, 14,* 694–708.

Stangor, C., Lynch, L., Duan, C., & Glass, B. (1992). Categorization of individuals on the basis of multiple social features. *Journal of Personality and Social Psychology, 62,* 207–218.

Storms, M. D. (1973). Videotape and the attribution process: Revising actors' and observers' points of view. *Journal of Personality and Social Psychology, 27,* 165–175.

Strauman, T. J. (1990). Self-guides and emotionally significant childhood memories: A study of retrieval efficiency and incidental emotional content. *Journal of Personality and Social Psychology, 59,* 869–880.

Strauman, T. J., & Higgins, E. T. (1987). Automatic activation of self-discrepancies and emotional syndromes: When cognitive structures influence affect. *Journal of Personality and Social Psychology, 53,* 1004–1014.

Strauman, T. J., & Higgins, E. T. (1988). Self-discrepancies as predictors of vulnerability to distinct syndromes of chronic emotional distress. *Journal of Personality and Social Psychology, 56,* 685–707.

Sullivan, H. S. (1940). *Conceptions in modern psychiatry.* New York: Norton.

Sullivan, H. S. (1953). *The interpersonal theory of psychiatry.* New York: Norton.

Swann, W. B., & Ely, R. J. (1984). A battle of wills: Self-verification versus behavioral confirmation. *Journal of Personality and Social Psychology, 46,* 1287–1302.

Taylor, S. E. (1981). Categorization approach to stereotyping. In D. L. Hamilton (Ed.), *Cognitive processes in stereotyping and intergroup behavior* (pp. 83–114). Hillsdale, NJ: Erlbaum.

Tesser, A. (1980). Self-esteem maintenance in family dynamics. *Journal of Personality and Social Psychology, 39,* 77–91.

Tesser, A., & Campbell, J. (1980). Self definition: The impact of the relative performance and similarity of others. *Social Psychology Quarterly, 43,* 341–347.

Tesser, A., & Campbell, J. (1982). Self-evaluation maintenance and the perception of friends and strangers. *Journal of Personality, 59,* 261–279.

Thorne, A. (1989). Conditional patterns, transference, and the coherence of personality across time. In D. M. Buss & N. Cantor (Eds.), *Personality psychology: Recent trends and emerging directions* (pp. 149–159). New York: Springer-Verlag.

Tomkins, S. S. (1979). Script theory: Differential magnification of affects. In H. E. Howe, Jr.,

& R. A. Dienstbier (Eds.), *Nebraska Symposium on Motivation* (Vol. 26, pp. 201–236). Lincoln: University of Nebraska Press.

Trope, Y. (1986). Identification and inferential processes in dispositional attribution. *Psychological Review, 93,* 239–257.

Tulving, E. (1972). Episodic and semantic memory. In E. Tulving & W. Donaldson (Eds.), *Organization of memory* (pp. 381–403). New York: Academic Press.

Tulving, E. (1985). How many memory systems are there? *American Psychologist, 40,* 385–398.

Tulving, E. (1993). What is episodic memory? *Current Directions in Psychological Science, 2,* 67–70.

Tversky, A. (1977). Features of similarity. *Psychological Review, 84,* 327–352.

Tversky, A., & Gati, I. (1978). Studies of similarity. In E. Rosch & B. B. Lloyd (Eds.), *Cognition and categorization* (pp. 79–98). Hillsdale, NJ: Erlbaum.

Uleman, J. S. (1989). A framework for thinking intentionally about unintended thoughts. In J. S. Uleman & J. A. Bargh (Eds.), *Unintended thought* (pp. 425–449). New York: Guilford Press.

Wachtel, P. L. (1981). Transference, schema, and assimilation: The relevance of Piaget to the psychoanalytic theory of transference. *Annual of Psychoanalysis, 8,* 59–76.

Westen, D. (1988). Transference and information processing. *Clinical Psychology Review, 8,* 161–179.

Winter, L., & Uleman, J. S. (1984). When are social judgments made? Evidence for the spontaneousness of trait inferences. *Journal of Personality and Social Psychology, 47,* 237–252.

Wright, J. C., & Mischel, W. (1988). Conditional hedges and the intuitive psychology of traits. *Journal of Personality and Social Psychology, 55,* 454–469.

Wyer, R. S., Jr., & Gordon, S. E. (1982). The recall of information about persons and groups. *Journal of Experimental Social Psychology, 18,* 128–164.

Wyer, R. S., Jr., & Martin, L. L. (1986). Person memory: The role of traits, group stereotypes and specific behaviors in the cognitive representation of persons. *Journal of Personality and Social Psychology, 50,* 661–675.

Wyer, R. S., Jr., & Srull, T. K. (1981). Category accessibility: Some theoretical and empirical issues concerning the processing of social information. In E. T. Higgins, C. P. Herman, & M. P. Zanna (Eds.), *The Ontario Symposium: Vol. 1. Social cognition.* (pp. 161–198). Hillsdale, NJ: Erlbaum.

Wyer, R. S., Jr., & Srull, T. K. (1986). Human cognition and its social context. *Psychological Review, 93,* 322–359.

Wyer, R. S., Jr., & Srull, T. K. (1988). Understanding social knowledge: If only the data could speak for themselves. In D. Bar-Tal & A. W. Kruglanski (Eds.), *The social psychology of knowledge* (pp. 142–193). Cambridge, England: Cambridge University Press.

Zajonc, R. B. (1980). Feeling and thinking: Preferences need no inferences. *American Psychologist, 35,* 51–75.

Zarate, M. A., & Smith, E. R. (1990). Person categorization and stereotyping. *Social Cognition, 8,* 161–185.

CHAPTER 9

Stereotyping as a Function of Personal Control Motives and Capacity Constraints
The Odd Couple of Power and Anxiety

SUSAN T. FISKE
BETH MORLING
University of Massachusetts at Amherst

In social interaction, people seek good enough understanding of each other. Attempting to be accurate enough for their current goals, they choose among several cognitive strategies, depending on two potentially conflicting factors: their needs to be accurate and situational constraints that prevent them from being accurate (Fiske, 1992, 1993b). People's motives to understand accurately are presumably based on their fundamental goal of predicting events and potentially controlling them, to obtain at least adequate outcomes from their social interactions. But conflict arises because people's understanding, prediction, and control are necessarily restricted by their limited capacity, both to attend to external events and to hold information in consciousness.

This chapter focuses on an "odd couple" of phenomena that both illustrate the tension between accuracy in the service of control and capacity constraints that prevent accuracy. First, we discuss how social structures, such as people's positions in power hierarchies, can affect the tension between people's need for prediction and control and their limited capacities. The tradeoff between these two situationally influenced variables affects how people form impressions of others. Next, we address how personal motivations (in particular, anxiety) can influence impression formation, through the same two variables of need for control and capacity limitations. Power relationships and personal anxiety, although importantly distinct, share the metatheoretical perspective that impression formation often involves a compromise between needs for accuracy and available resources. The interplay between control motivation and capacity limitations follows from a view of social perceivers as "motivated tacticians" (Fiske & Taylor, 1991), who strategically devote attention to others according to situational and personal constraints and motives.

TWIN THEMES: NEED FOR CONTROL MOTIVATES ACCURACY; LACK OF CAPACITY PROMOTES CATEGORIZATION

Impressions based on social categories—that is, stereotypes—serve as good enough mechanisms of impression formation much of the time. Category-based impressions serve as the automatic, default impression, according to recent models (Bargh, 1984; Brewer, 1988; Devine, 1989; Fiske & Neuberg, 1990; Fiske & Pavelchak, 1986; Stangor & Ford, 1992). Often perceivers can function adequately by using categories or subcategories, with their associated stereotypic content. However, real people do not perfectly fit stereotypes—a fact that appropriately motivated perceivers sometimes notice. Information that disputes the stereotype, along with motivation to be accurate, demonstrably undermines the reliance on stereotypes (Neuberg, 1989; Neuberg & Fiske, 1987).

One fundamental accuracy motive in person perception, guiding people beyond purely category-based impressions, is people's need for prediction and control (Pittman & Heller, 1987; Weary, Gleicher, & Marsh, 1993). When situations undermine people's ability to influence their own outcomes, people wish to be more accurate. Feelings of accuracy can enhance people's sense of predicting a future that is less connected to their own actions. Accuracy may also suggest avenues for potential influence that are idiosyncratic to particular individual characteristics of the target. In any case, control-deprived people generally go beyond initial categories in the interest of accuracy. By working harder at forming their impressions, people satisfy accuracy motives even if they are not being objectively more accurate. Motivated people pay more attention to others and attempt to use more information about them (Erber & Fiske, 1984; Pittman & Pittman, 1980). And toward the goal of prediction, people often infer dispositions or traits in others (Heider, 1958). Trait inferences may not be particularly rich, detailed, or objectively accurate, but they give perceivers a sense of predictability because they are tailored to individual persons and are perceived to be stable.

Whereas control motivations can lead people beyond default categorical impressions, capacity decrements can prevent them from straying too far. When too many tasks (or impression targets) compete for people's limited capacity, some of the tasks (or impressions) are necessarily done (or formed) with less effort (Kahneman, 1973). In general, when people are distracted, they form simpler impressions of others, depending more on initial categorizations and ignoring extra information. When people are distracted, categories are a pragmatic choice. They are informative, yet they are simply, perhaps even effortlessly, applied. But however pragmatic the categories may seem to a distracted perceiver, they do not completely fit any single real-world individual. Distracted people thus sacrifice accuracy when they stereotype.

SOCIAL STRUCTURES: CAPACITY AND CONTROL ISSUES IN POWER RELATIONSHIPS

Interdependence Motivates People to Be Accurate

Among the social structures that motivate accuracy through control deprivation is interdependence. For both theoretical and practical reasons, interdependence is a central motivational structure in social life. It is a core theoretical concept in social psychology, stemming from the earliest theoretical frameworks of Lewinian field theory (Kelley, 1990). Interdependence is a, if not the, fundamental feature of human social life. At work and at play, people's happiness largely depends on the behavior of other people, as well as on their own behavior toward these others.

Interdependence increases people's need for prediction and control, as people want to know whether their partners will help or hinder them in obtaining their desired outcomes. Interdependence thus motivates a goal of accurate impression formation. That is, interdependent people want to think they are forming veridical impressions of others on whom they depend. Interdependent people pay attention to the most informative attributes and make more dispositional attributions about them (Erber & Fiske, 1984; Neuberg, 1989; Neuberg & Fiske, 1987). What matters is interdependence per se (i.e., correlated outcomes) rather than team loyalty or ingroup bias, for competitive interdependence has the same individuating effects, at least in dyads (Ruscher & Fiske, 1990; but see Ruscher, Fiske, Miki, & Van Manen, 1991, for competition in teams). Although these effects do not always occur (e.g., for romantic interdependence, discussed shortly, and in Berscheid, Graziano, Monson, & Dermer, 1976; Omoto & Borgida, 1988), interdependence usually motivates accuracy in impression formation because it entails a certain loss of control.

Asymmetrical Interdependence Creates a Power Relationship

Interdependent partners often participate in a symmetrical situation, in which each person has equal stake in a shared outcome. But at other times, people have different amounts of control over one another's outcomes—a situation we term "asymmetrical interdependence," after Thibaut and Kelley (1959). In an asymmetrically interdependent arrangement, the person who has more control over another's outcomes has power over that person (Dépret & Fiske, 1993). This control-based definition of power is distinct from social status and social influence, two correlated but separate phenomena. Status (see Hogg & Abrams, 1988) may or may not be accompanied by control of others, such as when low-status people control outcomes of those in high status. Similarly, powerful people may not be able to influence the powerless, yet they can still control their outcomes (for definitions of power as influence, see Dahl, 1957; Huston, 1983; Pruitt, 1976).

Social-cognitive research has greatly neglected the study of power, just as it has generally neglected the larger social context that might confer power. With specific regard to social structure, people's roles have been essentially ignored. Possible exceptions include the work of Lord and Saenz (1985) on social perceptions by tokens; the work of Frable, Blackstone, and Scherbaum (1990) on social perceptions by stigmatized individuals; and the work of A. P. Fiske, Haslam, and Fiske (1991) and Sedikides, Olson, and Reis (1993) on how one's role vis-à-vis others can organize one's memory and actions toward those others (see also Higgins, McCann, & Fondacaro, 1982, for how roles can influence social encoding). Other work could be interpreted as relating to social structure—for example, Tetlock's (1991) extensive research program on accountability to third parties, and the work of Higgins and McCann (1984) on how authoritarians tailor their impressions to match those of a high-status audience. Nevertheless, these few exceptions stand out against a background of research that removes subjects from structural relationship with the specific targets they judge. In a review of 504 person perception articles published from 1975 to 1987, de la Haye (1991) concluded that few studies had focused on the perceiver–target relationship or the interpersonal context. Relatedly, she found that few researchers studied how perceivers react to targets' *behaviors* (instead of to written comments about them) in an interpersonal context. The role of social structure and vivid interpersonal contexts in shaping social cognitions of people in those contexts is hardly a mainstream enterprise. The present volume is a major step forward in acknowledging the important role of social context in motivation and social cognition.

To an even greater degree, there has been little or no explicit examination of power in social cognition or, for that matter, in social psychology more generally, according to various reviews (Apfelbaum, 1979; Billig, 1976; Brown, 1988; Cartwright, 1959; Condor & Brown, 1986; Dépret & Fiske, 1993; Deschamps, 1982; Hogg & Abrams, 1988; Ng, 1980, 1982; Sherif, 1962; Tajfel, 1982; for exceptions showing that power enables effective discrimination, see Ng, 1982; Sachdev & Bourhis, 1985). However, work on asymmetrical interdependence addresses power squarely. Furthermore, defining power as differential control of another's outcomes enables us to manipulate power straightforwardly in the laboratory, as we will describe.

Power relations have two potential roles: those of the powerful and the powerless. Our analysis emphasizes how each of these roles affects control motivation and available capacity, which in turn affect people's perceptions of others in that role relationship. To anticipate, powerful perceivers are vulnerable to stereotyping others. This occurs because (1) their outcomes are not so contingent on those subordinate others; (2) their capacities are limited by overload; and (3) they can be personally motivated by a dominance orientation, a personality trait analogue to power (Fiske, 1993a). Their control motivations (lack of contingency on others and possible dominance orientation), which make them less careful, combine with overloaded capacity to encourage stereotyping. In contrast, because others control their outcomes, powerless perceivers are control-deprived, so they may be more motivated to form accurate impressions of the powerful. Powerless people do not have many supervisors to compete for their attention, so subordinates have more capacity to devote to supervisors than vice versa. But although powerless people have the motivation and capacity to be accurate, they may also develop strategies to cope with anxiety associated with their loss of control—strategies that can lead to bias.

Powerful Perceivers Need Not, Cannot, or Choose Not to Attend

Powerful perceivers are vulnerable to stereotyping others (Fiske, 1993a) for at least three reasons. First, because their outcomes are less contingent on others, the powerful think that they need not attend to their subordinates (as much as vice versa) to control their own outcomes. Their perceived lack of interdependence allows them to neglect accuracy.[1] Second, they may not be able to attend to others because they are typically overloaded, given the pyramid structure of hierarchies. Lack of capacity promotes categorization. Third, one personality trait analogue to power is a high need for dominance. Dominant people may not be personally motivated to attend, regardless of their social role. Furthermore, powerful positions can enable any personality trait to wield extra influence; thus, in cases in which powerful people are also dominant, stereotyping may intensify.[2] In summary, for social and possibly personal reasons, the powerful may not need to, be able to, or want to attend to others, and so are vulnerable to using default stereotypic impressions.

The two critical underlying variables, capacity decrements and control motivation, drive the impression formation processes of the powerful. Because of their positions in the hierarchy, the powerful are responsible for more people than they are responsible to. As they control the fates of many others, they cannot necessarily pay individuating attention to each one—at least not to the same degree that those subordinates attend to them. In addition, the powerful are contingent on their own superiors or other third parties, but not, by definition, as much on the subordinates whose fates they control. Hence, their own motives for prediction and control will lead them to attend more elsewhere, and less to their subordinates.

Moreover, powerful people's lack of contingency on their subordinates means that their motivations are more autonomous in the context of their interactions with those subordinates. Personal motives, such as values (Goodwin & Fiske, 1995, Study 1), self-concept (Fiske & Von Hendy, 1992), and personality variables (Fiske, Canfield, & Von Hendy, 1994; Goodwin & Fiske, 1995, Study 2), thus become more relevant. For example, to the extent that they are also personally motivated by an orientation toward interpersonal dominance, they will be motivated to control a social interaction without accommodating the other. Dominance, with its attendant control motives, discourages individuated attention to the other. In brief, the dynamics of power relations can be explained by capacity limits and low control motivation, both of which lead powerful people to be less accurate about their subordinates.

Our ongoing research examines the effect of power in impression formation processes. In one paradigm, college students evaluate high school students for summer jobs, and all are in a position of power by virtue of making hiring decisions; none of the subjects are contingent on the targets. Moreover, their power is made less or more salient by informing them that their opinions will have either 0 or 30% weight in actual hiring decisions. This design thus manipulates power, according to our definition, in terms of outcome control. Subjects read applications from job candidates of different ethnic backgrounds, and their attention to the information about each candidate is measured. Having *more* power leads subjects to pay *less* attention to individuating information and *more* attention to stereotypic information in the applications they read, supporting the notion that powerful people are less accurate in attending to subordinates (Goodwin & Fiske, 1995). However, when powerful subjects are primed with egalitarian values, the effect is reversed and the powerful do attend more accurately. This finding suggests that powerful people hold the more flexible position in a hierarchy, so that their personal values and individual traits are more autonomously expressed.

Moreover, individual differences in dominance mimic situationally defined power. The Goodwin and Fiske (1995) data also showed that dominant subjects in ambiguous power situations attended more to stereotypic information about targets, suggesting a motivation to see subordinates in simple terms.

In another paradigm (Goodwin, Fiske, & Yzerbyt, 1995), subjects formed impressions of many targets, who held either powerful, powerless, or neutral roles. The targets were allegedly members of the subjects' own "work group." Work group members in powerful roles allocated work to members in powerless roles, who executed the plans of the powerful allocators. Other members, neutral with respect to power, simply observed the work group. Subjects paid more individuated attention to work group members who were in powerful roles, attending to stereotype-inconsistent information about them. Conversely, subjects' attention focused on consistent, stereotype-confirming information about powerless and neutral members of the work group. This research suggests that impressions formed of powerless people tend to be more stereotyped than impressions formed of the powerful.

Powerless Perceivers Use Various Strategies to Respond to Loss of Control

If power is defined as outcome control over other people (Dépret & Fiske, 1993), then being powerless entails the loss of outcome control. The powerless, like most control-deprived people, use a range of strategies to try to regain control.

The Powerless Use an Accuracy Strategy When Some Control Seems Possible

One strategy powerless people apparently use is seeking more information about the powerful, to operate effectively within the current power structure. Information seeking, in the form of attention to inconsistent information, is a common strategy in symmetrical interdependence (Erber & Fiske, 1984; Neuberg & Fiske, 1987; Ruscher & Fiske, 1990); in certain situations, powerless people similarly seek information about those who control their outcomes.

For example, Stevens and Fiske (1995) manipulated power within a joint task. All subjects believed they could win a prize for their performance on a joint task with a partner. Some were told that their partner (the target) would be paid regardless of her performance on the task, so the subject was dependent on the target, but not vice versa (asymmetrical interdependence, or power). Other subjects heard that their partner, like themselves, would win the prize only if the pair performed well (our paradigmatic symmetrical interdependence), and a third group heard that their eligibility for the prize would not depend on their partner's performance (no interdependence). Asymmetrically interdependent (i.e., powerless) subjects indeed paid more attention to inconsistent information about their (powerful) partners than did the noninterdependent subjects, suggesting an accuracy strategy. In another paradigm, the task-oriented work group of Goodwin et al. (1995), subjects' attention to the inconsistent information about powerful allocators also showed an accuracy strategy.

However, careful attention to the powerful mainly occurs when powerless people feel that they have some potential personal control (e.g., because they will perform some of the work). In task-oriented situations, the powerless may still perceive some impact on their outcomes—a situation more similar to symmetrical interdependence, and one that may foster similar accuracy-motivated strategies. Furthermore, in these symmetrical settings, only subjects who feel they are able to perform the task do bother with accuracy-oriented strategies (Ruscher & Fiske, 1990). In other power situations (such as evaluative situations, described later), powerless people use less accuracy-based and more motivationally biased strategies, perhaps because they perceive less possible opportunity for personal control.

In support of this notion, information seeking by the powerless may be mediated by their feelings of control in power situations. For example, some data show that when the powerful party is a homogeneous group, people seem to perceive an outgroup conspiracy: The powerful group may seem much less susceptible to influence, causing the powerless to feel much more out of control and to give up on information seeking as a strategy. In contrast, when the powerful party is a group of seemingly unconnected individuals, people perceive more potential for influence; consequently, they seek information by attending to inconsistent information about the individual group members (Dépret & Fiske, 1994).

The Anxiety of Powerlessness Can Promote Biased Strategies

Despite parallel strategies of information seeking in symmetrical and asymmetrical interdependence, the powerless position entails loss of control beyond that in symmetrical interdependence. And extreme loss of control, such as when powerless people perceive no possible influence over their own outcomes, leads to feelings of anxiety that do not typify more symmetrical control situations. In the laboratory, people who were deprived of personal control over their outcomes (when they were under control of a powerful outgroup individual or group) not only reported feeling that their outcomes were less under their own control; they also reported being more jittery, unhappy, and angry, and less calm and happy (Dépret, 1995). The converse was also true: People felt more in control and less anxious when they had some personal control. On a societal level, an external locus of control, which contradicts U.S. cultural norms for seeking prediction and personal control, is associated with feeling anxious (Amsbary, Dépret, Fiske, & Morling, 1994).

A powerless person, then, feels out of control and anxious. Besides seeking information, powerless people may use other strategies to regain feelings of control and cope with their anxiety. Outlined next are two coping strategies for which our laboratory has data: vicarious control through identification with the powerful, and positive thinking about incompetent but powerful evaluators. We also speculate on two other possible coping strategies: changing the social structure and attempting control in irrelevant domains.

THE POWERLESS MAY SEEK VICARIOUS CONTROL BY IDENTIFYING WITH A POWERFUL INGROUP   In one set of studies (Dépret, 1995), subjects expected to come up with titles for paintings, with the most creative titles eligible for prizes. Their titles were to be judged either by members of an outgroup or by members of their own ingroup. In addition, subjects' ratings of their own titles would account for either half of their creativity score or none of their score; that is, subjects either had some personal control over their chance at the prize or had no personal control. When subjects had some personal control, they reported feeling more in control and less anxious, as reported above. But when they had no personal control, they seemed to feel vicarious control *if* the powerful party (individual or group) was their ingroup. When subjects were under the control of powerful ingroup members, they felt more positive, less anxious, and more in control of their outcomes, even though they actually had no personal control themselves. In contrast, when they were under the control of powerful outgroup members, subjects felt much more anxious, unhappy, and angry, and much less in control of their outcomes. Furthermore, subjects with no personal control showed much more ingroup favoritism than subjects with some personal control (Dépret, 1995).

These studies suggest that when people's outcomes are totally controlled by ingroup members, they can regain a sense of control by identifying closely with them. In this strategy, people exploit group-based features of a power relationship: They use ingroup favoritism (e.g., Tajfel & Turner, 1986) to alleviate feelings of anxiety brought on by control deprivation.

PEOPLE TRY TO VIEW THEIR EVALUATORS POSITIVELY   Another strategy of the powerless is positive reframing, or "wishful thinking," occurring when power consists primarily of power to evaluate. People like to think that their evaluators are qualified, so they discount the negative and hope for the best (Stevens & Fiske, 1995). Powerless people prefer to trust powerful evaluators, often even in the face of contrary evidence, for two hypothesized reasons. In purely evaluative situations, the evaluated often perceive few opportunities to control their outcomes by influencing the evaluator, so they do not bother trying to be accurate. And evaluations of one's competence or one's person have potentially lasting effects on self-esteem—more so than many arbitrary tasks. Given that in this study subjects were led to expect to perform well, they were hypothesized to feel that a competent evaluator was most likely to evaluate them fairly (i.e., favorably). The data show that subjects attended more to negative information about evaluators, discounting this negative information,[3] and then elevating incompetent evaluators by judging them to be competent (Stevens & Fiske, 1995). Thus the powerless can employ a positively biased impression strategy when they lack control in an evaluative situation. In an opposite situation, in which powerless people do *not* expect to do well, they may form negatively biased impressions of their evaluators, creating a self-protective excuse for an unfavorable evaluation.

An intriguing parallel to this strategy occurs in a different social structure: romantic interdependence. Because initial dating situations are inherently evaluative, they can resemble evaluative power situations. Dating partners' evaluations also potentially affect self-esteem and may also be perceived as resistant to influence. In one study (Fiske, Goodwin, Rosen, & Rosenthal, 1995), men expected to date a woman and were also asked to evaluate some candidates in a videotaped performance task. Some men evaluated the same woman they expected to date; others did not. Men who expected to date the target in the evaluation task focused on negative information (presumably to discount it) and viewed her as competent even when she was not: They judged incompetent targets as favorably as competent ones. In another study, this pattern of results also held for women expecting to date men. Just as subjects reframe their impressions of evaluative supervisors to be more competent, people who anticipate a potentially evaluative initial dating relationship also prefer to form favorable impressions of their partners.

To summarize, in potentially evaluative situations such as performance review or the initial stages of dating relationships, the powerless may feel little personal control (or influence) over their evaluators, and may face potential threats to self-esteem. Focusing on and discounting negative information about evalua- tors, to form a favorable impression, may be the best strategy to use when self-es- teem is at stake and control is impossible.

THE POWERLESS MAY TRY TO CHANGE THE POWER STRUCTURE   The power- less may cope with their anxiety by trying to change the power structure—that is, the source of their anxiety. Social identity theory (e.g., Tajfel & Turner, 1986) suggests that certain social conditions precede social change attempts by power- less groups. Individual members of low-power groups sometimes protect their self-esteem by leaving the group (i.e., individual mobility). But when individuals do not desire to or cannot leave low-status groups, the group as a whole may re- ject their inferior social status. This is most likely, according to the theory, when the group perceives the social structure to be illegitimate or unstable (see also Ng, 1980). In short, on a group level, the powerless may be most likely to at- tempt to change the social structure when they identify strongly with their group despite its inferior social status, and when the group rejects this inferior status by viewing the powerful group as illegitimate and unstable.

THE POWERLESS MAY TRY TO CONTROL IRRELEVANT DOMAINS   If informa- tion seeking, feeling vicarious control through ingroup identification, evaluative reframing, or changing the power structure is not possible or not attempted, powerless people's control deprivation may spill over into irrelevant domains. Control motivation appears to be somewhat independent of its initial target (Pittman & Pittman, 1980): People who are control-deprived in one situation may try to exert control in a completely different domain. People's choices of these irrelevant control domains may depend on their sense of efficacy in par- ticular areas, on their current capacities, or on cultural norms. Some people may find it easier to direct control attempts outward by putting extra effort into work they can do well, as did control-deprived subjects in a study by Pittman and Pittman (1980), who worked extra hard at anagrams. Others may prefer to control people outside the power relationship, such as peers or family members. As we describe later, attempts to control other people can result when distract- ing, intrusive thoughts associated with anxiety interfere with attempts to regain control. Still others may direct their control attempts inward by controlling in- ternal reactions and processes that are affected by their powerless role, or inter- preting events to make meaning of their position (Weisz, Rothbaum, & Blackburn, 1984).

Summary

The characteristics of the particular power relationship seem to influence the strategies of powerless people. If the task-oriented nature of the relationship is salient, information seeking is likely. If the powerful are ingroup members, vic- arious control may be possible. When relationships are evaluative, people view the powerful optimistically. When powerless groups feel their position is unfair but unstable, they may revolt. Finally, powerless people may try to control irrelevant domains, depending on their own skills, capacities, or values.

Up and Down the Hierarchy: Parallels in Impression Processes of the Powerful and the Powerless

Impression formation proceeds pragmatically. People are motivated tacticians who seek good enough impressions to meet everyday goals (Fiske & Taylor, 1991; Fiske, 1993b). They form impressions according to their situational goals by using strategies that give them the accuracy they want, for the capacity they can afford to expend. Both the powerless and the powerful form impressions in line with their capacities and their motivations to do so. Powerful people are in a structural (and sometimes personally motivated) position of control, with reduced capacity to form individuating impressions. Hence, the powerful are vulnerable to stereotyping (Fiske, 1993a). The powerless may have fewer capacity limitations, but they sometimes use strategies other than accuracy-driven information seeking to cope with their lack of personal control.

In the common corporate structure, the same individuals may be simultaneously stereotyping and stereotyped. Although people with power may control their subordinates' outcomes, they do not necessarily control their own. Powerful people are usually supervised themselves. They simultaneously hold roles as powerful and powerless, so capacity deficits and control motivations may be compounded. As we have pointed out, their role in the hierarchy contributes to capacity decrements by directing their control-motivated attention upward in the hierarchy, distracting them from attending to those below. People's double roles affect their perception of people above and below them, through control motivations and challenges to capacity.

PERSONAL MOTIVES: CAPACITY AND CONTROL ISSUES IN ANXIOUS PEOPLE

Anxiety such as the powerless may experience can itself lead to stereotyping, according to a similar analysis of capacity decrements and control motivation. The basic idea is that people who are anxious experience a loss of mental control and may compensate by trying to control others. The proposed mechanism is that anxiety generates simultaneous capacity decrement and heightened control motivation, which both result from intrusive thoughts.

Our analysis of anxiety is unique because it examines personal motivations in impression formation in terms of capacity and control variables. In general, personal motives are only beginning to resurface as a source of influence on person perception (see Stevens & Fiske, 1995). In a return to classic concerns in social perception (Bruner, 1957), there is increasing work on goals, such as those that promote accuracy and those that promote quick decisions (for a review, see Fiske, 1993b). There are few studies of such personal motivations (e.g., anxiety states or self-esteem motivations) that may cause a specific, directional bias in person perception processes. But the bulk of the research on directional motivations has been applied to *self*-perception; for example, people are motivated to perceive themselves as worthy and in control (for reviews, see, e.g., Banaji & Prentice, 1994; Epstein, 1990; Greenwald & Banaji, 1993; Swann, 1990; Taylor & Brown, 1988). Fewer researchers have examined how these self-protective motivations play out in perceptions of other people. Threats to high collective self-esteem increase ingroup favoritism (e.g., Crocker & Luhtanen, 1990; Crocker, Thompson, McGraw, & Ingerman, 1987). But this work, as well as that derived from social identity and self-categorization theories (e.g., Hogg & Sunderland, 1991), focuses on collective rather than individual levels of self-esteem and perception.

Work by Klein and Kunda (1992) is closer to examining how personal needs affect perceptions of others. They indicate that people attempt to use available evidence to construct justifications for desired beliefs. Thus, when threatened with competition from others, people may attempt to protect their self-esteem by derogating their opponents (see also Higgins & Tykocinski, 1992). But outside of this work, the role of personal needs in person perception is underexamined in current social-cognitive research.

Background

Our analysis of personal motives (Fiske & Emery, 1993) focuses on a theory of the interpersonal dynamics of anxiety, as mediated by capacity decrements and control motivation. Although these are the same two fundamental variables as in our analysis of power dynamics, the capacity and control motives do not play out in precisely the same way, as we will describe.

The processes and effects of anxiety have been variously and extensively documented, and the evidence suggests that anxious people do not do well in complex situations; this may then hold for person perception. For example, anxiety is likely to cause arousal, which can limit the range of cues the anxious person notices (Easterbrook, 1959). Self-focused thoughts may distract the anxious person from another task, hurting performance (Bates, Campbell, & Burgess, 1991; Sarason, 1980; Sarason & Sarason, 1990; Wine, 1980). Expectations of failure at a task may cause an anxious person to withdraw physically or mentally from the task, again hurting performance (Carver & Scheier, 1988). Anxious people are bothered by worries that significantly interrupt their attention to other tasks (Borkovec, Robinson, Pruzinsky, & DePree, 1983; Clark & de Silva, 1985; Deffenbacher, 1980). These anxiety-related ruminations, like most unwanted thoughts, are extremely difficult to suppress, so anxious people may feel unable to control the interrupting thoughts (Clark & de Silva, 1985; Wegner, 1989; Wegner, Shortt, Blake, & Page, 1990). Any of these effects of anxiety may similarly interfere with complex person perception.

Fiske and Emery (1993) have described a theory of how mental control deprivation may lead to attempts at social control. The theory predicts how anxiety might cause people to simplify (i.e., categorize or fail to individuate) other people. They illustrated the theory in the original context with a psychoanalytic case study of a man remanded into therapy by the legal system. His "thinking was scattered and impulse driven" and his "stance toward other people was aggressively controlling. . . . His conscience took an 'immoral' stance toward others as things to be manipulated for his own good and supposedly theirs" (p. 183). The patient's scattered thinking left him feeling out of mental control, and he turned to controlling others as a substitute. He viewed others in stereotyped, categorical terms. On a less extreme level, many people have experienced an anxious colleague, acquaintance, or relative trying to manage his or her own anxiety by managing everyone else in the immediate vicinity. And as we have suggested in our discussion of power, the theory may also predict how powerless, anxious people can displace control motivations to others.

This theory deals with how people can react to being out of mental control, with anxiety as an important example of the phenomenon. Anxious people's uncontrollable, intrusive thoughts have two effects: They take up cognitive capacity, and they cause anxious people to feel out of mental control. While the control decrement motivates anxious people to want to regain control, the capacity decrement takes away resources with which to do so. As a result, anxious people may resort to unusual means to regain a sense of control. In particular, they may attempt to control others. Stereotyped thinking and categorization are abetted by an anxious person's depleted cognitive resources. Categories also make others seem simpler and, to the anxious person, may make them seem easier to control. Thus, like the analysis of power, this theory focuses on the twin variables of capacity decrements and control decrements.

Intrusive Thoughts Take Up Capacity

The intrusive ruminations that anxious people experience take up cognitive capacity. Both the literature on test anxiety (Deffenbacher, 1980; Sarason & Sarason, 1990) and research on general anxiety (Bates et al., 1991; Borkovec et al., 1983; Clark & de Silva, 1985) confirm that anxiety has a "worry" component consisting of intrusive thoughts, mostly focusing on the future, the self, or performance. The worry component is specified in anxiety research as a significant distractor from other tasks (Clark & de Silva, 1985; Wine, 1980).

Distracted people form simpler impressions of others. In relation to the present research, anxiety has been studied as a distractor in person perception. For example, as noted, solos (people who believe they are the only one of their gender or race in a group) are more preoccupied and anxious about others' attention to them, and they remember less information about others (Saenz & Lord, 1989). Also, when people are made anxious by expecting public criticism or embarrassment, they may adopt simplifying strategies for perceiving others, differentiating less among the members of an outgroup (Wilder & Shapiro, 1989a, 1989b).

These experiments and the test anxiety literature (Sarason & Sarason, 1990) indicate that anxious people are distracted by intrusive thoughts, and that they show deficits in memory, differentiation, and cognitive performance. Thus, the literature supports the idea that anxiety takes up mental capacity. But capacity decrements are not the whole story.

Intrusive Thoughts Are Uncontrollable, Causing Control Decrements

The intrusive thoughts that anxious people experience are difficult to control, especially as the thoughts become more emotional (Clark & de Silva, 1985; Salkovskis & Harrison, 1984). Even nonanxious people have great difficulty purposefully suppressing thoughts (Wegner, 1989), particularly when they are arousing (Wegner et al., 1990), which many of an anxious person's thoughts may be. Moreover, anxious people report special difficulty in thought control (Borkovec et al., 1983).

We hypothesize that anxious people's unsuccessful attempts at controlling their thoughts and feelings will make them feel control-deprived. No research to date has measured how out of control people feel when they try unsuccessfully to suppress thoughts. But unsuccessful attempts at thought control should mimic traditional outcome control situations: In both, people's efforts are unrelated to their outcomes. One study that supports our claim, by Kent and Gibbons (1987), demonstrated that perceived thought control is strongly related to distress in anxious people—more so than the frequency of their intrusive thoughts. The reported distress in that study is perhaps an indication of mental control deprivation.

So far, the reasoning suggests that anxious people's uncontrollable, intrusive thoughts leave them feeling out of control. Control deprivation in nonanxious people usually leads to control motivation, reflected in active information search. Will the control deprivation of anxious people also lead to control motivation? We believe so, but there is a potential problem in the reasoning, which lies in this distinction: All of the control deprivation paradigms mentioned, for example, in the review by Pittman and Heller (1987), concern *outcome* control (control over one's rewards and punishments). But the control deprivation in anxiety concerns *mental* control (control over one's thoughts and feelings). We believe that mental control deprivation will result in control motivation similar to that in outcome control deprivation. In support of this assumption, our data show that perceived loss of mental control can motivate effortful impression formation, in the form of more complex impressions and use of individuating information (Morling & Fiske, 1994); this parallels the results for outcome control deprivation.

Capacity Decrements and Control Decrements
Cause Competing Tendencies in Anxious People

In the last two subsections, we have argued that anxious people are likely to experience a capacity decrement and a control decrement. These two characteristics result in competing predictions for impression formation. People who are short on capacity are likely to form simpler impressions of others because they lack the capacity to be complex. People who are control-deprived will try to form more complex (or at least more effortful) impressions of others, because they are concerned about regaining prediction and control. Anxious people are caught in between: They want to regain control, but they lack the resources to do so. The simple combination of these two tendencies is likely to create a person who wants to get information about others, but who cannot attend to it or use it in meaningful ways.

An additional prediction from the theory is that anxious people respond to their lack of mental control and mental capacity by simplifying others in an attempt at social control. As we suggest next, anxious people can substitute the control of others, whom they perceive to be more neutral, controllable, and simple, for the control of the self, which they experience as more aversive, uncontrollable, and complex. This redirected control may be similar to powerless people's attempts to control irrelevant domains, discussed earlier. Anxious people, who are short on capacity and long on need for control, may thus prefer others as their objects of control for several social-cognitive reasons.

First, in anxiety the self is the source of negative states, and anxious people may find attention toward the self particularly aversive (Baumeister, 1990; Higgins, 1987). Anxious people should find it more pleasant to direct their attention outward than to focus it on themselves. Second, other people seem easier to control than the self because feedback from attempts at social control is more delayed, indirect, and ambiguous, whereas the anxious person's efforts at mental control give immediate (and often negative) feedback. Thus, unsuccessful attempts at mental control are immediately noticed, whereas unsuccessful attempts at social control can be reinterpreted or ignored. Third, people have less complex concepts of others than of themselves (Fiske & Taylor, 1991, Chs. 4 and 6), so other people seem simpler at the outset. The capacity decrements of anxiety accentuate a simple view of others: Categories are more likely to be the tools of a distracted mind (Gilbert, 1989; Pendry & Macrae, 1994; Wilder & Shapiro, 1989b). If anxious people are motivated to control their environment, another person who appears simple may seem an easy target.

Summary

Anxious people experience uncontrollable, intrusive thoughts. The uncontrollability of their thoughts makes anxious people control-deprived and accuracy-motivated. But the thoughts also take up cognitive capacity, robbing people of resources to act on their accuracy motives. In a social context, anxious people may want to perceive others carefully, but do not have the resources to do so. They channel their control efforts into controlling other people, who seem simpler and (ironically) more controllable. Table 9.1 summarizes the main steps of this new theory, including testable independent and dependent variables.

Our theory focuses on the social cognitions of anxious people, but some of the same mechanisms may apply to depressed individuals. Because depressed people also appear to suffer from thought intrusions or ruminations (Beck, 1976; Pyszczynski & Greenberg, 1987), particularly about unattained goals (Martin, Tesser, & McIntosh, 1993), they may also experience simultaneous distraction and loss of mental control. Anxiety and depression also frequently co-occur (Maser & Cloninger, 1990), making it difficult to distinguish symptomatic and hence theoretical aspects of the two. However, despite the similarities, we focus on anxiety in our theory because it has been understudied in social cognition compared to depression (but see Weary & Edwards, 1994, for some preliminary work). Our model is also unique in its particular focus on the intrusive thoughts of a clinical disorder, rather than the work on depression's well-developed schemas (Beck & Emery with Greenberg, 1985) and helplessness/hopelessness (Abramson, Metalsky, & Alloy, 1989). Finally, the agitation associated with anxiety may make people more likely to act on their control motivations, whereas the lack of energy associated with depression may make people less likely to act.[4]

Experimental Support

Two preliminary studies primarily address Steps 4, 5, and 6 in Table 9.1. According to the theory, two crucial components of anxiety are decreased mental control and decreased capacity. So in these studies we manipulated control motivation and cognitive load, and compared the results to those of an anxious comparison group (Fiske & Morling, 1994). The first study involved five groups of subjects. One group, selected for high trait anxiety, served as an external comparison group, the fifth cell of a $2 \times 2 + 1$ design. Of the remaining subjects, half were deprived of mental control and half were kept cognitively busy, forming a 2 (control-deprived or not) $\times$ 2 (cognitively busy or not) design. To manipulate mental control deprivation, we had subjects attempt to repress thoughts of a white bear (Wegner, Schneider, Carter, & White, 1987), and then gave them feedback that their performance indicated that they had trouble repressing such thoughts and told them to try again. Busyness was manipulated by having sub-

TABLE 9.1   Steps in the Fiske and Emery (1993) Theory of Mental Control and Exaggerated Social Control

Postulate/step	Related independent variable	Related dependent variable
1. Anxious people experience intrusive thoughts.	Manipulate or measure anxiety.	Monitor thought content.
2. The intrusive thoughts reduce cognitive capacity.	Manipulate thought intrusions.	Test cognitive performance.
3. The intrusive thoughts are uncontrollable.	Manipulate thought suppression efforts.	Measure control over thoughts.
4. Losing control over their thoughts makes people feel control-deprived.	Manipulate perceived mental control.	Ask about feelings of control.
5. Mental control deprivation leads to control motivation.	Manipulate perceived mental control.	Test information seeking.
6. Anxious people lack capacity for complex social cognition.	Add control deprivation and capacity deprivation.	Test for complexity of impressions, use of information.
7. The anxious self is aversive, so control attempts are not directed inward.	Manipulate or measure anxiety.	Measure aversiveness of self-focus.
8. Anxious people view other people as easier to control than the self, and thus target those others for control attempts.	Manipulate or measure anxiety.	Measure perceptions of and controllability of others.
9. To an anxious person, others seem good targets for control attempts.	Manipulate or measure anxiety.	Measure attempted control of others.

jects count beeps from a tape during the experiment. Anxiety was not manipulated; subjects in the comparison cell were selected on the basis of a prescreening
questionnaire on trait anxiety (the Trait Anxiety subscale of the State-Trait
Anxiety Inventory; Spielberger, Gorsuch, & Lushene, 1970) and their ratings of
anticipated state anxiety in this laboratory situation.

We expected the nonanxious subjects who were both mental-control-
deprived and cognitively busy to resemble our anxious comparison group.
Compared to subjects who were neither control-deprived nor busy, these two
groups should form less complex impressions of their partners. Results supported the hypothesis exactly in the first study. Mental-control-deprived subjects
wrote more complex essays about their partners than did baseline subjects, and
busy subjects' essays were slightly less complex. But when subjects were both
mental-control-deprived and busy, their essays were much less complex than
those of baseline subjects. The mental-control-deprived/busy subjects' essays
were as low in complexity as the anxious subjects'.

Analyses also supported a less central, yet theoretically important, prediction: Mental control deprivation by itself will lead to effortful impression formation. Mental-control-deprived subjects' trait ratings reflected expectancy-disconfirming information they obtained from their partners, and they used more
complexity in their essays (if they were not busy). Mental-control-deprived subjects seemed especially likely to put forth effort when they had lazy partners.
They wrote longer and more complex essays about lazy partners, and polarized
their trait ratings much less for lazy partners, indicating more integration of information (Morling & Fiske, 1994).

Although this design was factorial, correlational results comparing only the
anxious and baseline groups provide further support for the theory. Pretest anxiety scores, as well as how anxious subjects felt in the experiment, were related to
how distracting and uncontrollable they said their intrusive thoughts were, supporting the two hypothesized effects of intrusive thoughts in anxiety. Feeling
anxious was correlated with a desire to control the partner in the experiment;
mediational analyses suggested that this anxiety → partner control effect was
mediated by the uncontrollability of their thoughts. We also found that as subjects wanted *more* to control their partners, they paid *less* attention to information about them. More specifically, as subjects felt *more* anxious, they spent *less*
time reading inconsistent statements (the most informative ones). This constitutes an interesting parallel to Goodwin and Fiske's (1995) structurally powerful
and interpersonally dominant subjects, described earlier.

Our preliminary data thus support roles for capacity decrements and control motivation in anxiety. Anxious perceivers wanted to control their partners,
and seemed to do it by paying less attention to the most informative information about them and by forming simple impressions. The competing influences
of mental control deprivation and capacity decrements, then, may create a personal motivation in anxious people to form particularly simple impressions of
others.

SOCIAL STRUCTURE AND PERSONAL MOTIVES:
LINKING THE TWO

Although the dynamics of interpersonal power and personal anxiety are importantly distinct, they do share a metatheoretical perspective of an orientation toward social control, hobbled by capacity decrements. Power raises issues of socially sanctioned social control and capacity limits that result from hierarchical social structure. Anxiety raises issues of personally motivated social control and capacity limits that result from uncontrollable intrusive thoughts.

Addressing power and anxiety together reveals practical issues as well as theoretical advances, so there are interesting and important benefits to linking the two. One practical issue is that personal motives, such as those in anxiety, may have more or less influence, depending on the perceiver's social position. For example, the anxiety of a person in power necessarily affects more people's lives than does a subordinate's anxiety. And in the other direction, a perceiver's social position can contribute to feelings of anxiety. As already noted, being or feeling powerless over their own outcomes makes people anxious. One theoretical benefit of linking them is that powerful people's motives are relatively autonomous, and anxiety is one salient, motivating state likely to be relevant to people in high-stress powerful positions. Finally, as noted, the interpersonal mechanisms of power and anxiety turn out to have two central variables in common: capacity limitations and need for control. If a powerful person is also interpersonally dominant, then the parallel is complete: Both powerful dominant and anxious perceivers seek social control but have limited capacity to exercise it. And, unfortunately for their targets, stereotyping is likely to be the cognitive strategy of choice for powerful dominant and anxious perceivers.

People always have to budget their limited capacities to meet the many demands on their attention. They pragmatically use cognitive strategies that meet their motivational goals with the resources they have. People's dependence on or rejection of default categories apparently results from the tradeoff between capacity limits and control motivations, whether this tradeoff is necessitated by social structure, personal needs, or both.

Acknowledgments

The writing of this chapter was supported by National Institute of Mental Health (NIMH) Research Grant No. 41801 to Susan T. Fiske. Beth Morling was supported by NIMH Training Grant No. 18827.

Notes

1. However, neglecting their subordinates may be costly to powerful people in terms of

worker productivity and satisfaction (e.g., Roethlisberger, 1941). Reminding powerful people of their dependence on subordinates may be a remedy for some of the processes we discuss here.

2. Of course, not all people in powerful roles are also dominant; there is no necessary correlation between dispositional dominance and situational power, except to the extent that the former seeks the latter.

3. Subjects could not simply ignore this information, because they were required to read each piece of information aloud (see Stevens & Fiske, 1995).

4. One might wonder how our anxiety model extends to positive arousal more generally, because positive arousal can motivate effective, vigilant attention and performance (e.g., in achievement situations; McClelland, 1961). However, even positive arousal's effects on performance follow a well-known inverted-U-shaped function, suggesting that anxiety may be a case of too much arousal. Alternatively, although anxiety's arousal component motivates effort and attention, distracting self-focused thoughts interfere (see Eysenck & Calvo, 1992); this causes performance to fail, especially on complex tasks. We speculate that positive arousal may involve less self-focus, allowing task motivation to operate uninterrupted.

References

Abramson, L. Y., Metalsky, G. I., & Alloy, L. B. (1989). Hopelessness depression: A theory-based subtype of depression. *Psychological Review, 96*, 358–372.

Amsbary, D., Dépret, E., Fiske, S. T., & Morling, B. (1994, July). *Collectivistic values can mediate the adaptability of an external locus of control.* Poster presented at the meeting of the American Psychological Society, Washington, DC.

Apfelbaum, E. (1979). Relations of domination and movements for liberation: An analysis of power between groups. In W. G. Austin & S. Worchel (Eds.), *The social psychology of intergroup relations* (pp. 188–204). Belmont, CA: Wadsworth.

Banaji, M. R., & Prentice, D. A. (1994). The self in social contexts. *Annual Review of Psychology 45*, 297–332.

Bargh, J. A. (1984). Automatic and conscious processing of social information. In R. S. Wyer, Jr., & T. K. Srull (Eds.), *Handbook of social cognition* (Vol. 3, pp. 1–44). Hillsdale, NJ: Erlbaum.

Bates, G. W., Campbell, I. M., & Burgess, P. M. (1991). Assessment of articulated thoughts in social anxiety: Modification of the ATSS procedure. *British Journal of Clinical Psychology, 29*, 91–98.

Baumeister, R. F. (1990). Anxiety and deconstruction: On escaping the self. In J. M. Olson & M. P. Zanna (Eds.), *The Ontario Symposium: Vol. 6. Self-inference processes* (pp. 259–291). Hillsdale, NJ: Erlbaum.

Beck, A. T. (1976). *Cognitive therapy and the emotional disorders.* New York: International Universities Press.

Beck, A. T., & Emery, G., with Greenberg, R. L. (1985). *Anxiety disorders and phobias: A cognitive perspective.* New York: Basic Books.

Berscheid, E., Graziano, W., Monson, T., & Dermer, M. (1976). Outcome dependency: Attention, attribution, and attraction. *Journal of Personality and Social Psychology, 34*, 978–989.

Billig, M. (1976). *Social psychology and intergroup relations.* London: Academic Press.

Borkovec, T. D., Robinson, E., Pruzinsky, T., & DePree, J. A. (1983). Preliminary exploration of worry: Some characteristics and processes. *Behaviour Research and Therapy, 21*, 9–16.

Brewer, M. B. (1988). A dual process model of impression formation. In T. K. Srull & R. S. Wyer (Eds.), *Advances in social cognition* (Vol. 1, pp. 1–36). Hillsdale, NJ: Erlbaum.

Brown, J. D. (1988). Self-directed attention, self-esteem, and causal attributions for valenced outcomes. *Personality and Social Psychology Bulletin, 14*, 252–263.

Bruner, J. S. (1957). On perceptual readiness. *Psychological Review, 64*, 123–152.

Cartwright, D. (1959). *Studies in social power*. Ann Arbor, MI: Institute of Social Research.

Carver, C. S., & Scheier, M. F. (1988). A control-process perspective on anxiety. *Anxiety Research, 1*, 7–22.

Clark, D. A., & de Silva, P. (1985). The nature of depressive and anxious, intrusive thoughts: Distinct or uniform phenomena? *Behaviour Research and Therapy, 23*, 383–393.

Condor, S. G., & Brown, R. J. (1986). Psychological processes in intergroup conflicts. In W. Stroebe, A. W. Kruglanski, D. Bar-Tal, & M. Hewstone (Eds.), *The social psychology of intergroup conflicts* (pp. 3–26). New York: Springer.

Crocker, J., & Luhtanen, R. (1990). Collective self-esteem and in-group bias. *Journal of Personality and Social Psychology, 58*, 60–67.

Crocker, J., Thompson, L. L., McGraw, K. M., & Ingerman, C. (1987). Downward comparison, prejudice, and evaluation of others: Effects of self-esteem and threat. *Journal of Personality and Social Psychology, 52*, 907–916.

Dahl, R. A. (1957). The concept of power. *Behavioural Science, 2*, 201–215.

de la Haye, A. M. (1991). Problems and procedures: A typology of paradigms in interpersonal cognition. *European Bulletin of Cognitive Psychology, 11*, 279–304.

Deffenbacher, J. L. (1980). Worry and emotionality in test anxiety. In I. G. Sarason (Ed.), *Test anxiety: Theory, research, and applications* (pp. 111–128). Hillsdale, NJ: Erlbaum.

Dépret, E. F. (1995). *Feelings of personal control and the social categorization of powerful others*. Unpublished manuscript, Université de Grenoble, France.

Dépret, E. F., & Fiske, S. T. (1993). Social cognition and power: Some cognitive consequences of social structure as a source of control deprivation. In G. Weary, F. Gleicher, & K. Marsh (Eds.), *Control motivation and social cognition* (pp. 176–202). New York: Springer-Verlag.

Dépret, E. F., & Fiske, S. T. (1994). *Perceiving the powerful: Intriguing individuals versus threatening groups*. Unpublished manuscript, Université de Grenoble, France.

Deschamps, J.-C. (1982). Relations of power between groups. In H. Tajfel (Ed.), *Social identity and intergroup relations* (pp. 85–98). Cambridge, England: Cambridge University Press.

Devine, P. G. (1989). Stereotypes and prejudice: Their automatic and controlled components. *Journal of Personality and Social Psychology, 56*, 5–18.

Easterbrook, J. A. (1959). The effect of emotion on cue utilization and the organization of behavior. *Psychological Review, 66*, 183–201.

Epstein, S. (1990). Cognitive experiential self-theory. In L. A. Pervin (Ed.), *Handbook of personality: Theory and research* (pp. 165–192). New York: Guilford Press.

Erber, R., & Fiske, S. T. (1984). Outcome dependency and attention to inconsistent information. *Journal of Personality and Social Psychology, 47*, 709–726.

Eysenck, M. W., & Calvo, M. G. (1992). Anxiety and performance: The processing efficiency theory. *Cognition and Emotion, 6*, 409–434.

Fiske, A. P., Haslam, N., & Fiske, S. T. (1991). Confusing one person with another: What errors reveal about the elementary forms of social relations. *Journal of Personality and Social Psychology, 60*, 656–674.

Fiske, S. T. (1992). Thinking is for doing: Portraits of social cognition from daguerreotype to laserphoto. *Journal of Personality and Social Psychology, 63*, 877–889.

Fiske, S. T. (1993a). Controlling other people: The impact of power on stereotyping. *American Psychologist, 48*, 621–628.

Fiske, S. T. (1993b). Social cognition and social perception. *Annual Review of Psychology, 44*, 155–194.

Fiske, S. T., Canfield, J. E., & Von Hendy, H. (1994, June). *Stereotyping and prejudice across out-*

groups: A search for individual differences. Poster presented at the meeting of the American Psychological Society, Washington, DC.

Fiske, S. T., & Emery, E. J. (1993). Lost mental control and exaggerated social control: Social-cognitive and psychoanalytic speculations. In D. M. Wegner & J. W. Pennebaker (Eds.), *Handbook of mental control* (pp. 171–199). Englewood Cliffs, NJ: Prentice-Hall.

Fiske, S. T., Goodwin, S. A., Rosen, L. D., & Rosenthal, A. M. (1995). *Romantic outcome dependency and the (in)accuracy of impression formation: A case of clouded judgment.* Unpublished manuscript, University of Massachusetts at Amherst.

Fiske, S. T., & Morling, B. (1994, October). *Anxiety, mental control and social control.* Paper presented at the meeting of the Society of Experimental Social Psychology, Lake Tahoe, NV.

Fiske, S. T., & Neuberg, S. L. (1990). A continuum model of impression formation, from category-based to individuating processes: Influence of information and motivation on attention and interpretation. In M. P. Zanna (Ed.), *Advances in experimental social psychology* (Vol. 23, pp. 1–74). New York: Academic Press.

Fiske, S. T., & Pavelchak, M. A. (1986). Category-based versus piecemeal-based affective responses: Developments in schema-triggered affect. In R. M. Sorrentino & E. T. Higgins (Eds.), *Handbook of motivation and cognition: Foundations of social behavior* (Vol. 1, pp. 167–203). New York: Guilford Press.

Fiske, S. T., & Taylor, S. E. (1991). *Social cognition* (2nd ed.). New York: McGraw-Hill.

Fiske, S. T., & Von Hendy, H. M. (1992). Personality feedback and situational norms can control stereotyping processes. *Journal of Personality and Social Psychology, 62,* 577–596.

Frable, D. E. S., Blackstone, T., & Scherbaum, C. (1990). Marginal and mindful: Deviants in social interactions. *Journal of Personality and Social Psychology, 59,* 140–149.

Gilbert, D. T. (1989). Thinking lightly about others: Automatic components of the social inference process. In J. S. Uleman & J. A. Bargh (Eds.), *Unintended thought* (pp. 189–211). New York: Guilford Press.

Goodwin, S. A., & Fiske, S. T. (1993, June). *Effects of romantic outcome dependency on social judgments: Disentangling the possibilities.* Poster presented at the meeting of the American Psychological Society, Chicago.

Goodwin, S. A., & Fiske, S. T. (1995). *Power and motivated impression formation: How power holders stereotype by default and by design.* Manuscript submitted for publication.

Goodwin, S. A., Fiske, S. T., & Yzerbyt, V. (1995, August). *Social judgment in power relationships: A judgment-monitoring perspective.* Poster presented at the meeting of the American Psychological Association, New York.

Greenwald, A. G., & Banaji, M. R. (1993). *Implicit social cognition: Attitudes, self-esteem, and stereotypes.* Unpublished manuscript.

Heider, F. (1958). *The psychology of interpersonal relations.* New York: Wiley.

Higgins, E. T. (1987). Self-discrepancy: A theory relating self and affect. *Psychological Review, 94,* 319–340.

Higgins, E. T., & McCann, D. C. (1984). Social encoding and subsequent attitudes, impressions, and memory: "Context-driven" and motivational aspects of processing. *Journal of Personality and Social Psychology, 47,* 26–39.

Higgins, E. T., McCann, D. C., & Fondacaro, R. (1982). The "communication game": Goal-directed encoding and cognitive consequences. *Social Cognition, 1,* 21–37.

Higgins, E. T., & Tykocinski, O. (1992). Self-discrepancies and biographical memory: Personality and cognition at the level of psychological situation. *Personality and Social Psychology Bulletin, 18,* 527–535.

Hogg, M. A., & Abrams, D. (1988). *Social identifications: A social psychology of intergroup relations and group processes.* London: Routledge.

Hogg, M. A., & Sunderland, J. (1991). Self-esteem and intergroup discrimination in the minimal group paradigm. *British Journal of Social Psychology, 30,* 51–62.

Huston, T. L. (1983). Power. In H. H. Kelley, E. Berscheid, A. Christensen, J. H. Harvey, T. L. Huston, G. Levinger, E. McClintock, L. A. Peplau, & D. R. Peterson (Eds.), *Close relationships* (pp. 169-219). New York: W. H. Freeman.

Kahneman, D. (1973). *Attention and effort.* Englewood Cliffs, NJ: Prentice-Hall.

Kelley, H. H. (1990, August). *Lewin, situations, and interdependence.* Paper presented at the meeting of the American Psychological Association, Boston, MA.

Kent, G., & Gibbons, R. (1987). Self-efficacy and the control of anxious cognitions. *Journal of Behavior Therapy and Experimental Psychiatry, 18,* 33-40.

Klein, W. M., & Kunda, Z. (1992). Motivated person perception: Constructing justifications for desired beliefs. *Journal of Experimental Social Psychology, 28,* 145-160.

Lord, C. G., & Saenz, D. S. (1985). Memory deficits and memory surfeits: Differential cognitive consequences of tokenism for tokens and observers. *Journal of Personality and Social Psychology, 49,* 918-926.

Martin, L. L., Tesser, A., & McIntosh, W. D. (1993). Wanting but not having: The effects of unattained goals on thoughts and feelings. In D. M. Wegner & J. W. Pennebaker (Eds.), *Handbook of mental control* (pp. 552-572). Englewood Cliffs, NJ: Prentice-Hall.

Maser, J. D., & Cloninger, C. R. (Eds.). (1990). *Comorbidity in anxiety and mood disorders.* Washington, DC: American Psychiatric Press.

McClelland, D. C. (1961). *The achieving society.* Princeton, NJ: Van Nostrand.

Morling, B., & Fiske, S. T. (1994, July). *Mental control deprivation can motivate effortful person perception.* Poster presented at the meeting of the American Psychological Society, Washington, DC.

Neuberg, S. L. (1989). The goal of forming accurate impressions during social interactions: Attenuating the impact of negative expectancies. *Journal of Personality and Social Psychology, 54,* 374-386.

Neuberg, S. L., & Fiske, S. T. (1987). Motivational influences on impression formation: Outcome dependency, accuracy-driven attention, and individuating processes. *Journal of Personality and Social Psychology, 53,* 431-444.

Ng, S. H. (1980). *The social psychology of power.* New York: Academic Press.

Ng, S. H. (1982). Power and intergroup discrimination. In H. Tajfel (Ed.), *Social identity and intergroup relations* (pp. 179-206). Cambridge, England: Cambridge University Press.

Omoto, A. M., & Borgida, E. (1988). Guess who might be coming to dinner? Personal involvement and racial stereotyping. *Journal of Experimental Social Psychology, 24,* 571-593.

Pendry, L. F., & Macrae, C. N. (1994). Stereotypes and mental life: The case of the motivated but thwarted tactician. *Journal of Experimental Social Psychology, 30,* 303-325.

Pittman, T. S., & Heller, J. F. (1987). Social motivation. *Annual Review of Psychology, 38,* 461-489.

Pittman, T. S., & Pittman, N. L. (1980). Deprivation of control and the attribution process. *Journal of Personality and Social Psychology, 39,* 377-389.

Pruitt, D. G. (1976). Power and bargaining. In B. Seidenberg & A. Snadowsky (Eds.), *Social psychology: An introduction* (pp. 343-375). New York: Free Press.

Pyszczynski, T., & Greenberg, J. (1987). Self-regulatory perseveration and the depressive self-focusing style: A self-awareness theory of reaction depression. *Psychological Bulletin, 102,* 122-138.

Roethlisberger, F. J. (1941). *Management and morale.* Cambridge, MA: Harvard University Press.

Ruscher, J. B., & Fiske, S. T. (1990). Interpersonal competition can cause individuating processes. *Journal of Personality and Social Psychology, 58,* 832-843.

Ruscher, J. B., Fiske, S. T., Miki, H., & Van Manen, S. (1991). Individuating processes in competition: Interpersonal versus intergroup. *Personality and Social Psychology Bulletin, 17,* 595-605.

Sachdev, I., & Bourhis, R. Y. (1985). Social categorization and power differentials in group re-lations. *European Journal of Social Psychology, 15*, 415-434.

Saenz, D. S., & Lord, C. G. (1989). Reversing roles: A cognitive strategy for undoing memory deficits associated with token status. *Journal of Personality and Social Psychology, 56*, 698-708.

Salkovskis, P., & Harrison, J. (1984). Abnormal and normal obsessions—A replication. *Behaviour Research and Therapy, 22*, 549-552.

Sarason, I. G. (1980). Introduction to the study of test anxiety. In I. G. Sarason (Ed.), *Test anx-iety: Theory, research, and application* (pp. 3-14). Hillsdale, NJ: Erlbaum.

Sarason, I. G., & Sarason, B. R. (1990). Test anxiety. In H. Leitenberg (Ed.), *Handbook of social and evaluation anxiety* (pp. 475-496). New York: Plenum Press.

Sedikides, C., Olson, N., & Reis, H. T. (1993). Relationships as natural categories. *Journal of Personality and Social Psychology, 64*, 71-82.

Sherif, M. (1962). Intergroup relations and leadership: Introductory statement in M. Sherif (Ed.), *Intergroup relations and leadership* (pp. 3-21). New York: Wiley.

Spielberger, C. D., Gorsuch, R. L., & Lushene, R. E. (1970). *Manual for the State-Trait Anxiety Inventory*. Palo Alto, CA: Consulting Psychologists Press.

Stangor, C., & Ford, T. E. (1992). Accuracy and expectancy-confirming processing orienta-tions and the development of stereotypes and prejudice. In W. Stroebe & M. Hewstone (Eds.), *European review of social psychology* (Vol. 3, pp. 57-89). Chichester, England: Wiley.

Stevens, L. E., & Fiske, S. T. (1995). *Forming motivated impressions of a powerholder: Accuracy un-der task dependency and misperception under evaluation dependency*. Unpublished manu-script, University of Massachusetts at Amherst.

Stevens, L. E., & Fiske, S. T. (1995). Motivation and cognition in social life: A social survival perspective. *Social Cognition, 13*(3), 189-214.

Swann, W. B., Jr. (1990). To be adored or to be known? The interplay of self-enhancement and self-verification. In R. M. Sorrentino & E. T. Higgins (Eds.), *Handbook of motivation and cognition: Foundations of social behavior* (Vol. 2, pp. 408-448). New York: Guilford Press.

Taylor, S. E., & Brown, J. D. (1988). Illusion and well-being: A social psychological perspective on mental health. *Psychological Bulletin, 103*, 193-210.

Tajfel, H. (1982). Social psychology of intergroup relations. *Annual Review of Psychology, 33*, 1-39.

Tajfel, H., & Turner, J. C. (1986). The social identity theory of intergroup behavior. In S. Worchel & W. G. Austin (Eds.), *Psychology of intergroup relations* (2nd ed., pp. 7-24). Chicago: Nelson-Hall.

Tetlock, P. E. (1991). An alternative metaphor in the study of judgment and choice: People as politicians. *Theoretical Psychology, 1*, 451-475.

Thibaut, J. W., & Kelley, H. H. (1959). *The social psychology of groups*. New York: Wiley.

Weary, G., & Edwards, J. A. (1994). Social cognition and clinical psychology: Anxiety, depres-sion, and the processing of social information. In R. S. Wyer & T. K. Srull (Eds.), *Handbook of social cognition* (2nd ed., pp. 289-338). Hillsdale, NJ: Erlbaum.

Weary, G., Gleicher, F., & Marsh, K. (Eds.). (1993). *Control motivation and social cognition* (pp. 176-202). New York: Springer-Verlag.

Wegner, D. M. (1989). *White bears and other unwanted thoughts: Suppression, obsession, and the psy-chology of mental control*. New York: Viking.

Wegner, D. M., Schneider, D. J., Carter, S., III, & White, L. (1987). Paradoxical effects of thought suppression. *Journal of Personality and Social Psychology, 53*, 5-13.

Wegner, D. M., Shortt, J. W., Blake, A. W., & Page, M. S. (1990). The suppression of exciting thoughts. *Journal of Personality and Social Psychology, 58*, 409-418.

Weisz, J. R., Rothbaum, F. M., & Blackburn, T. C. (1984). Standing out and standing in: The psychology of control in America and Japan. *American Psychologist, 39*, 955-969.

Wilder, D. A., & Shapiro, P. N. (1989a). Effects of anxiety on impression formation in a group context: An anxiety–assimilation hypothesis. *Journal of Experimental Social Psychology, 25,* 481–499.

Wilder, D. A., & Shapiro, P. N. (1989b). Role of competition-induced anxiety in limiting the beneficial impact of positive behavior by an out-group member. *Journal of Personality and Social Psychology, 56,* 60–69.

Wine, J. D. (1980). Cognitive–attentional theory of test anxiety. In I. G. Sarason (Ed.), *Test anxiety: Theory, research, and application* (pp. 349–385). Hillsdale, NJ: Erlbaum.

CHAPTER 10

Seeing Groups as Entities
The Role of Perceiver Motivation

MARILYNN B. BREWER
AMY S. HARASTY
Ohio State University

In a now-classic article, Donald Campbell (1958) challenged social scientists to develop objective criteria by which social aggregates such as political units, groups, or social categories can be legitimately described as "entities." Borrowing from tenets of gestalt psychology, he proposed that the basic principles of perceptual organization—proxmity, similarity, common fate, and pattern—can be generalized to indices applicable to the assessment of group boundaries and internal coherence. With due apologies to linguistic purists, he coined the term "entitativity" to refer to "the degree of having the nature of an entity" (Campbell, 1958, p. 17), capturing the idea that group-as-entity represents a continuum rather than a strict dichotomy. He noted that social aggregates may be more or less "entitative," depending on such properties as clarity of boundaries, correlated movement of members in time and space, and intragroup similarity.

Although political scientists (and to some extent sociologists) grapple with the question of whether political units can be considered "actors," social psychologists have in general been little occupied with the epistemological status of groups as "real" entities. We have, however, been interested in the *consequences* of whether or not social groups are *perceived* as bounded units (see especially Wilder, 1981, 1986). To the extent that the principles of entitativity described by Campbell in 1958 influence how aggregates or social categories are cognitively represented, they are of relevance to current theories of group perception and stereotypes (cf. Mackie & Hamilton, 1993).

In a more recent treatise, David Hamilton (1991) has revived the concept of entitativity as a way of accounting for differences in results of social cognition research on forming impressions of persons and of groups. Apparent differences in the ways information about individuals and groups is processed and organized in memory have led Hamilton to conclude that perceivers do not assume the same degree of unity and coherence among members of a group as they expect in the personality of an individual person. In considering the implications of this assumption, however, he has acknowledged Campbell's concept of entitativity and suggested that some social groups may be perceived more as "individuals" than others are. To the extent that a social category is perceived to be high in entitativity, the processing of information and organization of impressions should resemble those characteristic of person perception.

Hamilton's review, together with theories of social categorization and stereotyping derived from social identity theory (Oakes & Turner, 1990), has raised renewed interest in the nature and antecedents of the perceived entitativity of social groups. How is entitativity reflected in the way information about category members is organized and interconnected in memory? What determines whether a social category is cognitively represented as a single coherent unit, as opposed to an associative link among individual group members?

RELATED CONCEPTUALIZATIONS

Posing the issue of group entitativity in terms of the structure of cognitive representations calls attention to the relationship between the entitativity concept and other recent lines of research and theory on group perception. Perceived entitativity is directly relevant to prototype- versus exemplar-based models of social categories; to research on perceived group variability and the outgroup homogeneity effect; to social identity theory's distinction between interpersonal and intergroup orientations; and to social categorization theories of intergroup relations. The concept of entitativity provides a connecting link among these otherwise disparate lines of research and theory.

Models of Category Representation: Prototypes versus Exemplars

One way to think about the relative entitativity of social categories is in terms of the difference between prototype- and exemplar-based models of category representation. In exemplar models, category information is stored in the form of representations of individual category members. In prototype models, category information is stored in the form of a representation of a "typical" category member, extracted and integrated from information about category instances. According to Rosch's (1978) model of category representation, the prototype represents those features that are most likely to be shared by category members and not shared by members of contrasting categories. The prototype of the category "apple," for instance, is a red, roundish, solid object with smooth skin. Not all individual instances of the apple category are exactly like this prototype; collectively, however, these features are the ones that distinguish apples from other fruits. The idea that categories are thought of as social entities resembles prototype models of category representation, in which a single mental representation captures information about the category as a whole.

Mixed models of category representation have been proposed that combine elements of prototype- and exemplar-based models. In mixed models, category labels are linked both to prototype representations and to individual instances, and both forms of category knowledge are presumed to be available (Medin, Altom, & Murphy, 1984; Park & Hastie, 1987; Smith & Zarate, 1990). Within the framework of such mixed models, perceived entitativity can be thought of as the relative strength and accessibility of a prototype representation of a social category, compared to exemplar representations.

A clear parallel between entitativity and prototype representations of social categories is evident in Brewer's (1988) characterization of the nature of social category prototypes. According to her model, prototypes are "pictoliteral" representations; that is, they are more like visual images than like semantic networks. In comparison to nonvisual concepts, pictoliteral images are more concrete, configural, and bounded. In other words, the form and content of category prototypes resemble those of images of single individuals. To the extent that a prototype representation of a social category is well developed, that group can be said to be high in perceived entitativity.

In a recent model of perception of majority and minority groups, Mullen (1991) also explicitly ties perceived entitativity to prototype representations of social categories. Based on the relative salience of minority as opposed to majority groups, Mullen proposes that information about minority group members will be processed in terms of category prototypes, whereas information about majority groups will be processed in terms of exemplars. As a consequence, minority groups are perceived as more homogeneous and depersonalized than are majority groups. To translate this idea into our terminology, minority groups are expected to be higher in perceived entitativity than are majority groups.

Perceived Variability in Category Representations

Hamilton's (1991) review of impression formation research focuses on the expectation of consistency as a critical feature of coherent impressions. At the level of the individual person, consistency is defined in terms of variability of behavior and preferences across time and settings. At the level of the social group, consistency refers to variability across *persons* in behavior, attitudes, and personality characteristics. Traditionally, the study of social category stereotypes has focused almost exclusively on the perception of group characteristics in terms of central tendency, the features of the average or typical group member. More recently, however, attention has turned to estimates of intragroup variability as an aspect of the representation of social groups or categories.

Measures of Perceived Variability

Perceived variability of social categories has been measured in a number of different ways, not all of which prove to be highly intercorrelated. Using structural-modeling analysis, Park and Judd (1990) compared 10 different measures of variability and identified two latent variables among those measures. One cluster of measures, represented by the first latent factor, pertained to the "dispersion" of category members along specific dimensions; range estimates and standard deviation measures loaded highly on this dimension. Most of the measures in this category derive from use of the "frequency distribution task" (Judd & Park, 1988; Linville, Fischer, & Salovey, 1989; Park & Hastie, 1987). In this task, subjects are provided with an array of six to eight boxes representing levels or gradations of a bipolar trait (e.g., "extremely intelligent" to "extremely stupid"). The respondent's task is to estimate the percentage of category members who fall at each level.

The second cluster of measures identified by Park and Judd (1990) was best represented by assessment of perceived prevalence of stereotypic versus counterstereotypic characteristics. In this group of measures, variability is operationalized in terms of estimates of what percentage of category members have stereotypical attributes, compared to what percentage have attributes that are atypical of or contrary to the category stereotype.

Other measures of perceived variability involve direct global judgments of similarity–dissimilarity among category members. For instance, some measures simply ask respondents to indicate how variable the category is on a Likert-type scale (e.g., ranging from "all the same" to "extremely different"). In Park and Judd's (1990) analysis, such global judgments loaded relatively weakly on both major factors, suggesting that such summary ratings do not reliably measure the same thing across occasions.

Because different measures of variability do not always produce the same results, it is a matter of speculation as to which measures are the best operationalizations of the perceived "entitativity" of a social category. However, given our conceptualization of entitativity in terms of the strength and accessibility of prototype representations of a category, it would seem that the measures captured by Park and Judd's second latent variable (perceived stereotypicality) come closest to our conceptualization. When such measures are used, category homogeneity is defined, in effect, as the tightness of fit of category members to the category prototype.

Ingroup versus Outgroup Variability

Interest in the perceived variability of social categories was stimulated by a persistent finding that outgroups (categories to which the perceiver does not belong) are judged to be less variable or more homogenous on stereotype-relevant characteristics than are ingroups. This so-called outgroup homogeneity effect has been demonstrated across a wide variety of social groups and measures of judged variability (Ostrom & Sedikides, 1992; Park & Judd, 1990). In his model of egocentric social categorization (ESC), Bernd Simon (1993) explicitly ties this difference between ingroup and outgroup perception to differences in the construal of ingroups and outgroups as social entities.

According to the ESC model, the perceiver's ingroup is usually construed as a heterogeneous aggregate of separate entities, and only outgroups are represented as homogeneous social categories. This asymmetry in cognitive construal generates what Simon refers to as "quasi-intergroup situations," in which inter-*group* relations with the outgroup (defined in terms of categorical differences from the self) coexist with inter*personal* relations with ingroup members (where differences among individuals are more salient).

Although Simon's ESC model focuses on differences between the construal of ingroup and outgroup categories, it does allow for the possibility that in-groups, too, will be represented as social entities when social identity is engaged. This aspect of the theory is consistent with recent work derived from self-cate-gorization theory, which places greater emphasis on the conditions under which *ingroups* will be perceived as homogeneous social units (Brewer, 1993; Haslam, Oakes, Turner, & McGarty, Chapter 6, this volume). According to this model, social identification with an ingroup is based on a process of self-categorization, which entails "a shift toward perception of the self as an interchangeable exem-plar of some social category and away from the perception of self as a unique person defined by individual differences from others" (Turner, Hogg, Oakes, Reicher, & Wetherell, 1987, p. 50). In other words, when social identity is acti-vated, the self and other ingroup members are construed as a single entity. On the other hand, when social identification with an ingroup category is not en-gaged, the ingroup serves as a reference for interpersonal rather than intergroup comparison. Thus, the concept of entitativity helps to articulate the relation-ship between perceived homogeneity and the distinction between intergroup and interpersonal orientations emphasized by social identity theory (Brown & Turner, 1981).

Ingroup Entitativity and Group Cohesiveness

According to self-categorization theory, the ingroup is cognitively represented in terms of a prototype incorporating those features that maximize the contrast between characteristics of the ingroup and all relevant outgroups. Furthermore, when social identity is engaged, the individual group member's self-perception is assimilated to this prototype representation. Hogg (1992, 1993) has suggested that the concept of group "cohesiveness" should be reinterpreted as the product of such self-categorization processes, as opposed to traditional approaches that define cohesiveness in terms of interpersonal attraction. Group cohesion lies in the shared perception by group members that they constitute a social entity. Again, the implication is that the perceived entitativity of the ingroup as a whole (not the interpersonal relations among group members) is what underlies group cohesiveness and associated intragroup behavior.

This self-categorization process is assumed to underlie many of the phe-nomena associated with group behavior, including conformity, group polariza-tion, and crowd behavior (Reicher, 1984; Turner, 1991; Turner et al., 1987). The basic idea is that self-categorization gives rise to a process of social influence that is translated into collective behavior. Each group member learns or forms a representation of the norms and attributes that distinguish the ingroup from

relevant others, and the members then adapt their own behavior to this definition of the social category. Self-categorization, in effect, provides a cognitive
mechanism for the concept of "group mind" as a shared definition of group
identity that directs and limits individual behavior. This generates an interesting
self-fulfilling prophecy, in that perceiving the ingroup as a social entity creates
the conditions under which collectives actually *behave* as a single entity. As
Abelson (1994) has pointed out, the concept of entitativity entails not only the
ascription of traits and features to groups as whole, but the attribution of motives, intents, and the capacity to act. The social influence processes associated
with self-categorization imply some validity for this conceptualization of social
collectives as behaving entities.

Categorization as a Mediator of Intergroup Contact Effects

Another application of the conceptualization of ingroups as social entities is
represented in Gaertner and Dovidio's approach to improving intergroup relations through recategorization (Gaertner, Dovidio, Anastasio, Bachman, &
Rust, 1993). Consistent with Hogg's conceptualization of group cohesiveness,
the recategorization model assumes that positive affect toward fellow group
members is a consequence (rather than a cause) of their shared definition as a
single group. Indeed, positive evaluations of the ingroup and its products have
been found to increase systematically with conditions that increase the perception of ingroup entitativity (L. Gaertner & Schopler, 1994).

Gaertner and Dovidio's prescription for improving intergroup relations is
based on forging a common group identity—one that extends to former outgroup members the cognitive and motivational processes that produce positive
attitudes toward ingroup members. In a series of experiments, Gaertner,
Dovidio, and their colleagues have drawn on the same perceptual principles proposed by Campbell (1958) to create conditions of intergroup contact that would
encourage recategorization from a two-group representation to a single, shared
group identity. Their results have demonstrated that environmental factors, such
as spatial arrangement of group members, group labels, and visual cues, influence whether a merged group is perceived as a single social entity (one-group
representation) (Gaertner, Mann, Murrell, & Dovidio, 1989). Furthermore, they
have found that the representation of the aggregate as one group or two is a significant mediator of the effects of cooperative intergroup contact on positive
evaluations of the former outgroup (Gaertner, Mann, Dovidio, Murrell, &
Pomare, 1990).

IMPLICATIONS OF PERCEIVED ENTITATIVITY

Cognitive representations of categories as entities are of interest only to the extent that differences in entitativity have implications for judgments and behav-

ior directed toward those categories or toward category members. In this section, we consider potential implications of the entitativity concept for research on stereotyping, person memory, intergroup behavior, and perceptions of social justice.

Stereotyping and Generalization

Perceived entitativity of social categories may be a mediator of the relationship between general beliefs about a social category and impressions of individual category members. This relationship is bidirectional. On the deductive side, *stereotyping* is the application of category knowledge to individual instances of the category; on the inductive side, *generalization* is the application of information about individual category members to representations of the category as a whole. Research on social stereotypes suggests that both of these relationships are tenuous at best. Impressions of individual category members are rarely equivalent to category stereotypes, and conversely, impressions based on experience with category exemplars do not always generalize to the category as a whole (Brewer, in press). The extent to which category representations influence processing of information about individual category members and vice versa (Quattrone & Jones, 1980) may depend on the extent to which the category is perceived as a social entity.

Stangor and McMillan (1992) have suggested that stereotyping of individuals as a function of category membership depends on the strength of the expectancy associated with the category belief or stereotype. The stronger the expectancy, the more information about category members should be processed in an expectancy-confirming manner. Stangor and Ford (1992) explicitly theorize that the development of strong expectancies and the motivation for expectancy-confirming information processing strategies are tied to the desire for a simple and coherent impression of the group as a whole. In our terms, as category entitativity increases, both expectancy strength and stereotyping of individual category members should also increase.

One implication of strength and accessibility of category prototypes is the increased likelihood that information about category members will be evaluated and interpreted in terms of dimensions or characteristics that are most relevant to the category stereotype. They should also increase the likelihood that behaviors of individual category members will be compared to the stereotype rather than to behaviors of other category members (Biernat, Manis, & Nelson, 1991). Given two category members who differ along a stereotype-relevant dimension, these two individuals should be judged to be more similar if they are compared to a strong category stereotype than if they are compared directly to each other.

Hilton and von Hippel (1990) have applied the entitativity concept to understanding assimilation and contrast of category members who are less extreme than the category prototype on attributes relevant to the group stereotype. They argue that perceivers expect relatively little internal consistency from loosely knit social groupings; as a consequence, intragroup comparisons result in *contrasting* midrange group members away from the group stereotype. However, when expectations of internal consistency are raised to a sufficiently high level (in our terms, when perceived entitativity is increased), moderately discrepant individuals will be *assimilated* to the group stereotype. Results of two experiments confirmed the hypothesis that assimilation versus contrast in judgments of midrange category members could be predicted from variations in expectations of internal consistency.

Memory for Expectancy-Incongruent Information

Of related interest is research on memory of category members whose behavior is either typical of (consistent with) or atypical of (inconsistent with) category stereotypes. In the literature on person-based expectancies (Hamilton, 1991; Hastie & Kumar, 1979), both expectancy-congruent and expectancy-incongruent behaviors tend to be better remembered than behaviors that are irrelevant to prior expectancies, and incongruent information is processed more extensively than other information. With expectancies that are based on category stereotypes, however, incongruent behavior by individuals is more likely to be ignored or forgotten (Hamilton, 1991; Stangor & McMillan, 1992) and engenders less attributional processing than behaviors that are incongruent with person-based expectancies (Weisz & Jones, 1994).

This difference between the effects of expectancies about individuals and expectancies about groups is what that led Hamilton (1991) to speculate that group perception assumes less entitativity than person perception. Presumably, then, differences in perceived entitativity of social categories should moderate the effect of a category-based expectancy on memory for incongruent individuals. Indeed, experiments have demonstrated that better memory for expectancy-congruent than for expectancy-incongruent information is obtained for relatively meaningless social aggregates, but that memory for incongruent information is enhanced for meaningful social groups (Srull, 1981, Experiment 1; Srull, Lichtenstein, & Rothbart, 1985, Experiment 7).

When category entitativity is high, perceivers should be more responsive to stereotype congruity–incongruity in processing information about category members than when entitativity is low. Some support for this speculation is available from results of two experiments by Lambert and Wyer (1990). In both studies, when a social category was judged to be heterogeneous (i.e., low in entitativity), liking for individual category members was undifferentiated; such liking was determined primarily by the perceiver's liking for the category as a whole, regardless of whether the member exhibited stereotypic or counterstereotypic traits. When the category was judged to be homogeneous, however, attitudes toward the category as a whole were extended only to group members who were typical of the category prototype. Atypical individuals were, in effect, treated as noncategory members. Apparently, when groups are perceived as homogeneous (i.e., high in entitativity), there is less tolerance for inconsistency, and atypical category members are likely to be attended to but dissociated from the category as a whole (see also Wilder, 1984).

Memory for stereotype-incongruent information may provide a basis for differentiating among different types of category expectancy effects. Stangor and McMillan (1992) reported a negative relationship between expectancy strength and memory for incongruent information, contrary to our assumption that higher entitativity (stronger reliance on category prototypes and expectation of consistency) should enhance memory for incongruencies. However, Stangor and McMillan operationalized strength of expectancy in terms of extent of prior experience with the target category. Expectancies based on frequency of exposure may be qualitatively different from expectancies derived from strength or coherence of a category prototype. Regardless of the length of time a specific stereotypic expectancy has been held, the perceiver's motivation to represent the category as a social entity should mediate sensitivity to incongruent information.

Another interesting question regarding memory for incongruent information as a function of perceived group entitativity is whether it is the incongruent individual or the behavior that is recalled. If entitativity implies that information is organized around the category prototype, then instances of incongruent behaviors should be well remembered, but not necessarily in association with the specific individual who produced the behavior.

Intergroup Behavior: The Individual–Group Discontinuity Effect

As mentioned earlier, social identity theory (e.g., Brown & Turner, 1981) places considerable emphasis on whether relationships among individuals are guided by an *interpersonal* or an *intergroup* perceptual orientation. This distinction is supported by results from one of the experiments conducted by Gaertner, Dovidio, and their colleagues (Gaertner et al., 1989). Evaluative ratings of fellow group members were significantly altered, depending on whether the interactive situation was construed as an aggregate of six individuals or as an interaction between two separate groups. In the former case, the social entity was the individual person; in the latter, it was the social category, with consequent enhancement of ingroup–outgroup differentiation.

Further evidence of the importance of the interpersonal-intergroup distinction comes from a series of experiments by Insko, Schopler, and their colleagues (e.g., Insko et al., 1987; Schopler et al., 1993). These studies have demonstrated a robust difference in competitive behavior in the Prisoner's Dilemma paradigm, depending on whether an individual is playing the game with another individual or with a social group. Consistently, intergroup interactions are significantly more competitive than interpersonal interactions. Furthermore, there is evidence that this individual-group discontinuity effect is mediated by a general group schema which "instigates expectations of such negative behaviors as competitiveness, deceit and distrust" (Schopler et al., 1993, p. 420). The discontinuity between individual and group perception is also supported by findings in the impression formation literature indicating that perception of individual persons is dominated by a general positivity bias, whereas perception of social categories is more likely to exhibit negativity effects (Sears, 1983). Sears argues that groups and the individuals who compose them are essentially independent attitude objects, products of different learning histories and bases of evaluation. In general, individuals are perceived as more similar to the perceiver (and hence more likeable) than are groups as a whole.

In the Prisoner's Dilemma experiments, a rough measure of perceived entitativity indicated that other players were more likely to be perceived as a single group rather than as individual players under group interaction conditions than in the individual interaction condition (Insko et al., 1987). Insko and associates also found that the intergroup competitiveness effect was particularly pronounced when subjects interacted with a single representative of the other group, rather than with all the members of the outgroup together. Presumably, the group representative condition made it easier to conceptualize the other group as a single social entity, and entitativity of the outgroup is apparently sufficient to elicit negative expectancies and distrust, even in the absence of any specific experience with or information about the group.

Perceptions of Social Justice

One final illustration of the consequences of perceived entitativity of social groups comes from the literature on social justice and procedural fairness. In research on perceptions of relative deprivation, an important distinction is made between "personal" and "fraternal" deprivation (Runciman, 1966). The former is based on social comparisons between outcomes achieved by oneself and those of others who are perceived to be similar to the self, whereas the latter is based on *intergroup* comparisons between one's ingroup as a whole and more advantaged outgroups. Feelings of personal deprivation and fraternal deprivation do not necessarily correspond closely. Indeed, it is frequently found that members of disadvantaged groups perceive that their groups are discriminated against, but report little or no experience of discrimination or deprivation at the personal level (Taylor, Wright, Moghaddam, & Lalonde, 1990). Feelings of personal relative deprivation may make individuals feel resentful and unhappy, but rarely result in collective action to bring about social change. Attitudes toward collective movements are more closely related to perceptions of fraternal deprivation (Walker & Pettigrew, 1984).

The role of intergroup versus interindividual social comparison is also directly relevant to perceived procedural justice in allocations of political power. The principle of proportionality (i.e., "one person, one vote") holds that allocation of power and political representation between social groups should be based on the number of group members, such that majority groups have more power and representation than minority groups. The principle of equality holds that each participating group should have equal power and representation. Clearly, the difference between these two allocation principles is related to differences in perception of social groups as wholistic entities or as aggregates of individuals. Judgments of procedural fairness will depend on which allocation rule is perceived to be more appropriate, which depends in turn on whether the focus is on individual-level or group-level concerns (Azzi, 1992).

Azzi's data suggest that the preferred allocation principle is related to the level of social comparison (individual or group) that is made salient by a particular political issue. Given that principles of procedural justice are mediated by whether or not intergroup social comparisons processes are engaged, our understanding of social justice may well depend on a better understanding of the determinants of perceived entitativity of social groups.

MOTIVATIONS OF THE PERCEIVER

To the extent that antecedents of perceived group entitativity have been investigated in the past, the emphasis has been on characteristics of the social category itself (e.g., similarity, proximity, relative group size) or characteristics of the intergroup context (e.g., spatial arrangements, salience of intergroup contrast) as causal variables. Objective indices of entitativity have been difficult to codify, possibly because the relevant features are necessarily subjectively defined. A more fruitful approach to understanding the determinants of perceived entitativity may be to look for perceiver variables that mediate group perception. These would include chronic individual differences in such traits as cognitive complexity and certainty orientation (Sorrentino & Short, 1986; Huber & Sorrentino, Chapter 18, this volume). Indeed, results of a study by Roney and Sorrentino (1987) indicate that certainty-oriented individuals generate person categories with more differentiation between categories and less differentiation within categories than do uncertainty-oriented individuals. This suggests that individuals high in certainty orientation may be particularly motivated to perceive social groups as internally consistent entities.

Perceived entitativity may also be influenced by situational factors, such as processing goals, expectancies, mood, and motivation. The role of processing goals in perceiver-induced consistency was demonstrated in a recent experiment by Park, DeKay, and Kraus (1994), where instructions to aggregate behavioral information about a target person increased perceptions of consistency, even though differential interpretation of single acts did not vary as a function of aggregation instructions. Aggregating across persons in processing information about social groups may be expected to have similar effects on judgments of internal consistency of the category.

The role of processing goals in determining category representations has also been suggested by Stangor and Ford (1992), who distinguish between accuracy and expectancy-confirming processes in the development of social stereotypes. Seta and Hayes (1994) reported results of an experiment demonstrating that different impression formation goals influence whether perceivers organize information about specific behaviors around a group prototype or represent behaviors as segregated units in memory. The remainder of this chapter is devoted to describing several experiments that illustrate how perceiver expectancies, goals, and motives related to group entitativity determine the way behaviors of individual group members are encoded and organized in memory.

Encoding Effects: Information Load

Prior to our own research in this area, experiments conducted by Rothbart, Fulero, Jensen, Howard, and Birrell (1978) provided an important paradigm for assessing different types of category representations. Their first experiment tested the effects of information load on how data from individual category members are organized in memory and affect subsequent impressions of the category as a whole. They distinguished between two representational models relying on exemplar-based versus category-based processing (see Figure 10.1). In one representation, perceivers organize their perceptions of a group around the characteristics of its individual members; in the other representation, trait information is organized in an undifferentiated way around the category as a whole.

In Figure 10.1, information about two members of the artificial "Dallonian" group (Bill and Joe) is presented twice as often as information about the other two group members. If that information is organized at the person level, frequency of exposure should have no effect on perceivers' estimates of the proportion of group members who have undesirable traits. However, if the trait information is stored in an undifferentiated way, frequency of exposure should influence proportionality judgments and subsequent impressions of group favorability. Under conditions of low information load (16 instances of person–trait pairings), Rothbart et al. (1978) found that subjects could distinguish between repeated occurrences of a trait in the same individual and occurrences of that trait in different individuals. Under conditions of high information load (64 instances), however, estimates were related to number of exposures in an undifferentiated way.

In our terms, the undifferentiated category representation described by Rothbart et al. should be more characteristic of groups that are perceived as high in entitativity. If data about traits and behavior of category members are encoded primarily as instances of *group* behavior, then the specific source of that information (whether the same individual or a different one) should make little difference. Information should be dissociated from the specific exemplar and stored directly with the group prototype (Pryor & Ostrom, 1987). This sort of organization at encoding should also produce the intracategory recognition errors that have been assessed in other studies of category-based processing of social information (Arcuri, 1982; Taylor, Fiske, Etcoff, & Ruderman, 1978). When information has been encoded at the category level, perceivers should avoid in-

ORGANIZATION BY INDIVIDUAL GROUP MEMBERS

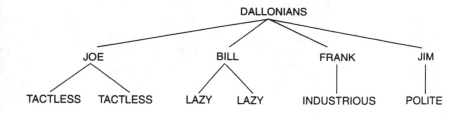

ORGANIZATION BY GROUP

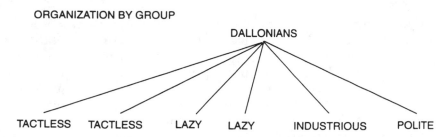

FIGURE 10.1 Two possible ways to organize trait information about four "Dallonians" (an artificial group) where two group members appear twice as often as the others. From Rothbart, Fulero, Jensen, Howard, and Birrell (1978, p. 240). Copyright 1978 by Academic Press, Inc. Reprinted by permission.

tercategory recognition errors, but should have relatively poor memory for intracategory distinctions. For this reason, we have used intracategory recognition confusions as a means of operationalizing perceived entitativity in a series of experiments in this area.

Entitativity of Minority versus Majority Groups

Earlier in this chapter, we have referred to Mullen's (1991) theory that the relative salience of minority groups makes such categories more likely to be represented in terms of category prototypes and hence to be perceived as more homogeneous than majority groups. One implication of Mullen's theory of group perception is that perceivers have a mental set to process information about minority groups differently from information about majority groups. This should be true even in situations in which the actual numbers of exemplars from minority groups and majority groups are held constant. In one experiment, we used the recognition error paradigm to test this hypothesis about differential entitativity of minority and majority groups (Brewer, Weber, & Carini, 1995).

On the basis of Mullen's theory, we hypothesized that the rate of intracategory confusions to intercategory recognition errors would vary as a function of perceiver expectations associated with category size. A videotaped group discussion was produced in which six same-sex college students participated, with three of the group members wearing red sweatshirts and three wearing blue sweatshirts. The format of the discussion was a group interview during which each of the six students provided information about their academic and social lives. Information from the six group members was interspersed throughout the interview, with each individual making four self-descriptive statements over the course of the discussion.

The discussion was scripted so that there were systematic differences between the individuals in red and blue sweatshirts, as well as systematic differences among individuals within each category. Sweatshirt color and academic major were correlated: The students in red sweatshirts all described themselves as pursuing science/math-related academic programs, whereas all the students in blue sweatshirts were self-described arts and humanities majors.. Within each category, however, each of the three students differed in level of academic performance, social relationships, and leisure activities. Thus, the videotape was constructed in such a way that information could be meaningfully organized either around the red–blue categories or around individuals.

Experimental participants viewed the videotape as part of an alleged study of perceptual style and personality. Prior to seeing the tape, they were told that the students in the group interview had been categorized on the basis of perceptual estimation tendencies and that the students wearing red sweatshirts had been classified as "overestimators" and those in blue were "underestimators." Furthermore, they were told that in the college population as a whole, one of the categories (whether overestimators or underestimators was counterbalanced) was much more prevalent than the other, with the majority being approximately 80% of the population and the minority representing less than 20%.

Thus, participants viewed the videotape believing that the two categories differed significantly in size within the population as a whole. However, the number of red and blue category members, and the degree of intragroup variability, were equivalent on the tape itself. Therefore, any differences in encoding and memory for information about the two categories would be a function of perceiver expectancies or processing set, independent of the stimulus information itself.

Following presentation of the stimulus tape (and after an irrelevant intervening task), subjects were given a surprise recognition test. Photographs of each of the six group members (with sweatshirt color visible) were provided, and subjects were shown a series of 24 slides, each containing one statement that had been made by one of the individuals on the videotape (four statements from each person, randomly ordered). The respondents' task was to identify which specific individual had made each statement. Slides were presented in rapid sequence, with respondents having 15 seconds to read each statement and make their identification selection.

Fifty-eight female college student subjects participated in the version of the recognition experiment described above. Recognition errors were scored according to whether they represented *inter*category confusions (a statement made by a red category member attributed to a blue group member, or vice versa) or *intra*category confusions (statements misattributed to an individual of the same subcategory). Intracategory errors were further broken down into minority group confusions and majority group confusions (depending on which color the subject believed to be in the minority).

As expected, overall intracategory errors (M = 2.30) exceeded intercategory confusions (M = 2.22), even though the number of possible intercategory errors exceeded possible intracategory errors by a ratio of 3:2. (When this difference was adjusted for, the corrected mean intercategory error was 1.48.) Of more interest, however, were differential confusions within categories identified as minority versus majority. These comparisons are presented in Figure 10.2. Consistent with the Mullen (1991) hypothesis, the average number of recognition errors among members of minority groups (M = 1.47) was significantly greater than those for majority group members (M = 0.83), F (1, 56) = 7.30, p < .01.

As the data represented in Figure 10.2 indicate, for information generated by majority group members, intracategory errors and intercategory errors were essentially equivalent (when the higher chance probability for intercategory errors was adjusted for). This suggests that information about majority group members was organized and stored at the individual level, and that failures of recognition were essentially random memory errors. For statements made by minority group members, however, recognition errors were systematically biased toward intracategory confusions, suggesting that the statements themselves were remembered as part of the information provided about the minority group, but not the specific individual who made them. In other words, information about minority group members was organized and stored at the category level rather than the individual level. These results support the idea that perceivers are "set" to perceive minority groups as higher in entitativity than majority groups, independent of any objective differences between groups in amount of information or in interindividual variability.

Entitativity and Intergroup Interdependence

In further experiments, we used the same videotape and recognition task to assess effects of intergroup relations on perceived entitativity (Brewer et al., 1995, Study 2). Prior to viewing the videotaped discussion, subjects themselves were given the perceptual estimation task and classified as overestimators or underes-

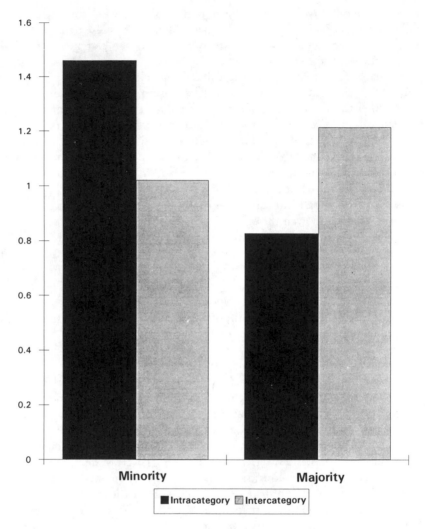

FIGURE 10.2   Intra- and intercategory recognition errors for minority and majority targets. Adapted from Brewer, Weber, and Carini (1995).

timators. For these subjects, then, the category distinction represented by red and blue sweatshirts in the videotape was also an ingroup–outgroup category distinction.

Before the videotape presentation, experimental sessions were varied to produce three different intergroup settings. In the "categorization only" condition, individual subjects were given feedback on their own estimation category, but no information was provided about the category identity of other participants in the session. Participants in this condition waited for a few minutes in the same room and then were shown the videotape. In the "salience" condition, participants were classified as overestimators or underestimators, given red or blue sweatshirts to wear for the remainder of the experiment, and separated into two rooms to engage in an individual problem-solving task prior to viewing the videotape. Subjects in this condition were made aware of their separate category identities, but no interdependence within or between categories was introduced. In the "interdependence" condition, participants were categorized and separated as in the salience condition, but then members of each group engaged in a cooperative problem-solving task and were told that their performance would be evaluated in comparison to the performance of groups from the other category. This condition created cooperative interdependence within groups and competitive interdependence between the two social categories.

Participants in all conditions (n = 61 male subjects) viewed the videotaped group interview, engaged in an intervening task, and then were given the statement recognition task. Recognition errors were classified as intragroup or intergroup confusions and compared across experimental conditions. Mean intercategory recognition errors did not differ as a function of intergroup context. Total intracategory errors, however, did differ significantly, $F (2, 58) = 3.46, p <$ .05. Post hoc paired comparisons indicated that the mean number of intracategory confusions in the interdependence condition was significantly higher than that for the other two conditions, which did not differ significantly from each other (see Figure 10.3). Across all conditions, intracategory errors were the same for ingroup and outgroup category information.

Enhanced salience of the ingroup–outgroup distinction alone was not sufficient to increase category-based processing and encoding of social information. However, the introduction of even a low level of intergroup competition did increase category-based processing of information about both the ingroup and the outgroup. The competitive condition apparently created an intergroup context, in which both ingroup and outgroup were construed as social entities (Simon, 1993). These results violate the general outgroup homogeneity effect and support the idea that there are conditions in which the ingroup is represented as a homogeneous category to the same extent as relevant outgroups (Brewer, 1993). Consistent with social identity theory, ingroup entitativity is evident when intergroup comparisons are particularly salient and on dimensions that best distinguish the ingroup from the outgroup (Haslam et al., Chapter 6, this volume).

POSSIBLE ORIGINS OF ENTITATIVITY MOTIVATION

The research described above suggests some general reasons why individuals may be motivated to perceive a social group as an entity. Different motivational factors may be engaged, depending on whether the group in question is an ingroup or an outgroup.

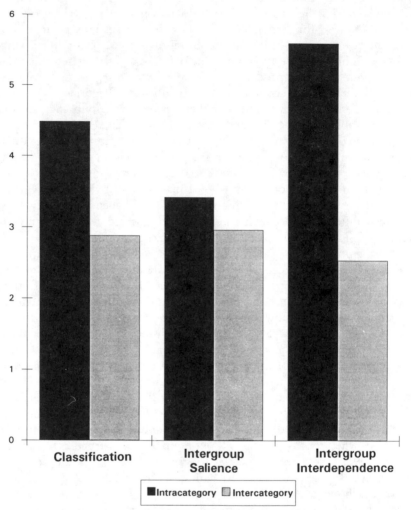

FIGURE 10.3   Total intra- and intercategory recognition errors as a function of inter-group context. Adapted from Brewer, Weber, and Carini (1995).

The Need for Coherence and Certainty

When the group in question is the perceiver's ingroup, needs for inclusion (Brewer, 1991) or collective action (Kelly, 1993) may engender a desire to see the ingroup as a cohesive social unit. Perceived ingroup entitativity should be associated with the social identity effects specified by self-categorization theory: assimilation of the self-concept to the group prototype, enhanced conformity to ingroup norms, ingroup cooperation, and ingroup favoritism (Turner et al., 1987).

To date, most of the research on social identity theory has focused on the consequences rather than the origins of self-categorization at the group level. Only recently has attention turned to consideration of what may motivate individuals to engage social identification processes in the first place. Two extensions of social identity theory have been advanced to explain the motivational underpinnings of ingroup identification. Brewer's (1991) "optimal distinctiveness theory" proposes that social identity originates with the need to resolve conflicting drives for inclusion and differentiation in the formation of a stable self-concept. Hogg and Abrams (1993) assume that ingroup formation ultimately derives from the need to reduce uncertainty. This theory focuses on the role of group consensus as the basis for coherence and subjective certainty. As Hogg and Abrams (1993) put it, "uncertainty-reduction is an individual motivation, but one that inevitably can only be realized by group belongingness" (p. 189). This conceptualization is consistent with the idea suggested earlier that perceived entitativity may be greater for certainty-oriented than for uncertainty-oriented individuals (Sorrentino & Short, 1986), and also suggests that certainty-oriented individuals may be particularly motivated to perceive ingroups as coherent social entities.

Ingroup Entitativity and Differentiation

Since social identification should enhance entitativity of ingroups as well as outgroups, the question remains as to why outgroups are often perceived as more homogeneous than the ingroup, even when ingroup membership is salient. One explanation lies in the greater degree of subtyping in definition of the ingroup as opposed to outgroups (Brewer, 1993; Park & Judd, 1990; Simon, 1993). Superordinate ingroup categories (such as gender, race, and age) are differentiated into more subgroups than are equivalent outgroup categories (Brewer & Lui, 1984).

In an interesting recent experiment, Wallace, Lord, and Ramsey (1995) demonstrated that this subtyping effect is particularly pronounced for group members who consider themselves *typical* members of the superordinate category. One interpretation of this finding is that such category members are motivated to perceive the ingroup as a coherent social entity. As a consequence, they are less tolerant of intracategory variability and more inclined to use subgrouping to dissociate others who differ from themselves from the specific ingroup category with which they identify. This interpretation is consistent with the previously discussed findings from the experiment by Lambert and Wyer (1990), indicating that perceived homogeneity of categories is associated with high sensitivity to typicality of category members in making category-based judgments.

Intergroup Behavior and Entitativity Motivation

Simon's (1993) model of egocentric social categorization holds that outgroups are generally construed as homogenous social entities. Perception of outgroups (social categories to which the perceiver does not belong) would seem to be less likely to be influenced by needs associated with self-definition. However, much of the research reviewed above indicates that there is considerable variation in the degree of entitativity ascribed to specific outgroups under different conditions. Some of this variation may be attributable to characteristics of the groups themselves, to context effects, or to cognitive processing factors. But various self-serving motives and biases may be implicated in the perceived entitativity of outgroups as well as ingroups.

In some cases, the motivation to perceive an outgroup as a social entity may arise from the existence of various forms of behavioral or outcome interdependence between the perceiver (or the perceiver's ingroup) and the outgroup. At the interpersonal level, the presence of cooperative or competitive interdependence induces greater individuation in impression formation (Fiske & Neuberg, 1990). At the intergroup level, this is paralleled by greater homogenization (less individuation) of perception of outgroups under competitive conditions (Judd & Park, 1988; Ruscher, Fiske, Miki, & van Manen, 1991). Research on the individual-group discontinuity effect (Schopler et al., 1993) and the results of the Brewer et al. (1995) experiment reported above also implicate the importance of competitive interdependence as a motivator of perceived outgroup entitativity.

Although it is intuitively obvious why intergroup competition should motivate perceiving the outgroup in generally negative terms, it is not so evident why such perceptions should involve enhanced entitativity. Interdependence at the group level, such as direct intergroup competition, implies that actions or decisions made by the perceiver (or the perceiver's ingroup) have some effect on the status or outcomes of the outgroup *as a whole*. It is our contention that this impact of one's own actions on the group is what motivates perceived entitativity.

There are many settings in which judgments, decisions, or policies are made that affect members of a social category in an undifferentiated way (e.g., mandatory retirement at age 65, trade agreements between nations, insurance rates based on demographic characteristics). Individuals, too, are sometimes called upon to take actions or make judgments about groups as a whole (e.g., supporting a sports team, disciplining a fraternity, comparing the ability of one class of students with that of another class). The question of interest is whether behaving toward a group in such a way increases the tendency to perceive that group as an entity. Making a judgment or decision about a group as a whole requires that some mental representation of that group be activated or formed. Thus, the act of treating a group as a "thing" may enhance the development of a group prototype and reliance on that prototype in future actions. From this perspective, perceived entitativity may be the consequence of actions directed toward the group as a whole, as much as a cause of such actions. When an individual treats a social aggregate *as if* it were an entity, perceiving that the group *is* an entity may be necessary to justify the action or its effects.

This behavior justification perspective explains why salience of category distinctions alone does not seem to be sufficient to induce high entitativity. The presence of intergroup competition or conflict increases salience, but it also creates a link between one's own interests and behaviors and outcomes that affect the outgroup as a whole. It may be this additional link that is critical to motivated perception of group entitativity. However, this analysis also suggests that negative interdependence is not a *necessary* condition for perceived entitativity. Anything that requires acting toward the category as a whole should have similar motivational consequences. This should include positive judgments, actions, or allocations as well as negative ones, as long as the consequences of those actions cannot be differentially directed to specific group members.

If our analysis of the motivational underpinnings of group perception is correct, then the concept of perceived entitativity should occupy a central position in theories of intergroup relations. Perceived entitativity may provide a critical link among cognitive, affective, and behavioral components of intergroup attitudes that could serve as the basis for an integrated theory of stereotypes, prejudice, and discrimination.

Acknowledgments

The research described in this chapter was funded by National Science Foundation Grant No. BNS-9120757 to Marilynn B. Brewer. This chapter was written while Amy S. Harasty was supported by National Institute of Mental Health Training Grant No. T32MH19728.

References

Abelson, R. (1994). *Have you heard what they did? Cognitions of the collective other.* Address at the Presidential Symposium at the annual meeting of the American Psychological Society, Washington, DC.

Arcuri, L. (1982). Three patterns of social categorization in attribution memory. *European Journal of Social Psychology, 12,* 271–282.

Azzi, A. E. (1992). Procedural justice and the allocation of power in intergroup relations: Studies in the United States and South Africa. *Personality and Social Psychology Bulletin, 18,* 736–747.

Biernat, M., Manis, M., & Nelson, T. (1991). Stereotypes and standards of judgment. *Journal of Personality and Social Psychology, 60,* 485–499.

Brewer, M. B. (1988). A dual process model of impression formation. In T. Srull & R. Wyer (Eds.), *Advances in social cognition* (Vol. 1, pp. 1–36). Hillsdale, NJ: Erlbaum.

Brewer, M. B. (1991). The social self: On being the same and different at the same time. *Personality and Social Psychology Bulletin, 17,* 475–482.

Brewer, M. B. (1993). Social identity, distinctiveness, and in-group homogeneity. *Social Cognition, 11,* 150–164.

Brewer, M. B. (1996). When stereotypes lead to stereotyping: The use of stereotypes in person

son perception. In N. Macrae, C. Stangor & M. Hewstone (Eds.), *Stereotypes and stereotyping* (pp. 254–275). New York: Guilford Press.

Brewer, M. B., & Lui, L. (1984). Categorization of the elderly by the elderly: Effects of perceiver's category membership. *Personality and Social Psychology Bulletin, 10*, 585–595.

Brewer, M. B., Weber, J. G., & Carini, B. (1995). Person memory in intergroup contexts: Categorization versus individuation. *Journal of Personality and Social Psychology, 69*, 29–40.

Brown, R., & Turner, J. C. (1981). Interpersonal and intergroup behaviour. In J. Turner & H. Giles (Eds.), *Intergroup behaviour* (pp. 33–65). Oxford: Blackwell.

Campbell, D. T. (1958). Common fate, similarity, and other indices of the status of aggregates as social entities. *Behavioral Science, 3*, 14–25.

Fiske, S. T., & Neuberg, S. L. (1990). A continuum of impression formation, from category-based to individuating processes: Influences of information and motivation on attention and interpretation. In M. Zanna (Ed.), *Advances in experimental social psychology* (Vol. 23, pp. 1–74). New York: Academic Press.

Gaertner, L., & Schopler, J. (1994). *Entitativity and intergroup prejudice and discrimination.* Paper presented at the Second International Congress on Prejudice, Discrimination, and Conflict, Jerusalem, Israel.

Gaertner, S., Dovidio, J., Anastasio, P., Bachman, B., & Rust, M. (1993). The common in-group identity model: Recategorization and the reduction of intergroup bias. In W. Stroebe & M. Hewstone (Eds.), *European review of social psychology* (Vol. 4, pp. 1–26). Chichester, England: Wiley.

Gaertner, S., Mann, J., Dovidio, J., Murrell, A., & Pomare, M. (1990). How does cooperation reduce intergroup bias? *Journal of Personality and Social Psychology, 59*, 692–704.

Gaertner, S., Mann, J., Murrell, A., & Dovidio, J. (1989). Reducing intergroup bias: The benefits of recategorization. *Journal of Personality and Social Psychology, 57*, 239–249.

Hamilton, D. L. (1991). *Perceiving persons and groups: A social cognitive perspective.* Address presented at the annual meeting of the American Psychological Association, San Francisco.

Hastie, R., & Kumar, P. (1979). Person memory: Personality traits as organizing principles in memory for behavior. *Journal of Personality and Social Psychology, 37*, 25–38.

Hilton, J. L., & von Hippel, W. (1990). The role of consistency in the judgment of stereotype-relevant behaviors. *Personality and Social Psychology Bulletin, 16*, 430–448.

Hogg, M. A. (1992). *The social psychology of group cohesiveness: From attraction to social identity.* London: Harvester/Wheatsheaf.

Hogg, M. A. (1993). Group cohesiveness: A critical review and some new directions. In W. Stroebe & M. Hewstone (Eds.), *European review of social psychology* (Vol. 4, pp. 85–111). Chichester, England: Wiley.

Hogg, M. A., & Abrams, D. (1993). Towards a single-process uncertainty-reduction model of social motivation in groups. In M. Hogg & D. Abrams (Eds.), *Group motivation: Social psychological perspectives* (pp. 173–190). London: Harvester/Wheatsheaf.

Insko, C., Pinkley, R., Hoyle, R., Dalton, B., Hong, G., Slim, R., Landry, P., Holton, B., Ruffin, P., & Thibaut, J. (1987). Individual versus group discontinuity: The role of intergroup contact. *Journal of Experimental Social Psychology, 23*, 250–267.

Judd, C. M., & Park, B. (1988). Out-group homogeneity: Judgments of variability at the individual and group levels. *Journal of Personality and Social Psychology, 54*, 778–788.

Kelly, C. (1993). Group identification, intergroup perceptions and collective action. In W. Stroebe & M. Hewstone (Eds.), *European review of social psychology* (Vol. 4, pp. 59–83). Chichester, England: Wiley.

Lambert, A. J., & Wyer, R. S. (1990). Stereotypes and social judgment: The effects of typicality and group heterogeneity. *Journal of Personality and Social Psychology, 59*, 676–691.

Linville, P. W., Fischer, G. , & Salovey, P. (1986). Perceived distributions of the characteristics of in-group and out-group members: Empirical evidence and a computer simulation. *Journal of Personality and Social Psychology, 57*, 165–188.

Mackie, D., & Hamilton, D. L. (Eds.). (1993). *Affect, cognition, and stereotyping: Interactive processes in group perception.* San Diego, CA: Academic Press.

Medin, D., Altom, M., & Murphy, T. (1984). Given versus induced category representations: Use of prototype and exemplar information in classification. *Journal of Experimental Psychology: Learning, Memory, and Cognition, 10,* 333–352.

Mullen, B. (1991). Group composition, salience, and cognitive representations: The phenomenology of being in a group. *Journal of Experimental Social Psychology, 27,* 297–323.

Oakes, P., & Turner, J. C. (1990). Is limited information processing capacity the cause of social stereotyping? In W. Stroebe & M. Hewstone (Eds.), *European review of social psychology* (Vol. 1, pp. 111–135). Chichester, England: Wiley.

Ostrom, T. M., & Sedikides, C. (1992). Out-group homogeneity effects in natural and minimal groups. *Psychological Bulletin, 112,* 536–552.

Park, B., DeKay, M., & Kraus, S. (1994). Aggregating social behavior into person models: Perceiver-induced consistency. *Journal of Personality and Social Psychology, 66,* 437–459.

Park, B., & Hastie, R. (1987). Perception of variability in category development: Instance-versus abstraction-based stereotypes. *Journal of Personality and Social Psychology, 53,* 621–635.

Park, B., & Judd, C. M. (1990). Measures and models of perceived group variability. *Journal of Personality and Social Psychology, 59,* 173–191.

Pryor, J. B., & Ostrom, T. M. (1987). Social cognition theory of group process. In B. Mullen & G. Goethals (Eds.), *Theories of group behavior* (pp. 147–183). New York: Springer-Verlag.

Quattrone, G., & Jones, E. E. (1980). The perception of variability within in-groups and out-groups: Implications for the law of small numbers. *Journal of Personality and Social Psychology, 38,* 141–152.

Reicher, S. (1984). The St. Paul's riot: An explanation of the limits of crowd action in terms of a social identity model. *European Journal of Social Psychology, 14,* 1–21.

Roney, C., & Sorrentino, R. M. (1987). Uncertainty orientation and person perception: Individual differences in categorization. *Social Cognition, 5,* 369–382.

Rosch, E. (1978). Principles of categorization. In E. Rosch & B. Lloyd (Eds.), *Cognition and categorization* (pp. 27–48). Hillsdale, NJ: Erlbaum.

Rothbart, M., Fulero, S., Jensen, C., Howard, J., & Birrell, P. (1978). From individual to group impressions: Availability heuristics in stereotype formation. *Journal of Experimental Social Psychology, 14,* 237–255.

Runciman, W. C. (1966). *Relative deprivation and social justice: A study of attitudes to social inequality in twentieth century England.* Berkeley: University of California Press.

Ruscher, J., Fiske, S. T., Miki, H., & van Manen, S. (1991). Individuating processes in competition: Interpersonal versus intergroup. *Personality and Social Psychology Bulletin, 17,* 595–605.

Schopler, J., Insko, C., Graetz, K., Drigotas, S., Smith, V., & Dahl, K. (1993). Individual–group discontinuity: Further evidence for mediation by fear and greed. *Personality and Social Psychology Bulletin, 19,* 419–431.

Sears, D. O. (1983). The person-positivity bias. *Journal of Personality and Social Psychology, 44,* 233–250.

Seta, C. E., & Hayes, N. (1994). The influence of impression formation goals on the accuracy of social memory. *Personality and Social Psychology Bulletin, 20,* 93–101.

Simon, B. (1993). On the asymmetry in the cognitive construal of ingroup and outgroup: A model of egocentric social categorization. *European Journal of Social Psychology, 23,* 131–147.

Smith, E. R., & Zarate, M. A. (1990). Exemplar and prototype use in social categorization. *Social Cognition, 8,* 243–262.

Sorrentino, R. M., & Short, J. C. (1986). Uncertainty, motivation, and cognition. In R. M. Sorrentino & E. T. Higgins (Eds.), *Handbook of motivation and cognition: Foundations of social behavior* (Vol. 1, pp. 379–403). New York: Guilford Press.

Srull, T. K. (1981). Person memory: Some tests of associative storage and retrieval models. *Journal of Experimental Psychology: Human Learning and Memory, 7,* 440–463.

Srull, T. K., Lichtenstein, M., & Rothbart, M. (1985). Associative storage and retrieval processes in person memory. *Journal of Experimental Psychology: Human Learning and Memory, 11,* 316–345.

Stangor, C., & Ford, T. E. (1992). Accuracy and expectancy-confirming processing orientations and the development of stereotypes and prejudice. In W. Stroebe & M. Hewstone (Eds.), *European review of social psychology* (Vol. 3, pp. 57–89). Chichester, England: Wiley.

Stangor, C., & McMillan, D. (1992). Memory for expectancy-consistent and expectancy-inconsistent information: A review of the social and social developmental literatures. *Psychological Bulletin, 111,* 42–61.

Taylor, D. M., Wright, S., Moghaddam, F., & Lalonde, R. (1990). The personal/group discrimination discrepancy: Perceiving my group but not myself to be a target of discrimination. *Personality and Social Psychology Bulletin, 16,* 254–262.

Taylor, S. E., Fiske, S. T., Etcoff, N. L., & Ruderman, A. (1978). Categorical and contextual bases of person memory and stereotyping. *Journal of Personality and Social Psychology, 36,* 778–793.

Turner, J. C. (1991). *Social influence.* Milton Keynes, England: Open University Press.

Turner, J. C., Hogg, M., Oakes, P., Reicher, S., & Wetherell, M. (1987). *Rediscovering the social group: A self-categorization theory.* Oxford: Blackwell.

Walker, I., & Pettigrew, T. F. (1984). Relative deprivation theory: An overview and conceptual critique. *British Journal of Social Psychology, 23,* 301–310.

Wallace, D., Lord, C., & Ramsey, S. (1995). Relationship between self-typicality and the ingroup subtypes effect. *Personality and Social Psychology Bulletin, 21,* 581–587.

Weisz, C., & Jones, E. E. (1994). Expectancy disconfirmation and dispositional inference: Latent strength of target-based and category-based expectancies. *Personality and Social Psychology Bulletin, 19,* 563–573.

Wilder, D. A. (1981). Perceiving persons as a group: Categorization and intergroup relations. In D. Hamilton (Ed.), *Cognitive processes in stereotyping and intergroup behavior* (pp. 213–257). Hillsdale, NJ: Erlbaum.

Wilder, D. A. (1984). Intergroup contact: The typical member and the exception to the rule. *Journal of Experimental Social Psychology, 20,* 177–194.

Wilder, D. A. (1986). Social categorization: Implications for creation and reduction of intergroup bias. In L. Berkowitz (Ed.), *Advances in experimental social psychology* (Vol. 19, pp. 291–355). New York: Academic Press.

CHAPTER 11

Making Stereotypes Better or Worse
Multiple Roles for Positive Affect in Group Impressions

DIANE M. MACKIE
SARAH QUELLER
University of California, Santa Barbara
STEVEN J. STROESSNER
Barnard College
DAVID L. HAMILTON
University of California, Santa Barbara

One of the most intuitively appealing ideas offered by social psychology is the notion that pleasant interaction between members of different groups can improve intergroup relations. Such a prescription for social change lies at the heart of the contact hypothesis, which suggests that the kind of pleasant interaction that may result from successful intergroup cooperation, for example, can improve mutual perceptions (see especially Amir, 1969; but also Allport, 1954; Brewer & Miller, 1984). Unlike many aspects of the contact hypothesis, which have been extensively revised in the light of empirical data (for reviews, see Hewstone & Brown, 1986; Pettigrew, 1986; Stephan, 1987), the idea that pleasant interaction promotes positive group perception has remained relatively unchallenged over the decades.

Recently, however, some questions have been raised even about this intuitively appealing proposition. The cause for concern is an unlikely one—the mildly pleasant affective state that may reasonably be thought to accompany pleasant interaction. Surely feeling good while interacting with someone else makes feeling good about that someone else more likely. Yet research evidence in other social judgment domains indicates that the presence of positive mood does not guarantee the production of positive judgments (Forgas, 1992; Mackie, Asuncion, & Rosselli, 1992; Petty, Gleicher, & Baker, 1991; Schwarz & Bless, 1991; Sinclair & Mark, 1992). Is the same true when it comes to group perception? If positive interaction is also accompanied by positive mood, will the impact of that positive affect on group perception necessarily be benign?

These were the questions that motivated the program of research we describe in this chapter. Our general interest is in the interaction of affective, cognitive, and motivational processes that contribute to group perception (Mackie & Hamilton, 1993). Our more specific concerns are with the effects of positive mood on group perception and with the conditions under which these effects may advance or impede the aims of pleasant intergroup contact.

In the first section of the chapter, we describe a series of studies documenting consistent effects of positive mood on various aspects of intergroup perception. Unfortunately, these effects indicate that positive mood may be likely to increase perceptions of homogeneity and stereotypicality, rather than to promote more differentiated, variable, or nonstereotypic views of other groups. These findings raise several important questions, both theoretical and practical, which we consider next: What processes mediate these effects of mood on stereotypic judgments? Under what conditions can the less-than-beneficial effects of positive mood on group perception be eliminated? Are there in fact some conditions under which the presence of positive mood may have a salutary effect on judgments about other groups? Finally, we return to the issue with which we began: What are the costs and benefits of positive affect for group perception? In this last section, we discuss the implications of our work for the contact hypothesis, and we suggest some directions that future work might profitably take in order to expand our understanding of successful and unsuccessful intergroup contact.

HOW DOES POSITIVE MOOD INFLUENCE GROUP PERCEPTION?

When intergroup contact is cooperative, successful, or friendly, it is assumed that the positive feelings thus generated will translate into liking, at least for fellow interactants and ideally for other members of the group as well (Hewstone & Brown, 1986; Pettigrew, 1986; Rothbart & John, 1985; Wilder, 1984). One mechanism by which this transformation can be achieved is classical conditioning (Staats & Staats, 1958). If interactions with another group repeatedly involve pleasant activity, the positive affect invoked by the activity can become associated with the group. Alternatively, being in a positive mood (as a result of pleasant activity) may activate positively toned cognitions, which may in turn color people's perceptions of an individual or group with whom they interact (Isen, 1987; Bower, Gilligan, & Montiero, 1981).

Although the actual mechanisms that accomplish this translation are still not well specified, the assumption that positive feelings will increase liking clearly has implications for how positive affective states should influence the encoding, interpreting, elaborating, and evaluating of social information. Although there has been a long tradition of studying emotion and prejudice in social psychology (Adorno, Frenkel-Brunswik, Levinson, & Sanford, 1950; Dollard, Miller, Doob, Mowrer, & Sears, 1939; Stephan & Stephan, 1985), a research focus on the interface of the relevant affective and cognitive processes is a relatively recent enterprise. In fact, when we initiated our program of research on affective influences on group perception, no other studies had taken such an approach. Our first task, then, was to ascertain exactly what impact positive affect has on some of the processes thought to be central to the formation of impressions—especially stereotypic impressions—of groups.

To do so, we attempted to induce a positive affective state while preventing subjects from suspecting either our interest in the consequences of mood or any possible connection between mood state and subsequent exposure to group information. Our procedures thus involved a "two-experiment ruse," in which subjects first perform a task designed to manipulate their affective state and then in a second (ostensibly unrelated) experiment are exposed to information about either a known or an unknown group.

Our first investigation, designed to assess the impact of positive mood on subjects' perceptions of group variability (Stroessner & Mackie, 1992, Experiment 1), followed just such a procedure. In the first part of the two-experiment ruse, we randomly assigned subjects to watch one of two 4-minute video segments, ostensibly so they could evaluate the segment's suitability for use in a future study. In fact, of course, we intended the videos to change subjects' affective states. After viewing the segments, subjects responded to inquiries about their current happiness or sadness, among other items. Subjects who watched a segment on wine corking rated themselves near the midpoint on scales asking about happiness and sadness, whereas those assigned to watch a segment from a comedy special rated themselves as significantly happier, verifying that our manipulation had successfully induced the intended mood states.

In the ostensibly unrelated second study, subjects were presented with 28 statements (taken from Park & Hastie, 1987), each describing a behavior performed by a different member of an unnamed group. Each behavior had implications for the actor's intelligence or sociability, and the subjects' task was to form an impression of the group as a whole. Half of the subjects in a positive mood and half of the subjects in a neutral mood read a set of sentences in which the behaviors described were quite low in variability. In this condition, the activities of the 28 members of the group suggested moderate levels of both intelligence and sociability, and none of the group members engaged in extremely intelligent, extremely stupid, extremely sociable, or extremely unfriendly behaviors.

The rest of the subjects in each of the induced mood conditions read a set of behaviors reflecting a high degree of variability on these traits. Although on average the group portrayed by this second stimulus set again appeared to have moderate levels of intelligence and sociability, some group members in this condition were described as performing extremely intelligent or extremely sociable actions, whereas the activities of other members suggested rather extreme stupidity or extreme unfriendliness. One member, for example, was described as having "joined a group of strangers playing Frisbee" while another member of the group "went to the Saturday matinee alone." Whereas one member of the group "failed to pass the written driver's test," another member of the group "presented a paper to experts in the field." Thus, crossing mood induction with stimulus set variability meant that subjects in either happy or neutral moods were presented with information about either a highly variable or a relatively homogeneous group.

After reading the group descriptions, subjects used a number of items to indicate the degree of variability they saw in the group they had just read about. The results (collapsed across three relevant items) are shown in Figure 11.1. As can be seen, affect had a considerable impact on subjects' perceptions. Subjects in neutral moods quite appropriately reported higher variability when exposed to information about the high variability group and less variability when presented with information about the low variability group. In contrast, subjects in positive moods saw targets in both groups as equally homogeneous. Although the ratings of the low variability group were similar, regardless of subjects' affective states, being in a positive mood apparently made perceivers less aware of the variability in the highly variable group.

Given the centrality of perceptions of variability to issues of stereotyping, the results of this study suggest that positive mood may *not* have routinely benign consequences for group impressions. The fact that perceivers in positive moods failed to take account of the variability present in the group information suggested to us that they might well have perceived both the behaviors performed by group members, and those who performed them, as more "consistent" and "typical" than did those subjects who became fully aware of the vari-

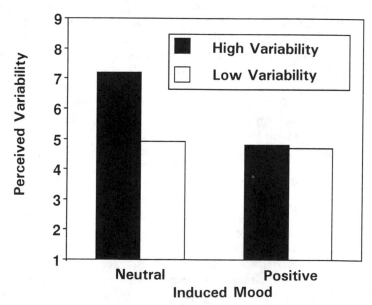

FIGURE 11.1   Perceived variability as a function of induced mood and variability of group description. From Stroessner and Mackie (1992, Experiment 1). Copyright 1992 by the Society for Personality and Social Psychology. Reprinted by permission.

ability of group behavior. Thus it seems a short step from happy perceivers seeing groups as homogeneous to their seeing behaviors as more uniformly "consistent" with, and group members as more uniformly "typical" of, their overall impressions of a group.

To examine this idea, we borrowed a well-known paradigm for presenting information about group members that usually increases perceptions of group members and their behaviors as atypical, and we analyzed what impact positive mood had on such perceptions (Mackie, Queller, & Stroessner, 1994). In this study, a positive or a neutral mood was first induced by having subjects read uplifting or neutral newspaper articles, ostensibly so that we could assess the way people process information presented in news articles. Self-report measures again confirmed the success of our intended mood manipulation: Subjects who read a story about getting together with old friends reported feeling significantly happier than subjects who read about a city's economic recovery.

Subjects were then presented information about members of a group for whom our University of California, Santa Barbara subjects had fairly well-defined stereotypes: surfers. Subjects received a mixture of stereotype-consistent information ("As soon as the other guys were gone, he and his friends started joking again" as an example of "cliquish") and stereotype-inconsistent information ("He takes his date to art films so they can have lengthy discussions about the movie later" as an example of "intellectual") under one of two different conditions. Following the technique introduced by Gurwitz and Dodge (1977) and used subsequently by Weber and Crocker (1983) and Johnston and Hewstone (1992), we presented subjects with descriptions of group members in which all the inconsistent behaviors were said to have been performed by only a few members of the group, or descriptions in which these same inconsistent behaviors were dispersed more widely across many members of the group. In the former, "concentrated" condition, group members were rather similar to one another, except for a few very atypical individuals. In the latter, "dispersed" condition, many group members were slightly atypical. Such a manipulation typically results in subjects perceiving greater inconsistency of behaviors and atypicality of group members in the dispersed condition than in the concentrated condition (Johnston & Hewstone, 1992; Weber & Crocker, 1983). In our experiment, subjects in happy or neutral moods were asked to estimate the percentage of group-consistent or group-inconsistent behaviors they had read about, as well as the number of typical and atypical group members they had seen. We formed indices from these dependent measures by subtracting percentage estimates of inconsistent behaviors from estimates of consistent ones, and by subtracting frequency estimates of atypical members from estimates of typical members. Thus higher numbers reflected greater perceived behavioral consistency and greater perceived typicality. We analyzed these indices to see whether affective state influenced group perceptions, and, if so, how.

As can be seen in Figure 11.2, receiving concentrated versus dispersed descriptions of a variable group produced quite different perceptions depending on the perceivers' mood state. The top panel summarizes subjects' perceptions

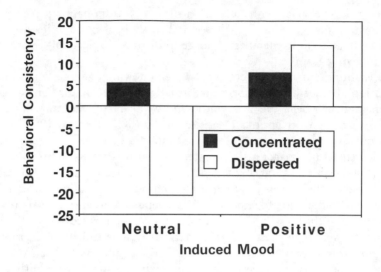

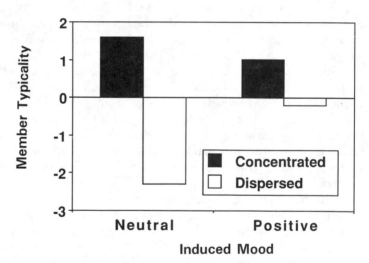

FIGURE 11.2 Perceived consistency of behaviors performed by group (upper panel) and perceived typicality of group members (lower panel) as a function of induced mood and concentrated versus dispersed presentation of inconsistent behaviors. From Mackie, Queller, and Stroessner (1994).

of group behavior. The pattern in the neutral mood condition replicated previous findings: Dispersed presentation of the inconsistent behaviors led subjects to perceive that inconsistency more fully. But the results in the positive mood condition stood in stark contrast: Rather than increasing perceived inconsistency, dispersed presentation made the behaviors seem more consistent.

Similar differences between neutral mood and happy subjects' responses were apparent in subjects' perceptions of group members, shown in the bottom panel of Figure 11.2. Subjects in neutral moods again showed a pattern of results consistent with those found in previous studies. Although the same number of inconsistent behaviors were present in each group condition, the distribution of those inconsistent behaviors across many group members increased subjects' perceptions of the number of group members who were atypical. Yet this manipulation had much less impact on happy subjects: The number of typical relative to atypical group members they perceived did not differ significantly in the concentrated and dispersed conditions. In addition, within the dispersed condition, happy subjects perceived significantly more group members as typical than did subjects in neutral moods. As a result of their failure to perceive the variability in group members' behavior, happy subjects appeared to come away from exposure to group information with perceptions of group behavior as significantly more consistent and of group members as significantly more typical, compared to the perceptions of subjects in neutral moods.

If positive mood increases both perceptions of homogeneity and perceptions of typicality, it also seems likely to increase perceptions of stereotypicality—ironically, of course, just the opposite outcome of that intended by the contact hypothesis. Not surprisingly, then, evidence that happy subjects are also more likely to make stereotypic judgments of groups was obtained in another experiment using the variability paradigm (Stroessner & Mackie, 1992, Experiment 2). Neutral or positive mood was induced, this time by asking female subjects to view a different set of video clips. In what they thought was an unrelated experiment, subjects were presented with descriptions of either a group whose behavior was highly variable in terms of intelligence and sociability, or a group whose behavior was relatively homogeneous on those dimensions. Because we were interested in stereotypicality of judgments, the described group this time was identified as a campus sorority, about whose members our female subjects held clear stereotypes: Sorority members were believed to be highly sociable but not very intelligent.

After reading the behaviors, subjects were asked how different from one another the members of the group were. Their responses to this question replicated our initial findings (Stroessner & Mackie, 1992, Experiment 1): Whereas those in neutral moods correctly saw more variability in the high than in the low variability condition, those in positive moods perceived both groups as homogeneous, and equally so. Again, the presence of positive mood appeared to reduce the perception of variability in the stimulus materials.

What impact did positive mood have on the stereotypicality of their perceptions of the group? To answer this question, subjects were asked to rate the extent to which two stereotypic traits (one positive and one negative—sociability and promiscuity, respectively) characterized the group and the extent to which two nonstereotypic traits (again, one positive and one negative—intelligence and lack of responsibility, respectively) characterized the group. Figure 11.3 demonstrates that mood state had a considerable impact on these trait judgments about the group. Regardless of whether they saw a variable or a homogeneous

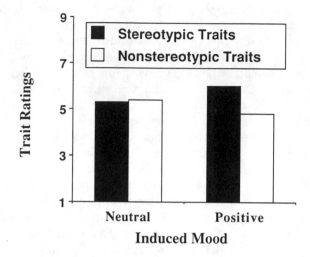

FIGURE 11.3 Perceived stereotypicality of target group as a function of induced mood and trait type. From Stroessner and Mackie (1992, Experiment 2). Copyright 1992 by the Society for Personality and Social Psychology. Reprinted by permission.

group, subjects in neutral moods saw stereotypic and nonstereotypic traits as equally characteristic of the group. This is perhaps not surprising, given that the group descriptions included stupid and sociable (stereotype-consistent) as well as intelligent and nonsociable (stereotype-inconsistent) behaviors. In contrast, the happy subjects' perceptions of the group were much more stereotypical: Compared to the subjects in neutral moods, they dramatically overestimated the extent to which stereotypic traits characterized the group and underestimated the extent to which nonstereotypic traits did so.

The greater role of stereotypic expectancies in happy subjects' judgments is consistent with more recent research on the effects of positive affect on group perception. Bodenhausen, Kramer, and Susser (1994), for example, have demonstrated that happy subjects render more stereotypic judgments than do those in neutral moods. These findings are also consistent with the results of Mackie et al.'s (1989) research demonstrating the impact of induced mood on responses made in expectancy-based illusory correlation. In this study, a mood induction was followed by presentation of statements that described members of four occupations (e.g., accountants, construction workers) with an equal number of stereotypic and nonstereotypic traits. After seeing the sentences, the subjects' task was to estimate the number of times each occupation appeared with a stereotypic trait and with a nonstereotypic trait. The correct answer in both cases was twice. Whereas subjects in neutral moods slightly overestimated the frequency with which stereotypic traits were associated with occupational labels (demonstrating an illusory correlation; Hamilton & Rose, 1980), this effect was much more pronounced for the happy subjects.

In summary, then, the results from this program of research tell a consistent story. Despite different techniques of inducing positive mood, and despite the fact that group-relevant information was presented in several different paradigms, the experience of positive mood led subjects to perceive greater homogeneity and greater typicality, to make more stereotypic judgments, and to show greater expectancy-based illusory correlation. Despite the intuitively obvious appeal of the idea that being in a good mood while learning about a negatively stereotyped outgroup should improve perceptions of that group, our results suggest a note of caution. From reduced variability estimates to increased stereotypic perceptions, the consequences of positive mood seem more likely to impede than to improve intergroup relations.

WHY DOES POSITIVE MOOD INCREASE PERCEPTIONS OF HOMOGENEITY AND STEREOTYPICALITY?

What is it about the experience of positive mood that may produce such effects? This question is especially important because of the presumption that positive mood states may improve intergroup relations. By understanding the antecedents of the less-than-benign effects of positive mood on group perceptions, we hoped to discover situations in which these negative consequences might be eliminated, as well as to uncover situations in which positive mood could indeed facilitate positive intergroup perceptions. From theoretical developments in other social judgment domains and the pattern of data in our initial studies, we identified two (perhaps complementary) possible causal mechanisms.

First, research in other domains has demonstrated that positive mood often reduces careful processing of available information (Batra & Stayman, 1990; Bless, Bohner, Schwarz, & Strack, 1990; Bodenhausen et al., 1994; Fiedler, 1988; Isen, 1987; Sinclair & Mark, 1992; Worth & Mackie, 1987). Whether solving problems, making decisions, engaging in attribution, or processing the content of a persuasive message, people in positive moods appear to show more evidence of superficial or less resource-intensive processing, and less evidence of systematic, deliberative, and comprehensive consideration of available information, than do people in neutral moods. Although the motivational and cognitive mechanisms that seem likely to underlie this effect in different conditions are still being specified (for summaries, see Forgas, 1992; Mackie et al., 1992; Petty et al., 1991; Schwarz & Bless, 1991; Sinclair & Mark, 1992), there is little debate that one frequent consequence of a positive mood is a decrease in this kind of careful processing. Given that perceivers in happy moods process information less carefully, it is not surprising that their judgments of groups tend toward the simpler and less complex when compared to those of perceivers in neutral moods.

Second, this lack of careful processing may take a particular toll on the processing of material that conveys distinctiveness information. Information about what groups have in common—information about typicality, what is usual, or "the norm"—may be easier to process or may suggest an easier route to an adequate judgment, and thus may absorb the majority of the attention that happy perceivers allocate to the group perception task. Perceivers' initial or default expectations are that group members will be more similar than different (Worth, 1988), and perhaps happy subjects do not go very far beyond these initial expectations in processing group-relevant information. At the same time, information about inconsistencies, information that violates preconceptions, or information that suggests the existence of distinctions or differentiations between group members may be more difficult to process, may require more cognitive capacity, or may simply not seem worth processing (Bodenhausen, 1993; Bodenhausen & Lichtenstein, 1987; Macrae, Hewstone, & Griffiths, 1993; Stangor & Duan, 1991). For any or all of these reasons, such information may receive relatively less processing attention.

Some evidence from the studies already described is consistent with this idea. In our initial experiments on perceptions of variability, for example, we asked subjects to recall as many behaviors as they could from the descriptions they had received about the groups (Stroessner & Mackie, 1992). Compared to the behaviors remembered by subjects in neutral moods, the most accessible behaviors recalled by happy subjects were ones reflecting the group's central tendency. The more extreme behaviors, those that represented deviations from the central tendency, were underrepresented among happy subjects' most accessible memories.

Findings conceptually consistent with the idea that happy subjects pay less attention to or are less influenced by information conveying distinctiveness have also emerged in research conducted by Isen and her colleagues. Isen and Daubman (1984), for example, induced happy or neutral mood states in their subjects. They then presented subjects with a variety of nonsocial stimuli that had previously been rated with respect to how well they represented certain categories. For example, a chair was a good example within the category of furniture, whereas a telephone was a poor example within the category of furniture. Subjects rated how good an example each item was of its corresponding category. The results indicated that subjects in happy moods included significantly more poor examples within the corresponding categories than did subjects in neutral moods; the happy subjects apparently saw what the objects had in common, rather than what differentiated them (see Murray, Sujan, Hirt, & Sujan, 1990, for a different interpretation). Even when they did not include the poor examples within the category, subjects in happy moods rated the poor examples as more similar to the corresponding categories than the subjects in neutral moods rated them.

Thus, it appears that the unexpectedly negative impacts of positive mood on group perceptions emerging from our initial studies could be attributable at least in part to happy subjects' tendency to engage in reduced processing, particularly of the kind of information that may convey distinctiveness. If so, then manipulating happy subjects' desire or opportunity to process more fully, and altering the amount of attention they pay to differentiating, distinguishing, or distinctiveness information, should have a dual purpose. If such manipulations prove capable of eliminating some of the negative effects of positive mood on group perception, they should, on the one hand, implicate the amount of processing and the amount of distinctiveness processing as causal agents of our earlier findings. At the same time, eliminating the more pernicious effects of positive mood on group perception should have practical implications for the kinds of contact situations from which more favorable intergroup perceptions might be expected to emerge.

ELIMINATING THE NEGATIVE CONSEQUENCES OF POSITIVE MOOD ON GROUP PERCEPTION

If reduced processing of available information interferes with happy subjects' ability to extract differentiating information about group members, then manipulations that increase opportunity for these subjects to process the information more thoroughly should rectify this situation. Our initial test of this idea (Stroessner & Mackie, 1993, Experiment 3) used the variability paradigm already described in some detail (Stroessner & Mackie, 1992). After happy or neutral moods were successfully induced by having subjects watch appropriate video segments, subjects were shown the descriptions of either the highly variable or the relatively homogeneous group. The behavioral descriptions appeared one at a time on a computer screen, and the opportunity to process more extensively was manipulated by varying the item presentation time. Half the subjects in each mood condition saw each behavioral statement for 3 seconds (just enough time to ascertain the meaning of the item); other subjects were allowed to study each item for 7 seconds. After all 28 items had appeared, subjects were asked how similar to one another the members of the group they had read about were, and their responses on a 9-point scale were reverse-scored to produce indices of variability.

The results of the study can be seen in Figure 11.4. The graphs on the left show the results from the brief 3-second exposure condition, and the pattern clearly replicates our previous findings. Although subjects in a neutral mood made a clear distinction between the highly variable group and the more homogeneous group, subjects in positive moods did not. Instead, they saw both groups as relatively homogeneous. The difference between happy and neutral-mood subjects' responses disappeared, however, in the 7-second condition, which gave perceivers more time to consider the information. The only apparent effect in this condition was that of stimulus group. Both happy and neutral-mood subjects correctly saw the highly variable group as significantly more variable than the homogeneous group. Thus, given enough time to process thoroughly, happy subjects produced variability judgments as differentiated as the judgments of subjects in neutral moods.

Encouraged by our ability to eliminate one of the negative effects of positive mood by allowing happy subjects to process more thoroughly, we then test-

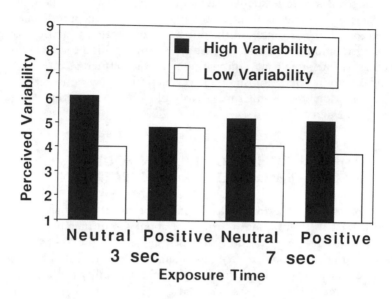

FIGURE 11.4   Perceived variability as a function of induced mood, variability of group description, and presentation exposure. From Stroessner and Mackie (1993). Copyright 1993 by Academic Press, Inc. Reprinted by permission.

ed the idea that specifically drawing subjects' attention to distinctiveness information might have a similar effect. Whereas our previous experiments had simply asked subjects to process the group information, some subjects in this experiment were specifically asked to think about the ways in which the group members they read about were similar or different. In this experiment (Queller, Mackie, & Stroessner, 1994), undergraduates read either the uplifting or the neutral newspaper story described earlier. Responses designed to assess the effectiveness of this manipulation again showed that reading the first story successfully induced positive moods, whereas reading the second story left subjects in neutral moods.

After moving to a separate room, subjects followed a second experimenter's instructions to form an impression of a group of "Big Brothers." The Big Brothers were described as a group of young men whose goal is to provide positive male role models to children who lack such role models in their home environments. Subjects were then given 16 index cards, each of which provided a three-sentence description of a different member of the group. The first sentence in these descriptions always described the individual performing a helpful behavior, and the second sentence always described the individual as having lenient parents (Park, Ryan, & Judd, 1992). For example, one individual "helped his sister move into a new apartment" and "was allowed to have parties at his parents' house when growing up."

The third sentence on each card was intended to allow subjects to differentiate among the 16 target individuals. For eight of the group members, the third sentence described an athletic behavior, whereas it described a musical behavior for the other eight group members. Of the eight athletic statements, four described competitive athletic behaviors (e.g., "chipped a tooth on a hockey puck last season"), whereas the other four described casual athletic behaviors (e.g., "played tennis with a friend on Wednesdays"). Of the eight musical statements, four described involvement in classical music studies (e.g., "practices the violin at least three times a week"), whereas the other four described a casual involvement with music (e.g., "turned the radio on before he sat down to study"). Thus, four of the group members were described as competitive athletes, four as casual athletes, four as students of classical music, and four as casual music listeners.

We manipulated the amount of attention we hoped subjects would pay to this differentiating information by giving subjects different tasks as they formed their impressions of the group. Half the subjects were merely instructed to form their impressions by reading the cards to learn about the members of the Big Brother group. The other half were instructed to form their impressions by sorting the cards into piles that put together group members who were "similar to each other in some way(s) and different from the members in other piles in some way(s)." Subjects in both conditions were told they could look at each card as many times as they liked. When subjects felt they had finished their assigned task satisfactorily, they were asked to indicate the extent to which they felt members of the group were similar to one another. These responses (on 9-point scales) were reverse-scored and the resulting indices of perceived variability were analyzed.

How did the different processing tasks influence the group perceptions formed by subjects in neutral and positive moods? The answer can be seen in Figure 11.5. When subjects were merely instructed to read about the group members to form an impression of the group (the filled bars on the graph), the results were similar to those of previous research. Subjects in neutral moods perceived the group as significantly more variable than did subjects in positive moods, despite the fact that all subjects saw identical information. The effect of explicitly asking subjects to deal with the ways in which group members might be similar or different, however, can be seen in the open bars. Apparently, the sorting task was sufficient to allow happy subjects to extract the same degree of differentiating information from the material as did subjects in neutral moods. When subjects sorted similar and different group members as they formed their impressions, subjects perceived equal amounts of variability, regardless of their mood state.

Taken together, then, these two experiments indicate that when happy subjects were encouraged to process all available information more thoroughly, their perceptions of group variability were very similar to those formed by subjects in neutral moods. Thus, giving subjects the opportunity to process more extensively, and encouraging them (through the sorting task) to take into account information conveying differences as well as similarities eliminated the relatively

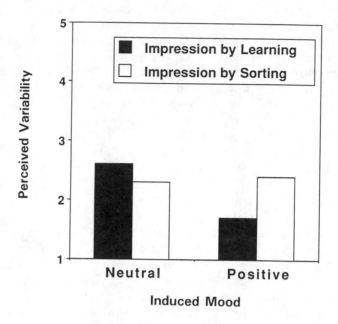

FIGURE 11.5 Perceived variability as a function of induced mood and processing task. From Queller, Mackie, and Stroessner (1994).

detrimental effects of positive mood on perception found in earlier studies. Notice, however, that these manipulations had the effect only of bringing the perceptions of subjects in positive moods into line with those of subjects whose mood state was neutral. There is no sign in these results of any advantage that positive mood may bring to the processing of intergroup information.

Can we think of conditions in which positive mood is an advantage (relative to neutral mood) when it comes to group impressions? If positive affect reduces the extensive processing of available information, and if it reduces the processing of distinctive information in particular, are there intergroup contexts in which such tendencies may reduce rather than exacerbate stereotypic perceptions? One such condition arises when processing of distinctive information is necessary for the formation of stereotypic judgments. Under these conditions, subjects who pay less attention to distinctive information should fail to form stereotypic perceptions.

Just such a situation is established by the materials commonly used in a distinctiveness-based illusory-correlation paradigm (Hamilton & Gifford, 1976). In this paradigm, processing of distinctive information is required for stereotypes—differential perceptions of groups—to be formed. Our interest, then, was in the effect of induced positive mood on perceptions formed in a distinctiveness-based illusory-correlation paradigm.

We (Stroessner, Hamilton, & Mackie, 1992; Hamilton, Stroessner, & Mackie, 1993) induced positive and neutral moods by means of our video presentation technique before moving subjects to a separate room, where a new experimenter presented them with standard illusory-correlation materials. Subjects saw 36 sentences in all: 16 describing desirable behaviors performed by members of an unnamed Group A; 8 describing undesirable behaviors performed by members of Group A; 8 describing desirable behaviors performed by members of an unnamed Group B; and 4 describing undesirable behaviors performed by Group B members. In this stimulus set, then, descriptions of Group B are numerically infrequent, as are the instances of undesirable behaviors. In addition, the intersection of these two infrequent events—the undesirable behaviors performed by Group B—is particularly distinctive. Although each group actually performs the same ratio of desirable to undesirable behaviors, the attention given to these especially distinctive behaviors usually means that subjects overassociate Group B with the performance of undesirable behaviors. An illusory correlation forms between group membership and behavior desirability, and the consequence is more favorable perceptions of Group A than of Group B.

Because we were interested in tracking the formation of such stereotypes among subjects in happy or neutral moods, we included a number of process as well as outcome measures in our study. First, because illusory correlations and their resultant stereotypes apparently depend on processing of distinctive information, we presented the group information on a computer screen and measured how long subjects spent processing desirable and undesirable behaviors about Group A and Group B. Second, after they had read the descriptions, subjects were asked to estimate how many behaviors of each kind they had read, from which we assessed the formation of illusory correlations. Third, subjects were asked how much they liked members of Group A and Group B, to determine whether differential evaluations of the group had resulted.

We looked first at the attention subjects in the different mood conditions paid to the four different kinds of information (processing times were averaged across different items of the same kind). Figure 11.6 shows processing latencies in seconds for each of the four kinds of information for subjects in a neutral mood (on the left) and those in a positive mood (on the right). Increased attention to the distinctive (Group B undesirable) behaviors is assumed to underlie formation of an illusory correlation. This was exactly what happened when subjects in neutral moods processed the sentences: Compared to the other kinds of information, Group B undesirable behaviors attracted significantly more attention from neutral-mood subjects. In contrast, our expectations regarding the effect of positive mood were borne out: Happy subjects paid no special attention to the distinctive Group B undesirable information.

Given the pattern of results in the processing data, we expected that subjects in neutral moods would form illusory correlations, whereas those in positive moods would not. Examination of indices of association between group

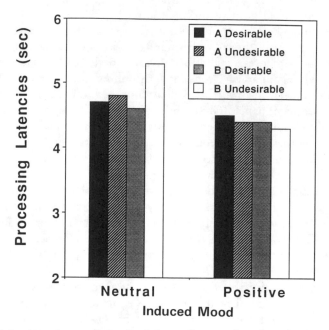

FIGURE 11.6 Attention to distinctive information as a function of induced mood and information type. From Stroessner, Hamilton, and Mackie (1992, Experiment 2). Copyright 1992 by the American Psychological Association. Reprinted by permission.

membership and behavior type in subjects' frequency estimates revealed exactly this pattern. Whereas a significant association (due primarily in this case to overestimation of the number of Group B undesirable behaviors) formed in the neutral mood condition, there was no such association in the positive mood condition. These differences in frequency estimates should also, of course, translate into differences in group perceptions. On the basis of their extra attention to distinctive information and the biased associations they formed, perceivers in neutral moods might be expected to like Group A more than Group B. The left-hand bars in Figure 11.7 reveal such a pattern. Because of their failure to process distinctive information extensively, and their subsequent failure to form biased associations between group membership and behavior type, however, subjects in positive moods should fail to form differential perceptions of the groups. As can be seen from the right-hand bars in Figure 11.7, Group A and Group B were liked equally by happy subjects. In this experiment, then, the presence of a positive mood undermined the processes that typically result in the formation of different perceptions of the two groups. In other words, this was a case where being in a positive mood actually had a beneficial effect on intergroup perceptions, compared to being in a neutral mood.

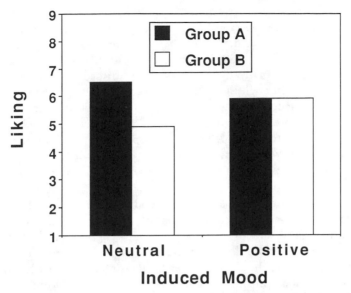

FIGURE 11.7   Differential liking for Group A and Group B as a function of induced mood. From Stroessner, Hamilton, and Mackie (1992, Experiment 2). Copyright 1992 by the American Psychological Association. Reprinted by permission.

POSITIVE MOOD AND GROUP PERCEPTIONS: COSTS OR BENEFITS?

We initiated this program of research to determine what effect the experience of a positive mood state has on the processing of group-relevant information, in an attempt to gauge the costs and benefits of positive mood during intergroup contact. The majority of our findings give no cause for particular optimism. In general, the presence of positive mood increased perceptions of group homogeneity; it heightened the extent to which behavior was seen as consistent with expectations; it enhanced the perception of individual group members as being typical of the group; and it increased the likelihood that expectancy-based stereotypic judgments about groups would be made. Thus, especially for negatively valued groups, positive mood seems to have predominantly detrimental effects.

To account for this pattern of findings, we have considered the importance of two possible mediating mechanisms. The first is that positive mood reduces the extent to which subjects process information thoroughly and carefully—an effect that is well documented in the literature. The second is that this diminished processing is particularly consequential for information that conveys the distinctive, atypical, or stereotype-inconsistent properties of the group (or its members).

Some of our experimental findings provide support for the importance of these mediating effects. Specifically, when happy subjects were given an opportunity to process in greater depth, or when they were specifically asked to think about similarities and differences among group members, their perceptions of other groups were virtually the same as those formed by subjects in neutral moods. Moreover, although the tendency to process in less depth most often led to detrimental outcomes for group perceptions, it did produce more positive outcomes in one case. When forming group stereotypes depended on differential processing of distinctive information, happy subjects did not form differential perceptions of two previously unknown groups, whereas those in neutral moods did. All of these results are consistent with the interpretation we have offered.

Of course, the finding that positive mood undermines the formation of illusory correlations was obtained in a situation in which no prior stereotypes existed—not the typical state of affairs when groups engage in intergroup contact, and certainly not the conditions of negative intergroup relations that contact is designed to alleviate. Although our other findings point to more costs than benefits of positive mood during intergroup interactions, they do begin to demonstrate conditions under which such costs can be minimized or reversed. This brings us back to where we began, but also suggests questions for the future. Just what are the implications of positive mood for intergroup contact situations? In which directions could future research be profitably extended to increase our understanding of those implications?

The first question that might be asked is whether positive affect ever arises in intergroup contact situations. If it does not, then our findings are of purely theoretical interest, without much practical application. Previous research has indicated that both the anticipation and the actual experience of intergroup interaction are usually accompanied by negative emotions, such as irritation and anxiety (Stephan & Stephan, 1985; Dijker, 1987; Vanman & Miller, 1993).

Despite this potential for negative affect in intergroup contexts, we nevertheless suspect that there are at least two kinds of situations where positive affect does occur during intergroup information processing, and to which our findings are directly relevant. First, although empirical evidence is scant, the kinds of interaction envisaged by contact theorists—typically, cooperation that leads to success—should be capable of generating positive affect. Intergroup interaction that proceeds smoothly, and interaction that is friendly and affable, have both been shown to engender positive feelings (Fiske & Ruscher, 1993). Similarly, successful outcomes induce positive mood states in individuals, and to the extent that one identifies with a group, group successes and failures should have the same effect (Cialdini & Richardson, 1980; Smith, 1993). Thus, despite the fact that the direct affective consequences of intergroup success, cooperation, or friendly interaction remain unmeasured, there is at least reason to believe that such interactions may involve positive affect if the circumstances are right. Second, there are no doubt many more situations in which intergroup information is received when perceivers are in a positive mood for quite incidental or irrelevant reasons—the kind of situation that directly parallels our experimental situation. When people watch situation comedies that include members of stigmatized groups, when sexist or racist remarks are made during an otherwise pleasant occasion, or even when people share a joke with a spouse and then turn to read the newspaper, group perceptions can be affected by the mood state of the processor. Thus, the kinds of situations in which quite incidental positive affect can influence the processing of information about one's own and other groups are likely to be quite commonplace.

The second question that then needs to be answered is whether the kind of positive affect aroused as a result of intergroup interaction has the same effects as the mood states induced in our studies here. Affect aroused as an integral part of an intergroup situation may have properties and consequences for the interactants that incidental and interaction-irrelevant mood states like those induced here do not (Bodenhausen, 1993). Of course, affect that is integral to intergroup relations can be present long before any particular group interaction takes place. In an experiment currently underway, we are attempting to induce integral affective states by manipulating whether our subjects' ingroup is praised or disparaged by another group (Queller, Mackie, & Neddermeyer, 1994). Our subjects, most of whom are social science majors, are asked to evaluate a story supposedly appearing in a student newspaper. An engineering student interviewed in the article describes the contribution of social science majors to his own work in terms that are either positive (praising the perceptiveness, creativity, and cooperativeness of the social science students he has encountered) or negative (disparaging the social science students as incompetent, uninformed, and unhelpful).

Pretest responses to various items designed to assess the effect of this manipulation indicate that it does successfully induce differences in mood state. When the ingroup is praised, subjects report feeling significantly happier than when the ingroup is derogated. Perhaps because our operationalization in the derogation condition is not very extreme, because the relevant groups are not crucially interdependent, or because our students are particularly well defended, the disparagement condition has so far induced a neutral rather than a negative mood. Nevertheless, these preliminary data suggest that such manipulations are capable of inducing integral positive affect, just as other manipulations successfully produce incidental affect.

Does integral affect have the same impact on perceptions of variability, typicality, and stereotypicality as manipulations of incidental mood? We know of only one research program that has allowed for such a comparison, and the emotion manipulated was negative rather than positive. Wilder (1984; Wilder & Shapiro, 1989a, 1989b) manipulated incidental anxiety in one experiment by asking some subjects to imagine engaging in embarrassing activities (e.g., having their photos taken while dressed in baby clothes) and manipulated integral affect in a second experiment (by leading subjects to anticipate intergroup competition). Both incidental and integral anxiety had an identical effect on dependent measures, decreasing perceptions of differentiation in the target group in both cases. Despite the fact that there are currently no direct comparisons of the impact of incidental and integral affect, Wilder's studies provide some precedent for predicting that they might have similar effects. Such predictions would be consistent with theories suggesting that the experience of mood should have similar consequences, regardless of why it is aroused (Bower, 1981; Isen, 1984, 1987; see Schwarz & Clore, 1988, for an exception).

On the other hand, others have argued that the reductions in processing typically produced by positive mood reflect lack of motivation to process (e.g., because positive affect is a sign that everything is fine in the environment; Schwarz, 1990), and thus that increases in motivation will eliminate mood-induced processing deficits. Given that any affect aroused as an integral consequence of group interaction has implications for the interactants, processing decrements usually induced by positive mood should not occur. In this view, then, integrally aroused positive mood need not have detrimental effects on group perception (Bodenhausen et al., 1994). It is not clear, however, why this should be so. It is possible, of course, that any cues suggesting that a situation is self-relevant may override the effects of positive affect. However, if the intergroup situation itself is successful enough to induce positive affect, it is not clear why the informational value of that affect ("everything is all right") is not valid (after all, everything *is* all right). Regardless of why the mood state is induced, then, its presence may well activate the same procedures with the same consequences.

Other theoretical positions also suggest differences between integral and incidental affect, but for different reasons. One possibility is that affect influences processing differently at different levels of motivation. Thus high motivation may initiate thorough processing, but the presence of a positive mood may bias that processing in a favorable direction (Petty et al., 1991; Forgas, 1991). From this perspective, integral positive affect may produce more favorable perceptions of other groups. Not only should more information be processed, but resulting judgments should be positively tinged.

A second possibility is that mood has different informational value, depending on the processing task. For example, Martin, Ward, Achee, and Wyer (1993) found that tasks that focused subjects on the adequacy of their judgments apparently led those in good moods to feel that they had done enough and to cease processing. On the other hand, tasks that made subjects think about whether they were having a good time led to continued processing. In the context of a successful intergroup interaction, then, integral positive mood may operate to keep participants actively processing information, as long as "enjoyment" consequences rather than "confidence" consequences of mood remain salient.

Thus, there are reasons to predict either that the effects of integral and incidental positive affect will differ or that they will not. The empirical resolution of this issue obviously has important implications for whether positive affect arising from intergroup interaction is a help or a hindrance to stereotype change. Such research will also clarify when and under what conditions incidental and integral affect will have similar or different effects.

When positive affect is considered as an integral part of an intergroup interaction, a third issue becomes focal. It is clear that positive affect may be aroused at different times in different interactions. Although intergroup interaction is often accompanied by negative emotions, friendly interaction may displace such emotions almost immediately. In this case, positive affect may influence the processing of group-relevant information. On the other hand, participants may not experience any positive emotion until well into the interaction, and, in the case of intergroup cooperation, perhaps not until the interaction has concluded successfully. This may mean that most intergroup information is processed under neutral conditions at best—a situation our results suggest is likely to produce more variable and less stereotypic group perceptions.

Such a possibility lowers the relevance of our results for the majority of contact situations; the consequences of processing decrements induced by positive mood are not a problem if perceivers are not in a positive mood. But it does raise another set of interesting questions. What is the effect on group impressions of positive affect aroused after most of the group-relevant information has been processed? Can subsequent positive mood have some retroactive effect on information previously processed in a different mood state (Srull, 1983)? Are judgmental processes influenced by mood state in a similar manner to encoding processes, or not (Bless, Mackie, & Schwarz, 1992)? These are obviously empirical questions, and need to be answered if we are to gain a more complete understanding of affect's many possible consequences, even in successful intergroup interactions.

The focus of our research on the effects of positive mood naturally leads to another question: Do positive and negative affect have similar or different consequences for intergroup perceptions? Given that we have found predominantly unfavorable effects of positive mood, we might expect similar outcomes: Experiencing negative mood states during interactions with members of other groups would not seem any more likely to produce improved intergroup perceptions. In fact, some research findings support this expectation. Bodenhausen (1993) reported that induced anger had effects similar to those reported here, particularly in an increased reliance on stereotypic judgments. Wilder and Shapiro (1989a, 1989b) found that anxiety tended to decrease perceptions of variability in the outgroup, paralleling our effects for positive mood.

Other studies have investigated the impact of sadness on group perceptions, although sadness is no doubt less likely in intergroup interactions than anger, frustration, anxiety, and perhaps even happiness. Some studies have found that incidentally induced sadness produces effects very similar to those we have summarized as being provoked by happiness. For example, subjects in negative moods perceived greater homogeneity, even in objectively heterogeneous groups. In three different studies they responded in the same way that happy subjects did (Stroessner & Mackie, 1992, Experiments 1 and 2; Stroessner

& Mackie, 1993, Experiment 3). The responses of happy and sad subjects were also identical in our two studies of distinctiveness-based illusory correlation, with sad subjects failing to process information carefully enough to produce biased perceptions of the two groups (Hamilton, Stroessner, & Mackie, 1993; Stroessner, Hamilton, & Mackie, 1992). Moreover, when subjects in a negative mood were asked to categorize exemplars as category members, they also tended to overinclude unusual members, though not to the significant degree that those in a positive mood did (Isen & Daubman, 1984). However, not all of the effects of negative mood parallel those of positive mood. Stroessner and Mackie (1992, Experiment 2) found that although subjects in negative moods perceived increased homogeneity in judging the variability of a group, they did not make any more stereotypic judgments about the group than did subjects in neutral moods. This finding foreshadows a more recent demonstration by Bodenhausen (1993) of the same effect: Subjects in a sad mood appeared no more likely to rely on stereotypes in making judgments than did subjects in a nonaffective control condition. More research is clearly needed to specify the conditions under which different kinds of negative emotional states may promote or prevent either more favorable or more differentiated views of groups.

Finally, future research might consider the kind of group-relevant information that is best suited to change impressions of groups during successful interactions. In the experimental paradigms we used, the most varied and least stereotypic perceptions of groups usually depended on extensive processing of information (not in the distinctiveness-based illusory-correlation study, of course). The assumption that this kind of thorough, extensive, systematic processing is necessary to overturn superficial, incomplete, and inaccurate stereotypes permeates theorizing about group perception; as a result, it influences the paradigms that are typically used. Although the kind of information we presented is quite similar to the information available when stereotypes are formed, maintained, or changed through real observation or interactions, it is not clear that it is the best way to change group perceptions when perceivers are in a good mood. If positive interaction elicits positive affect, and if positive affect increases the tendency to process superficially rather than extensively, descriptions of groups that allow positive impressions to be formed via heuristic processing may be more effective. Presenting positive information initially, making it especially salient, or presenting it in group-level, summary, or central-tendency format might make it even more impactful for the happy perceiver, producing more positive perceptions. Under such conditions, the heuristic processing that seems to characterize happy perceivers' approach to information may help improve group relations where extensive processing has failed.

Until these issues can be resolved by further research, our findings sound a note of warning about the apparently straightforward notion that pleasant interaction routinely promotes positive perceptions. Our results demonstrate that if such interaction also induces positive mood, it runs the risk of promoting perceptions of homogeneity and of increased reliance on established stereotypes. Further investigation of the affective, cognitive, and motivational processes that produce these counterintuitive findings should increase both our theoretical understanding of intergroup perception and our practical ability to improve the outcomes of intergroup contact. This work serves as a powerful reminder of the many benefits, both theoretical and applied, of studying the interaction among cognitive, motivational, and affective systems in a domain as central to social psychology as group perception.

Acknowledgments

Some of this work was presented in an invited address by Diane M. Mackie at the annual meeting of the Western Psychological Association, Kona, Hawaii, 1994, and by Sarah Queller at the annual convention of the American Psychological Society, Washington, DC, 1994. This research was supported by National Science Foundation (NSF) Grant No. SBR-9209995 to Diane M. Mackie; National Institute of Mental Health Grant No. MH-40058 to David L. Hamilton; an NSF Graduate Student Fellowship to Sarah Queller; and a Jacob K. Javits National Graduate Student Fellowship to Steven J. Stroessner.

References

Adorno, T. W., Frenkel-Brunswik, E., Levinson, D. J., & Sanford, R. N. (1950). *The authoritarian personality*. New York: Harper.

Allport, G. W. (1954). *The nature of prejudice*. Reading, MA: Addison-Wesley.

Amir, Y. (1969). Contact hypothesis in ethnic relations. *Psychological Bulletin, 71*, 319–342.

Batra, R., & Stayman, D. M. (1990). The role of mood in advertising effectiveness. *Journal of Consumer Research, 17*, 203–214.

Bless, H., Bohner, G., Schwarz, N., & Strack, F. (1990). Mood and persuasion: A cognitive response analysis. *Personality and Social Psychology Bulletin, 16*, 331–345.

Bless, H., Mackie, D. M., & Schwarz, N. (1992). Mood effects on attitude judgments: The independent effects of mood before and after message elaboration. *Journal of Personality and Social Psychology, 63*, 585–595.

Bodenhausen, G. V. (1993). Emotions, arousal, and stereotypic judgments: A heuristic model of affect and stereotyping. In D. M. Mackie & D. L. Hamilton (Eds.), *Affect, cognition, and stereotyping: Interactive processes in group perception* (pp. 13–37). San Diego, CA: Academic Press.

Bodenhausen, G. V., Kramer, G., & Susser, K. (1994). Happiness and stereotypical thinking in social judgment. *Journal of Personality and Social Psychology, 66*, 621–632.

Bodenhausen, G. V., & Lichtenstein, M. (1987). Social stereotypes and information-processing strategies: The impact of task complexity. *Journal of Personality and Social Psychology, 52*, 871–880.

Bower, G. H. (1981). Mood and memory. *American Psychologist, 36*, 129–148.

Bower, G. H., Gilligan, S. G., & Montiero, K. P. (1981). Selectivity of learning caused by affective states. *Journal of Experimental Psychology: General, 110*, 451–473.

Brewer, M. B., & Miller, N. (1984). Beyond the contact hypothesis: Theoretical perspectives on desegregation. In N. Miller & M. B. Brewer (Eds.), *Groups in contact: The psychology of desegregation* (pp. 281–302). Orlando, FL: Academic Press.

Cialdini, R. B., & Richardson, K. D. (1980). Two indirect tactics of image management: Basking and blasting. *Journal of Personality and Social Psychology, 39*, 406–415.

Dijker, A. J. M. (1987). Emotional reactions to ethnic minorities. *European Journal of Social Psychology, 17*, 305–325.

Dollard, J., Miller, N. E., Doob, L. W., Mowrer, O. H., & Sears, R. R. (1939). *Frustration and aggression*. New Haven, CT: Yale University Press.

Fiedler, K. (1988). Emotional mood, cognitive style, and behavior regulation. In K. Fiedler & J. P. Forgas (Eds.), *Affect, cognition, and social behavior* (pp. 100–119). Toronto: Hogrefe.

Fiske, S. T., & Ruscher, J. B. (1993). Negative interdependence and prejudice: Whence the affect? In D. M. Mackie & D. L. Hamilton (Eds.), *Affect, cognition, and stereotyping: Interactive processes in group perception* (pp. 63–86). San Diego, CA: Academic Press.

Forgas, J. P. (1991). Affect and social judgments: An introductory review. In J. P. Forgas (Ed.), *Emotion and social judgments* (pp. 3–29). Elmsford, NY: Pergamon Press.

Forgas, J. P. (1992). Affect and social perception: Research evidence and an integrative theory. In W. Stroebe & M. Hewstone (Eds.), *European review of social psychology* (Vol. 3, pp. 183–223). Chichester, England: Wiley.

Gurwitz, S. B., & Dodge, K. A. (1977). Effect of confirmations and disconfirmations on stereotype-based attributions. *Journal of Personality and Social Psychology, 35*, 495–500.

Hamilton, D. L., & Gifford, R. K. (1976). Illusory correlation in interpersonal perception: A cognitive basis of stereotypic judgments. *Journal of Experimental Social Psychology, 12*, 392–407.

Hamilton, D. L., & Rose, T. L. (1980). Illusory correlation and the maintenance of stereotypic belief. *Journal of Personality and Social Psychology, 39*, 832–845.

Hamilton, D. L., Stroessner, S. J., & Mackie, D. M. (1993). The influence of affect on stereotyping: The case of illusory correlations. In D. M. Mackie & D. L. Hamilton (Eds.), *Affect, cognition, and stereotyping: Interactive processes in group perception* (pp. 39–61). San Diego, CA: Academic Press.

Hewstone, M., & Brown, R.(1986). Contact is not enough: An intergroup perspective on the 'contact hypothesis'. In M. Hewstone & R. Brown (Eds.), *Contact and conflict in intergroup encounters* (pp. 169–195). Oxford: Basil Blackwell.

Isen, A. M. (1984). Toward understanding the role of affect in cognition. In R. S. Wyer & T. K. Srull (Eds.), *Handbook of social cognition* (pp. 179–236). Hillsdale, NJ: Erlbaum.

Isen, A. M. (1987). Positive affect, cognitive processes, and social behavior. In L. Berkowitz (Ed.), *Advances in experimental social psychology* (Vol. 20, pp. 203–253). New York: Academic Press.

Isen, A. M., & Daubman, K. A. (1984). The influence of affect on categorization. *Journal of Personality and Social Psychology, 47*, 1206–1217.

Johnston, L., & Hewstone, M. (1992). Cognitive models of stereotype change: 3. Subtyping and the perceived typicality of disconfirming group members. *Journal of Experimental Social Psychology, 28*, 360–386.

Mackie, D. M., Asuncion, A. G., & Rosselli, F. (1992). The impact of positive mood on persuasion processes. In M. S. Clark (Ed.), *Emotion and social behavior* (pp. 247–270). Newbury Park, CA: Sage.

Mackie, D. M., & Hamilton, D. L. (Eds.). (1993). *Affect, cognition, and stereotyping: Interactive processes in group perception*. San Diego, CA: Academic Press.

Mackie, D. M., Hamilton, D. L., Schroth, H. A., Carlisle, C. J., Gersho, B. F., Meneses, L. M., Nedler, B. F., & Reichel, L. D. (1989). The effects of induced mood on expectancy-based illusory correlations. *Journal of Experimental Social Psychology, 25*, 524–544.

Mackie, D. M., Quellcr, S., & Stroessner, S. J. (1994). *The impact of positive mood on perceptions of behavioral consistency and member typicality in social groups.* Unpublished manuscript, University of California, Santa Barbara.

Macrae, C. N., Hewstone, M., & Griffiths, R. J. (1993). Processing load and memory for stereotype-based information. *European Journal of Social Psychology, 23*, 77–87.

Martin, L. L., Ward, D. W., Achee, J. W., & Wyer, R. S., Jr. (1993). Mood as input: People have to interpret the motivational implications of their moods. *Journal of Personality and Social Psychology, 64*, 317–326.

Murray, N., Sujan, H., Hirt, E. R., & Sujan, M. (1990). The influence of mood on categorization: A cognitive flexibility interpretation. *Journal of Personality and Social Psychology, 59*, 411–425.

Park, B., & Hastie, R. (1987). The perception of variability in category development: Instance- versus abstraction-based stereotypes. *Journal of Personality and Social Psychology, 53*, 621–635.

Park, B., Ryan, C. S., & Judd, C. M. (1992). Role of meaningful subgroups in explaining differences in perceived variability for in-groups and out-groups. *Journal of Personality and Social Psychology, 63,* 553-567.

Pettigrew, T. F. (1986). The intergroup contact hypothesis reconsidered. In M. Hewstone & R. Brown (Eds.), *Contact and conflict in intergroup encounters* (pp. 169-195). Oxford: Basil Blackwell.

Petty, R. E., Gleicher, F., & Baker, S. M. (1991). Multiple roles for affect in persuasion. In J. Forgas (Ed.), *Emotion and social judgments* (pp. 181-200). Elmsford, NY: Pergamon Press.

Queller, S., Mackie, D. M., & Neddermeyer, K. D. (1994). *Perceptions of group variability: An investigation of the effects of integrally induced affect.* Unpublished manuscript, University of California, Santa Barbara.

Queller, S., Mackie, D. M., & Stroessner, S. J. (1994). *Positive affect and perceptions of homogeneity: Reversing the effects.* Unpublished manuscript, University of California, Santa Barbara.

Rothbart, M., & John, O. (1985). Social cognition and behavioral episodes: A cognitive analysis of the effect of intergroup contact. *Journal of Social Issues, 41*(3), 81-104.

Schwarz, N. (1990). Feeling as information: Informational and motivational functions of affective states. In R. Sorrentino & E. T. Higgins (Eds.), *Handbook of motivation and cognition: Foundations of social behavior* (Vol. 2, pp. 527-561). New York: Guilford Press.

Schwarz, N., & Bless, H. (1991). Happy and mindless, but sad and smart? The impact of affective states on analytic reasoning. In J. Forgas (Ed.), *Emotion and social judgments* (pp. 55-71). Elmsford, NY: Pergamon Press.

Schwarz, N., & Clore, G. L. (1988). How do I feel about it? Informative functions of affective states. In K. Fiedler & J. Forgas (Eds.), *Affect, cognition, and social behavior* (pp. 44-62). Toronto: Hogrefe.

Sinclair, R. C., & Mark, M. M. (1992). The influence of mood state on judgment and action: Effects on persuasion, categorization, social justice, person perception, and judgmental accuracy. In L. L. Martin & A. Tesser (Eds.), *The construction of social judgments* (pp. 165-193). Hillsdale, NJ: Erlbaum.

Smith, E. R. (1993). Social identity and social emotions: Toward new conceptualizations of prejudice. In D. M. Mackie & D. L. Hamilton (Eds.), *Affect, cognition, and stereotyping: Interactive processes in group perception* (pp. 63-86). San Diego, CA: Academic Press.

Srull, T. K. (1983). Memory, mood, and consumer judgment. In M. Wallendorf & P. Anderson (Eds.), *Advances in consumer research* (Vol. 14, pp. 404-407). Provo, UT: Association for Consumer Research.

Staats, A. W., & Staats, C. K. (1958). Attitudes established by classical conditioning. *Journal of Abnormal and Social Psychology, 57,* 37-40.

Stangor, C., & Duan, C. (1991). Effects of multiple task demands on memory for information about social groups. *Journal of Experimental Social Psychology, 27,* 357-378.

Stephan, W. G. (1987). The contact hypothesis in intergroup relations. In C. Hendrick (Ed), *Review of personality and social psychology* (Vol. 9, pp. 13-40). Newbury Park, CA: Sage.

Stephan, W. G., & Stephan, C. W. (1985). Intergroup anxiety. *Journal of Social Issues, 41*(3), 157-175.

Stroessner, S. J., Hamilton, D. H., & Mackie, D. M. (1992). Affect and stereotyping: The effect of induced mood on distinctiveness-based illusory correlations. *Journal of Personality and Social Psychology, 62,* 564-576.

Stroessner, S. J., & Mackie, D. M. (1992). The impact of induced affect on the perception of variability in social groups. *Personality and Social Psychology Bulletin, 18,* 546-554.

Stroessner, S. J., & Mackie, D. M. (1993). Affect and perceived group variability: Implications for stereotyping and prejudice. In D. M. Mackie & D. L. Hamilton (Eds.), *Affect, cognition, and stereotyping: Interactive processes in group perception* (pp. 63-86). San Diego, CA: Academic Press.

Vanman, E. J., & Miller, N. (1993). Applications of emotion theory and research to stereotyping and intergroup relations. In D. M. Mackie & D. L. Hamilton (Eds.), *Affect, cognition, and stereotyping: Interactive processes in group perception* (pp. 213-238). San Diego, CA: Academic Press.

Weber, R., & Crocker, J. (1983). Cognitive processes in the revision of stereotypic beliefs. *Journal of Personality and Social Psychology, 45,* 961–977.

Wilder, D. A. (1984). Intergroup contact: The typical member and the exception to the rule. *Journal of Experimental Social Psychology, 20,* 177–194.

Wilder, D. A., & Shapiro, P. (1989a). The role of competition-induced anxiety in limiting the beneficial impact of positive behavior by an out-group member. *Journal of Personality and Social Psychology, 56,* 60–69.

Wilder, D. A., & Shapiro, P. (1989b). Effects of anxiety on impression formation in a group context: An anxiety–assimilation hypothesis. *Journal of Experimental Social Psychology, 25,* 481–499.

Worth, L. T. (1988). *The outgroup homogeneity effect: Information processing causes and consequences.* Unpublished doctoral dissertation, University of California, Santa Barbara.

Worth, L. T., & Mackie, D. M. (1987). Cognitive mediation of positive affect in persuasion. *Social Cognition, 5,* 76–94.

CHAPTER 12

Incidental and Integral Affect as Triggers of Stereotyping

DAVID A. WILDER
ANDREW F. SIMON
Rutgers—The State University of New Jersey

Virtually all of social psychology involves the interplay among three constructs: affect, cognition, and behavior. In the domain of intergroup relations, these constructs wear the masks of prejudice, stereotype, and discrimination, respectively. Common sense suggests consistency among these constructs. For example, persons who harbor prejudice against a group may also be expected to possess unfavorable stereotypes about the group and to behave hostilely toward members of that group. However, actual consistency among these constructs falls far short of this "psycho-logic" (e.g., Allport, 1954; Ajzen & Fishbein, 1980). Moreover, much of the research in the broad field of intergroup relations has looked at prejudice, stereotypes, and discrimination separately.

During the last two decades, a considerable body of research has focused on stereotypes as cognitive constructs, subject to principles of development, use, and change in the same manner as cognitions or beliefs in general (e.g., Hamilton & Trolier, 1986). In response to the dominance of social-cognitive and information-processing models in mainstream social psychology, researchers have become increasingly interested in the interaction of affect with cognition and consequent influences on behavior (e.g., Zajonc, 1980; Higgins & Sorrentino, 1990; Isen, 1984). Interest in the interaction of affect and cognition can be seen in the nascent literature that examines the relationship between affect and stereotyping. This chapter reviews that literature, and proposes a model to explain the findings as well as to suggest avenues for additional exploration.

STEREOTYPES

Following Lippman's (1922) reference to stereotypes as pictures in people's heads, social psychologists have posed multiple definitions of the construct. According to Allport (1954, p. 187), a stereotype is "an exaggerated belief associated with a category." The phrase "exaggerated belief" suggests that a stereotype is bound to be in error. More recently, Hamilton and Sherman (1994, p. 2) have defined a stereotype as a "cognitive structure that contains the perceiver's knowledge, beliefs, and expectations about a human group." In this later definition the question of accuracy is omitted; rather, emphasis is placed on the potential complexity of the stereotype as a cognitive entity.

Ashmore and Del Boca (1981) have identified three approaches to the definition and use of stereotypes. One approach envisions stereotypes as motivational constructs that frequently serve intergroup attitudes (prejudice). This orientation has its roots in psychodynamic theories and is typified by Allport's (1954, p. 187) contention that stereotypes are used to "justify (rationalize) our conduct." The sociocultural approach has focused on stereotypes as means of transmitting knowledge and folklore about groups. Finally, from a social-cognitive perspective, stereotypes are structured cognitions about groups, as typified by Hamilton and Sherman's definition above. Recently, Oakes, Haslam, and Turner (1994) have questioned the rigidity of stereotypes. They have argued that stereotypes are more fluid and changeable than many past researchers have supposed (e.g., Allport, 1954; Brigham, 1971; Stangor & Lange, 1994).

Regardless of how one conceptualizes a stereotype, most research can be sorted into a few inevitable categories. Beginning with the classic work by Katz and Braly (1933), some researchers have concentrated on cataloguing the content of stereotypes. They have surveyed stereotypes attributed to a variety of groups (e.g., gender, race, nationality, occupation). A second line of research has focused on stereotypes as justifications for attitudes, especially for prejudice (e.g., Ashmore & Del Boca, 1981). A third literature has examined the role of stereotypes in person perception (e.g., Hamilton, 1979, 1981; Hamilton & Trolier, 1986). Topics addressed by this approach have included, for instance, the role of stereotypes in creating self-fulfilling prophecies and recall bias for stereotype-consistent information. A fourth line of research has addressed the impact of counterstereotypic information. Specifically, under what circumstances are stereotypes likely to be modified in response to inconsistent information (e.g., Hamilton & Sherman, 1994; Weber & Crocker, 1983)? A fifth area of work has focused on conditions under which stereotypes are likely to affect a person's judgments and actions. For instance, Turner and colleagues have examined the role of social context in the formation and salience of group stereotypes (Oakes et al., 1994).

Although each of these topics has merit, it seems to us that the issue of when stereotypes are likely to be used is critical to an evaluation of the importance of stereotype research as a whole. Critics of laboratory-based social research rightfully question the external validity of its findings. Often the most troubling question is not whether the findings are "real," but whether that reality is a creature of the laboratory, unable to thrive on the outside. As researchers, we tend to regard our findings with Promethean awe even as outsiders see them as Frankenstein's children, alien to the natural world. Although few would question the existence of stereotypic beliefs outside the lab, reasonable concerns may be raised about the ways in which researchers have made stereotypes salient and have assessed them in the laboratory.

In most studies of stereotypes, the experimental procedure explicitly prompts the stereotype of interest. Thus, subjects may be provided with information about members of a group and then asked to form an impression. Subsequently, they make judgments about one or more group members. Alternatively, subjects may be presented with a target person about whom little is known except for the target's membership in a particular social group. Dependent measures assess the subjects' reliance on stereotypes when making judgments of the target. One may reasonably question whether stereotypes are as frequently or as explicitly made salient outside the lab. In other words, although this research may be valid, it may also be limited to those instances in which persons are directly induced to think of (or to construct) their stereotypes of a given target group. Thus, the issue of when stereotypes are likely to be used is of importance, not merely as a topic in its own right, but also as a forum to assess the validity of much stereotype research.

STEREOTYPE USAGE

When are stereotypes likely to be used? The simplest response is that they are used when they are cued by the situational context, especially the actions of others (e.g., Bodenhausen & Wyer, 1985; Fazio, 1986, 1990). Once made salient, stereotypes can influence what a person attends to and how he or she processes social information (Berman, Read, & Kenny, 1983; Hamilton & Trolier, 1986). An interesting issue is how conscious or automatic the influence of stereotypes is. Some investigators (e.g., Devine, 1989; Macrae & Shepherd, 1989) report evidence for automatic or involuntary arousal of stereotypes. Subjects in this research were typically exposed to words associated with social stereotypes at durations below conscious awareness. In comparison to control subjects, they made more stereotype-consistent interpretations of the ambiguous actions of a target. On the other hand, when stereotypic words were made more obvious, subjects made fewer stereotypic judgments, perhaps so as not to appear to be biased by their use of stereotypes.

Research on the automaticity of stereotyping indicates that stereotypes may influence people's judgments without their making a conscious decision to use them. By implication, then, people may have to make a conscious decision not to use stereotypes if the default action is to use a stereotype when a stimulus cue associated with it has been detected. From this perspective, stereotypes can be likened to conditioned responses that will automatically be elicited by associated stimuli.

Second, stereotypes may be actively employed when no information is available about the target aside from the target's membership in a social group. Under this circumstance, people may consider a stereotype to be a best guess about the target and use it to interpret the target's actions as well as to form their own judgments and responses. In essence, the stereotype is employed as a default strategy in the absence of individuating information about the target (e.g., Locksley, Borgida, Brekke, & Hepburn, 1980; Locksley, Hepburn, & Ortiz, 1982).

Third, stereotypes are also likely to be brought into play when they are relevant to one's self-identity. To the extent that a particular self-identity is salient, one is likely to categorize others along dimensions relevant to that identity. Stereotypes associated with those outgroup categories should then be more readily accessed. For example, when contemplating a political decision, an individual may classify acquaintances in terms of relevant political ingroups and outgroups. Expectations and stereotypes associated with those groups should then become salient and may influence subsequent interactions with them. Similarly, salience of an outgroup may cue a complementary ingroup identity and the corresponding stereotypes associated with both groups (McGuire, McGuire, Child, & Fujioka, 1978; McGuire & Padawer-Singer, 1978; Wilder & Shapiro, 1986). To take a personal example, in a room full of women, gender is a highly salient self-categorization for either of us. Moreover, we are likely to infer that our presence makes the category of gender salient for the women as well. Consequently, we will be perceived and judged by how our behavior corresponds to expectations associated with our gender category.

Fourth, stereotypes are likely to be employed as a means of defending one's self-concept. This is the classic motivation position (Allport, 1954; Ashmore & Del Boca, 1981; Turner & Giles, 1981). People may employ stereotypes (particularly negative ones) of an outgroup in order to feel good about themselves or to protect us from perceived threats. For example, the belief that members of an outgroup are intellectually inferior can help sustain a positive view of one's own abilities. Encountering an outgroup member who behaves intelligently may trigger an explanation that preserves the self-enhancing stereotype (e.g., that person has benefited from enrichment programs; that person is an exception to the rule).

Fifth, stereotypes may be employed as well-learned habits or heuristics that are accessed when careful processing of social information is not feasible. Under conditions of cognitive overload induced by task complexity or stress, people may fall back on their stereotypes as a guide for social interaction. In this manner, stereotypes function like the dominant responses of social facilitation. An experiment by Gilbert and Hixon (1991) illustrates this argument. They manipulated the degree to which subjects were made cognitively "busy" by having to attend to multiple tasks. Cognitive demand was manipulated before or after subjects viewed an Asian or a Caucasian experimenter. Subjects who were initially exposed to the Asian experimenter and were then made cognitively "busy" rated her more stereotypically than did subjects under low cognitive demand.

Sixth, stereotypes are likely to be used as a cognitive shortcut that frees one to focus on other matters. This is the complement to our fifth point. Rather than using stereotypes because their attention is constrained, people may employ stereotypes to free up their attention. Categorization of persons into a social group makes salient the expectations, including stereotypes, associated with that group. To the extent that those stereotypes are firmly believed, a perceiver may assume that the group members' actions will be congruent with expectations and consequently may monitor them less closely. This in turn frees processing capacity for other uses. Moreover, individuals may differ in their need for certainty (e.g., Roney & Sorrentino, 1987) or closure (e.g., Kruglanski, Peri, & Zakai, 1991) in any given setting. Certainly personality differences such as these may augment or diminish the likelihood of an individual's relying on stereotypes as a cognitive device for interpretation of and response to the social world.

Finally, and of central importance to this chapter, reliance on stereotypes may increase following affective arousal. Three lines of argument can be marshaled to support this hypothesis. Two of these arguments are essentially different interpretations of the same process, whereas the third one differs fundamentally from the others. Following an overview of these arguments, we will review the few studies that have directly examined the relationship between affect and stereotyping. Then we offer a model that summarizes these data, along with the implications of this work for intergroup relations.

1. Cognitive limitation hypothesis. Affect will foster increased reliance on stereotypes to the extent that the affect consumes a person's attention or capacity for active processing of information. This argument is based on the premise that attention is finite and selective. The more an individual's affective state garners attention, the less capacity should be available for other tasks. Consequently, the person will rely on available schemas or expectations (such as social stereotypes) to compensate for the reduction in available attention. This hypothesis is essentially the "cognitive overload" argument (the fifth point raised just above) applied to affective states. Strong affect is hypothesized to consume degrees of freedom in active processing, with the result that perceivers fall back on habits and cognitive schemas, such as stereotypes, rather than attending fully to their social environment. For instance, when aroused at the prospect of an impending fear-producing stimulus, a perceiver may focus on coping with that affect, and thus may have less available attention free to monitor on other aspects of the situation. In an intergroup context, this process should encourage reliance on stereotypes associated with the outgroup.

2. Affect consistency hypothesis. Affect should trigger similarly valenced cognitions: Pleasant affect should make pleasant cognitions salient whereas unpleasant affect should trigger negative cognitions. By implication, positive affect should increase the availability of positive social stereotypes, and negative affect ought to make negative stereotypes more salient. This hypothesis follows from two large literatures that have examined consistency as an organizing and motivating principle for cognitions. Social psychologists have argued for more than a generation that persons are motivated to maintain consistency among their beliefs and between their beliefs and their behavior (Abelson et al., 1968; Aronson, 1969). Motivation for consistency is thought to be particularly strong when beliefs are relevant to one's self-concept. In addition, spreading-activation models of cognitive organization have maintained that associated networks of cogni-

tions are created on the basis of affect and belief consistency. Stimulation of a particular feeling or belief triggers others that have been associated, and this activation spreads outward from the source along pathways created by past association (e.g., Bower, 1981).

3. Affect attribution hypothesis. Awareness of affect should instigate an attempt to explain it. To the extent that the source of the affect is not immediately obvious, the affect is likely to be used as information to direct and interpret subsequent cognitions (Schwarz & Clore, 1988). To cite an example used by Schwarz (1990), if I am feeling good because of pleasant weather and I am asked to recall events from kindergarten, I should be more likely to recall positive events if I have not already attributed my good mood to the weather. The affect attribution argument can be applied to stereotyping as follows: Affect is likely to trigger valence-consistent cognitions, including stereotypes, when the source of the affect has not been clearly labeled.

The cognitive limitation, affect consistency, and affect attribution hypotheses are clearly not incompatible and perhaps not even independent. For instance, affect may distract a person from carefully attending to the behavior of members of an outgroup (cognitive limitation hypothesis). At the same time, affect may trigger similarly valenced cognitions (affect consistency and affect attribution hypotheses), which in turn may be the source of further distractions.

RESEARCH ON AFFECT AND STEREOTYPING

Before we review the literature on affect and stereotyping, it may be useful to define "affect." In this chapter, "affect" is defined as either a mood or an emotion. "Emotion" refers to a specific feeling state that usually has an easily identifiable source and a target (Isen, 1984). In addition, we often use the term "emotion" to refer to a feeling state that impels people to some action or coping strategy. In other words, emotions are often hard to ignore; they are "hot." On the other hand, the term "mood" refers to a more diffuse feeling state (e.g., general pleasantness or unpleasantness) that may be both less intense and less focused than an emotion. Because of the difficulty in separating emotion and mood beyond the application of common sense and consensus of opinion, we do not force a rigid distinction unless it is important to interpretation of the literature reviewed here. We employ the term "affective state" to refer generally to both emotions and moods.

Relatively few studies have directly examined the effect of affect on stereotyping. Consequently, it is difficult to come to any strong, sweeping conclusion about that relationship. To confound us further, even when experimenters have endeavored to create the same affective state across studies, they have often employed different operationalizations. In addition, both target stereotypes and dependent measures have usually varied from experiment to experiment.

Mackie et al. (1989) manipulated the mood of subjects who then read a series of trait statements about target persons. Later, the subjects estimated the frequency of the traits they had seen. As the first of two allegedly separate experiments, subjects watched a videotape containing either a comedy excerpt (happy or positive mood), interviews with cancer patients (sad or negative mood), or a description of how cork is selected for wine bottles (neutral mood). Then their mood was assessed. For the second experiment, they read statements about fictitious persons who were either accountants, construction workers, lawyers, or policemen. Two attributes were ascribed to each stimulus person. Half of the subjects saw positive attributes associated with each occupation, while the others saw negative traits. After exposure to the stimulus set, subjects estimated the number of times each trait had described the members of each job category.

The main finding was an interaction between mood and estimates of trait occurrence. Subjects showed an illusory-correlation effect (Hamilton & Rose, 1980) when their mood was inconsistent with the valence of the traits they had read. In other words, subjects overestimated the frequency of positive stereotypic traits when they had received the negative mood induction, and overestimated the frequency of negative traits when they had received the positive mood induction.

In a follow-up experiment, Mackie et al. (1989) reported that subjects took longer to read sentences that contained stereotype-unrelated attributes than sentences that contained stereotype-confirming information. They interpreted their findings as evidence for mood effects on the encoding of information. Mood that is incongruent with information biases encoding against that information. Consequently, subjects are more likely to use existing stereotypes or expectations when trying to recall whether that information was present.

Bodenhausen and Kramer (1990) manipulated mood state by asking subjects to recall events that were either happy, sad, or angry. Following the mood induction, subjects were asked to make a judgment about the guilt of a student who had been accused either of cheating or of committing an assault. In the case of cheating, the student was either identified as an athlete or not. For the assault, the student was given a name that either suggested he was Latino (Robert Garcia) or not. Subjects in the happy and angry conditions judged the stereotypic defendant (athlete for the cheating scenario and Latino for the assault) as more likely to be guilty than subjects in either the sad or control conditions judged him to be. Thus, happy and angry subjects made more stereotypic judgments of the target, but no such effect was observed for sad subjects.

Baron, Burgess, Kao, and Logan (1990) examined the impact of affect on stereotyping in a dental setting. In the first of two experiments, subjects completed a mood measure assessing their anxiety while waiting for a dentist appointment. Then they read a series of sentences involving members of occupational groups (e.g., "Sue, a librarian, is wise and gentle"). The statements systematically varied the stereotypicality of the actors' behaviors, using a variation of the Hamilton and Rose (1980) illusory-correlation paradigm. Anxious subjects significantly overestimated the correlation between stereotypic traits and members of the corresponding occupation.

In Baron et al.'s second study, subjects were provided with information about dental procedures that was designed to generate either high or low fear. Then they were exposed to a weak persuasive message that was presented with superficial cues suggesting a strong message (e.g., applauding audience). Baron et al. reasoned that subjects who examined the message carefully would rate it poorly, whereas those who superficially examined the message would judge it to be more convincing. The latter subjects would be more affected by the peripheral cues and presentation style of the speaker. As expected, subjects in the high-fear condition rated the message as more persuasive than subjects in the low-fear condition rated it. These findings suggest that affect generated by the fear manipulation encouraged superficial processing of the message.

Forgas and Moylan (1991) showed subjects films that provoked different moods: a popular comedy series for positive mood; a film dealing with a cancer death for negative mood; a program on architecture for neutral mood. As part of an ostensibly second and unrelated experiment, subjects viewed drawings of heterosexual dyads in which both persons were members of the same race (Caucasian or Asian) or one person was Asian and one was Caucasian. Subjects then rated the stimulus persons on a set of traits. Overall, subjects in a pleasant mood rated the targets more positively than subjects in an unpleasant mood did. In addition, there was a significant interaction between mood and the racial pairing: Subjects in a good mood rated the same-race and mixed-race pairs similarly; however, subjects in an unpleasant mood rated the mixed-race pairs as less competent and likeable than the matched-race pairs. According to Forgas and Moylan, the mixed-race pairs presented a more complex unusual stimulus for subjects, and therefore demanded greater processing when evaluations were made. Consequently, a subject's mood was likely to influence judgments in a manner consistent with the literature on affect–cognition consistency (e.g., Bower, 1981; Isen, 1984). A negative mood made salient more negative conditions than a positive mood did.

A set of experiments by Wilder and Shapiro (1989a, 1989b, 1991) investigated the impact of anxiety on judgments of an outgroup member who behaved contrary to expectations about his group. Following Stephan and Stephan (1985), Wilder and Shapiro reasoned that intergroup contact may be ineffective in improving relations between groups when anxiety is generated by anticipation of contact. Such anxiety (and attempts to cope with it) may poison the interaction, not only because the negative affect is associated with the outgroup, but also because it interferes with information processing in the contact setting. To the extent that anxiety distracts individuals, they should be more likely to interpret the contact experiences in terms of their expectations or stereotypes of the outgroup. In short, anxiety at the prospect of interacting with an outgroup may diminish the effectiveness of the contact experience because of the distraction created by coping with the negative affect.

In a series of experiments conducted to test this line of reasoning, subjects were made anxious at the prospect of either making an embarrassing speech, posing for some embarrassing pictures, or receiving a set of electric shocks. Then they viewed a tape of a group interaction in which one of the four group members behaved quite differently from the majority (e.g., he behaved incompetently while the other members behaved competently). Subjects who were anxious underestimated the degree to which the deviant differed from the majority. Thus, anxious subjects were more likely than nonanxious subjects to judge the deviant to be acting according to expectations about the group, based on the majority's behavior. Moreover, self-reported anxiety was significantly correlated with judgments that assimilated the deviant's behavior in the direction of the majority.

In one of these experiments, following the mood induction, subjects viewed a set of humorous cartoons designed to reduce anxiety. These subjects did not make more stereotypic judgments of the deviant outgroup member. This finding, coupled with the strong correlations between self-reported anxiety and stereotypic judgments in these studies, suggests that anxiety was a causal factor in subjects' stereotypic evaluations of the outgroup member despite his counterstereotypic actions.

Finally, Kim and Baron (1988) manipulated level of physiological arousal rather than a specific mood or affect. Arousal was induced by physical exertion (subjects exercised on a stationary bicycle). Then the subjects viewed word pairs, some of which were stereotypically associated (e.g., "practical" and "serious"). When asked to recall word pairings, aroused subjects showed an illusory-correlation effect. They overestimated the occurrence of stereotypic word pairs.

SUMMARY AND EVALUATION OF THE RESEARCH

The pattern of findings from these diverse research programs defies a single summary statement. Overall, the evidence suggests that positive affect enhances reliance on stereotypes (Bodenhausen & Kramer, 1990; Mackie et al., 1989), although this relationship was limited to negative traits in the Mackie et al. research. A simple conclusion for negative affect is even more problematic. Anger and anxiety/fear facilitated greater reliance on stereotypes in several studies (Bodenhausen & Kramer, 1990; Baron et al., 1990; Wilder & Shapiro, 1989a, 1989b, 1991). However, findings have been least consistent for sadness. Mackie et al. (1989) reported greater stereotyping when sad subjects made estimates of negative stereotypic traits. Bodenhausen and Kramer (1990) failed to find an effect for sadness. Forgas and Moylan (1991) reported that sad subjects made less positive judgments of mixed racial groups (which may be interpreted as evidence for an ethnocentric, if not stereotypic, response).

In evaluating these findings, we should note some aspects of the methodologies. To begin with, in all of these studies the manipulation of affect was independent of the target group about which stereotypic judgments were later made. In other words, affect was incidental rather than integral to the later judgments (Bodenhausen, 1993). This was done, understandably, to assess the independent role of affect as a cause of stereotyping. If the target group had directly aroused the affect, it would have been difficult to ascertain the role of affect per se in subsequent judgments of that group. Later judgments may have reflected the cognitions that were made salient by the target's role in the instigation of the affect. But precisely because of this concern for control, we must be careful in generalizing this body of work to situations where the target group is the source of the affect.

A second point that bears mention about the affect–stereotyping research is that assessment of the affect manipulation usually occurred after affect was induced and before subjects were presented with the target group. In the typical procedure, subjects were presented with the second judgment task as a separate experiment from the earlier affect induction. This cover story was reinforced by the explicit measurement of affect before the second experiment began (usually via self-report rating scales). An exception to this pattern can be found in one of the studies by Wilder and Shapiro (1991). So that the potential reactivity of the mood measures could be assessed, some subjects did not complete a manipulation check for affect following its induction. Data from these subjects did not differ from results obtained from subjects who had completed the mood check before making judgments of the target person. This finding suggests that the potential reactivity of the manipulation check may not be a significant concern in this research. Nevertheless, it is worth pointing out that most of the studies did not assess the impact that the manipulation check may have had on the affect it was designed to measure.

We raise the issue of the manipulation check because of two concerns. First, a manipulation check for affect focuses subjects' attention on their feelings. Attending to their affect may inflate the impact of the manipulation as subjects make a behavioral commitment (responses on the mood inventory) to that state. Second (and more important to an interpretation of this literature), by focusing subjects on their feeling states, the manipulation check may distract them from attending to the second task. This possibility leads us to an interpretation of the affect–stereotyping research. Our explanation is based largely on the role of attention as a critical mediator.

In the next two sections, we present a model of the relationship between affect and stereotyping. We have divided the model into two versions, one for incidental affect and one for integral affect. "Incidental affect" is affect that has been created apart from the target group. Most of the research reviewed above has employed manipulations of incidental affect. For example, subjects watch a videotape that makes them sad; then they make some judgments about the target group. "Integral affect" refers to affect whose source is attributed directly to the target group. For example, when subjects are frustrated by criticism from another group, the ensuing anger is attributed to that group.

MODEL OF THE RELATIONSHIP BETWEEN INCIDENTAL AFFECT AND STEREOTYPING

With the exception of sadness, experimental evidence points to incidental affect as a facilitator of stereotypic judgments. Whether this relationship is monotonic or not is open to question. It seems reasonable to suppose that strength of affect ought to be correlated with reliance on stereotypes, but this issue has not yet been addressed.

Figure 12.1 depicts a model of the relationship between incidental affect and stereotyping. We propose that incidental affect can have two consequences relevant to the eventual use of stereotypes. First, incidental affect can generate physiological arousal, which in turn constrains attention as an individual attempts to monitor and explain that arousal (far right column of Figure 12.1). By "physiological arousal," we refer to body reactions that result from either pleasant or unpleasant affect (e.g., activation of sympathetic responses). This arousal can distract a perceiver from external stimuli, in addition to amplifying the affective experience.

As reviewed earlier, Kim and Baron (1988) reported that subjects aroused by physical exercise displayed an increase in stereotypic judgments. Aroused subjects may be distracted in a number of ways. First, they may attend to internal cues created by their arousal state. To the extent that any emotional state creates physiological arousal, the arousal can be a distraction from careful attention to

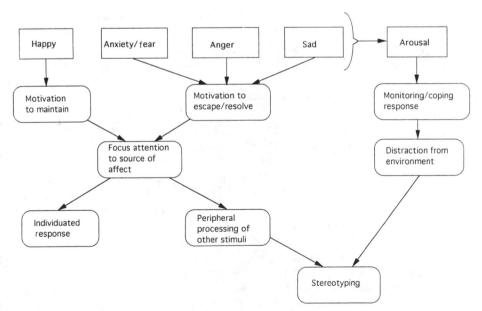

FIGURE 12.1   Model of the relationship between incidental affect and stereotyping.

the external world. Distraction ought to be particularly likely when the external environment appears to be irrelevant to the source of the arousal, as in the affect–stereotyping studies in which the stereotypic judgments are made during a task that is apparently not connected to the task that created the arousal. In addition, aroused individuals may ruminate on their performance in an attempt to assess how well they did (e.g., performance on the exercise bike in the Kim & Baron work). Such thoughts can distract them from careful attention to subsequent information. When judgments are later made about that subsequent information, the individuals rely on expectations, including social stereotypes, to fill in the missing information.

Second, affect can instigate coping reactions as the individuals respond to motivation induced by the affect and act either to cultivate positive feelings or to escape negative feelings. We are not in the position to argue which of these two avenues is more potent. Nor do we maintain that they are independent, even though they are depicted as such for the sake of clarity in Figure 12.1.

Attention to any of these reactions consumes individuals' finite cognitive capacity and should diminish their ability to attend closely to other stimuli. In other words, having their minds on the affective state encourages superficial processing of information about other external stimuli. Persons who are distracted should show increased reliance on pre-existing schemas such as stereotypes when making judgments (Gilbert & Hixon, 1991). In coursing through the model of Figure 12.1, we consider the following affective states: happiness, fear/anxiety, anger, and sadness.

For most persons, pleasant affect is desirable, and behavior is directed toward maintaining and enriching it (cf. Isen, 1984). Positive affect can be maintained in several related ways. First, people often dwell on the source of that affect (e.g., pleasant reminiscence, humorous anecdote). With some attention allocated to affect maintenance, they may be less vigilant on subsequent tasks unrelated to the source of the pleasant affect (Figure 12.1). Second, the content of the positive affect may directly distract people by triggering similarly valenced thoughts and memories (cf. Bower, 1981).

Third, Schwarz and Bless (1991) have argued that pleasant affect induces mindlessness whereas negative affect fosters more thoughtfulness. When people are steeped in positive feelings, they tend to be less focused and intense than when feelings run sour. Consequently, they may process new information that could threaten their pleasant feelings superficially, as a means of preserving our positive affective state. Peripheral attention to external stimuli should foster greater dependence on stereotypes when judgments are made.

Subjects experiencing the negative emotions of fear/anxiety or anger should also be distracted, but by different means than those basking in positive affect (Figure 12.1). Fear, anxiety, and anger are emotional states for which there are usually specific sources or threats available (Schwarz, 1990). We expect that persons experiencing those emotions are likely to focus on the perceived source or threat and allocate attention in that direction. Consequently, they too may be distracted from the subsequent stereotype judgment task.

When we consider sadness (Figure 12.1), the simple distraction hypothesis is still applicable, but in an inverted form. Subjects who have been reminded of personal sad events (e.g., failure to land a job, doomed romance) or those who have been exposed to a depressing scene (e.g., a film of cancer patients) might well be motivated to distract themselves from these events as a means of escaping the aversive affect. An escape response should be particularly attractive when there are no means available to remedy the source of the affect (e.g., subjects cannot help the cancer patients or change past personal events). The second judgment task in these experiments provides a welcome opportunity to avoid thinking about the sad events, so subjects may focus closely on this task. Increased vigilance is manifested in careful, thorough attention to that task. As a result, sad subjects' stereotyping of the targets declines, relative to sterotyping by happy, angry, or anxious subjects. It should be noted that distraction induced by a desire to escape negative affect is not unique to sadness. Certainly, anger can also generate a desire to escape, particularly if there are no apparent means of dealing with the perceived cause of that emotion. However, to the extent that sad individuals attend to the feelings generated by their sadness, they should be as open to distraction as persons experiencing other affective states. Thus, we might expect greater variability among sad subjects than among happy, angry, or anxious subjects in their use of stereotypes. This may account for the mixed results obtained in studies examining sadness and stereotyping.

Another possibility, of course, is that the manipulations of sadness in these experiments were not as potent as the manipulations of the other affective states. This possibility again demonstrates the necessity of multiple manipulations of these affective states with different levels within the experiments.

Both Mackie et al. (1989) and Forgas and Moylan (1991) reported some evidence for a relationship between sadness and stereotyping. In both cases, however, their findings were more complex than we would like. In the Mackie et al. research, sad subjects stereotyped target persons on positive traits but not on negative ones. In the Forgas and Moylan work, sad subjects lowered their evaluation of a mixed-race pair (Caucasian and Asian), which the authors interpreted as consistent with Caucasian students' stereotypes about Asians. However, Bodenhausen and Kramer (1990, Experiment 1) reported no increased reliance on stereotypes among sad subjects.

As we sort out this conflicting pattern of results, it is instructive to consider differences in the manipulations of mood. Bodenhausen and Kramer asked each subject to recall a sad personal event. Because past events cannot be changed, it is unlikely that ruminating about a sad event helped a subject to cope with the negative affect. Rather, direction of attention outward toward the second task (stereotyping task) provided a means of coping with the aversive affect. Thus, subjects should have been more focused on the "distracting" information about the target person, who was irrelevant to the subjects' sad state. This should have yielded a more careful analysis of the target and less reliance on stereotypes when making judgments.

On the other hand, in the studies where sadness was created by having subjects view a tape of cancer patients (Mackie et al., 1989; Forgas & Moylan, 1991), mood effects on focus of attention become less clear to us. One possibility is that the information as well as the affect generated by the videotapes in those studies distracted subjects as they either dwelled on that information or attempted to cope with the induced mood. However, they also may have felt helpless in the face of the depressing information and focused on the second task as a distractor. The net result, when averaged across subjects, was a more variable pattern of behavior with greater stereotyping on some traits but not on others (Mackie et al., 1989).

Our reading of the sparse literature that has examined the relationship between sadness and stereotyping suggests greater variability in subjects' behavior when they experience sadness as compared to other affective states (e.g., anger, anxiety, happiness). This conclusion fits with the observation that sadness and depression can cause an inward or an outward shift in attention as a person attempts to alleviate the negative mood (Isen, 1984). Attention may be focused outward as a means of distracting oneself from a negative memory. In an intergroup context, attention focused externally should facilitate the acquisition of available information about present outgroup members, and should lessen the impact of stereotypes on judgments of them. To the extent their behavior violates stereotypes of the outgroup, this in turn ought to lessen the impact of group stereotypes on judgments of those members. However, rumination on the source of the negative affect should focus attention internally. In that case, one is likely to overlook or miss some specific behaviors by those outgroup members and to rely instead on group stereotypes when making judgments of those individuals.

MODEL OF THE RELATIONSHIP BETWEEN INTEGRAL AFFECT AND STEREOTYPING

As already noted, the affect–stereotyping research has mostly employed manipulations of incidental affect. We believe that the independence of the affect manipulation from the target group enhances the distractiveness of those manipulations, and thereby encourages subsequent stereotypic judgments of the target. An exception to this pattern of using incidental affect can be found in a set of studies by Wilder and Shapiro (1989a) in which affect was induced directly by the target outgroup. Subjects received hostile feedback from members of a competing outgroup. Anxious subjects were more likely to judge counterstereotypic behavior by an outgroup member as stereotypic than were nonanxious subjects who had not been provoked by the outgroup.

Figure 12.2 depicts one plausible chain of events for integral affect. Major differences between the models in Figures 12.1 and 12.2 occur at two steps. First, in the case of integral affect, attention should be focused on the target group as the source of the affect. Second, attributions to the target group will cue expec-

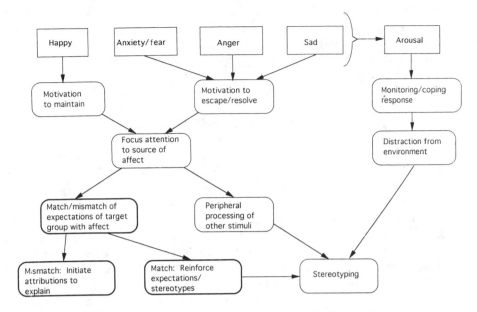

FIGURE 12.2   Model of the relationship between integral affect and stereotyping.

tations (including stereotypes) associated with that group. A match in valence between the stereotypes and the affect should reinforce the stereotypes even if the behavior engaged in by the outgroup is not directly relevant to the stereotype. A mismatch between the valence of a subject's affect and the stereotypes cued by an outgroup should provoke an attribution. In other words, a mismatch triggers a search for an explanation.

If an individual possesses generally positive stereotypes about an outgroup, and the outgroup appears to have induced positive affect, this sequence should reinforce existing positive stereotypes even though the content of the stereotypes may not necessarily be manifested in the specific action of that group. For instance, if one believes that a group is untrustworthy and that its members behave cruelly, negative feelings induced by this perceived cruelty should reinforce the negative stereotype of untrustworthiness. This argument follows the logic of Kelly's (1955) principle of evaluative consistency: If a perceiver believes that a person has a favorable (or an unfavorable) trait, the perceiver is likely to infer other traits of similar valence. The end product should be a strengthening of positive (or negative) stereotypes of the target person's group.

On the other hand, if a perceiver has generally negative (or positive) stereotypes about an outgroup and this group appears to be responsible for positive (or negative) affect, then the perceiver will search for an explanation for this apparent inconsistency. Increased vigilance, in turn, should foster a more careful examination of the actions of the outgroup that have aroused the unexpected affect (i.e., unpleasant affect from a positively evaluated outgroup or pleasant affect from a negatively evaluated outgroup). Consequently, the perceiver will attend closely to the outgroup's behavior, make more individuated judgments of behavior, and be less inclined to rely on group stereotypes, whether favorable or unfavorable.

SUMMARY OF THE MODELS

As indicated in Figures 12.1 and 12.2, the models relating incidental and integral affect to stereotyping share several factors and could well be combined in a single diagram. We have chosen to separate them, both to clarify our presentation and to emphasize the importance of how the perceived source of affect guides an individual's attention and coping responses. In general, incidental affect is likely to distract the perceiver, thereby increasing reliance on heuristics such as social stereotypes. On the other hand, integral affect focuses attention on the outgroup and should tap stereotypes associated with that group. A match between those expectations and the affect attributed to the outgroup should reinforce stereotypes. A mismatch will provoke a more thorough, individuated examination of the outgroup's behavior. This in turn may lead to reinforcement of outgroup stereotypes or to a change in the stereotypes, depending on the outcome of the attributions generated by the mismatch of affect and expectations.

To the extent that affect generates arousal, the arousal can be a source of distraction, regardless of whether the affect is integral or incidental in origin. Any such distraction can foster peripheral processing of information about the outgroup. Consequently, we would predict that the "hotter" or more urgent the affect, the greater should be the potential for distraction caused by the physiological arousal per se. Therefore, strength of affect should be positively correlated with reliance on stereotypes when a person is making judgments of outgroup members. Certainly, it is a common observation that strong emotions are associated with extreme, often simplistic responses. For example, when cut off by a fellow driver, one of us (who will remain anonymous) admits to always noting the age of the driver and to attributing the miscreant's deeds to membership in that age category (e.g., "old geezers," "wild and crazy teens"). This often occurs as a seemingly automatic response to traffic terror, even though when calm he realizes that age is an unreliable predictor of driving habits for any given individual. The social facilitation literature is also consistent with this line of reasoning. This literature has shown a relationship between arousal (induced by an audience or co-actors) and the facilitation of dominant or well-learned responses (e.g., Wilder & Shapiro, 1991). To the extent that stereotypes can be regarded as dominant responses to a social category, we would expect from the facilitation literature to find an association between arousal generated by affect and the use of stereotypes.

APPLICATION TO INTERGROUP CONTACT

One situation that is likely to produce affect, especially negative emotions and moods, occurs when hostile groups are brought together. If relations between groups are poor, then contact (or the prospect of contact) is likely to generate negative affect, including anger, anxiety, or fear (e.g., Stephan & Stephan, 1985; Wilder, 1993a, 1993b). Negative affect can distract the perceiver from careful processing of information in the contact setting (a likely response to incidental affect—see Figure 12.1) and/or can trigger negative stereotypes (a likely response to integral affect—see Figure 12.2). Either reaction should result in greater reliance on stereotypes and less success for the contact experience (Wilder & Shapiro, 1989a, 1989b, 1991). By implication, we might expect that reduction of negative affect in the contact setting should enhance the benefits of the contact experience. Although this is a tempting inference, we believe that the relationship between a reduction in negative affect and improvement of intergroup relations is more complex, as we discuss in the next several paragraphs.

The notion that a pleasant environment will facilitate successful contact follows readily from classic principles of conditioning. Indeed, contact in a pleasant setting can be thought of as the social analogue of individual desensitization therapy. But the track record of positive contact by itself is poor. As many researchers have pointed out (e.g., Amir, 1969; Brewer & Miller, 1984; Hewstone & Brown, 1986; Sherif & Sherif, 1973), mere contact, even in an ostensibly pleasant circumstance, is insufficient to ensure a favorable interaction between the groups and a lessening of intergroup hostility. Contact may be successful when the groups are accorded equal status and interact in cooperative pursuit of a common goal. Contact is also more likely to be successful when it involves intimate interaction and when it has the support of institutions and reference others respected by the groups. In addition to these factors, we believe that a perceiver's affective state can be influential in determining the outcomes of a contact experience. This can occur in three ways.

First, the valence of the affect generated in the contact setting can trigger similarly valenced cognitions (including outgroup stereotypes), which in turn reinforce or disconfirm expectations of the outgroup. Second, attributions made for arousal can be influential when the source of affect is attributed, at least in part, to the outgroup. Third, affect can become a draw on attention that distracts a perceiver from focusing on the behavior of outgroup members in the contact setting.

Consistent with the models that we have sketched in this chapter, these three consequences of affect can either increase or decrease the likelihood of using stereotypes. In general, negative (or positive) stereotypes of an outgroup are likely to be cued by negative (or positive) affect. However, this cuing may be tempered by the perceiver's interpretation of the source of his or her affect. For instance, positive affect experienced in the presence of a disliked outgroup may have little impact on negative evaluations of the outgroup if this positive affect is judged not to be caused by that group and is therefore incidental to the outgroup. Moreover, whether it is incidental or integral, affect that distracts the perceiver from attending to the behavior of the outgroup (e.g., strong arousal that demands internal coping, or cognitions generated by affect that focus the perceiver on memories of distant events) will diminish the impact of the outgroup's behavior in the contact setting. If this behavior disconfirms negative stereotypes of the outgroup, its effect will be largely lost on the distracted perceiver (e.g., Wilder & Shapiro, 1989a, 1989b, 1991).

We believe that integral and incidental affect can help explain the failure of contact to reduce bias in an apparently pleasant context. To begin with, manipulations of pleasant contact often involve incidental affect. Part of the rationale behind the contact hypothesis is that hostile ingroup and outgroup members must be brought together under favorable conditions (equal status, cooperation, intimacy). The ensuing interaction will produce both positive affect and stereotype-disconfirming information. The weakness in this reasoning, however, lies with the attributions persons make of the positive affect generated by pleasant contact. If this affect is perceived as incidental (attributed to an agent other than the outgroup), then it may function as a distraction, so that pre-existing attitudes and beliefs about the outgroup remain unchallenged.

On the other hand, if the outgroup is perceived to be responsible for the pleasant setting (integral affect), then the pleasant mood created may very well lessen hostility to the outgroup and pave the way for changes in negative stereotypes. Of course, the success of this tactic depends greatly on the ease with which persons can discount the positive affect generated by the outgroup. To the extent that the outgroup's pleasant actions can be judged as exceptions to the rule or as having been forced by an outside authority, the outgroup's association with the pleasant affect should be discounted.

Some research on cooperative intergroup contact by Worchel and his colleagues (see Worchel, 1986) is consistent with the ideas advanced here. Worchel points out that the success of a contact experience is influenced both by its outcomes and by the past relations between the groups. When the groups have a history of poor relations, and they cooperate on a task but that cooperation ends in failure, relations between the groups do not improve. Cooperative contact per se is not sufficient to lessen bias when the groups have experienced the frustration of failure. Although Worchel and colleagues did not assess any role that affect and stereotyping played in their findings, we believe that their results are quite consistent with the affect–stereotyping model outlined in this chapter. When relations between groups have been poor, it is very likely that members of each group harbor negative expectations about the respective outgroup. Frustration, anger, or disappointment experienced following failure of a cooperative venture should cue existing negative beliefs about the outgroup (as in the model of integral affect and stereotyping; see Figure 12.2). Although the failure experience may not be part of the history of relations between the groups, and therefore may not reinforce beliefs about how the groups work together, the negative affect created by the failure should reinforce negative affect associated with the outgroup, and thereby should strengthen existing unfavorable beliefs about that group. The result should be a strengthening of negative stereotypes of the outgroup even if the outgroup behavior does not relate directly to those stereotypes. The path for this reinforcement of stereotypes follows from the shared negative affect associated with both the outgroup and the failed contact experience.

In a similar vein, Wilder and Shapiro (1989a) demonstrated that when subjects were experiencing integral anxiety, negative expectations about an outgroup colored their judgments of the objectively favorable behavior of an individual outgroup member. In those experiments, subjects who expected to compete with a hostile outgroup experienced increased anxiety and rated the positive behavior of an outgroup member as more negative (consistent with their expectations about the outgroup) than when their anxiety was low because they did not expect to compete with the outgroup. Furthermore, the greater the level of self-reported anxiety, the more subjects relied on negative expectations about the outgroup, and the less they used the actual behavior of the target person to form their judgments of him.

FINAL THOUGHTS

In this chapter, we have presented three lines of reasoning that posit a relationship between affect and the use of social stereotypes. First, affect encourages the use of outgroup stereotypes when that affect is incidental to the target outgroup and thereby is a potent source of distraction from careful examination of the outgroup members' actions. In this circumstance, the perceiver relies on pre-existing stereotypes to construct and interpret perceptions of the situation. Second, affect encourages the use of outgroup stereotypes when the affect is integral to the target group and the valence of this affect is consistent with the valence of outgroup stereotypes. Third, when affect attributed to the outgroup (integral affect) violates expectations (positive feelings generated by a negative outgroup and vice versa), it should instigate a causal search. That search will focus attention on the specific actions of the outgroup members thought to be responsible for the affect. This should encourage a more individuated, less stereotypic evaluation of them—an evaluation based more on their perceived actions and less on general stereotypes associated with their group.

Throughout the chapter we have treated the relationship between affect and stereotyping as a general principle, regardless of the personality of the perceiver or the nature of the target group. We have hypothesized that reliance on stereotypes should increase to the extent that affect cues similarly valenced cognitions and to the extent that it distracts persons from careful examination of the actions of outgroup members. Conversely, we expect that perceivers are less likely to utilize outgroup stereotypes to the extent that affect directs attention toward the outgroup members and to the extent that careful scrutiny reveals a mismatch between their behavior and outgroup stereotypes.

In addition to these broad predictions, we also expect to find differences among persons based on their idiosyncratic skills for coping with affect, as well as on more stable personality differences. One candidate from personality research is a person's uncertainty orientation (Brouwers & Sorrentino, 1993; Sorrentino, Bobocel, Gitta, Olson, & Hewitt, 1988; Roney & Sorrentino, 1987). Sorrentino and his colleagues have reported a stable difference among persons in their reaction to uncertainty. On the basis of their research, we would expect that persons with a high need for certainty ought to be particularly likely to rely on stereotypes and other heuristics that simplify the world when they are under the pressure of strong affect. Those with a high need for certainty should devote more resources to coping with the affect or trying to escape it, thereby leaving less attention for monitoring the specific actions of outgroup members. The net result should be greater reliance on outgroup stereotypes when judgments are being made in an intergroup context. Roney and Sorrentino (1987) reported that certainty-oriented subjects had person categories less rich than those of uncertainty-oriented subjects. This finding suggests to us that certainty-oriented persons ought to be more likely to use outgroup stereotypes when interpreting the actions of outgroup members. We further expect this difference to be accentuated when the persons are affectively aroused.

As another example of a relevant personality moderator, let us consider Kruglanski's research on the need for closure (Heaton & Kruglanski, 1991; Kruglanski et al., 1991). Again, we would expect that the greater a person's need for closure, the more likely he or she will be to employ stereotypes (and other simplifying heuristics) to tie up the loose ends of social perception. In addition, we would expect differences between those high versus low in need for closure to be exaggerated under conditions of affective arousal. Thus, persons high in need for closure should show an even greater use of outgroup stereotypes when they are experiencing strong affect than should persons low in need for closure.

In conclusion, we believe that affect plays a deceptively complex role in the use of stereotypes when judgments are being made about members of an outgroup. As indicated in Figures 12.1 and 12.2, a given affective state (whether incidental or integral) can enhance the use of stereotypes, but this depends in part on the impact of the affect on the perceiver's direction of attention, the priming of similarly valenced cognitions about the outgroup, and the perceiver's attribution for the source of his or her affective state. In studying the role of stereotypes in intergroup behavior, we believe that increased attention to affect will usefully complement the dominant cognitive approach of the past two decades.

References

Abelson, R. P., Aronson, E., McGuire, W. J., Newcomb, T. M., Rosenberg, M. J., & Tannenbaum, P. H. (1968). *Theories of cognitive consistency.* Chicago: Rand McNally.

Ajzen, I., & Fishbein, M. (1980). *Understanding attitudes and predicting social behavior.* Englewood Cliffs, NJ: Prentice-Hall.

Allport, G. W. (1954). *The nature of prejudice.* Reading, MA: Addison-Wesley.

Amir, Y. (1969). Contact hypothesis in ethnic relations. *Psychological Bulletin, 71,* 319-342.

Aronson, E. (1969). The theory of cognitive dissonance: A current perspective. In L. Berkowitz (Ed.), *Advances in experimental social psychology* (Vol. 2, pp. 2-32). New York: Academic Press.

Ashmore, R. D., & Del Boca, F. K. (1981). Conceptual approaches to stereotypes and stereotyping. In D. L. Hamilton (Ed.), *Cognitive processes in stereotyping and intergroup behavior* (pp. 1-33). Hillsdale, NJ: Erlbaum.

Baron, R. S., Burgess, M. L., Kao, C. F., & Logan, H. (1990). *Fear and superficial social processing: Evidence of stereotyping and simplistic persuasion.* Paper presented at the annual convention of the Midwestern Psychological Association, Chicago.

Berman, J. S., Read, S. J., & Kenny, D. A. (1983). Processing inconsistent social information. *Journal of Personality and Social Psychology, 45,* 1211-1224.

Bodenhausen, G. V. (1993). Emotions, arousal, and stereotypic judgments: A heuristic model of affect and stereotyping. In D. M. Mackie & D. L. Hamilton (Eds.), *Affect, cognition, and stereotyping: Interactive processes in group perception* (pp. 13-37). San Diego, CA: Academic Press.

Bodenhausen, G. V., & Kramer, G. P. (1990). *Affective states trigger stereotypic judgments.* Paper presented at the annual convention of the American Psychological Society, Dallas.

Bodenhausen, G. V., & Wyer, R. S., Jr. (1985). Effects of stereotypes on decision making and information-processing strategies. *Journal of Personality and Social Psychology, 48,* 267-282.

Bower, G. H. (1981). Mood and memory. *American Psychologist, 36,* 129-148.

Brewer, M. B., & Miller, N. (1984). Beyond the contact hypothesis: Theoretical perspectives on desegregation. In N. Miller & M. B. Brewer (Eds.), *Groups in contact: The psychology of desegregation* (pp. 281-302). Orlando, FL: Academic Press.

Brigham, J. C. (1971). Ethnic stereotypes. *Psychological Bulletin, 76,* 15-38.

Brouwers, M. C., & Sorrentino, R. M. (1993). Uncertainty orientation and protection motivation theory: The role of individual differences in health compliance. *Journal of Personality and Social Psychology, 65*(1), 102-112.

Devine, P. G. (1989). Stereotypes and prejudice: Their automatic and controlled components. *Journal of Personality and Social Psychology, 56,* 5-18.

Fazio, R. H. (1986). How do attitudes guide behavior? In R. M. Sorrentino & E. T. Higgins (Eds.), *Handbook of motivation and cognition: Foundations of social behavior* (Vol. 1, pp. 204-243). New York: Guilford Press.

Fazio, R. H. (1990). Multiple processes by which attitudes guide behavior: The MODE model as an integrative framework. In M. P. Zanna (Ed.), *Advances in experimental social psychology* (Vol. 23, pp. 75-109). New York: Academic Press.

Forgas, J. P., & Moylan, S. (1991). Affective influences on stereotype judgments. *Cognition and Emotion, 5*(5-6), 379-395.

Gilbert, D. T., & Hixon, J. G. (1991). The trouble of thinking: Activation and application of stereotypic beliefs. *Journal of Personality and Social Psychology, 54,* 193-202.

Hamilton, D. L. (1979). A cognitive-attributional analysis of stereotyping. In L. Berkowitz (Ed.), *Advances in experimental social psychology* (Vol. 12, pp. 53-84). New York: Academic Press.

Hamilton, D. L. (1981). *Cognitive processes in stereotyping and intergroup behavior.* Hillsdale, NJ: Erlbaum.

Hamilton, D. L., & Rose, T. L. (1980). Illusory correlation and the maintenance of stereotypic beliefs. *Journal of Personality and Social Psychology, 39,* 832-845.

Hamilton, D. L., & Sherman, J. W. (1994). Stereotypes. In R. S. Wyer & T. K. Srull (Eds.), *Handbook of social cognition* (Vol. 2, pp. 1-68). Hillsdale, NJ: Erlbaum.

Hamilton, D. L., & Trolier, T. (1986). Stereotypes and stereotyping; An overview of the cognitive approach. In J. F. Dovidio & S. L. Gaertner (Eds.), *Prejudice, discrimination, and racism* (pp. 127-164). Orlando, FL: Academic Press.

Heaton, A. W., & Kruglanski, A. W. (1991). Person perception by introverts and extraverts under time pressure: Effects of need for closure. *Personality and Social Psychology Bulletin, 17* (2), 161–165.

Hewstone, M., & Brown, R. (1986). Contact is not enough: An intergroup perspective. In M. Hewstone & R. Brown (Eds.), *Contact and conflict in intergroup encounters* (pp. 1–44). Oxford: Blackwell.

Higgins, E. T., & Sorrentino, R. M. (Eds.). (1990). *Handbook of motivation and cognition: Foundations of social behavior* (Vol. 2). New York: Guilford Press.

Isen, A. M. (1984). Toward understanding the role of affect in cognition. In R. S. Wyer & T. J. Srull (Eds.), *Handbook of social cognition* (pp. 179–236). Hillsdale, NJ: Erlbaum.

Katz, D., & Braly, K. W. (1933). Racial stereotypes of one hundred college students. *Journal of Abnormal and Social Psychology, 61,* 82–86.

Kelly, G. A. (1955). *The psychology of personal constructs: A theory of personality.* New York: Norton.

Kim, H. S., & Baron, R. S. (1988). Exercise and illusory correlation: Does arousal heighten stereotypic processing? *Journal of Experimental Social Psychology, 24,* 366–380.

Kruglanski, A. W., Peri, N., & Zakai, D. (1991). Interactive effects of need for closure and initial confidence on social information seeking. *Social Cognition, 9*(2), 127–148.

Lippman, W. (1922). *Public opinion.* New York: Harcourt, Brace.

Locksley, A., Borgida, E., Brekke, H., & Hepburn, C. (1980). Sex stereotypes and judgment. *Journal of Personality and Social Psychology, 39,* 821–831.

Locksley, A., Hepburn, C., & Ortiz, V. (1982). Social stereotypes and judgments of individuals: An instance of the base rate fallacy. *Journal of Experimental Social Psychology, 18,* 23–42.

Mackie, D. M., Hamilton, D. L., Schroth, H. A., Carlisle, C. J., Gersho, B. F., Meneses, L. M., Nedler, B. F., & Reichel, L. D. (1989). The effects of induced mood on expectancy-based illusory correlations. *Journal of Experimental Social Psychology, 25,* 524–544.

Macrae, C. N., & Shepherd, J. W. (1989). Stereotypes and social judgments. *British Journal of Social Psychology, 28,* 319–325.

McGuire, W. J., McGuire, C. U., Child, P., & Fujioka, T. (1978). Salience of ethnicity in the spontaneous self-concept as a function of one's ethnic distinctiveness in the social environment. *Journal of Personality and Social Psychology, 36,* 511–520.

McGuire, W. J., & Padawa-Singer, A. (1978). Trait salience in the spontaneous self-concept. *Journal of Personality and Social Psychology, 33,* 743–754.

Oakes, P. J., Haslam, S. A., & Turner, J. C. (1994). *Stereotyping and social reality.* Oxford: Blackwell.

Roney, C. J. R., & Sorrentino, R. M. (1987). Uncertainty orientation and person perception: Individual differences in categorization. *Social Cognition, 5*(4), 369–382.

Schwarz, N. (1990). Feelings as information: Informational and motivational functions of affective states. In E. T. Higgins & R. M. Sorrentino (Eds.), *Handbook of motivation and cognition: Foundations of social behavior* (Vol. 2, pp. 527–561). New York: Guilford Press.

Schwarz, N., & Bless, H. (1991). Happy and mindless, but sad and smart? The impact of affective states on analytic reasoning. In J. P. Forgas (Ed.), *Emotion and social judgments* (pp. 55–71). Elmsford, New York: Pergamon Press.

Schwarz, N., & Clore, G. L. (1988). How do I feel about it? The informative function of affective states. In K. Fiedler & J. Forgas (Eds.), *Affect, cognition, and social behavior* (pp. 44–62). Toronto: Hogrefe.

Sherif, M., & Sherif, C. W. (1973). *Groups in harmony and tension: An integration of studies on intergroup relations.* New York: Octagon Books.

Sorrentino, R. M., Bobocel, D. R., Gitta, M. Z., Olson, J. M., & Hewitt, E. C. (1988). Uncertainty orientation and persuasion: Individual differences in the effects of personal relevance on social judgments. *Journal of Personality and Social Psychology, 55*(3), 357–371.

Stangor, C., & Lange, J. E. (1994). Mental representations of social groups: Advances in understanding stereotypes and stereotyping. In M. P. Zanna (Ed.), *Advances in experimental social psychology* (Vol. 26, pp. 357–405). San Diego, CA: Academic Press.

Stephan, W. G., & Stephan, C. W. (1985). Intergroup anxiety. *Journal of Social Issues, 41*(3), 157–175.

Turner, J. C., & Giles, H. (1981). *Intergroup behavior*. Chicago: University of Chicago Press.

Weber, R., & Crocker, T. (1983). Cognitive processes in the revision of stereotypic beliefs. *Journal of Personality and Social Psychology, 45*, 961–977.

Wilder, D. A. (1993a). The role of anxiety of facilitating stereotypic judgments of outgroup behavior. In D. M. Mackie & D. L. Hamilton (Eds.), *Affect, cognition, and stereotyping: Interactive processes in group perception* (pp. 87–109). San Diego, CA: Academic Press.

Wilder, D. A. (1993b). Freezing intergroup evaluations: Anxiety fosters resistance to counter-stereotypic information. In M. A. Hogg & D. Abrams (Eds.), *Group motivation: Social psychological perspectives* (pp. 68–86). New York: Harvester/Wheatsheaf.

Wilder, D. A., & Shapiro, P. (1986). The role of outgroup salience in determining social identity. *Journal of Personality and Social Psychology, 47*, 342–348.

Wilder, D. A., & Shapiro, P. (1989a). Role of competition-induced anxiety in limiting the beneficial impact of positive behavior by an outgroup member. *Journal of Personality and Social Psychology, 56*, 60–69.

Wilder, D. A., & Shapiro, P. (1989b). Effects of anxiety on impression formation in a group context: An anxiety-assimilation hypothesis. *Journal of Experimental Social Psychology, 25*, 481–499.

Wilder, D. A., & Shapiro, P. (1991). Facilitation of outgroup stereotypes by enhanced ingroup identity. *Journal of Experimental Social Psychology, 27*, 431–452.

Worchel, S. (1986). The role of cooperation in reducing intergroup conflict. In S. Worchel & W. G. Austin (Eds.), *Psychology of intergroup relations* (2nd ed., pp. 288–304). Chicago: Nelson-Hall.

Zajonc, R. B. (1980). Feeling and thinking: Preferences need no inferences. *American Psychologist, 35*, 151–175.

PART III

Group Dynamics: Getting to Know You

CHAPTER 13

Exploring the Interpersonal Dynamics of Intergroup Contact

PATRICIA G. DEVINE
SOPHIA R. EVETT
KRISTIN A. VASQUEZ-SUSON
University of Wisconsin–Madison

The United States is becoming an increasingly multicultural society. Contact with people who are different from oneself (e.g., with regard to race, sexual orientation) is a virtually inevitable feature of contemporary American life. With calls for the celebration of diversity and multiculturalism, as well as legislative mandates such as affirmative action, interpersonal intergroup contact is occurring with greater frequency than ever before. As social scientists look forward to the 21st century, one of their primary challenges will be to understand the nature of interpersonal intergroup dynamics and to develop interventions that will enable smooth and positive intergroup relations. Upon a moment's reflection, however, it is clear that this has been a primary objective of students of intergroup relations for at least the second half of the 20th century (e.g., Allport, 1954; Jones et al., 1984; Mackie & Hamilton, 1993; Myrdal, 1944; Pettigrew, 1979; Rokeach, 1973; Sherif & Sherif, 1953; Stephan, 1985, 1987; Tajfel & Turner, 1979, 1986; Williams, 1947; Worchel & Austin, 1986). Following the landmark *Brown v. Board of Education* decision, which created opportunities for intergroup contact through school desegregation, social psychologists have been concerned with the origin and nature of tension arising in intergroup settings. Indeed, both theoreticians and practitioners have generally acknowledged that intergroup contact settings are fraught with tension, and have been concerned with the problem of how to overcome this tension so as to promote positive interpersonal relations in these situations.

Although the existence of tension in intergroup settings has been widely recognized, there has been very little analysis of the origin or nature of tension experienced by members of either majority or minority groups. We believe that a key step in achieving positive intergroup relations is to understand the different forms of tension that majority and minority group members feel in intergroup encounters. The literature has typically characterized intergroup tension as arising from majority group members' prejudice and minority group members' victimization. Elaborating on these themes, Stephan and Stephan (1985) identified a number of other possible sources of intergroup tension, which they referred to as "intergroup anxiety." They suggested that intergroup anxiety may result from sources such as ignorance about the other group, perceived dissimilarity of the groups, group composition (e.g., being in a numerical minority), type of interdependence demanded by the interaction, and participation in an unstructured rather than a structured interaction. We agree with Stephan and Stephan that such factors can contribute to tension in intergroup contact situations. However, we believe that the qualitative experiences of tension may differ both between groups and within groups. As such, the term "intergroup anxiety" may be too broad. To date, there has been no systematic delineation of the qualitatively distinct forms of tension that may arise in intergroup contact settings. The primary purpose of the present chapter is to explore the different sources and forms of intergroup tension, in order to achieve a fuller understanding of their possible impact on interpersonal intergroup interactions.

In this chapter, we review and evaluate what social psychologists have learned about the nature of intergroup dynamics and intergroup tension. Some of the advances made by social scientists are impressive. However, it is our position that by and large the field has failed to examine people's goals and concerns in intergroup situations, and their subsequent influence on the interpersonal dynamics of intergroup contact. Because the existing theories concerning intergroup contact have generally failed to consider such issues, they have left us ill equipped to understand the practical challenges and difficulties faced by both majority and minority group members as they try to negotiate their day-to-day intergroup encounters. In a thoughtful article on the pragmatics of social thinking, Fiske (1992) reminds social psychologists that people's thinking about interpersonal situations is embedded in a practical context: Social thinking is guided by a person's specific goals and by his or her role in the situation (see also Higgins, 1981, 1992; Hilton & Darley, 1991; Miller & Turnbull, 1986; Neuberg, 1989 and Chapter 7, this volume; Snyder, 1992). Fiske's reminder was exceedingly timely for our work and for the overall themes and goals of this chapter, for it was through a consideration of the pragmatics of interpersonal intergroup contact that we found the existing theoretical approaches to intergroup tension lacking.

A central theme of our approach is that a key obstacle to positive intergroup relations is the potential for miscommunication between majority and minority group members, which arises out of the expectations and concerns each interactant brings to the encounter. Both majority and minority interactants come into the interaction with a set of motivations (e.g., the impression they would like to create, the kind of interaction they want to have) and cognitions (e.g., expectations about the other group and about their own likely responses). These motivations and cognitions determine the nature of the dynamics of the interaction by influencing the behaviors, affective responses, and perceptions of both interactants (cf. Jones et al., 1984; Miller & Turnbull, 1986;

Neuberg, Chapter 7, this volume). Below, we present a theoretical framework in progress aimed at understanding how individuals from majority and minority groups think about and approach dynamic interpersonal intergroup situations.

In this framework, we consider the motives participants bring to intergroup interactions, their concerns and expectations, and the implications of these motivations and cognitions for the outcome of the encounter. Specifically, these motivations and cognitions are likely to affect majority and minority group members' thoughts and feelings about themselves, their interaction partner, and the interaction in general. We present preliminary data concerning the way in which majority and minority group members construe intergroup contact situations, and we outline what we believe is a productive research agenda in the domain of interpersonal intergroup relations. Only by understanding majority and minority group members' specific motivations and cognitions about interpersonal intergroup contact can we explore the reciprocal dynamics of these interactions. And only by understanding the dynamic nature of real intergroup encounters can we develop strategies to promote harmonious intergroup relations at the interpersonal level.

When we looked to the literature on intergroup relations to glean insights concerning how individuals think about and negotiate specific interpersonal intergroup encounters, we found little guidance. That is, the research literature on intergroup contact has little to offer concerning the nature of the interpersonal dynamics of intergroup contact. Previous research has typically examined majority groups (such as whites and heterosexuals) and minority groups (such as blacks and homosexuals) separately. The majority group literature has focused on the origin and nature of prejudiced attitudes and stereotypes about minority group members, with an underlying goal of developing interventions to reduce prejudice (see Devine, 1995, and Duckitt, 1992, for reviews). The minority group literature has examined the consequences for self-esteem and adjustment of being a member of a stigmatized group (e.g., Crocker & Major, 1989; Jones et al., 1984). As a result, social psychology has basically studied prospective interactants rather than the full nature of intergroup interactions. Indeed, for a literature concerned with intergroup issues, it is remarkably intrapersonal. In reviewing the extant literature to provide the relevant background, we consider the majority and minority group literatures separately. However, our ultimate goal is to bring these typically separate literatures together in an analysis of the interpersonal challenges involved in intergroup contact situations.

CLASSIC CONCEPTIONS OF THE PROBLEM OF INTERGROUP PREJUDICE AND TENSION

Social psychologists have generally conceived of the problem of intergroup tension and conflict in terms of majority group members' negative attitudes (i.e., prejudice) toward minority group members (see Ashmore, 1970). According to this analysis, intergroup tension stems from the hostility majority group members feel toward minority group members. Thus, the main goal for early prejudice reduction strategies was to change the negative attitudes of majority group members as a tactic to alleviate tension. Only then, it was thought, could the stage be set for less antagonistic and more harmonious intergroup relations. Proceeding from these assumptions, social scientists explored the effectiveness of a variety of techniques (e.g., propaganda, education, psychotherapy) to change majority group members' negative attitudes toward minority group members. In this tradition, perhaps the most extensively investigated strategy for reducing intergroup prejudice was the "contact hypothesis," which argues that intergroup contact leads majority group members to develop more positive attitudes toward minority group members (Allport, 1954; Amir, 1969; Cook, 1984, 1985; Herek, 1984; Stephan, 1985).

Research on the contact hypothesis has been productive in identifying a number of situational conditions that encourage attitude change among majority group members, such as equal status for members of each group, cooperative rather than competitive interactions, and institutional support for contact (see Stephan, 1985, for a review). However, the contact hypothesis has a number of shortcomings that limit its power as a solution to the problem of intergroup tension. First, the necessary conditions for positive attitudes to develop among majority group members are rather restrictive and are typically unrepresentative of most contact situations. Consider, for example, that the classroom setting—an arena in which there was great hope for contact to improve intergroup relations—typically encourages competition for grades or for the teacher's attention. Similarly, most employment settings are not only competitive but hierarchically organized as well, violating the equal-status condition of the contact hypothesis.

Second, because of interdependencies among the "necessary conditions," contact is likely to have propitious effects only under a set of highly specialized (or perhaps ideal) circumstances. For example, cooperation is beneficial, but only when it leads to successful outcomes. When cooperative endeavors end in failure, conflict can be intensified (Worchel, 1986; Worchel & Norvel, 1980). In a review of the contact literature, Stephan (1987) concluded that the most succinct and accurate summary of research on the contact hypothesis is that contact *sometimes* produces positive effects in the form of reducing negative attitudes. Moreover, the positive effects of contact, when obtained, rarely generalize beyond the specific contact situation in the form of a general reduction in prejudice (Miller & Brewer, 1986; Stephan, 1985, 1987; but see Pettigrew, 1994a).

LIMITATIONS TO THE CLASSIC CONCEPTIONS OF INTERGROUP PREJUDICE AND TENSION

Even if contact were universally effective in promoting positive attitudes among majority group members, we believe that the analysis of the problem and solution of intergroup conflict offered by the contact hypothesis is too global and incomplete for understanding the complex nature of interpersonal intergroup dynamics. Specifically, the contact hypothesis is limited in what it can reveal about intergroup dynamics because of its focus on (1) majority group members as the targets of change, and (2) attitude change as the ultimate goal of contact. The contact hypothesis work is clearly not unique in these regards. Indeed, most of the theorizing and research concerning the origins of prejudice and intergroup conflict, as well as proposed solutions to these problems, have focused almost exclusively on majority group members and their negative attitudes.

Overemphasis on Majority Group Members

We believe that the emphasis on majority group members and their negative attitudes in the contact hypothesis obscures the complexities associated with intergroup contact. Although majority group members' negative attitudes clearly contribute to the problem of intergroup tension, any analysis of intergroup contact must consider (1) the perspectives of both majority and minority group members, and (2) the dynamics between these individuals when they come together in intergroup contact settings. Sigelman and Welch (1991) recently noted that in uncounted thousands of pages about racial inequality, black people's views are "conspicuous by their absence" (p. 1). The major volumes on racial issues, for example, examine the values, attitudes, opinions, and behavior of white Americans (e.g., Adorno, Frenkel-Brunswik, Levinson, & Sanford, 1950; Apostle, Glock, Piazza, & Suezele, 1983; Kluegel & Smith, 1986; Myrdal, 1944; Schuman, Steeth, & Bobo, 1985; Sniderman with Hagen, 1985). Sigelman and Welch (1991) argued that the disparity in attention to whites' compared with blacks' views on racial issues stems from "the basic intellectual and political assumption motivating research on racial attitudes" (p. 3). They suggested that dating back to Myrdal's (1944) writings on the American racial dilemma as fundamentally "a white man's problem," social scientists have been consumed with exploring the nature of and changes in white people's attitudes toward blacks. Minority group members in such analyses are viewed as rather passive targets of prejudice. Similar disparities are found in the study of other majority–minority group combinations, such as heterosexuals and homosexuals (Herek, 1984; Kite & Deaux, 1986) and the physically abled and disabled (Katz, 1981). These concerns are particularly serious because, for example, in the case of race relations, whites and blacks have disparate views on the extent to which white racial attitudes have improved and the extent to which blacks are treated fairly in contemporary U.S. society (Hochschild & Herk, 1990; Sigelman & Welch, 1991).

If people come to the contact setting with different expectations for how the interaction will ensue, their construals may affect the very nature of the interaction. However, little is known about either majority or minority group members' expectations regarding interpersonal intergroup contact. Surprisingly few studies in social psychology have afforded the opportunity to study the interpersonal dynamics of interactions between majority and minority group members, or the nature of the tensions that arise in intergroup contact situations (those that have are considered below). As a result, we believe social psychologists need to expand their conceptualization of intergroup contact to be more inclusive in the analysis of the interpersonal dynamics of such contact.

Overemphasis on Attitude Change as the Ultimate Goal of Contact

A second concern we have with the contact hypothesis is that it is too narrowly focused on attitude change of majority group members as the ultimate goal of contact. This limitation is also characteristic of the other classic strategies aimed at achieving harmonious intergroup relations. Although attitude change may be a necessary element of long-term improvement of intergroup relations, it is not sufficient to produce it. For example, despite widespread evidence that majority group members' racial attitudes have become more positive over the last 50 years (e.g., Hochschild & Herk, 1990; Schuman et al., 1985), minority group members continue to experience significant discrimination (see Crosby, Bromley, & Saxe, 1980; Dovidio & Gaertner, 1986; Feagin, 1989; Herek, 1984; Jones et al., 1984; Moses & Hawkins, 1982), and intergroup tension persists (Stephan & Stephan, 1985).

In attempts to reconcile the disparity between expressed attitudes and persistent discriminatory responses, several contemporary theorists have developed models to explain such paradoxical reactions (Crosby et al., 1980; Gaertner & Dovidio, 1986; Kinder & Sears, 1981; McConahay, 1986). A common theme in the models of aversive racism, modern racism, and symbolic racism is that although attitudes have changed to become more consistent with egalitarian principles, prejudice has not been truly reduced. Instead, the expression of prejudice has shifted from overt to more covert, subtle forms of prejudice. Inherent in these models is an assumption that prejudice reduction is an "all-or-none" event; if prejudice is truly reduced, no discriminatory responses should occur. A second theme common in these contemporary models is that majority group members either are unaware of their prejudiced attitudes or are lying about them so as to present a socially desirable, nonprejudiced identity to others. In one form or another (e.g., repression, rationalization), they hide their prejudices from themselves and others. According to such frameworks, prospects for further prejudice reduction and improvement in intergroup relations are dim.

Although we do not deny the presence of paradoxical reactions among majority group members, we find the assumptions of aversive racism, modern racism, and symbolic racism to be somewhat troubling. First, we believe that an all-or-none approach to prejudice reduction is naive and does not allow for the possibility that prejudice reduction may be a process in which attitude change is a necessary but preliminary step in the process (cf. Devine, 1989). Second, in each of these models, the fact that discriminatory responses persist despite self-reported changes in attitudes is taken as manifest evidence of prejudice. This assumption falls into the trap of equating discriminatory responses with prejudice. We believe that it is important to distinguish between "discrimination," which means differential treatment based on group membership, and "prejudice," which implies some type of antipathy or hostility directed toward people because of their group membership. Indeed, according to many of the contemporary approaches, any discriminatory response—whether it benefits or harms minority group members—is interpreted as a manifestation of prejudice (Crosby et al., 1980; Gaertner & Dovidio, 1986; McConahay, 1986; Sears & Kinder, 1985). Furthermore, any positive or non-negative response is assumed to be motivated by social desirability considerations (Crosby et al., 1980) or to occur in response to normative guidelines for appropriate behavior (Gaertner & Dovidio, 1986). Such responses are seen as strategies to "cover up" unacceptable responses, rather than as evidence of an internal motivation to overcome prejudice. Thus, majority group members can find themselves in a "Catch-22" of sorts: If any response is seen as prejudiced, how can low prejudiced majority group members effectively communicate nonprejudiced values or goals?

This type of interpretational bias is clearly evident in the few studies that have examined the responses of majority group members (whites and heterosexuals) in real contact situations with minority group members (blacks and homosexuals). The typical procedure for such studies is to place a majority group member in an interaction with a minority group member and to measure an array of nonverbal behaviors displayed by the majority group member.[1] Nonverbal measures have been preferred in these studies because they are more difficult to control intentionally than verbal responses, and thus have been assumed by the experimenters to be more trustworthy. In virtually none of these studies have subjects' self-reported attitudes been assessed. The results from these studies suggest two general conclusions: (1) majority group members generally display more "avoidant" nonverbal behaviors (e.g., decreased eye contact, greater interpersonal distance, more speech errors, briefer durations of contact) when interacting with minority group members than with other majority group members (Cuenot & Fugita, 1982; Dennis & Powell, 1972; Hendricks & Bootzin, 1976; Ickes, 1984; Weitz, 1972; Willis, 1966; Word, Zanna, & Cooper, 1974); and (2) majority group members find such interactions to be uncomfortable, awkward, and strained (Cuenot & Fugita, 1982; Henley, 1977; Ickes, 1984; LaFrance & Mayo, 1976; Moses & Hawkins, 1982; Strommen, 1989). The pervasive conclusion drawn from these studies has been that majority group members' avoidant behaviors reveal the underlying antipathy or prejudice felt by majority group members toward minority group members. This interpretation is based on the logical fallacy that because greater dislike leads to responses such as increased interpersonal distance, such negative responses must indicate greater dislike or prejudice (Hendricks & Bootzin, 1976; Word et al., 1974).

We believe that it is too simplistic, and rather pessimistic, to conclude that all majority group members are prejudiced toward minority group members (cf. Devine, 1989). Moreover, basing such important conclusions solely on the types of nonverbal measures most commonly used in this research is problematic and potentially misleading, because such measures are not uniquely associated with negative attitudes (cf. Schlenker & Leary, 1982). Nowhere in these contemporary approaches is it suggested that discriminatory responses might result from positive intentions or internal motivations to respond in nonprejudiced ways. This possibility was anticipated, however, by Poskocil (1977) in his discussion of the difficulties faced by whites in their interactions with blacks. Poskocil argued that many whites are attitudinally nonprejudiced but uncertain about how to manage specific interpersonal encounters with blacks. As illustrated in Figure 13.1, this lack of effective social skills for managing intergroup interactions may make some whites feel anxious and awkward in their dealings with blacks.

According to Poskocil, then, anxiety rather than hostility may account for many instances of apparent racial discrimination. Thus, there may be different forms of tension associated with intergroup contact for majority group members who report low versus high levels of prejudice toward minority group members. Although this idea is intriguing, Poskocil provided no empirical work to support his claims that many whites have good intentions but are unskilled, and his analysis has received little theoretical or empirical attention. We believe that there is some merit to Poskocil's analysis and that some discriminatory responses may be rooted in good intentions gone awry (i.e., failure to translate nonprejudiced attitudes into corresponding behaviors). In what follows, we develop an analysis suggesting that individual differences in self-reported prejudice may be related to qualitatively distinct forms of intergroup tension. We argue that for

FIGURE 13.1 Doubts and uncertainties experienced by some majority group members. Cartoon by C. Headrick.

majority group members, individual differences in prejudice affect the motivations and cognitions they bring into intergroup contact situations, and that these factors determine the nature of the tension experienced.

INDIVIDUAL DIFFERENCES IN PREJUDICE LEVEL AND THE NATURE OF INTERGROUP TENSION

Our theoretical analysis differs from the other contemporary models of prejudice in two important ways. First, we do not make the assumption that prejudice reduction is an all-or-none event; second, we do not assume that discriminatory behavior is direct evidence of underlying prejudice. In contrast to the frameworks of aversive racism, modern racism, and symbolic racism, Devine (1989; Devine & Monteith, 1993) has proposed that prejudice reduction does not occur all at once, but rather is a process involving both motivation and ability components. In this analysis, the prejudice reduction process is likened to the breaking of a habit. As in the breaking of any habit, one must first develop the resolve (i.e., the motivation) to overcome the habit, and then develop the skills to overcome the habit (i.e., ability). In an intergroup context, therefore, it is possible that after internalizing nonprejudiced standards, one may still be prone to failure experiences—the violation of those standards—until one develops the skills or abilities to comply with the standards. Thus, discriminatory treatment is not *necessarily* a direct reflection of prejudiced attitudes.

In our recent work on prejudice reduction, we have found that self-reported prejudice is systematically related to people's personal standards for how to treat members of minority groups and to the consequences of failing to live up to those standards (Devine, 1989; Devine & Monteith, 1993; Devine, Monteith, Zuwerink, & Elliot, 1991; Monteith, Devine, & Zuwerink, 1993; Zuwerink, Monteith, Devine, & Cook, in press). Specifically, we have found that low prejudiced people have established and internalized personal standards that require nonprejudiced responses; as a result, they are highly motivated to respond without prejudice. Low prejudiced people report that it is important to respond consistently with their standards, and that their standards represent an important aspect of their self-concept. In contrast, high prejudiced people have less well-internalized personal standards; their standards are not self-defining or particularly important. In addition, although low prejudiced people are highly motivated to respond without prejudice toward minority group members, they sometimes fail in their efforts by responding with more prejudice than they personally find acceptable. Such failures typically lead to feelings of guilt and self-criticism (Devine & Amodt, 1994; Devine et al., 1991; Monteith, 1993; Monteith et al., 1993; Pressly & Devine, 1992; Zuwerink et al., in press). For higher prejudiced people, failure to respond consistently with their standards does not lead to feelings of guilt. Instead, such failures lead to negative affect directed toward others, most often in the form of antipathy toward minority group members (Monteith et al., 1993). We believe that these differences between low and high prejudiced people will determine which concerns and motivations become most salient to them in contact situations with minority group members, and will affect their responses in such situations.

Although our work to date has focused primarily on the nature of intrapersonal conflict associated with violating personal standards, we have recently begun to explore how differences in motivation to respond without prejudice affects people's expectations regarding intergroup encounters. Specifically, we are developing an analysis of how majority group members of varying levels of prejudice expect to manage their interpersonal encounters with minority group members, and of the implications of such expectations for the type of tension experienced in intergroup contact situations. In what follows, we delineate the theoretical analysis and briefly present the results from a series of studies lending support to the analysis.

Let us consider, first, the analysis for high prejudiced people. Existing research suggests that they would prefer not to interact with members of particular minority groups and would experience discomfort when interacting with them (e.g., Devine et al., 1991; Hudson & Ricketts, 1980; Lance, 1987; Monteith et al., 1993). Thus, it seems logical to assume that their avoidant behaviors (e.g., greater interpersonal distance, briefer duration of contact) directly reflect their negative attitudes or antipathy toward minority group members.[2]

We began the analysis for low prejudiced people with Devine's (1989; see also Devine & Monteith, 1993) motivation and ability analysis of prejudice reduction. The key to Devine's analysis is that motivation is not sufficient to overcome prejudice. Even when equally motivated, low prejudiced people may vary in their ability to respond consistently with their standards (Devine et al., 1991). The ability to translate low prejudiced standards into behaviors consistent with those standards is likely to depend on a variety of factors, including the number and quality of previous personal experiences with minority group members. We propose that the reactions of low prejudiced people in intergroup interactions are likely to be determined jointly by their motivation and by their self-perceived ability to respond consistently with their nonprejudiced standards.

Leary and his colleagues (Leary, 1983a, 1983b; Leary & Atherton, 1986; Schlenker & Leary, 1982) have developed an analysis of the intrapersonal consequences when high motivation to convey a particular impression is coupled with uncertainty regarding one's ability to convey the impression. Self-perceived ability to convey an impression can be partitioned into two components derived from self-efficacy theory: self-presentational efficacy expectancy and self-presentational outcome expectancy (Leary & Atherton, 1986). In order to convey an impression successfully to others, one needs to believe, first, that one is able to perform the appropriate behaviors (i.e., self-presentational efficacy expectancy); and, second, that the other person is willing to accept the presentation (i.e., self-presentational outcome expectancy).

The specific intrapersonal consequences of concern to Leary and colleagues are self-focused attention (Duval & Wicklund, 1972; Wicklund, 1975) and social anxiety. Generally, "anxiety" is defined as a state of physiological arousal accompanied by "apprehension or dread regarding an impending negative outcome that the person believes he or she is unable to avert" (Leary, 1983b, p. 15). More specifically, "social anxiety" is anxiety that arises in real or imagined social situations under conditions of potentially negative personal evaluation (Schlenker & Leary, 1982). It can result from self-focused attention (Buss, 1980), or can occur when either or both of the self-presentational expectancies (i.e., efficacy or outcome) are low (Leary & Atherton, 1986). These intrapersonal consequences are important because of their implications for how people attempt to manage interpersonal interactions. For example, when people are highly self-focused, they carefully monitor their behaviors and compare them to currently salient standards, resulting in efforts to bring their behaviors in line with their standards (Carver & Scheier, 1981, 1990; Scheier & Carver, 1988).

These self-regulatory efforts, coupled with the social anxiety arising from such people's uncertainties about the success of their efforts, result in interaction styles that are awkward and strained. For example, socially anxious people often attempt to control their nonverbal behaviors, trying to respond "normally" in the situation. They begin to monitor the amount of eye contact they make in the interaction, and they wonder what the other person is thinking about their interaction style. Overall, they become distracted by their efforts to control aspects of the interaction that typically are unavailable to conscious awareness (DePaulo, 1992; Polanyi, 1962) or are not carefully monitored during ordinary interactions. These conscious efforts, even when made with the best of intentions, actually disrupt the typically smooth nature of social interactions. The ultimate implication is that those who are socially anxious tend to engage in a number of nervous behaviors (e.g., hesitant speech, fidgeting, stuttering) and disaffiliative tendencies (e.g., decreased eye contact, increased interpersonal distance, efforts to escape the situation). As previously noted, these nervous and disaffiliative outcomes are exactly the same types of outcomes that have typically been taken as evidence of antipathy and prejudice.

If we use the analysis of Leary and his colleagues to explore an intergroup encounter, it becomes plausible that, as Poskocil (1977) suggested, a well-intentioned majority group member may be unsure that he or she is able to act in a nonprejudiced way, because, for example, he or she does not know what behaviors constitute nonprejudiced treatment. Or, alternatively, even if the majority group member feels that he or she can behave in a perfectly "natural" or nonprejudiced manner, there may be some doubt as to whether the minority group member will accept the presentation. Following Leary's model, differences in the self-presentational expectancies of low prejudiced majority group members are likely to result in qualitatively different experiences in an intergroup encounter.

When motivation and self-perceived ability to convey a nonprejudiced impression are both high, intergroup interactions should pose no particular interpersonal difficulties. Under these circumstances, people should expect to feel comfortable in the interaction and should expect positive outcomes (Leary & Atherton, 1986; Schlenker & Leary, 1982). However, when motivation is high and self-perceived ability is low, the stage is set for possible interpersonal difficulties (Schlenker & Leary, 1982). That is, for low prejudiced people who are uncertain about their ability to convey a nonprejudiced image, their high motivation to respond without prejudice may actually interfere with their efforts to accurately convey their nonprejudiced intentions. Their task is further complicated because they may recognize the potential for minority group members to misinterpret their intentions—that is, to perceive their behaviors as prejudiced despite their efforts to behave without prejudice (Duke & Morin, 1992; Norris, 1991; Poskocil, 1977; Stephan & Stephan, 1985).

This type of interpersonal intergroup dilemma has been the topic of recent publications, which have characterized the experience of some college students and professors as having to be constantly on guard about whether they are saying or doing the "wrong thing" in intergroup situations (e.g., Adler et al., 1990; Taylor, 1991). One faculty member explained why he felt the need to censor what he said around homosexuals as follows: "Although I have a few gay friends, I don't feel as though I've become sensitive to their needs well enough to know when they might be slighted. I know that they are more easily insulted than I am and probably with good reason" (quoted in Norris, 1991, p. 93). Students at the University of Wisconsin have complained that there are not good guidelines for how to "do the intergroup thing right."[3] They report feeling that they will be perceived as prejudiced regardless of what they do, and that they are in a "damned if they do and damned if they don't" situation. As a result, they feel uncertain and awkward in intergroup settings. Moses and Hawkins (1982) concluded that for heterosexuals interacting with homosexuals, "sometimes this awkwardness is simply because of ignorance about what to expect from a gay person or about what is socially 'appropriate' as a response" (p. 66).

In sum, the reactions of low prejudiced people in intergroup interactions are likely to be determined jointly by their motivation and their ability to respond consistently with their nonprejudiced standards. Although some low prejudiced individuals may feel quite comfortable interacting with minority group members, low prejudiced people may experience social anxiety owing to their concern about being perceived as prejudiced, which can lead to avoidant nonverbal behaviors. The key point for the present analysis is that the same avoidant nonverbal behaviors can be indicators of two very different psychological experiences: social anxiety and antipathy. If this analysis is valid, it would appear that differential treatment (discrimination) can occur in the absence of antipathy or hostility. Considering attitude change as the lone measure of success in reducing prejudice has left us unprepared to address the challenges of many low prejudiced people who have *changed* their attitudes, and thus are highly motivated to respond without prejudice, but are uncertain about how to express those attitudes.

MAJORITY GROUP MEMBERS' SELF-REPORTED EXPECTANCIES IN AN INTERGROUP INTERACTION

To explore the efficacy of the present analysis, we conducted three studies examining heterosexuals' expectations about the experiences they would have in an interaction with a homosexual. Before we discuss the studies, a few comments on the selection of heterosexuals and homosexuals as the majority-minority group combination are in order.

Selection of Majority–Minority Group Combination

Although we believe that there are likely to be some differences between prejudice toward homosexuals and prejudice toward other stigmatized groups (e.g., the concealability of the stigma), we believe that the heterosexual-homosexual combination serves as a good model of majority-minority relations for a number of reasons. Historically, homosexuals, like other minority group members, have been subjected to discrimination at the hands of majority group members. In recent years, the gay and lesbian community has become increasingly visible in American society with the introduction of both pro- and anti-homosexual legislation in a number of states as well as at the federal level (see Henry, 1994). As more gays and lesbians publicly reveal their sexual orientation, alleviating tensions that may arise in interpersonal intergroup encounters is becoming a pressing social concern.

A review of the literatures on heterosexual-homosexual relations and white-black relations reveals a number of theoretical and empirical parallels, such as the sources of prejudice, the strategies to reduce prejudice, and the consequences of being a member of a stigmatized group. These parallels lead us to believe that the forms of intergroup tension experienced by majority and minority group members in interpersonal encounters should be similar across these different majority-minority group combinations. For example, in both literatures, one of the key sources of prejudice is the perception that minority group members violate cherished or traditional values, although the specific values violated differ for the two groups. For blacks, it is the violation of the Protestant work ethic (cf. Katz, Wackenhut, & Hass, 1986); for homosexuals, it is the violation of traditional sex roles (cf. Herek, 1984). Moreover, both literatures posit that defensiveness can play a causal role in negative attitudes toward minority group members.

In terms of the empirical literatures on majority group members' attitudes, both literatures have focused on developing attitude scales and identifying the correlates of high and low prejudiced attitudes (e.g., age, socioeconomic status, personality characteristics). Parallels are also observed in the strategies proposed to reduce intergroup hostilities, most specifically in trying to improve majority group members' attitudes through contact with minority group members under the conditions specified by the contact hypothesis. There are also similarities in the literatures on black and homosexual minority groups. Each literature suggests that minority group members are suspicious of majority group members' intentions and motivations in intergroup situations. However, in neither literature is there much discussion of how such concerns and suspicions will affect intergroup dynamics. Finally, much of our previous work concerns heterosexuals' personal standards for how to treat homosexuals. We believe that in using this specific majority–minority group combination, we are on the strongest ground to extend our theoretical ideas into the interpersonal intergroup arena.[4]

Overview of Studies

In each of the three studies presented below, people of varying levels of prejudice imagined an interaction with a homosexual whom they did not know well, and reported their expectations regarding the interaction. The instructions in each study stressed that participants' responses would be kept confidential and that there were no right or wrong answers. Participants' prejudice level was assessed using the Heterosexual Attitudes Toward Homosexuals scale (HATH; Larsen, Reed, & Hoffman, 1980), which we have used in our previous research. Participants were introductory psychology students who completed the HATH as part of a larger set of questionnaires administered at the beginning of the semester. They rated each of the 20 HATH items on a 5-point Likert-type scale ranging from "strongly agree" (1) to "strongly disagree" (5), and their total HATH score could range from 20 (low prejudice) to 100 (high prejudice). Because participants lower in prejudice were expected to be further along in the prejudice reduction process, we expected that those lowest in prejudice would be most likely to have both the motivation and the perceived ability to convey a nonprejudiced impression. Therefore, we examined separately the responses of participants who scored very low in prejudice, and those who scored moderately low.[5]

Study 1

The goals of the first study (Devine & Vasquez-Suson, 1994) were (1) to test explicitly the assumption that very low and moderately low prejudiced participants are equally motivated to respond without prejudice in an interaction with a homosexual but differ in their self-perceived ability to do so, either because they have low self-presentational efficacy expectancies or low self-presentational outcome expectancies; and (2) to determine whether high prejudiced people expect predominantly to experience antipathy in the interaction, whereas moderately low prejudiced people expect predominantly to experience social anxiety. A third ancillary goal was to assess whether the amount and nature of participants' previous experience with homosexuals contribute to differences in their expectancies in the interaction, above and beyond the effects of prejudice level. Participants completed the questionnaire at the same session in which they completed the HATH at the beginning of the semester. On the basis of their HATH scores, participants were divided into four prejudice levels: very low (n = 159, HATH range = 20–32); moderately low (n = 115, HATH range = 33–46); moderate (n = 136, HATH range = 47–72); and high (n = 18, HATH range = 73–100). To highlight the similarities and differences between these groups, we will present analyses of variance. However, because of the unequal cell sizes, multiple-regression analyses were also conducted and yielded very similar results.

Participants completed a 33-item questionnaire designed to measure the theoretical constructs of interest (sample items are described below). For each item, participants read a statement about the experiences they might have during an interaction with a homosexual student, and indicated the extent to which they agreed with the statement on a scale from 1 ("strongly disagree") to 7 ("strongly agree"). Participants' responses to the items were submitted to a factor analysis with varimax rotation. On the basis of the factor analysis, the following six indices were formed by averaging items with loadings greater than .40 (reverse scoring when necessary): Motivation to appear nonprejudiced (e.g., whether it is important to behave and be seen as nonprejudiced; whether they would try to respond without prejudice); Self-Efficacy Expectancy (e.g., whether they would feel confident and would know how to behave in a nonprejudiced manner); Outcome Expectancy (e.g., whether the homosexual interactant would expect the subject to be prejudiced); Self-Awareness (e.g., whether they would pay attention to their own thoughts, feelings, and behaviors); Anxiety (e.g., whether they would feel awkward, nervous, and uncomfortable during the interaction); and Antipathy and Suspicion in the interaction (e.g., whether they would feel annoyed and hostile during the interaction; whether they would think the homosexual interactant would be watching for signs of prejudice). In addition, an index was formed to assess participants' previous experience with homosexuals (e.g., whether they had a lot of experience; whether that experience was generally positive). Each index was highly reliable (mean Cronbach's **a** = .77).

There was a significant main effect for prejudice level on all six indices; the means for each group are presented in Table 13.1. These results support the analysis derived from the synthesis of our work on prejudice reduction with work by Leary and his colleagues on social anxiety. Although the very low and moderately low prejudiced participants were highly and equally motivated to respond without prejudice, they differed in their self-perceived ability to do so. Specifically, moderately low prejudiced participants reported both lower self-efficacy expectancies and lower outcome expectancies than very low prejudiced participants. Thus, moderately low prejudiced participants were less sure about whether they could behave in a nonprejudiced manner and whether the homosexual interactant would perceive them to be nonprejudiced. We also found that moderately low prejudiced participants expected to be more self-focused and to

TABLE 13.1 Mean Scores on the Six Indices as a Function of Prejudice Level

Index	Prejudice level			
	Very low	Moderately low	Moderate	High
Motivation	5.47$_a$	5.43$_a$	4.45$_b$	2.32$_c$
Self-Efficacy Expectancy	5.23$_a$	4.71$_b$	4.53$_{bc}$	4.11$_c$
Outcome Expectancy	4.44$_a$	4.14$_b$	3.66$_c$	3.58$_c$
Self-Awareness	3.93$_a$	4.68$_b$	4.64$_b$	4.22$_b$
Anxiety	2.69$_a$	3.97$_b$	4.80$_c$	5.54$_d$
Antipathy and Suspicion	1.51$_a$	2.10$_b$	2.82$_c$	4.07$_d$

Note. For each row, means not sharing a subscript differ at $p < .01$. The data are from Devine and Vasquez-Suson (1994).

feel more anxiety in the intergroup interaction than their very low prejudiced counterparts. Importantly, neither the very low prejudiced nor the moderately low prejudiced participants expected to experience particularly high levels of antipathy in the interaction.

Not surprisingly, high prejudiced participants reported expecting the lowest levels of motivation to respond without prejudice; they also reported expecting to experience high levels of antipathy during the intergroup interaction. These participants reported low levels of self-efficacy expectancies and outcome expectancies and high levels of anticipated anxiety. The anxiety experienced by high prejudiced participants appears to have been at least partly attributable to their antipathy and suspicion. Regression analyses indicated that the higher Anxiety scores among high prejudiced participants (predicted mean = 5.3) diminished substantially after the effects of Antipathy and Suspicion were covaried out (predicted mean = 4.1), whereas the scores for the other participants were unaffected.[6] We have begun to speculate on the origin of the residual anxiety anticipated by high prejudiced people. It seems likely that the anxiety anticipated by moderately low prejudiced and high prejudiced individuals is fundamentally different in nature. Whereas moderately low prejudiced people are positively motivated toward minority group members, high prejudiced people are not. Generally speaking, anxiety arises in psychological situations involving the "presence of a negative" (Higgins, 1987). For low prejudiced people, the negative is the difficulty of communicating their nonprejudiced feelings; for high prejudiced people the negative may be having to interact with the disliked minority group member. It is also possible that the anxiety anticipated by high prejudiced people arises from self-presentational concerns associated with the anticipated disapproval from others for responding in a prejudiced manner (cf. Dovidio & Gaertner, 1986). Thus, it is presently unclear whether the anxiety anticipated by high prejudiced people is *social* anxiety. What is clear is that high prejudiced people expect to experience antipathy in addition to any anxiety they may experience; this antipathy makes their experiences qualitatively distinct from the experiences of low prejudiced people.

The responses of our moderately prejudiced participants either fell between the responses of the moderately low and the high prejudiced participants or were equivalent to the responses of the high prejudiced participants. Their responses suggest that people with moderate levels of prejudice may be at the earliest stages of renouncing prejudice, because they appear to be fairly motivated to respond without prejudice and expect to experience relatively low levels of antipathy. However, this suggestion is merely speculative.

Although prejudice level was an important determinant of participants' anticipated concerns and feelings, previous experiences with homosexuals also played an important role. The effects of experience were assessed by means of hierarchical regression analyses in which experience was entered into the regression equation after participants' sex and prejudice score. On several of the indices, previous experience accounted for significant additional variance not accounted for by prejudice and sex. Consistent with our expectations, participants who had more positive previous experiences with homosexuals had higher self-efficacy and outcome expectancies. In addition, they expected to be less self-aware and to feel less anxiety and less hostility than did participants who had fewer, less positive experiences with homosexuals. Interestingly, previous experience did not contribute to participants' motivation to behave and be seen as nonprejudiced. This motivation appears to have been fully accounted for by differences in participants' prejudice level.

Overall, these data strongly support our theory that people of varying prejudice levels have different expectations and concerns about intergroup interactions. Although very low and moderately low prejudiced people are equally motivated to convey a nonprejudiced impression in an interaction with a homosexual, they differ in their self-perceived ability to do so. Whereas very low prejudiced people anticipate being successful in their efforts to convey a nonprejudiced identity, moderately low prejudiced people doubt their ability to behave and be perceived as nonprejudiced. Consequently, they expect to experience heightened self-focus and anxiety during the interaction. The overall pattern of their responses suggests that they expect to experience social anxiety in intergroup interactions. Higher prejudiced individuals lack the motivation to appear nonprejudiced to a minority group member. It appears that their negative attitudes toward the minority group member are at the root of their expected antipathy and anxiety. Thus, although moderately low prejudiced and high prejudiced people have very different underlying concerns, these concerns may be manifested in very similar avoidant interaction styles.

Study 2

The main goal of our second study study was to determine whether participants varying in prejudice would spontaneously report the different types of experiences predicted by our theoretical analysis. Participants were asked to describe in an open-ended format their expectations for how they would feel, think, and behave in an interaction with a gay male (Evett & Devine, 1993). Twenty participants were randomly selected from each of four different levels of prejudice and were recruited for the study: very low (HATH range = 20–32); moderately low (HATH range = 33–46); moderately high (HATH range = 73–86); and very high (HATH range = 87–100). Participants were then asked to describe, *in as much detail as possible,* the types of feelings they might have, the thoughts that might go through their minds, and the ways they might behave. They were also asked to explain why they might have these types of responses.

Judges who were unaware of participants' prejudice level coded protocols for the presence or absence of various feelings (e.g., anxious, comfortable, disgusted, hostile), thoughts about the interaction and homosexuality (e.g., not knowing what to do or say, wanting to escape the situation, thinking that homosexuality is unnatural or that gays should be treated equally), and behaviors (e.g., act normally, be nervous and appear awkward, be rude). Judges agreed on 93% of their ratings; a third judge resolved discrepancies. These data were submitted to a discriminant-function analysis in which linear combinations of the independent variables (i.e., codes from the protocols) were formed and served as the basis for classifying cases into groups (i.e., prejudice level). To the extent that participants' protocols revealed distinct themes, there should have been few classification errors. Indeed, a large percentage of cases were correctly classified: 71.4% for very low prejudiced participants, 65.0% for moderately low prejudiced participants, and 76.2% for very high prejudiced participants (chance rate = 25%). Moderately high prejudiced participants' protocols produced the greatest amount of ambiguity, with only 55.0% correctly classified. The themes along which participants' protocols differed were consistent with our theoretical analysis and are illustrated below. It was somewhat striking how clearly participants explained how they would feel in such situations, and perhaps even more striking (if not disconcerting) how intense some of the descriptions were.

The predominant themes for very low prejudiced participants were that they would feel comfortable in the interaction and would treat a homosexual just like anyone else. For example, "It doesn't matter if he's gay," "I'd behave the same and wouldn't feel uncomfortable," "My feelings and thoughts would be no different than with any person." Moderately low prejudiced participants most often indicated that they should act "normally" but that it would be difficult to do so. Their protocols revealed themes of social anxiety about managing the interaction. For example, "I would try to interact the way I would with anyone. I would feel uncomfortable and worry that it shows," "In interacting I would be concerned with trying to act completely normally so that he would not feel that I was prejudiced," "I would feel nervous and be cautious about what I said so as not to offend him . . . but I would be focusing on that, so it wouldn't be natural." The protocols of the very high prejudiced participants revealed high levels of antipathy, disgust, and a desire to end the interaction as quickly as possible. For example, "I would be highly disgusted with the way the person chose to live. I would feel very hostile. I would not be friendly, I might look at them with contempt, or be short with them," "I would try to avoid the person as much as possible. I would act in a rude manner," "I would try to hurry up and leave." These distinct themes suggest that the expectations and concerns that participants varying in prejudice bring to an intergroup encounter are likely to be very different from one another.

Study 3

The two previous studies examined participants' expected feelings and behavioral responses in an interaction with a homosexual. The goal of our third study was to examine more closely the feelings participants expected to have in such an interaction, using a closed-ended format (Devine & Evett, 1993). A 23-item questionnaire that asked participants to indicate on 7-point scales whether they would experience a variety of different feelings (see sample items below) when interacting with a homosexual was completed by 1,194 participants as part of a larger set of questionnaires administered at the beginning of the semester. These items were submitted to a factor analysis with varimax rotation, which yielded two factors. Two indices were formed by combining items with loadings of at least .57 (reverse scoring when necessary): Anxiety (e.g., nervous, apprehensive, comfortable, confident, uneasy) and Antipathy/Negativity (e.g., hostile, annoyed, bothered). Both scales were highly reliable (mean Cronbach's a = .92). Hierarchical regression analyses were conducted to examine the linear and quadratic effects of HATH on these two indices.

Participants' prejudice level was linearly related to their scores on the Antipathy/Negativity index, such that higher prejudiced participants reported that they would feel more bothered, annoyed, and hostile during an interaction with a homosexual than lower prejudiced participants, F (1, 1,191) = 856.20, p < .001 (β = .05). This pattern remained even after the effect of Anxiety was covaried out, F (1, 1,190) = 262.61, p < .001. Prejudice level was curvilinearly related to Anxiety, with very low prejudiced participants reporting very little anxiety, moderately low prejudiced participants reporting much more anxiety, and moderate and high prejudiced participants reporting the highest levels of anxiety, F (1, 1,190) = 61.98, p < .001 (β = -6.42). Interestingly, after the effect of Antipathy/Negativity was covaried out, the Anxiety scores for moderately low prejudiced participants remained high but diminished substantially for higher prejudiced participants, suggesting that their negative emotions were predominantly attributable to the antipathy and negativity they felt toward homosexuals, F (1, 1,189) = 62.14, p < .001.

Discussion

Taken together, the results from these three studies suggest that majority group members with varying levels of prejudice bring different motivations (e.g., to appear nonprejudiced, to avoid the interaction) and cognitions (e.g., expectancies about one's own behavior, expectancies about the minority group member's perceptions) into the interaction. Consequently, they anticipate experiencing qualitatively distinct forms of tension in such encounters. The findings are highly consistent across the three studies and strongly support our theoretical analysis. It is, however, important to recognize that these data rely on participants' self-reported expectations for how they believe they will feel, think, and behave when interacting with a minority group member. Although these findings represent a crucial part of this research program, it is extremely important to move beyond self-report data to determine whether these concerns and different forms of tension are realized in actual interactions between majority and minority group members. Do moderately low and high prejudiced people show similar patterns of avoidant nonverbal behaviors for different reasons? Are very low prejudiced people as comfortable and skilled in such interactions as they believe they are?

The next step in this program of research will enable us to explore these issues. Heterosexual participants will be placed in an interaction with a confederate who (they are led to believe) is either heterosexual or homosexual. Although this will not represent a true dynamic interaction, for this stage of the research program we believe that the experimental control afforded by the use of a confederate interactant is necessary to help pave the way for studying natural intergroup interactions. It is important to note that to test our hypotheses that people with varying levels of prejudice experience qualitatively distinct forms of tension in intergroup settings, we cannot rely exclusively on the types of measures of nonverbal behavior most commonly used in previous studies on interpersonal intergroup contact, because these measures are not sensitive to differences between anxiety and antipathy.[7]

Therefore, our empirical strategy will be to use measures that will enable us to examine the psychological experiences (i.e., thoughts, feelings, concerns, intentions) and overt behavioral responses of low versus high prejudiced people during interpersonal interactions with minority group members. In addition, we intend to examine a number of nonverbal measures, such as Ekman and Friesen's (1978) Facial Action Coding System (FACS), which may help to distinguish between people experiencing anxiety and those experiencing antipathy or disgust during the interaction with a minority group member. Distinct patterns of facial movements are associated with anxiety and disgust, as well as other emotional states. Similarly, we can use Gottman and Krokoff's (1989) Specific Affect Coding System (SPAFF), which involves coding verbal content, voice tone, facial expression, gestures, and body movement to derive an overall judgment of the person's emotional experience. Such measures, although not previously used in intergroup contact studies, have proven to be useful elsewhere to validate participants' self-reported emotional experiences during interpersonal encounters (Levenson & Gottman, 1983, 1985). Thus, our strategy is to obtain converging evidence, through a variety of verbal and nonverbal measures, that majority group members with varying levels of prejudice have qualitatively distinct psychological experiences during interactions with minority group members.

We do not expect systematic differences on any of the verbal or nonverbal measures as a function of participants' prejudice toward homosexuals in the heterosexual-confederate condition. In the homosexual-confederate condition, global nonverbal behaviors (i.e., eye contact and interpersonal distance) are not expected to differ for those who expect to be socially anxious (i.e., moderately low prejudiced people) and those who expect to experience antipathy (i.e., high prejudiced people). However, we expect both their verbal responses (i.e., thoughts and self-reported feelings) and their more specific nonverbal behaviors (as coded with FACS or SPAFF) to differ for these two groups. We expect, for example, that moderately low prejudiced participants, whose expectations for the interaction reveal themes of social anxiety, should show facial expressions of fear and embarrassment, and that high prejudiced participants' facial expressions should reveal subtle signs of contempt and disgust. The very low prejudiced people, who report that they have both the motivation and ability to respond without prejudice, should not show facial signs of fear, embarrassment, or disgust.

IMPLICATIONS AND THE NEED TO CONSIDER THE MINORITY GROUP PERSPECTIVE

If these patterns of data are obtained, we would have further converging evidence to support our theory that majority group members can have very different psychological experiences in intergroup contact situations, and that their self-reported level of prejudice is an important factor underlying these differences. The findings for low prejudiced participants should provide some reason for encouragement and optimism about the potential for reducing intergroup tensions. That is, some low prejudiced people should expect to be comfortable in interactions with minority group members. Other low prejudiced people, although they may become socially anxious in intergroup contact settings, should be motivated to respond without prejudice. These findings would support the analysis that we have been developing for a number of years that low prejudiced people are sincere in their efforts to behave without prejudice (Devine, 1989; Devine et al., 1991; Devine & Monteith, 1993), even if the efforts of some are not particularly skillful or smooth (see also Poskocil, 1977).

Although majority group members may come to intergroup encounters with vastly differing expectations and motivations that may affect the outcome of the interaction, our enthusiasm and optimism about the impact that low prejudiced people's good intentions will have on intergroup relations must be somewhat tempered. Interactions, by definition, are not static. Because minority group members are active participants in the dynamics of the interaction and not passive targets, we need to understand the perspective (i.e., the goals, concerns, and motivations) they bring to the interaction. In a very real sense, the good intentions of majority group members are only useful if they are accurately interpreted by the targets of the intentions. Intentions, however, cannot be seen directly and must be inferred from others' behaviors. This could be problematic if minority group members rely primarily on the types of nonverbal behaviors that do not differentiate between majority group members who are high in prejudice and those who are low in prejudice but socially anxious. For example, some minority group members may *mis*interpret the anxious behavior of some low prejudiced individuals as a sign of antipathy or prejudice. For this reason, it is crucial that we examine and understand how minority group members respond to the behaviors of majority group members with different types of intentions.

Historically, the social-psychological literature has virtually ignored the effect of minority group members' expectations and concerns on the dynamics of interpersonal intergroup contact. Indeed, in interaction studies, the minority group member has typically been a confederate with a scripted role whose presence was needed to examine the behavior of majority group members (see Frable, Blackstone, & Scherbaum, 1990, and Ickes, 1984, for exceptions). When social-psychological research has concerned minority group members, it has focused on the long-term self-esteem and adjustment consequences of being in a disadvantaged or otherwise stigmatized group (e.g., Crocker & Major, 1989; Jones et al., 1984; Major & Crocker, 1993). People who are stigmatized, either by social group membership (e.g., race, sexual orientation) or by possession of particular characteristics (e.g., facial disfigurement, paralysis), are often labeled as deviant and targeted for prejudice and discrimination (Goffman, 1963; Jones et al., 1984). Jones et al. (1984) noted, however, that the stigmatized person "is neither interpersonally powerless nor bereft of beliefs or expectations of his own" (p. 180).

A growing literature suggests that a stigma assumes a central role in the way a stigmatized person construes and responds to his or her social world (Dion & Earn, 1975; Frable et al., 1990; Goffman, 1963; Jones et al., 1984; Kleck & Strenta, 1980; Wright, 1960). For example, Frable et al. (1990) argued that stigmatized people are more "mindful" in social interactions than are their nonstigmatized counterparts (cf. Langer, 1989). More specifically, Frable et al. (1990) suggested that stigmatized people pay close attention to how an interaction with another develops and envision the possible paths it may take. To this end, stigmatized people are likely to attend to the other's perspective and to details of the situation. Frable et al. posited that such mindfulness is adaptive because it enables stigmatized people to be more responsive during the interaction. As a result, they can negotiate potentially problematic social interactions more effectively.

The mindful strategy would work well if stigmatized people were unbiased and objective in the evaluation of others' behavior and if the behavioral cues of others were unambiguous. However, the evidence suggests that neither of these conditions is typical in intergroup situations. For example, those who are self-conscious about being stigmatized sometimes misinterpret others' behaviors

FIGURE 13.2 Doubts and uncertainties experienced by some minority group members. Cartoon by Don Wright, *The Palm Beach Post.* Copyright 1994 by Don Wright. Reprinted by permission.

and mannerisms, misattributing them to the stigma; in other words, people who expect bias often see bias (Kleck & Strenta, 1980; Jones et al., 1984). Indeed, Frable et al. (1990) argued that mindfulness is a defensive strategy that results, at least partly from uncertainty about how others will respond to one's stigma.

Thus, a theme that consistently emerges in the literature, and is particularly relevant for the interpersonal dynamics of intergroup interactions, is that socially stigmatized members of society are generally mistrusting and suspicious of majority group members' intentions and motives (Crocker & Major, 1989; Crocker, Voekl, Testa, & Major, 1991; Duke & Morin, 1992; Feagin, 1989; Hacker, 1992; Major & Crocker, 1993; Moses & Hawkins, 1982; Pettigrew & Martin, 1987; Schneider, 1986; Sears, 1991; Townsend, 1992). As illustrated in Figure 13.2, these suspicions may guide minority group members' perceptions of the behavior of others. Some of their suspicion derives from an awareness that members of their group are often targets of prejudice, discrimination, and oppression (Jones et al., 1984). Indeed, there is ample evidence to suggest that members of minority or stigmatized groups are aware of the stereotypes held by others about them and of discrimination against them (Taylor, Wright, Moghaddam, & Lalonde, 1990) because they are black (Hochschild & Herk, 1990; Rosenberg, 1979; Sigelman & Welch, 1991), female (Crosby, 1982), or homosexual (D'Emilio, 1983).[8]

Many homosexuals, for example, report feeling a need to be "on guard" and cautious about revealing their sexual orientation (Schneider, 1986). Specifically, they report fearing a variety of negative outcomes, including everything from physical abuse and overt discrimination to feelings of social isolation and rejection (e.g., Moses & Hawkins, 1982; Norris, 1991; Schneider, 1986; Tierney, 1992; Weinberg & Williams, 1974). Sears (1991) reported the experience of one student who was reluctant to tell a counselor about being homosexual because "people just kind of go bonkers when they hear that word or find out somebody is homosexual. . . . They don't know how to handle it. . . .I can't trust anybody with this information" (p. 37). Another student indicated that revealing his sexual orientation would involve "risking them not liking me" (p. 37).

In addition to the concerns about potential negative responses from majority group members, intergroup interactions are complicated for minority group members because, as Crocker, Major, and their colleagues (Crocker et al., 1991; Major & Crocker, 1993) have suggested, they live in a chronic state of attributional ambiguity with regard to the causes of others' behavior toward them. According to Major and Crocker (1993, p. 346), "this attributional ambiguity occurs because when the stigmatized and the nonstigmatized interact, the behavior of the nonstigmatized may be in response to the individual, personal qualities or behavior of the stigmatized person, or it may reflect the stereotypes and prejudices that the nonstigmatized person holds about the stigma." Such attributional ambiguity renders any feedback, whether positive or negative, cause for suspicion.

In a provocative set of studies, Crocker et al. (1991) showed that when black participants were being evaluated by a white person who was aware of their race (i.e., stigma was known), the black participants attributed both negative and positive feedback to the majority group member's negative attitudes. Crocker et al. argued that negative feedback is attributed directly to the majority group member's negative attitudes. Positive feedback, however, is attributed to the desire not to *appear* prejudiced. When the minority group member's race was unknown by the majority group evaluator, minority group members were more accepting of the feedback. Crocker et al. (1991) were primarily interested in the affective and self-evaluation implications of attributional ambiguity. They found that attributing negative feedback to one's stigma buffers one's self-esteem, because minority group members can discount personal dispositional qualities as responsible for the negative feedback. Affective reactions to positive feedback depend on whether the feedback is viewed as occurring in spite of the stigma (i.e., augmentation) or because of membership in the stigmatized group. In the former case, affect and self-evaluation should be enhanced; in the latter case, more depressed affect and more negative self-evaluation may occur.

If, as Frable et al. (1990) suggest, a minority group member is very mindful in an intergroup interaction, then the interaction may be affected by the minority group member's suspicion of the majority group member's intentions and by attributional ambiguity about whether the majority group member is responding to him or her as an individual or as a member of a stigmatized group. How such expectations of bias and prejudice and attributional ambiguity affect the actual dynamics of interpersonal intergroup contact has received scant attention. It is our contention that such suspicions and concerns, as well as attributional ambiguity, are likely to lead minority group members to experience a fair amount of stress and uncertainty about how to handle interpersonal encounters with majority group members (Crocker et al., 1991; Dion & Earn, 1975; Jones et al., 1984; Major & Crocker, 1993). Are their suspicions valid in a given situation (and how can they tell)? Should they act in accordance with their suspicions? What if they are wrong? What if they are right?! Such trepidation is quite understandable in the context of a history of prejudice and discriminatory treatment. However, it could have adverse effects on the interpersonal aspects of intergroup contact. For example, some minority group members may be prepared to see prejudice whether it is intended or not, particularly when the behavioral cues are ambiguous. Thus, the cognitions minority group members bring to intergroup settings may affect their expectations for how they will be treated by majority group members, their interpretations of the majority group members' behaviors and mannerisms, and their own interpersonal strategies. Taken together, these factors may influence the outcome of an interaction, the minority group member's feelings about the interaction, and his or her expectations regarding the likely success or failure of future interactions with majority group members.

Lest we fall prey to the same problem we have identified as prevalent in the majority group literature, we believe it is misleading to characterize *all* minority group members as suspicious and mistrusting of majority group members (Weinberg & Williams, 1974). That is, just as there is variability in majority group members' prejudice levels, which may have implications for how they approach intergroup contact, we expect that minority group members will also show variability in their level of suspicion and trust of majority group members. To explore this possibility, we collected data from gay men and lesbian women concerning their expectations about an interaction with a heterosexual person they did not know well (Devine, Conley, & Evett, 1993).

MINORITY GROUP MEMBERS' SELF-REPORTED EXPECTANCIES IN AN INTERGROUP INTERACTION

Gay men ($n = 44$) and lesbians ($n = 41$) were recruited from local organizations for a study on interactions with heterosexuals. This study parallels Study 3 in the majority group research (see above). The questionnaire consisted of the same 23 items, but the instructions were revised to be appropriate for gay and lesbian participants. Specifically, participants indicated the feelings they anticipated experiencing during an interaction with a heterosexual whom they did not know very well, and who was aware of their sexual orientation. The goal of the study was to determine whether individual-difference measures were related to the quality of the emotional experiences of minority group members during an intergroup interaction. To this end, we collected a number of potentially useful individual-difference measures, including how comfortable participants were with their sexual orientation, the nature of their previous experiences with heterosexuals (i.e., the amount of positive experience minus the amount of negative experience), and whether they thought people would respond negatively to them on the basis of their sexual orientation (i.e., whether people would like them less and evaluate their work more negatively because of their sexual orientation). All responses were made on 7-point scales.

The affect items were submitted to a factor analysis with varimax rotation, which yielded three factors. Indices were formed by combining items with loadings of at least .43 (reverse scoring when necessary): Discomfort (e.g., nervous, awkward, comfortable, suspicious, uneasy); Negative (e.g., afraid, hostile, annoyed, bothered); and Positive (e.g., trusting, sympathetic, friendly). The scales were all highly reliable (mean Cronbach's α = .84). Two of the items, guarded and confident, did not load strongly onto any of the indices, so separate analyses were done for these items. Hierarchical regression analyses were conducted to examine whether any of the predictor variables were associated with the feelings participants expected to have in the interaction. One predictor variable was added to the equation at each step, in the following order: gender, comfort with sexual orientation, past experience, and concern about negative evaluation.

The results of the regression analyses are presented in Table 13.2. One important determinant of participants' expectancies for how they would feel in the intergroup interaction was how comfortable they were with their own sexual orientation. Participants who were more comfortable with their sexual orientation expected to feel less discomfort, less negative, more confident, and less guarded during the interaction than did participants less comfortable with their sexual orientation. Participants' past experience with heterosexuals was also significantly related to their expected feelings. Specifically, participants with more positive past experiences with heterosexuals expected to feel less discomfort, less negative, more positive, and more confident than did participants with more negative past experiences. The extent to which participants were concerned that their sexual orientation would lead to more negative evaluations from others only significantly predicted participants' scores on the Positive index. Specifically, participants who thought they would be liked less and that their work would be more negatively evaluated if others knew their sexual orientation expected to feel less positive in the interaction than did participants who thought their sexual orientation would have less negative consequences. Participant gender was significantly related to scores on the negative index, such that lesbians expected to feel more negative than did gay males. Gender was not related to any of the other dependent variables.

These data suggest that some minority group members are less comfortable, less trusting, and more guarded in intergroup interactions than others. The variability in these expectancies is sensibly related to individual differences in how comfortable minority group members are with their stigmatized characteristic (in this case, sexual orientation) and the nature of their past experiences with majority group members. These factors are likely to affect not only the ex-

TABLE 13.2 Significant Effects in Hierarchical Regression Analyses on Five Affect Measures

	β	*df*	*F*	*p*
Discomfort				
Comfort with orientation	−.39	(1, 84)	6.41	.02
Positive past experience	−.11	(1, 83)	4.14	.05
Negative				
Gender	.61	(1, 85)	4.76	.05
Comfort with orientation	−.52	(1, 84)	15.16	.001
Positive past experience	−.13	(1, 83)	7.88	.01
Positive				
Positive past experience	.10	(1, 83)	4.75	.05
Concern about negative evaluation	−.17	(1, 82)	4.09	.05
Confident				
Comfort with orientation	.55	(1, 84)	10.42	.002
Positive past experience	.20	(1, 83)	12.41	.001
Guarded				
Comfort with orientation	−.55	(1, 84)	7.28	.01

Note. Variables were entered into the regression equation in the following order: gender, comfort with sexual orientation, past experience, and concern about negative evaluation. The data are from Devine, Conley, and Evett (1993).

pectancies of minority group members, but also their perceptions of and responses to a majority group member's behavior in an actual interaction. As we have noted in regard to our work on majority group members, we intend to extend our empirical work on minority group members beyond self-reported expectancies to actual interaction settings. Specifically, our subsequent empirical work is designed to examine whether minority group members, who vary in their overall level of trust and suspicion of majority group members, are sensitive to the characteristics that may distinguish high prejudiced people from low prejudiced people in intergroup contact situations. Our primary concern is whether minority group members who expect hostile or negative treatment may misperceive social anxiety as antipathy. Anticipation of negative reactions from majority group members and suspicion about majority group members' intentions or motives, however justified they may be from a historical vantage point, are likely to be sources of tension in intergroup contact settings.

THE RECIPROCAL DYNAMICS OF INTERPERSONAL INTERGROUP CONTACT

It seems clear that both majority and minority group members bring expectancies about intergroup contact and about their interaction partner to the interaction setting. Our challenge at this point is to examine the implications of these expectancies for the interaction dynamics that evolve. We must be somewhat speculative here, because we have not yet collected data bearing on these issues. Our focus is on the initial phases of intergroup contact between people who do not know each other well. In addition, we are interested in interactions for which there are no prescribed roles. Such roles (e.g., teacher and student) provide each interactant with a script to follow; although these situations are interesting, unstructured interactions between strangers provide the clearest opportunities for the ambiguities of social dynamics to reveal themselves (Stephan & Stephan, 1985). The greatest potential for bias and miscommunication is present early in a relationship, before a great deal of information about the interaction partner has been obtained. In addition, examining the earliest phases of an intergroup interaction is important because these phases set the stage for what type of relationship (if any) will develop between the majority and minority group members.

Before we proceed with an analysis of the interpersonal aspects of intergroup contact, several comments on the complexity of studying social interaction are appropriate. In social psychology, the term "interaction" is typically used to refer to the interdependent actions of two or more persons (Jones et al., 1984). In studying interactions, it is important to examine overt behaviors, but Jones et al. point out that it is also important to understand the cognitive, affective, and motivational factors within each interactant because these influence the reciprocal dynamics of an interaction. Hence, a researcher needs to keep track of intrapersonal processes (i.e., cognitions, affect) and interpersonal processes (i.e., the mutual influence of the interactants on each other) simultaneously. One of the things that makes interactions so complicated to study is their ongoing and sequential nature. As the interaction unfolds over time, the interactants update their impressions, form new expectancies, and plan new behaviors. These intrapersonal updates affect each interactant's subsequent behaviors. Devising ways to keep track of the complexities of these dynamic aspects of social interaction introduces methodological dilemmas (if not nightmares) for the social scientist interested in these processes. We believe that these complexities are largely responsible for the dearth of empirical work on the reciprocal dynamics of social interaction.

Expectancy Confirmation in Social Interaction

Although there is a relative shortage of empirical work specifically addressing the reciprocal dynamics of social interaction (and even less concerning intergroup interactions), there is a fairly extensive literature on impression formation, attribution, and expectancy confirmation biases that may shed light on how people's expectancies shape the early stages of social interaction (for reviews, see Darley & Fazio, 1980; Hilton & Darley, 1991; Miller & Turnbull, 1986; Neuberg, Chapter 7, this volume; Snyder, 1992). Although they may differ in some details, expectancy confirmation models have in common the notion that interpersonal expectancies, through their effect on a variety of information processing and behavioral strategies (e.g., information gathering, encoding, interpretation of behavior), exert a powerful influence on social interactions. To illustrate how expectancies can affect social interactions, we review Darley and Fazio's (1980) model of expectancy confirmation processes in some detail. The model highlights how inherently complicated interaction sequences are to model and to study.

Darley and Fazio (1980) outlined the steps in a general interaction sequence as follows:

1. The perceiver develops an expectancy regarding the target person, based either on past experience or on knowledge of the category to which the target belongs.
2. The perceiver then behaves toward the target in accordance with the expectancy.
3. The target interprets the meaning of the perceiver's action.
4. On the basis of the interpretation, the target responds to the perceiver's action.
5. The perceiver then interprets the target's action and updates his or her expectancy. At this point, the perceiver re-enters the interaction sequence at Step 2.

Darley and Fazio argue that it is useful to consider the sequence as containing a sixth step: After responding to the perceiver's action, the target interprets the meaning of his or her own action. Often the target will recognize that his or her action was a direct response to the perceiver's action and is therefore situationally appropriate. However, at times the target may not recognize that his or her action is constrained by the perceiver's behavior, and will therefore infer something new about himself or herself as a result of the action. In this manner, the target's action may have implications for his or her own self-concept (Fazio, Effrein, & Falender, 1981; Miller & Turnbull, 1986).

When this model is applied to any interaction sequence, two caveats are in order. First, Darley and Fazio (1980) note that selecting one person to be labeled the "perceiver" and the other the "target" is arbitrary. It is important to recognize that the process is symmetric; both interactants are both perceivers and targets. This observation is critical when we consider the intergroup contact setting. Both majority and minority group members bring expectancies to the intergroup setting and it is important to consider both perspectives simultaneously when imagining how an interaction sequence will unfold. Thus, the comments about the perceiver's expectancies and the target's reactions are relevant to both majority and minority group participants in an intergroup interaction. Second, perception of another's behavior is an active and constructive process. Actions do not directly convey meanings, but rather are given meanings by a perceiver. This point takes on added significance when perceivers are biased and behaviors are ambiguous.

Darley and Fazio (1980) were particularly concerned with how perceivers' expectancies could bias the entire interaction sequence, particularly in expectancy-confirming ways. Expectancy confirmation theorists (Darley & Fazio, 1980; Hilton & Darley, 1991; Miller & Turnbull, 1986; Neuberg, Chapter 7, this volume; Snyder, 1992) have identified two major sources of expectancy confirmation effects: (1) cognitive processing biases and (2) self-fulfilling prophecies. Cognitive processing biases include a variety of perceptual, attentional, and interpretational biases that lead to the persistence of a perceiver's expectancies, even when the evidence clearly contradicts the expectancy (see Hilton & Darley, 1991, and Neuberg, Chapter 7, this volume, for reviews). For example, perceivers are selective in their attention to and evaluation of the actions of a target (Fiske & Neuberg, 1990). This type of information screening limits the actions that are attended to, and hence simplifies observation of a target (Darley & Gross, 1983; Zadny & Gerard, 1974). When a target's action is consistent with expectancies, perceivers readily accept the behavioral evidence and attribute it to dispositional qualities of the target (e.g., Darley & Gross, 1983; Evett, Devine, Hirt, & Price, 1994; Gilbert, 1989; Hastie, 1984; Jones & Davis, 1965). In contrast, when information is inconsistent with expectancies, the perceiver's information-processing flexibility diminishes the impact of the information, enabling persistence of the original expectancy. That is, expectancy-inconsistent behavior, if attended to at all, is often explained away by attributing it to situational forces or otherwise rationalizing the behavior (e.g., Crocker, Hannah, & Weber, 1983; Darley & Gross, 1983; Evett et al., 1994). Contributing to the tenacity of expectancies is the well-documented finding that when a target's behavior is ambiguous, perceivers interpret the behavior in expectancy-congruent ways (e.g., Darley & Gross, 1983; Dion, 1972; Deaux, 1976; Duncan, 1976; Hastorf & Cantril, 1954; Sagar & Schofield, 1980).

The second major source of expectancy confirmation effects occurs in the context of ongoing interaction sequences between perceivers and targets in the form of self-fulfilling prophecies. Specifically, many studies have shown that expectancies influence a perceiver's actions toward a target in ways that lead the target to behave consistently with the perceiver's initial expectancies. For example, Snyder and Swann (1978; see also Kelley & Stahelski, 1970a, 1970b) demonstrated that when a perceiver is led to expect that a target is hostile in the context of a competitive game, the perceiver, expecting the target to be competitive, makes a pre-emptive competitive move. The target, who is not privy to the perceiver's expectancy, reciprocates with a competitive action, hence confirming the perceiver's initial expectancy. In this sense, a perceiver's expectancy can become a reality. Such self-fulfilling prophecy effects are particularly important and interesting, because very often neither the perceiver nor the target appreciates how the target's behavior is constrained by the perceiver's actions (e.g., Fazio et al., 1981; Jones & Panitch, 1971; Ross, Amabile, & Steinmetz, 1977; Snyder & Swann, 1978; Snyder, Tanke, & Berscheid, 1977; Word et al., 1974). Once the target responds to the perceiver's action, the interaction sequence cycles back to the perceiver, who must now interpret the target's behavior, update his or her expectancies, plan a new behavior, and so on. The perceiver's interpretations of the target's behavior are likely to influence future behaviors toward the target and may result in continuing confirmation of the perceiver's expectancy.

Reciprocal Dynamics in Interpersonal Intergroup Settings

With Darley and Fazio's (1980) model of expectancy confirmation processes as background, we can proceed to an analysis of intergroup interactions. One clear implication of many of the expectancy confirmation models is that expectancies brought to the interaction setting are likely to affect participants' interaction goals and strategies. Furthermore, early in an intergroup exchange, responses to the other may be based more on group membership than on individual identity (Allport, 1954; Brewer, 1988; Devine, 1989; Fiske & Neuberg, 1990). Indeed, mere knowledge that an impending interaction is an *intergroup* interaction may set in motion processes for both the majority and minority participants that will have important consequences for how the interaction unfolds.

Our data concerning how people construe intergroup interactions suggest that both majority and minority group members have expectancies about intergroup interactions, and that within each group there is variability in the nature of the expectancies. The variability can be attributed to individual differences in prejudice among majority group members and to individual differences in trust or suspicion among minority group members. Such differences are very likely to be linked to goals and plans for action. For example, a low prejudiced majority group member may set up a goal to "communicate my nonprejudiced identity." In a similar vein, a suspicious minority group member may set in motion a plan to "protect myself from the adverse consequences of majority group prejudice." These goals in turn will affect each person's expectancies for the interaction, what the person does, and interpretations of the other's behavior.

In all interactions, particularly those in the intergroup context, not only do each of the interactants have expectancies and goals; they also have cognitive representations of the other person's expectancies, goals, and likely attributions (cf. Asch, 1952). These representations may or may not be accurate. Because interactants do not often overtly share their expectancies or interaction goals with each other, the stage is set for various levels of misunderstanding, particularly at the outset of an interaction. In the intergroup context, we contend that such misunderstandings may contribute to miscommunication between interactants and may lead to heightened intergroup tension.

To illustrate the applicability of the Darley and Fazio (1980) analysis to the intergroup setting, we consider only a few of the myriad of possibilities for dynamic exchanges between majority and minority group members. Whether miscommunication and/or tension results depends strongly on the extent to which the goals of the interactants match or clash. For example, an interaction between a high prejudiced majority group member and a suspicious minority group member may go relatively smoothly, if not positively. In this case, the majority group member may plan his or her interaction strategy so as to terminate the interaction as quickly as possible.[9] The minority group member may set in motion attributional biases to protect his or her self-esteem (Crocker et al., 1991). Under these circumstances, little miscommunication occurs, but tension is likely to be high. Alternatively, the majority group member may be a low prejudiced person who possesses the requisite skills to convey his or her standards, and the minority group member may not be suspicious of majority group members. Under these circumstances, miscommunication is also unlikely, and we can anticipate a smooth and positive exchange between the interactants.

Miscommunication and intergroup conflict are likely to arise when the interactants' goals and expectancies clash. For example, in our analysis of prejudice reduction, we have been particularly concerned with interactions in which the goals and expectancies of low prejudiced people clash with those of minority group interactants. More specifically, we have discussed the plight of well-intentioned, highly motivated, nonprejudiced majority group members who believe they lack the skills necessary to convey that identity to a minority group member. This situation is likely to be particularly problematic if the minority group member is suspicious of majority group members. Here the goals and concerns of the interactants conflict.

Consider the development of this type of interaction from the perspective of Darley and Fazio's (1980) interaction model:

1. The low prejudiced majority group member is highly motivated to respond without prejudice, but is uncertain about his or her ability to do so.

2. In an effort to respond consistently with these important standards, the majority group member is likely to become highly self-conscious and socially anxious. Thus, despite his or her good intentions, the majority group member is likely to display avoidant nonverbal behaviors such as decreased eye contact and increased speech errors.

3. Because the minority group member cannot directly see the interaction partner's good intentions, and because the meaning of such avoidant nonverbal behaviors is ambiguous, these behaviors are likely to be interpreted in line with the minority group member's expectation of prejudice from majority group members. That is, the minority group member's expectancies may lead him or her to see hostile rather than anxious behavior.

4. Having interpreted the majority group member's actions as prejudiced and hostile, the minority group member may respond with withdrawal, aloofness, or hostility.

5. If the majority group member is unaware that his or her behavior has been interpreted as hostile, he or she may consider the minority group member's responses to be unreasonable and reflective of the minority group member's dispositional dislike of majority group members (Jones & Panitch, 1971; Ross et al., 1977; Snyder et al., 1977). The majority group member then re-enters the interaction sequence at Step 2: He or she may reciprocate the negative behavior or withdraw from the interaction.

6. Meanwhile, the minority group member's negative beliefs and suspicions about majority group members are reinforced and perhaps even elevated.

Thus, even when low prejudiced individuals have the best of intentions in the intergroup setting, there is the potential for miscommunication between interactants. Because of the dynamic nature of interactions and the inherent ambiguity of much social behavior, this miscommunication can lead to the escalation rather than the alleviation of intergroup tension, as *perceived* hostility is transformed into *actual* hostility on the part of both interactants.

It is important to recognize that any intergroup interaction has implications for each interactant's expectancies concerning future intergroup interactions. If majority and minority group members come to expect that intergroup interactions will go badly, they most assuredly will go badly. Under these circumstances a cycle of spiraling mistrust can be established, leading both majority and minority group members to expect and create failed intergroup interactions. Indeed, one of our main concerns is that because intergroup interactions are often difficult to negotiate, many majority and minority group members may decide to retreat from intergroup contact settings rather than put themselves at risk of a negative interaction. Recent evidence suggests that when intergroup interactions are awkward, strained, or uncomfortable, people avoid intergroup contact, resulting in a new form of separatism (Pettigrew, 1994b). Such separatism, even when voluntary, seems an unsatisfactory resolution to the problem of intergroup tension (Celis, 1994). It clearly violates the spirit of the *Brown v. Board of Education* decision, the goal of which was to facilitate contact between majority and minority group members. A much more positive and satisfactory resolution to this problem would to be to identify means to avoid miscommunication between majority and minority group members in intergroup contact settings.

CONCLUDING COMMENTS

The goal of this chapter and of our present program of research is to explore the origins and nature of intergroup tension that may create obstacles for harmonious intergroup relations. In contrast to the traditional approaches, our analysis suggests that simply changing the prejudiced attitudes of majority group members is necessary but insufficient for improving intergroup relations. We have argued that intergroup tension can be experienced by low and high prejudiced majority group members, as well as by their minority group interaction partners. This tension can arise from the motivations and cognitions that both majority and minority group members bring to an intergroup interaction, as well as from the dynamics of the interaction itself. In this chapter, we have outlined a preliminary analysis of the psychological experiences and practical challenges that may underlie the tension felt by both majority and minority group interactants. Furthermore, we address the consequences that such tension may have for the interpersonal dynamics of interactions between majority and minority group members.

Tension in intergroup settings may take many forms, including prejudice and hostility, fear of victimization and negative evaluation, and social anxiety about negotiating the intergroup interaction. Of particular concern is the type of intergroup tension that arises despite the best intentions of the participants. Specifically, we have proposed that some low prejudiced majority group members are highly motivated to respond without prejudice in the interaction but doubt their ability to do so successfully. As a result, they may display avoidant nonverbal behaviors—behaviors that are also associated with prejudice and antipathy. When the interaction partner is a minority group member who expects most majority group members to be prejudiced, these ambiguous behaviors are likely to be misinterpreted as signs of prejudice. The subsequent perceptions and responses of both interactants are likely to influence one another in a cycle of miscommunication and escalating tension.

Despite this somewhat gloomy scenario, we believe that the proposed theoretical framework, unlike other contemporary approaches, offers reason for considerable optimism regarding the potential to reduce intergroup tension and promote harmonious intergroup relations. First, we recognize that there are key individual differences in majority group prejudice. This is important because it suggests that many majority group members (i.e., those low in prejudice) are motivated to work toward smooth intergroup relations. Some low prejudiced majority group members may be confident that they are able to convey their nonprejudiced standards successfully. For these individuals, the prospects for establishing a cycle of nonthreatening intergroup contact are good. Those low prejudiced people who lack confidence may be able to develop the skills needed to act and feel more comfortable and less anxious in intergroup encounters, increasing the likelihood that these interactions will be successful. By developing these skills, they may be able to break the cycle of miscommunication that disrupts their intergroup encounters.

Second, we recognize that the problem of intergroup tension is not simply a "majority group problem." Ultimately, intergroup tension is experienced by both majority and minority group members involved in intergroup encounters. Our analysis highlights the importance of considering the minority group perspective in developing a complete understanding of the problem of intergroup tension and conflict. The positive implication of this analysis is that minority group members can also be viewed as part of the solution. Although some minority group members understandably have negative expectations about majority group members, and these expectations may lead to biased perceptions of majority group members' behavior, presumably such biases can be overcome with effort and practice. We contend that if tension is experienced by both majority and minority group members, one-sided efforts to remediate the problem, such as the traditional focus on changing majority group members' attitudes, are destined to fail. We believe that the present framework, because it includes an analysis of the practical challenges and obstacles faced by both majority and minority group members, serves as a point of departure for developing effective interventions for reducing intergroup tension and improving interpersonal communication between majority and minority group members.

Without such interventions, the difficulties of intergroup contact pose significant problems at both micro and macro levels. For both of the individuals involved in an encounter that "goes sour," there may be stress, damage to self-esteem, and a reluctance to attempt further intergroup meetings. These consequences are damaging for society as well. Although there is clearly less risk to the interactants if they stay within their own groups, the increasingly multicultural United States can scarcely afford to revert to a separatist society of groups unable to communicate with one another. By recognizing the interdependence of majority and minority group members in intergroup interactions, we can begin to alleviate the concerns and distrust underlying intergroup tension and to promote harmony between groups.

Acknowledgments

The preparation of this chapter, and the research reported herein, were supported in part by grants from the Wisconsin Alumni Research Foundation, the Vilas Associates Program, and the Hilldale Faculty Fellowship Program to Patricia G. Devine. We would like to thank Terri Conley for her insightful feedback and her assistance with data collection, and the members of our research team for their participation in spirited discussions that contributed to the development of these ideas. We would also like to thank Tory Higgins and Dick Sorrentino for their helpful comments on a previous draft of this chapter.

Notes

1. Note once again, that the emphasis is placed on the behaviors of the majority group members and the likelihood that majority group members display bias in their responses to minority group members. In most of these studies, the minority group member was a confederate with scripted behaviors and responses (for exceptions, see Ickes, 1984, and Frable, Blackstone, & Scherbaum, 1990). Thus, these studies did not afford the opportunity to study the reciprocal nature of the interpersonal dynamics between majority and minority group members.

2. We do not mean to suggest that high prejudiced people never try to present a nonprejudiced image. However, when they do make such efforts, we expect that they do so simply for strategic impression management reasons. The important audience for high prejudiced people is the outside audience, not themselves (i.e., it is not *personally* important for them to present a nonprejudiced image).

3. These reports were collected by Richard Tyler in his role as the head of the Minority Affairs Program on the University of Wisconsin–Milwaukee campus in 1990. Tyler often held focus groups and counseled students on how to deal with intergroup contact situations for a variety of different minority groups on campus, including blacks, homosexuals, Latinos, Asians, and women.

4. An additional, more practical reason contributed to our decision to study homosexuals and heterosexuals. Because of the nature of the subject samples available on our campus, the heterosexual–homosexual combination is better suited to our present purposes. Our research requires majority group members at all levels of prejudice toward minority group members. It is only for the heterosexual–homosexual combination that we have reliably identified majority group members at all levels of prejudice toward minority group members (from very low to very high). In our work on prejudice toward blacks, for example, we typically have identified only a small number of whites with strongly prejudiced attitudes toward blacks (e.g., Devine et al., 1991).

5. Recent research on the accessibility of participants' personal standards provides additional support for the notion that very low prejudiced individuals may be further along in the prejudice reduction process than those who score slightly higher in prejudice (Zuwerink & Devine, 1993). In this study, although all participants who scored on the low prejudiced end of the HATH continuum reported low prejudiced personal standards, the standards were more highly accessible for very low prejudiced (HATH range = 20–32) than for moderately low prejudiced (HATH range = 33–46) participants. Moreover, the standards of moderately low prejudiced participants were no more accessible than the standards of moderate and high prejudiced participants.

6. It is also important to note that the higher Anxiety scores were not attributable to greater dispositional social anxiety. In a different data collection on a smaller sample (n = 148), we gave the same questionnaire as well as Leary's Interaction Anxiousness and Audience Anxiousness scales (Leary 1983a, 1983b) which measure dispositional social anxiety. Although HATH was linearly related to anxiety, it was uncorrelated with the Interaction anxiousness (r = .01, n.s.) and Audience Anxiousness (r = .07, n.s.) scales.

7. It is important to note that one study did obtain measures of participants' psychological experiences in an intergroup contact situation between blacks and whites (Ickes, 1984). Ickes found that in comparison to black participants, white participants reported higher levels of social anxiety (e.g., tried to avoid offending the other). Moreover, whites who indicated that they typically avoided interactions with blacks reported higher levels of social anxiety than did whites who indicated that they typically initiated interactions with blacks. Ickes assumed that the "avoidant" participants in his research were motivated by prejudice, but he did not explicitly measure prejudice, nor was he able to compare interracial dyads with same-race dyads. Consequently, it is possible that the "avoidant" participants in Ickes's research were generally avoidant people who would have treated both minority and majority group members to the same pattern of avoidant behaviors.

8. Members of other stigmatized groups, such as the blind, mentally ill, obese, and physically handicapped, are also aware of the negative connotations of their labels (see Scott, 1969; Link, 1987; Jarvie, Lahey, Graziano, & Framer, 1983; and Avillion, 1986, respectively). Although we believe that the analysis we are developing could apply well to the experiences of majority-minority group combinations involving these stigmatized groups, our immediate concern is to present the analysis in terms of majority-minority group combinations for which the stigma is primarily socially, rather than physically, defined.

9. Keep in mind that this is only one of many possible interaction strategies available to a high prejudiced majority group member; we have selected it for illustrative purposes. Clearly, under some circumstances, high prejudiced majority group members may attempt to adopt a nonprejudiced interaction style (e.g., under clear normative pressure for nonprejudiced behavior or the possibility of negative sanctions for high prejudiced behavior). These situations will be critical to explore. Are high prejudiced people able to manage a nonprejudiced identity effectively? Can minority group members detect such efforts as insincere? How does such deception affect the unfolding of the interaction or the developing relationship between the interaction participants? We plan to examine these possibilities, as well as many others, in our intergroup interaction research.

References

Adler, J., Starr, M., Chiedeya, F., Wright, L., Wingert, P., & Hacc, L. (1990, December 24). Taking offense. *Newsweek*, pp. 48-54.

Adorno, T. W., Frenkel-Brunswik, E., Levinson, D. J., & Sanford, R. N. (1950). *The authoritarian personality*. New York: Harper.

Allport, G. W. (1954). *The nature of prejudice*. Reading, MA: Addison-Wesley.

Amir, Y. (1969). Contact hypothesis of ethnic relations. *Psychological Bulletin, 71,* 319-343.

Apostle, R. A., Glock, C. Y., Piazza, T., & Suezele, M. (1983). *The anatomy of racial attitudes*. Berkeley: University of California Press.

Asch, S. E. (1952). *Social psychology*. Englewood Cliffs, NJ: Prentice-Hall.

Ashmore, R. D. (1970). The problem of intergroup prejudice. In B. E. Collins (Ed.), *Social psychology* (pp. 246-296). Reading, MA: Addison-Wesley.

Avillion, A. E. (1986). Barrier perception and its influence on self-esteem. *Rehabilitation Nursing, 11,* 11-14.

Brewer, M. B. (1988). A dual process model of impression formation. In T. K. Srull & R. S. Wyer, Jr. (Eds.), *Advances in social cognition: Vol. 1. A dual model of impression formation* (pp. 1-36). Hillsdale, NJ: Erlbaum.

Buss, A. H. (1980). *Self-consciousness and social anxiety*. San Francisco: W. H. Freeman.

Carver, C. S., & Scheier, M. F. (1981). *Attention and self-regulation: A control theory approach to behavior*. New York: Springer-Verlag.

Carver, C. S., & Scheier, M. F. (1990). Origins and functions of positive and negative affect: A control process view. *Psychological Review, 97,* 19-35.

Celis, W., III. (1994, May 18). 40 years after *Brown*, segregation persists. *The New York Times*, p. A1.

Cook, S. W. (1984). Cooperative interaction in multiethnic contexts. In N. Miller & M. B. Brewer (Eds.), *Groups in contact: The psychology of desegregation* (pp. 155-185). New York: Academic Press.

Cook, S. W. (1985). Experimenting on social issues: The case of school desegregation. *American Psychologist, 40,* 452-460.

Crocker, J., Hannah, D. B., & Weber, R. (1983). Person memory and causal attributions. *Journal of Personality and Social Psychology, 40,* 441-452.

Crocker, J., & Major, B. (1989). Social stigma and self-esteem: The self-protective properties of stigma. *Psychological Review, 96,* 608-630.

Crocker, J., Voekl, K., Testa, M., & Major, B. (1991). Social stigma: The affective consequences of attributional ambiguity. *Journal of Personality and Social Psychology, 60,* 218-228.

Crosby, F. (1982). *Relative deprivation and working women*. New York: Oxford University Press.

Crosby, F., Bromley, S., & Saxe, L. (1980). Recent unobtrusive studies of black and white discrimination and prejudice: A literature review. *Psychological Bulletin, 87,* 546-563.

Cuenot, R. G., & Fugita, S. S. (1982). Perceived homosexuality: Measuring heterosexual attitudinal and nonverbal reactions. *Personality and Social Psychology Bulletin, 8,* 100-106.

Darley, J. M., & Fazio, R. H. (1980). Expectancy confirmation processes arising in the social interaction sequence. *American Psychologist, 35,* 867-881.

Darley, J. M., & Gross, P. H. (1983). A hypothesis-confirming bias in labeling effects. *Journal of Personality and Social Psychology, 44,* 20-33.

Deaux, K. (1976). Sex: A perspective on the attribution process. In J. H. Harvey & R. F. Kidd (Eds.), *New directions in attribution research* (Vol. 1, pp. 335-352). Hillsdale, NJ: Erlbaum.

D'Emilio, J. (1983). *Sexual politics, sexual communities: The making of a homosexual minority in the United States, 1940-1970*. Chicago: University of Chicago Press.

Dennis, V. C., & Powell, E. R. (1972). Nonverbal communication in across-race dyads. *Proceedings of the 80th Annual Convention of the American Psychological Association, 7*(Part 2), 557-558.

DePaulo, B. M. (1992). Nonverbal behavior and self-presentation. *Psychological Bulletin, 111,* 203-243.

Devine, P. G. (1989). Stereotypes and prejudice: Their automatic and controlled components. *Journal of Personality and Social Psychology, 56,* 5-18.

Devine, P. G. (1995). Prejudice and outgroup perception. In A. Tesser (Ed.), *Advanced social psychology* (pp. 466-524). New York: McGraw-Hill.

Devine, P. G., & Amodt, I. (1994, May). *When personal standards collide with social pressure: Competing motivations and affective consequences.* Paper presented at the meeting of the Midwestern Psychological Association, Chicago.

Devine, P. G., Conley, T., & Evett, S. R. (1993). Unpublished raw data, University of Wisconsin-Madison.

Devine, P. G., & Evett, S. R. (1993). Unpublished raw data, University of Wisconsin-Madison.

Devine, P. G., & Monteith, M. J. (1993). The role of discrepancy associated affect in prejudice reduction. In D. M. Mackie & D. L. Hamilton (Eds.), *Affect, cognition, and stereotyping: Interactive processes in intergroup perception* (pp. 317-344). New York: Academic Press.

Devine, P. G., Monteith, M. J., Zuwerink, J. R., & Elliot, A. J. (1991). Prejudice with and without compunction. *Journal of Personality and Social Psychology, 60,* 817-830.

Devine, P. G., & Vasquez-Suson, K. A. (1994). Unpublished raw data, University of Wisconsin-Madison.

Dion, K. K. (1972). Physical attractiveness and evaluation of children's trangressions. *Journal of Personality and Social Psychology, 24,* 207-213.

Dion, K. L., & Earn, B. M. (1975). The phenomenology of being a target of prejudice. *Journal of Personality and Social Psychology, 32,* 944-950.

Dovidio, J. F., & Gaertner, S. L. (1986). Prejudice, discrimination and racism: Historical trends and contemporary approaches. In J. F. Dovidio & S. L. Gaertner (Eds.), *Prejudice, discrimination, and racism* (pp. 1-34). San Diego, CA: Academic Press.

Duckitt, J. (1992). *The social psychology of prejudice.* New York: Praeger.

Duke, L., & Morin, R. (1992, March 8). Focusing on race: Candid dialogue, elusive answers. *The Washington Post,* pp. A1, A24, A25.

Duncan, S. L. (1976). Differential social perception and attribution of intergroup violence: Testing the lower limits of the stereotyping of blacks. *Journal of Personality and Social Psychology, 34,* 590-598.

Duval, S., & Wicklund, R. A. (1972). *A theory of objective self-awareness.* New York: Academic Press.

Ekman, P., & Friesen, W. V. (1978). *Facial Action Coding System.* Palo Alto, CA: Consulting Psychologists Press.

Evett, S. R., & Devine, P. G. (1993, April). *Prejudice and the nature of intergroup tension.* Paper presented at the meeting of the Midwestern Psychological Association, Chicago.

Evett, S. R., Devine, P. G., Hirt, E. R., & Price, J. (1994). The role of the hypothesis and the evidence in the trait hypothesis testing process. *Journal of Experimental Social Psychology, 30,* 456-481.

Fazio, R. H., Effrein, E. A., & Falender, V. J. (1981). Self-perceptions following social interaction. *Journal of Personality and Social Psychology, 41,* 232-242.

Feagin, J. R. (1989). The continuing significance of race: Antiblack discrimination in public places. *American Sociological Review, 56,* 101-116.

Fiske, S. T. (1992). Thinking is for doing: Portraits of social cognition from daguerreotype to laserphoto. *Journal of Personality and Social Psychology, 63,* 877-889.

Fiske, S. T., & Neuberg, S. L. (1990). A continuum of impression formation, from category-based to individuating processes: Influences of information and motivation on attention and interpretation. In M. P. Zanna (Ed.), *Advances in experimental social psychology* (Vol. 23, pp. 1-63). San Diego, CA: Academic Press.

Frable, D., Blackstone, T., & Scherbaum, C. (1990). Marginal and mindful: Deviants in social interaction. *Journal of Personality and Social Psychology, 59,* 140-149.

Gaertner, S. L., & Dovidio, J. F. (1986). The aversive form of racism. In J. F. Dovidio & S. L.

Gaertner (Eds.), *Prejudice, discrimination, and racism* (pp.1-34). San Diego, CA: Academic Press.

Gilbert, D. T. (1989). Thinking lightly about others: Automatic components of the social inference process. In J. S. Uleman & J. A. Bargh (Eds.), *Unintended thought* (pp. 189-211). New York: Guilford Press.

Goffman, E. (1963). *Stigma: Notes on the management of a spoiled identity.* Englewood Cliffs, NJ: Prentice-Hall.

Gottman, J. M., & Krokoff, L. J. (1989). Marital interaction and satisfaction: A longitudinal view. *Journal of Consulting and Clinical Psychology, 57,* 47-52.

Hacker, A. (1992). *Two nations: Black and white, separate, hostile, unequal.* New York: Ballantine Books.

Hastie, R. (1984). Causes and effects of causal attribution. *Journal of Personality and Social Psychology, 37,* 25-38.

Hastorf, A. H., & Cantril, H. (1954). They saw a game: A case study. *Journal of Abnormal and Social Psychology, 49,* 129-134.

Hendricks, M., & Bootzin, R. (1976). Race and sex as stimuli for negative affect and physical avoidance. *Journal of Social Psychology, 98,* 111-120.

Henley, N. M. (1977). *Body politics: Power, sex, and nonverbal communication.* Englewood Cliffs, NJ: Prentice-Hall.

Henry, W. A., III. (1994, June 27). Pride and prejudice. *Time,* pp. 54-59.

Herek, G. M. (1984). Beyond "homophobia": A social psychological perspective on attitudes toward lesbians and gay men. *Journal of Homosexuality, 10,* 1-21.

Higgins, E. T. (1981). The "communication game": Implication for social cognition and persuasion. In E. T. Higgins, C. P. Herman, & M. P. Zanna (Eds.), *The Ontario Symposium: Vol. 1. Social cognition* (pp. 343-392). Hillsdale, NJ: Erlbaum.

Higgins, E. T. (1987). Self-discrepancy: A theory relating self and affect. *Psychological Review, 94,* 319-340.

Higgins, E. T. (1992). Achieving 'shared reality' in the communication game: A social action that creates meaning. *Journal of Language and Social Psychology, 11,* 107-131.

Hilton, J. L., & Darley, J. M. (1991). The effects of interaction goals on person perception. In M. P. Zanna (Ed.), *Advances in experimental social psychology* (Vol. 24, pp. 235-267). San Diego, CA: Academic Press.

Hochschild, J. L., & Herk, M. (1990). "Yes, but . . .": Principles and caveats in American racial attitudes. In J. W. Chapman & A. W. Wertheimer (Eds.), *Majorities and minorities* (pp. 308-335). New York: New York University Press.

Hudson, W. W., & Ricketts, W. A. (1980). A strategy for the measurement of homophobia. *Journal of Homosexuality, 5,* 357-372.

Ickes, W. (1984). Compositions in black and white: Determinants of interaction in interracial dyads. *Journal of Personality and Social Psychology, 47,* 330-341.

Jarvie, G. J., Lahey, B., Graziano, W., & Framer, E. (1983). Childhood obesity and social stigma: What we know and what we don't know. *Developmental Review, 3,* 237-273.

Jones, E. E., & Davis, K. E. (1965). A theory of correspondent inference: From acts to dispositions. In L. Berkowitz (Ed.), *Advances in experimental social psychology* (Vol. 2, pp. 219-266). New York: Academic Press.

Jones, E. E., Farina, A., Hastorf, A. H., Markus, H., Miller, D. T., & Scott, R. A. (1984). *Social stigma: The psychology of marked relationships.* New York: W. H. Freeman.

Jones, S. C., & Panitch, D. (1971). The self-fulfilling prophecy and interpersonal attraction. *Journal of Experimental Social Psychology, 7,* 356-366.

Katz, I. (1981). *Stigma: A social psychological analysis.* Hillsdale, NJ: Erlbaum.

Katz, I., Wackenhut, J., & Hass, R. G. (1986). Racial ambivalence, value duality, and behavior. In J. F. Dovidio & S. L. Gaertner (Eds.), *Prejudice, discrimination, and racism* (pp. 35-60). San Diego, CA: Academic Press.

Kelley, H. H., & Stahelski, A. J. (1970a). Errors in perception of intentions in a mixed-motive game. *Journal of Experimental Social Psychology, 6,* 379-400.

Kelley, H. H., & Stahelski, A. J. (1970b). Social interaction basis of cooperators' and competitors' beliefs about others. *Journal of Personality and Social Psychology, 16,* 6-19.

Kinder, D. R., & Sears, D. O. (1981). Prejudice and politics: Symbolic racism versus racial threats to the good life. *Journal of Personality and Social Psychology, 40,* 414-431.

Kite, M. E., & Deaux, K. (1986). Attitudes toward homosexuality: Assessment and behavioral consequences. *Basic and Applied Social Psychology, 7,* 137-162.

Kleck, R. E., & Strenta, A. (1980). Perceptions of the impact of negatively valued physical characteristics on social interaction. *Journal of Personality and Social Psychology, 39,* 861-873.

Kluegel, J. R., & Smith, E. R. (1986). *Beliefs about inequality: Americans' views of what is and what ought to be.* New York: Aldine/de Gruyter.

LaFrance, M., & Mayo, C. (1976). Racial differences in gaze behavior during conversations: Two systematic observational studies. *Journal of Personality and Social Psychology, 33,* 547-552.

Lance, L. M. (1987). The effects of interactions with gay persons on attitudes toward homosexuality. *Human Relations, 40,* 329-336.

Langer, E. J. (1989). *Mindfulness.* Reading, MA: Addison-Wesley.

Larsen, K. S., Reed, M., & Hoffman, S. (1980). Attitudes of heterosexuals toward homosexuality: A Likert-type scale and construct validity. *Journal of Sex Research, 16,* 245-257.

Leary, M. R. (1983a). Social anxiousness: The construct and its measurement. *Journal of Personality Assessment, 47,* 66-75.

Leary, M. R. (1983b). *Understanding social anxiety: Social, personality and clinical perspectives.* Beverly Hills, CA: Sage.

Leary, M. R., & Atherton, S. C. (1986). Self-efficacy, social anxiety, and inhibition in interpersonal encounters. *Journal of Social and Clinical Psychology, 4,* 256-267.

Levenson, R. W., & Gottman, J. M. (1983). Marital interaction: Physiological linkage and affective exchange. *Journal of Personality and Social Psychology, 45,* 587-597.

Levenson, R. W., & Gottman, J. M. (1985). Physiological and affective predictors of change in relationship satisfaction. *Journal of Personality and Social Psychology, 49,* 85-94.

Link, B. G. (1987). Understanding labeling effects in the area of mental disorders: An assessment of the effects of expectations of rejection. *American Sociological Review, 52,* 96-112.

Mackie, D. M., & Hamilton, D. L. (Eds.). (1993). *Affect, cognition, and stereotyping: Interactive processes in group perception.* San Diego, CA: Academic Press.

Major, B., & Crocker, J. (1993). Social stigma: The consequences of attributional ambiguity. In D. M. Mackie & D. L. Hamilton (Eds.), *Affect, cognition, and stereotyping: Interactive processes in group perception* (pp. 345-370). San Diego, CA: Academic Press.

McConahay, J. B. (1986). Modern racism, ambivalence, and the Modern Racism Scale. In J. F. Dovidio & S. L. Gaertner (Eds.), *Prejudice, discrimination, and racism* (pp. 91-125). San Diego, CA: Academic Press.

Miller, D. T., & Turnbull, W. (1986). Expectancies and interpersonal processes. *Annual Review of Psychology, 37,* 233-256.

Miller, N., & Brewer, M. B. (1986). Categorization effects on ingroup and outgroup perception. In J. F. Dovidio & S. L. Gaertner (Eds.), *Prejudice, discrimination, and racism* (pp. 209-230). San Diego, CA: Academic Press.

Monteith, M. J. (1993). Self-regulation of prejudiced responses: Implications for progress in prejudice reduction efforts. *Journal of Personality and Social Psychology, 65,* 469-485.

Monteith, M. J., Devine, P. G., & Zuwerink, J. R. (1993). Self-directed vs. other-directed affect as a consequence of prejudice-related discrepancies. *Journal of Personality and Social Psychology, 64,* 198-210.

Moses, A. E., & Hawkins, R. O. (1982). *Counseling lesbians and gay men: A life-issues approach.* St. Louis, MO: C. V. Mosby.

Myrdal, G. (1944). *An American dilemma.* New York: Harper.

Neuberg, S. L. (1989). The goal of forming accurate impressions during social interactions: Attenuating the impact of negative expectancies. *Journal of Personality and Social Psychology, 56,* 374-386.

Norris, W. P. (1991). Liberal attitudes and homophobic acts: The paradoxes of homosexual experience in a liberal institution. *Journal of Homosexuality, 22,* 81–120.

Pettigrew, T. F. (1979). The ultimate attribution error: Extending Allport's cognitive analysis of prejudice. *Personality and Social Psychology Bulletin, 5,* 461–476.

Pettigrew, T. F. (1994a). *The deprovincialization hypothesis: Generalized intergroup contact effects on prejudice.* Unpublished manuscript, University of California at Santa Cruz.

Pettigrew, T. F. (1994b, September). *Intergroup prejudice and discrimination on the campus.* Paper presented at the University of Massachusetts conference: Racism—The Problem and the Response: Seven Social Psychologists Speak Out, Amherst, MA.

Pettigrew, T. F., & Martin, J. (1987). Shaping the organizational context for black American inclusion. *Journal of Social Issues, 43,* 41–78.

Polanyi, M. (1962). *Personal knowledge.* Chicago: University of Chicago Press.

Poskocil, A. (1977). Encounters between blacks and white liberals: The collision of stereotypes. *Social Forces, 55,* 715–727.

Pressly, S. L., & Devine, P. G. (1992, April). *Sex, sexism, and compunction: Group membership or internalization of standards?* Paper presented at the meeting of the Midwestern Psychological Association, Chicago.

Rokeach, M. (1973). *The nature of human values.* New York: Free Press.

Rosenberg, M. (1979). *Conceiving the self.* New York: Basic Books.

Ross, L. D., Amabile, T. M., & Steinmetz, J. L. (1977). Social roles, social control, and biases in social perception processes. *Journal of Personality and Social Psychology, 35,* 485–494.

Sagar, H. A., & Schofield, J. W. (1980). Racial and behavioral cues in black and white children's perceptions of ambiguously aggressive acts. *Journal of Personality and Social Psychology, 39,* 590–598.

Scheier, M. F., & Carver, C. S. (1988). A model of behavioral self-regulation: Translating intention into action. In L. Berkowitz (Ed.), *Advances in experimental social psychology* (Vol. 21, pp. 303–346). New York: Academic Press.

Schlenker, B. R., & Leary, M. R. (1982). Social anxiety and self-presentation: A conceptualization and model. *Psychological Bulletin, 92,* 641–669.

Schneider, B. E. (1986). Coming out at work: Bridging the private/public gap. *Work and Occupations, 13,* 463–487.

Schuman, H., Steeth, C., & Bobo, L. (1985). *Racial attitudes in America: Trends and interpretation.* Cambridge, MA: Harvard University Press.

Scott, R. A. (1969). *The making of blind men: A study of adult socialization.* New York: Russell Sage Foundation.

Sears, D. O., & Kinder, D. R. (1985). Whites' opposition to busing: On conceptualizing and operationalizing group conflict. *Journal of Personality and Social Psychology, 48,* 1141–1147.

Sears, J. T. (1991). Educators, homosexuality, and homosexual students: Are personal feelings related to professional beliefs? *Journal of Homosexuality, 22,* 29–79.

Sherif, M., & Sherif, C. W. (1953). *Groups in harmony and tension.* New York: Harper.

Sigelman, L., & Welch, S. (1991). *Black Americans' views of racial inequality: The dream deferred.* New York: Cambridge University Press.

Sniderman, P. M., with Hagen, M. G. (1985). *Race and inequality: A study in American values.* Chatham, NJ: Chatham House.

Snyder, M. (1992). Motivational foundations of behavioral confirmation. In M. P. Zanna (Ed.), *Advances in experimental social psychology* (Vol. 25, pp. 67–114). San Diego, CA: Academic Press.

Snyder, M., & Swann, W. B. (1978). Behavioral confirmation in social interaction. *Journal of Experimental Social Psychology, 14,* 148–162.

Snyder, M., Tanke, E. D., & Berscheid, E. (1977). Social perception and interpersonal behavior: On the self-fulfilling nature of social stereotypes. *Journal of Personality and Social Psychology, 35,* 656–666.

Stephan, W. G. (1985). Intergroup relations. In G. Lindzey & E. Aronson (Eds.), *Handbook of social psychology* (3rd ed., Vol. 2, pp. 599–658). New York: Random House.

Stephan, W. G. (1987). The contact hypothesis in intergroup relations. In C. Hendrick (Ed.), *Review of personality and social psychology: Vol. 9. Processes and intergroup relations* (pp. 13–40). Newbury Park, CA: Sage.

Stephan, W. G., & Stephan, C. W. (1985). Intergroup anxiety. *Journal of Social Issues, 41,* 157–175.

Strommen, E. F. (1989). "You're a what?": Family member reactions to the disclosure of homosexuality. *Journal of Homosexuality, 18,* 37–58.

Tajfel, H., & Turner, J. C. (1979). An integrative theory of intergroup conflict. In W. G. Austin & S. Worchel (Eds.), *The social psychology of intergroup relations* (pp. 33–47). Monterey, CA: Brooks/Cole.

Tajfel, H., & Turner, J. C. (1986). The social identity theory of intergroup behavior. In S. Worchel & W. G. Austin (Eds.), *Psychology of intergroup relations* (2nd ed., pp. 7–24). Chicago: Nelson-Hall.

Taylor, D. M., Wright, S. C., Moghaddam, F. M., & Lalonde, R. N. (1990). The personal/group discrimination discrepancy: Perceiving my group, but not myself, to be a target for discrimination. *Personality and Social Psychology Bulletin, 16,* 254–262.

Taylor, J. (1991, January 21). Are you politically correct? *New York Magazine,* pp. 33–40.

Tierney, W. G. (1992). Building academic communities of difference. *Change, 24,* 40–46.

Townsend, J. (1992). The private life of a teacher. *The Progressive, 57,* 37.

Weinberg, M., & Williams, C. (1974). *Male homosexuals: Their problems and adaptations.* New York: Oxford University Press.

Weitz, S. (1972). Attitude, voice, and behavior: A repressed affect model of interracial behavior. *Journal of Personality and Social Psychology, 24,* 14–21.

Wicklund, R. A. (1975). Objective self-awareness. In L. Berkowitz (Ed.), *Advances in experimental social psychology* (Vol. 8, pp. 233–275). New York: Academic Press.

Willis, F. N., Jr. (1966). Initial speaking distance as a function of the speakers' relationship. *Psychonomic Science, 5,* 221–222.

Williams, R. M., Jr. (1947). *The reduction of intergroup tensions: A survey on research problems of ethnic, racial, and religious group relations.* New York: Plenum Press.

Worchel, S. (1986). The role of cooperation in reducing intergroup conflict. In S. Worchel & W. G. Austin (Eds.), *Psychology of intergroup relations* (2nd ed., pp. 288–304). Chicago: Nelson-Hall.

Worchel, S., & Austin, W. G. (Eds.). (1986). *Psychology of intergroup relations* (2nd ed.). Chicago: Nelson-Hall.

Worchel, S., & Norvel, N. (1980). Effects of perceived environmental conditions during cooperation on intergroup attraction. *Journal of Personality and Social Psychology, 38,* 764–772.

Word, C. O., Zanna, M. P., & Cooper, J. (1974). The verbal mediation of self-fulfilling prophecies in interracial interaction. *Journal of Experimental Social Psychology, 10,* 109–120.

Wright, B. A. (1960). *Physical disability: A psychological approach.* New York: Harper & Row.

Zadny, J., & Gerard, H. G. (1974). Attributed intentions of informational selectivity. *Journal of Experimental Social Psychology, 10,* 34–52.

Zuwerink, J. R., & Devine, P. G. (1993, May). *Prejudice, internalization, and the accessibility of personal standards.* Paper presented at the meeting of the Midwestern Psychological Association, Chicago.

Zuwerink, J. R., Monteith, M. J., Devine, P. G., & Cook, D. (in press). Prejudice towards Blacks: With and without compunction. *Basic and Applied Social Psychology.*

CHAPTER 14

A Motivated Gatekeeper of Our Minds
Need-for-Closure Effects on Interpersonal and Group Processes

ARIE W. KRUGLANSKI
University of Maryland–College Park

The construction of knowledge is among the most ubiquitous human activities, intimately tied to our social nature as a species. Its manifestations are manifold, including a newborn child's striving to make sense of the "buzzing confusion" threatening to engulf him or her (James, 1890), and a trauma victim's desperately seeking "meaning" in the devastating events to which he or she has fallen prey (Baumeister, 1991; Tat & Silver, 1989). On the collective level, it is ensconced in time-honored cultural institutions such as religion or academe, where countless individuals, like masons on a cathedral, build on their predecessors' foundations to erect new knowledge on major questions of interest to humankind.

The human proclivity toward knowledge construction may have contributed a great deal to our evolution. From the social-biological perspective (see Buss, in press), it may have constituted a serious coping advantage, selected for in the struggle for survival: Individuals who possessed it may have fared markedly better than those who did not. They may have designed better shelters, built better weapons, and have been more adept at securing nutrition, thus ultimately improving their chances at procreation.

Although the predilection to construct knowledge may characterize humans as a group, as with any human tendency, and some individuals may possess it and some situations may elicit it to a greater degree than others. As an activity, knowledge construction may compete with various alternative pursuits persons may wish to engage in (e.g., acting on the knowledge, daydreaming, or performing such bodily maintenance functions as feeding or resting). For some individuals and in some circumstances, knowledge construction may take a back seat to these alternative pursuits, and hence may be manifested less in behavior.

How the knowledge construction process is carried out may have profound implications for various aspects of information processing and social interaction. For example, en route to knowledge formation, individuals may process information more or less extensively. They may inspect a considerable or only a limited body of facts before arriving at a judgment, and they may generate numerous hypotheses to account for those facts or only a few. They may pay a great deal of attention to new information provided situationally or "on line," or may largely ignore it and base their judgments instead on information available in memory. They may expend considerable efforts on retrieving "deeply buried" information, or may utilize readily accessible, "top-of-the-head" notions. Finally, they may examine information and engender hypotheses impartially, or may be directionally biased in their processing toward some particular desirable conclusions.

Such knowledge construction effects may not be restricted to cognition or judgment per se, but may extend to a variety of social-psychological phenomena. After all, human cognition occurs in a social context (Vygotsky, 1978; Wyer & Srull, 1986). Other persons may variously constitute the targets of judgmental activity, sources of information utilized toward the construction of individual knowledge, or partners in a collective knowledge construction endeavor whose particular views (consistent or inconsistent with one's own) need to be taken into account and dealt with in the course of forging commonly shared knowledge.

Indeed, social psychologists have long been interested in knowledge construction processes on both the individual and the collective levels of analysis. In fact, most major social-psychological phenomena have been examined at one time or another from an epistemic perspective. As early as the 1890s, Durkheim (1897/1951) commented on the adverse effects on the individual's well-being of a societal state of normlessness ("anomie")—the lack of culturally shared knowledge concerning means–ends relations. Le Bon (1895/1896) analyzed the conditions under which a leader can induce widespread suggestibility in a crowd, creating common knowledge through his or her persuasive personality and rhetoric. Since then, the topic of persuasion has become a mainstay of social psychological research (Allport, 1935; Chaiken, Liberman, & Eagly, 1989; Hovland, Janis, & Kelley, 1953; Petty & Cacioppo, 1986), yielding numerous insights as to how various knowledge structures (opinions, judgments, or attitudes) are interpersonally molded during the communication process. Recently, the domain of group processes (group decision making, consensus striving, and information processing in groups) has also become increasingly concerned with knowledge construction phenomena (cf. Levine, Resnick, & Higgins, 1992), and epistemic issues of social identity (Tajfel & Turner, 1979; Turner, 1991; Turner, Hogg, Oakes, Reicher, & Wetherell, 1987; Turner & Oakes, 1989) have come to play a central role in explaining social influence (Levine & Thompson, in press).

EPISTEMIC MOTIVATIONS: NEEDS FOR NONSPECIFIC AND SPECIFIC CLOSURE

A fundamental aspect of knowledge construction concerns its underlying motivation. A motivational analysis of such process may elucidate the antecedent conditions of its engagement, its specific course, and its psychological and socio psychological consequences (e.g., for individuals' affective states or their reactions to others who facilitate or impede their knowledge construction efforts). The present chapter describes theory and research relevant to one epistemically relevant motivation, labeled the "need for cognitive closure."

The need for cognitive closure is an individual's desire for a firm answer to a question and an aversion to ambiguity. As employed here, the term "need" denotes a motivated tendency or a proclivity rather than a tissue deficit (for a similar use, see Cacioppo & Petty, 1982). Furthermore, the need for cognitive closure as discussed in this chapter refers to an individual's need for nonspecific closure—that is, the desire for "an answer on a given topic, any answer . . . compared to confusion and ambiguity" (Kruglanski, 1990, p. 337). Imagine, for example, a psychological tester engaged in calculating an unknown student's IQ score. The tester is probably motivated primarily to arrive at a correct calculation, without excessive concern about what the actual score may be. By contrast, the student or his or her parents may care a great deal about the particular score. They may experience a need for specific closure (Kruglanski, 1989, 1990a)—in this case, a directional motivational bias toward the desirable judgment that the student's IQ is high.

Various needs for specific closure have received ample attention in the social-psychological literature. In fact, the entire issue of motivational influence on social cognition has centered on the question of whether such directional effects have an impact on judgment (Bem, 1967, 1972; Zanna & Cooper, 1976; Miller & Ross, 1975; Tetlock & Levi, 1982; Zuckerman, 1979). "Dissonance theory," for example (Festinger, 1957), stresses the motivation to justify one's unfortunate decisions—that is, to adopt the specific closure that the decisions were judicious and well advised. Similarly, research on "defensive attributions" (Johnson, Feigenbaum, & Weiby, 1964) has examined the directional motivation to reach specific causal closures (personal causal assignments for success and situational causal assignments for failure) that are self-protective or ego-enhancing in. Finally, recent research on "motivated reasoning" (Kunda, 1990) has looked at the need to reach specific desirable closures of various kinds—for example, the need to conclude that one's personality predisposes one toward academic success, or that one's personal habits, such as coffee drinking (Kunda & Sherman-Williams, 1993) or tooth-brushing (Ross, McFarland, & Fletcher, 1981) are compatible with the maintenance or promotion of good health.

By contrast with the considerable efforts invested in the study of directional motivational effects on judgment, nondirectional effects have received relatively little attention from social and personality psychologists. Furthermore, whereas the former effects have often been conceptualized in terms of general situationally inducible tendencies, the latter have been thought of primarily as individual-difference dimensions. For instance, the concept of "intolerance for ambiguity" (Frenkel-Brunswik, 1949; Eysenck, 1954) denotes a stable personality-based aversion of cognitive uncertainty or unclarity—that is, a nondirectional motivated tendency to form definite conclusions of whatever content. Sorrentino's notions of "certainty orientation" and "uncertainty orientation" (Sorrentino & Short, 1986) similarly refer to stable individual differences in nondirectional (or non specific with regard to content) motivational tendencies of judgmental consequence. So does Cacioppo and Petty's (1982) construct of "need for cognition," representing an individual-difference dimension in the tendency to engage in and enjoy thinking.

Although the present motivational construct of the need for cognitive closure may also be thought of as a stable individual-difference dimension (Webster & Kruglanski, 1994), it has also been assumed to be capable of situational arousal in a wide range of circumstances. In what follows, the antecedent conditions of this need and its cognitive and social consequences are discussed at some length. First, however, the general properties of the construct are described.

APPROACHING AND AVOIDING CLOSURE: A MOTIVATIONAL CONTINUUM

Though in many circumstances persons may desire clear-cut knowledge, in other conditions they may be less interested in closure, and in still other situations they may even prefer a lack of closure over closure. Thus, persons' degree of motivation for cognitive closure may be depicted as located on a continuum ranging from a strong need for closure to a strong need to avoid closure. A person at the former end of the continuum may display cognitive impatience or impulsivity: He or she may "leap" to judgment on the basis of inconclusive evidence, and exhibit rigidity of thought and reluctance to consider views other than his or her own. At opposite end of the continuum—signifying a high need to avoid closure—a person may experience considerable doubt and unwillingness to make a commitment to a opinion on an issue. Such a person may tend to suspend judgment instead, and may be quick to come up with competing alternatives to any definite interpretation or opinion that is offered.

Finally, it is assumed that the effects of the motivation for closure are monotonic along the continuum. That is, at any two points the direction of the effect is assumed to be the same: Higher (vs. lower) need for closure may result in a higher or lower degree of a phenomenon, but the direction of this difference should be constant, regardless of these points' specific location on the need-for-closure continuum.

ANTECEDENT CONDITIONS OF THE MOTIVATION
FOR CLOSURE

The need-for-closure notion represents a broad motivational construct applicable across diverse contents of judgment. That is, one's motivation to attain or avoid closure is assumed to be independent of the topic of the judgment. Correspondingly, the antecedent conditions of the motivation for closure are assumed to be "content-free," having to do with the perceived costs or benefits of closure as such. More specifically, magnitude of the need for closure is assumed to be proportionate to the perceived benefits of closure and the perceived costs of lacking closure. For instance, potential benefits of cognitive closure include the affordance of predictability and the provision of guidance for action. Thus, where the subjective importance of predictability and action loom large, need for closure is likely to be elevated. A potential cost of lacking closure is failing to act or decide on an issue in time to meet an important deadline. Thus, need for closure should be heightened under time pressure. Alternate costs of lacking closure may relate to the perceived effortfulness of continued information processing (the possession of closure would obviate this), perceiver-based reluctance to expend the required effort (e.g., because the perceiver is fatigued), or task-based aversiveness of information processing (e.g., the task is unpleasant or dreary).

As we move in the opposite direction along our motivational continuum, the need for closure may be lowered and the need to avoid closure elevated by conditions highlighting the costs of having closure and the benefits of retaining an open mind. In some situations, costs of closure may be made salient by a "fear of invalidity" or by a concern about making a judgmental mistake for which a high price may have to be paid. Under such conditions, the person may desire to suspend judgment—that is, to avoid premature closure.

Closure and Validity

The preceding discussion implies, in effect, that validity concerns can conflict with those of closure. Obviously, however, no one would *consciously* choose to adopt a closure he or she deems invalid. In fact, the notion of subjective knowledge connotes the simultaneous sense of closure and validity. To *know*, for example, that "London is the capital of England" is at once to have closure on this issue *and* to believe it to be true. All this notwithstanding, the concerns for closure and validity may arise fairly independently of each other; moreover, they may pull information processing in opposite directions.

When closure concerns loom large, for example, an individual may engage in activities that will result in a sense of closure without sacrificing the sense of validity. Thus, under heightened need for closure, the person may generate fewer competing hypotheses and/or suppress attention to information inconsistent with his or her hypothesis. Both may result in a sense of valid closure, uncontested by alternative interpretations or inconsistent evidence.

By contrast, when validity concerns are aroused, the person may engage in thorough and extensive information processing and may generate multiple alternative interpretations to account for known facts. In short, he or she may process information in exactly the opposite way to that which a heightened need for closure would induce. In fact, when validity concerns loom large, the individual may be motivated to postpone closure, or in extreme case to avoid it altogether. Admittedly, however, this need not always be so. If a given closure appears to be of indubitable validity (e.g., because of the impeccable credibility of its source), the fear of invalidity may increase the tendency to embrace it rather than prompting the avoidance (or postponement) of closure.

Alternate Bases of the Need to Avoid Closure

The need to avoid or postpone closure may arise for reasons unrelated to accuracy concerns. For instance, this need may be felt when the judgmental task is intrinsically enjoyable and interesting (compared to possible alternative pursuits), because closure would terminate the pleasant activity.

In some interpersonal situations, any definite commitment may be perceived as fraught with negative consequences. In a conflict between friends, for example, taking one friend's side may risk offending the other party. To avoid this predicament, the individual may be motivated to avoid closure altogether. A different, and occasionally serious, cost of closure stems from the constraints it imposes on the individual; it may imply a threat to his or her freedom and a narrowing of options. Where freedom of maneuvering and option maintenance are of paramount importance (to a professional diplomat or negotiator, for example), the individual may experience the need to avoid closure. This may be particularly true in cases when current options are unattractive, and the individual hopes that more appealing possibilities will present themselves in the future.

The need to avoid closure may also stem from a motive to maintain a self-image or self-presentation of an open minded and flexible person. Finally, a prolonged state of closure may foster excessive predictability and stability, which may be experienced as stultifying. To generate excitement, individuals may seek uncertainty (Sorrentino & Short, 1986) and hence strive to avoid closure, at least temporarily. Uncertainty-engendered excitement may be the principal underlying cause for the immense attraction of the suspense genre—thrillers selling millions of copies and keeping viewers glued to TV screens the world over.

To take stock of what has been said thus far: (1) The need for cognitive closure represents a desire for definite knowledge and an aversion to ambiguity. (2) A motivational continuum is assumed to exist, ranging from a strong need for closure to a strong need to avoid closure. (3) The antecedent conditions of the need for closure relate to any perceived costs or benefits associated with closure or the absence of closure. Accordingly, numerous situational antecedents of the need for closure may exist, and the magnitude of this need may vary also as a stable individual-difference dimension. Another way of stating this is that diverse circumstances should be functionally equivalent with regard to phenomena affected by the need for closure.

COGNITIVE CONSEQUENCES OF THE NEED FOR CLOSURE

Because it constitutes a desire for a particular epistemic state, the need for closure should appropriately affect the knowledge formation process. This process involves numerous cognitive activities individuals may perform on the way to arriving at final judgments. Because of the essentially social nature of human knowledge (Vygotsky, 1978; Wyer & Srull, 1986), need for closure should have social as well as cognitive consequences. In fact, such social consequences constitute the main focus of the present chapter. Prior to discussing them in detail, however, I briefly review the cognitive consequences.

Extent of Information Processing

An individual with a high need for closure should be inclined to act quickly to terminate the aversive motivational state of lacking closure. This could mean less extensive information processing prior to forming a judgment. Indeed, subjects high in the need for closure appear to search less extensively for "external" information prior to forming a judgment, and to generate fewer competing hypotheses to account for available data (Mayseless & Kruglanski, 1987).

Subjective Confidence

Lowered extent of information processing under heightened need for closure may suggest that subjects in this motivational state "satisfice" rather then "optimize" in forming judgments; that is, they may lower their judgmental "threshold" and be prepared to form less confident opinions. In fact, the evidence suggests quite the opposite. Elevated confidence of subjects under heightened need for closure has been replicated by now in several studies using widely ranging methods of inducing this motivation—for example, noise (Kruglanski & Webster, 1991; Kruglanski, Webster, & Klem, 1993), instructions stressing the value of clarity (Mayseless & Kruglanski, 1987), task attractiveness (Webster, 1993), and time pressure (Kruglanski & Webster, 1991). Similar results have also been obtained in studies where need for closure was assessed via a personality scale (Webster & Kruglanski, 1994). It is thus of interest to consider what possible mechanisms may mediate the seemingly paradoxical coupling of elevated confidence with the restricted information processing observed under heightened need for closure.

Note, first, that such coupling may appear paradoxical only if it is assumed that subjects with a heightened need for closure are *consciously aware* that their information processing is especially restricted. In fact, such an assumption may be quite unwarranted. That individuals are often unaware of the underlying causes of their actions and judgments has been compellingly demonstrated in past research (Nisbett & Wilson, 1977). They may be similarly unaware that their need for closure is particularly elevated, or that this curtails the extent of their processing.

Furthermore, curtailed information processing as such (rather than the *awareness* of curtailment) may well contribute to the boosting of confidence. To apply the reverse version of the "discounting" principle (Kelley, 1971), the generation of fewer alternative hypotheses on a topic may increase an individual's confidence in each hypothesis (Mayseless & Kruglanski, 1987). In addition, subjects with a heightened need for closure may process information asymmetrically, paying more attention to or admitting more into awareness information that is consistent (vs. inconsistent) with an expectancy, again, this may boost the subjects' confidence in the hypothesis.

Some support for the latter notion was recently provided by Dijksterhuis (1994). Subjects in this research, Dutch college students, were presented with target information that was either consistent or inconsistent with the stereotype of a "soccer hooligan"; the stereotype was activated either before or after subjects viewed the information. In both cases, subjects dispositionally high in the need for closure (Webster & Kruglanski, 1994) subsequently recalled a greater proportion of stereotype-consistent versus inconsistent information, whereas the opposite was the case for subjects low in the need for closure.

Type of Information Sought

Restricted generation of competing hypotheses under heightened need for closure (Mayseless & Kruglanski, 1987) should also affect the type of information sought, not merely its amount. Specifically, individuals with a high need for closure may seek prototypical information about a category, whereas those with a high need to avoid closure may seek diagnostic information (Trope & Bassok, 1983) capable of discriminating among competing categories. Research (Kruglanski & Mayseless, 1988) has obtained results consistent with this proposition.

Cue Utilization

The proclivity of individuals with a high need for closure to formulate some judgment (any judgment) quickly may dispose them toward early "freezing"— that is, an overutilization of early judgmental cues and an underadjustment in light of subsequent relevant information. This fundamental process may underlie a variety of effects that on the surface may appear quite disparate and unrelated.

Primacy Effects in Impression Formation

Among such effects are "primacy effects" in impression formation (Asch, 1946; Luchins, 1957)—that is, the tendency to base one's impressions of a social target on early rather than late information. Augmentation of primacy effects under heightened need for closure has been found by now in several studies (Heaton & Kruglanski, 1991; Kruglanski & Freund, 1983; Freund, Kruglanski, & Schpitzajzen, 1985; Webster & Kruglanski, 1994) varying in the specific operational definitions used to manipulate or measure the need for closure.

Anchoring and Adjustment

A different instance of cue-utilization may underlie the classic phenomenon of "anchoring and insufficient adjustment" (Tversky & Kahneman, 1974). In this case, a hypothesis engendered by an early cue may serve as an "anchor" whose adjustment varies inversely with the need for closure. Results consistent with this interpretation have been obtained (Kruglanski & Freund, 1983).

The Correspondence Bias

Overutilization of early cues and insufficient adjustment may also underlie the "correspondence bias" in person perception (Jones, 1979)—that is, observers' tendency to overascribe actors' behavior to personal inclinations even in the presence of clear situational pressures prompting the behavior. In the original demonstration of the phenomenon, Jones and Harris (1967) presented subjects with essays expressing either an expected or an unexpected opinion, allegedly written by a person who either had or did not have a free choice in preparing the essay. Under both the free-choice and the no-choice instructions, subjects assumed that the writer's attitudes were more consistent with the essay content when the opinion expressed in the essay was unexpected as opposed to expected.

How might the correspondence bias be explained? Different theorists have implied that the underlying mechanism may involve the phenomenon of anchoring and insufficient adjustment (Gilbert, Pelham, & Krull, 1988; Jones, 1979, Quattrone, 1982): When subjects come to rate the actor's attitude, the most salient evidence they have is the behavior that has occurred. A natural hypothesis this brings to mind is that the behavior expresses the actor's attitude. This attitude-correspondence hypothesis pops to mind almost "automatically," and serves as an initial anchor from which the estimate is further adjusted in a "controlled" process based upon additional evidence (e.g., that the actor was situationally constrained to engage in the behavior)

Such controlled adjustment may require significant cognitive effort. For instance, Gilbert et al. (1988) found that when perceivers were cognitively busy, the correspondence bias was enhanced. This may mean that the increased effort required by the adjustment process was more than they were willing to put out. The finding suggests that motivational considerations may be highly relevant to the correspondence bias.

Research by Tetlock (1985) supports this possibility. Specifically, he found that subjects made to feel accountable (vs. non accountable) for their inferences about an essay writer demonstrated a markedly reduced overattribution bias. Presumably, manipulation of accountability motivated subjects to process information in a more discriminating manner, which afforded greater adjustments for their initial bias. Thus, Tetlock's research identifies specific motivational conditions that may mitigate the overattribution effect.

The foregoing evidence is consistent with the notion that, just like the primacy or anchoring effects, the correspondence bias represents cue overutilization—that is, the tendency to rely excessively on early hypotheses or estimates, and to fail to correct these sufficiently in the light of available information. This suggests that the correspondence bias should be appropriately affected by the motivation for closure. Indeed, in a recent series of experiments, Webster (1993) obtained support for this proposition by manipulating the need for closure through task attractiveness.

Specifically, Webster reasoned that the need for cognitive closure should be heightened if subjects perceive a task as dull and unattractive, because task-related information processing should appear costly under those conditions. Similarly, the need for closure should be lowered (or the need to avoid closure should be heightened) if subjects perceive a task as attractive. The attitude attribution task involving the essay writer, described above, was made to appear unattractive by informing the subjects that the subsequent task was much more attractive (watching comedy videos); the task was made to appear attractive by informing subjects that the subsequent task was less attractive (watching a video of a statistics lecture). Indeed, Webster (1993) found that the tendency to rate the writer's attitude in line with the position expressed in the essay was greater in the unattractive than in the neutral condition, and lesser in the attractive than in the neutral condition. Of particular interest was the finding that when the initial cues suggested a situational rather than a personal attribution, the tendency to overattribute the essay to the writer's personality was less under high need for closure (manipulated via an unattractive task) than in a neutral condition, and *more* under high need to avoid closure (manipulated via an attractive task) than in a neutral condition. This last result is of particular importance, as it demonstrates that need-for-closure effects are content-free, depending on the order in which the cues are considered (the early bird gets the judgmental "worm") rather than on their specific substance.

Interactive Effects of Initial Knowledge and Need for Closure on Social Information Seeking

In the research described so far, heightened need for cognitive closure generally appeared to inhibit epistemic activity. However, this effect may depend on the information-processing phase at which this need is induced, and more specifically on whether when this happens the individual has fairly confident initial knowledge on a topic or is experiencing relative ambiguity. When a person with a high need for closure possesses confident knowledge, that which he or she already has matches that which he or she desires; this may foster epistemic freezing and suppress further information seeking. Indeed, in the previously described studies, curtailment of epistemic activity was typically observed after some preliminary hypothesis (e.g., concerning the target's personality or attitude) had already crystallized.

The case may be different, however, if an individual lacks initial hypotheses on a topic. In such circumstances, a person with a high need for closure should experience a mismatch between the actual and desired epistemic states. This may stimulate an intense informational search intended to yield clear knowledge. These notions were supported in two experiments (Kruglanski, Peri, & Zakai, 1991). Both studies varied orthogonally subjects' initial confidence in a hypothesis and the need for closure. In both cases, those variables interacted statistically in affecting information seeking: When initial confidence was high, subjects with a high (vs. low) need for closure looked at fewer information items, and exhibited longer latencies of seeking the first such item. In contrast, when initial confidence was low, subjects with a high (vs. low) need for closure looked at a greater number of information items and exhibited shorter latencies of seeking out the first such item.

Stereotypes as Cues

The evidence reviewed so far suggests that under high need for cognitive closure, individuals may tend to rely on early cues affording the formation of judgment, and in the absence of such cues may search for them intensively. From a social-psychological perspective, a particularly interesting source of early judgmental cues consists of previously stored knowledge structures (e.g., stereotypes, prejudices, or attitudes readily accessible in memory). When an individual comes to form a judgment about a member of a known social category, such knowledge structures may compete for influence with individuating information about the target. In those circumstances, it is possible to predict that when an individual's need for closure is heightened, such accessible pre-existing structures may exert the dominant influence on judgments, as the extensive processing of individuating information may uncomfortably delay closure. Increased tendency to base judgments on stereotypes under heightened need for closure (manipulated via time pressure) has been demonstrated (Kruglanski & Freund, 1983; Bechtold, Zanna, & Nacarratto, cited in Jamieson & Zanna, 1989).

Accessibility Effects

Presumably, the increased tendency under heightened need for closure to employ pre-conceptions and stereotypes results from their being highly accessible in memory, popping to mind immediately when a person focuses on the stimulus. Evidence that need for closure indeed increases the assimilation of judgments to primed constructs has been recently obtained (Ford & Kruglanski, in press; Thompson, Roman, Moscovitz, Chaiken, & Bargh, in press).

NEED-FOR-CLOSURE EFFECTS ON INTERPERSONAL PHENOMENA

Persuasion

The phenomena considered so far have been effects of the need for the closure on intraindividual cognitive processes (e.g. the tendency to rely on readily available cues in making judgments). However, individual cognitive processes do not typically occur in social isolation; rather, they are intricately tied to social interaction contexts (Vygotsky, 1978; Wyer & Srull, 1986). For example, judgmental cues are often made accessible through one's partner's utterances resulting in persuasion. It is therefore of interest to ask how need for closure may affect an individual's reaction to persuasion. A possible answer is that this may depend on how early or late in the closure formation process does the communication arrives. If it arrives late—that is, after a person has already formed an opinion—need for closure is likely to promote freezing, increasing resistance to persuasion. However, if it arrives early enough, before an opinion has crystallized, need for closure is likely to promote seizing on cues and thus to reduce resistance to persuasion: Because they may miss closure badly, persons high (vs. low) in the need for closure may readily embrace any opinion offered them, exhibiting greater persuadability. We examined these notions in research (Kruglanski et al., 1993, Studies 2 and 3).

We used a modified form of a procedure originally devised by London (1973). Dyads were formed, each consisting of a naive subject and a confederate. The experimenter introduced the study as an investigation into the workings of juries. Each subject and confederate were presented with the essentials of a legal case (a civil suit of an airline company by a lumber company). For half the subjects, the materials also included a "legal analysis" affording the formation of a fairly definite opinion favoring the defendant or the plaintiff. The remaining subjects received no comparable analysis; hence, they lacked a firm informational basis for an opinion.

The presence or absence of an opinion base was crossed orthogonally with the need for closure, which was manipulated through environmental noise introduced by a rackety computer printer. Each subject read the case materials, recorded an opinion (or hunch) concerning the appropriate verdict, and confronted a confederate who argued for the opposite verdict. When in possession of the legal analysis, subjects were more resistant to persuasion by the confederate (they tended less to shift their pre discussion verdicts, and took longer to deliberate the verdict) under the noisy condition (assumed to induce the need for closure) than under the quiet condition. However, when the legal analysis was excluded, subjects were in fact less resistant to persuasion in the noisy than in the quiet environment.

In a subsequent study, rather than manipulating the need for closure, we assessed it via our individual-difference measure (Webster & Kruglanski, 1994). The data pattern of the first experiment was replicated: Subjects high (vs. low) in the need for closure tended to be more resistant to persuasion in the presence of prior information, yet less resistant to persuasion in its absence. Apparently, in the latter condition subjects' desire to form an opinion impelled them to embrace the persuasive message readily as a means of securing closure.

The need for closure may have additional intriguing implications for the persuasion process. These are outlined briefly below.

Heuristic/Peripheral versus Systematic/Central Processing

Major models of persuasion and attitude change (Chaiken et al., 1989; Petty & Cacioppo, 1986) distinguish between persuasion accomplished through careful and systematic attention to message arguments and persuasion driven by attention to various "peripheral" cues or "heuristics" (e.g., cues related to source expertise or attractiveness). Because typically the latter (peripheral or heuristic) cues are relatively simple and easy to process, whereas the processing of arguments contained in the message may be more laborious, individuals with a high (vs. low) need for closure may lean toward the heuristic mode of processing. Specifically, when a heuristic cue is available, persons with a a high need for cognitive closure should utilize it more than those with a low need. Consequently, they may pay lesser attention to argument quality (i.e., they may be less swayed by high-quality and more by low-quality arguments). It is possible to hypothesize further that not all heuristic cues should exert equal influence upon persuasion: A "positive heuristic" (e.g., the source is an expert to be trusted) may be expected to be more influential (and hence reduce more the impact of argument quality) than a "negative heuristic" (e.g., the source may not be trustworthy). The reason is that only a positive heuristic, not a negative one, affords closure. After all, learning that a source cannot be trusted does not indicate who can be trusted or on what basis may one form an opinion. Under those conditions, and also in the absence of any heuristic cues, persons with a high need for closure may pay particularly close attention to message arguments—perhaps even more than individuals with a low need for closure—and consequently may be more convinced by high-quality and less by low-quality arguments.

"Positive" and "Negative" Heuristics, Prior Opinions, and Need for Closure

In the research described earlier, we (Kruglanski et al., 1993) found that in the presence of prior opinion subjects with a high (vs. low) need for closure were more resistant to persuasion whereas in the absence of prior opinion high (vs.

low) need for closure were less resistant to persuasion. These tendencies may interact in interesting ways with the presence of positive versus negative heuristics to affect persuasion. Consider a situation where a communicator of low or high expertise endorses an opinion. Subjects with a high (vs. low need for closure may pay particular attention to heuristic cues, but their tendency to accept the persuader's opinion may vary, depending on the presence or absence of their own prior opinion. As a result, for high-need-for-closure subjects lacking an opinion, the presence of a positive heuristic (i.e., high communicator expertise) should act in concert with their tendency to seize upon any offered opinion to augment their persuadability further, as compared to a case where no heuristic cue is being given. However, the presence of a negative heuristic (i.e., low communicator expertise) should be in conflict with the seizing tendency, reducing high-need-for-closure subjects' persuadability as opposed to that of subjects in a no-heuristic control condition.

A mirror image of these predictions may be expected for subjects with a well-formed prior opinion. Here, the tendencies to freeze upon prior knowledge and to attend to heuristic cues should augment each other when the persuader is of low expertise, resulting in an even *greater* resistance to persuasion in high-need-for-closure individuals as compared to those in a no-heuristic control condition. The same tendencies should conflict with each other when the persuader is of high expertise, decreasing the tendency of high-need-for-closure subjects to be more resistant to persuasion than subjects in the no-heuristic control condition.

Persuasiveness and Need for Closure

In our research (Kruglanski et al., 1993, Study 1), dyads were formed, each consisting of one member who was dispositionally high and another dispositionally low in the need for closure. These two individuals were led to hold initial opposing views concerning a legal case they were to discuss. Under these circumstances, the final consensus represented in the majority of cases the opinion of the high-need-for-closure individual. Subsequent research (Kruglanski et al., 1993, Studies 2 and 3) demonstrated that this data pattern could represent in part the greater resistance to persuasion of high-need-for-closure persons in conditions where they enter the situation with a relatively well-formed prior opinion. However, it is also possible that individuals with a high need for closure are also *more persuasive* rather than merely *less persuadable*, than their low-need-for-closure counterparts. This could occur in either one or both of two possible ways. First, because of their tendency to freeze and to be insensitive to inconsistent information, subjects with a high (vs. low) need for closure may have higher confidence in their opinions (Mayseless & Kruglanski, 1987; Webster, 1993; Webster & Kruglanski, 1994). Such confidence may be perceived by the audience and contribute to persuasiveness. Moreover, the more intense quest for consensus exhibited by high-need-for-closure individuals may lead them to exert greater persuasive efforts, prompting them to generate stronger, more persuasive arguments.

Whereas both higher confidence and better arguments may characterize high-need-for-closure persuaders, different types of audience may be differentially responsive to these two communicative dimensions. Specifically, high-need-for-closure audiences may be more responsive to the peripheral or heuristic cue of a communicator's confidence (Miller, Maruyama, Beaber, & Valone, 1976) and less responsive to argument quality requiring central or systematic processing.

How might these ideas be tested experimentally? A possible paradigm would be to devise a situation where subjects with a high or low need for closure would be assigned the role of communicator or "recipient" of a communication. The communicator's role would be to familiarize himself or herself with some materials (e.g., essentials of a legal case) and subsequently to impart this information to the recipient so that the latter would be able to form an opinion. From the present analysis, it could be predicted that high-need-for-closure communicators would be more persuasive to both high- and low-need-for-closure recipients, albeit for different reasons: For high-need-for-closure recipients this effect would be mediated by communicator confidence, and for low-need-for-closure recipients it would be mediated by the argument quality.

Interpersonal Communication

The tendency of individuals with a high (vs. low) need for closure to reach judgments quickly and to overutilize early cues or hypotheses may lower their ability to communicate effectively with others. Specifically, need for closure may adversely affect the individuals' tendency to take into account (1) the conversational context of social discourse, and (2) communicatively relevant characteristics of the audience. These issues are now discussed in turn.

Considering the Communication Context

How do communication recipients decide what issue to address in response to their partners' communications? Theories of social discourse suggest that they pay attention to the conversational context in which messages are embedded (Grice, 1975; Sperber & Wilson, 1986). A major contextual principle stressed by those theories is that speakers make their messages exactly as informative as but no more informative than required. Thus, every bit of information in a message is assumed to be there for a reason; different types of contextual information may lead to different inferences of communicative intent, and ultimately to different responses to the communication.

Recently, Schwarz, Stack, Hilton, and Naderer (1991) applied such an analysis to identify conditions under which subjects based their judgments of likelihood that a target was an engineer on individuating information about the target, or on relevant population base rates. Specifically, Schwarz et al. demonstrated that (1) framing the problem as *psychological* implied to subjects the "conversational" relevance of individuating information, whereas framing it as *statistical* implied the relevance of base rate information; and (2) having each subject receive different individuating information about two targets from the same sample distribution (i.e., with the same base rates) implied the relevance of individuating information, whereas having them receive the same individuating information with two different base rates implied the relevance of base rate information. In support of their analysis, Schwarz et al. (1991) found that subjects tended to utilize individuating or base rate information in accordance with its implied relevance in the conversational context.

The Schwarz et al. (1991) conversational interpretation imposes an important qualification on previous theorizing as to conditions in which base rate (vs. individuating) information is utilized (e.g., Kahneman, Slovic, & Tversky, 1982). However, additional insights may be gained by recognizing that the extent of the conversational analysis itself may vary, depending upon the circumstances.

Specifically, such an analysis is governed by the listener's judgmental process, in which cognitive and motivational variables play a key role. Listeners may attempt to form judgments about their conversational obligation through using information provided by the speaker. To that end, they may generate initial hypotheses about the nature of the obligation and adjust these on the basis of subsequent information. The ultimate outcome of the process may depend upon: (1) the nature of the initial hypotheses and (2) the individual's motivation, which determines the extent to which these hypotheses are adjusted.

In turn, the nature of the initial hypothesis may depend on the *sequence* in which the relevant context information reaches the individual. Consider the Schwarz et al. (1991) study, where subjects were told that their task was to make judgments about the target's profession (i.e., his or her being an engineer). Suppose, that such instructions are immediately followed by individuating information about the target, followed by base rate information followed by framing the problem as statistical or psychological. Because it appears early in the sequence, the individuating information may lead subjects to hypothesize that their conversational obligation is to use it for judgmental purposes. If subjects have a high (vs. low) need for closure, they may accept this hypothesis uncritically, and hence may strongly rely on the individuating information in their likelihood judgments. If subjects have a low need for closure, however, they may reassess the initial hypothesis in light of the subsequent framing information. Psychological framing should corroborate the hypothesis that their obligation is to use the individuating information, but statistical framing may imply that they should be using the base rate information instead.

The situation may be very different if, following task instructions, subjects receive first the (psychological or statistical) framing information, followed by base rate information, with the individuating information last. The framing information may suggest an initial hypothesis regarding the subjects' obligation.

A statistical framing may suggest that some kind of numerical information is to be utilized, whereas a psychological framing may suggest that the useful information should relate to the target's personal properties. Subjects with a high need for closure are likely to freeze on such an initial hypothesis. By contrast, subjects with a low need for closure may adjust their initial hypothesis on the basis of subsequent information. They may, for example, stray from a statistical framing hypothesis and utilize the individuating information, and/or stray from a psychological framing hypothesis and utilize the base rate information.

Considering Characteristics of the Audience

MESSAGE FORMATION CONTEXT Reduced motivation to engage in an extensive adjustment of initial hypotheses may affect individuals' sensitivity not only to the conversational context, but also to communicatively relevant characteristics of the audience. Communication theory generally assumes that in designing messages, communicators consider their audiences' points of view (Clark, 1985; Grice, 1975). As Krauss and Fussell (1991, p. 4) pointed out, however, speakers' knowledge may be regarded as "hypotheses that participants continuously modify and reformulate on the basis of additional evidence." Such hypothesis testing may occur with respect to both the encoding of communications by speakers and their decoding by listeners. Furthermore, this process is likely to be affected jointly by participants' own knowledge and the motivation to adjust it in accordance with presumed knowledge differences between themselves and their audience. It seems reasonable to assume that often participants will use their own knowledge as the initial hypothesis about their partners' knowledge, displaying a kind of "false consensus effect" (Ross, Greene, & House, 1977). They may then adjust this hypothesis on the basis of further considerations. Extent of such adjustment is likely to depend on individuals' need for closure: Subjects with a high (vs. low) need for closure may seize and freeze more upon the initial hypothesis and may adjust it less. Consequently, under high (vs. low) need for closure, both communicators and addressees should be less sensitive to differences in perspective (knowledge) between themselves and their audiences, and hence should be less efficient at the encoding and decoding of communications.

Those issues could be investigated within the "audience design" paradigm developed by Fussell and Krauss (1989). In that research, subjects performed a two-stage referential task in which they created expressions for referring to abstract visual figures consisting of simple geometric combinations of lines and circles. Specifically, subjects were instructed to provide a name or description for each figure that would enable either "another student" (social condition) or themselves (nonsocial condition) to identify the stimulus at a later time. If subjects took into account their audience's characteristics, communications in the nonsocial and social conditions should differ. This indeed was the case: Messages in the nonsocial condition were shorter and more figurative, reflecting more idiosyncratic bias, than were messages in the social condition. Apparently, such tailoring of messages can be highly effective: Identification success was greatest for messages created for oneself by oneself (self nonsocial condition), was less for messages created by oneself for others (self social condition), was even less for messages created by others for different others (other social condition), and was least of all for messages created by others for themselves (other nonsocial condition).

If the audience design phenomenon involves a motivated judgmental process, its extent and efficacy should be affected by the need for closure. Generally, greater adherence to one's own perspective is predicted for high- than for low-need-for-closure individuals. Thus, message length is expected to be shorter and its contents to be more figurative under high than under low need for closure. Need for closure (high vs. low) may also suppress the difference in message length and contents (figurative vs. literal) between the nonsocial and social conditions. As a consequence of these processes, the efficacy of communication may suffer. Specifically, identification success may be less for messages *created* under high versus low need for closure, particularly with respect to messages created by other communicators, because of their reduced tendency in such a motivational state to match messages to audiences.

MESSAGE RECEPTION CONTEXT   Need for closure may affect not only the formation of messages, but also their reception. Specifically, under a high degree of this motivation, a receiver may decode a message in terms of constructs that happen to be particularly accessible to him or her (Ford & Kruglanski, 1995; Thompson et al., 1994). Whether such decoding will be successful should depend on the extent to which the receiver's accessible constructs match the notions employed by the communicator in the message.

Indeed, descriptions in the different naming conditions may vary systematically in the extent to which they employ constructs that are generally accessible to message receivers. Messages in the self/nonsocial condition—that is, those created by oneself for oneself—may contain the most (chronically) accessible constructs (Higgins, King, & Mavin, 1982), followed by messages in the self/social, other/social, and other/nonsocial conditions. As noted earlier, identification success may vary as a function of need for closure and construct accessibility. When the messages use highly accessible constructs, subjects with a high need for closure should be quite successful in identifying the referents—probably as successful as subjects with a low need for closure—simply because accessible constructs have clear, immediately obvious referents that do not require extensive cognitive work to be divined. However, subjects with a high need for closure should do less well when the descriptive constructs employed in the message are relatively inaccessible. Correct decoding of such messages may require fairly extensive cognitive effort, which high-need-for-closure subjects are less inclined to put out.

If the various foregoing ideas are supported empirically, it should be demonstrated that the processes of judgment and communication are closely intertwined. Specifically, the quality and efficacy of the communication may depend on the quality of judgments whereby the communication context is assessed, which in turn may depend on various cognitive and motivational factors, such as construct accessibility and need for closure.

Accuracy of Social Perception

In much of the discussion so far, need for closure has been portrayed as a kind of motivational "villain" whose effects tend to bias judgments (e.g., Jamieson & Zanna, 1989; Kruglanski & Freund, 1983; Sanbomatsu & Fazio, 1990) or to reduce the efficacy with which communicative messages are formed or received. This may not be invariably so, however. In fact, in some circumstances, need-for-closure effects may be downright positive. The fundamental effect of the need for closure is the tendency to base judgments upon readily accessible constructs (Ford & Kruglanski, 1995; Thompson et al., 1994). Whether this results in accurate or inaccurate judgments should depend entirely upon whether the accessible constructs happen to match some external reality—for example, characteristics of the target about whom one is making judgments (Kruglanski, 1989).

Accordingly, it is possible that in some conditions need for closure may actually contribute to the accuracy of social perception! Specifically, persons with a high (versus low) need for closure may freeze on readily processed nonverbal cues (Gilbert & Krull, 1988) that often convey the target's true feelings (DePaulo & Coleman, 1987), and may be relatively impervious to more normatively controlled (and hence less authentic) verbal communications whose processing requires greater effort (Gilbert & Krull, 1988). Furthermore, as a special case of social perception, the meta-perception accuracy of high-need-for-closure subjects—that is, their ability to discern how they are perceived by others—should be high.

High-need-for-closure persons may also constitute more accurately perceptible *targets* of social perception. Consider that in many social situations, individuals' direct reactions to persons and events are subjected to self-critical evaluation and adjustment in accordance with situational norms. Individuals with a high (vs. low) need for closure may be more likely to seize and freeze on their initial impulses, and less likely to engage in extensive adjustment of their reactions. If so, they should be more "transparent" or accurately perceptible. In short, high-need-for-closure subjects may be at once more accurately perceptible to others and capable of perceiving others more accurately, particularly in contexts where individuals' true feelings deviate from normative expectations, so that the more spontaneous and veridical nonverbal reactions may appreciably differ from the more normatively driven verbal expressions.

One wonders what implications such differences in accuracy may have for social interaction. For instance, a couple in which both members are high in the need for closure, and hence are more sensitive social perceivers as well as more "transparent" targets, may therefore develop a more accurate appreciation of each other's attitudes and preferences than partners who are low in the need for closure. As a consequence, high-need-for-closure partners may be more willing to act on each other's behalf. They may also develop greater confidence in each other's judgments: Because of the sense that they accurately perceive each other, they may come to trust the accuracy of each other's perceptions in other domains. Those unobvious implications of need-for-closure effects on social judgment accuracy may be profitably investigated in subsequent research.

NEED-FOR-CLOSURE EFFECTS ON GROUP PHENOMENA: MOTIVATED EMERGENCE OF A CONSERVATIVE GROUP CULTURE

The need for closure represents a desire for firm knowledge. In turn, knowledge can be of paramount relevance to group processes in that (1) interaction with members of one's group may play an important role in knowledge acquisition (Festinger, 1954), and (2) appropriate types of knowledge (e.g., knowledge of group norms and rules) may play a major role in effective group interaction. Because of its centrality to the knowledge formation process, need for closure may exert wide-ranging effects on group phenomena, including the emergence and perpetuation of group structure, interpersonal relations within and between groups, groups' attitudes to subgroups and minorities, and status allocation phenomena within groups. Indeed, as elaborated subsequently, need-for-closure effects on group processes may be broadly hypothesized to contribute to the emergence of a conservative group culture.

Webster's Ninth New Collegiate Dictionary (1985) defines "conservatism" as "a disposition to preserve what is established, philosophy based on social stability, stressing established institutions, the tendency to prefer an existing or traditional situation to change"(p. 279). One psychological reason why change may be aversive to some people is that it typically entails a state of epistemic ambiguity; thus, need for closure may induce an abhorrence of change, leading to conservatism. This may manifest itself in several fundamental features of group life, such as preferences for types of leadership and decision-making structures within the group, patterns of status allocation, reactions to minorities and majorities, reactions to attempts at changing group norms, and reactions to ingroup versus outgroup members.

Leadership and Decision-Making Preferences

A group with a high (vs. low) need for closure may prefer authoritarian or "closed" over liberal or "open" leadership. Such a tendency may be properly labeled "conservative," because a liberal leadership is by definition open to new ideas, carrying the seed of potential change. By contrast, authoritarian leadership may be expected to preserve the status quo, primarily the leaders' privilege and power base. In addition, an authoritarian leader typically reaches decisions quickly and consults little with others. This may minimize the inherent ambiguity of the predecisional phase, further promoting cognitive stability within the group. Recall that in our research (Kruglanski et al., 1993), high-need-for-closure individuals who lacked an initial opinion were more readily persuaded by their partners. In a similar vein, high-need-for-closure individuals may be more ready to accept a leader's authority and influence.

Admittedly, high-need-for-closure individuals who possessed an initial opinion were less persuadable, or more resistant to influence. Presumably, however, this was because they felt their partners were persuadable and that getting the partners to change their minds would allow them to maintain their own prior opinion, or closure. However, if a group contains numerous members expected to hold diverse views, the potential debate may appear considerable, creating a great deal of ambiguity and forestalling the attainment of closure. Under such conditions, high-need-for-closure members may prefer to accept a leader's authority rather than sticking to their own opinion if this raises the specter of a prolonged debate. For exactly the same reasons, a group whose members have a high need for closure may promote the adoption of nonegalitarian and "lenient" rules (e.g., a vote by majority vs. a decision by consensus) that ease the decision-making process and avoid ambiguity.

Those effects are particularly likely to emerge when group members appear to differ in task-relevant ability or expertise. Specifically, such differences provide the informational basis for creating a hierarchy or adopting nonegalitarian rules, and hence provide a ready justification for persons with a high need for closure to do just that. Previous research (for a review, see Kunda, 1990) suggests that in the absence of such informational justification, the motivation to create a hierarchy may not suffice; in order for it to have an impact on judgments, motivation may need informational "grist" for its "mill."

Furthermore, in cases where an absence of apparent ability or expertise differences may obstruct the formation of a hierarchy, group members with a high need for closure may experience more dissatisfaction with the group process than their low-need-for-closure counterparts. Similar affective reactions may be present when a particular (i.e, a hierarchical or an egalitarian) group structure is imposed externally upon a group, rather than evolving internally within it. Such a situation may be quite typical, in fact, in the many societal institutions or organization-types where members enter groups with pre-existing norms and rules for carrying out the group tasks. In terms of the present analysis, members with a high need for closure should be particularly dissatisfied with a situation where an egalitarian process is imposed despite a natural basis for creating a hierarchy (e.g., clear-cut knowledge, ability, or expertise differences), and they should be particularly pleased when a hierarchical system exists conjointly with a compelling basis for a hierarchy. Individuals who feel uncomfortable with closure, on the other hand, may be particularly frustrated with an imposed hierarchy devoid of a rational base, and particularly pleased with an egalitarian system.

Status Allocation

The hypotheses outlined in the preceding section might be taken to imply that group members with a high need for closure may allocate leadership status rather reasonably, according to members' perceived ability, expertise, or task-relevant knowledge. However, need-for-closure effects on status allocation may often be less than wholly reasonable. In fact, need for closure may often bias status assignments in the direction of diffuse social characteristics (e.g., age, sex, or race) that are largely unrelated to members' actual contributions to the task. That diffuse characteristics may serve as a basis for status allocation in groups has been long documented in the sociological literature (Bales, Strodbeck, Mills, & Roseborough, 1951). In fact, such assignments have been known to occur almost "instantaneously" (Berger, Rosenholtz, & Zeldich, 1980) and to exert significant influence on the course and outcomes of group interaction. According to the present analysis, these effects may occur in part because group members strive to dispel the ambiguity that typically exists concerning the structure and process of group interaction in the initial phases of group formation. Diffuse features (e.g., sex or race) may be linked to pre-existing stereotypes about leadership competence; thus, they may serve as initial cognitive "anchors" for status assignments. Groups whose members are high on the need for closure may seize these status anchors and freeze upon them, paying less attention to individuating information about participants' actual contributions to the group task.

It is of interest that the predicted tendency under high (vs. low) need for closure to allocate status on the basis of diffuse social characteristics may stem from one or both of two possible sources. As already noted, group members may exhibit these trends in regard to assignments made to others. Even more interesting, however, is the possibility that under high need for closure group members may also assign status to themselves on the basis of diffuse characteristics. In such a condition, notions such as "I am a woman," "I am young," or "I am black" may determine an individual's perception of his or her own status relative to that of others in the group. Such self-labeling may subsequently affect the individual's own group-relevant behavior (e.g., the degree of initiative, assertiveness, or intellectual independence) in a label-congruent direction. Such phenomena may properly be labeled "conservative" in that they enhance the power of pre-existing stereotypes and prejudices, thus maintaining the existing "pecking order" within the group, and forestalling the possibility of structural change even if it might ultimately benefit the group.

Groups' Reactions to Normative Change

Increased group conservatism under high need for closure may augment resistance to other types of change—for example change in the prevalent normative climate in the group. Such change may often be effected by changes in group composition, particularity the entry of new members whose ideas deviate from existing group norms. To the extent that the group atmosphere is open and accepting, new members may be listened to and may influence the evolution of group norms in the direction of their own views. However, when the group atmosphere is closed, new ideas may be resisted, and new members lacking in status may be treated with relatively little respect compared to "old-timers." In such conditions, group norms may remain stable across considerable shifts in membership even if the incoming members do not initially share the assumptions or values underlying those particular norms.

According to the present analysis, need for closure is likely to contribute to just such a closed-minded group atmosphere. This may be particularly likely where a formal differentiation exists between new and old members, as may be typical in many organizations or institutions (e.g., the military, academic departments) where most new members enter at low rungs on the hierarchical ladder and in time ascend to higher organizational levels. A formal differentiation between new and old members may thus furnish the informational justification for discrimination, supplying the needed "grist" for the motivational "mill." Those ideas could be empirically tested via the "generations design" (Jacobs & Campbell, 1961), in which old members leave the group and new ones enter after each interaction cycle. To create the potential for normative change, the norm initially established in the group (e.g. via the use of confederates) might be opposed to the prevailing view among the incoming members. The present analysis suggests that normative stability across generational cycles would be greater for groups under high (versus low) need for closure and that this tendency should be more pronounced when the group structure contains a hierarchy weighted in favor of the old-timers versus the newcomers.

Functional Rigidity of Leadership across Tasks: The "Once a Leader, Always a Leader" Phenomenon

Efficient utilization of a group's resources may often require that members who perform leadership functions in regard to one type of task, requiring their unique expertise, assume a subordinate role when the task changes and their expertise is no longer relevant. Such flexibility in leadership functions may be less likely to be present in conservative groups, because these are generally opposed to change, including rotation of leadership functions across different members. The present analysis suggests that the flexibility loss may be particularly pronounced in groups whose members have a high need for closure. Furthermore, because a motivated freezing on a given leadership structure is more likely when an informational justification exists for its emergence, such functional rigidity may be augmented when the group members differ in competence with respect to the initial task.

Again, the phenomenon of functional rigidity could arise from two possible sources: other members' perceptions of an individual's leadership status (determined by an initially created structure), and the member's own perceptions, which may affect his or her leadership behavior. For example, under high need for closure a member who lacks expertise on an initial group task may decide that he or she is a follower rather than a leader, and may persist in that perception even though he or she possesses the requisite skills for leadership on subsequent tasks. Finally, under high need for closure an individual's freezing on a perceived leadership status (i.e., that of a leader or a follower) may persist not only across tasks in the same group but across different groups as well. Those ideas could be investigated using "rotation designs" (Kenny, Hallmark, Sullivan, & Kashy, in press), in which the group composition is kept constant while the tasks are varied, the group composition is varied while the task is constant, or both are varied.

Rejection of Deviates

A particularly interesting psychological property of groups is members' ability to define the group boundaries in various ways, so that particular other members are either included or excluded from the group. Such flexibility may allow the group to maintain consensus in its midst by placing opinion deviates outside the group boundaries (Festinger, 1950; Schachter, 1951). Once the deviates are redefined as non members, their dissenting opinions apparently cease to matter to existing members. It is as if at this point they cease to be part of the "social reality" relevant to the members' opinions.

A point relevant to the present discussion is that if need for closure increases group members' desire for normative stability, this should be apparent not only across generational cycles but also within each cycle, manifesting itself via the striving for an intragroup consensus. One consequence of such strivings should be an increased tendency under heightened need for closure to reject deviants whose opinions undermine consensus. These notions were investigated in a series of experiments (Kruglanski & Webster, 1991).

In the first study, need for closure was operationally defined in terms of time pressure, or temporal proximity of the group decision deadline. We assumed that with the deadline relatively remote, members' prepotent concern would be to safeguard the quality of their decision. This might induce a need to avoid premature closure and increase the tolerance for ambiguity that dissenting views might create. With the deadline drawing near, however, the implied time pressure might induce an overriding need for closure. This might reduce group members' tolerance for dissent, and increase their tendency to reject the deviates.

In a field experiment designed to test those ideas (Kruglanski & Webster, 1991, Study 1), groups of Boy and Girl Scouts in Tel Aviv were presented with the decision of choosing a location for their annual "working camp" of 2 weeks' duration. Two kibbutz settlements were presented as choices. One was an affluent, centrally located kibbutz (Naan) amply endowed with such luxurious accoutrements as swimming pools, tennis courts, and color TVs. The other choice was a fledgling kibbutz (Ktora) in the Judean desert, lacking (at the time) even such basic amenities as in-house bathrooms.

Despite what to some might appear the obvious choice, the idealistically motivated Scouts predominantly preferred the rugged little settlement over its luxurious alternative. This fact was known to us, and was treated as the group's consensual opinion. To introduce our deviancy manipulation, we asked one member in each group (whose sociometric standing was at the median of the distribution) to argue either for the consensual choice (the conformist role) or for the unpopular alternative (the deviate role), and to do so either early in the deliberation process or late, near the putative deadline.

Actually, there existed three experimental conditions related to the timing of opinion expression. In the "objectively early" condition, the confederate announced his or her (conforming or deviate) opinion near the commencement of discussion. In the "objectively late" condition; he or she did so near the expected deadline. In the "subjectively early" condition, the confederate announced an opinion at the same actual time as in the objectively late condition; yet, because the deadline was appropriately postponed, subjects believed they had as much discussion time remaining as did participants in the objectively early condition.

The available evidence confirmed that subjects' need for closure was proportionate to the remaining discussion time subjects believed they had. Specifically, subjects' differentiation between attractiveness of the two choice alternatives was significantly lower in both early conditions (objective as well as subjective) than in the (objectively) late condition. This suggests that subjects were more open-minded to both alternatives when they felt little (vs. much) time pressure to make up their minds. Those findings were paralleled by expressed confidence in the attractiveness ratings which was significantly higher at the late point than at either early point. Both findings support the notion that time pressure, induced by perceived proximity of the deadline, contributed in the expected manner to need-for-closure arousal.

The main dependent variable of interest was an evaluative shift toward the confederate in the deviate and conformist roles. The evaluative shifts toward the conformist were negligible and did not appreciably vary as a function of timing. The shifts toward the deviate exhibited a strikingly different pattern: They were progressively more negative as a function of proximity to the deadline.

We (Kruglanski & Webster, 1991, Study 2) conceptually replicated this experiment, manipulating the need for closure through ambient noise. Groups of University of Maryland students were instructed to discuss and reach a consensus on compulsory drug testing for campus athletes. Subjects were preselected to favor such testing. Two members of each group were confederates, whose behavior during the discussion varied systematically as a function of our experimental manipulations. One confederate enacted a conformist's role and expressed opinions consistent with the prevailing consensus (in favor of drug testing). The other confederate enacted a deviate's role and expressed opinions at odds with the consensus (arguing against drug testing). To control for possible effects due to the confederates' personalities, we had them rotate the conformist and deviate roles across the experimental sessions.

As in the Kruglanski et al. (1993) research described earlier, the noise was produced by a computer printer. We assumed that in a noisy environment information processing would be more laborious (and hence more subjectively costly), and that this would elevate subjects' need for closure, leading to greater rejection of the deviate. This was precisely what happened.

To examine the possible alternative interpretation that derogation of the deviate under noisy conditions stemmed from irritability induced by the noise rather than from the need for closure, we replicated our experiment (Kruglanski & Webster, 1991, Study 3) with one exception. Subjects in one condition were provided an alternative way of safeguarding collective closure: the possibility of formally excluding the deviate from the decision-making process. Specifically, subjects in this condition were allowed to reach their decision by a majority rather than a consensus rule. Indeed, no rejection occurred in any of the majority rule conditions. Instead, the only condition where the deviate was downgraded was the noise consensus rule cell. It appears, then, that in and of itself, noise-induced irritability did not account for derogation of the deviate. Only when the deviate undermined the other members' sense of closure, by voicing a dissenting opinion in a significant reference group, did his or her deviance seem upsetting enough to cause rejection.

The present analysis has an additional intriguing implication: If rejection under noise was attributable to heightened need for closure frustrated by the deviate's dissent, the conformist should have been evaluated more positively under noise (vs. no noise), for his or her opinions would have facilitated the gratification of this need. The reason this may not have been apparent in research described thus far is that in those experiments the conformist merely reiterated the normative opinion; hence her or his statements may have been lacking in salience. To overcome this problem, in our last study (Kruglanski & Webster, 1991, Study 4) the conformist was made to assume a leader's role (including initiation of conversations with the deviate, and provision of repeated reminders to the group of the consensus objective). The results were illuminating: Whereas the deviant continued being downgraded more under noise (vs. no noise) the conformist was actually applauded more in this condition. Considered collectively, then, the findings reviewed here support the notion that need for closure increases subjects' desire for consensus, and that this may lead to the derogation of persons who threaten consensus and the approbation of those who strive to consolidate it.

Intragroup Relations between Majorities and Minorities

The flexibility in the setting of group boundaries (e.g., as seen in the rejection of deviates) may account for Asch's (1946) classic finding that to have a single "ally" sharing in an individual's minority opinion is sufficient to markedly reduce the individual's tendency to conform to the majority. It is as if the individual is capable of redefining what constitutes the relevant reference group in terms of a *single* other member, and thus of conferring an irrelevancy status on the entire remainder of the group! In other words, individuals do seem to need "social reality" to validate their opinions (Festinger, 1950, 1954) but what constitutes it may be defined flexibly and include as little as a single individual other than oneself.

These notions have interesting implications for how newcomers into a group (e.g., new immigrants into a country) may be integrated into the host group as a function of their need for closure. Consider a relatively isolated newcomer or "lone immigrant," devoid of ties to members of the old culture. If we assume that such an individual will need some "social reality" to refer to, he or she may well find it in the new majority culture. If we assume further that the need to have firm, socially validated knowledge increases as a function of the need for closure, we may predict for the lone immigrant greater integration within the majority culture as a direct function of the need for closure.

The case may be very different, however, for the "collective immigrant," who enters the new culture as a member of a larger body of similar newcomers sharing his or her attitudes and values. It seems plausible that this type of immigrant will find an immediate "social reality" in the minority culture by which he or she is surrounded. Again, to the extent that the need for socially validated knowledge may increase as a function of the need for closure, we may predict for the collective immigrant greater adherence to the (old) minority culture, and hence ultimately less integration into the majority culture.

Although the foregoing processes are assumed to be localized in the newcomers as such, they may be even augmented by differential reactions of the majority culture to the lone immigrant versus the collective immigrant. Specifically, the lone immigrant may be treated more as an individual and objected to less than the collective immigrant, who is seen as part of a larger category. This category may be seen as an outgroup from which the ingroup may wish to distance itself—for example, by encouraging well-demarcated spatial boundaries between the majority and minority, or even a "ghetto" in which the minority may be kept at bay. Such tendencies on the part of the majority may be intensified under a high need for closure, because of the stronger presumed tendency under such a motivation to preserve a clear distinction between the ingroup and the outgroup. The reason for sharpening this distinction may derive from the particular value that the ingroup acquires under heightened need for closure as a source of "social reality." In other words, heightened need for closure intensifies the individuals' need for firm knowledge. Firm knowledge, in turn, often requires social reality for its validation. Hence, it becomes particularly important, under heightened need for closure, to establish a clear demarcation between the ingroup and the outgroup.

Ingroup versus Outgroup Favoritism

Such demarcation may not be merely perceptual, but may be accompanied by an affective differentiation manifested in greater favoritism toward ingroup versus outgroup members. Specifically, the maintenance of a firm social reality may render agreement among ingroup members particularly important for individuals. This may induce an expectation of agreement, as well as positive affect and a sense of communion with ingroup members. Under these circumstances, a communal orientation may develop toward ingroup members whereas the outgroup members, may be treated according to an exchange scheme—that is, in a "strictly business" manner (Clark & Mills, 1993). Specifically, individuals with a heightened need for closure may be more sensitive to *needs* of the ingroup members versus the outgroup members, and more conscious of the *relative contributions* toward task accomplishment of outgroup versus ingroup members (Clark, 1984).

For the same reasons, individuals with a heightened need for closure may prefer an *equality* allocation rule when interacting with ingroup members, and an *equity* allocation rule when interacting with outgroup members. The stronger feelings of cohesion with respect to the ingroup may lead members to select an equality rule with respect to other ingroup members, because it highlights the commonality among members, rather than their differences. By contrast, the desire to demarcate the ingroup (including oneself) from the outgroup may lead to selection of an equity rule when interacting with outgroup members because it highlights interpersonal differences.

CONCLUSION

If the elaborate construction of knowledge pervasively characterizes humans as a species; *if* knowledge construction is an inherently social enterprise to which judgmental processes are central; and, finally, *if* epistemic motivation plays a pivotal role in judgment, then understanding such motivation may yield insights into fundamental aspects of human social behavior. Those assumptions constituted the premises upon which the research described in this chapter has been based. The central theoretical construct under investigation, the need for (nonspecific) cognitive closure, represents the desire for a particular epistemic state—a state of firm and definite knowledge. Extant evidence suggests that such a desire may be induced situationally, via various perceived benefits of closure or costs of lacking closure, and that it also constitutes a dimension of individual differences.

Regardless of how the need for closure is aroused, its systematic effects on the judgmental process appear to be the same. They include early "seizing" and "freezing" upon accessible cues and insensitivity to subsequent relevant information. These mechanisms have been documented in research on impression formation, stereotyping, anchoring, and attributional correspondence bias, among others. However, the social-psychological phenomena affected by the need for closure do not seem limited to intrapersonal aspects of social perception. Instead, they seem to extend to various interpersonal and group phenomena of major significance. The chapter has outlined hypotheses regarding the role need for closure may play in interpersonal communication, the accuracy of interpersonal impressions, and communication.

On the group level of analysis, the present discussion suggests that heightened need for closure may prompt the emergence of a conservative group culture, characterized by hierarchical power and decision-making structure, resistance to normative change, and ingroup favoritism. Admittedly, many of the hypotheses concerning the interpersonal and group-level consequences of the need for closure are at present speculative and remain to be investigated empirically. However, they do illustrate the promise of a "motivated social cognition" approach as a new general paradigm for the study of social psychology.

References

Allport, G. W. (1935). Attitudes. In C. Murchison (Ed.), *Handbook of social psychology* (Vol. 2). Worcester, MA: Clark University Press.

Asch, S. E. (1946). Forming impressions of personality. *Journal of Abnormal and Social Psychology, 41,* 258-290.

Bales, R. F., Strodbeck, F. L., Mills, T. M., & Roseborough, M. E. (1951). Channels of communication in small groups. *American Sociological Review, 16,* 461-468.

Baumeister, R. F. (1991). *Meanings of life.* New York: Guilford Press.

Bem, D. J. (1967). Self-perception: An alternative interpretation of cognitive dissonance phenomena. *Psychological Review, 74,* 183-200.

Bem, D. J. (1972). Self-perception theory. In L. Berkowitz (Ed.), *Advances in experimental social psychology* (Vol. 6, pp. 1-62). New York: Academic Press.

Berger, J., Rosenholtz, A., & Zeldich, M. (1980). Status organizing processes. *American Review of Sociology, 6,* 479-508.

Buss, D. (in press). Evolutionary mechanisms of social interaction. In E. T. Higgins & A. W. Kruglanski (Eds.), *Social psychology: Handbook of basic principles.* New York: Guilford Press.

Cacioppo, J. T., & Petty, R. E. (1982). The need for cognition. *Journal of Personality and Social Psychology, 42,* 116-131.

Chaiken, S., Liberman, A., & Eagly, A. H. (1989). Heuristic and systematic information processing within and beyond the persuasion context. In J. S. Uleman & J. A. Bargh (Eds.), *Unintended thought* (pp. 212-252). New York: Guilford Press

Clark, H. H. (1985). Language use and language users. In G. Lindzey & E. Aronson (Eds.), *Handbook of social psychology* (3rd ed., Vol. 2, pp. 179-232). New York: Random House.

Clark, M. S. (1984). Record keeping in two types of relationships. *Journal of Personality and Social Psychology, 47,* 549-557.

Clark, M. S., & Mills, J. (1993). The differences between communal and exchange relationships: What it is and is not. *Personality and Social Psychology Bulletin, 19*(6), 684-691.

DePaulo, B. M., & Coleman, L. M. (1987). Verbal and nonverbal communication of warmth to children, foreigners, and retarded adults. *Journal of Nonverbal Behavior, 11,* 75-88.

Dijksterhuis, A. (1994). [Effects of need for closure on recall of stereotype-consistent and inconsistent information]. Unpublished raw data, University of Nijmegen, The Netherlands.

Durkheim, E. (1951). *Suicide* (G. Simpson, Ed.; J. A. Spaulding & G. Simpson, Trans.). Glencoe, IL: Free Press. (Original work published 1897)

Eysenck, H. J. (1954). *The psychology of politics.* New York: Praeger.

Festinger, L. (1950). Informal social communication. *Psychological Review, 57,* 271–282.

Festinger, L. (1954). A theory of social comparison processes. *Human Relations, 7,* 117–140.

Festinger, L. (1957). *A theory of cognitive dissonance.* Stanford, CA: Stanford University Press.

Ford, T. E., & Kruglanski, A. W. (1995). Effects of epistemic motivations on the use of accessible constructs in social judgment. *Personality and Social Psychology Bulletin, 21*(9), 950–962.

Frenkel-Brunswik, E. (1949). Intolerance of ambiguity as an emotional and perceptual personality variable. *Journal of Personality, 18,* 108–143.

Freund, T., Kruglanski, A. W., & Schpitzajzen, A. (1985). The freezing and unfreezing of impressional primacy: Effects of the need for structure and the fear of invalidity. *Personality and Social Psychology Bulletin, 11,* 479–487.

Fussell, S. R., & Krauss, R. M. (1989). The effects of intended audience on message production and comprehension: Reference in a common ground framework. *Journal of Experimental Social Psychology, 25,* 203–219.

Gilbert, D. T., & Krull, D. S. (1988). Seeing less and knowing more: The benefits of perceptual ignorance. *Journal of Personality and Social Psychology, 54,* 193–202.

Gilbert, D. T., Pelham, B. W., & Krull, D. S. (1988). On cognitive busyness: When person perceivers meet persons perceived. *Journal of Personality and Social Psychology, 54,* 733–740.

Grice, H. (1975). Logic and conversation. In P. Cole & J. L. Morgan (Eds.), *Syntax and semantics: Vol. 3. Speech acts.* New York: Academic Press.

Heaton, A. W., & Kruglanski, A. W. (1991). Person perception by introverts and extroverts under time pressure. *Personality and Social Psychology Bulletin, 17,* 161–165.

Higgins, E. T., King, G. A., & Mavin, G. H. (1982). Individual construct accessibility and subjective impressions and recall. *Journal of Personality and Social Psychology, 43,* 35–47.

Hovland, C. I., Janis, I. L., & Kelley, H. H. (1953). *Communication and persuasion.* New Haven: Yale University Press.

Jacobs, R. C., & Campbell, D. T. (1961). The perpetuation of an arbitrary tradition through several generations of laboratory microculture. *Journal of Abnormal and Social Psychology, 62,* 649–658.

James, W. (1890). *Principles of psychology* (2 vols.). New York: Holt.

Jamieson, D. W., & Zanna, M. P. (1989). Need for structure in attitude formation and expression. In A. Pratkanis, S. Breckler, & A. G. Greenwald (Eds.), *Attitude structure and function* (pp. 73–89). Hillsdale, N J: Erlbaum.

Johnson, T. J., Feigenbaum, R., & Weiby, M. (1964). Some determinants and consequences of teachers' perception of causation. *Journal of Educational Psychology, 55,* 237–246.

Jones, E. E. (1979). The rocky road from acts to dispositions. *American Psychologist, 34,* 107–117.

Jones, E. E., & Harris, V. A. (1967). The attribution of attitudes. *Journal of Experimental Social Psychology, 3,* 1–24.

Kahneman, D., Slovic, P., & Tversky, A. (Eds.). (1982). *Judgment under uncertainty: Heuristics and biases.* New York: Cambridge University Press.

Kelley, H. H. (1971). Attribution in social interaction. In E. E. Jones, D. E. Kanause, H. H. Kelley, R. E. Nisbett, S. Valins, & B. Weiner (Eds.), *Attribution: Perceiving the causes of behavior* (pp. 1–27). Morristown, NJ: General Learning Press.

Kenny, D. A., Hallmark, B. W., Sullivan, P., & Kashy, D. A. (in press). The analysis of designs in which individuals are in more than one group. *British Journal of Social Psychology.*

Krauss, R. M., & Fussell, S. R. (1991). Perspective-taking in communication: Representations of others' knowledge in reference. *Social Cognition, 9,* 2–24.

Kruglanski, A. W. (1989). *Lay epistemics and human knowledge: Cognitive and motivational bases.* New York: Plenum Press.

Kruglanski, A. W. (1990). Motivations for judging and knowing: Implications for causal attribution. In E. T. Higgins & R. M. Sorrentino (Eds.), *Handbook of motivation and cognition: Foundations of social behavior* (Vol. 2, pp. 333-368). New York: Guilford Press.

Kruglanski, A. W., & Freund, T. (1983). The freezing and unfreezing of lay-inferences: Effects on impressional primacy, ethnic stereotyping and numerical anchoring. *Journal of Experimental Social Psychology, 19,* 448-468.

Kruglanski, A. W., & Mayseless, O. (1988). Contextual effects in hypothesis testing: The role of competing alternatives and epistemic motivations. *Social Cognition, 6,* 1-21.

Kruglanski, A.W., Peri, N., & Zakai, D. (1991). Interactive effects of need for closure and initial confidence on social information seeking. *Social Cognition, 9,* 127-148.

Kruglanski, A. W., & Webster, D. M. (1991). Group members' reactions to opinion deviates and conformists at varying degrees of proximity to decision deadline and of environmental noise. *Journal of Personality and Social Psychology, 61,* 212-225.

Kruglanski, A. W., Webster, D. M., & Klem, A. (1993). Motivated resistance and openness to persuasion in the presence or absence of prior information. *Journal of Personality and Social Psychology, 64,* 861-876.

Kunda, Z. (1990). The case for motivated reasoning. *Psychological Bulletin, 108*(3), 480-498.

Kunda, Z., & Sherman-Williams, B. (1993). Stereotypes and the construal of individuating information. *Personality and Social Psychology Bulletin, 19,* 90-99.

LeBon, G. (1896). *The crowd.* London: T. Fisher Unwin. (Original work published 1895)

Levine, J. M., Resnick, L., & Higgins, E. T. (1993). Social foundations of cognition. *Annual Review of Psychology, 44,* 585-612.

Levine, J. M., & Thompson, L. (in press). Conflict in groups. In E. T. Higgins & A. W. Kruglanski (Eds.), *Social psychology: Handbook of basic principles.* New York: Guilford Press.

London, H. (1973). Psychology of the persuader. Morristown, N.J: General Learning Press.

Luchins, A. S. (1957). Primacy-recency in impression formation. In C. E. Hovland (Ed.), *The order of presentation* (pp. 33-61). New Haven, CT: Yale University Press.

Mayseless, O., & Kruglanski, A.W. (1987). What makes you so sure? Effects of epistemic motivations on judgmental confidence. *Organizational Behavior and Human Decision Processes, 39,* 162-183.

Miller, D. T., & Ross, M. (1975). Self-serving biases in the attribution of causality: Fact or fiction? *Psychological Bulletin, 82,* 213-225.

Miller, N. N., Maruyama, G., Beaber, R.J., & Valone, K. (1976). Speed of speech and persuasion. *Journal of Personality and Social Psychology, 34,* 615-624.

Nisbett, R. E., & Ross, L. (1980). *Human inference: strategies and shortcomings of human judgment.* Englewood Cliffs, NJ: Prentice-Hall.

Nisbett, R. E., & Wilson, T.D. (1977). Telling more than we can know: Verbal reports on mental processes. *Psychological Review, 84,* 231-259.

Petty, R. E., & Cacioppo, J. T. (1986). The elaboration likelihood model of persuasion. In L. Berkowitz (Ed.), *Advances in experimental social psychology* (Vol. 19, pp. 123-205). New York: Academic Press.

Quattrone, G. A. (1982). Overattribution and unit formation: When behavior engulfs the person. *Journal of Personality and Social Psychology, 42,* 593-607.

Ross, L., Greene, D., & House, P. (1977). The "false consensus effect": An egocentric bias in social perception and attribution processes. *Journal of Experimental Social Psychology, 13,* 279-301.

Ross, M., McFarland, C., & Fletcher, G. J. O. (1981). The effect of attitude on recall of past histories. *Journal of Personality and Social Psychology, 10,* 627-634.

Sanbomatsu, D. M., & Fazio, R. H. (1990). The role of attitudes in memory-based decision making. *Journal of Personality and Social Psychology, 59,* 614-622.

Schachter, S. (1951). Deviation, rejection and communication. *Journal of Abnormal and Social Psychology, 46,* 190-207.

Schwarz, N., Strack, F., Hilton, D., & Naderer, G. (1991). Base rates, representativeness and the logic of conversation: The contextual relevance of "irrelevant" information. *Social Cognition, 9,* 67–84.

Sorrentino, R. M., & Short, J. C. (1986). Uncertainty, motivation, and cognition. In R.M. Sorrentino & E.T. Higgins (Eds.), *Handbook of motivation and cognition: Foundations of social behavior* (Vol. 1, pp. 370–403). New York: Guilford Press.

Sperber, D., & Wilson, D. (1986). *Relevance: Communication and cognition.* Cambridge, MA: Harvard University Press.

Tait, R., & Silver, R. C. (1989). Coming to terms with major negative life-events. In J. S. Uleman & J. A. Bargh (Eds.), *Unintended thought* (pp. 351–382). New York: Guilford Press.

Tajfel, H., & Turner, J.C. (1979). An integrative theory of intergroup conflict. In W. G. Austin & S. Worchel (Eds.), *The social psychology of intergroup relations* (pp. 33–47). Monterey, CA: Brooks/Cole.

Tetlock, P. E. (1985). Accountability: A social check on the fundamental attribution error. *Social Psychology Quarterly, 48,* 227–236.

Tetlock, P. E. & Levi, A. (1982). Attribution bias: On the inconclusiveness of the cognition-motivation debate. *Journal of Experimental Social Psychology, 18,* 68–88.

Thompson, E. P., Roman, R. J., Moscovitz, G. B., Chaiken, S., & Bargh, J. A. (1994). *Journal of Personality and Social Psychology 66,* 474–489.

Trope, Y., & Bassok, M. (1983). Information gathering strategies in hypothesis testing. *Journal of Experimental Social Psychology, 19,* 560–576.

Turner, J. C. (1991). *Social influence.* Pacific Grove, CA: Brooks/Cole.

Turner, J. C., Hogg, M. A., Oakes, P. J., Reicher, S. D., & Wetherell, M. S. (1987). *Rediscovering the social group: A self-categorization theory.* Oxford: Blackwell.

Turner, J. C., & Oakes, P. J. (1989). Self-categorization theory and social influence. In P. B. Paulus (Ed.), *Psychology of group influence* (2nd ed., pp. 233–275). Hillsdale, NJ: Erlbaum.

Tversky, A., & Kahneman, D. (1974). Judgment under uncertainty: Heuristics and biases. *Science, 185,* 1124–1131.

Vygotsky, L. S. (1978). *Mind in society: The development of higher psychological processes.* Cambridge, MA: Harvard University Press.

Webster, D. M. (1993). Motivated augmentation and reduction of the overattribution bias. *Journal of Personality and Social Psychology, 65*(2), 261–271.

Webster, D. W., & Kruglanski, A. W. (1994). Individual differences in need for cognitive closure. *Journal of Personality and Social Psychology, 67*(6), 1049–1062.

Webster's Ninth New Collegiate Dictionary. (1985). Springfield, MA: Merriam-Webster.

Wyer, R. S., & Srull, T. K. (1986). Human cognition in its social context. *Psychological Review, 93,* 322–359.

Zanna, M. P., & Cooper, J. (1976). Dissonance and the attribution process. In J. Harvey, W. I. Ickes, & R. F. Kidd (Eds.), *New directions in attribution research* (Vol. 1, pp. 199–217). Hillsdale, NJ: Erlbaum.

Zuckerman, M. (1979). Attribution of success and failure revisited, or: The motivational bias is alive and well in attribution theory. *Journal of Personality, 47,* 245–287.

CHAPTER 15

Ambivalence in Close Relationships
Conflicted Cognitions as a Catalyst for Change

MEGAN M. THOMPSON
Defence and Civil Institute of Environmental Medicine
Toronto, ON

JOHN G. HOLMES
University of Waterloo
Waterloo, ON

As the initial elation of a romantic relationship subsides, and interdependence increases, individuals start to learn more about their partners' more negative qualities. The specter of potential faults often leads to a certain amount of internal conflict, requiring that the previously unblemished positive view of a partner be reconciled with these newly discovered negative qualities. Is experiencing such ambivalence a warning that a relationship is at risk, or rather an indication that individuals are in touch with the realities of intimacy? Might ambivalence function as a catalyst that moves a relationship in one direction or another because of individuals' basic discomfort with "the babble of competing inner voices" (Jones & Gerard, 1967, p. 181)? If ambivalence does function in this manner, are there psychological forces that can determine whether it ultimately has a constructive or destructive role in the relationship?

The psychological dynamics of ambivalence in close relationships require a focus on the interface of motivation and cognition, for several reasons. First, feelings of ambivalence may require a distinctive configuration of cognitive representations of a partner. The mere presence of positive and negative assessments need not be experienced as ambivalence. In some cases, the existence of conflicting positive and negative partner perceptions may be denied or carefully compartmentalized. However, as many theorists have previously proposed (e.g., Freud, 1923/1962; Festinger, 1957; Heider, 1944; Lewin, 1951), latent cognitive inconsistency can result in a state of intense discomfort as conflicts among cognitions become manifest. Like Brickman (1987), whose model we explore more fully later in the chapter, we propose that experiencing an "unstable dialectic" of

(Holmes & Rempel, 1989, p. 210) positive and negative evaluations can in and of itself motivate an individual to resolve the internal conflict, either by leaving the relationship or by coming to terms with the ambivalence through cognitive and affective changes (Berscheid, 1983; Holmes & Rempel, 1989). Thus, ambivalence can create a motivational state that is a catalyst for change in relationships.

Second, Sorrentino and Higgins (1986) have used the term "synergism" to describe the complex and symmetrical interdependence between motivation and cognition. Tetlock and Levi (1982) have framed this issue in terms of "how people reconcile their desires with their beliefs" (p. 84). Consistent with this theme, we explore how people reconcile their desires about the future of their relationships with their beliefs about their partners—evaluations that may include various amounts of ambivalence. More specifically, we demonstrate that individuals' commitment to the future of their relationships serves to transform their experience of ambivalence.

Perhaps surprisingly, ambivalence is a relatively new avenue of exploration in the area of close relationships. Thus, the beginning of the chapter describes the historical background of the ambivalence concept in general. We then review the relevant research conducted in the field of close relationships. After setting the stage, we present the results of our research concerning the nature and long-term impact of ambivalence in dating relationships. We conclude by exploring potential sources of ambivalence, including the conflicts that arise when individuals' romantic ideals diverge from the actual attributes of their partners.

AMBIVALENCE: THE HISTORICAL BACKGROUND

The idea of conflicted impulses has long held an intuitive appeal for scholars. Indeed, discussions of the nature of ambivalence appear as early as the writings of Aristotle, who described humankind's ongoing struggle between passion and reason (Epstein, 1980). Freud (1923/1962) considered the presence of underlying and unconscious conflicts as the crucial element in understanding the human psyche. Within the realm of social psychology, field theory (Lewin, 1951) posited that a state of tension often results when the positive and negative aspects associated with a goal are in conflict. These conflicts were thought to lead to changes in relevant cognitions and behavior, to restore clarity to the psychological field. However, conflict theorists provided the most detailed operationalization of what it meant to be ambivalent.

Conflict theory (Brown & Farber, 1951; Dollard & Miller, 1950; Epstein, 1980; Hovland & Sears, 1938; Janis, 1982; Janis & Mann, 1968; Miller, 1944), based in the behaviorist tradition, viewed conflict as arising from incompatible response tendencies. Motivational orientations, based on attraction and fear, were thought to have distinct internal mechanisms and were measured as separate entities. The basic tenets of the theory are reflected in the most obvious of these conflicts, termed "approach–avoidance conflict"—the wish to pursue a goal while simultaneously wishing to flee from the same goal. Miller (1944) suggested that both approach and avoidance impulses are a function of the drives upon which they are based and grow stronger as proximity to the goal increases. Miller also believed that a critical intersection between approach and avoidance impulses exists. Specifically, the drive to avoid a goal should become stronger more quickly than should the drive to approach a goal as proximity to the goal increases. Thus, although the consequent behavior was assumed to be based on which of the two underlying drives ultimately has the stronger force, ambivalent responses were ultimately seen as a function of the impeding or weaker force.

These ideas have found support in diverse experimental settings. In animal studies (e.g., Miller, Brown, & Lipofsky, cited in Miller, 1944), for example, approach motivations were induced by presenting food sources to hungry rats. Results indicated that the strength of the approach responses (i.e., the degree of force with which a harness was pulled) increased as the rats drew closer to the food goal. Avoidance motivations, generated via electric shock, led to a tendency to hesitate and avoid the point of prior shock, even when shocks were no longer administered to the rats. Furthermore, when the recorded approach and avoidance gradients were compared, it was apparent that the avoidance gradient was steeper than the approach gradient. Also, stronger approach motivations (greater hunger) or weaker avoidance motivations (weaker shocks) affected the extent to which the rats would approach the food.

In experiments applying the principles of conflict theory to humans (see Miller, 1959), subjects were trained to draw a line from a central point in front of them to an opposite corner of a piece of paper in response to the presence or absence of a light. The approach–avoidance conflict condition required subjects to draw the line to the corner containing a red light and away from the corner containing a green light. The conflict-inducing trial involved flashing a combination of lights simultaneously to induce incompatible responses. The main behavioral responses to each conflict were analogous to those obtained in the earlier animal studies and included a single response (e.g., continuing to draw the line according to training), a double response (drawing the line to both lights), compromise (drawing the line down the center of the paper), or blocking (no response). Certain responses were more characteristic of particular conflicts. For instance, approach–approach conflicts were marked by single responses, and double approach–avoidance conflicts were much more likely to result in blocking.

Epstein (1980) subsequently refined the original formulations of conflict theory to increase their applicability to the cognitive and emotional realms of human experience. He hypothesized that conceptual conflicts—inconsistencies between beliefs or between values and beliefs—are as powerful among humans as, and even more prevalent than, behaviorally based conflicts. Epstein also suggested redefining Miller's simple approach and avoidance tendencies in terms of a hierarchy of weaker and stronger responses. Epstein's contributions have meant that many purely mental processes can also be thought of in terms of distinct and sometimes orthogonal processes. For instance, his formulations have expanded the notion of ambivalence to include conflicts between positive and negative beliefs, and discrepancies between what one thinks and what one feels. As we shall see later, they also allow for a conceptualization of conflicts as discrepancies between ideal and actual assessments of a romantic partner.

Various literatures have demonstrated the existence and importance of conceptual conflicts. Interestingly, however, these conflicts have rarely been termed "ambivalence." For example, there is a wealth of research in the area of subjective well-being indicating the distinctiveness of positive and negative affect (see Bradburn, 1969; Diener, 1984; Diener & Emmons, 1985; Reich & Zautra, 1983; Warr, Barter, & Brownbridge, 1983; Watson & Tellegen, 1985). These studies found that the presence of positive emotions did not necessarily imply the absence of negative emotions. Rather, positive moods were typically associated with desires, and negative moods with demands (Bradburn, 1969; Zautra & Reich, 1983) or undesirable events.

Most social-psychological theories have focused upon consistency and the restoration of consistency between attitude components (e.g., balance theory, Heider, 1944; cognitive dissonance theory, Festinger, 1957). Thus, it is perhaps not surprising that theories articulating the multidimensionality of attitudes are a relatively recent development in attitude theory. According to this perspective, certain attitudes may have positive and negative or affective and cognitive components that are relatively independent of each other (Breckler, 1984; Breckler, in press; Breckler & Wiggins, 1989; Chaiken & Baldwin, 1981; Chaiken & Yates, 1985; Hass, Katz, Rizzo, Bailey, & Eisenstadt, 1991; Katz, Wackenhut, & Hass, 1986; Norman, 1975; Parisi & Katz, 1986; Thompson, Griffin, & Zanna, 1994; Thompson & Zanna, 1995; Thompson, Zanna, & Griffin, 1995; Zanna & Rempel, 1988).

Recent research has shown that certain people are more likely to possess both positive and negative attitudes toward a range of social issues—that is, to chronically exhibit ambivalent attitudes. Moreover, these predispositions have been linked to particular individual-difference constructs in predictable ways. Specifically, those people having a high chronic concern with error, termed high "personal fear of invalidity" (Thompson, Naccarato, Parker, & Moskowitz, 1993), were more likely to possess ambivalent attitudes than individuals who were low in this attribute. Also, those people high in "need for cognition" typically had less ambivalent attitudes than those people low in need for cognition (Thompson & Zanna, 1995; Thompson et al., 1995).

Another line of research was designed to explore response amplification theory (Hass et al., 1991; Katz et al., 1986). In these studies, white students rated as either high or low in ambivalence on the basis of the composition of their racial attitudes (sympathetic vs. hostile toward blacks) interacted with a black person whose behavior was either positive or negative. When the black target acted in a positive manner, the evaluations of the high-ambivalence respondents were the most positive of all subjects. However, when the black target's behavior was negative, the evaluations of the high-ambivalence group were the most negative. Thus, the attitudes of ambivalent individuals were the most polarized, and their reactions depended upon which component of their intergroup attitude was activated.

In another study, Parisi and Katz (1986) found that attitudes concerning organ donation were also characterized by both positive and negative sentiments. The degree of positivity and negativity of these attitudes distinguished novices (those who had yet to sign their organ donor cards) from people who had committed themselves to organ donation. Furthermore, those who were ambivalent toward organ donation were more hesitant to sign their organ donor cards.

Despite the evidence from these various lines of research, concerns about the validity of results suggesting the independence of attitude components have emerged of late. Green and colleagues (Green, 1988; Green, Goldman, & Salovey, 1993) have argued that such results may be attributable to measurement artifacts of correlational analyses or derivatives of these analyses (e.g., multiple regression). They advise that confirmatory factor analysis (CFA) is the only technique that adequately addresses these measurement issues. Indeed, their reanalysis of existing mood and well-being data led Green et al. (1993) to conclude that although some independence may exist in the measured variables, the latent constructs underlying the measured variables are bipolar in nature. On the other hand, Thompson et al. (1994) have used CFA techniques to reanalyze their data concerning the relative independence of attitude components. They continued to find evidence for the distinctiveness of the positive and negative components, even after sources of random and nonrandom error had been controlled. Moreover, the findings of Katz and colleagues cited above indicate the potentially important implications of ambivalence for both the attitude holder and the target of such attitudes.

AMBIVALENCE IN CLOSE RELATIONSHIPS

Conflicted attitudes concerning a romantic partner have been the focus of a variety of studies. Such attitudes concerning a spouse have been associated with greater marital discord and dissatisfaction (Jacobson, Follette, & McDonald, 1982; Jacobson, Waldron, & Moore, 1980; Weiss, 1976). A separate line of research has characterized ambivalent reactions to a partner as having their origins in early attachment deficits (Bartholomew, 1990; Collins & Read, 1990; Epstein, 1980; Hazan & Shaver, 1987). Experiencing intense and conflicted feelings concerning a romantic partner has thus been assumed to reflect interpersonal or personal problems. Although this has not been directly tested in these studies, there also appears to be an assumption that the effects of ambivalence are largely linear: The greater the ambivalence, the more extreme the distress.

However, we have speculated that the presence of both positive and negative attitudes toward a romantic partner may not always be indicative of interpersonal or intrapersonal disturbance. Specifically, ambivalent attitudes may sometimes reflect the natural and ongoing development of interdependence in a relationship, particularly when the terms of endearment in a relationship are being negotiated (see Braiker & Kelley, 1979; Brickman, 1987; Eidelson, 1980). Indeed, a moderate level of ambivalence may actually indicate a balanced, realistic assessment of a partner. Moreover, we have speculated whether very low levels of ambivalence may indicate an unreflectively positive and perhaps primitive attitude structure—an idealized image that may be fragile in the face of the natural upheavals of the accommodation stages of relationships, as sometimes disappointing realities are revealed. Thus, we introduce a distinct type of ambivalence in romantic relationships, with origins in the natural (and, indeed, even healthy) process of relational accommodation. Such a perspective is not new to developmental psychologists, who assume that some amount of conflict with parents and peers is common in adolescent development and is often functional for interpersonal regulation and identity formation.

This perspective complements existing theory that views ambivalence as stemming from intrapsychic or interpersonal distress. Undoubtedly, at high levels, ambivalence does reflect serious doubts and dissatisfaction with a relationship. Some of this ambivalence is probably warranted, mirroring actual relational incompatibility, personal issues (e.g., insecure attachment styles), or real doubts about the partner. These processes should be reflected by a linear effect of ambivalence. We add to this traditional interpretation of ambivalence a type of ambivalence that is related more to the normal challenges of maintaining high levels of interdependence (Kelley, 1983). These effects should be represented by an additional "inverted-U curve" or quadratic ambivalence component.

Several studies support the idea that experiencing some ambivalence is a normal feature associated with changes in interdependence. Braiker and Kelley (1979) had married couples plot the progress of their relationships from inception through engagement in terms of the amount of love, conflict, and ambivalence they experienced. Respondents recalled that their ambivalence grew as their dating relationship progressed, although ambivalence appeared to subside at the time of engagement. Kelly, Huston, and Cate (1985) tracked married individuals through the first year of marriage. They found continued evidence of ambivalence, as measured by the Braiker and Kelley measure. Importantly, reports of ambivalence were relatively orthogonal to feelings of love for a partner in both the Braiker and Kelley (1979) and the Kelly et al. (1985) studies. Finally, Holmes and Rempel (1989) found that married individuals with only moderate trust levels appeared reluctant to attribute their partners' positive behaviors to positive motives and were highly reactive to the negative behaviors of their partners. However, the tendency to experience this sort of internal conflict was not necessarily associated with global negative evaluations of the relationship. In fact, these ambivalent respondents indicated that they were almost as happy and satisfied with their relationships as were high-trust partners. Hence, ambivalence may not be an inevitable sign that a relationship is at risk and need not be immediately equated with diminished overall satisfaction.

Some theorists have even considered ambivalence to be a property that can enhance and revitalize a commitment. The leading proponent of this view has been Brickman (1987; see also Braiker & Kelley, 1979; Holmes & Rempel, 1989), who believes that ambivalence and commitment are contingent upon each other. Based in the tradition of dialectic contradiction, he has suggested that inconsistent or contradictory ideas often coexist, even if uncomfortably and only temporarily. In applying these notions to the dynamics of close relationships, he has assumed that a person is initially drawn to the positive qualities that the partner possesses. As time goes on and the relationship deepens, the person comes to realize the almost inevitable costs and sacrifices that are part of increased interdependence. Personal schedules must be coordinated, the likes and dislikes of the partner must be taken into account, and compromises must be made. Most importantly, the person may begin to realize that the previously "ideal" partner and relationship may not be so perfect after all. The person may be left with distressing second thoughts about the partner, and perhaps even doubts about the quality of his or her own judgments.

For Brickman, it is precisely the discomfort generated by ambivalence that provokes efforts to resolve these inconsistencies. He has suggested that mechanisms for achieving resolutions include varying amounts of cognitive distortion, ranging from the outright denial of a partner's negative attributes, through the masking of negativity, through the realistic and adaptive integration of negativity into coherent attitude structures. Thus, ambivalence is viewed as the stimulus for change in a relationship—a recurring catalyst that can either erode or deepen intimacy. Viewed from this perspective, ambivalence becomes a much richer construct: It is a necessary and perhaps cyclical element in continuing involvements, rather than an inevitably destructive force in relationships. Our research reported in this chapter represents the first empirical tests of these intriguing notions.

THE DEVELOPMENT OF THE AMBIVALENCE IN RELATIONSHIPS SURVEY (AIRS)

To date, the Braiker and Kelley (1979) scales have been the only published measures that tap the degree of ambivalence experienced in a relationship. As effective as these scales are in many respects, we felt that the development of our own measure of ambivalence was warranted for at least two reasons. First, the Braiker and Kelley Ambivalence subscale reflects the traditional view of ambivalence as generalized confusion and negativity concerning a relationship. The five items in this scale include statements such as "How confused were you about your feelings toward [your partner]?" and "How ambivalent or unsure were you about continuing your relationship with [your partner]?" Second, the questions ask for a summative representation of a relationship—an overall assessment that requires integration of beliefs about the relationship as a whole. Presumably, respondents scoring high on the Braiker and Kelley Ambivalence subscale are aware of their conflicted reactions and know that they feel torn and confused.

In contrast, our approach was to measure individuals' evaluations of a wide variety of specific partner attributes. Furthermore, our theoretical perspective (Thompson et al., 1995), as well as those of Katz and conflict theorists, argues for the separate assessment of positive and negative components of attitudes. Thus, when we explore perceptions of partner attributes, we separate what have previously been considered opposite ends of a bipolar continuum, attempting to distinguish the positive from the negative aspects of experience.

The Braiker and Kelley operationalization of ambivalence has some overlap with the conceptualization we propose here. For instance, generalized confusion or uncertainty may often be an outcome of ambivalent feelings concerning a

---

How expressive or self-disclosing, that is, open with feelings as opposed to closed with feelings, would you say that your partner is?

—   —   —   —   —   —   —

Not at All Expressive   Quite Expressive   Extremely Expressive

1. Focus on only the best aspects of your partner's degree of expressiveness, and ignore the worst aspects: To what extent do you believe your partner's degree of expressiveness is beneficial to your relationship?

—   —   —   —   —   —   —

Not at All   Quite   Extremely

2. Now, focus on only the worst aspects of your partner's degree of expressiveness, and ignore the best aspects: To what extent do you believe your partner's degree of expressiveness is harmful to your relationship?

—   —   —   —   —   —   —

Not at All   Quite   Extremely

3. Focus on only the best aspects of your partner's degree of expressiveness, and ignore the worst aspects: To what extent does your partner's degree of expressiveness make you feel good?

—   —   —   —   —   —   —

Not at All   Quite   Extremely

4. Now, focus on only the worst aspects of your partner's degree of expressiveness, and ignore the best aspects: To what extent does your partner's degree of expressiveness make you feel bad?

—   —   —   —   —   —   —

Not at All   Quite   Extremely

FIGURE 15.1   Exemplar of Ambivalence in Relationships Survey (AIRS).

partner. However, we feel that such confusion may as easily be the result of a very different phenomenological experience—relative indifference in the form of a lack of very positive feelings toward a partner. Moreover, in our approach ambivalence is regarded as a latent state indexed by the accessibility of positive and negative elements. Thus, we conceptualize ambivalence as a derivative variable, in that our measure of the construct does not require the a priori integration of cognitive elements. We essentially obtain a microanalysis of relationship perceptions, which ideally may reveal relationship concerns—the potential weak points in a relationship—before they are necessarily integrated into an overall assessment of the relationship. As such, this approach may result in a measure that is diagnostic of future instability in a relationship. Furthermore, by eliciting reactions to a wide variety of specific properties of the relationship, the measure may also better pinpoint potentially problematic aspects.

Specifically, our procedure first asks respondents to focus on only the positive aspects of each partner attribute, while ignoring the negative aspects, and to indicate on a 7-point scale (ranging from "not at all" to "extremely") the extent to which the attribute is regarded as beneficial to the relationship. Respondents then focus only on the negative aspects of the partner attribute, ignoring the positive aspects, and are asked to indicate the extent to which each attribute was harmful to the relationship. We then compare the degree to which a partner is considered to be both positive and negative on an attribute. For instance, a partner may be quite closed concerning his or her feelings and be difficult to read at times. Thus, the worst aspects of that partner's expressiveness may be seen as somewhat harmful to the relationship. On the other hand, when that partner does discuss an important relationship issue, he or she may always be very honest and sincere. Thus, when the respondent focuses only upon the best aspects, this same partner's expressiveness may be seen as quite beneficial to the relationship. This separate measurement of positivity and negativity conforms more closely to our conceptualization of ambivalence and allows for more precise indicators of complex attitudes and derivative measures of ambivalence (see Kaplan, 1972).

We originally set out to tap the affective components separately from the cognitive aspects of partner representations. As indicated in Figure 15.1, we also asked questions concerning how good versus bad each partner attribute made respondents feel. However, in each of our studies there was a very high correlation between the affective and cognitive components as tapped by our present measure. There may be several reasons for this finding. First, questions indexing the affective and cognitive aspects of each of the partner attributes were presented together. We might have had greater success measuring the potentially distinct constructs if the cognitive items for all attributes have been presented separately from the affective items. Furthermore, Breckler and colleagues (Breckler & Wiggins, 1989; Breckler & Berman, 1991) have suggested that affective representations differ from cognitive representations in that they are nonpropositional in nature. This means that oral or written affective ratings may be less successful in tapping a construct distinct from cognition. Future research geared toward measuring a separate affective component would probably benefit from the inclusion of nonverbal measures such as intensity ratings (e.g., physiological measures or manual intensity rating dials; see Breckler & Berman, 1991). Thus, the Ambivalence in Relationships Survey (AIRS) is best regarded as a measure of individuals' cognitive representations concerning their romantic partners.

Partner Attributes

To ensure that our ambivalence measure accurately depicted the complexity of close relationships, we drew a wide variety of partner attributes from three major models of interpersonal relations. From the interpersonal circumplex model (Kiesler, 1983; Wiggins, 1979), we selected the following traits: partner's degree of independence versus dependence on the relationship, degree of comfort with emotional closeness, and partner's tendencies to be critical and to be controlling. Attributes were also selected to represent the "Big Five" model of personality (John, 1990; McCrae & Costa, 1989): partner's degree of expressiveness and general sociability, and partner's tendencies to be conventional and to be passionate. Partner attributes were also chosen from the intimacy process dimensions suggested by Reis and Shaver (1988): partner's degree of responsiveness, dependability, affirmation of respondent as unique and valued, emotional support, encouragement of shared activities, and effectiveness in dealing with conflict in the relationship.

We also wanted to avoid infusing our measure of ambivalence with value judgments concerning the attributes. After all, while one person may consider a great deal of expressiveness as a positive partner quality, another person may well find the same level of expressiveness to be excessive and thus problematic for the relationship. We accomplished this by simply phrasing questions in terms of the degree to which a partner possesses each of the interpersonal attributes.

Computational Formula for the Measurement of Ambivalence

Several formulas are available to estimate ambivalence (Hass et al., 1991; Kaplan, 1972; Scott, 1966, 1968; Thompson et al., 1995; Thompson & Zanna, 1995), though some controversy surrounds which is the optimal formula (Breckler, 1994; Hass & Eisenstadt, 1993; Thompson et al., 1995). In the present research program, we have used a formula rooted in the conflict theory tradition. Ambivalence is defined as the weaker attitude component squared divided by the stronger component of an attitude: $Amb = $ weaker attitude component^2/stronger attitude component (Scott, 1966). For instance, the example of the private yet sincere partner we have presented earlier may produce a score of 4 out of 7 on our scale concerning the harmful aspects of a partner's degree of expressiveness, but a 6 out of 7 concerning the beneficial aspects of his or her expressiveness. According to our formula, in this case ambivalence would be $4^2/6$, or 2.67.

There are several reasons why we have chosen this particular computational formula. Note first that because the formula is a ratio of the weaker to the stronger of the attitude components it measures the relative similarity or balance between the two components—that is, the relative "pushes and pulls" associated with an attitude. Second, squaring the weaker or minimum component enhances attitudes of higher total intensities and characterizes ambivalence as a function of the intensity of the weaker component. The latter point translates a central tenet of conflict theory that ambivalent responses are largely a function of the weaker response, and that the weaker response must surpass some threshold before it is considered a source of ambivalence (Miller, 1944). This feature of the formula distinguishes ambivalent from indifferent attitudes—an area of potential concern we identified with the Braiker and Kelley (1979) measure.

An alternative formula for measuring ambivalence can also be derived from the separate assessments of positivity and negativity. Thompson et al. (1995) define an ambivalent attitude as one wherein both attitude components are similar in magnitude and where the overall attitude is of at least moderate intensity:

Amb = | positive component − negative component |
+ mean (of positive and negative components).

However, our research shows that ambivalence as calculated by the Scott and the Thompson et al. formulas is virtually identical ($r = .97$). Indeed, in this domain there is a high correlation between the Scott measure, which magnifies the intensity of the lesser component and a measure of ambivalence derived from a simple ratio between the negative and positive attitude components ($r = .89$).

PSYCHOMETRIC STUDIES OF THE AIRS

We conducted two studies to test and refine the psychometric properties of the AIRS, using both dating and married samples of respondents. The initial study was exploratory in nature, to test the methodology and the attributes selected for the inventory. The second study was designed to provide psychometric refinement of the AIRS and to test the generalizability of the inventory to nonuniversity dating and married samples. We conducted the second study outside a university setting at the Ontario Science Centre (OSC). In addition to the AIRS, each study also included traditional relationship measures, such as the Braiker and Kelley (1979) scales tapping love, conflict, and ambivalence (generalized confusion), as well as measures of trust (Boon & Holmes, 1991), satisfaction, and commitment (Lund, 1985).

Subjects and Procedure

Exploratory Study

Respondents in the pilot study were 46 introductory psychology students (23 females and 23 males). In this study, the AIRS consisted of the original seventeen attributes described earlier. Respondents were recruited for a study concerning, "Perspectives on Close Relationships." After a brief introduction to the study, participants completed the AIRS in individual testing rooms.

OSC Study

We constructed two conceptually equivalent forms of the AIRS for use in the second study in order to meet time restrictions at the OSC. For instance, where Form A of the AIRS included partner's degree of expressiveness, Form B included partner's degree of comfort with emotional closeness. In the analyses of the OSC dating and married samples presented below, the results of Form A attributes are presented before the slash, and the results of "Form B" attributes are presented after the slash. Correlations between Form A and Form B based on the data from the exploratory study indicated that they were essentially equivalent measures ($r = .91, p < .001$).

OSC DATING SAMPLE   Participants in this study volunteered to take part in the "Perspectives on Close Relationships" study in response to a poster located just outside the study area at the OSC. The dating sample was composed of 69 males and 56 females (mean age = 23 years). Ninety-three participants listed their involvement as "exclusively dating," 27 were "casually dating," and 5 were engaged to their partners. The average length of relationship in this dating sample was 15 months.

OSC MARRIED SAMPLE   We also recruited a sample of 36 males and 40 females who were either living on a common-law basis with (25 respondents) or married to (51 respondents) their partners. The average length of these relationships was 10 years.

Instructions

In all studies, instructions to subjects stated:

> In a close relationship, we come to know all aspects of our partners' character, that is, both their positive and negative qualities. As close relationships are complex . . . this complexity may be reflected in both positive and negative perceptions. . . . These sorts of perceptions do not necessarily reflect inconsistencies . . . but rather

reveal the complexity inherent in your relationship. Thus, we are interested in your unique perceptions of your partner. . . .

In order to give you an opportunity to explore and reflect on the various aspects of your partner, you will be presented with questions that are both positively and negatively worded. These questions will ask you to focus on either the positive (or negative) aspects while ignoring the negative (or positive) aspects of specific attributes of your partner. . . .We want to know about the various characteristics which your partner may possess, your estimation of the impact of these characteristics upon your relationship, or what your head tells you, and how these characteristics make you feel, or what your heart tells you.

Results

According to the computational formula, the lowest possible ambivalence score would be 0.14. This would indicate the absolute polarization of perceptions of a partner attribute—for example, believing that the positive aspects of a partner's degree of responsiveness were extremely beneficial to the relationship and believing that the negative aspects were not at all harmful to the relationship. The highest ambivalence score possible would be 7.0. This could occur, for example, if the positive aspects of a partner's degree of responsiveness were rated as extremely positive and the negative aspects were rated as extremely negative. We calculated ambivalence at the level of the attribute and then averaged ambivalence scores across the partner attributes.

The individuals who participated in our studies were typically quite satisfied with their relationships (mean score of 7.77 on a 9-point scale). Not surprisingly, then, positivity scores across attributes were quite high across both the dating and the married samples (mean positivity across attributes: Study 1, 5.51; OSC dating sample, 5.73/4.42; OSC married sample, 5.61/4.96). However, some negativity was also acknowledged with respect to many of the same partner attributes (mean negativity: Study 1, 2.83; OSC dating sample, 2.89/2.59; OSC married sample, 2.69/3.06). We also found that the positive and negative aspects of the partner characteristics were uncorrelated in Study 1, ($r = -.14$, n.s.). In the OSC study, we derived a measure of the average amount of positivity across forms of the AIRS by dividing the total positivity and total negativity within each form of the AIRS by the number of attributes in that form. Positivity and negativity were moderately negatively correlated with each other in both cases (OSC dating sample, $r = -.43$, $p < .001$; OSC married sample, $r = -.53$, $p < .001$). Further psychometric results showed that the AIRS achieved a reasonable degree of reliability (Study 1, $\alpha = .93$; OSC dating sample: $\alpha = .78/.82$; OSC married sample, $\alpha = .81/.75$). Factor analyses of the ambivalence scores yielded a unifactorial structure, accounting for at least 35% of the variance in ambivalence scores (Study 1, 46.8%; OSC dating sample, 36.4%/46.5%; OSC married sample, 41.8%/38.6%). Mean ambivalence scores across attributes were 1.93 in Study 1,

1.57/1.31 in the OSC dating, sample and 1.49/1.59 for the OSC married sample. In summary, these results are consistent with our conceptualization of ambivalence. It was apparent that the positive and negative aspects of these partner attributes were at least somewhat distinct from and not merely the polar opposites of, each other. Furthermore, the AIRS itself was found to be a reliable measure for both dating and married samples.

THE STRUCTURE OF EXPERIENCE IN CLOSE RELATIONSHIPS

Our psychometric studies also had scales tapping positive feelings about the relationship such as love, commitment, trust, and communication (Braiker & Kelley's [1979] Maintenance subscale), and measures tapping potentially negative experiences, such as conflict and ambivalence (Braiker & Kelley's Ambivalence subscale). The convergent and divergent validity of the AIRS was explored through the use of multitrait matrix analyses. We also conducted LISREL CFAs (Joreskog & Sorbom, 1984) to understand how ambivalence, as measured by the AIRS, fits within the structure of experience in close relationships.

The literature presents two general models concerning the structure of experience in intimate relationships. One suggests that intimacy is characterized by a relatively undifferentiated set of partner perceptions (e.g., Bentler & Huba, 1979; Berscheid & Walster, 1978; the Spearman model in Sternberg & Grajeck, 1984). This model specifies that the presence of positive feelings tends to preclude the existence of negativity, and it describes the structure of experience in close relationships as unidimensional in nature. Positive feelings should load highly and positively, and negative perceptions highly and negatively, on the same factor.

The alternative model that we propose involves greater dimensionality. Scales measuring positive perceptions should load on a separate factor from the scales assessing negative perceptions in relationships. Furthermore, the model allows certain measures to load on both the positive and negative factors. This perspective is reflected in research that separately assessed the rewards and costs in a relationship and showed their differential effects upon satisfaction (Cate, Lloyd, Henton, & Larson, 1982; Jacobson et al., 1980; Rusbult, 1983; Simpson, 1987; Wills, Weiss, & Patterson, 1974). This multidimensional model is also evident in research showing that feelings of love are often relatively independent of reports of conflict, at least among dating couples and newlyweds (Braiker & Kelley, 1979; Kelly, Cate, & Huston, 1985). Other research has demonstrated that the presence or absence of negativity becomes more closely tied to love and satisfaction in a relationship over time (Huston & Vangelisti, 1991; Jacobson et al., 1980; Kelly et al., 1985; Wills et al., 1974). This suggests that the multidimensional model may be more applicable to our dating samples, and that the unidimensional model may be more descriptive of our married sample.

TABLE 15.1 Pearson Correlations and Reliabilities of Relationship Variables for the Combined Dating Sample in Study 1 and the OSC Study (*n* = 165)

	1	*2*	*3*	*4*	*5*	*6*	*7*	*8*
1. Love	(.91)							
2. Satisfaction	.65	(.89)						
3. Maintenance	.66	.45	(.78)					
4. Commitment	.69	.71	.53	(.89)				
5. Trust	.68	.66	.48	.62	(.87)			
6. Braiker & Kelley Ambivalence	-.52	-.56	-.41	-.62	-.54	(.80)		
7. AIRS	-.31	-.37	-.23	-.45	-.50	.52	(.87)	
8. Conflict	-.27	-.50	-.16	-.41	-.57	.58	.49	(.73)

Note. Numbers in parentheses are reliabilities for each scale.

The Structure of Experience in Dating Relationships

In order to maximize the size of our dating sample, we added the data from the first study to those from the OSC dating-sample, resulting in a combined dating sample size of 165 respondents. Results of the multitrait matrix analyses for the combined dating sample were consistent with our expectations (see Table 15.1). Ambivalence was unrelated to gender, age of respondent, or length of dating relationship, and was only minimally related to the self-reports of status of the relationship. Moreover, the AIRS was only moderately and negatively related to feelings of love, satisfaction, and commitment, and showed more evidence of discriminant validity than did the Braiker and Kelley Ambivalence subscale. In terms of convergent validity, the AIRS was positively and more strongly related to the incidence of conflict and confusion, as measured by the Braiker and Kelley Ambivalence scale. The pattern of correlations revealed that all positivity scales tended to cluster together and all negativity measures tended to correlate most strongly with each other.

We next conducted a CFA in order to test our model of the structure of experience in dating relationships. This model included two factors representing positivity and negativity in the relationship. Theory and inspection of the data led us to place correlated errors between all the Braiker and Kelley measures, between the measure of love and trust, and between the Braiker and Kelley Ambivalence subscale and the trust measure. Results of this analysis indicated that our model fit the data quite well. As expected, love, satisfaction, maintenance, and commitment all loaded quite highly on the positivity factor, while the AIRS and conflict loaded highly on the negativity factor. Furthermore, the trust measure and the Braiker and Kelley Ambivalence subscale loaded on both the positivity and negativity factors, consistent with our expectations that these constructs reflect an integration of both types of experiences.

Although the degree of relation between the two latent constructs of positivity and negativity was fairly high ($\varphi = -.73$), it was substantially less than the value indicative of a unidimensional model, where φ would more closely approach -1.0. Moreover, although the chi-square value associated with the two-dimensional model was significant, χ^2 (9) = 17.21, $p = .05$, suggesting some slippage between the model and the data, other indices of the goodness of fit showed that on the whole, the model fit that data quite well: For example, goodness-of-fit index (GFI) = .98; adjusted goodness-of-fit index (AGFI) = .91; root mean square residual (RMR) = .03 (see Judd, Jessor, & Donovan, 1986). A direct comparison of the unidimensional and multidimensional models also showed the statistically superior fit of the multidimensional model, χ^2 (6) = 44.49, $p < .001$.

The Structure of Experience in Marital Relationships

As in to the dating sample, neither the gender nor the age of respondents was related to ambivalence as measured by the AIRS. Ambivalence was more likely to be a feature of the relationships of individuals who were living with their partners than for respondents who were married to their partners ($r = -.30, p = .01$). Results of the multitrait matrix analysis (see Table 15.2) suggested that all variables were more related to each other than was the case with the dating sample. This unidimensional pattern was also evident in the results of the LISREL CFA on the data χ^2 (15) = 22.85, n.s.; GFI = .93; AGFI = .84; RMR = .03. Thus, individuals in our married sample had more unified representations of their partners. Despite this more unified cognitive structure, the AIRS was the only variable that showed any discriminant validity, correlating only $-.45$ with love and $-.51$ with satisfaction.

TABLE 15.2 Pearson Correlations and Reliabilities of Relationship Variables for the Married Sample ($n = 165$)

	1	2	3	4	5	6	7	8
1. Love	(.88)							
2. Satisfaction	.71	(.80)						
3. Maintenance	.56	.36	(.75)					
4. Commitment	.78	.75	.38	(.86)				
5. Trust	.70	.80	.40	.70	(.92)			
6. Braiker & Kelley Ambivalence	−.78	−.75	−.42	−.84	−.74	(.80)		
7. AIRS	−.45	−.51	−.26	−.51	−.55	.46	(.78)	
8. Conflict	−.55	−.69	−.22	−.58	−.73	.68	.56	(.84)

Note. Numbers in parentheses are reliabilities for each scale. The AIRS correlations are based upon an aggregate index representing the average ambivalence of Form A and Form B. The associated reliability is the average of Form A ($\alpha = .81$) and Form B ($\alpha = .75$).

AMBIVALENCE, COMMITMENT, AND THE DISSOLUTION OF DATING RELATIONSHIPS

Although the previous results illustrate that positive and negative experiences in dating relationships are relatively independent, a more critical question concerns the potential long-term impact of ambivalence. According to Braiker and Kelley's (1979) results, ambivalence appeared to be a minor theme in relationships and to have no lasting consequences. This finding seems to be at odds with longitudinal research on marital relationships. These studies have shown that negativity, indexed by self-reported conflict or negative reactions to partners during discussions, is relatively independent of love at the point of marriage. However, these same studies demonstrated that the longer-term effects of these initial reports of negativity are more powerful. Indeed, initial negativity has been found to be the most important predictor of subsequent relationship stability and satisfaction (Kelly et al., 1985; Markman, 1979, 1981).

Thus there are reasons why we might want to re-examine the conclusions of Braiker and Kelley regarding the role of ambivalence in relationships. First, their study was retrospective, asking presently happily married couples to recall the course of their dating relationships. Biases in reconstructive memory processes leave the accuracy of such accounts open to question (Ross, 1989). Respondents may have unwittingly provided their theories about happy marriages, and such accounts may yield little information about the actual course of ambivalence. Second, the Braiker and Kelley respondents had all weathered the ambivalence they experienced during courtship, and we do not know the course of ambivalence for those whose dating relationships dissolved.

In contrast to this prior perspective, we have hypothesized that ambivalence in dating relationships should be predictive of subsequent dissolution, over and above the effects of a lack of positivity. If this hypothesis is borne out, then we will have identified a new and valuable diagnostic marker of the future of a relationship—one not redundant with feelings of positivity in the relationship. Indeed, research exploring the outcomes of dating relationships has in large part only been able to identify predictive variables associated with a general positivity factor; the "sleeper effects" of negativity in the form of conflict occurred only in married samples. However, conflict in dating relationships may be relatively orthogonal to satisfaction, because it is usually explained away by attributing it to unstable sources (cf. Bradbury & Fincham, 1990); disagreements are not acknowledged as having negative implications. Only over a period of time, after offending behaviors prove to be recurrent, may conflict be transformed into feelings of ambivalence. If our measure of ambivalence is a more sensitive marker of negative feelings than reports of conflict are, then initial reports of ambivalence may show a "sleeper effect" pattern in dating relationships.

As we have argued earlier, ambivalence has a variety of origins, some of which are likely to have obvious negative implications for a relationship. For instance, negative assessments may reflect incompatible needs, the residue of personal issues, or a partner who truly warrants one's doubts. In such cases, the greater the intensity of doubts, the more potentially destructive ambivalence may be for a relationship. This logic would lead to a prediction of a linear effect of reported ambivalence on relationship dissolution.

On the other hand, we have suggested that a certain degree of ambivalence is a relatively "normal" aspect of interpersonal accommodation as interdependence grows. Indeed, the willingness to acknowledge some negative aspects of a partner, reflected in a moderate amount of ambivalence, is expected to be least predictive of relationship dissolution. Consistent with this view, Brickman (1987) has argued that cognitive resolutions of doubt involve a positive synthesis or integration that requires at least the tacit acknowledgment of some negativity. Thus, a certain amount of ambivalence, not exceeding some theoretical threshold, becomes an important catalyst for integrative resolutions. In contrast, a very low amount of ambivalence may reflect a more primitive coping style emphasizing idealization and denial—a style likely to be challenged eventually by the harsher realities of interdependence. Thus we would predict an "inverted U curve" effect over and above the linear effect of ambivalence, with a moderate amount of ambivalence having potentially the most constructive implications for the future of a relationship.

We tested out these ideas in a prospective study of the progress of dating relationships over the course of respondents' first year at a university. We chose to focus on this sample because the first university term often represents a major time of transition in dating relationships. Students are often experiencing their first physical separation from their high school dating partners, family members, and friends. This, coupled with exposure to new people and experiences, often provides individuals with new options while reducing the barriers for the dissolution of their existing relationships.

Commitment

Ambivalence often heightens a sense of vulnerability and uncertainty—an aversive state that individuals will be motivated to reduce. In their desire to put uncertainties to rest, individuals may more carefully monitor interactions with a partner, or in some cases even create situations to test a partner's degree of affection and character (Brickman, 1987; Holmes & Rempel, 1989). Eventually, however, most people must make a "leap of faith" in the face of evidence that can never be conclusive (Rempel, Holmes, & Zanna, 1985). We have speculated that this process of laying concerns to rest requires a critical interplay between ambivalent partner representations and some positive motivational elements. Brickman (1987) has discussed the interplay of motivation and cognition in this context, suggesting that ambivalence includes both feelings of uncertainty (an emotional or motivational element) and an ambivalent choice (a cognitive aspect). He suggests that its resolution requires a constructive force to promote a shift that removes the ambivalence (a motivational element that instigates some cognitive change) (Brickman, 1987). To date, however, little is known of the exact nature of the forces that enable people to surmount their doubts. We suspect that individuals' commitment to their relationships may be just such a motivational force.

Commitment to a relationship is both an assessment of, and a private pledge to, the future of a relationship (Rusbult, 1983). Feelings of commitment reflect the investments made in a relationship, including time, effort, sacrifices, mutual friends, and so on. Commitment has been conceptualized as having stable causal features, which distinguish it from variables such as love and satisfaction (see Kelley, 1983; Lund, 1985; Rusbult, 1983). Most importantly, Rusbult and colleagues (Rusbult & Buunk, 1992; Rusbult & Van Lange, 1992) have suggested that commitment motivates people to act in ways that ensure the future of a relationship, especially during periods of stress. Commitment "importantly shapes stable tendencies to engage in pro-relationship behaviors, even when such behaviors are (a) costly, (b) stand in opposition to primitive self-interest, or (c) to some degree fly in the face of reality" (Rusbult & Van Lange, 1992, p. 5). We have hypothesized that commitment processes have a similar stabilizing role in individuals' efforts to resolve ambivalence, motivating individuals to integrate negative evaluations into an overall positive account of a partner.

In contrast to this analysis, Brickman (1987) has argued that commitment is the result of the resolution of ambivalence—a resolution that is possible only after a threat to a relationship has been encountered and negotiated. We have extended this thinking by arguing that commitment, the investment in the continuation of a relationship in spite of its negative aspects, may be a critical motivational factor in the resolution of ambivalence in close relationships. That is, just as the resolution of ambivalence may lead to increased commitment, so too may commitment lead to a reduction in ambivalence and a strengthened relationship. Hence commitment should moderate the potential ill effects of ambivalence, with fewest breakups occurring for individuals with high commitment regardless of the level of ambivalence. In the absence of the motivational benefits of a strong commitment, the curvilinear effect of ambivalence should be most apparent.

Subjects and Procedure

Sixty-five participants (20 males and 25 females; mean age = 19.5 years) were recruited for the "Perspectives on Close Relationships" study during the fall term of the academic year. The mean length of relationship was 17 months. Thirteen respondents were "casually dating," 47 were "exclusively dating," and 5 respondents were living with their partners.

Individual respondents completed the AIRS and measures of love, trust, commitment, and conflict during the first wave of the study. We phoned respondents 4 months later to determine the status of their relationships. At that time 34 respondents were continuing to see the same romantic partners, while 28 people had broken up with their partners. Three subjects could not be located. All subjects whose relationships were ongoing agreed to complete a follow-up set of questionnaires, which included the same measures administered at Time 1.

Results

Preliminary Analyses

Initial analyses of the data from this third sample yielded similar average positivity (5.46), negativity (2.76), and ambivalence (1.45) scores, and similar reliability ($\alpha = .78$) and factor-analytic characteristics to those of the previous studies. However, a higher correlation existed between the positive and negative aspects of partner attributes for this sample ($r = -.58$, $p < .001$). Indeed, the overall pattern of correlations among the relationship variables was somewhat higher than had previously been the case, although the general pattern of convergent and discriminant validity of the AIRS remained. The AIRS was largely unrelated to respondents' gender ($r = .19$, $p = .08$), or the length ($r = -.11$, n.s.) or status ($r = .14$, n.s.) of their relationships. Higher ambivalence on the AIRS was related to less love ($r = -.47$, $p < .001$), satisfaction ($r = -.42$, $p < .001$), maintenance behavior ($r = -.18$, $p = .04$), commitment ($r = -.33$, $p < .001$), and trust ($r = -.33$, $p < .001$). The AIRS was again related to greater conflict in the relationship ($r = .47$, $p < .001$) and confusion as measured by the Braiker and Kelley Ambivalence subscale ($r = .62$, $p < .001$).

The Effects of Ambivalence and Commitment upon Relationship Dissolution

We used logistic regression to test the curvilinear effects of our continuous predictor variables upon the categorical outcome variable of relationship dissolution (dissolution vs. survival). All variables were first z-score-transformed. In addition, the linear and curvilinear effects of ambivalence were entered in the same block of the logistic regression, so that the linear component of ambivalence was partialed out from the effects of the quadratic component. In this way the two measures of ambivalence measured independent effects. Next, we grouped variables into blocks categorized by positive and negative valences, based on results of the CFA we have reported earlier. In hierarchical regression equations, we reversed the order of these blocks of variables to illustrate the unique contributions of positivity and negativity in predicting relationship dissolution (see Table 15.3).

As expected, the positive group of variables predicted relationship dissolution, even when entered second into the regression equation ($\chi^2 = 11.38$, $p < .001$), and this effect was largely attributable to the effects of commitment ($\beta = -1.06$, $p < .05$). Also as predicted, the negative block of variables predicted relationship dissolution, even after the effects of positivity had been taken into ac-

TABLE 15.3 Logistic Regressions of Positive and Negative Blocks upon Relationship Dissolution ($n = 62$)

	Order: AB			*Order: BA*		
	χ^2	β	*% of cases correctly classified*	χ^2	β	*% of cases correctly classified*
A. Love 1	19.64***	−1.25**	72.58	11.38***	−0.477	77.42
Trust 1		0.478			1.35*	
Commitment 1		−0.911			−1.06**	
B. Ambivalence 1[a]	10.52***	1.11**	77.42	18.78***	1.02**	69.35
Ambivalence 1[b]		−1.20**			−1.30**	
Conflict 1		−0.12			−0.20	

Note. The "1" after each variable name indicates that the variable at time 1 is meant.
[a]Linear component.
[b]Curvilinear component.
*$p < .10$. **$p < .05$. ***$p < .01$.

count ($\chi^2 = 10.52$, $p < .001$). Importantly, this effect was attributable to the independent effects of both the linear ($\beta = 1.11$, $p < .05$) and curvilinear ($\beta = -1.20$, $p < .05$) components of ambivalence. Just as interesting was the finding that amount of conflict did not predict relationship dissolution in this sample.

We also conducted a separate analysis in which the main effect for commitment and the linear and curvilinear effects of ambivalence were entered on the first block of a regression equation, with the interactions between commitment and the linear and quadratic components of ambivalence entered on a second step. As predicted, these results showed significant effects for the interaction of commitment and ambivalence. The block of the regression equation containing the interaction terms explained significant amounts of the variance in relationship dissolution, even after the main effects of commitment and the linear and curvilinear effects of ambivalence were taken into account ($\chi^2 = 4.13$, $p < .01$).

The pattern of this interaction of commitment and ambivalence becomes clear when we examine the proportion of breakups that occurred under high and low commitment and high, moderate, and low ambivalence (see Table 15.4). Highly committed individuals remained in their relationships even when they also experienced high levels of ambivalence concerning their partners' attributes. For the high-ambivalence group, only 25% of the relationships ended, the same as occurred when individuals reported low ambivalence. The fewest breakups occurred when moderate ambivalence was coupled with high commitment (14% dissolution). In stark contrast, the results for the low-commitment group conformed to the expected inverted-U curve pattern. Those people less committed to their relationships showed the deleterious effects of ambivalence, with fully 88% of these relationships dissolving under the strain of high ambivalence. Even the presence of low ambivalence did not ensure the stability of

TABLE 15.4 Proportion of Breakups by Ambivalence and Commitment Levels at Time 1 (*n* = 62)

	Commitment 1		
Ambivalence 1	*Low*	*High*	*Overall*
Low	.56	.25	.41
	(9)	(12)	
Moderate	.43	.14	.29
	(7)	(14)	
High	.88	.25	.57
	(16)	(4)	
Overall	.62	.21	

Note. Numbers in parentheses are cell *n*'s.

respondents' relationships if their commitment was also low. Over 50% of the low ambivalence, low commitment group broke up over the 4-month period.

"Survivor" Analyses

We also conducted multiple-regression analyses of the interaction of initial commitment and ambivalence upon Time 2 love and conflict for individuals whose relationships survived, controlling for the effects of these criterion variables at Time 1(see Table 15.5). Because of the low sample size (*n* = 34), these analyses are clearly exploratory in nature. Despite a lack of power, results showed a trend for the interaction of commitment and ambivalence to be related to increases in love (*t* = -1.876, *p* = .07) and decreases in conflict (*t* = 1.676, *p* = .11) for survivors.

Commitment Processes in Ambivalence Reduction

These analyses rather convincingly demonstrate the role of commitment in moderating the effects of ambivalence on both the stability and quality of dating relationships. Our results showed that, as predicted, the presence of commitment served in some way to transform or at least to minimize the impact of respondents' ambivalence. We speculate that commitment to the goal of maintaining a relationship motivates people to engage in a variety of processes that ensure the future of the relationship, despite any doubts they may have about it. On an interpersonal level, greater commitment may result in more sustained efforts to work out problems and to compromise when disagreements arise. On an intrapersonal level, commitment may motivate a person to cognitively transform the meaning and implications of negative elements.

Some speculation as to the nature of this transformation process seems warranted. At the most basic level, commitment may simply promote charitable

TABLE 15.5 Mean Levels of Love and Conflict at Follow-Up for Survivors by Ambivalence and Commitment at Time 1 (*n* = 34)

	Commitment 1		
Ambivalence 1	*Low*	*High*	*Overall*
Low	7.60	8.64	8.12
	(5)	(7)	(12)
	4.27	2.57	3.42
Moderate	8.29	8.50	8.40
	(6)	(7)	(13)
	3.44	2.33	2.89
High	6.95	8.38	7.65
	(5)	(4)	(9)
	6.07	2.50	4.29
Overall	7.61	8.50	
	(16)	(18)	
	4.59	2.47	

Note. Numbers in parentheses are cell *n*'s. Numbers above cell *n*'s refer to self-reported amount of love in the relationship at the time of the follow-up, whereas numbers below cell *n*'s refer to conflict in the relationship. Higher scores indicate greater love and greater conflict. Cell means are presented in raw scores.

attributions about a partner's negative qualities, limiting their meaning without necessarily denying them. Similarly, highly committed individuals may be motivated to make temporally constrained attributions ("We are going through a difficult time right now"). These time-delineated "accounts" of relationship difficulties may be the least threatening and damaging to the relationship. In addition, the desire to maintain the relationship may lead individuals to minimize the significance of negative features in their personal theories about the qualities that are important for a successful relationship ("Yes, my partner is not particularly expressive, but that isn't important to me"). Accounts may even change over time to accommodate the realities of a partner ("Yes, my partner isn't particularly expressive, but I find it less important now than I used to before I understood his [her] nature").

Commitment may further provide the impetus to specifically focus on and accentuate those features of the partner that are most attractive or worthwhile ("My partner may not be particularly demonstrative, but he [she] is one of the kindest people I have known"). Indeed, Brickman (1987) has even argued that idealization occurs not in spite of imperfections, but because of them. Finally, a strong commitment to the future of the relationship may also provide the motivation simply to "grit one's teeth" and hang on through difficult times in a relationship. Thus, high commitment works in a variety of ways to cushion the full impact of a partner's less-than-perfect realities and to limit the implications of negative perceptions. The specific means by which individuals' cognitive representations of their partners incorporate their doubts, and how these representations are affected by commitment processes, will be the topics of our future research.

SOURCES OF AMBIVALENCE

The studies reported above have focused on the balance between positive and negative assessments of partners' attributes as one manifest indication of ambivalence. However, the wide variety of potential sources of ambivalence suggests that the construct could be measured in other ways. In this section we describe some ongoing research on this issue, and then speculate on other potential sources of ambivalence.

Real–Ideal Discrepancies in Partner Assessments

One source of ambivalence that we are exploring was derived from considering Higgins's (1989, 1990) self-discrepancy theory. According to Higgins, social judgments are made by comparing a target (usually the self) with some relevant standard reflecting either "ideal" or "ought" expectations. People are motivated to achieve a match between a given self-state and a relevant guide. Failing to meet the standard leads to predictable patterns of psychological distress (Higgins, 1989, 1990; Higgins, Bond, Klein, & Strauman, 1986; Higgins, Klein, & Strauman, 1985; Higgins, Tykocinski, & Vookles, 1990). Higgins and colleagues have demonstrated that discrepancies between self-ratings and self-guides have significant implications for self-esteem above and beyond self-concept alone (Moretti & Higgins, 1990; Van Hook & Higgins, 1988). The wider the gap between the actual self and the self-guide, the greater the resultant level of discomfort. The type of discrepancy determines the nature of the psychological distress the individual should experience. For instance, discrepancies between actual self-ratings (i.e., representations of attributes actually possessed) and ideal self-ratings (i.e., representations of hopes and aspirations) lead to dejection-related motivational problems such as sadness, disappointment, and dissatisfaction, whereas discrepancies between actual self-ratings and ought self-guides (i.e., representations of responsibilities, obligations, duty) are related to agitation and anxiety (Higgins, 1989; Higgins, Vookles, & Tykocinski, 1992). Most recently, discrepancies between self-assessments and self-guides have been differentially linked to anorexia and bulimia (Higgins et al., 1992) and to the immunological precursors of illness (Strauman, Lemieux, & Coe, 1993).

Given the important effects of these sorts of self-discrepancies, we have speculated that judgments about partners may follow similar cognitive principles. That is, individuals' evaluations of the "actual" attributes possessed by their often all-too-human partners may be compared to their romantic ideals, their hopes for the relationship. To the extent that a partner falls short of this standard, dissatisfaction should result. To this end, we asked the respondents who participated in the dissolution study to rate their partners in terms of the degree to which they possessed each relationship attribute (real or actual partner assessments). We also had respondents rate how much of each attribute they wished their partners ideally possessed (romantic ideals or ideal partner assessments). "Real–ideal (R-I) discrepancy" was defined as the absolute difference between these real and ideal partner assessments. These discrepancies were calculated for each attribute and then averaged across attributes.

Discrepancies between what is perceived and what is ideally hoped for in the interpersonal domain may constitute an important source of ambivalence. Overall, we expected that R-I discrepancies would show effects similar to ambivalence upon relationship dissolution and quality. An additional benefit of this line of inquiry is that we may come closer to understanding the effects of idealization upon dating relationships. For instance, we have speculated earlier that low ambivalence may be associated with relationship schemas based largely upon idealization, and that such schemas may prove to be more primitive and fragile in the face of the realities of interdependence. The measurement of romantic ideals and real or actual partner assessments has allowed us to explore this issue more directly. Because of space constraints, we present only selected results of these analyses in the following section.

Results and Discussion

First of all, Time 1 R-I discrepancies were indeed associated concurrently with ambivalence as measured by the AIRS ($r = .48$). The argument that discrepancies are not only a form of ambivalence but a source of it was strengthened by the finding that Time 1 R-I discrepancies also predicted increases in ambivalence over time for those relationships that survived (partial $r = .19$). Regression analyses further demonstrated an interaction between discrepancies and commitment on increases in ambivalence ($b = 1.41$, $p = .07$). Thus it appears that early discrepancies between actual partner assessments and romantic ideals forecast the growth of ambivalence about a dating partner's qualities. Also, parallel to patterns we observed earlier, Time 1 discrepancies predicted increases in ambivalence only when individuals reported lower levels of commitment to their relationship. This finding is consistent with our perspective that commitment represents a motivational force that shapes changes in cognitive representations.

Second, discrepancies appear to have effects paralleling those of ambivalence in predicting breakups. Results of logistic regressions revealed that both Time 1 R-I discrepancies ($b = -1.602$, $p = .05$) and commitment ($b = 0.455$, $p = .02$) were significantly related to subsequent relationship dissolution ($v^2 = 15.18$, $p < .001$). In order to provide the most rigorous test of the role of discrepancies in relationship dissolution, we conducted an additional logistic regression in which R-I discrepancies were entered as one block, with variables indicating positivity (e.g., love, commitment) and negativity (e.g., conflict) entered as two further blocks. The order of entry of the three blocks was varied in order to determine the unique impact of each block. Regardless of order of entry, R-I discrepancies emerged as the most consistent predictor of relationship dissolution, even after the effects of positivity had been taken into account (b = -2.058, p = .05). Of the other variables, only love was rather consistently associated with relationship dissolution, even when discrepancies were entered first (b = 0.877, p = .06).

Thus, R-I discrepancies appear to be a source of ambivalence that has an important impact upon the stability of dating relationships. These effects occurred over and above the effects of relationship positivity, traditionally seen as the paramount feature for predicting change in the quality of close relationships. And as Higgins (1990) suggests, it was the degree of discrepancy that produced effects on dissatisfaction, rather than the levels of real or ideal evaluations alone (see also Moretti & Higgins, 1990; Van Hook & Higgins, 1988). When the latter variables were entered as a block, they did not predict dissolution, probably because they were more collinear with positive sentiment variables.

It is also of interest to contrast the role of romantic ideals and R-I discrepancies in the relationship schemas for those individuals whose relationships ended (leavers) versus those whose relationships survived (survivors). The ideal relationship schemas of leavers were strongly related to their Time 1 feelings of love (r = .65), commitment (r = .53), and trust (r = .49). They seem essentially to have been in love with their fantasies of an ideal partner. These associations were much weaker for survivors (love, .20; commitment, .24; trust, .22). A further indication that leavers were blinded by their initial hopes was that R-I discrepancies, which took account of "actual" characteristics, were unrelated to feelings of love for those who broke up (r = -.04). In contrast, for those whose relationships continued, greater R-I discrepancies were related to less love (r = -.36).

R-I discrepancies also figured more prominently in perceptions of negativity for those whose relationships continued. For survivors, higher discrepancies were related to greater concurrent conflict (b = 0.357, p = .03) and ambivalence (b = 0.457, p = .002), whereas for leavers, R-I discrepancies were only marginally related to conflict (b = 0.393, p = .09). Finally, conflict appeared to be a precursor of discrepancies for survivors, much as it was for ambivalence. For survivors, only greater Time 1 conflict predicted increases in R-I discrepancies (partial r = .42). This strong connection suggests that conflict is an interpersonal platform that reveals how a partner falls short of one's hopes.

Overall then, the positive sentiments of leavers were initially strongly related to their romantic ideals, whereas discrepancies had no impact on the feelings they reported. It was as if leavers constructed too large a proportion of their relationships in their hearts, somewhat divorced from the perhaps disappointing realities of their partners' qualities. Consequently, the relationship schemas of these individuals appeared to be much more fragile; the initial discrepancies later proved to be an important marker of relationships that would not survive. Thus, low ambivalence indeed sometimes reflected excessive idealization that ultimately put individuals' relationships at risk. The normal upheavals of accommodation on the road to interdependence appear to have highlighted the meaning of the discrepancies and overridden their hopes. In contrast, those people whose relationships survived seemed to be more "realistic" in incorporating discrepancies in their assessments of their relationships and their perceptions of their partners' attributes.

AMBIVALENCE AS AN INDIVIDUAL DIFFERENCE

We have introduced the notion that ambivalence may at times be a natural outcome of increased interdependence and not the result of personality issues or other types of dysfunction, as prior theory in the area has suggested. However, we look upon our perspective as complementary to these previous findings concerning ambivalence in close relationships. Certainly there are types of ambivalence resulting from chronic tendencies that heighten interpersonal and intrapersonal distress.

Attachment Styles

Using attachment scales developed by Bartholomew (1990), we found correlations in the present studies indicating that to the extent that individuals had anxious–ambivalent, fearful, or dismissive attachment styles, they experienced more ambivalence concerning their partners' attributes, whereas a secure attachment style was not related to ambivalence (Thompson & Holmes, 1992). These results are perhaps not surprising, in that concerns about trust and rejection have been shown to be less of a chronic concern to those people possessing a secure attachment style (cf. Collins & Read, 1990). Secure individuals thus may be less threatened by some evidence of negativity and more likely to successfully integrate the potentially negative aspects of their partners' attributes into their relationship schemas. On the other hand, individuals with insecure attachment styles have mental models of the interpersonal world in which rejection and abandonment are important chronic concerns. Such concerns may lead individuals possessing these styles to be vigilant for signs of negative behavior on the part of their partners. Once discovered, such behavior may be assigned disproportional weight in their representations of their partners. Indeed, their doubts and worries may be chronically accessible if self-protective motivations are primed by feelings of vulnerability.

Chronic Cognitive Tendencies

In the introduction to this chapter, we have noted that certain cognitive styles have been associated with the levels of ambivalence experienced concerning social attitudes. Specifically, individuals with a high personal fear of invalidity (Thompson et al., 1993) were chronically more ambivalent, whereas those people high in need for cognition (Cacioppo & Petty, 1982) experienced less ambivalence concerning a number of social issues (Thompson & Zanna, 1995). Similarly, a tendency to prefer structure in one's life, termed high "personal need for structure" (Thompson et al., 1993), may also be related to reporting less ambivalence but being more troubled by its presence.

This line of reasoning is supported by research linking the chronic cognitive style of uncertainty orientation to perceptions of close relationships. "Uncertainty orientation" reflects a tendency to frame issues in complex ways and resist cognitive closure, whereas "certainty orientation" results in simplified cognitive structures and a desire for cognitive clarity (Sorrentino, Short, & Raynor, 1984). Sorrentino, Holmes, Hanna, and Sharp (1995) found that uncertainty oriented individuals typically reported having only moderate trust in their partners, though they were more comfortable living with a certain degree of ambivalence and saw some negative partner perceptions as less of a cause for concern. In contrast, certainty-oriented individuals reported either high or low levels of trust in their partners. They apparently preferred cognitive clarity concerning their relationships, whether that clarity promoted a positive or negative view of their partners. However, those with high trust exhibited a positive bias in the recall of negative relationship events, in an apparent attempt to reduce potential ambivalence and sustain cognitive closure.

A final personality variable that could affect one's tendency to experience ambivalence may be level of self-awareness. "Objective self-awareness" refers to the degree to which a person is conscious or aware of his or her inner states (Duval & Wicklund, 1972). It has been proposed that chronic tendencies to be self-aware are tapped by the Private Self-Consciousness Scale (Fenigstein, Scheier, & Buss, 1975). An increased awareness of one's inner states may result in more sensitivity to conflicted beliefs or feelings about a romantic partner. The subsequent ability to tolerate or to resolve this ambivalence may involve some interaction between self-consciousness and the other cognitive styles discussed above. For instance, when high private self-consciousness is coupled with high need for cognition, there should be a readiness to apprehend ambivalent reactions when they become manifest, and an accompanying ability to resolve the inconsistencies encountered. On the other hand, high private self-consciousness and a high personal fear of invalidity should be associated with an awareness of ambivalence but less ability to achieve an integrative resolution.

When ambivalence originates from personality or attachment style predispositions, the amount and duration of positive relationship evidence necessary for maintaining relationship stability may be greater than they are when ambivalence originates largely from normal features of interdependence. Individuals possessing these predispositions may need more constant reassurance, and weaker evidence of negativity may be sufficient to undermine their feelings of security in the relationship. Consequently, when other sources of ambivalence interact with predispositions, the intensity, impact, and consequences of the "normal" experience of ambivalence may be more severe.

We believe that the AIRS will prove to be a useful diagnostic tool for exploring these various sources of ambivalence. The specificity inherent in the AIRS measurement procedures should aid in the identification of the particular sources and types of ambivalence associated with both cognitive styles and attachment styles. For instance, the analysis of perceptions at the level of specific attributes permits idiographic sources of ambivalence to be identified—instances where a partner is evaluated positively on most traits but evaluated negatively on a few traits that may reflect personality issues.

CONCLUSION: AMBIVALENCE AS AN EARLY-WARNING SYSTEM

Our results have shown that ambivalence is a better predictor of the dissolution of dating relationships than is interpersonal conflict. This is a rather interesting result, given prior research suggesting that early marital conflict determines the subsequent quality of the relationship. However, in dating relationships, conflict has been shown (in a retrospective study) to be essentially orthogonal to concurrent feeling of love for a partner (Braiker & Kelley, 1979), and this result was replicated in the present studies. Apparently, dating partners do not always attach much significance to their conflicts in their relationships. Instead, disagreements might be seen as a temporary feature of growing interdependence and mutual adjustment (Levinger, 1983). Therefore, conflict in the course of relationship development might best be viewed as a somewhat distal interpersonal event—one that is not always reflected in interpersonal evaluations or diagnostic of the future of a dating relationship. Indeed, when conflicts are resolved, they often serve to strengthen a relationship (Braiker & Kelley, 1979).

A broader theme that can be abstracted from this analysis is that in reaching evaluative conclusions about relationships, individuals may often be slow to integrate negative perceptions or give weight to what impartial observers might construe as "negative evidence." We believe that it is in such circumstances that the AIRS may prove to be a very useful diagnostic tool, identifying potential relationship issues before they have significantly colored individuals' overall appraisals. Therefore, reports of ambivalence, as measured by the AIRS may serve as an important early-warning sign, forecasting potentially deeper issues within the relationship. Just as importantly, however, our results also underscore the powerful moderating effects of a strong commitment in ameliorating the full force of ambivalence about a romantic partner. So, although ambivalence may be a valuable early warning system, our findings show that it is not an inevitable harbinger of doom for relationships. Indeed, the results of the R-I discrepancy analyses suggest that commitment, combined with a certain degree of doubt based on "realistic" appraisals, leads to a more optimistic prognosis than do low ambivalence and love rooted in idealization of a partner. Continued work directed toward understanding how motivational factors transform signs of doubt in representations of partners will greatly enhance our knowledge of the processes serving to maintain satisfying close relationships.

References

Bartholomew, K. (1990). Avoidance of intimacy: An attachment perspective. *Journal of Social and Personal Relationships, 7,* 147–178.

Bentler, P. M., & Huba, G. J. (1979). Simple minitheories of love. *Journal of Personality and Social Psychology, 37,* 124–130.

Berscheid, E. (1983). *Emotion.* In H. H. Kelley, E. Berscheid, A. Christensen, J. H. Harvey, T. L. Huston, G. Levinger, E. McClintock, L. A. Peplau, & D. R. Peterson (Eds.), *Close relationships* (pp. 110–168). New York: W. H. Freeman.

Berscheid, E., & Walster, E. (1978). *Interpersonal attraction.* Reading: MA: Addison-Wesley.

Boon, S. D., & Holmes, J. G. (1991). *Interpersonal trust, attachment and emotion: Implications for coping with insecurity in marriage.* Paper presented at the meeting of the International Society for the Study of Personal Relationships, Oxford.

Bradburn, N. M. (1969). *The structure of psychological well-being.* Chicago: Aldine.

Bradbury, T. N., & Fincham, F. D. (1990). Attributions in marriage: Review and critique. *Psychological Bulletin, 107,* 3–33.

Braiker, H. B., & Kelley, H. H. (1979). Conflict in the development of close relationships. In R. Burgess & T. L. Huston (Eds.), *Social exchange in developing relationships* (pp. 135–168). New York: Academic Press.

Breckler, S. J. (1984). Empirical validation of affect, behavior, and cognition as distinct components of attitudes. *Journal of Personality and Social Psychology, 47,* 1191–1205.

Breckler, S. J. (1994). A comparison of numerical indices for measuring attitude ambivalence. *Educational and Psychological Measurement, 54*(2), 350–365.

Breckler, S. J., & Berman, J. S. (1991). Affective responses to attitude objects: Measurement and validation. *Journal of Social Behavior and Personality, 6,* 529–544.

Breckler, S. J., & Wiggins, E.C. (1989). Affect versus cognition in the structure of attitudes. *Journal of Experimental Social Psychology, 25,* 253–271.

Brickman, P. (1987). *Commitment, conflict and caring.* Englewoods Cliffs, NJ: Prentice-Hall.

Brown, J. S., & Farber, I. E. (1951). Emotions conceptualized as intervening variables with suggestions toward a theory of frustration. *Psychological Bulletin, 48,* 465–480.

Cacioppo, J. T., & Petty, R. E. (1982). The need for cognition. *Journal of Personality and Social Psychology, 42,* 116–131.

Cate, R. M., Lloyd, S., Henton, J. M., & Larson, J. (1982). Fairness and reward levels as predictors of relationship satisfaction. *Social Psychology Quarterly, 45,* 177–181.

Chaiken, S., & Baldwin, M. H. (1981). Affective–cognitive consistency and the effect of salient behavioral information on the self-perception of attitudes. *Journal of Personality and Social Psychology, 41,* 1–12.

Chaiken, S., & Yates, S. (1985). Affective–cognitive consistency and thought–induced polarization. *Journal of Personality and Social Psychology, 49,* 1470–1481.

Collins, N. L., & Read, S. J. (1990). Adult attachment, working models, and relationship quality in dating couples. *Journal of Personality and Social Psychology, 58*(4), 644–663.

Diener, E. (1984). Subjective well-being. *Psychological Bulletin, 95,* 542–575.

Diener, E., & Emmons, R. A. (1985). The independence of positive and negative affect. *Journal of Personality and Social Psychology, 47,* 1105–1117.

Dollard, J., & Miller, N. E. (1950). *Personality and psychotherapy: An analysis in terms of learning, thinking, and culture.* New York: McGraw-Hill.

Duval, S., & Wicklund, R. A. (1972). *A theory of objective self-awareness.* New York: Academic Press.

Eidelson, R. J. (1980). Interpersonal satisfaction and level of involvement: A curvilinear relationship. *Journal of Personality and Social Psychology, 39,* 460–470.

Epstein, S. (1980). Conflict and stress. In L. Goldberger & S. Breznitz (Eds.), *The handbook of stress: Theoretical and clinical aspects* (pp. 49–68). New York: Free Press.

Festinger, L. (1957). *A theory of cognitive dissonance.* Stanford, CA: Stanford University Press.

Fenigstein, A., Scheier, M. F., & Buss, A. H. (1975). Public and private self-consciousness: Assessment and theory. *Journal of Consulting and Clinical Psychology, 43,* 522-527.

Freud, S. (1962). *The ego and the id* (J. Strachey, Ed. and Trans.). New York: Norton. (Original work published 1923)

Green, D. P. (1988). On the dimensionality of public sentiment toward partisan and ideological groups. *American Journal of Political Science, 32,* 758-780.

Green, D. P., Goldman, S. L., & Salovey, P. (1993). Measurement error masks bipolarity in affect ratings. *Journal of Personality and Social Psychology, 64,* 1029-1041.

Hass, R. G., & Eisenstadt, D. (1993, August). *Comparing theories and measures of ambivalent attitudes: A three-dimensional surface plot analysis and a reanalysis of experimental data.* Paper presented at the annual meeting of the American Psychological Association, Toronto.

Hass, R. G., Katz, I., Rizzo, N., Bailey, J., & Eisenstadt, D. (1991). Cross-racial appraisal as related to attitude ambivalence and cognitive complexity. *Personality and Social Psychology Bulletin, 17,* 83-92.

Hazan, C., & Shaver, P. (1987). Romantic love conceptualized as an attachment process. *Journal of Personality and Social Psychology, 52,* 511-524.

Heider, F. (1944). Social perception and phenomenal causality. *Psychological Review, 51,* 358-374.

Higgins, E. T. (1989). Self-discrepancy theory: What patterns of self-beliefs cause people to suffer? In L. Berkowitz (Ed.), *Advances in experimental social psychology* (Vol. 22, pp. 93-136). New York: Academic Press.

Higgins, E. T. (1990). Personality, social psychology, and person–situation relations. Standards and knowledge activation as a common language. In L. A. Pervin (Ed.), *Handbook of personality: Theory and research* (pp. 301-338). New York: Guilford Press.

Higgins, E. T., Bond, R. N., Klein, R., & Strauman, T. (1986). Self-discrepancies and emotional vulnerability: How magnitude, accessibility and type of discrepancy influence affect. *Journal of Personality and Social Psychology, 51,* 1-15.

Higgins, E. T., Klein, R., & Strauman, T. J. (1985). Self-concept discrepancy theory: A psychological model for distinguishing among different aspects of depression and anxiety. *Social Cognition, 3,* 51-76.

Higgins, E. T., Tykocinski, O., & Vookles, J. (1990). Patterns of self-beliefs: The psychological significance of relations among the actual, ideal, ought, can, and future selves. In J. M. Olsen & M. P. Zanna (Eds.), *The Ontario Symposium: Vol. 6. Self-inference processes* (pp. 148-180). Hillsdale, NJ: Erlbaum.

Higgins, E. T., Vookles, J., & Tykocinski, O. (1992). Self and health: How "patterns" of self-beliefs predict types of emotional and physical problems. *Social Cognition, 10,* 125-150.

Holmes, J. G., & Rempel, J. K. (1989). Trust in close relationships. In C. Hendrick (Ed.), *Review of personality and social psychology: Vol. 10. Close relationships* (pp. 187-220). Newbury Park, CA: Sage.

Hovland, C. I., & Sears, R. R. (1938). Experiments on motor conflict: I. Types of conflict and their modes of resolution. *Journal of Experimental Psychology, 23,* 477-493.

Huston, T. L., & Vangelisti, A. L. (1991). Socioemotional behavior and satisfaction in marital relationships: A longitudinal study. *Journal of Personality and Social Psychology, 61,* 721-733.

Jacobson, N. S., Follette, W. C., & MacDonald, D. W. (1982). Reactivity to positive and negative behavior in distressed and nondistressed couples. *Journal of Consulting and Clinical Psychology, 50,* 706-714.

Jacobson, N. S., Waldron, H., & Moore, D. (1980). Toward a behavioral profile of marital distress. *Journal of Consulting and Clinical Psychology, 48,* 696-703.

Janis, I. L. (1982). Decision making under stress. In L. Goldberger & S. Brenitz (Eds.), *The handbook of stress: Theoretical and clinical aspects* (pp. 69-86). New York: Free Press.

Janis, I. L., & Mann, L. (1968). A conflict-theory approach to attitude change and decision making. In A. G. Greenwald, T. C. Brock, & T. M. Ostrom (Eds.), *Psychological foundations of attitudes* (pp. 327–360). New York: Academic Press.

John, O. P. (1990). The "Big Five" factor taxonomy: Dimensions of personality in natural language and in questionnaires. In L. A. Pervin (Ed.), *Handbook of personality: Theory and research* (pp. 66–100). New York: Guilford Press.

Jones, E. E., & Gerard, H. B. (1967). *Foundations of social psychology.* New York: Wiley.

Joreskog, K. G., & Sorbom, D. (1984). LISREL: *Analysis of linear structural relationships by the method of maximum likelihood.* Chicago: SPSS.

Judd, C. M., Jessor, R., & Donovan, J. E. (1986). Structural equation models and personality research. *Journal of Personality, 54,* 149–198.

Kaplan, K. J. (1972). On the ambivalence–indifference problem in attitude theory and measurement: A suggested modification of the semantic differential technique. *Psychological Bulletin, 77,* 361–372.

Katz, I., Wackenhut, J., & Hass, G. (1986). Racial ambivalence, value duality, and behavior. In S. L. Gaertner & J. Dovidio (Eds.), *Prejudice, discrimination, and racism* (pp. 35–60). New York: Academic Press.

Kelley, H. H. (1983). Love and commitment. In H. H. Kelley, E. Berscheid, A. Christensen, J. H. Harvey, T. L. Huston, G. Levinger, E. McClintock, L. A. Peplau, & D. R. Peterson (Eds.), *Close relationships* (pp. 265–314). New York: W. H. Freeman.

Kelly, C., Huston, T. L., & Cate, R. M. (1985). Premarital correlates of the erosion of satisfaction in marriage. *Journal of Social and Personal Relationships, 2,* 167–178.

Kiesler, D. J. (1983). The 1982 interpersonal circle: A taxonomy for complementarity in human transactions. *Psychological Review, 90,* 185–214.

Levinger, G. (1983). Development and change. In H. H. Kelley, E. Berscheid, A. Christensen, J. H. Harvey, T. L. Huston, G. Levinger, E. McClintock, L. A. Peplau, & D. R. Peterson (Eds.), *Close relationships* (pp. 315–359). New York: W. H. Freeman.

Lewin, K. (1951). *Field theory in social science: Selected theoretical papers* (R. Cartwright, Ed.). New York: Harper & Row.

Lund, M. (1985). The development of investment and commitment scales for predicting continuity of personal relationships. *Journal of Personal and Social Relationships, 2,* 3–23.

Markman, H. J. (1979). Application of a behavioral model of marriage in predicting relationship satisfaction of couples planning marriage. *Journal of Consulting and Clinical Psychology, 47,* 743–749.

Markman, H. J. (1981). Prediction of marital distress: A 5-year follow-up. *Journal of Clinical and Consulting Psychology, 49,* 760–762.

McCrae, R. R., & Costa, P. T., Jr. (1989). The structure of interpersonal traits: Wiggins' circumplex and the five-factor model. *Journal of Personality and Social Psychology, 56*(4), 586–595.

Miller, N. E. (1944). Experimental studies of conflict. In J. Hunt (Ed.), *Personality and the behavior disorders* (Vol. 1, pp. 431–465). New York: Ronald Press.

Miller, N. E. (1959). Liberalization of S-R concepts: Extension to conflict behavior, social learning and motivation. In S. Koch (Ed.), *Psychology: A study of a science* (Vol. 2, pp. 196–292). New York: McGraw-Hill.

Moretti, M., M., & Higgins, E. T. (1990). Relating self-discrepancy to self-esteem: The contribution of discrepancy beyond actual self-ratings. *Journal of Experimental Social Psychology, 26,* 108–123.

Norman, R. (1975). Affective-cognitive consistency, attitudes, conformity, and behavior. *Journal of Personality and Social Psychology, 32,* 83–91.

Parisi, N., & Katz, I. (1986). Attitudes toward posthumous organ donation and commitment to donate. *Health Psychology, 5,* 565–580.

Reich, J. W., & Zautra, A. J. (1983). Demands and desires in daily life. Some influences on well-being. *American Journal of Community Psychology, 11,* 41–58.

Reis, H. T., & Shaver, P. (1988). Intimacy as an interpersonal process. In S. W. Duck (Ed.), *Handbook of personal relationships* (pp. 367–389). New York: Wiley.

Rempel, J. K, Holmes, J. G., & Zanna, M. P. (1985). Trust in close relationships. *Journal of Personality and Social Psychology, 49,* 95–112.

Ross, M. (1989). Relation of implicit theories to the construction of personal histories. *Psychological Review, 96,* 341–357.

Rusbult, C. E. (1983). A longitudinal test of the investment model: The development (and deterioration) of satisfaction and commitment in heterosexual involvement. *Journal of Personality and Social Psychology, 45,* 101–117.

Rusbult, C. E., & Buunk, B. P. (1992). *Commitment processes in close relationships: An interdependence analysis.* Unpublished manuscript, University of North Carolina at Chapel Hill.

Rusbult, C. E., & Van Lange, P. A. M. (1992, July). *Perceived superiority in close relationships.* Paper presented at the Sixth Annual Conference on Personal Relationships, Orono, ME.

Scott, W. A. (1966). Measures of cognitive structure. *Multivariate Behavior Research, 1,* 391–395.

Scott, W. A. (1968). Attitude measurement. In G. Lindzey & E. Aronson (Eds.), *The Handbook of social psychology* (Vol. 2, pp. 204–273). Reading, MA: Addison-Wesley.

Simpson, J. A. (1987). The dissolution of romantic relationships: Factors in relationship stability and emotional distress. *Journal of Personality and Social Psychology, 53,* 683–692.

Sorrentino, R. M., & Higgins, E. T. (Eds.). (1986). *Handbook of motivation and cognition: Foundations of social behavior* (Vol. 1). New York: Guilford Press.

Sorrentino, R. M., Holmes, J. G., Hanna, S., & Sharp, A. (1995). Uncertainty orientation and trust in close relationships: Individual differences in cognitive styles. *Journal of Personality and Social Psychology, 68*(a), 314–327.

Sorrentino, R. M., Short, J. C., & Raynor, J. O. (1984). Uncertainty orientation: Implications for affective and cognitive views of achievement behavior. *Journal of Personality and Social Psychology, 47,* 312–329.

Sternberg, R. J., & Grajeck, S. (1984). The nature of love. *Journal of Personality and Social Psychology, 47,* 312–329.

Strauman, T. J., Lemieux, A. M., & Coe, C. L. (1993). Self-discrepancy and natural killer cell activity: Immunological consequences of negative self-evaluation. *Journal of Personality and Social Psychology, 64,* 1042–1052.

Tetlock, P. E., & Levi, A. (1982). Attribution bias: On the inconclusiveness of the cognition-motivation debate. *Journal of Experimental Social Psychology, 18,* 68–88.

Thompson, M. M., Griffin, D. W., & Zanna, M. P. (1994). *The dimensional structure of attitudes: Beyond bipolarity.* Unpublished manuscript, University of Waterloo.

Thompson, M. M., & Holmes, J. G. (1992, July). *Ambivalence, commitment and the dissolution of dating relationships.* Paper presented at the sixth annual meeting of the International Society for the Study of Personal Relationships, University of Maine, Orono.

Thompson, M. M., Naccarato, M. E., Parker, K., & Moskowitz, G. B. (1993). *Measuring cognitive needs: The development and validation of the Personal Need for Structure (PNS) and Personal Fear of Invalidity (PFI) measures.* Manuscript submitted for publication.

Thompson, M. M., & Zanna, M. P. (1995). The conflicted individual: Personality-based and domain-specific antecedents of ambivalent social attitudes. *Journal of Personality, 63,* 259–288.

Thompson, M. M., Zanna, M. P., & Griffin, D. W. (1995). Let's not be indifferent about (attitudinal) ambivalence. In R. E. Petty, & J. A. Krosnick (Eds.), *Attitude strength: Antecedents and consequences.* Hillsdale, NJ: Erlbaum.

Van Hook, E., & Higgins, E. T. (1988). Self-related problems beyond the self-concept: Motivational consequences of discrepant self-guides. *Journal of Personality and Social Psychology, 55,* 625–633.

Warr, P., Barter, J., & Brownbridge, G. (1983). On the independence of positive and negative affect. *Journal of Personality and Social Psychology, 44,* 644–651.

Watson, D., & Tellegen, A. (1985). Toward a consensual structure of mood. *Psychological Bulletin, 98,* 219–235.

Weiss, R. S. (1976). The emotional impact of marital separation. *Journal of Social Issues, 32*(1), 135–145.

Wiggins, J. S. (1979). A psychological taxonomy of trait-descriptive terms: The interpersonal domain. *Journal of Personality and Social Psychology, 37,* 395–412.

Wills, T. A., Weiss, R. L., & Patterson, G. R. (1974). A behavioral analysis of the determination of marital satisfction. *Journal of Consulting and Clinical Psychology, 42,* 802–811.

Zanna, M. P., & Rempel, J. K. (1988). Attitudes: A new look at an old concept. In D. Bar-Tal & A. W. Kruglanski (Eds.), *The social psychology of knowledge* (pp. 315–334). New York: Cambridge University Press.

Zautra, A. J., & Reich, J. W. (1983). Life events and perceptions of life quality: Developments in a two factor approach. *Journal of Community Psychology, 11,* 121–132.

CHAPTER 16

Impact of Anticipated Group Membership on Cognition

JOHN M. LEVINE
LAURA M. BOGART
BOZENA ZDANIUK
University of Pittsburgh

Although students of human cognition have tended to focus their attention on how socially isolated individuals perceive, interpret, and manipulate information, there is good reason to view cognition as a socially embedded activity (see Higgins, 1992a; Levine, Resnick, & Higgins, 1993; Resnick, Levine, & Teasley, 1991). There are several ways in which social processes can affect cognitive processes.

The most rudimentary type of social influence on cognition involves the mere presence of others. Even when the responses of others are not observed or cognitively represented and there is no opportunity for interaction, others' physical presence can affect a person's cognitive activity, sometimes improving and sometimes worsening it. For example, work on social facilitation indicates that others' presence elicits dominant cognitions such as common word associations (Matlin & Zajonc, 1968), which can either facilitate or impair performance, depending on whether these cognitions are correct for the task at hand. And some theories of social facilitation suggest that the mere presence of others produces distraction, attentional conflict, and cognitive overload (see Baron, 1986, and Geen, 1989). Work on social loafing indicates that believing one's contributions will be pooled with others' contributions can reduce effort on cognitive tasks, such as evaluating written materials, brainstorming, and performing judgment tasks (Harkins & Petty, 1983; Weldon & Gargano, 1988). And research on group composition reveals that the mix of people in a group can affect several types of social information processing, including stereotype-based memory and judgment, social projection, and perception of ingroup–outgroup homogeneity (Higgins & King, 1981; Mullen, 1991).

Cognitive activity is also affected by the way people construe their social situations. These construals, in turn, are influenced by people's perceptions of how others view them and expect them to behave. Evidence indicates that cognitions can be influenced by the social roles a person plays (Anderson & Pichert, 1978; Zukier & Pepitone, 1984). Similarly, cognitions can be affected by the social positions a person occupies (Snyder, 1992) and the social identities he or she adopts (Frable, Blackstone, & Scherbaum, 1990).

Often an individual is not in the physical presence of others, but nevertheless has knowledge about their responses. This mental representation of others can affect cognition via such routes as role taking (Mead, 1934) and social comparison (Festinger, 1954). In addition, individuals' opinions are often influenced by the assumed opinions of reference groups that they value (Siegel & Siegel, 1957). Recent evidence indicates that susceptibility to social influence depends on categorizing oneself as a group member and conforming to the norms defining the group (Abrams & Hogg, 1990; Turner & Oakes, 1989). These findings are consistent with the idea that people differentially process messages from ingroup and outgroup members (Mackie, Gastardo-Conaco, & Skelly, 1992; Van Knippenberg & Wilke, 1992).

Several additional lines of work stress the relationship between social interaction and cognitive change. Research on conflict as a source of cognitive growth indicates that social interaction can facilitate children's intellectual development, if sociocognitive conflict between the interactants is generated and resolved in appropriate ways (Azmitia & Perlmutter, 1989; Doise & Mugny, 1984; Perret-Clermont, 1980). Studies of minority influence suggest that disagreement from a minority can produce cognitive changes in majority members (Moscovici, 1980; Mugny & Perez, 1991; Nemeth, 1986; Wood, Lundgren, Ouellette, Busceme, & Blackstone, 1994). And research on group decision making shows that participation in collective decision making can have cognitive consequences for group members, including private opinion change and acquisition of problem-solving strategies (Kaplan, 1987; Laughlin & Ellis, 1986; Stasser & Davis, 1981).

Finally, a number of studies treat cognition as an emergent product of social interaction, in which the dyad or the group, rather than the individual, is the unit of analysis. Several lines of work involve the development of shared cognitions in groups. These include research on norm formation (Sherif, 1935; Weick & Gilfillan, 1971); studies of individual versus group performance (Hastie, 1986); research on group decision making (Hastie & Pennington, 1991; Stasser, Kerr, & Davis, 1989); and studies of groupthink (Janis, 1982; Tetlock, Peterson, McGuire, Chang, & Feld, 1992). Other work involves group memory, including research on transactive memory (Wegner, 1987) and studies on collaborative recall in groups (Clark & Stephenson, 1989; Hinsz, 1990; Vollrath, Sheppard, Hinsz, & Davis, 1989). Finally, there is a substantial literature on communication and linguistic interaction, which explores the often complex relationships between what people say to one another and what they think (Billig, 1987; Clark & Brennan, 1991; Higgins, 1981; Krauss & Fussell, 1991). Much of this work deals with how people establish and maintain common ground during conversation.

ANTICIPATED GROUP MEMBERSHIP

As the discussion above indicates, a good deal of research attention has been devoted to how social factors affect cognition. Very little attention, however, has been devoted to the cognitive consequences of *anticipated* group membership. Why might this be? We believe that the lack of interest in anticipatory processes can be attributed to the rather narrow way in which researchers have traditionally thought about and studied groups. Most group studies use laboratory groups that exist for only an hour or two. Because the experimenter determines group composition, prospective members have no choice about whether to join the group. And because the group has no history, prospective members have no knowledge about how they should behave after they join and no opportunity to prepare for membership. All members enter the group at the same time, and everyone is a charter member. When the interaction is over, all members leave at the same time, and the group ceases to exist. In these situations, then, an individual can occupy only two roles vis-à-vis the group (nonmember or member). Moreover, only behavior in the member role is interesting, and all individuals associated with the group occupy the same role at any point in time.

Laboratory groups of this kind are very useful for answering certain questions, but they have some important disadvantages as well. Because of their restricted temporal perspective, these groups impose constraints on the kinds of questions that researchers ask. In order to understand the nature and magnitude of these contraints, it is useful to compare the typical laboratory group with a typical natural group. Rather than existing for an hour or two, many natural groups exist for months or years. Prospective members often have substantial choice about whether to join the group. And, because the group has a history, prospective members typically have knowledge about how they should behave after they join and an opportunity to prepare for membership. People enter the group at different times, and after the group has existed for a while, most of the members are not charter members. People also leave the group at different times, and the group continues to exist after its charter members depart.

This analysis suggests that membership in natural groups is not an all-or-none affair. Instead, one can think of membership as varying along an ingroup–outgroup dimension (see Figure 16.1). According to this analysis, the relationship between a group and its members changes over time, and members occupy different roles in the group, depending on the length and quality of their relationship with it. Five such roles can be differentiated (Levine & Moreland, 1994; Moreland & Levine, 1982). "Prospective members" have not yet joined the group, but may do so in the future. "New members" have recently joined the group and are undergoing socialization in order to acquire the knowledge and skills needed for full membership. "Full members" have successfully completed socialization and thereby earned all the privileges and responsibilities of membership. "Marginal members" once had full member status, have lost this status because they violated group norms, and are undergoing resocialization. Finally, "ex-members" once belonged to the group, have left it, but may

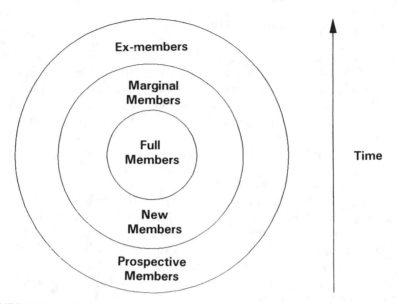

FIGURE 16.1   Roles that group members can occupy, depending on the length and quality of their relationship with the group.

still be influenced by their group experiences. It is worth noting that both prospective members and ex-members are nonmembers of the group, but they are very different kinds of nonmembers. Similarly, both new members and marginal members are quasi-members of the group, but they are very different kinds of quasi-members.

According to this analysis, an individual can occupy several roles vis-à-vis the group. Moreover, all of these roles are potentially interesting, and different individuals can occupy different roles in the group at a given point in time (e.g., some people are full members, while others are prospective members). This analysis emphasizes the temporal dimension of group life, and suggests a number of interesting research questions that are not salient if one focuses on laboratory groups of the sort discussed earlier.

In this chapter, we discuss several ways in which the expectation of impending group membership can influence the cognitions of prospective members and current (typically full) members. First, we talk about how prospective and current members decide whether or not to establish a relationship in the first place. Here we focus on the cognitive processes that occur during the investigation phase of group membership, when prospective members decide whether they want to join an existing group and current members decide whether they want this role transition to occur (Levine & Moreland, 1994; Moreland & Levine, 1982). In the next section, we assume that this investigation has been successful—that is, the prospective and current members agree that the prospective members' joining is a good idea and expect it to happen in the near future. Here, we discuss two ways in which impending group membership can affect the cognitions of both prospective and current members. One concerns changes in prospective and current members' understanding of the group culture, including task and social knowledge. The other concerns changes in prospective and current members' cognitions about people, including themselves, other members of their present or future group, and members of other groups that are related (either negatively or positively) to that group. In both of these sections, we focus on small, autonomous, voluntary groups, whose members interact on a regular basis, have affective ties with one another, share a common frame of reference, and are behaviorally interdependent. Finally, we shift our attention to the case in which prospective members expect to form a new group that has not been in existence before. Here, we discuss how prospective members' cognitions are altered by the expectation that after entering such a group, they will encounter disagreement from other members and will have to defend their opinions.

DECIDING WHETHER A PROSPECTIVE MEMBER SHOULD JOIN AN EXISTING GROUP

In their model of group socialization, Moreland and Levine (1982; Levine & Moreland, 1994) have proposed that the relationships between groups and their members change in systematic ways over time. They suggest that individuals pass through five phases of group membership ("investigation," "socialization," "maintenance," "resocialization," and "remembrance"), separated by four role transitions ("entry," "acceptance," "divergence," and "exit"). They have argued that (1) groups and individuals continually evaluate the rewardingness of their own and alternative relationships; (2) these evaluations lead to increases or decreases in commitment to the other party; and (3) when commitment reaches a specific level (decision criterion) warranting a qualitative change in the relationship between the two parties, a role transition occurs. Following a role transition, the individual's relationship with the group is jointly relabeled, and the parties alter their expectations for each other's behavior. Evaluation continues, producing further changes in commitment and subsequent role transitions.

The first phase of group membership, investigation, concerns us here. During investigation, the prospective member engages in reconnaissance, seeking groups that might contribute to the satisfaction of his or her personal needs. Similarly, the group engages in recruitment, seeking people who are likely to contribute to the attainment of the group's goals. If, as a result of the evaluation process, both parties' commitment levels rise to their respective entry criteria, then the role transition of entry occurs, and the individual moves from the role of prospective member to that of new member.

Prospective Members

In order for reconnaissance to succeed, a prospective member must do three things. First, the person has to identify potentially attractive groups. This involves deciding which groups he or she wishes to join and determining whether such groups are available in the environment. Locating an appropriate group may be more or less difficult, depending on the person's attractiveness as a potential member and the uniqueness of his or her selection criteria. Second, the person must evaluate whether membership in these groups will satisfy his or her personal needs. This involves obtaining information about the probable rewards and costs of membership in these groups. This task may be difficult, especially if the groups have been in existence for only a short time and are not actively seeking new members. Finally, if the individual's commitment to a particular group reaches his or her entry criterion, the person must make some effort to enter the group. If the group is reluctant to allow this role transition, the person will try to convince current members to alter their position (e.g., by engaging in anticipatory assimilation in order to become more rewarding). All three of these steps require cognitive activity on the part of the prospective member.

In seeking to identify, evaluate, and enter new groups, prospective members can use many sources of information. One source is official recruitment materials disseminated by groups that are looking for new members. Although sometimes quite useful, this kind of information is often biased to highlight the potential rewards of group membership and to downplay the potential costs. A related source of information about new groups is current or past members of these groups. Informal discussions with these people can often elicit "inside" information about a group that would not be emphasized, or even mentioned, in its official recruiting material. Finally, a third source of information about a new group is the prospective member's prior experience in other groups. The idea here is that people generalize their group experiences from one context to another, making inferences about future groups on the basis of their experiences in past groups. Although there is evidence that prior group experience predicts later group participation (e.g., Hanks, 1981; Hanks & Eckland, 1978), the psychological mechanisms underlying this relationship are not well understood. Two studies using natural groups provide evidence for the operation of one mechanism—namely, the influence of prior group memberships on the subsequent reconnaissance activities of former members.

In one study, Pavelchak, Moreland, and Levine (1986) examined the impact of high school group experiences on the reconnaissance activities of freshmen at a large university. These investigators predicted that students whose experiences in high school groups were more positive would expend more effort in identifying potentially desirable college groups and that this effort would be mediated by the belief that memberships in such groups were useful for achieving personal goals. Subjects' perceptions of the enjoyableness and importance of their high school group memberships, beliefs about the value of college group memberships for achieving personal goals, and the names of the campus groups they were considering joining were obtained from questionnaires completed by 1,134 students just prior to the beginning of their freshman year. Structural-equation analyses indicated that, as predicted, students whose experiences in high school groups were more positive (i.e., important and enjoyable) tried harder to identify potentially desirable college groups, primarily because of their belief that membership would be useful for achieving personal goals.

Pavelchak et al. (1986) also investigated the second phase of the reconnaissance process—namely, how prospective members who have identified potentially desirable groups evaluate the probable rewardingness of belonging to these groups. They predicted that experienced students, who had belonged to high school groups that were similar to the college groups they were considering joining, would provide more balanced evaluations of the college groups than would inexperienced students, who had not belonged to such groups. They also predicted that, for experienced students, the more positive their experiences had been in a relevant high school group, the more optimistic they would be about belonging to a similar college group. Relevant questionnaire data were obtained from 499 students who indicated that they were likely to join a particular college group. Results indicated that students were generally optimistic about their chosen group, expecting more and stronger rewards than costs. In addition, consistent with predictions, experienced students were more balanced in their expectations than were inexperienced students (i.e., they listed more costs as well as more rewards of group membership), and experienced students whose experiences in a relevant high school group were more positive were more optimistic about belonging to a similar college group.

Finally, Pavelchak et al. (1986) examined prospective members' efforts to enter the college groups they wished to join. They predicted that one factor stimulating prospective members to join desirable college groups would be previous experience in relevant high school groups. This is because membership in a relevant high school group can be viewed as a form of direct experience with its college equivalent, and attitudes formed through direct experience predict subsequent behavior better than do attitudes formed by indirect means (Fazio & Zanna, 1981). Relevant data were obtained from telephone interviews conducted with 30 students who had initially indicated a campus group they wished to join and then attended an Activities Fair where they had an opportunity to contact their chosen group. As expected, students who wanted to join a campus group were more likely to approach their chosen group if they had belonged to a relevant high school group than if they had not.

In a second study, Brinthaupt, Moreland, and Levine (1991) investigated three possible reasons why prospective members may have positive expectations about their future group experiences. First, prospective members' optimism may be based on the recruitment efforts of the groups they plan to join. Because groups seeking new members want to present themselves in a favorable light, they are inclined to provide positively biased information about themselves, which in turn may raise prospective members' expectations about how they will fare after they join. Second, prospective members' optimism may reflect their efforts to resolve dissonance about the group they plan to join. Prior to joining, prospective members may exert substantial effort in learning about the group and participating in its activities, which in turn may produce feelings of dissonance when negative aspects of the group are discovered. Desire to reduce this dissonance may cause prospective members to seek and remember positive information about the group and to avoid and forget negative information. Finally, the optimism of prospective members may stem from a general need for self-enhancement. There is evidence that many people harbor self-serving illusions (Taylor & Brown, 1988), which include unrealistic optimism about the future in such domains as health, marriage, and career (e.g., Alloy & Ahrens, 1987; Hoorens, 1993; Weinstein, 1980). Perhaps this optimism also influences prospective members' expectations about the rewards and costs associated with group membership.

In this study, 200 college freshmen were asked to list, for both themselves and the average student, the rewards and costs of membership in a campus group they were interested in joining. They were also asked to answer questions about the recruitment activities of the group and possible reasons for feeling dissonant about the group. Brinthaupt et al. (1991) found, consistent with prior data, that students were generally optimistic about membership in their chosen college groups. In addition, results suggested that this optimism was attributable to a general need for self-enhancement, rather than to group recruitment effort or dissonance.

Of course, a general need for self-enhancement is unlikely to be the only factor that affects optimism about future group experiences. Individual-difference factors may also be important. Two such factors are affiliation motivation and achievement motivation, which have been shown to influence participation in group activities and leadership emergence (e.g., Sorrentino, 1973; Sorrentino & Field, 1986). The work of Sorrentino and his colleagues suggests that people who are both affiliation-oriented and success-oriented will be more optimistic about future group experiences than will others.

Current Members

So far, our discussion of cognitive activity during the investigation phase of group socialization has focused on prospective members engaging in reconnaissance (i.e., looking for groups that might contribute to the satisfaction of their personal needs). It is also true, of course, that current members engaging in recruitment (i.e., looking for people who might contribute to the attainment of group goals) exhibit substantial cognitive activity. In fact, in deciding whether or not to establish a relationship, current members go through a set of cognitive activities that are quite similar to those described above for prospective members. First, current members must identify prospective members—a task that may be assigned to recruitment specialists who are knowledgeable about the population of available candidates. Second, current members must evaluate prospective members in terms of their potential contributions to group goals. This evaluation process may be more or less formal, depending on the level of agreement among current members regarding the valued characteristics of new-comers, the extent to which these characteristics can be easily assessed, and the perceived consequences of making errors. Information about prospective mem-bers can be obtained from various sources, including records and applications, people who know the prospective members, and face-to-face contacts with the prospective members. Finally, if current members' commitment to a prospective member reaches their entry criterion, they will extend an offer of membership to the person. If the person is reluctant to join at this point, current members will try to persuade him or her to do so (e.g., by promising inducements, such as money or status).

Current members' cognitions about the advisability of prospective mem-bers' joining the group may be influenced by a number of factors. One impor-tant factor is the group's need for new members, which is affected by its "staffing level" (Barker, 1968; Schoggen, 1989; Wicker, 1979). A group's staffing level involves a comparison between the number of people who actually belong to the group and the number needed for optimal performance. Thus, groups that have just the right number of members are adequately staffed, whereas those that have too few or too many members are understaffed and overstaffed, respectively. Evidence indicates that understaffing places special demands on group members: As groups become more understaffed, their members work harder, perform a wider variety of tasks, take more responsibility for the group's performance, and feel more involved in it (e.g., Arnold & Greenberg, 1980; Perkins, 1982; Petty & Wicker, 1974; Wicker, Kirmeyer, Hanson, & Alexander, 1976; Wicker & Mehler, 1971). One would expect, therefore, that members of understaffed groups would perceive problems associated with the group's size. In addition, one would expect that members of understaffed groups would de-sire to recruit new members and, in order to do so, might adopt relatively low standards for these people.

Cini, Moreland, and Levine (1993) examined the impact of group staffing level on current members' cognitions about group problems and recruitment practices. They asked leaders of 93 campus groups about the actual and ideal sizes of their group, how small or large the group would have to become before staffing problems arose and what kinds of problems would develop, and the group's recruitment activities toward prospective members. Although leaders agreed that both understaffing and overstaffing were possible, they were more sensitive to having "too few" than "too many" members. In discussing problems associated with understaffing, leaders were most likely to mention poor group performance, fatigue and burnout, loss of resources, and member homogeneity. The most commonly mentioned solutions to these problems were to recruit new members or reorganize the group. Finally, Cini et al. (1993) found that groups that were more understaffed (1) wanted more recruits and were more likely to al-low these people to enter the group at any time, and (2) were less selective about who could join and required fewer special qualities in their recruits. These findings indicate, as predicted, that current members' beliefs about group problems and their efforts to resolve these problems by recruiting new members are influenced by group staffing level.

PREPARING FOR A PROSPECTIVE MEMBER'S ENTRY INTO AN EXISTING GROUP

Once the commitment levels of prospective and current members reach their respective entry criteria, they will seek to produce the role transition of entry.[1] Deciding whether this transition should occur is not always easy, particularly when prospective and current members feel different levels of commitment to one another and/or have different entry criteria (Moreland & Levine, 1984). Moreover, even if both parties favor the transition, joining an existing group is often a very stressful experience for newcomers (Moreland & Levine, 1982, 1989). For one thing, the "true" nature of the group is revealed to the newcomer for the first time. Given the optimistic expectations that prospective members have about the groups they plan to join (e.g., Brinthaupt et al., 1991; Wanous, 1980), learning about the heretofore secret costs of group life can be quite disturbing (Louis, 1980; Van Maanen, 1977). For another thing, entry is often a demeaning experience, in that a newcomer generally has low status and little control over how he or she is treated. The negative experiences that newcomers face are quite varied, ranging from being ignored and devalued to being forced to participate in unpleasant and even dangerous initiation ceremonies (e.g., Kanter, 1968; Nuwer, 1978; Schein, 1964; Van Maanen & Schein, 1979; Vaught & Smith, 1980). Such ceremonies may have several benefits, which include increasing newcomers' commitment to the group as a result of dissonance reduction (Aronson & Mills, 1959; Gerard & Matthewson, 1966), providing the group with useful information about newcomers' motivation and ability to become full members (Clark, 1983; Haas, 1972), and demonstrating to newcomers the extent of their dependence on current members (Pascale, 1984; Schopler & Bateson, 1962).

Several factors can influence the amount of stress associated with entry into a group, including newcomers' similarity and attractiveness to current members (Blau, 1960; Ziller, Behringer, & Goodchilds, 1960), their status (Zander & Cohen, 1955), and their skill level (Ziller & Behringer, 1960; Ziller, Behringer, & Jansen, 1961). Also important is the number of newcomers relative to the number of current members. In general, the lower the ratio of newcomers to current members, the more difficult entry is likely to be. Entry is particularly stressful when a person is the only newcomer to a group, because "solo" newcomers often evoke high levels of attention from current members (cf. Taylor & Fiske, 1978), which in turn increases newcomers' objective self-awareness and their concern about conforming to group standards (cf. Wicklund & Frey, 1980). In contrast, entry is easier when newcomers join a group together. Fellow newcomers can reduce stress by permitting social comparison, providing emotional support, and warding off harassment from current members.

There is also evidence that, prior to actually joining an existing group, prospective members anticipate that their group experience will be stressful. Moreland (1985) found that people who expected to be newcomers in an existing group were more pessimistic about group membership than were people who expected that they and everyone else would be participating in the group for the first time.

Of course, newcomers are not the only ones who find entry stressful. Current members are often threatened by the entry of newcomers, and hence they too experience stress when new people enter the group (Ziller, 1965). For example, newcomers may ask hard or embarrassing questions about group practices, which force current members to re-examine many of their cherished assumptions and behaviors. In addition, newcomers may destabilize the group by producing changes in current members' relationships with one another (e.g., the entry of newcomers may alter the status hierarchy among current members).

Acquiring and Transmitting Group Culture

Given the stressful nature of entry for newcomers and current members, both parties are typically motivated to ensure that the shift from prospective member to new member proceeds smoothly and that the new members obtain the knowledge they need to succeed in the group. One way to facilitate this transition is to transmit task and social knowledge to prospective members before they actually join (producing what Merton, 1957, termed "anticipatory socialization"). Task knowledge is useful in helping a prospective member prepare for the specific job he or she will carry out, whereas social knowledge is useful in helping a prospective member prepare to win acceptance from current members and gain power in the group.[2] These two kinds of knowledge are embodied in the group's "culture," which involves a set of thoughts shared by members and a set of customs, or behavioral expressions of these thoughts (Levine & Moreland, 1991).

The shared thoughts that prospective members must learn are of three types: knowledge about the group as a whole, knowledge about group members, and knowledge about the group's tasks. Regarding knowledge about the group as a whole, prospective members want to know the following: What makes the group different from other groups? What are the group's past, present, and future? How good is the group? What is the climate within the group? What are the norms of the group? How does the group relate to other groups? Regarding knowledge about group members, prospective members want to know these things: What kind of person belongs to the group? How do members differ from one another? How will they themselves fit into the group? What are the relationships among members? How should members' behaviors be interpreted?

Finally, regarding knowledge about the group's tasks, prospective members want to know the following: What kinds of motivation do members have? What kinds of tasks does the group perform? How are these tasks carried out? What does it mean to do a good job? What are the group's working conditions?

The customs that prospective members must learn are of five types: "routines," "accounts," "jargon," "rituals," and "symbols." Routines involve standardized procedures that group members use in interacting with one another and with outsiders. An example is the standard telephone greeting used by secretaries in a company. Accounts involve verbal descriptions of, or explanations for, issues that group members find particularly interesting (e.g., what happens when a group member behaves dishonestly?). These are often embedded in stories members tell. Jargon involves words, phrases, or gestures that mean a good deal to group members, but mean little to outsiders. An example is the special language that kitchen workers use to describe the food they are preparing (e.g., "two over easy with spuds"). Rituals are ceremonies that group members use to mark the occurrence of special events, including anniversaries, victories, changes in members' status, and arrivals in or departures from the group. Many groups, for example, use special rituals to initiate new members. Finally, symbols are material objects that possess a special meaning only group members can understand. Examples in military groups include special weapons, uniforms, and insignia.

Prospective Members

Little research attention has been devoted to how prospective members acquire group culture, so our discussion of this process is necessarily speculative. We suggest that the likelihood that a prospective member will try to learn the group's culture and will succeed in doing so depends on two sets of factors. One set involves the motivation and ability of the prospective member; the other involves the motivation and ability of the current members in the group.

It seems plausible to assume that a prospective member's effort to acquire cultural information depends on his or her motivation to obtain this information. This motivation, in turn, is likely to vary inversely with the prospective member's level of current knowledge about the group. That is, the higher the current knowledge, the lower the motivation to acquire additional knowledge. Several kinds of experiences may affect how much prospective members already know about a group. These experiences include exposure to stereotypes about similar groups, prior memberships in similar groups, and contacts with previous and current group members. In addition, a prospective member's motivation to acquire cultural information is likely to be influenced by his or her assessment of the probable rewardingness of membership. A person who believes that membership will be very rewarding should exert more effort to learn the group's culture than should a person who believes that membership will be relatively neutral.

A prospective member's success in acquiring cultural information is likely to be dependent on his or her task and social skills. For example, prospective members who already possess task skills should find it easier to understand and remember task-related information than should those who lack these skills. And prospective members who possess social skills (e.g., empathy, sensitivity to non-verbal cues) should find it easier to obtain information from current members than should those who are socially unskilled. In addition, socially skilled prospective members may be more likely to use techniques that are helpful in obtaining cultural information, such as seeking patrons within the group and collaborating with other prospective members.

Of course, prospective members do not have total control over their access to cultural knowledge. Current members, because of their higher status and power, often control the type of information that prospective members receive, as well as when and how that information is transmitted. Therefore, current members' motivation and ability to transmit such information no doubt influence prospective members' ability to acquire cultural knowledge.

Current members' motivation to transmit cultural knowledge is probably influenced by the group's success at attaining its goals and by current members' estimates of prospective members' future contributions to goal attainment. When a group is failing because it has too few members or its members lack necessary skills, current members should feel greater commitment to prospective members and should want to provide information about group culture. This commitment to prospective members and motivation to share information with them should be particularly strong when current members believe that prospective members possess skills that the group needs or can develop these skills. Of course, current members are not always motivated by the desire to help prospective members learn about the group's culture. In some cases, current members may be motivated to withhold rather than share information. This may occur, for example, when current members want to maintain power by possessing "secret" information, or when they want to shield prospective members from information that might weaken their interest in the group.

Current members' ability to transmit cultural knowledge may be influenced by several factors, including the strength of the group culture, the group's prior experience with prospective members, and current members' task and social skills. Some groups have strong cultures, in the sense that knowledge is codified, widely shared among current members, and embodied in customs, whereas other groups have weak cultures. In general, the stronger a group's culture, the easier it probably is for current members to transmit cultural knowledge to prospective members. In addition, groups vary in their experience with prospective members, because some recruit new members more often than others do. It seems likely that current members in experienced groups will be better able to transmit cultural knowledge to prospective members, because these current members will be more aware of what prospective members need to learn. Finally, even within a given group, current members may vary in their knowledge of group culture and their ability to communicate this information to prospective members.

Current Members

Above, we have discussed the critical role that current members play in transmitting group culture to prospective members. It is important to note, however, that current members often do not escape unscathed from their tutorial role. Instead, the responsibility for transmitting group culture may have profound effects on their own cognitions.

A major way in which the imminent entry of prospective members may influence current members' cognitions is by altering their understanding of group culture. That is, the need to explain the group's shared thoughts and customs to prospective members may cause current members to think more carefully about aspects of group culture that they normally take for granted. This may have several consequences. For example, in thinking about the culture, members may discover inconsistencies between shared thoughts and customs that they have never noticed before. This, in turn, may stimulate them to engage in cognitive work designed to reduce these inconsistencies. If these efforts are successful, members' understanding of the group culture will change. If these efforts are unsuccessful, members may "forget" some (less important) aspects of the culture that conflict with other (more important) aspects. In addition, even if no inconsistencies are discovered, members may anticipate that certain cultural elements will be difficult to transmit to prospective members. This perception, in turn, may cause members to invent new ways of imparting cultural knowledge, which may then change how they represent this knowledge. In general, consistent with work on cognitive tuning reviewed below, current members' expectation that they will have to transmit cultural information to prospective members should produce more organized and polarized cognitive structures regarding this information (cf. Zajonc, 1960).

In addition to expecting to transmit cultural information, actually imparting this information may affect current members' cognitions. Consistent with this hypothesis, Higgins and his colleagues have demonstrated that the act of communicating a message to an audience can influence a communicator's message-relevant cognitions. They have shown, for example, that speakers' verbal encoding of information during transmission to an audience affects how the speakers remember the information (e.g., Higgins & McCann, 1984; Higgins, McCann, & Fondacaro, 1982; Higgins & Rholes, 1978; McCann & Hancock, 1983; McCann, Higgins, & Fondacaro, 1991; see Higgins, 1992b, for a review). Given this robust finding, it seems likely that current members' memory for cultural information they have previously communicated to prospective members will be affected by how they have verbally encoded this information during transmission.

Under what circumstances are current members' cognitions likely to change as a result of efforts to impart cultural knowledge to prospective members? One determinant of this cognitive change may be current members' motivation to enculturate prospective members. It seems plausible that the higher this motivation is, the more cognitive effort current members will exert in seeking to impart cultural knowledge. This increased effort, in turn, should lead to cognitive change when current members are forced to resolve cultural inconsistencies or to invent new ways to transmit cultural information. Several factors may increase motivation to enculturate prospective members, including the group's recent success at attaining its goals and current members' estimates of prospective members' future contributions to goal attainment. It seems likely that current members' motivation to enculturate prospective members will increase if the group has recently failed to attain its goals and if prospective members are perceived to have skills that the group needs.

Another determinant of cognitive change on the part of current members may be their self-perceived ability to transmit group culture. It seems likely that the lower members' self-perceived ability is, the more cognitive change they will experience as a result of trying to impart cultural knowledge, at least when cultural inconsistencies must be resolved or new ways of imparting cultural information must be invented. This is because, in transmitting cultural knowledge, low-ability members will feel it necessary to process cultural information in a relatively thoughtful (or controlled) manner, whereas high-ability members will think it sufficient to process this information in a relatively thoughtless (or automatic) manner. The more thoughtful their information processing is, the more likely current members are to experience cognitive change. Members' self-perceived ability to transmit group culture is probably affected by several factors, including their prior experience with prospective members, their task and social skills, the strength of the group culture, and prospective members' assumed desire to become enculturated. Current members' self-perceived ability will probably be low when they have had little experience with prospective members, when their task and social skills are low, when the culture is weak (e.g., knowledge is not codified), and when prospective members are viewed as resistant to enculturation.

Some Caveats

In our discussion of the acquisition and transmission of group culture, we have made two implicit assumptions that deserve examination. First, we have assumed that group culture is instrumental for carrying out group tasks, and hence that it is valuable for prospective members to acquire as much cultural knowledge as possible prior to entering the group. However, this rosy view of group culture may not always be warranted. For example, newly formed groups and groups with high member turnover may not have an opportunity to develop "useful" cultures, and therefore prospective members' efforts to acquire cultural knowledge may not have a strong payoff. In addition, if the group's environment is changing rapidly, cultural prescriptions developed to cope with earlier (and different) environmental contingencies may prove to be maladaptive in the current situation (cf. Gray, Bougon, & Donnellon, 1985; Wilkins & Ouchi, 1983). Thus, although prospective group members are often well advised to absorb a group's culture prior to entering it, there may be cases in which such activity confers no special benefit and is even harmful.

Second, we have assumed that all prospective (and current) group members should share the same task and social knowledge. That is, we have assumed that groups function best when their members possess identical information and think alike. The assumption that shared knowledge facilitates group performance is quite common (e.g., Argote, 1989; Hackman, 1987; Lawler & Mohrman, 1987; Mackie & Goethals, 1987; Stasser & Titus, 1985). However, several lines of research suggest that maximally shared information can hinder group performance, whereas heterogeneity in task-relevant knowledge can enhance performance (e.g., Isenberg, 1986; Janis, 1982; Wegner, 1987). Clearly, then, more effort should be made to identify factors that influence the utility of different distributions of knowledge within groups. It may be, for example, that knowledge should be broadly distributed when a group faces an uncertain environment, all members do the same task, and status differences between members are small, whereas knowledge should be narrowly distributed in other cases.

Perceiving People

There is another way in which the cognitions of prospective and current members of existing groups may be influenced by the expectation of impending membership. When prospective members expect to enter a group, they may change their cognitions about various categories of people, including themselves, members of their future group, and members of other groups that are related (either negatively or positively) to their future group. And parallel changes may occur in the cognitions of current members.

Prospective Members

In regard to changes in cognitions about themselves, prospective members may come to believe that they possess the prototypical attributes that group members apply to themselves. If a typical group member is thought to be very athletic, for example, a prospective member may come to see himself or herself as more athletic. These distortions of one's characteristics in the direction of the prototypical group member are probably constrained by other information about oneself (e.g., "I never participate in sports"). Nevertheless, rather dramatic changes in self-perceptions may occur when people expect to join a group, particularly when the behavioral implications of group members' characteristics are vague or nonexistent.

In regard to changes in cognitions about the members of one's future group and the members of other groups, a number of hypotheses can be derived from research on the consequences of ingroup–outgroup categorization. It has been found, for example, that information about outgroup members is represented more simply than information about ingroup members, and that the outgroup is often (though not always) seen as more homogeneous than the in-group (e.g., Judd & Park, 1988; Linville, Fischer, & Salovey, 1989; Mullen & Hu, 1989; Park, Ryan, & Judd, 1992; Simon, 1992). In addition, people process infor-mation differently about ingroups and outgroups—for example, by perceiving il-lusory correlations that associate their ingroup with favorable behaviors (Schaller, 1991). And they also tend to recall less negative information about their ingroup than about an outgroup (Howard & Rothbart, 1980). Finally, peo-ple show a preference for information that indicates ingroup similarity and out-group dissimilarity to themselves (Wilder & Allen, 1978).

We would expect that prospective members' cognitions regarding their fu-ture group will mirror current members' cognitions regarding their ingroup. Similarly, we would expect that prospective members' cognitions regarding ene-my groups, which have hostile relations with their future group, will mirror cur-rent members' cognitions about their outgroup. Finally, it seems plausible that prospective members' cognitions regarding allied groups, which have friendly re-lations with their future group, will be similar to (but less extreme than) current members' cognitions regarding their ingroup. Thus, prospective members are likely to see their future group in more complex terms and as more heteroge-neous than allied groups, which in turn will be seen in more complex terms and as more heterogeneous than enemy groups (cf. Brown & Wootton-Millward, 1993). In addition, prospective members should process information about their future group in group-enhancing ways; this tendency should be weaker in the case of allied groups; and information about enemy groups should be processed in group-denigrating ways. Prospective members should also recall less negative information about their future group than about allied groups, which in turn should be remembered less negatively than enemy groups. Finally, prospective members should show a strong preference for information indicating that they are similar to their future group, a weaker preference for similarity to allied groups, and a preference for dissimilarity to enemy groups.

Several variables are likely to affect how anticipated group membership will affect prospective members' cognitions about people. One such variable is the degree to which prospective members expect that the role transition from non-member to member will necessitate major changes in how they must behave. The more profound the disjunction between current and anticipated role expec-tations, the more members' cognitions are likely to shift in the directions sug-gested above. A second variable is the probable rewardingness of group member-ship. The more rewarding group membership is expected to be, the more likely prospective members are to change their cognitions about their future group, al-lied groups, and enemy groups. Finally, a third variable is the imminence of the role transition from nonmember to member. The more imminent this transi-tion, the more likely prospective members are to change their cognitions about people.

So far, we have implicitly assumed that prospective members are "group-less" prior to joining an existing group, and therefore that any anticipatory cog-nitive changes they experience will focus on their future group and other groups related to it (as allies or enemies). In many cases, however, prospective members of one group are simultaneously planning to leave another group. When this occurs, prospective members' cognitions about their present (soon to be past) group and other groups related to it should also change. We might expect, for example, that prospective members will come to perceive the group they are leaving as lower in complexity and higher in homogeneity, and that they will be less likely to process information about it in group-enhancing ways.

Current Members

Of course, current members' cognitions may also be influenced by the anticipated entrance of prospective members. The expectation that new members will join the group may cause current members to alter their cognitions about various categories of people, including themselves, current members of their own and other groups, and the prospective members who will soon enter the group. The expected entrance of new members, and the assumption that these people will need enculturation, may well increase the salience of the group culture for current members. This increased cultural salience, in turn, may cause current members to focus on differences between their ingroup and various outgroups.

This heightened ingroup–outgroup categorization may have several cognitive consequences. For example, current members may become more likely to see themselves as possessing the prototypical attributes of group members. In addition, current members may become more susceptible to various cognitive biases elicited by ingroup–outgroup categorization. For example, they may show an increased tendency to represent the outgroup in simpler terms than the ingroup and to perceive the outgroup as more homogeneous than the ingroup. Finally, current members may come to see prospective members as possessing the prototypical characteristics of group members. These tendencies are likely to be affected by the same variables that influence prospective members' cognitive changes about people, including current members' assumptions about how much a prospective member's role expectations will shift after he or she joins the group, how rewarding the new member's presence will be for the group, and how soon the prospective member will enter the group.

PREPARING FOR ENTRY INTO A NEW GROUP

In the preceding section, we have argued that the imminent entry of new members into an existing group can affect the cognitions of both prospective and current members. But cognitive changes can also be stimulated by anticipated membership in a new group that has not existed before, particularly when prospective members expect that they will encounter disagreement from others and will have to defend their opinions. An example might be a person who expects to participate in a discussion on a controversial topic with several strangers who have not interacted before (e.g., a jury member prior to deliberation). In such cases, the person may seek to prepare for the discussion by engaging in various cognitive activities. Some of these may focus on the persons with whom one expects to interact, whereas others may focus on the expected discussion topic. For example, the prospective member may develop particular impressions about interaction partners that are presumed to facilitate interaction with them, or may learn new information supporting his or her position.

The literature reviewed at the beginning of the preceding section indicates that entry into an exisiting group is often a stressful experience for newcomers, and we may assume that similar stress is experienced by people who enter a new group in which they and others are charter members. But do prospective members of such groups anticipate this stress, and do they prepare for it prior to entry? Several lines of work suggest that anticipated interaction with others can indeed be anxiety-provoking. For example, Hoyle, Pinkley, and Insko (1989) found that subjects who expect to interact with a group anticipate a more abrasive encounter than do subjects who expect to interact with an individual. In addition, there is evidence that subjects who expect a competitive interaction with outgroup members are more anxious than those who expect a cooperative interaction (Wilder & Shapiro, 1989), and that subjects who expect to negotiate with an outgroup member have lower outcome expectancies than those who expect to negotiate with an ingroup member (Thompson, 1993). It has also been found that subjects who believe that their chances of winning a monetary prize are contingent on how much attitude change they can produce in a partner exhibit higher blood pressure than do subjects who do not perceive such a contingency (Smith, Allred, Morrison, & Carlson, 1989). Finally, data indicate that subjects who believe there is a 100% probability that they will have an aversive interaction with another person (listening to criticism while silently generating rebuttals) feel more depressive affect, anxiety, and hostility than do subjects who think there is a lower probability of such an interaction (Andersen & Lyon, 1987).

Given that anticipated interaction can induce stress, it should not be surprising if, prior to the interaction, people make some effort to increase the future rewards and decrease the future costs of their relationship. Several lines of work suggest that this kind of anticipatory activity does indeed occur. In some cases, people can influence the identity of their interaction partners, and, when this kind of control is available, careful selection of partners can substantially influence the rewardingness of future interaction. For example, Swann and his colleagues have found a self-verification effect in partner choice, such that people with positive self-views tend to select partners who perceive them favorably, and people with negative self-views tend to select partners who perceive them unfavorably (e.g., Hixon & Swann, 1993; Swann, Stein-Seroussi, & Giesler, 1992). In other cases, the identity of the interaction partner is fixed, but people can nevertheless influence the nature of the interaction they will have with the partner. For example, Clark (1986) found that subjects' desire for a communal versus exchange relationship with another person varied as a function of the partner's characteristics (see also Glick, 1985). And Clark and Taraban (1991) and Kaplan,

Schaefer, and Zinkiewicz (1994) found that subjects' preferred topic for an up-coming discussion varied as a function of the kind of interaction they expected to have. Several other kinds of responses to anticipated interaction have also been found, including self-disclosure (Shaffer & Ogden, 1986; Taylor & Belgrave, 1986) and strategic self-presentation (Kowalski & Leary, 1990; Whitehead & Smith, 1990); evaluations of the interaction partner (Morf & Rhodewalt, 1993); sensitivity to a partner's need for help (Clark, Mills, & Powell, 1986) and will-ingness to extend help (Schoenrade, Batson, Brandt, & Loud, 1986); preferences regarding who should play a leadership role (Fleischer & Chertkoff, 1986); social comparison choices (Smith & Insko, 1987); selection of task performance goals (Hinsz, 1992); contributions to a public good (Yamagishi & Sato, 1986); and pre-ferred rules for allocating a scarce resource (Azzi, 1993).

As this list suggests, anticipation of future interaction can be a powerful motivator of perception and behavior prior to the interaction. In the following subsections, we examine two major types of cognitive activity stimulated by an-ticipated interaction that are particularly relevant to the case in which a person expects to encounter disagreement from fellow group members. The first deals with the persons with whom one expects to interact; the second deals with the topic one expects to discuss.

Cognitions about Future Interaction Partners

An early study investigating cognitions about future interaction partners was conducted by Berscheid, Graziano, Monson, and Dermer (1976). They varied perceivers' outcome dependency on opposite-sex target persons by leading sub-jects to expect that they would date one person and would not date two others. Subjects then had an opportunity to watch a videotape of the three people. Berscheid et al. found that perceivers paid more attention to prospective dates, remembered more information about them, evaluated them more extremely and confidently, and liked them better than prospective nondates.

In recent years, there has been an explosion of interest in goal-driven social cognition, with particular emphasis on how outcome dependency affects atten-tion to and processing of information about other people. Numerous studies have investigated these issues (e.g., Devine, Sedikides, & Fuhrman, 1989; Erber & Fiske, 1984; Fiske & Von Hendy, 1992; Flink & Park, 1991; Forgas, 1991; Harkness, DeBono, & Borgida, 1985; Klein & Kunda, 1992; Neuberg & Fiske, 1987; Omoto & Borgida, 1988; Osborne & Gilbert, 1992; Pendry & Macrae, 1994; Ruscher & Fiske, 1990; Ruscher, Fiske, Miki, & Van Manen, 1991; Sedikides, Devine, & Fuhrman, 1991; Snyder, Berscheid, & Glick, 1985).

In seeking to interpret much of this literature, Fiske and Neuberg (1990) have argued that outcome dependency can facilitate either individuating or cate-gory-based impression formation, depending on the specific interdependence structure that is activated. They have suggested that short-term, task-oriented outcome dependency on targets (e.g., anticipated cooperation or competition) causes perceivers to desire accurate impressions, which in turn leads to individuating impression formation. In contrast, committed outcome dependency on targets (e.g., anticipated marriage) causes perceivers to desire specific kinds of impressions (e.g., the partner is wonderful), which in turn leads to category-based impression formation. Clearly, both kinds of outcome dependency are possible when prospective members anticipate joining a group. For the short-term groups that concern us here, however, it seems likely that prospective members' desire for accurate impressions will be stronger than their desire for specific kinds of impressions, which in turn will cause them to develop individuated impressions of their anticipated discussion partners.

Cognitions about the Discussion Topic

Several lines of work indicate that people who expect to send and/or receive information on a topic often engage in anticipatory cognitive activity about the topic prior to the exchange. Both the amount and type of this activity are likely to vary as a function of the kind of interaction that is expected, the presumed characteristics of the interaction partner(s), and the subject's goals. For example, a person may expect only to receive information, only to transmit information, or both to receive and to transmit information. In addition, a person may know nothing about the interaction partner's position or may believe that the partner either agrees or disagrees with his or her position. Finally, a person may be motivated to ensure that his or her position prevails, or that the best possible position wins no matter who initially advocated it.

One source of information about anticipatory cognitive activity derives from work on "cognitive tuning." Initial research on this topic was done by Zajonc (1960), who discovered that people who expect to transmit information to others develop more organized and polarized cognitive structures concerning the information than do those who expect to receive information from others. Since Zajonc's early work, cognitive tuning has continued to elicit research attention (e.g., Boninger, Brannon, & Brock, 1993; Boninger, Brock, Cook, Gruder, & Romer, 1990; Brock & Fromkin, 1968; Boudreau, Baron, & Oliver, 1992; Cohen, 1961; Harkins, Harvey, Keithly, & Rich, 1977; Harvey, Harkins, & Kagehiro, 1976; Hennigan, Cook, & Gruder, 1982; Higgins et al., 1982; Hoffman, Mischel, & Baer, 1984; Holt & Watts, 1969; Inman, Reichl, & Baron, 1993; Lassiter, Pezzo, & Apple, 1993; Leventhal, 1962; Mazis, 1973; Powell, 1974; Watts & Holt, 1970). In summarizing most of this literature, Guerin and Innes (1989) state that (1) a transmitter set causes people to form a more unified and complex impression, whereas a receiver set causes people to form a more loose and simply structured impression; (2) receivers suspend judgment, whereas transmitters polarize their judgments; (3) transmitters' unified impressions lead to more attribution errors and more extreme trait attributions; (4) receivers are generally more receptive to additional information, whereas transmitters prefer to listen to supportive information and reject inconsistent information; and (5) transmitters are more likely to believe in the position they are summarizing. In seeking to explain the effects of cognitive tuning, Guerin and Innes emphasize the role of motivation, particularly transmitters' concerns about self-presentation.

The hypothesis that preparing to *transmit* information to others produces special kinds of cognitive activity has been tested in other contexts. For example, studies show that individuals who expect to present a persuasive message shift their position in the direction of the position they expect to advocate (Jellison & Mills, 1969) and remember information that is congruent with the position of their anticipated audience (Zimmerman & Bauer, 1956). In addition, research indicates that people learn material better when they expect to teach it to others (e.g., Annis, 1983; Bargh & Schul, 1980; Benware & Deci, 1984) and when they expect to be called on in class (Stahl & Clark, 1987). Moreover, the particular target audience for a communication (e.g., peers vs. teacher) can influence how well the communication is constructed (Cohen & Riel, 1989). Finally, several studies on the "next-in-line" effect show that people who anticipate a public performance show memory deficits for information available just prior to their performance (e.g., Bond, 1985; Bond & Omar, 1990; Bond, Pitre, & Van Leeuwen, 1991).

In seeking to clarify the cognitive consequences of preparing to transmit information, particular attention has been devoted to the role of accountability. A number of studies show that people who expect to justify their views to others engage in more careful information processing than do people who do not have this obligation (e.g., Chaiken, 1980; Davis, Stasser, Spitzer, & Holt, 1976; Kroon, Van Kreveld, & Rabbie, 1992; Kruglanski & Freund, 1983; Sanbonmatsu, Akimoto, & Biggs, 1993; Simonson & Nye, 1992; Weldon & Gargano, 1988). The consequences of this effortful processing are complex, however, as indicated by the work of Tetlock and his colleagues. On the positive side, accountability reduces the likelihood that perceivers will make the fundamental attribution error (Tetlock, 1985) or fall prey to primacy effects (Tetlock, 1983a) and increases the likelihood that they will form accurate and complex impressions (Tetlock & Kim, 1987). On the negative side, accountability magnifies the dilution effect (Tetlock & Boettger, 1989) and the status quo effect (Tetlock & Boettger, 1994). In a recent review, Tetlock (1992) suggested that people who feel accountable to others for their decisions respond in three ways: (1) by shifting their views toward those of the audience, (2) by pre-emptively criticizing their own position (which stimulates cognitive complexity), and (3) by generating justifications for this position. The first strategy is used when people know the views of the audience and are not committed to their own position; the second strategy is chosen when people do not know the views of the audience and are not committed to their own position; and the third strategy is adopted when people are accountable for a position to which they feel committed (Tetlock, 1983b; Tetlock, Skitka, & Boettger, 1989).

A good deal of research attention has also been devoted to the other side of the coin—namely, how preparing to *receive* information affects cognitive activity.

Much of this work has been done under the rubric of forewarning and anticipatory attitude change (see reviews by Cialdini & Petty, 1981, and McGuire, 1985). McGuire and Millman (1965) proposed an ego-defensive explanation of anticipatory change, in which the target of a persuasive communication saves face or self-esteem by shifting in the direction of the communication before it is delivered, thereby implying that he or she has agreed all along rather than capitulated. This explanation is consistent with evidence that (1) different kinds of shifts occur when the forewarning mentions the side to be advocated or does not do so (i.e., movement toward the advocated position in the first case, movement toward neutrality in the second case); (2) anticipatory change is greater when the attack is expected to be immediate rather than delayed; and (3) anticipatory change on uninvolving issues dissipates when the attack is canceled (see McGuire, 1985).

The psychological mechanisms underlying anticipatory attitude change have been clarified by the Elaboration Likelihood Model of persuasion (Petty & Cacioppo, 1986). According to this model, when motivation and/or ability to think about an issue are low, forewarning effects on attitude change should not depend on issue-relevant thinking. In contrast, when motivation and/or ability are high, forewarning effects should be mediated by such thinking. Consistent with the latter prediction, evidence indicates that expecting to receive a counterattitudinal message on a personally involving topic causes subjects to engage in anticipatory argumentation against the message (e.g., Brock, 1967; Petty & Cacioppo, 1977; see also Chen, Reardon, Rea, & Moore, 1992). In addition, data suggest that under certain circumstances, expecting to receive a counterattitudinal message can elicit anticipatory argumentation in favor of the message (McFarland, Ross, & Conway, 1984).

So far, our discussion has focused on cases in which a person expects either to transmit information or to receive information, but not both. There are many situations, however, in which an individual expects to participate in a discussion with disagreeing others, during which he or she will both transmit and receive information. Research indicates that such expected two-way communication can produce anticipatory attitude change (e.g., Cialdini, Levy, Herman, & Evenbeck, 1973; Sears, 1967; Snyder & Swann, 1976). In addition, there is evidence that expected discussion with a disagreeing other can also stimulate anticipatory argumentation (e.g., Cialdini, Levy, Herman, Kozlowski, & Petty, 1976; Fitzpatrick & Eagly, 1981; but see Kerr & Watts, 1982). Finally, research indicates that people who expect to join a group can be influenced by the opinions of group members (Kerr, MacCoun, Hansen, & Hymes, 1987), and that anticipation of future interaction with disagreeing others can increase conformity to the group's position (Lewis, Langan, & Hollander, 1972) and can affect the tendency to reciprocate prior support from the group (Hancock & Sorrentino, 1980).

Two recent studies from our laboratory have investigated how anticipated disagreement in a group affects prospective members' cognitive activity regarding the discussion topic. Although a good deal of theoretical and empirical attention has been devoted to the cognitive consequences of disagreement from majority and minority sources (e.g., Moscovici, 1980, 1985; Mugny & Perez, 1991; Nemeth, 1986), little attention has been given to how *anticipated interaction* with majorities and minorities of various sizes affects the cognitions of prospective group members.

In the first experiment, Levine and Russo (in press) assessed how subjects' attention to issue-relevant information was influenced by the relative number of people who would allegedly agree and disagree with their position during an upcoming discussion of a controversial issue. Subjects were brought together in six-person groups and led to believe that they either belonged to a minority (and were going to confront a majority) or belonged to a majority (and were going to confront a minority). In both cases, the minority faction ostensibly consisted of either one person or two persons. Thus, the subject was either in a one-person minority opposing a five-person majority, a two-person minority opposing a four-person majority, a four-person majority opposing a two-person minority, or a five-person majority opposing a one-person minority. In a fifth (control) condition, subjects expected a group discussion, but did not receive information about the distribution of opinions in their group. Prior to the discussion, subjects in all conditions were given an opportunity to read computer-stored arguments supporting and opposing their position.

Data revealed that within both minority and majority factions, the more people there were supposed to be in the opposing faction (and the fewer in the supporting faction), the more biased subjects were in reading information that supported (rather than opposed) the position they expected to defend. Levine and Russo (in press) interpreted these findings as indicating that within both majority and minority factions, the greater the relative size of the opposing faction, the more motivated subjects were to prepare for the discussion, which in turn caused them to spend a disproportionate amount of time reading information that strengthened (rather than weakened) the position they expected to defend. Subjects in the control condition were asked to estimate how many group members agreed with their position, and they guessed that they had support from three others. Thus, control subjects expected to be part of a four-person majority opposing a two-person minority. Consistent with this perception, reading times in the control condition were similar to those in the experimental condition where subjects were explicitly told that they were part of a four-person majority opposing a two-person minority.

In the second experiment (Zdaniuk & Levine, in press), a similar methodology was used, with two differences. First, the control condition was eliminated, and a new "even-split" condition was included to assess the impact of membership in a three-person faction opposed by another three-person faction. Second, and more important, a different dependent variable was used to assess anticipatory cognitive activity. Rather than measuring information acquisition (operationalized as reading time), Zdaniuk and Levine measured information generation (operationalized as thought listing). Subjects in six-person groups were led to believe that the other five people in the group disagreed with their position, that one person agreed and four people disagreed, that two people agreed and three disagreed, that three people agreed and two disagreed, or that four people agreed and one person disagreed. Prior to the anticipated discussion, subjects were asked to list their thoughts concerning the discussion topic. It was assumed that the thought-listing procedure might stimulate more attention to opposing arguments than occurred in Levine and Russo's (in press) study, where subjects had no reason to believe that learning the opposing arguments stored in their computers would be useful (because there was no evidence that these arguments would actually be used by members of the opposing faction; cf. Canon, 1964; Freedman, 1965; Frey, 1986).

Findings indicated that subjects in all conditions wrote more thoughts supporting their position than opposing their position. In addition, there was a positive linear relationship between subjects' faction size and their bias toward supporting thoughts. That is, the smaller the subjects' faction (and the larger the opposing faction), the less biased subjects were in thinking about their own position. There are at least three possible explanations for these results: Compared to subjects in larger factions, those in smaller factions may have been more motivated to think about opposing arguments because these arguments could help them rebut their opponents' statements, because the arguments could facilitate a shift toward their opponents' position, or because the subjects wanted to arrive at the best possible answer to the question under consideration.[3]

The results of these two experiments indicate that a prospective member's response to anticipated disagreement can be influenced by the relative number of people who support versus oppose the individual's position. Other variables may also be important. For example, anticipatory cognitive activity presumably will be greater if (1) disagreers are experts on the issue and highly committed to their position; (2) the issue has only one correct answer; (3) the anticipated interaction will involve face-to-face discussion (rather than, e.g., exchange of written messages); (4) the anticipated interaction will happen very soon; (5) the anticipated discussion will last for a long time; and (6) group members will be required to reach consensus (rather than, e.g., merely exchange opinions). These variables may be influential because they increase the amount of social and cognitive conflict that the prospective member expects. In general, greater conflict should elicit more anticipatory cognitive activity.

Also important may be the prospective member's judgment of the probability that he or she can convince others to change their positions. This judgment, in turn, is likely to influence the prospective member's dominant goal for the upcoming discussion (cf. Fitzpatrick & Eagly, 1981). When the subjective probability of convincing others is high, the prospective member will probably be motivated to win. Winning involves convincing others who disagree to change their position and convincing others who agree to maintain their position. Thus, winning involves gaining converts and retaining allies. When the subjective probability of convincing others is moderate, the prospective member will probably be motivated to avoid capitulation without winning. Avoiding capitulation without winning involves maintaining one's position without necessarily gaining converts or retaining allies. And when the subjective probability of convincing others is low, the prospective member will probably be motivated to capitulate in a face-saving manner. Capitulating in a face-saving manner involves changing one's position while conveying the impression that one is thoughtful and sincere.

Each of these motives is likely to produce a different form of anticipatory cognitive activity. When people desire to win, they will probably develop arguments that are biased toward their own position, and these arguments are likely to differ as a function of the perceived expertise of those they are trying to influence. Thus, it is probable that complex, two-sided arguments will be developed when opponents are experts, whereas simple, one-sided arguments will be developed when opponents are nonexperts (cf. Hovland, Lumsdaine, & Sheffield, 1949; Sorrentino, Bobocel, Gitta, Olson, & Hewitt, 1988). When people desire to avoid capitulation without winning, they will probably develop simple, one-sided arguments that are biased toward their own position, regardless of their opponents' expertise. The major utility of such arguments may reside in their self-persuasion rather than other-persuasion capability. That is, rather than being designed to convince others that one's position is valid, such arguments may be generated primarily to convince oneself of this fact. And when people desire to capitulate in a face-saving manner, they will probably develop arguments that are biased toward their opponents' position, so as to convince both themselves and others that they are moving for "rational" reasons rather than simply succumbing to social pressure (cf. McFarland et al., 1984; McGuire & Millman, 1965). It is likely that these arguments will be complex and two-sided when opponents are experts, and simple and one-sided when opponents are nonexperts.[4]

Although the two studies described above demonstrated that anticipated interaction with disagreers can stimulate cognitive activity, they did not address the relative impact of this form of disagreement versus other forms, such as mere awareness that others hold a different position or actual interaction with these people. Some variables may be expected to have similar effects on cognitive activity for all three types of disagreement. For example, in all cases cognitive activity will presumably be greater if the disagreers are experts on the issue and committed to their position, and if the issue is a matter of fact rather than opinion. Other variables may be expected to have similar effects on cognitive activity only in the anticipated-interaction and actual-interaction cases. For example, cognitive activity will presumably be greater if the anticipated or actual interaction involves face-to-face discussion (rather than exchange of written messages), if it lasts for a long (rather than a short) period of time, and if group members are required to reach consensus (rather than simply exchange opinions).

In general, disagreement is probably more likely to elicit cognitive activity in the cases of anticipated and actual interaction than in the case of mere awareness, because the social implications of disagreement are more salient in the former two cases. That is, in addition to the negative cognitive connotations of holding a divergent position (which occur in all three cases), various social motives are operative in the anticipated- and actual-interaction cases. As suggested above, these motives include (1) the desire to win, (2) the desire to avoid capitulation without winning, and (3) the desire to capitulate in a face-saving manner.

Of course, anticipating interaction with disagreeing others and actually interacting with these people is not the same thing. For example, in the anticipated-interaction case, the imminence of the discussion can vary, which may well affect anticipatory cognitive activity. In the actual-interaction case, group members exchange arguments with people who both disagree and agree with their position and observe their nonverbal responses. The arguments that members of each faction present, as well as paralinguistic aspects of their speech and their facial expressions, may all affect the amount and type of cognitive activity that occurs. For example, people may assume that opponents are most susceptible to the types of arguments that they themselves use, which in turn may elicit imitation of the style of these arguments.[5]

CONCLUSION

In this chapter, we have discussed several ways in which the expectation of impending group membership can influence the cognitions of prospective and current members. First, we have talked about the cognitive processes that occur during the investigation phase of group membership, when prospective members decide whether they want to join an existing group and current members decide whether they want this role transition to occur. Next, assuming that investigation leads both prospective and current members to desire the role transition of entry, we have discussed two ways in which impending group membership can affect members' cognitions—by altering their understanding of the group culture and by altering their perceptions of various categories of people (e.g., themselves, other group members). Finally, we have shifted our attention from existing groups to newly forming groups and examined how the cognitions of prospective members are affected by probable disagreement from others. It must be acknowledged that much of our analysis is speculative and in need of empirical test. We hope that the ideas we have presented will stimulate investigators to consider seriously the motivational and cognitive consequences of anticipated group membership and to conduct studies that will shed light on these processes.

Acknowledgment

Preparation of this chapter was supported by a grant from the Office of Educational Research and Improvement of the U.S. Department of Education to the Learning Research and Development Center at the University of Pittsburgh.

Notes

1. Although we focus on cases in which a prospective member's desire to join a group is reciprocated by current members, people sometimes want to join groups that do not want them as members. Group boundaries can thus vary in permeability, and this permeability may affect the anticipatory responses of prospective members (cf. Ellemers, Wilke, & Van Knippenberg, 1993; Lalonde & Silverman, 1994; Wright, Taylor, & Moghaddam, 1990).

2. Evidence indicates that high stress narrows one's focus of attention and thereby impedes the acquisition of new information (Easterbrook, 1959). In the present context, we assume that because prospective members desire to enter the group and look forward to this role transition, their stress level is moderate rather than high, which in turn produces openness to new information about the group.

3. Supporting thoughts were defined as those that agreed with the subject's position or disagreed with the alternative position; opposing thoughts were defined as those that agreed with the alternative position or disagreed with the subject's position. Although generation of opposing thoughts may reflect a desire to rebut the alternative position, the data do not provide direct evidence for this motive. For one thing, the category of opposing thoughts did not include arguments *against* the alternative position. For another thing, thoughts could not be coded in terms of specific rebuttals of the alternative position, because the subjects were not exposed to arguments for this position and hence could not "rebut" it.

4. We have highlighted three social motives that may operate in anticipated interaction situations—desire to win, desire to avoid capitulation without winning, and desire to capitulate in a face-saving manner. It is also possible, of course, that people in such situations will have nonsocial motives, such as the "need for nonspecific cognitive closure," defined as desire for definite knowledge on an issue (Kruglanski, 1989). This need may be expected to produce a range of anticipatory cognitive activities serving two primary functions: (1) seizing closure quickly, and (2) maintaining closure once it is achieved (see Kruglanski & Webster, in press).

5. Our discussion has emphasized preparation for anticipated disagreement. Of course, in many group settings (e.g., those used by Levine & Russo, in press, and Zdaniuk & Levine, in press), people expect to encounter disagreement from some people and agreement from others. In these cases, caution must be exercised in attributing anticipatory effects to either disagreement or agreement alone. Moreover, it is worth noting that just as people sometimes move away from disagreers in order to restore their threatened freedom (e.g., Brehm, 1966; Brehm & Mann, 1975), they may also move away from agreers (i.e., abandon their own position) in order to demonstrate their uniqueness (e.g., Codol, 1984; Lemaine, 1974; Snyder & Fromkin, 1980; Ziller, 1964). And anticipation of agreement may stimulate position shift and cognitive activity for additional reasons—for example, the belief that agreers hold their opinion for the "wrong" reason or have negative personal characteristics.

References

Abrams, D., & Hogg, M. A. (1990). Social identification, self-categorization and social influence. In W. Stroebe & M. Hewstone (Eds.), *European review of social psychology* (Vol. 1, pp. 195–228). Chichester, England: Wiley.

Alloy, L. B., & Ahrens, A. H. (1987). Depression and pessimism for the future: Biased use of statistically-relevant information in predictions for self and others. *Journal of Personality and Social Psychology, 52,* 366–378.

Andersen, S. M., & Lyon, J. E. (1987). Anticipating undesired outcomes: The role of outcome certainty in the onset of depressive affect. *Journal of Experimental Social Psychology, 23,* 428–443.

Anderson, R. C., & Pichert, J. W. (1978). Recall of previously unrecallable information following a shift in perspective. *Journal of Verbal Learning and Verbal Behavior, 17,* 1–12.

Annis, L. F. (1983). The processes and effects of peer tutoring. *Human Learning, 2,* 39-47.

Argote, L. (1989). Agreement about norms and work-unit effectiveness: Evidence from the field. *Basic and Applied Social Psychology, 10,* 131-140.

Arnold, D., & Greenberg, C. (1980). Deviate rejection within differentially manned groups. *Social Psychology Quarterly, 43,* 419-424.

Aronson, E., & Mills, J. (1959). The effect of severity of initiation on liking for a group. *Journal of Abnormal and Social Psychology, 59,* 177-181.

Azmitia, M., & Perlmutter, M. (1989). Social influences on children's cognition: State of the art and future directions. In H. W. Reese (Ed.), *Advances in child development and behavior* (Vol. 22, pp. 89-144). New York: Academic Press.

Azzi, A. E. (1993). Implicit and category-based allocations of decision-making power in majority-minority relations. *Journal of Experimental Social Psychology, 29,* 203-228.

Bargh, J. A., & Schul, Y. (1980). On the cognitive benefits of teaching. *Journal of Educational Psychology, 72,* 593-604.

Barker, R. G. (1968). *Ecological psychology.* Stanford, CA: Stanford University Press.

Baron, R. S. (1986). Distraction/conflict theory: Progress and problems. In L. Berkowitz (Ed.), *Advances in experimental social psychology* (Vol. 19, pp. 1-40). New York: Academic Press.

Benware, C. A., & Deci, E. L. (1984). Quality of learning with an active versus passive motivational set. *American Educational Research Journal, 21,* 755-765.

Berscheid, E., Graziano, W., Monson, T., & Dermer, M. (1976). Outcome dependency: Attention, attribution, and attraction. *Journal of Personality and Social Psychology, 34,* 978-989.

Billig, M. (1987). *Arguing and thinking.* Cambridge, England: Cambridge University Press.

Blau, P. M. (1960). A theory of social integration. *American Journal of Sociology, 65,* 545-556.

Bond, C. F., Jr. (1985). The next-in-line effect: Encoding or retrieval deficit? *Journal of Personality and Social Psychology, 48,* 853-862.

Bond, C. F., Jr., & Omar, A. S. (1990). Social anxiety, state dependence, and the next-in-line effect. *Journal of Experimental Social Psychology, 26,* 185-198.

Bond, C. F., Jr., Pitre, U., & Van Leeuwen, M. D. (1991). Encoding operations and the next-in-line effect. *Personality and Social Psychology Bulletin, 17,* 435-441.

Boninger, D. S., Brannon, L. A., & Brock, T. C. (1993). Effects of transmitter tuning on attitude change persistence: An examination of alternative explanations. *Psychological Science, 4,* 211-213.

Boninger, D. S., Brock, T. C., Cook, T. D., Gruder, C. L., & Romer, D. (1990). Discovery of reliable attitude change persistence resulting from a transmitter tuning set. *Psychological Science, 1,* 268-271.

Brehm, J. W. (1966). *A theory of psychological reactance.* New York: Academic Press.

Brehm, J. W., & Mann, M. (1975). Effects of importance of freedom and attraction to group members on influence produced by group pressure. *Journal of Personality and Social Psychology, 31,* 816-824.

Brinthaupt, T. M., Moreland, R. L., & Levine, J. M. (1991). Sources of optimism among prospective group members. *Personality and Social Psychology Bulletin, 17,* 36-43.

Brock, T. C. (1967). Communication discrepancy and intent to persuade as determinants of counterargument production. *Journal of Experimental Social Psychology, 3,* 296-309.

Brock, T. C., & Fromkin, H. L. (1968). Cognitive tuning set and behavioral receptivity to discrepant information. *Journal of Personality, 36,* 108-125.

Brown, R., & Wootton-Millward, L. (1993). Perceptions of group homogeneity during group formation and change. *Social Cognition, 11,* 126-149.

Boudreau, L. A., Baron, R. M., & Oliver, P. V. (1992). Effects of expected communication target expertise and timing of set on trait use in person description. *Personality and Social Psychology Bulletin, 18,* 447-451.

Canon, L. K. (1964). Self-confidence and selective exposure to information. In L. Festinger (Ed.), *Conflict, decision, and dissonance* (pp. 83-96). Stanford, CA: Stanford University Press.

Chaiken, S. (1980). Heuristic versus systematic information processing and the use of source versus message cues in persuasion. *Journal of Personality and Social Psychology, 39,* 752-766.

Chen, H. C., Reardon, R., Rea, C., & Moore, D. J. (1992). Forewarning of content and involvement: Consequences for persuasion and resistance to persuasion. *Journal of Experimental Social Psychology, 28,* 523-541.

Cialdini, R. B., Levy, A., Herman, C. P., & Evenbeck, S. (1973). Attitudinal politics: The strategy of moderation. *Journal of Personality and Social Psychology, 25,* 100-108.

Cialdini, R. B., Levy, A., Herman, C. P., Kozlowski, L. T., & Petty, R. E. (1976). Elastic shifts of opinion: Determinants of direction and durability. *Journal of Personality and Social Psychology, 34,* 663-672.

Cialdini, R. B., & Petty, R. E. (1981). Anticipatory opinion effects. In R. E. Petty, T. M. Ostrom, & T. C. Brock (Eds.), *Cognitive responses in persuasion* (pp. 217-235). Hillsdale, NJ: Erlbaum.

Cini, M. A., Moreland, R. L., & Levine, J. M. (1993). Group staffing levels and responses to prospective and new group members. *Journal of Personality and Social Psychology, 65,* 723-734.

Clark, H. H., & Brennan, S. E. (1991). Grounding in communication. In L. B. Resnick, J. M. Levine, & S. D. Teasley (Eds.), *Perspectives on socially shared cognition* (pp. 127-149). Washington, DC: American Psychological Association.

Clark, M. S. (1986). Evidence for the effectiveness of manipulations of communal and exchange relationships. *Personality and Social Psychology Bulletin, 12,* 414-425.

Clark, M. S., Mills, J., & Powell, M. C. (1986). Keeping track of needs in communal and exchange relationships. *Journal of Personality and Social Psychology, 51,* 333-338.

Clark, M. S., & Taraban, C. (1991). Reactions to and willingness to express emotion in communal and exchange relationships. *Journal of Experimental Social Psychology, 27,* 324-336.

Clark, N. K., & Stephenson, G. M. (1989). Group remembering. In P. B. Paulus (Ed.), *Psychology of group influence* (2nd ed., pp. 357-391). Hillsdale, NJ: Erlbaum.

Clark, R. P. (1983). Patterns in the lives of ETA members. *Terrorism: An International Journal, 6,* 423-454.

Codol, J. P. (1984). Social differentiation and non-differentiation. In H. Tajfel (Ed.), *European developments in social psychology: Vol. 1. The social dimension* (pp. 314-337). Cambridge, England: Cambridge University Press.

Cohen, A. R. (1961). Cognitive tuning as a factor affecting impression formation. *Journal of Personality, 29,* 235-245.

Cohen, M., & Riel, M. (1989). The effect of distant audiences on students' writing. *American Educational Research Journal, 26,* 143-159.

Davis, J. H., Stasser, G., Spitzer, C. E., & Holt, R. W. (1976). Changes in group members' decision preferences during discussion: An illustration with mock juries. *Journal of Personality and Social Psychology, 34,* 1177-1187.

Devine, P. G., Sedikides, C., & Fuhrman, R. W. (1989). Goals in social information processing: The case of anticipated interaction. *Journal of Personality and Social Psychology, 56,* 680-690.

Doise, W., & Mugny, G. (1984). *The social development of the intellect.* Oxford: Pergamon Press.

Easterbrook, J. A. (1959). The effect of emotion on the utilization and the organization of behavior. *Psychological Review, 66,* 183-201.

Ellemers, N., Wilke, H., & Van Knippenberg, A. (1993). Effects of the legitimacy of low group or individual status on individual and collective status-enhancement strategies. *Journal of Personality and Social Psychology, 64,* 766-778.

Erber, R., & Fiske, S. T. (1984). Outcome dependency and attention to inconsistent information. *Journal of Personality and Social Psychology, 47,* 709-726.

Fazio, R. H., & Zanna, M. P. (1981). Direct experience and attitude-behavior consistency. In L. Berkowitz (Ed.), *Advances in experimental social psychology* (Vol. 14, pp. 161-202). New York: Academic Press.

Festinger, L. (1954). A theory of social comparison processes. *Human Relations, 7,* 117–140.

Fiske, S. T., & Neuberg, S. L. (1990). A continuum of impression formation, from category-based to individuating processes: Influences of information and motivation on attention and interpretation. In M. P. Zanna (Ed.), *Advances in experimental social psychology* (Vol. 23, pp. 1–74). San Diego, CA: Academic Press.

Fiske, S. T., & Von Hendy, H. M. (1992). Personality feedback and situational norms can control stereotyping processes. *Journal of Personality and Social Psychology, 62,* 577–596.

Fitzpatrick, A. R., & Eagly, A. H. (1981). Anticipatory belief polarization as a function of the expertise of a discussion partner. *Personality and Social Psychology Bulletin, 7,* 636–642.

Fleischer, R. A., & Chertkoff, J. M. (1986). Effects of dominance and sex on leader selection in dyadic work groups. *Journal of Personality and Social Psychology, 50,* 94–99.

Flink, C., & Park, B. (1991). Increasing consensus in trait judgments through outcome dependency. *Journal of Experimental Social Psychology, 27,* 453–467.

Forgas, J. P. (1991). Affective influences on partner choice: Role of mood in social decision. *Journal of Personality and Social Psychology, 61,* 708–720.

Frable, D. E. S., Blackstone, T., & Scherbaum, C. (1990). Marginal and mindful: Deviants in social interactions. *Journal of Personality and Social Psychology, 59,* 140–149.

Freedman, J. L. (1965). Confidence, utility, and selective exposure: A partial replication. *Journal of Personality and Social Psychology, 2,* 778–780.

Frey, D. (1986). Recent research on selective exposure to information. In L. Berkowitz (Ed.), *Advances in experimental social psychology* (Vol. 19, pp. 41–80). New York: Academic Press.

Geen, R. G. (1989). Alternative conceptions of social facilitation. In P. B. Paulus (Ed.), *Psychology of group influence* (2nd ed., pp. 15–51). Hillsdale, NJ: Erlbaum.

Gerard, H. B., & Matthewson, G. C. (1966). The effects of severity of initiation on liking for a group: A replication. *Journal of Experimental Social Psychology, 2,* 278–287.

Glick, P. (1985). Orientations toward relationships: Choosing a situation in which to begin a relationship. *Journal of Experimental Social Psychology, 21,* 544–562.

Gray, B., Bougon, M. G., & Donnellon, A. (1985). Organizations as constructions and destructions of memory. *Journal of Management, 11,* 83–98.

Guerin, B., & Innes, J. M. (1989). Cognitive tuning sets: Anticipating the consequences of communication. *Current Psychology: Research and Reviews, 8,* 234–249.

Haas, J. (1972). Binging: Educational control among high steel iron workers. *American Behavioral Scientist, 16,* 27–34.

Hackman, J. R. (1987). The design of work teams. In J. Lorsch (Ed.), *Handbook of organizational behavior* (pp. 315–342). Englewood Cliffs, NJ: Prentice-Hall.

Hancock, R. D., & Sorrentino, R. M. (1980). The effects of expected future interaction and prior group support on the conformity process. *Journal of Experimental Social Psychology, 16,* 261–269.

Hanks, M. (1981). Youth, voluntary associations, and political socialization. *Social Forces, 60,* 211–223.

Hanks, M., & Eckland, B. (1978). Adult voluntary associations and adolescent socialization. *Sociological Quarterly, 19,* 481–490.

Harkins, S. G., Harvey, J. H., Keithly, L., & Rich, M. (1977). Cognitive tuning, encoding, and the attribution of causality. *Memory and Cognition, 5,* 561–565.

Harkins, S. G., & Petty, R. E. (1983). Social context effects in persuasion: The effects of multiple sources and multiple targets. In P. B. Paulus (Ed.), *Basic group processes* (pp. 149–175). New York: Springer-Verlag.

Harkness, A. R., DeBono, K. G., & Borgida, E. (1985). Personal involvement and strategies for making contingency judgments: A stake in the dating game makes a difference. *Journal of Personality and Social Psychology, 49,* 22–32.

Harvey, J. H., Harkins, S. G., & Kagehiro, D. K. (1976). Cognitive tuning and the attribution of causality. *Journal of Personality and Social Psychology, 34,* 708–715.

Hastie, R. (1986). Review essay: Experimental evidence on group accuracy. In G. Owen & B. Grofman (Eds.), *Information pooling and group decision making* (pp. 129-157). Greenwich, CT: JAI Press.

Hastie, R., & Pennington, N. (1991). Cognitive and social processes in decision making. In L. B. Resnick, J. M. Levine, & S. D. Teasley (Eds.), *Perspectives on socially shared cognition* (pp. 308-327). Washington, DC: American Psychological Association.

Hennigan, K. M., Cook, T. D., & Gruder, C. L. (1982). Cognitive tuning set, source credibility, and temporal persistence of attitude change. *Journal of Personality and Social Psychology, 42*, 412-425.

Higgins, E. T. (1981). The "communication game": Implications for social cognition and persuasion. In E. T. Higgins, C. P. Herman, & M. P. Zanna (Eds.), *The Ontario Symposium: Vol. 1. Social cognition* (pp. 343-392). Hillsdale, NJ: Erlbaum.

Higgins, E. T. (1992a). Social cognition as a social science: How social action creates meaning. In D. N. Ruble, P. R. Costanzo, & M. E. Oliveri (Eds.), *The social psychology of mental health: Basic mechanisms and applications* (pp. 241-278). New York: Guilford Press.

Higgins, E. T. (1992b). Achieving "shared reality" in the communication game: A social action that creates meaning. *Journal of Language and Social Psychology, 11*, 107-131.

Higgins, E. T., & King, G. (1981). Accessibility of social constructs: Information processing consequences of individual and contextual variability. In N. Cantor & J. Kihlstrom (Eds.), *Personality, cognition, and social interaction* (pp. 69-121). Hillsdale, NJ: Erlbaum.

Higgins, E. T., & McCann, C. D. (1984). Social encoding and subsequent attitudes, impressions, and memory: "Context-driven" and motivational aspects of processing. *Journal of Personality and Social Psychology, 47*, 26-39.

Higgins, E. T., McCann, C. D., & Fondacaro, R. (1982). The "communication game": Goal-directed encoding and cognitive consequences. *Social Cognition, 1*, 21-37.

Higgins, E. T., & Rholes, W. S. (1978). "Saying is believing": Effects of message modification on memory and liking for the person described. *Journal of Experimental Social Psychology, 14*, 363-378.

Hinsz, V. B. (1990). Cognitive and consensus processes in group recognition memory performance. *Journal of Personality and Social Psychology, 59*, 705-718.

Hinsz, V. B. (1992). Social influences on the goal choices of group members. *Journal of Applied Social Psychology, 22*, 1297-1317.

Hixon, J. G., & Swann, W. B., Jr. (1993). When does introspection bear fruit? Self-reflection, self-insight, and interpersonal choices. *Journal of Personality and Social Psychology, 64*, 35-43.

Hoffman, C., Mischel, W., & Baer, J. S. (1984). Language and person cognition: Effects of communicative set on trait attribution. *Journal of Personality and Social Psychology, 46*, 1029-1043.

Holt, L. E., & Watts, W. A. (1969). Salience of logical relationships among beliefs as a factor in persuasion. *Journal of Personality and Social Psychology, 11*, 193-203.

Hoorens, V. (1993). Self-enhancement and superiority biases in social comparison. In W. Stroebe & M. Hewstone (Eds.), *European review of social psychology* (Vol. 4, pp. 113-140). Chichester, England: Wiley.

Hovland, C. I., Lumsdaine, A. A., & Sheffield, F. D. (1949). *Experiments on mass communication*. Princeton, NJ: Princeton University Press.

Howard, J. H., & Rothbart, M. (1980). Social categorization and memory for in-group and out-group behavior. *Journal of Personality and Social Psychology, 38*, 301-310.

Hoyle, R. H., Pinkley, R. L., & Insko, C. A. (1989). Perceptions of social behavior: Evidence of differing expectations for interpersonal and intergroup interaction. *Personality and Social Psychology Bulletin, 15*, 365-376.

Inman, M. L., Reichl, A. J., & Baron, R. S. (1993). Do we tell less than we know or hear less than we are told? Exploring the teller-listener extremity effect. *Journal of Experimental Social Psychology, 29*, 528-550.

Isenberg, D. J. (1986). Group polarization: A critical review and meta-analysis. *Journal of Personality and Social Psychology, 50,* 1141-1151.

Janis, I. L. (1982). *Groupthink* (2nd ed.). Boston: Houghton Mifflin.

Jellison, J. M., & Mills, J. (1969). Effect of public commitment upon opinions. *Journal of Experimental Social Psychology, 5,* 340-346.

Judd, C. M., & Park, B. (1988). Out-group homogeneity: Judgments of variability at the individual and group levels. *Journal of Personality and Social Psychology, 54,* 778-788.

Kanter, R. M. (1968). Commitment and social organization: A study of commitment mechanisms in utopian communities. *American Sociological Review, 33,* 499-517.

Kaplan, M. F. (1987). The influencing process in group decision making. *Review of Personality and Social Psychology, 8,* 189-212.

Kaplan, M. F., Schaefer, E. G., & Zinkiewicz, L. (1994). Member preferences for discussion content in anticipated group decisions: Effects of type of issue and group interactive goal. *Basic and Applied Social Psychology, 15,* 489-508.

Kerr, N. L., MacCoun, R. J., Hansen, C. H., & Hymes, J. A. (1987). Gaining and losing social support: Momentum in decision-making groups. *Journal of Experimental Social Psychology, 23,* 119-145.

Kerr, N. L., & Watts, B. L. (1982). After division, before decision: Group faction size and pre-deliberation thinking. *Social Psychology Quarterly, 45,* 198-205.

Klein, W. M., & Kunda, Z. (1992). Motivated person perception: Constructing justifications for desired beliefs. *Journal of Experimental Social Psychology, 28,* 145-168.

Kowalski, R. M., & Leary, M. R. (1990). Strategic self-presentation and the avoidance of aversive events: Antecedents and consequences of self-enhancement and self-depreciation. *Journal of Experimental Social Psychology, 26,* 322-336.

Krauss, R. M., & Fussell, S. R. (1991). Constructing shared communicative environments. In L. B. Resnick, J. M. Levine, & S. D. Teasley (Eds.), *Perspectives on socially shared cognition* (pp. 172-200). Washington, DC: American Psychological Association.

Kroon, M. B. R., van Kreveld, D., & Rabbie, J. M. (1992). Group versus individual decision making: Effects of accountability and gender on groupthink. *Small Group Research, 23,* 427-458.

Kruglanski, A. W. (1989). *Lay epistemics and human knowledge: Cognitive and motivational bases.* New York: Plenum Press.

Kruglanski, A. W., & Freund, T. (1983). The freezing and unfreezing of lay-inferences: Effects on impressional primacy, ethnic stereotyping, and numerical anchoring. *Journal of Experimental Social Psychology, 19,* 448-468.

Kruglanski, A. W., & Webster, D. M. (in press). Motivated closing of the mind: "Seizing" and "freezing." *Psychological Review.*

Lalonde, R. N., & Silverman, R. A. (1994). Behavioral preferences in response to social injustice: The effects of group permeability and social identity salience. *Journal of Personality and Social Psychology, 66,* 78-85.

Lassiter, G. D., Pezzo, M. V., & Apple, K. J. (1993). The transmitter-persistence effect: A confounded discovery? *Psychological Science, 4,* 208-210.

Laughlin, P. R., & Ellis, A. L. (1986). Demonstrability and social combination processes on mathematical intellective tasks. *Journal of Experimental Social Psychology, 22,* 177-189.

Lawler, E. E., & Mohrman, S. A. (1987). Quality circles: After the honeymoon. *Organizational Dynamics, 15,* 42-54.

Lemaine, G. (1974). Social differentiation and social originality. *European Journal of Social Psychology, 4,* 17-52.

Leventhal, H. (1962). The effects of set and discrepancy on impression change. *Journal of Personality, 30,* 1-15.

Levine, J. M., & Moreland, R. L. (1991). Culture and socialization in work groups. In L. B. Resnick, J. M. Levine, & S. D. Teasley (Eds.), *Perspectives on socially shared cognition* (pp. 257-279). Washington, DC: American Psychological Association.

Levine, J. M., & Moreland, R. L. (1994). Group socialization: Theory and research. In W. Stroebe & M. Hewstone (Eds.), *European review of social psychology* (Vol. 5, pp. 305-336). Chichester, England: Wiley.

Levine, J. M., Resnick, L. B., & Higgins, E. T. (1993). Social foundations of cognition. *Annual Review of Psychology, 44,* 585-612.

Levine, J. M., & Russo, E. (in press). Impact of anticipated interaction on information acquisition. *Social Cognition.*

Lewis, S. A., Langan, C. J., & Hollander, E. P. (1972). Expectation of future interaction and the choice of less desirable alternatives in conformity. *Sociometry, 35,* 440-447.

Linville, P. W., Fischer, G. W., & Salovey, P. (1989). Perceived distributions of the characteristics of in-group and out-group members: Empirical evidence and a computer simulation. *Journal of Personality and Social Psychology, 57,* 165-188.

Louis, M. R. (1980). Surprise and sense making: What newcomers experience in entering unfamiliar organizational settings. *Administrative Science Quarterly, 25,* 226-251.

Mackie, D. M., Gastardo-Conaco, M. C., & Skelly, J. J. (1992). Knowledge of the advocated position and the processing of in-group and out-group persuasive messages. *Personality and Social Psychology Bulletin, 18,* 145-151.

Mackie, D. M., & Goethals, G. R. (1987). Individual and group goals. In C. Hendrick (Ed.), *Review of personality and social psychology: Vol. 8. Group processes* (pp. 144-166). Newbury Park, CA: Sage.

Matlin, M. W., & Zajonc, R. B. (1968). Social facilitation of word associations. *Journal of Personality and Social Psychology, 10,* 455-460.

Mazis, M. B. (1973). Cognitive tuning and receptivity to novel information. *Journal of Experimental Social Psychology, 9,* 307-319.

McCann, C. D., & Hancock, R. D. (1983). Self-monitoring in communicative interactions: Social-cognitive consequences of goal-directed message modification. *Journal of Experimental Social Psychology, 19,* 109-121.

McCann, C. D., Higgins, E. T., & Fondacaro, R. A. (1991). Primacy and recency in communication and self-persuasion: How successive audiences and multiple encodings influence subsequent evaluative judgments. *Social Cognition, 9,* 47-66.

McFarland, C., Ross, M., & Conway, M. (1984). Self-persuasion and self-presentation as mediators of anticipatory attitude change. *Journal of Personality and Social Psychology, 46,* 529-540.

McGuire, W. J. (1985). Attitudes and attitude change. In G. Lindzey & E. Aronson (Eds.), *Handbook of social psychology* (3rd ed., Vol. 2, pp. 233-346). New York: Random House.

McGuire, W. J., & Millman, S. (1965). Anticipatory belief lowering following forewarning of a persuasive attack. *Journal of Personality and Social Psychology, 2,* 471-479.

Mead, G. H. (1934). *Mind, self, and society.* Chicago: University of Chicago Press.

Merton, R. K. (1957). *Social theory and social structure* (rev. ed.). Glencoe, IL: Free Press.

Moreland, R. L. (1985). Social categorization and the assimilation of "new" group members. *Journal of Personality and Social Psychology, 48,* 1173-1190.

Moreland, R. L., & Levine, J. M. (1982). Socialization in small groups: Temporal changes in individual-group relations. In L. Berkowitz (Ed.), *Advances in experimental social psychology* (Vol. 15, pp. 137-192). New York: Academic Press.

Moreland, R. L., & Levine, J. M. (1984). Role transitions in small groups. In V. L. Allen & E. van de Vliert (Eds.), *Role transitions: Explorations and explanations* (pp. 181-195). New York: Plenum Press.

Moreland, R. L., & Levine, J. M. (1989). Newcomers and oldtimers in small groups. In P. B. Paulus (Ed.), *Psychology of group influence* (2nd ed., pp. 143-186). Hillsdale, NJ: Erlbaum.

Morf, C. C., & Rhodewalt, F. (1993). Narcissism and self-evaluation maintenance: Explorations in object relations. *Personality and Social Psychology Bulletin, 19,* 668-676.

Moscovici, S. (1980). Toward a theory of conversion behavior. In L. Berkowitz (Ed.), *Advances in experimental social psychology* (Vol. 13, pp. 209-239). New York: Academic Press.

Moscovici, S. (1985). Social influence and conformity. In G. Lindzey & E. Aronson

(Eds.), *Handbook of social psychology* (3rd ed., Vol. 2, pp. 347-412). New York: Random House.

Mugny, G., & Perez, J. A. (1991). *The social psychology of minority influence.* Cambridge, England: Cambridge University Press.

Mullen, B. (1991). Group composition, salience, and cognitive representations: The phenomenology of being in a group. *Journal of Experimental Social Psychology, 27,* 297-323.

Mullen, B., & Hu, L. (1989). Perceptions of ingroup and outgroup variability: A meta-analytic integration. *Basic and Applied Social Psychology, 10,* 233-252.

Nemeth, C. (1986). Differential contributions of majority and minority influence. *Psychological Review, 93,* 23-32.

Neuberg, S. L., & Fiske, S. T. (1987). Motivational influences on impression formation: Outcome dependency, accuracy-driven attention, and individuating processes. *Journal of Personality and Social Psychology, 53,* 431-444.

Nuwer, H. (1978, October). Dead souls of hell week. *Human Behavior,* pp. 53-56.

Omoto, A. M., & Borgida, E. (1988). Guess who might be coming to dinner? Personal involvement and racial stereotyping. *Journal of Experimental Social Psychology, 24,* 571-593.

Osborne, R. E., & Gilbert, D. T. (1992). The preoccupational hazards of social life. *Journal of Personality and Social Psychology, 62,* 219-228.

Park, B., Ryan, C. S., & Judd, C. M. (1992). Role of meaningful subgroups in explaining differences in perceived variability for in-groups and out-groups. *Journal of Personality and Social Psychology, 63,* 553-567.

Pascale, R. (1984, May 28). Fitting new employees into the company culture. *Fortune,* pp. 28-43.

Pavelchak, M. A., Moreland, R. L., & Levine, J. M. (1986). Effects of prior group memberships on subsequent reconnaissance activities. *Journal of Personality and Social Psychology, 50,* 56-66.

Pendry, L. F., & Macrae, C. N. (1994). Stereotypes and mental life: The case of the motivated but thwarted tactician. *Journal of Experimental Social Psychology, 30,* 303-325.

Perkins, D. V. (1982). Individual differences and task structure in the performance of a behavior setting: An experimental evaluation of Barker's manning theory. *American Journal of Community Psychology, 10,* 617-634.

Perret-Clermont, A.-N. (1980). *Social interaction and cognitive development in children.* London: Academic Press.

Petty, R. E., & Cacioppo, J. T. (1977). Forewarning, cognitive responding, and resistance to persuasion. *Journal of Personality and Social Psychology, 35,* 645-655.

Petty, R. E., & Cacioppo, J. T. (1986). *Communication and persuasion: Central and peripheral routes to attitude change.* New York: Springer-Verlag.

Petty, R. M., & Wicker, A. W. (1974). Degree of manning and degree of success of a group as determinants of members' subjective experiences and their acceptance of a new group member. *Psychological Documents, 4,* 1-22.

Powell, F. A. (1974). Cognitive tuning and differentiation of arguments in communication. *Human Communication Research, 1,* 53-61.

Resnick, L. B., Levine, J. M., & Teasley, S. D. (Eds.). (1991). *Perspectives on socially shared cognition.* Washington, DC: American Psychological Association.

Ruscher, J. B., & Fiske, S. T. (1990). Interpersonal competition can cause individuating processes. *Journal of Personality and Social Psychology, 58,* 832-843.

Ruscher, J. B., Fiske, S. T., Miki, H., & Van Manen, S. (1991). Individuating processes in competition: Interpersonal versus intergroup. *Personality and Social Psychology Bulletin, 17,* 595-605.

Sanbonmatsu, D. M., Akimoto, S. A., & Biggs, E. (1993). Overestimating causality: Attributional effects of confirmatory processing. *Journal of Personality and Social Psychology, 65,* 892-903.

Schaller, M. (1991). Social categorization and the formation of group stereotypes: Further evidence for biased information processing in the perception of group-behavior correlations. *European Journal of Social Psychology, 21,* 25–35.

Schein, E. H. (1964). How to break in the college graduate. *Harvard Business Review, 42,* 93–101.

Schoenrade, P. A., Batson, C. D., Brandt, J. R., & Loud, R. E., Jr. (1986). Attachment, accountability, and motivation to benefit another not in distress. *Journal of Personality and Social Psychology, 51,* 557–563.

Schoggen, P. (1989). *Behavior settings: A revision and extension of Roger G. Barker's ecological psychology.* Stanford, CA: Stanford University Press.

Schopler, J., & Bateson, N. (1962). A dependence interpretation of the effects of a severe initiation. *Journal of Personality, 30,* 633–649.

Sears, D. O. (1967). Social anxiety, opinion structure, and opinion change. *Journal of Personality and Social Psychology, 7,* 142–151.

Sedikides, C., Devine, P. G., & Fuhrman, R. W. (1991). Social perception in multitarget settings: Effects of motivated encoding strategies. *Personality and Social Psychology Bulletin, 17,* 625–632.

Shaffer, D. R., & Ogden, J. K. (1986). On sex differences in self-disclosure during the acquaintance process: The role of anticipated future interaction. *Journal of Personality and Social Psychology, 51,* 92–101.

Sherif, M. (1935). A study of some social factors in perception. *Archives of Psychology,* No. 187.

Siegel, A. E., & Siegel, S. (1957). Reference groups, membership groups, and attitude change. *Journal of Abnormal Social Psychology, 55,* 360–364.

Simon, B. (1992). The perception of in-group and out-group homogeneity: Reintroducing the intergroup context. In W. Stroebe & M. Hewstone (Eds.), *European review of social psychology* (Vol. 3, pp. 1–30). Chichester, England: Wiley.

Simonson, I., & Nye, P. (1992). The effect of accountability on susceptibility to decision errors. *Organizational Behavior and Human Decision Processes, 51,* 416–446.

Smith, R. H., & Insko, C. A. (1987). Social comparison choice during ability evaluation: The effects of comparison publicity, performance feedback, and self-esteem. *Personality and Social Psychology Bulletin, 13,* 111–122.

Smith, T. W., Allred, K. D., Morrison, C. A., & Carlson, S. D. (1989). Cardiovascular reactivity and interpersonal influence: Active coping in a social context. *Journal of Personality and Social Psychology, 56,* 209–218.

Snyder, C. R., & Fromkin, H. L. (1980). *Uniqueness: The human pursuit of difference.* New York: Plenum Press.

Snyder, M. (1992). Motivational foundations of behavioral confirmation. In M. P. Zanna (Ed.), *Advances in experimental social psychology* (Vol. 25, pp. 67–114). San Diego, CA: Academic Press.

Snyder, M., Berscheid, E., & Glick, P. (1985). Focusing on the exterior and the interior: Two investigations of the initiation of personal relationships. *Journal of Personality and Social Psychology, 48,* 1427–1439.

Snyder, M., & Swann, W. B., Jr. (1976). When actions reflect attitudes: The politics of impression management. *Journal of Personality and Social Psychology, 34,* 1034–1042.

Sorrentino, R. M. (1973). An extension of theory of achievement motivation to the study of emergent leadership. *Journal of Personality and Social Psychology, 26,* 356–368.

Sorrentino, R. M., Bobocel, D. R., Gitta, M. Z., Olson, J. M., & Hewitt, E. C. (1988). Uncertainty orientation and persuasion: Individual differences in the effects of personal relevance on social judgments. *Journal of Personality and Social Psychology, 55,* 357–371.

Sorrentino, R. M., & Field, N. (1986). Emergent leadership over time: The functional value of positive motivation. *Journal of Personality and Social Psychology, 50,* 1091–1099.

Stahl, S. A., & Clark, C. H. (1987). The effects of participatory expectations in classroom discussion on the learning of science vocabulary. *American Educational Research Journal, 24,* 541–555.

Stasser, G., & Davis, J. H. (1981). Group decision making and social influence: A social inter-action sequence model. *Psychological Review, 88,* 523-551.

Stasser, G., Kerr, N. L., & Davis, J. H. (1989). Influence processes and consensus models in decision-making groups. In P. B. Paulus (Ed.), *Psychology of group influence* (2nd ed., pp. 279-326). Hillsdale, NJ: Erlbaum.

Stasser, G., & Titus, W. (1985). Pooling of unshared information in group decision making: Biased information sampling during discussion. *Journal of Personality and Social Psychology, 48,* 1467-1478.

Swann, W. B., Jr., Stein-Seroussi, A., & Giesler, R. B. (1992). Why people self-verify. *Journal of Personality and Social Psychology, 62,* 392-401.

Taylor, D. A., & Belgrave, F. Z. (1986). The effects of perceived intimacy and valence on self-disclosure reciprocity. *Personality and Social Psychology Bulletin, 12,* 247-255.

Taylor, S. E., & Brown, J. D. (1988). Illusion and well-being: A social psychological perspective on mental health. *Psychological Bulletin, 103,* 193-210.

Taylor, S. E., & Fiske, S. T. (1978). Salience, attention, and attribution: Top of the head phenomena. In L. Berkowitz (Ed.), *Advances in experimental social psychology* (Vol. 11, pp. 249-288). New York: Academic Press.

Tetlock, P. E. (1983a). Accountability and perseverance of first impressions. *Social Psychology Quarterly, 46,* 285-292.

Tetlock, P. E. (1983b). Accountability and complexity of thought. *Journal of Personality and Social Psychology, 45,* 74-83.

Tetlock, P. E. (1985). Accountability: A social check on the fundamental attribution error. *Social Psychology Quarterly, 48,* 227-236.

Tetlock, P. E. (1992). The impact of accountability on judgment and choice: Toward a social contingency model. In M. P. Zanna (Ed.), *Advances in experimental social psychology* (Vol. 25, pp. 331-376). San Diego, CA: Academic Press.

Tetlock, P. E., & Boettger, R. (1989). Accountability: A social magnifier of the dilution effect. *Journal of Personality and Social Psychology, 57,* 388-398.

Tetlock, P. E., & Boettger, R. (1994). Accountability amplifies the status quo effect when change creates victims. *Journal of Behavioral Decision Making, 7,* 1-23.

Tetlock, P. E., & Kim, J. (1987). Accountability and judgment processes in a personality prediction task. *Journal of Personality and Social Psychology, 52,* 700-709.

Tetlock, P. E., Peterson, R. S., McGuire, C., Chang, S., & Feld, P. (1992). Assessing political group dynamics: A test of the groupthink model. *Journal of Personality and Social Psychology, 63,* 403-425.

Tetlock, P. E., Skitka, L., & Boettger, R. (1989). Social and cognitive strategies for coping with accountability: Conformity, complexity, and bolstering. *Journal of Personality and Social Psychology, 57,* 632-641.

Thompson, L. (1993). The impact of negotiation on intergroup relations. *Journal of Experimental Social Psychology, 29,* 304-325.

Turner, J. C., & Oakes, P. J. (1989). Self-categorization theory and social influence. In P. B. Paulus (Ed.), *Psychology of group influence* (2nd ed., pp. 233-275). Hillsdale, NJ: Erlbaum.

Van Knippenberg, D. V., & Wilke, H. (1992). Prototypicality of arguments and conformity to ingroup norms. *European Journal of Social Psychology, 22,* 121-155.

Van Maanen, J. (1977). Experiencing organization: Notes on the meanings of careers and socialization. In J. Van Maanen (Ed.), *Organizational careers: Some new perspectives* (pp. 15-45). New York: Wiley.

Van Maanen, J., & Schein, E. H. (1979). Toward a theory of organizational socialization. In B. Staw (Ed.), *Research in organizational behavior* (Vol. 1, pp. 209-264). Greenwich, CT: JAI Press.

Vaught, C., & Smith, D. L. (1980). Incorporation and mechanical solidarity in an underground coal mine. *Sociology of Work and Occupations, 7,* 159-187.

Vollrath, D. A., Sheppard, B. H., Hinsz, V. B., & Davis, J. H. (1989). Memory performance by decision-making groups and individuals. *Organizational Behavior and Human Decision Processes, 43,* 289–300.

Wanous, J. P. (1980). *Organizational entry: Recruitment, selection, and socialization of newcomers.* Reading, MA: Addison-Wesley.

Watts, W. A., & Holt, L. E. (1970). Logical relationships among beliefs and timing as factors in persuasion. *Journal of Personality and Social Psychology, 16,* 571–582.

Wegner, D. M. (1987). Transactive memory: A contemporary analysis of group mind. In B. Mullen & G. Goethals (Eds.), *Theories of group behavior* (pp. 185–208). New York: Springer-Verlag.

Weick, K. E., & Gilfillan, D. P. (1971). Fate of arbitrary traditions in a laboratory microculture. *Journal of Personality and Social Psychology, 17,* 179–191.

Weinstein, N. D. (1980). Unrealistic optimism about future life events. *Journal of Personality and Social Psychology, 39,* 806–820.

Weldon, E., & Gargano, G. M. (1988). Cognitive loafing: The effects of accountability and shared responsibility on cognitive effort. *Personality and Social Psychology Bulletin, 14,* 159–171.

Whitehead, G. I., III, & Smith, S. H. (1990). The use of consensus-raising excuses as a function of the manipulation of publicness: The role of expectations of future interaction. *Personality and Social Psychology Bulletin, 16,* 562–572.

Wicker, A. W. (1979). *An introduction to ecological psychology.* Monterey, CA: Brooks/Cole.

Wicker, A. W., Kirmeyer, S. L., Hanson, L., & Alexander, D. (1976). Effects of manning levels on subjective experiences, performance, and verbal interaction in groups. *Organizational Behavior and Human Performance, 17,* 251–274.

Wicker, A. W., & Mehler, A. (1971). Assimilation of new members in a large and a small church. *Journal of Applied Psychology, 55,* 151–156.

Wicklund, R. A., & Frey, D. (1980). Self-awareness theory: When the self makes a difference. In D. M. Wegner & R. R. Vallacher (Eds.), *The self in social psychology* (pp. 31–54). New York: Oxford University Press.

Wilder, D. A., & Allen, V. L. (1978). Group membership and preference for information about others. *Personality and Social Psychology Bulletin, 4,* 106–110.

Wilder, D. A., & Shapiro, P. N. (1989). Role of competition-induced anxiety in limiting the beneficial impact of positive behavior by an out-group member. *Journal of Personality and Social Psychology, 56,* 60–69.

Wilkins, A. L., & Ouchi, W. G. (1983). Efficient culture: Exploring the relationship between culture and organizational performance. *Administrative Science Quarterly, 28,* 468–481.

Wood, W., Lundgren, S., Ouellette, J. A., Busceme, S., & Blackstone, T. (1994). Minority influence: A meta-analytic review of social influence processes. *Psychological Bulletin, 115,* 323–345.

Wright, S. C., Taylor, D. M., & Moghaddam, F. M. (1990). Responding to membership in a disadvantaged group: From acceptance to collective protest. *Journal of Personality and Social Psychology, 58,* 994–1003.

Yamagishi, T., & Sato, K. (1986). Motivational basis of the public goods problem. *Journal of Personality and Social Psychology, 50,* 67–73.

Zajonc, R. B. (1960). The process of cognitive tuning in communication. *Journal of Abnormal and Social Psychology, 61,* 159–167.

Zander, A., & Cohen, A. R. (1955). Attributed social power and group acceptance: A classroom experimental demonstration. *Journal of Abnormal and Social Psychology, 51,* 490–492.

Zdaniuk, B., & Levine, J. M. (in press). Anticipated interaction and thought generation: The role of faction size. *British Journal of Social Psychology.*

Ziller, R. C. (1964). Individuation and socialization. *Human Relations, 17,* 341–360.

Ziller, R. C. (1965). Toward a theory of open and closed groups. *Psychological Bulletin, 64,* 164–182.

Ziller, R. C., & Behringer, R. D. (1960). Assimilation of the knowledgeable newcomer under conditions of group success and failure. *Journal of Abnormal and Social Psychology, 60,* 288-291.

Ziller, R. C., Behringer, R. D., & Goodchilds, J. D. (1960). The minority newcomer in open and closed groups. *Journal of Psychology, 50,* 75-84.

Ziller, R. C., Behringer, R. D., & Jansen, M. J. (1961). The newcomer in open and closed groups. *Journal of Applied Psychology, 45,* 55-58.

Zimmerman, C., & Bauer, R. A. (1956). The effect of an audience upon what is remembered. *Public Opinion Quarterly, 20,* 238-248.

Zukier, H., & Pepitone, A. (1984). Social roles and strategies in prediction: Some determinants of the use of base-rate information. *Journal of Personality and Social Psychology, 47,* 349-360.

CHAPTER 17

The Individual–Group Distinction in Assessments of Strategies to Reduce Prejudice and Discrimination
The Case of Affirmative Action

VICTORIA M. ESSES
CLIVE SELIGMAN
University of Western Ontario

Programs designed to reduce prejudice toward certain groups and to improve their status in society have often been based on the assumption that favorable outcomes for groups and for individual group members will coincide. That is, we often assume that whether we are successful at changing perceptions of specific individuals or of a group as a whole, both will benefit. For example, it is assumed that if we change perceptions of a sample of blacks, perceptions of blacks as a group will also be affected. Thus, when prejudice-reducing strategies are implemented and evaluated, the issue of whether groups or individual group members are the intended beneficiaries is often overlooked.

For example, one approach to reducing prejudice and discrimination is through intergroup contact. This has been attempted through programs such as forced busing of school children and legislated desegregation at work and play. The assumption underlying the presumed benefits of contact is that people will come to have favorable attitudes toward individual members of other groups and, by association, toward the groups as a whole (for a review of the psychology of intergroup contact, see Miller & Brewer, 1984). Another approach to reducing prejudice is through educational and mass media programs. For example, the declaration of February as "Black History Month" is a salient effort to remind Americans of the role that black people have played in U.S. history and in the growth of the nation. In this case, attempts are being made to improve perceptions of black people as a group, with the implicit hope that individual blacks will also benefit. These examples demonstrate that we often assume that perceptions of groups and of individual group members will coincide.

In contrast, both the social-psychological literature on prejudice and the more applied research on the effects of strategies to reduce prejudice and discrimination suggest that it may be important to distinguish between the individual level and the group level of analysis. This has important practical relevance, because our assessment of the value of social programs to reduce prejudice and discrimination may then differ as a function of whether we focus on the benefits and costs to individuals or to groups.

In this chapter, we begin by briefly discussing social-psychological theories of prejudice that describe the relation between perceptions of groups and of individual group members. These theories suggest that there are times when perceptions of groups and their individual members will be similar and times when they will not. This serves to highlight the importance of distinguishing between factors that may influence a group as a whole and those that may influence individual group members.

Next, we propose a framework for examining the effectiveness of strategies designed to improve intergroup relations. Our framework incorporates the individual–group distinction: It distinguishes between outcomes for specific individuals and those for a group as a whole. The model also differentiates outcomes according to their source—whether they originate from members of other groups or from members of the intended target group (i.e., intended beneficiaries). For example, one outcome of a program to reduce prejudice and discrimination might be more positive attitudes toward women (i.e., women as the target). A program might produce more positive attitudes toward women among men (members of other group as source) and/or more positive attitudes toward women among women themselves (members of target group as source).

We demonstrate the value of this model by applying it to a rather controversial social program, affirmative action. In particular, we fit the findings on the effects of affirmative action into the four cells of the proposed model. Not only does this demonstration point out the value of the model for organizing the outcomes of strategies to reduce prejudice and discrimination, but we suggest that it may highlight one reason why affirmative action and many other related programs elicit so much controversy. That is, we suggest that public discussions of the costs and benefits of such programs often flounder because the discussants are talking at cross-purposes, failing to distinguish between individual and group outcomes or to clarify sources of these outcomes. In addition, we discuss the implications of our proposed model for the successful implementation and evaluation of prejudice-reducing strategies.

THEORIES OF PREJUDICE

Reciprocal Relations between Perceptions of Groups and of Individual Group Members

It is indeed the case that perceptions of groups and of individual group members can affect each other. First, perceptions of groups can influence perceptions of and behavior toward group members. In fact, this is one of the main reasons why stereotypes and prejudice are considered to be major social problems and have received considerable research attention. Over the years, psychologists have predominantly been concerned with the effects of social categorization on responses to individual members of a group.

Within the framework of the cognitive approach to stereotyping and prejudice, perceptions of social categories have been described as schemas or expectancies that guide subsequent information processing (e.g., Hamilton & Trolier, 1986; Stephan, 1985; see also Olson, Roese, & Zanna, in press). In this context, it has been demonstrated that perceptions of social groups can influence attention to and encoding of the behavior of an individual group member. For example, stereotypes about a group set up expectations about the behavior of individuals. In addition, people tend to pay particular attention to expectancy-confirming behavior[1] and to interpret behavior as confirming their expectations, especially when it is objectively ambiguous. Thus, stereotypes about a group tend to lead to stereotype-consistent perceptions of individual group members (see Hamilton, Sherman, & Ruvolo, 1990, for a review).

It has also been demonstrated that self-fulfilling prophecies may occur, such that one's initial expectancies about a group may influence one's behavior when interacting with an individual from that group. In turn, this may elicit behavior from the individual that confirms the initial expectancies. As a result, the initial expectancies about the group are reinforced by the individual group member's behavior (for reviews of when self-fulfilling prophecies are likely to occur, see Jussim, 1986; Miller & Turnbull, 1986; Snyder, 1992).

People may also use their initial impressions of a group in forming causal attributions about the behavior of particular group members (Hewstone, 1990; Pettigrew, 1979). For example, successful achievement by a member of a disliked group may be attributed to good luck, an easy task, or exceptional effort, whereas failure by a member of the same group may be attributed to lack of ability (Hewstone, 1990).

Information about individual group members can also influence perceptions of a group as a whole. Perhaps the clearest example of this is the development of stereotypes of a group on the basis of interaction with or information about a few individual members. An interesting example of this process is the formation of stereotypes on the basis of the co-occurrence of distinctive individuals (e.g., members of visible minority groups) and distinctive behavior (e.g., infrequently observed behavior; Hamilton, 1981; see also Hamilton, Stroessner, & Mackie, 1993). It has been demonstrated that even if the proportional representation of minority and majority group members displaying the distinctive behavior is equal, an illusory correlation (i.e., false association) is likely to form between the minority group and the behavior. The observers will then overestimate the frequency with which minority group members perform the behavior in question, and will overestimate the strength of the association between the minority group and the behavior. More general evaluations of the group will be similarly affected (Hamilton, 1981). Given that socially undesirable behaviors are likely to be relatively infrequent and distinctive, the formation of illusory correlations between visible minority groups and undesirable behavior is especially unfortunate.

To summarize, there are two main paths to consistency. First, perceptions of groups can influence perceptions of individual group members by setting up expectancies that tend to be confirmed. Processes underlying this tendency to confirm expectations include selective attention to and interpretation of the behavior of the individual members of the group. Second, through such processes as the formation of illusory correlations, perceptions of individual group members can influence perceptions of the group as a whole.

When Perceptions of Groups and of Individual Group Members Will Not Necessarily Coincide

Of special relevance to the present chapter is an understanding of when perceptions of groups and of individual group members are unlikely to affect each other. This is, of course, the basis for suggesting that perceptions of groups and of individual group members will not necessarily coincide.

Category-based expectancies or stereotypes will not strongly influence perceptions of an individual group member when the perceiver is motivated to use individuating information and has sufficient attentional resources to do so (Brewer, 1988; Fiske & Neuberg, 1990). Brewer (1988) suggests that when a situation or characteristics of a target person engage self-involvement (i.e., have high personal relevance), a perceiver will be motivated to form an impression of the target on the basis of specific information presented about the target. Self-involvement may be engaged because of the target's relevance to the perceiver's goals (e.g., outcome interdependency; Erber & Fiske, 1984) or relevance to the perceiver's identity (e.g., similarity; Park & Rothbart, 1982). Similarly, Fiske and Neuberg (1990) suggest that individuating information is more likely to be used when the formation of an accurate impression of a target is important to a perceiver (see also Hilton & Darley, 1991). A perceiver may thus be especially motivated to pay attention to individuating information under such conditions as task-oriented outcome dependency (in a situation of either cooperation or competition; e.g., Neuberg & Fiske, 1987; Ruscher & Fiske, 1990) or accountability to a third party for the impression formed (e.g., Kruglanski & Freund, 1983).

It is also the case that, once formed, perceptions of a group tend to be relatively impervious to change, even when new disconfirming information is presented (e.g., Higgins & Bargh, 1987; Stephan, 1985). Thus, individual group members who disconfirm a stereotype may have little effect on perceptions of the group as a whole. Instead, they may be separated into a subtype and dismissed as unrepresentative of the group as a whole (Brewer, Dull, & Lui, 1981; Taylor, 1981; Weber & Crocker, 1983). For example, a man who stays at home to take care of his children may not affect a strongly held stereotype that men are the "breadwinners" in a family; instead, a new subcategory of "daddy-track" men may be formed. In this way, the disconfirming evidence does not generalize to the group as a whole, and the stereotype that men are breadwinners is maintained. It has been demonstrated that the subtyping of atypical group members is most likely to occur when disconfirming, stereotype-inconsistent behavior is concentrated in a relatively small number of individuals and when additional information about these individuals makes it possible to assume that they are not representative of the group in other ways (Hewstone, Johnston, & Aird, 1992; Johnston & Hewstone, 1992; Kunda & Oleson, 1995; Weber & Crocker, 1983).

It has also been suggested that individual group members who disconfirm a stereotype may, for that reason, not be considered prototypical members of that group (i.e., not be considered a good fit with the prototype), and thus will not be strongly associated in memory with the group label. Instead, these individuals will be more strongly associated with an alternative label. As a result, the initial group stereotype will not be altered (Rothbart & John, 1985). For example, professional blacks may not be as strongly associated with the category label "blacks" as with the category label "professionals." As a result, the stereotype of blacks as poor and unsuccessful will not be altered. Like subtyping, this recategorization is especially likely to occur when the individuals in question may be considered unrepresentative of the initial group (e.g., blacks) in other ways (Rothbart & Lewis, 1988).

In a similar vein, it has been suggested that causal attributions about individual group members serve to maintain initial perceptions of a group. In particular, positive behavior by a member of a disliked group is likely to be explained away rather than resulting in improved perceptions of the group in general (the "ultimate attribution error," Pettigrew, 1979; see Hewstone, 1990, for a review of relevant literature). Thus, expectancy-disconfirming positive behavior may be attributed to external factors such as (1) luck and special advantage or (2) a manipulable situational context. Alternatively, the positive behavior may be attributed to internal factors that are unique to the individual and not generalizable to the group, such as (1) the exceptional-case individual who proves the rule (possibly a subtype) or (2) high motivation and effort by that individual (Pettigrew, 1979). In any case, these attributions serve to protect perceptions of the group in general from change.

As a result of the processes that serve to maintain perceptions of groups, it is possible that attempts to improve intergroup relations may actually influence perceptions of individuals and of their group in opposite directions. For example, in an attempt to improve attitudes toward the individuals in a group who are initially viewed in a more favorable light, these individuals may be caused to be subtyped or recategorized. As a result, these individuals may be perceived more positively, but when these individuals are removed as regular group members, the remainder of the group may be perceived more negatively.

To summarize, perceptions of groups and of individual group members are not always mutually reinforcing. When sufficient motivation and attentional resources are available, perceivers will not apply their stereotypes of groups to individual members. In addition, once perceptions of a group are formed, experience with a few stereotype-disconfirming individuals is unlikely to have a major impact on these perceptions. As a result, perceptions of groups and of individual group members may come to differ radically. Having made the point that perceptions of groups and of individual group members need not affect each other or coincide, we next apply the individual–group distinction to our analysis of strategies to reduce prejudice and discrimination.

A MODEL FOR EXAMINING COSTS AND BENEFITS OF STRATEGIES TO REDUCE PREJUDICE AND DISCRIMINATION

In order to weigh the costs and benefits of strategies designed to reduce prejudice and discrimination, we propose a framework for organizing these outcomes. We suggest that, rather than attempting to consider all outcomes together, it is more useful to break them down into categories and then attempt to balance them accordingly. Based on the social-psychological theories and supporting research we have reviewed, an important distinction to make is that between outcomes for individual members of a target group and outcomes for the group as a whole. For example, affirmative action in hiring may improve the status of individual blacks, but if they are subtyped as "successful blacks," the group as a whole may not benefit. Similarly, affirmative action programs may elicit negative reactions, leading to the unfavorable perception of blacks in general as requiring special advantages in order to succeed. However, perceptions of individual blacks who have been hired under such programs will not necessarily be detrimentally affected if conditions such as outcome interdependency ensure that individuating information is attended to. Thus, in organizing costs and benefits of prejudice-reducing strategies, we suggest that it is necessary to distinguish between outcomes for individuals and those for a group as a whole. Outcomes may include changes in both attitudes and behavior toward individuals and groups.

A second important distinction to make is that between two different sources of outcomes. First, outcomes may derive from members of groups other than the potential beneficiaries. In fact, prejudice-reducing strategies are primarily aimed at these other groups who are considered to be the main problem, or source of prejudice. In addition, however, the source of the outcomes may be members of the target group in question. A successful program to reduce prejudice and discrimination also depends on favorable reactions from its intended beneficiaries. For example, in part because of affirmative action programs, women are now represented in management positions in greater numbers than they were in the past (Turner & Pratkanis, 1994b). One positive consequence or outcome of this may be that men are now more accepting of women in positions of authority. In this case, the source of the outcome is members of a group other than the intended beneficiaries. Another outcome, however, may be that successful women discount their achievements because they attribute them in part to the special treatment accorded them. Here, the source of the negative outcome is members of the target group itself.

It is logical to assume that outcomes originating from members of other groups and those originating from members of the target group will often affect each other. For example, women may be more likely to discount their achievements when they know that men are also doing so. However, the distinction between these sources of outcomes is necessary in order to pinpoint the specific causes of successful and unsuccessful programs.

As a result of this line of reasoning, we suggest a model composed of four cells in which outcomes of strategies to reduce prejudice and discrimination may be placed (see Figure 17.1). Individual members of a target group can experience costs and benefits originating from members of other groups (Cell A; e.g., men's perceptions that specific women are competent) and those originating from members of their own group, including themselves (Cell B; e.g., specific women's self-perceptions of competence). In addition, a target group as a whole may prosper or suffer because of reactions from members of other groups (Cell C; e.g., men's stereotypes of women's competence) and reactions from members of the target group itself (Cell D; e.g., women's stereotypes of their own group's competence). Whereas the individual-level outcomes may be considered impor-

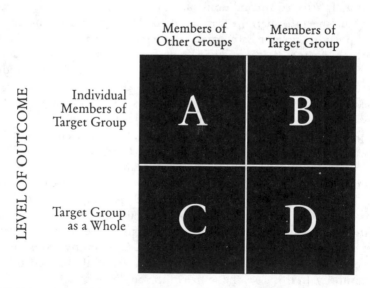

FIGURE 17.1   A model for assessing outcomes of strategies to reduce prejudice and discrimination toward target groups.

tant on a personal level, the group-level outcomes may be important in determining future social policies involving groups, which are likely to be based at least in part on perceptions of the groups as such.

APPLICATION OF THE MODEL TO AFFIRMATIVE ACTION

The Goal of Affirmative Action

"Affirmative action is just that: action; it is an employer doing something to remedy the effects of past discrimination against women, minority group members, persons with disabilities . . . " (Holloway, 1989, p. 18). On a superficial level, this seems like a straightforward and worthy goal. Yet the implementation of affirmative action programs has been controversial, to a large extent because there has been disagreement as to how society should go about remedying the effects of past and present prejudice and discrimination. Affirmative action generally involves the setting of goals and timetables for achieving representation of minority group members and women in jobs, in proportion to their availability in the relevant pool of potential candidates (e.g., Holloway, 1989). In working toward this goal, affirmative action may involve differential treatment in the recruitment, training, selection, or promotion of target group members (Crosby, 1994). There has been considerable disagreement as to whether this is the fairest and most effective way of obtaining justice.

At the crux of the disagreement is the legal and moral debate as to whether society should apply "compensatory" or "distributive" principles of justice to redress the problems of discrimination (Greene, 1989). A brief discussion of this issue is appropriate in the present context, because the application of compensatory versus distributive justice to affirmative action coincides with the distinction we have drawn between outcomes for individual members of a group and those for the group as a whole.

Compensatory justice is concerned with rectifying or compensating particular individuals for injustices that they have suffered. Thus, it can be seen as an individualistic view of justice, in which reparations are made to an *individual* victim of discrimination. Distributive justice is concerned with the just distribution of resources among members of society. An application at the group level is eliminating patterns of discrimination, which may be identified on the basis of statistical evidence of percentages of various groups receiving benefits and costs from society. In this case, justice is sought at the *group* level, through a fair distribution of group representation in various facets of society. Thus, compensatory justice is primarily concerned with outcomes for particular individual members of a minority group, whereas group-based distributive justice is primarily concerned with outcomes for the group as a whole (Greene, 1989). A similar distinction may be made between "microjustice" and "macrojustice" (Brickman, Folger, Goode, & Schul, 1981; for an application to affirmative action, see Clayton & Tangri, 1989).

Compensatory principles of justice have mainly been used to argue against the implementation of affirmative action, on the grounds that affirmative action does not necessarily benefit those individuals who have actually been victims of discrimination. In fact, it has been argued that the individual minority group members who are most likely to benefit from affirmative action are those who are least likely to be disadvantaged, because they have the education and skills necessary to qualify them for the jobs in question (Greene, 1989; Steele, 1990).

In contrast, group-based distributive principles of justice have been at the heart of arguments in favor of affirmative action. It is suggested that the distributive inequities among groups would not be as great as they currently are if discrimination against members of certain groups did not exist. Therefore, affirmative action is justified on the grounds that it helps to eliminate distributive inequities among groups (Greene, 1989).

A review of U.S. Supreme Court decisions on affirmative action suggests that Title VII, which prohibits discrimination in employment, has mainly been interpreted in terms of group-based distributive justice (Greene, 1989). Thus, in terms of the legislated purpose of affirmative action, the focus has been on a *group* level of analysis rather than an *individual* level. In other words, affirmative action has a group-based goal: It is directed at benefitting groups as a whole.

Research Findings Regarding Costs and Benefits to Groups and to Individual Group Members

As recent social-psychological volumes on affirmative action make clear (Blanchard & Crosby, 1989; Turner & Pratkanis, 1994c), in addition to issues of justice, questions have been raised as to whether affirmative action is effective in reducing prejudice and discrimination toward members of minority groups. In this section, we provide examples of research that has addressed the issue from the perspective of the model we have suggested. In other words, we describe what sort of research has been undertaken in each of the cells defined by the level and source of outcome dimensions of the proposed model.

Cell A: Level, Individual Members of Target Group; Source, Members of Other Groups

In Cell A, research has addressed the question of how individual members of the intended target groups have been affected by the responses of outgroup members.

Research on this issue has predominantly dealt with the question of whether members of other groups will discount the qualifications of individuals whose success can be at least partially attributed to the implementation of affirmative action programs (see also Pettigrew & Martin, 1987; Crosby & Clayton, 1990). It has been suggested that affirmative action may initiate application of the discounting principle (Kelly, 1972): Given that two possible causes of the success are possible (personal qualifications and group membership), each cause will be given less weight in determining the outcome (e.g., Garcia, Erskine, Hawn, & Casmay, 1981). Several studies have indeed demonstrated that outgroup members see target group members as less competent and less qualified to have achieved the positions they have attained (e.g., being admitted to graduate school, hired for a job, or promoted to a managerial position) when an affirmative action program is in place than when it is not (Garcia et al., 1981; Heilman, Block, & Lucas, 1992; Summers, 1991).

In all of these studies, affirmative action was not defined for subjects. However, it can be assumed that affirmative action was interpreted by these subjects in line with the common perception that affirmative action relies heavily on strict preferential selection of target group members—that is, selection based largely on the individuals' group membership (so-called "reverse discrimination"; Holloway, 1989; Taylor, 1994; Turner & Pratkanis, 1994b). This is not how affirmative action has typically been implemented (Clayton & Crosby, 1992; Taylor, 1994), perhaps to a large extent because it is generally illegal in the United States to implement affirmative action through quotas (i.e., the setting aside of a prescribed number of positions for target group members; Newman, 1989; Robinson, Allen, & Abraham, 1992). Nevertheless, it is perhaps not surprising that individuals who *believe* that this is how affirmative action has been implemented will tend to assume the relative incompetence of individuals hired through such programs.

Cell B: Level, Individual Members of Target Group; Source, Members of Target Group

Research that fits into Cell B of the model has primarily examined the self-perceptions of individuals who are the direct beneficiaries of affirmative action programs.

This research has addressed the frequent claim that affirmative action serves to undermine the self-esteem of the very individuals who are intended to benefit from the programs (e.g., Bloom, 1987; Steele, 1990). It has been suggested that individuals who succeed in the presence of affirmative action programs will discount their own qualifications in obtaining that success. Indeed, much of the initial experimental research seemed to support the assertion that affirmative action has adverse effects on beneficiaries in areas such as evaluations of own qualifications and performance (e.g., Nacoste, 1989; Heilman, Simon, & Repper, 1987), job satisfaction and commitment (e.g., Chacko, 1982), and evaluation apprehension (e.g., Nacoste & Lehman, 1987; see Turner & Pratkanis, 1994a, and Taylor, 1994, for reviews).

However, when we look more closely at this research, there is reason to question its validity. In particular, in many of the studies cited, affirmative action was specifically operationalized as set-aside preferential treatment for target group members (i.e., selection based mainly on membership in a target group).

For example, the affirmative action condition in Heilman et al. (1987) involved informing women that they were assigned a leadership role on the basis of their sex and regardless of their qualifications. Although, as mentioned previously, this tends to be the misperception frequently held by members of the general public, it is not a misperception held by a majority of blacks—a primary target of affirmative action in the United States (Taylor, 1994). Thus, a more valid operationalization of affirmative action, both from the point of view of how it is actually implemented and based on how it is perceived by blacks to be implemented, is selection based on *both* qualifications and group status. Under these experimental conditions, qualifications have not been found to be discounted, and individuals selected through affirmative action do not typically view themselves in negative terms (Arthur, Doverspike, & Fuentes, 1992; Major, Feinstein, & Crocker, 1994; Nacoste, 1985).

Consistent with these findings, in analyzing data from a U.S. national survey, Taylor (1994) found no adverse effects in such areas as job satisfaction, ambition, and life satisfaction for blacks and women who reported that their employers practiced affirmative action. In fact, the one significant finding indicated that blacks whose employers practiced affirmative action reported *more* job-related ambition than did blacks whose employers did not practice affirmative action. Similarly, Ponterotto, Martinez, and Hayden (1986) found that minority graduate students at a university practicing affirmative action in admissions generally held high academic self-efficacy and thought that they were somewhat more capable than most white students.

Cell C: Level, Target Group as a Whole; Source, Members of Other Groups

Research that fits into Cell C of the model examines how target groups as a whole have been affected by the responses of outgroup members. Two types of outcomes may fit in here: (1) changes in target group representation in valuable positions in society, and (2) attitudes of outgroup members toward the beneficiary groups.

In line with our earlier discussion of the purpose of affirmative action, changes in target group representation in various positions may best be considered a group outcome. In describing the purpose of affirmative action, we have noted above that affirmative action programs have primarily been upheld in the courts to obtain a group level of justice involving fair representation of group members in various positions in society. Thus, statistics on change in representation may be taken as an outcome for the group at a global level. In addition, the argument can be made that statistics on representation of group members in various positions may be interpreted as an indicator of how the group in general is faring. In terms of the source of this outcome, at a proximal level it may be best categorized as originating from members of other groups, because these individuals are more likely to have had the power to implement such changes. That is, women and minorities (target group members) probably provided the impetus for change in their representation in society, whereas men and majority group members in positions of authority actually implemented, at least initially, the changes that have occurred.

What do the statistics suggest about the success of affirmative action programs in improving representation of minority groups and women in relevant employment situations? The answer to this question may be addressed at two levels. First, at a broad level, the economic gap between employed whites and blacks and between men and women in the United States has decreased since 1970 (Crosby, 1994). This improvement in target group status may be partially attributable to affirmative action programs, but it may also be tied to more general changes in society (Heckman, 1986). Thus, in order to pinpoint the improvement directly attributable to affirmative action, it is also necessary to examine the effects of specific programs.

Research focusing on specific affirmative action programs suggests that affirmative action has been reasonably successful in increasing target group representation in employment (Huckle, 1983; Leonard, 1985; Taylor, 1989). For example, Taylor (1989) compared employment of minorities and women by federal contractor establishments and noncontractor establishments for the period 1974 to 1980. The federal contractors were subject to affirmative action requirements, whereas the noncontractors were not. Results revealed that the federal contractors displayed a greater rise in employment of minorities and women than did the noncontractors. In addition, the federal contractors showed a greater shift in distribution of minorities and women to higher-level positions than did the noncontractors.

In terms of attitudes toward beneficiary groups, has affirmative action served to enhance or worsen attitudes held by outgroup members toward minorities and women? Much of the speculation and relevant research on this issue has focused on potential effects on attitudes toward blacks.

In particular, it has been suggested that the presence of affirmative action programs confirms some whites' perception that blacks are inferior to whites and require assistance to succeed (Steele, 1990). Relevant research has dealt with this issue only indirectly by examining the relation between prejudice toward blacks and attitudes expressed about affirmative action for blacks. Indeed, it has been found that policy- or justice-focused explanations do not completely account for opposition to affirmative action (Murrell, Dietz-Uhler, Dovidio, Gaertner, & Drout, 1994). Rather, prejudice toward blacks also predicts opposition to affirmative action for blacks (e.g., Jacobson, 1985; Kinder & Sears, 1981; Kluegel & Smith, 1983). Similarly, in a survey of white undergraduates, it was found that affirmative action programs for blacks were opposed more than were similar programs for physically handicapped and elderly people, especially when no explicit justifications for the program were provided (Murrell et al., 1994).

One explanation for this finding is provided by the theory of "aversive racism" (Dovidio, Mann, & Gaertner, 1989). In particular, the theory suggests that many whites feel superior to blacks but also believe in egalitarian values. Thus, they are unlikely to discriminate against blacks unless it is possible to rationalize this negative response on the basis of a factor other than race. Affirmative action provides such an opportunity to rationalize a negative response to blacks, because principles of justice and the "competence issue" with respect to selection procedures can be called upon to justify opposition to affirmative action programs without seeming to be prejudiced (Dovidio et al., 1989). Thus, affirmative action may provide an opportunity for many whites to express negative attitudes toward blacks. It may also confirm and perhaps strengthen perceptions already held of blacks as inferior to whites and as requiring outside assistance to succeed. Indeed, Eberhardt and Fiske (1994) suggest that many whites may view affirmative action for blacks as help and perceive blacks as requiring this help, because these perceptions fit with their stereotypes of blacks as lazy and incompetent.[2]

Cell D: Level, Target Group as a Whole; Source, Members of Target Group

In Cell D, research addresses the question of how target groups as a whole have been affected by the reactions to affirmative action by members of these same groups. In particular, the most obvious question is whether affirmative action has influenced the attitudes held by target group members toward their own groups (i.e., ingroup esteem). Attitudes held by target group members toward their groups may clearly differ from their individual self-perceptions, discussed previously (Cell B). For example, a successful woman may believe that she clearly deserves her success, but that other women do not (the "Queen Bee" phenomenon).

A commonly expressed view is that affirmative action programs may be seen as trying "to compensate for inadequacies in people" (Crosby, 1994, p. 32), and thus may encourage target group members to suspect the inferiority of their own group (e.g., Steele, 1990). Thus, for example, in colleges and universities practicing affirmative action in admissions, black students may come to suspect that their group must be intellectually less deserving to warrant such treatment, and these students may fear personally confirming this stereotype (Steele, 1992).

The suspicion of inferiority may be especially likely to exist among group members when affirmative action is seen as remedial treatment for the group, rather than as a means to counteract prejudice and discrimination (Steele, 1992). In support of this suggestion, Barnes Nacoste (1994) found that, in estimating the grade point averages of white and black students generally admitted to colleges and universities with affirmative action policies, the responses of black students were related to their perceptions of whether affirmative action procedures were necessary to balance out the effects of racial prejudice. In particular, black students who believed that there were not enough affirmative action procedures to compensate for discrimination (i.e., who perceived undercompensation), and who also believed that affirmative action was acceptable, indicated a discrepancy in group qualifications favoring blacks: They estimated higher grade point averages for blacks than for whites entering the colleges and universities. However, black students who believed that there were more affirmative action procedures than were necessary to compensate for discrimination (i.e., who perceived over-compensation) indicated a discrepancy in group qualifications favoring whites: They estimated higher grade point averages for whites than for blacks entering the institutions. Thus, affirmative action may be most likely to induce a suspicion of inferiority among group members when they see it as overcompensating for effects of prejudice and discrimination. In this regard, it is interesting to note that, on average, the black students in the Barnes Nacoste (1994) study perceived affirmative action as slightly undercompensating for discrimination.

Also relevant to the present discussion is a measure of black ingroup esteem included in the U.S. national survey discussed earlier for Cell B (Taylor, 1994). In particular, this measure assessed differences between ratings of blacks as a group and whites as a group on several dimensions. The measure revealed no differences in ingroup esteem between blacks whose employers practiced affirmative action and those whose employers did not (Taylor, 1994). Thus, these results provide no indication that affirmative action programs induce a suspicion of group inferiority among target group members for whom affirmative action should be especially salient (see Barnes Nacoste, 1994, and Nacoste, 1994, for discussions of activation of policy schemas for affirmative action).

Summary of Research on Costs and Benefits of Affirmative Action

As our review of the literature indicates, much of the social-psychological research on affirmative action has focused on outcomes for *individual* members of target groups. In particular, much of this work has looked for evidence of discounting in assessments of the qualifications and abilities of affirmative action beneficiaries.

When the source of these assessments is outgroup members, there is considerable evidence to suggest that discounting indeed occurs. Outgroup members are likely to misperceive that affirmative action beneficiaries have succeeded mainly because of their group membership, and thus assume that they are not very competent or qualified. Similarly, in studies in which affirmative action has been defined in line with this misperception (i.e., individuals are told that they have been selected because of their group membership alone), beneficiaries themselves discount their own qualifications and competence. However, when affirmative action is more appropriately defined as selection based on both qualifications and group membership, and when actual beneficiaries of affirmative action are surveyed, no adverse effects on self-perceptions are evident. Thus, at the individual level, the costs of affirmative action seem to derive predominantly from outgroup members.

At the group level, the research suggests that affirmative action may produce both benefits and costs. In terms of benefits, affirmative action has led to an increase in employment of women and minorities at various levels. Thus, affirmative action has been somewhat successful in achieving one of its primary goals. However, very little research has examined the issue of the effects of affirmative action on attitudes toward target groups. This would seem to be an important question to address if the effects of affirmative action are expected to persist beyond the actual practice of affirmative action. It seems likely that, once established, favorable attitudes toward target groups would go far to maintain equitable representation in society.

The research conducted to date has demonstrated that whites may express opposition to affirmation action for blacks at least in part because of prejudice toward blacks. This suggests that affirmative action may provide an opportunity for whites to express negative attitudes toward blacks in a socially acceptable way. Thus, affirmative action programs may, in fact, have *no* effect on attitudes toward blacks. Instead, prior attitudes toward blacks may determine how people respond to affirmative action programs, and their response to these programs may simply support their prior attitudes. In terms of ingroup esteem, the scant research on this issue suggests that a suspicion of inferiority of the group is most likely to occur when members of target groups believe that affirmative action overcompensates for discrimination. However, this belief in overcompensation may not be common among beneficiary groups. Thus, although there is a suggestion that affirmative action may result in less favorable attitudes toward target groups, a great deal of additional research is required to determine the validity of this claim.

IMPLICATIONS OF THE MODEL

In this chapter, we have proposed a model to organize the outcomes of strategies to reduce prejudice and discrimination. This model distinguishes between two levels of outcomes (those for individuals vs. groups) and between two sources of outcomes (those originating from other groups and those originating from intended target groups). The application of the model to affirmative action, we believe, demonstrates that it provides a meaningful and convenient way to organize the costs and benefits of such strategies.

The model can similarly be applied to other strategies to reduce prejudice and discrimination. For example, under specified conditions, intergroup contact has been considered to be a useful means to improve intergroup relations (Miller & Brewer, 1984). However, it may be the case that contact improves attitudes held by majority group members toward specific minority group members—in particular, those with whom they have come into contact—without generalizing to improved attitudes toward the group as a whole (Cook, 1984; Rothbart & John, 1985). In addition, such contact may have very different effects on minority group members' self-perceptions and ingroup esteem (see also Devine, Evett, & Vasquez-Suson, Chapter 13, this volume). Thus, the application of our model to other strategies for improving intergroup relations may similarly prove useful.

At the level of research, the model allows us to identify areas in which research questions have been most fully played out, and it helps us to identify new research questions that need to be addressed. For example, our application of the model to affirmative action suggests that individual outcomes, and particularly the issue of discounting of abilities and qualifications, have been well researched. Thus, it may be time to move beyond the individual level to examine the effect of affirmative action on attitudes toward groups as a whole—both attitudes of outgroups toward beneficiary groups, and beneficiary ingroup esteem. Certainly there has been much speculation on this issue, and empirical data would be useful.

At the level of implementation of programs to reduce prejudice and discrimination, the model may also provide some guidelines. In order to implement such programs successfully, it is of primary importance to define what is meant by "success." That is, we must identify the primary goals in terms of both level and source of outcomes. A question to consider is whether a program primarily intends to improve attitudes and behavior toward individuals or toward groups as a whole. In addition, it is important to consider whether favorable reactions from outgroups or from target groups are of greater concern. If the designers of a program consider these issues, the program may be more focused, and thus may have a greater likelihood of success in achieving its primary goals.

Once a program to reduce prejudice and discrimination is in place, it is important to evaluate its success within each cell of the model. In this way, all costs and benefits, and not only the potential benefits that were initially intended, can be assessed. For example, consider a program developed to improve the self-perceptions of individual members of a group that has historically been a target of prejudice and discrimination. This program is thus primarily aimed at the level of individuals, and the intended source of outcomes is target group members (i.e., Cell B). In addition to examining outcomes in this cell, however, it is also important to examine outcomes derived from outgroup members and outcomes for the group as a whole (i.e., Cells A, C, and D). If it is found that the program has its intended effects on self-perceptions but produces significant costs in other cells of the model, one may conclude that the program requires alteration. In addition, the particular cells into which the critical costs fall will presumably indicate what type of changes are necessary to improve the program.

We are thus suggesting that once a program to reduce prejudice and discrimination is in place, outcomes in all four cells of the model need to be assessed. However, we also emphasize that there are reasons to distinguish among these outcomes and to consider them separately. First, in an attempt to balance costs and benefits to determine whether a social program is worth continuing, outcomes in different cells of the model may be weighted differently. An obvious example is that outcomes falling into the cell that was initially the primary target of change may be weighted more heavily than outcomes occurring in the other cells.

Second, the public discussion of costs and benefits of social programs such as affirmative action will prove more productive if outcomes in the different cells of the model are delineated. The application of the model to affirmative action indicates that the relative costs and benefits may differ, depending on which cell of the model is the primary focus. In Cell A (outcomes for individuals derived from members of other groups), significant costs are evident, whereas in Cell C (outcomes for a group derived from members of other groups), benefits may outweigh any costs. Thus, conclusions about the overall value of affirmative action may be biased by a focus on a particular level and source of outcomes. A person who focuses on Cell A may conclude that affirmative action has proven to be of little value, whereas a person who focuses on Cell C may reach the opposite conclusion.

We would suggest that this is one reason why affirmative action and many other related programs have elicited so much controversy. Public discussions of the costs and benefits of these programs flounder and prove frustrating for discussants and observers alike because the discussants end up talking at cross-purposes, failing to distinguish between levels and sources of outcomes. As a consequence, discussants often rely on the level and source of outcome that best support their position, and may argue against the value of a benefit at one level by calling forth a cost at the other level. This is unlikely to prove productive. In contrast, public discussion that distinguishes between levels and sources of outcomes may provide a more focused and rational forum for assessing the value of social programs intended to improve intergroup relations.

SUMMARY

A review of the literature suggests that perceptions of groups and of individual group members do not always coincide. Thus, in assessments of the outcomes of strategies to reduce prejudice and discrimination, we suggest that it is useful to distinguish between costs and benefits for groups as a whole and those for individual group members. We also suggest that it is important to distinguish between outcomes derived from outgroup members and outcomes derived from target group members, the intended beneficiaries.

On the basis of these distinctions, we propose a model for organizing the costs and benefits of strategies to improve intergroup relations that comprises both levels of outcomes and sources of outcomes. An application of this model to affirmative action highlights its utility both for organizing research and for implementing social programs that are intended, in the long run, to improve society for groups and for their individual members.

Acknowledgments

Preparation of this chapter was supported by a grant from the Social Sciences and Humanities Research Council of Canada to Victoria M. Esses. We would like to thank Tory Higgins, Lynne Jackson, Jim Olson, Doug Palmer, David Sherry, and Dick Sorrentino for their helpful comments on an earlier version of this chapter.

Notes

1. People also attend to behavior that is clearly expectancy-disconfirming, presumably in an attempt to resolve the inconsistency (Olson et al., in press).

2. Affirmative action programs for physically handicapped people and for elderly people may be viewed more favorably because these groups may be seen as more deserving of assistance. Whereas blacks may be perceived as needing help because they are believed to be lazy and therefore undeserving, physically handicapped and elderly people may be seen as needing help because of conditions beyond their control and therefore as more deserving of assistance (Murrell et al., 1994).

References

Arthur, W., Doverspike, D., & Fuentes, R. (1992). Recipients' affective responses to affirmative action interventions: A cross-cultural perspective. *Behavioral Sciences and the Law, 10,* 229-243.

Barnes Nacoste, R. (1994). If empowerment is the goal . . . : Affirmative action and social interaction. *Basic and Applied Social Psychology, 15,* 87-112.

Blanchard, F. A., & Crosby, F. J. (Eds.). (1989). *Affirmative action in perspective.* New York: Springer-Verlag.

Bloom, A. (1987). *The closing of the American mind.* New York: Simon & Schuster.

Brewer, M. B. (1988). A dual process model of impression formation. In T. K. Srull & R. S. Wyer (Eds.), *Advances in social cognition: Vol. 1. A dual model of impression formation* (pp. 1-36). Hillsdale, NJ: Erlbaum.

Brewer, M. B., Dull, V., & Lui, L. (1981). Perceptions of the elderly: Stereotypes as prototypes. *Journal of Personality and Social Psychology, 41,* 656-670.

Brickman, P., Folger, R., Goode, E., & Schul, Y. (1981). Microjustice and macrojustice. In M. J. Lerner & S. C. Lerner (Eds.), *The justice motive in social behavior* (pp. 173-202). New York: Plenum Press.

Chacko, T. I. (1982). Women and equal employment opportunity: Some unintended effects. *Journal of Applied Psychology, 67,* 119-123.

Clayton, S. D., & Crosby, F. J. (1992). *Justice, gender, and affirmative action.* Ann Arbor: University of Michigan Press.

Clayton, S., & Tangri, S. S. (1989). The justice of affirmative action. In F. A. Blanchard & F. J. Crosby (Eds.), *Affirmative action in perspective* (pp. 177-192). New York: Springer-Verlag.

Cook, S. W. (1984). Cooperative interaction in multiethnic contexts. In N. Miller & M. B. Brewer (Eds.), *Groups in contact: The psychology of desegregation* (pp. 155-185). Orlando, FL: Academic Press.

Crosby, F. J. (1994). Understanding affirmative action. *Basic and Applied Social Psychology, 15,* 13-41.

Crosby, F., & Clayton, S. (1990). Affirmative action and the issue of expectancies. *Journal of Social Issues, 46*(2), 61-79.

Dovidio, J. F., Mann, J., & Gaertner, S. L. (1989). Resistance to affirmative action: The implications of aversive racism. In F. A. Blanchard & F. J. Crosby (Eds.), *Affirmative action in perspective* (pp. 83-102). New York: Springer-Verlag.

Eberhardt, J. L., & Fiske, S. T. (1994). Affirmative action in theory and practice: Issues of power, ambiguity, and gender versus race. *Basic and Applied Social Psychology, 15,* 201-220.

Erber, R., & Fiske, S. T. (1984). Outcome dependency and attention to inconsistent information. *Journal of Personality and Social Psychology, 47,* 709-726.

Fiske, S. T., & Neuberg, S. L. (1990). A continuum of impression formation, from category-based to individuating processes: Influences of information and motivation on attention and interpretation. In M. P. Zanna (Ed.), *Advances in experimental social psychology* (Vol. 23, pp. 1-74). San Diego, CA: Academic Press.

Garcia, L. T., Erskine, N., Hawn, K., & Casmay, S. R. (1981). The effect of affirmative action on attributions about minority group members. *Journal of Personality, 49,* 427-437.

Greene, K. W. (1989). *Affirmative action and principles of justice.* New York: Greenwood Press.

Hamilton, D. L. (1981). Illusory correlation as a basis for stereotyping. In D. L. Hamilton (Ed.), *Cognitive processes in stereotyping and intergroup behavior* (pp. 115-144). Hillsdale, NJ: Erlbaum.

Hamilton, D. L., Sherman, S. J., & Ruvolo, C. M. (1990). Stereotype-based expectancies: Effects on information processing and social behavior. *Journal of Social Issues, 46*(2), 35-60.

Hamilton, D. L., Stroessner, S. J., & Mackie, D. M. (1993). The influence of affect on stereotyping: The case of illusory correlations. In D. M. Mackie & D. L. Hamilton (Eds.), *Affect, cognition, and stereotyping: Interactive processes in group perception* (pp. 39-61). San Diego, CA: Academic Press.

Hamilton, D. L., & Trolier, T. K. (1986). Stereotypes and stereotyping: An overview of the cognitive approach. In J. F. Dovidio & S. L. Gaertner (Eds.), *Prejudice, discrimination, and racism* (pp. 127-163). Orlando, FL: Academic Press.

Heckman, J. (1986). Affirmative action and black employment. *Social Science, 71,* 125-129.

Heilman, M. E., Block, C. J., & Lucas, J. A. (1992). Presumed incompetent? Stigmatization and affirmative action efforts. *Journal of Applied Psychology, 77,* 536-544.

Heilman, M. E., Simon, M. C., & Repper, D. P. (1987). Intentionally favored, unintentionally harmed? Impact of sex-based preferential selection on self-perceptions and self-evaluations. *Journal of Applied Psychology, 72,* 62-68.

Hewstone, M. (1990). The 'ultimate attribution error'? A review of the literature on intergroup causal attribution. *European Journal of Social Psychology, 20,* 311-335.

Hewstone, M., Johnston, L., & Aird, P. (1992). Cognitive models of stereotype change: 2. Perceptions of homogeneous and heterogeneous groups. *European Journal of Social Psychology, 22,* 235-249.

Higgins, E. T., & Bargh, J. A. (1987). Social cognition and social perception. *Annual Review of Psychology, 38,* 369-425.

Hilton, J. L., & Darley, J. M. (1991). The effects of interaction goals on person perception. In M. P. Zanna (Ed.), *Advances in experimental social psychology* (Vol. 24, pp. 235-267). San Diego, CA: Academic Press.

Holloway, F. A. (1989). What is affirmative action? In F. A. Blanchard & F. J. Crosby (Eds.), *Affirmative action in perspective* (pp. 9-19). New York: Springer-Verlag.

Huckle, P. (1983). A decade's difference: Mid-level managers and affirmative action. *Public Personnel Management, 12,* 249-257.

Jacobson, C.K. (1985). Resistance to affirmative action: Self-interest or racism? *Journal of Conflict Resolution, 29,* 305-329.

Johnston, L., & Hewstone, M. (1992). Cognitive models of stereotype change: 3. Subtyping and the perceived typicality of disconfirming group members. *Journal of Experimental Social Psychology, 28,* 360-386.

Jussim, L. (1986). Self-fulfilling prophecies: A theoretical and integrative review. *Psychological Review, 93,* 429-445.

Kelly, H. H. (1972). Attribution in social interaction. In E. E. Jones, D. E. Kanouse, H. H. Kelly, R. E. Nisbett, S. Valins, & B. Weiner (Eds.), *Attribution: Perceiving the causes of behavior* (pp. 1-26). Morristown, NJ: General Learning Press.

Kinder, D. R., & Sears, D. O. (1981). Prejudice and politics: Symbolic racism versus racial threats to the good life. *Journal of Personality and Social Psychology, 40,* 414-431.

Kluegel, J. R., & Smith, E. R. (1983). Affirmative action attitudes: Effects of self-interest, racial affect, and stratification beliefs on whites' views. *Social Forces, 61,* 797-824.

Kruglanski, A. W., & Freund, T. (1983). The freezing and unfreezing of lay-inferences: Effects of impressional primacy, ethnic stereotyping, and numerical anchoring. *Journal of Experimental Social Psychology, 19*, 448-468.

Kunda, Z., & Oleson, K. C. (1995). Maintaining stereotypes in the face of disconfirmation: Constructing grounds for subtyping deviants. *Journal of Personality and Social Psychology, 68*, 565-579.

Leonard, J. S. (1985). What promises are worth: The impact of affirmative action goals. *Journal of Human Resources, 20*, 3-20.

Major, B., Feinstein, J., & Crocker, J. (1994). Attributional ambiguity of affirmative action. *Basic and Applied Social Psychology, 15*, 113-141.

Miller, D. T., & Turnbull, W. (1986). Expectancies and interpersonal processes. *Annual Review of Psychology, 37*, 233-256.

Miller, N., & Brewer, M. B. (Eds.). (1984). *Groups in contact: The psychology of desegregation.* Orlando, FL: Academic Press.

Murrell, A. J., Dietz-Uhler, B. L., Dovidio, J. F., Gaertner, S. L., & Drout, C. (1994). Aversive racism and resistance to affirmative action: Perceptions of justice are not necessarily color blind. *Basic and Applied Social Psychology, 15*, 71-86.

Nacoste, R. W. (1985). Selection procedure and responses to affirmative action: The case of favorable treatment. *Law and Human Behavior, 9*, 225-242.

Nacoste, R. W. (1989). Affirmative action and self-evaluation. In F. A. Blanchard & F. J. Crosby (Eds.), *Affirmative action in perspective* (pp. 103-109). New York: Springer-Verlag.

Nacoste, R. W. (1994). Policy schemas for affirmative action. In L. Heath et al. (Eds.), *Applications of heuristics and biases to social issues* (pp. 205-221). New York: Plenum Press.

Nacoste, R. W., & Lehman, D. (1987). Procedural stigma. *Representative Research in Social Psychology, 17*, 25-38.

Neuberg, S. L., & Fiske, S. T. (1987). Motivational influences on impression formation: Outcome dependency, accuracy-driven attention, and individuating processes. *Journal of Personality and Social Psychology, 53*, 431-444.

Newman, J. D. (1989). Affirmative action and the courts. In F. A. Blanchard & F. J. Crosby (Eds.), *Affirmative action in perspective* (pp. 31-49). New York: Springer-Verlag.

Olson, J. M., Roese, N. J., & Zanna, M. P. (in press). Expectancies. In E. T. Higgins & A. W. Kruglanski (Eds.), *Social psychology: Handbook of basic principles.* New York: Guilford Press.

Park, B., & Rothbart, M. (1982). Perception of out-group homogeneity and levels of social categorization: Memory for the subordinate attributes of in-group and out-group members. *Journal of Personality and Social Psychology, 42*, 1051-1068.

Pettigrew, T. F. (1979). The ultimate attribution error: Extending Allport's cognitive analysis of prejudice. *Personality and Social Psychology Bulletin, 5*, 461-476.

Pettigrew, T. F., & Martin, J. (1987). Shaping the organizational context for black American inclusion. *Journal of Social Issues, 43*(1), 41-78.

Ponterotto, J. G., Martinez, F. M., & Hayden, D. C. (1986). Student affirmative action programs: A help or hindrance to development of minority graduate students? *Journal of College Student Personnel, 27*, 318-325.

Robinson, R. K., Allen, B. M., & Abraham, Y. T. (1992). Affirmative action plans in the 1990s: A double-edged sword? *Public Personnel Management, 21*, 261-272.

Rothbart, M., & John, O. P. (1985). Social categorization and behavioral episodes: A cognitive analysis of the effects of intergroup contact. *Journal of Social Issues, 41*(3), 81-104.

Rothbart, M., & Lewis, S. (1988). Inferring category attributes from exemplar attributes: Geometric shapes and social categories. *Journal of Personality and Social Psychology, 55*, 861-872.

Ruscher, J. B., & Fiske, S. T. (1990). Interpersonal competition can cause individuating impression formation. *Journal of Personality and Social Psychology, 58*, 832-842.

Snyder, M. (1992). Motivational foundations of behavioral confirmations. In M. P. Zanna

(Ed.), *Advances in experimental social psychology* (Vol. 25, pp. 67-114). San Diego, CA: Academic Press.

Steele, C. M. (1992, April). Race and the schooling of black Americans. *Atlantic Monthly*, pp. 68-78.

Steele, S. (1990). *The content of our character: A new vision of race in America.* New York: St. Martin's Press.

Stephan, W. G. (1985). Intergroup relations. In G. Lindzey & E. Aronson (Eds.), *The handbook of social psychology* (3rd ed., Vol. 2, pp. 599-658). New York: Random House.

Summers, R. J. (1991). The influence of affirmative action on perceptions of a beneficiary's qualifications. *Journal of Applied Social Psychology, 21,* 1265-1276.

Taylor, D. A. (1989). Affirmative action and presidential executive orders. In F. A. Blanchard & F. J. Crosby (Eds.), *Affirmative action in perspective* (pp. 21-29). New York: Springer-Verlag.

Taylor, M. C. (1994). Impact of affirmative action on beneficiary groups: Evidence from the 1990 general social survey. *Basic and Applied Social Psychology, 15,* 143-178.

Taylor, S. E. (1981). A categorization approach to stereotyping. In D. L. Hamilton (Ed.), *Cognitive processes in stereotyping and intergroup behavior* (pp. 83-114). Hillsdale, NJ: Erlbaum.

Turner, M. E., & Pratkanis, A. R. (1994a). Affirmative action as help: A review of recipient reactions to preferential selection and affirmative action. *Basic and Applied Social Psychology, 15,* 43-69.

Turner, M. E., & Pratkanis, A. R. (1994b). Affirmative action: Insights from social psychological and organizational research. *Basic and Applied Social Psychology, 15,* 1-11.

Turner, M. E., & Pratkanis, A. R. (Eds.). (1994c). Social psychological perspectives on affirmative action [Special issue]. *Basic and Applied Social Psychology, 15*(1-2).

Weber, R., & Crocker, J. (1983). Cognitive processes in the revision of stereotypic beliefs. *Journal of Personality and Social Psychology, 45,* 961-977.

CHAPTER 18

Uncertainty in Interpersonal and Intergroup Relations
An Individual-Differences Perspective

GÜNTER L. HUBER
Universität Tübingen

RICHARD M. SORRENTINO
University of Western Ontario

> The twentieth century has been colored by the principle of uncertainty, taken both in its original Heisenberg meaning of 1927, to refer to a fundamental incommensurability, and in its broadest sense, as a general characteristic of the life of modern man since Einstein's miracle year of 1905 and the killing of the archduke in 1914. Along with relativity, uncertainty is a sort of charismatic concept, exciting those who filter conventional concepts and data through its perspectives.
>
> —*Fiddle* (1980, p. 3)

The notion that uncertainty has become a major characteristic of the 20th century is borne out by numerous books and articles on the subject. The Library of Congress lists 246 books published from 1968 to 1994 for which "uncertainty" is part of the title. These include books on uncertainty modeling, coping with uncertainty in the face of chaos, self-organization and complexity, uncertain motherhood, economics, dynamic timing, bargaining, trade reform, leadership, risk management and risk taking, environmental policy, medical choices, multidisciplinary conceptions, emerging paradigms, political science and science policy, and information and communication. Closer to home, we find that Psyclit2, from 1987 to the end of 1994, lists 341 books or chapters and 1,199 journal articles for which "uncertainty" is a key word.

Clearly, then, uncertainty is a concept that reaches far beyond the laboratory walls of social psychology and is considered a major force in the world today. In our examination of uncertainty, we find that the domain of interpersonal and intergroup relations is no exception. In this chapter, we show that many theories propose that both the problems of and the solutions to interpersonal and intergroup conflict lie in uncertainty and its reduction. Although we do not disagree with these approaches, we also argue that they are limited by their underlying assumption that all persons approach uncertainty in the interpersonal and intergroup domain on an equal footing. It is our major contention that individual differences in how people approach and/or cope with uncertainty must be considered if there is to be any hope of resolving much of the conflict prevalent in our world as it nears the 21st century. Following a brief review of the theory of uncertainty orientation, we attempt to show how it is relevant to interpersonal and intergroup processes. We then examine some of the current theories in both interpersonal communication and intergroup relations, showing how they often apply to only a small segment of the population, to the relative neglect of the majority. Finally, we attempt some suggestions for remedial action.

THE THEORY OF UNCERTAINTY ORIENTATION[1]

In attempting to resolve several lingering issues involved in research on the initial (Atkinson, 1964) and general (Atkinson & Raynor, 1974) theory of achievement motivation, Sorrentino and Short (1986) focused on a single dimension that they felt pervades all achievement-oriented situations, and in fact all situations in general. The dimension is the uncertainty of the situation itself. These authors contended that along with any other motivational or affective component that may be inherent in a given situation, there is also an informational component—the extent to which the situation will resolve uncertainty about the self, the environment, or the outcome of any tendency to act in the situation. They also contended that there are clear individual differences in the way people approach or avoid, attend to or ignore, such uncertainty. As a consequence, Sorrentino and Short (1986) developed a measure of uncertainty orientation in order to investigate these differences (see Sorrentino, Roney, & Hanna, 1992).

The general hypothesis is that uncertainty-oriented persons are motivated in situations where there is uncertainty about the self and the environment for them to resolve; by contrast, certainty-oriented persons are more motivated where there is no uncertainty about the self or the environment. Several findings support this hypothesis. For example, Sorrentino and Hewitt (1984) found that uncertainty-oriented people chose to engage in an activity (i.e., construct a test) that would resolve uncertainty about the self, regardless of the potential outcome (one condition could resolve uncertainty about having high ability; another, uncertainty about having low ability). Certainty-oriented people, however, chose to engage in an activity that would not resolve such uncertainty, also without regard to the outcome. It did not matter whether the resolution would reveal high or low ability. Certainty-oriented people apparently did not want to know anything new about themselves, regardless of the affective value of the information.

This tendency for certainty-oriented persons to maintain the certainty or clarity associated with their existing cognitions, rather than striving to resolve uncertainty, carried over into research on information processing and persuasion. In two studies, Sorrentino, Bobocel, Gitta, Olson, and Hewitt (1988) found that uncertainty-oriented persons followed current models of information processing (Chaiken, 1980; Petty & Cacioppo, 1981), whereas certainty-oriented persons behaved in a manner opposite to what these theories would predict. Uncertainty-oriented persons increased their processing of issue quality and decreased their use of specific heuristic cues as personal relevance increased. Certainty-oriented persons, however, were actually *more* likely to use heuristics and engaged in *less* systematic processing when personal relevance increased. The latter people thus did not strive to resolve the issue themselves, relying on heuristics (e.g., an expert) when the issue was important. Conceptually similar findings were reported in research on health-protective behavior (Brouwers & Sorrentino, 1993) under varying conditions of threat and efficacy. Uncertainty-oriented persons showed the expected linear relationship between these variables: They were most likely to undertake activity that would tell them whether or not they had a disease when it was life-threatening (high personal relevance) and high in efficacy (highly diagnostic), and least likely under low threat and low efficacy. Surprisingly, certainty-oriented persons showed an inverted-U relationship between the two variables: They were actually more likely to undertake the activity under low threat and high efficacy or high threat and low efficacy than when both were at low or high levels!

Other research suggests that certainty-oriented persons maintain certainty and clarity by avoiding or ignoring inconsistency or ambiguity. Roney and Sorrentino (1987) found that when certainty-oriented persons were asked to categorize traits of persons in different roles, they perceived fewer traits within categories, and, more importantly, less overlap of traits across categories. In other words, certainty-oriented people were less likely to conceive that a person in one category (e.g., a homemaker) could have traits in common with a person in another category (e.g., a student). Also, Driscoll, Hamilton, and Sorrentino (1991) found that uncertainty-oriented people recalled more information that had been presented if it was expectancy-incongruent than if it was expectancy-congruent, as predicted by current research on memory (e.g., Hastie, 1980; Srull, Lichtenstein, & Rothbart, 1985). Certainty-oriented people showed no such difference, however, suggesting that incongruent information was less likely to be encoded into memory than these theories would predict.

The notion of uncertainty as a major psychological dimension that is domain-nonspecific was supported in a study by Sorrentino, Hewitt, and Raso (1992). These investigators demonstrated that whether a situation dealt with uncertainty about the self (performance at a skilled activity) or sheer uncertainty about the outcome (gambling in a chance situation), uncertainty-oriented people were motivated to resolve the uncertainty, whereas certainty-oriented people were motivated to avoid that situation. In different ways, then, all of these studies suggest that uncertainty-oriented people attend to and deal directly with uncertainty or inconsistency, whereas certainty-oriented people attend to and deal with the familiar and certain.

RESEARCH ON UNCERTAINTY ORIENTATION FROM AN INTERPERSONAL PERSPECTIVE

Given that individual differences in uncertainty orientation appear to have a powerful influence in the way one approaches uncertainty, at every level from playing a game of chance (Sorrentino et al., 1988) to dealing with life-threatening events (Brouwers & Sorrentino, 1993), it seems an appropriate step to expand the research to the area of interpersonal and intergroup processes. On the basis of the studies described above, this research has already been extended to the domain of close relationships (Sorrentino, Holmes, Hanna, & Sharp, 1995) and to cross-cultural research on cooperative learning (Huber, Sorrentino, Davidson, Eppler, & Roth, 1992).

In the close-relationship study (Sorrentino et al., 1995), 77 married couples were placed under close scrutiny. From a multitude of self-report, diary, and actual-memory data, it became clear that uncertainty-oriented men and women constantly tested their relationships with their partners. As predicted, they were more likely to have only moderate trust in their partners than to have low or high trust. Certainty-oriented men and women, however, in order to avoid the ambivalence associated with moderate trust, were more likely to have very low or very high trust in their partners than to have moderate trust. More importantly, whereas uncertainty-oriented men and women appeared to be quite satisfied with having moderate trust in their partners, certainty-oriented men and women experienced a great deal of discomfort with such relationships. Indeed, certainty-oriented women were more likely to exhibit symptoms of depression, psychoses, obsessive–compulsive behavior, and neuroticism when they had moderate trust in their partners than when they had *either* low *or* high trust. In other words, they were more disturbed when they were ambivalent toward their partners than when they didn't trust them at all. Although certainty-oriented men did not reveal such symptoms, they showed greater distortion of memory and denial of their feelings under moderate as opposed to low or high trust. It is also important to note that when asked to recall their feelings regarding an actual event that took place earlier during the study, certainty-oriented men and women were much more likely to distort their memories, relying on the heuristic of trust in their recall, than were uncertainty-oriented men and women.

The cross-cultural research on cooperative learning (Huber et al., 1992) was based on our assumption that whereas uncertainty-oriented students would enjoy the atmosphere of discovery-based learning situations, in which they and their peers would share their knowledge with one another, certainty-oriented students would not enjoy this type of atmosphere, preferring typical expository teaching situations that were either competitive or individualistic in nature. As predicted, uncertainty-oriented university students in Germany, Iran, and Canada were significantly more likely to prefer cooperative learning to individualistic or competitive learning than were certainty-oriented students (Study 1); this was also true for grade school students (Study 2). In addition, whereas uncertainty-oriented student teachers enjoyed cooperative problem-solving situations, certainty-oriented student teachers did not (Study 3). Finally, it was found that whereas uncertainty-oriented sixth- and seventh-grade students performed better when using the jigsaw method developed by Aronson (1978) than when using traditional expository methods, certainty-oriented persons actually performed less well with the jigsaw method than with traditional methods (Study 4).

These studies suggest strongly that some theories of interpersonal communication and others related to intergroup relations need to be re-examined in light of individual differences in uncertainty orientation. Such an attempt takes place below.

UNCERTAINTY IN INTERPERSONAL COMMUNICATION

Linguistic uncertainty seems to be a normal feature of communication. Sender and receiver must understand their mutual messages, despite the fact that their semantic encoding and decoding of signs are never perfectly congruent. Beyond the linguistic level, uncertainty appears to play a key role for understanding the interpersonal functions of communication. When two people meet for the first time, one might argue that they are primarily concerned with learning to understand and thus to predict each other's interactive behavior. At least the onset of social interactions seems to be a clear example of concern with uncertainty in interpersonal relations. Also, when one person meets another repeatedly, he or she may be more interested in finding out new information about this other person than in listening to the same stories again and again. The continuation of interpersonal relations, then, also seems to be related to uncertainty and its reduction.

The role of uncertainty in the communication process has been discussed in detail by Berger and Calabrese (1975; see also Berger, 1979; Berger & Bradac, 1982; Berger & Kellerman, 1983). These authors have criticized the limited validity of various theoretical approaches for explaining interaction processes, particularly social-psychological and sociological exchange theories, reinforcement theories, attribution theories, and social-linguistic approaches. Berger and Calabrese (1975) note the limits of theoretical power whenever such an approach is used to describe and explain how interpersonal relations develop and how they break, because these approaches are not focused on communicative behavior. This judgment seems to be especially true for social-linguistic models (e.g., Mishler, 1975), which normally concentrate on relations of communicative behavior and general social rules or norms instead of the specifics of particular interpersonal relations.[2] Therefore, Berger and Calabrese (1975) have outlined a general axiomatic model of communication processes, which they relate to characteristics of the communicative behavior of persons in interaction. In this model, interpersonal communication is defined as a three-step process: (1) an introductory or entry phase, determined by implicit and explicit communication rules; (2) a more spontaneous personal phase of communication, during which normative regulations play a minor role; and (3) an exit phase, shaped by personal decisions as to whether further contacts will be desirable.

During the entry phase, the partners in social interaction attempt above all to reduce mutual uncertainty. This is the central assumption in Berger and Calabrese's (1975) model, on which the other axioms of social interaction are based. "Uncertainty" is defined in this model according to Shannon and Weaver's (1949) construct of information; the primary concern of communication is to increase the predictability of one's partner's actions or to reduce uncertainty about these actions. Two particular meanings of "reduction of uncertainty" in social relations follow from this assumption: "In the first sense of uncertainty reduction, the individual is engaged in a proactive process of creating predictions. The second sense of uncertainty [reduction] concerns the problem of retroactively explaining the other's behavior" (Berger & Calabrese, 1975, p. 101). In other words, the uncertainty of social-interactive processes is reduced to the extent that one succeeds in predicting the other's behavior and in explaining it later. Berger (1979) has discussed this aspect in more detail. He suggests that more attention should be paid "to the ways in which communicative behavior is employed to gain knowledge and understanding in relationships. In the present view, the communicative processes involved in knowledge generation and the development of understanding are central to the development and disintegration of most interpersonal relationships" (p. 123).

The fundamental assumptions of this approach seem to contradict many experiences from everyday social interaction. When two strangers start to communicate for the first time—that is, when they are in the entry phase of the Berger and Calabrese (1975) model—neither the topics they talk about nor the types of information they exchange in this process seem to be very appropriate to reducing mutual uncertainties. Typical topics and information often do not greatly augment each person's knowledge or understanding of the other. Indeed, in their analyses of the social penetration process, Altman and Taylor (1973) note that initial interactions typically begin with rather meaningless, inconsequential discourse. The notorious small talk during parties is a good example of interpersonal processes of this kind. Altman and Taylor do, however, discuss the "stranger-on-the-train" phenomenon, in which conversations between strangers in airplanes or railways may consist of relatively intimate details of their personal lives (e.g., details about their families, their jobs, and even their love lives).

In order to resolve this contradiction, Berger (1979) introduces the influence of additional variables on readiness for or interest in reduction of uncertainty, such as the probability of future encounters or the degree to which the actual relation is determined by the attribution of situation-specific norms. However, he also distinguishes between "cognitive" and "behavioral" uncertainty. According to this distinction, cognitive states of uncertainty and the uncertainty level of verbal exchange are not necessarily correlated. The obvious redundancy of many talks during the entry phase of social interactions, as well as the lack of effort to understand each other (i.e., to retroactively explore each other's behavior), produces a high amount of certainty or predictability on the behavioral level without reducing the partners' cognitive uncertainty about each other.

These arguments are meant to defend the premise in the model of Berger and Calabrese (1975) that all individuals strive principally to reduce (cognitive) uncertainty in social relations. However, they cannot resolve the problem that probably not all persons strive for uncertainty reduction in interpersonal communication. Others have, in fact, questioned whether there is a general tendency toward uncertainty reduction in social-interactive situations. For example, Planalp and Honeycutt (1985) have noted that studies on the subject of interpersonal communication conceive of acquisition of knowledge about the other person as equivalent to reduction of uncertainty, and that communication and acquisition of knowledge are seen as necessarily interrelated. These authors point instead to the possibility that information mediated by communication, but inconsistent with pre-existing knowledge and/or implicit theories, may increase uncertainty in interpersonal relations. A simple example should be sufficient to illustrate this situation. Imagine that someone finds out that a closely related person is lying about him or her. This incident will increase the uncertainty of communication between these two persons. We may expect that the belied person will alter his or her implicit assumptions about the liar, as well as his or her emotional reactions; at the same time, the further process of communications and the fate of this relationship may change.

Although empirical findings have demonstrated strong social-cognitive (e.g., Lachman, Lachman, & Butterfield, 1979) and affective (e.g., Dyer, 1983) effects of inconsistent information, no general communicative strategy for handling this experience can be found. From Berger and Calabrese's (1975) model, we would conclude that people try to reduce the uncertainty of communicative inconsistency either by seeking further information or by avoiding further unpleasant experiences of this kind. In an experimental study, Planalp and Honeycutt (1985) found five ways in which communication was used in uncertainty-increasing interpersonal situations: talking over the issue, arguing over the issue, talking around the issue, avoiding the issue, and avoiding the other person. The average frequencies of these strategies differed only slightly. As a result of a common factor analysis of these variables, Planalp and Honeycutt (1985) expected a single factor of approaching or avoiding the issue or the source of uncertainty. However, they found two factors. Both factors were characterized by "avoidance of the critical topic" at the one pole; the opposite pole of one factor was characterized by "talking about the issue," and the other factor's opposite pole was characterized by "arguing about the issue." Both factors were slightly negatively correlated ($r = -.18$), but the authors did not report whether this coefficient was significant.

Although there may be communicative strategies that either negate or prevent inconsistencies, we cannot presume that all people who focus on an inconsistent issue in their communication with another person will seek information through this process in order to find out more about the other person and his or her point of view. That is, we cannot presume that all people try to reduce

TABLE 18.1   Axioms of Uncertainty Reduction by Communication

High level of uncertainty	Low level of uncertainty
Is produced by dissimilarity of partners	Is produced by similarity of partners
Produces decrease of mutual liking	Produces increase of mutual liking
Is reduced by verbal communication	Increases verbal communication
Is reduced by increasing nonverbal expressions of affiliation	Increases nonverbal expressions of affiliation
Increases information seeking	Decreases information seeking
Decreases the intimacy level of communication	Increases the intimacy level of communication
Produces high rates of reciprocity	Produces low rates of reciprocity

the uncertainty (of perceiving, predicting, or understanding the other person) caused by inconsistent information. The strategy "talking about the issue," for instance, may reduce uncertainty by integration of information. However, there seem to be individuals who prefer strategies of communication (i.e., strategies of information selection) that allow them to maintain knowledge or "certainty" about the critical issue without any changes. The pole "arguing about the issue" in Planalp and Honeycutt's (1985) second factor seems to indicate such a tendency of information selection. Clearly, then, there appear to be important individual differences in the way people approach uncertainty with regard to interpersonal communication; research on uncertainty orientation may aid in accounting for such differences, as we describe below.

THE UNCERTAINTY BIAS IN THEORIES OF INTERPERSONAL COMMUNICATION

The assumptions about general principles underlying interpersonal communication are summarized by Berger and Calabrese (1975) as "axioms of uncertainty reduction by communication," and are shown in Table 18.1. These principles clearly suggest that everybody is interested in communication in order to attain more information and to construct new certainties about others. Interpersonal states of uncertainty, which are likely when partners are dissimilar or do not know each other yet, stimulate information seeking, verbal and nonverbal communication, and high rates of reciprocity.[3] Once uncertainty is reduced, according to Berger and Calabrese (1975), the partners tend to like each other more; they exchange more verbal communications and more nonverbal expressions of affiliation; and the rate of reciprocity decreases.

Clearly, our theory and past research indicate that this table seems to apply only to the uncertainty-oriented person. Only such a person is interested in reducing uncertainty by seeking out information. Only he or she is interested in finding out new things that may increase ambivalence or confusion regarding the status quo (cf. Sorrentino & Hewitt, 1984; Roney & Sorrentino, 1987;

Driscoll et al., 1991). In addition to the study on close relationships (Sorrentino et al., 1995) which shows the differential reactions to ambivalence in interpersonal relations, and our research on cooperative learning (Huber et al., 1992), which shows the differential reactions to reducing uncertainty by means of cooperative learning techniques (both discussed earlier), a more recent study demonstrates how uncertainty-oriented and certainty-oriented students interact with each other. This experimental study was performed jointly at the University of Tübingen and at the University of Jena (Huber & Scholz, 1995). A total of 209 students aged 14 and 15, from nine classrooms and of the eighth grade of "gymnasium" (representing the upper level of the three-part German school system), were observed during processes of decision making while learning to solve problems. Students were placed in three-person groups, which were homogeneous with regard to the students' level of uncertainty orientation. All subjects dealt with a decision-making task individually and as part of a group. Results confirmed expectations as regards the different behavior tendencies of uncertainty-oriented versus certainty-oriented students when confronted with alternatives. Although there were no significant differences under the condition of individual learning and decision making, the team condition seemed to inhibit certainty-oriented students' task-relevant behavior. For example, in teams, uncertainty-oriented students produced significantly more ideas (on the average, 49 vs. 31 alternative ideas), asked more questions (7.3 vs. 1.2), gave more explanations (44 vs. 14), and rejected more alternatives (36 vs 15) than certainty-oriented students.

Because this study compared students in situations of individual versus team learning, several indicators of social preference versus rejection in the classrooms were assessed with the *Diagnostisches Soziogramm* (Diagnostic Sociogram, DSO; Müller, 1980). Moreover, in each classroom a science teacher and a teacher of a nonscience subject rated each of the students in terms of their willingness to cooperate, their readiness to assume social obligations, and their dominance in situations of decision making. Generally, it was found that uncertainty-oriented students enjoyed a significantly more positive social image than certainty-oriented students. They were more often selected as team members and less often rejected as team members by their classmates. Most interesting was the finding that both uncertainty-oriented students and certainty-oriented students rated their uncertainty-oriented classmates as more popular than their certainty-oriented classmates. A complementary qualitative analysis of individual explanations for ratings (pro or con) of particular classmates as partners for cooperation confirmed the expectation. Uncertainty-oriented students explained their own membership in a particular group more frequently than certainty-oriented students by referring to the possibility of exchange and mutual support, whereas certainty-oriented students reported more often than uncertainty-oriented students that they felt forced to cooperate and would rather learn individually.

Also revealing was the analysis of cliques in the classroom. "Cliques" were defined as subgroups whose members showed a minimal ratio of mutual positive votes and no mutual rejection. Uncertainty-oriented students outnumbered certainty-oriented students in cliques by a margin of 2 to 1. This finding could be interpreted as another confirmation of uncertainty-oriented students' greater cooperativeness versus certainty-oriented students' individualistic tendencies. The teachers' ratings supported this interpretation, particularly those of teachers who were in regular interaction with the students.

These results thus suggest that instructional situations in which students are not passive recipients of information, but contribute actively to reach their learning goals, have to provide ample room for students to make decisions about their own learning activities. However, this room seems to be utilized differently by different learners. Individual differences in uncertainty orientation seem to be crucial in this regard. In addition to their openness to controversial interpersonal communications and to information-processing strategies that may provide new insights in these situations, uncertainty-oriented students seem to be advantaged by characteristics of their social-interactive strategies. Their greater engagement and higher dominance in group decision making, combined with certainty-oriented students' reluctance to initiate activities in new or controversial domains, may reinforce existing differences in cognitive processing. Similar conclusions may be derived from the following section on intergroup relations.

UNCERTAINTY IN INTERGROUP RELATIONS

In the European context, the topic of intercultural relations is receiving increasing attention, because of migratory pressures from outside and the increase of xenophobia and rejection within many of the European states over the last few years. In fact, the headline of a lead article in the *International Herald Tribune* (Robinson, 1993, p. 1) warned, "Flood of Migrants May Be 'Crisis of the Age.' " However, as Campani and Gundara (1994, p. 7) summarize their view of intercultural policies within the European Union, "the notion of a multicultural or plural society [is] not widely accepted and governmental policies may in fact oscillate between assimilation and segregation."

Unlike the United States and Canada, the European countries have attempted to deal with intercultural relations only from the 1960s on. In the beginning, they focused almost exclusively on the linguistic differences and specific sociocultural problems of migrant workers' children. These children were fully expected to return to their home countries relatively quickly (Perotti, 1994; Wittek, Nijdam, & Kroeger, 1993). With permanent settlement of migrant workers and the birth of a second generation of their children, however, the educational systems are being challenged to cope with growing intolerance and racism. The Council of Europe made recommendations promoting intercultural education in 1984, but "intercultural education principles have not been enthusiastically embraced in European countries" (Perotti, 1994, p. 16), for a number of reasons. These include fears from the political right that national cultures may suffer from attempts to legitimize minorities, as well as suspicions from the left that minority cultures may be undermined by the application of these principles (Coulby, 1993).

Despite the general reluctance to adopt the principles of intercultural education, teachers have to cope with prejudice and rejection of minority groups in their classrooms. On the level of concrete classroom management, they cannot circumvent the questions of intergroup relations, whether official policies and social science support their efforts or not. This support and its doubtful contribution to life in ethnically mixed classrooms are at the core of our considerations. We say "doubtful," because teachers looking for help find themselves in a puzzling situation: Although science shows various possible ways of achieving the goal of positive intercultural relations, there appears to be no clear or coherent indication as to which of these directions teachers should follow.

Condor and Brown (1988) describe three levels of analysis that social scientists have utilized in their attempts to make recommendations for resolving intergroup conflict. First, there are those who advocate treatment of universal psychological characteristics of individuals—that is, their motivational and cognitive processes—as causes of intergroup problems. Explaining intergroup problems by referring to individual motives, lack of knowledge, or biased perceptions of others tends to focus attention almost exclusively on individuals involved in an intergroup problem. Of course, individuals' motives and cognitions play an important role, but an individualistic approach may prevent analysis of the potential contribution of collective norms to the problem.

A second group of theories also explains intergroup problems in terms of individual psychological processes that are expected to vary from person to person; however, the perspective is broadened. This group of theories takes account of the fact that individual differences in reactions to social problems can be traced to general features of social situations that may have influenced the development of individual characteristics in the past. These now promote or impede an individual's readiness to get involved in an intergroup problem. An example is the consideration of intergroup problems from the viewpoint of interindividual differences in authoritarianism, which are seen as emerging from particular family situations in a specific society and as influencing the rigidity of ingroup-outgroup boundaries experienced by an individual.

A third group of theories does not deal primarily with individual characteristics, but with characteristics of social situations that give rise to intergroup problems. The situation is also seen as containing keys to solving the problem. For example, according to "realistic-conflict theory" (Campbell, 1965), relations between groups depend on collaborative versus antagonistic goal interdependence. Intergroup problems, in the form of antagonistic goal interdependencies of the people involved, arise from a scarcity of particular situational components—water, food, energy, and the like, but also popularity or prestige. The solution is seen as establishing cooperative goal interdependence. Likewise, Tajfel and Turner's (1979) "social identity theory" describes how membership in a particular group mediates the members' social identity and thus their interpretation of themselves and others. (Both these theories are discussed in more detail later.)

Practical recommendations for handling intercultural problems in the classroom also conceive of the educational challenge of cultural heterogeneity in different ways. In an analysis of the curricula for German elementary schools (Huber & Roth, 1994), three typical points of view on ethnically heterogeneous classrooms were found. Problems were seen in (1) students' deficient knowledge of each other, according to Stephan and Stephan's (1984) notion of ignorance as a mediator of prejudice in conflicting values; (2) differing value orientations, as described by Batelaan and Gundara (1993); and (3) controversial decisions for action to be taken in the same situation. Consequently, influential educational suggestions have been focused mainly on supplying adequate information about cultural minorities, providing opportunities for personal experience with the minorities' way of life, or creating situations for dialectic decision making and joint action (Huber & Roth, 1994).

Unfortunately, a review by Axhausen and Feil (1984) of six long-term projects designed along various lines described above gives a discouraging view of the efficacy of projects designed to reduce prejudice and intergroup conflict. These projects were begun during the early 1970s in the metropolitan area of Munich, Germany. During this time, people from other countries, mostly southern European countries and Turkey, were invited to come to Germany and to work there as so-called *Gastarbeiter* (guest workers). This status was meant as a signal that they were coming for a temporary stay to alleviate a temporary shortage of workers in Germany, not for immigration. Therefore, there were controversial ideas regarding the nature of acculturation of these people and, above all, of their children. Intercultural education as a task related to social diversity in general was not discussed, nor was the problem space mapped out theoretically. Some children of migrant workers were simply put into regular classrooms; others attended preparatory classes where they were taught the German language and introduced to the German curriculum; and still others attended German schools in the morning and classes run by teachers hired from their home countries in the afternoon (Reich, 1994).

Since school-based programs were not established at this time (today, "intercultural education has become an issue of theoretical debate and analysis among academics, but changes within the school system or higher education are still in their infancy"; Campani & Gundara, 1994, p. 8), Axhausen and Feil (1984) selected projects dedicated to reducing prejudice among German and foreign children and adolescents in the schools as well as in community-based social initiatives outside the classroom. Thus, the activities designed to foster interpersonal relations spanned a wide range. Included were reports from multinational play groups in kindergartens, as well as reports from so-called "children's shops" where mostly primary school children were invited to meet in the afternoon for joint social activities in multicultural groups, but also to get assistance in doing their homework assignments or to attend special courses in German, math, and so on.

The experiences of educators in regular classrooms or in their everyday encounters with prejudices of native and foreign children against members of the other group complemented the reports from the six projects. According to Axhausen and Feil (1984),

> The catalog of activities that should diminish prejudices in these projects is illustrated by our abstract summary: German children (and educators) receive information about the countries where their new group-mates come from. The children learn about geographical, social, economical and political conditions in the countries where the "others" come from, and about cultural and religious aspects of living in these countries. The goal is not only that children become aware of differing everyday habits, but that they come to understand the causes and accept these differences—and that they experience them as mutual enrichment of their respective own ways of life. (p. 21; translation by G. L. Huber)

In cases of real conflict, discussions were initiated and information was given to assist the children in reflecting and solving their problems.

According to Axhausen and Feil (1984), this mainly cognitive approach was not very successful. In a "children's shop" project, a group of German and (in those days) Yugoslavian girls tried together to establish a hierarchy of nationalities in order to put a group of Turkish girls in a subordinate position. One day one of the German girls wrote *"Türken raus"* ("Turks, go home") on the blackboard. The educator tried to initiate reflection by writing *"Deutsche raus"* ("Germans, go home") on the blackboard and asking the German girls how they would feel if they encountered this inscription on a wall in Italy during a vacation. The developing discussion did not lead to better understanding; the criticized German girls simply left the project.

Equally unsuccessful, as attempts to decrease existing prejudices, were the common efforts to bring German and foreign children and adolescents in contact with each other and to instigate joint experiences. Accompanying "public relations" actions—for instance, street festivals in a neighborhood—were very popular. However, it is unclear whether these activities contributed to reduce prejudices.

Axhausen and Feil (1984) summarized their findings by stating that the nature of prejudice as a social phenomenon may account for the ineffectiveness of endeavors such as these. That is, false and negative appraisals, along with biased generalizations of reality, may resist even strong efforts to disprove them because of their solid emotional foundations. This conclusion, especially the failure of contact approaches, is unfortunately confirmed by many other studies (e.g., Rogers, Miller, & Hennigan, 1981; Pettigrew, 1986; Stephan, 1987; Gundara, 1993).

Axhausen and Feil's (1984) evaluation of attempts to improve social relations in the field, as opposed to efforts in rigorous experimental settings, suggests at least two important things. First, interventions that concentrate on individuals, without taking into account critical conditions of the social system, are likely to fail. Group members whose behaviors are criticized and who feel compelled to comply with specific interpersonal norms will leave a project if there are no structural constraints against doing so. This may be even more likely for members of the dominant group, who do not lose status or access to resources by their departure. Second, although interventions may be effective when children are motivated to gain from each other, it is not clear that this is the case. Even if it is, to perceive group and personal differences under a perspective of "mutual enrichment" seems to be a requirement that cannot be generally met.

Although Axhausen and Feil (1984) reported that the projects they examined were primarily failures in terms of reducing prejudice, we feel that the authors may have overlooked an important point. That is, it cannot be determined from the data whether nothing changed at all, or whether the interventions actually may have increased some children's prejudices while decreasing other children's partiality and intolerance. From Axhausen and Feil's (1984) differentiation between "open" and "organized" intercultural contacts (e.g., meetings on playgrounds vs. weekend stays on a camp site), it occurs to us that interindividual differences may have played an important role. Axhausen and Feil (1984, p. 50) described open situations of contact as relatively problematic because of individual reservations, whereas organized situations mediated contacts between children who came "prepared" and brought "a readiness to learn more about each other."

As we can see, both personal prerequisites and social situations are areas where causes for interpersonal problems can be located and where interventions seem to be necessary. However, it is difficult to name examples of problematic or satisfying interpersonal relations where the social system level can be separated from the personal level of analysis. It is the contention of this chapter that we must take into account characteristics of social situations as well as characteristics of persons in examining interpersonal and intergroup relations, and must elaborate on the interactive ties between them. Only then can we begin to give educators the advice they so sorely need. The theory of uncertainty orientation (Sorrentino & Short, 1986) seems to be an adequate conceptual tool to analyze existing approaches to promote intercultural relations in education and to develop new insights into their strengths and their shortcomings.

THE UNCERTAINTY BIAS IN THEORIES OF INTERCULTURAL RELATIONS

A look at the various approaches to explaining biased intercultural relations and to intervening in a socially desirable way also reveals, ironically, a bias of these approaches toward persons attracted by uncertainty. Miller and Harrington (1990) have provided a review of approaches to intergroup behavior that were recommended and tested in experiments. This review is summarized in Table 18.2.

Because of mostly ambiguous findings, the authors conclude that these approaches may represent important elements of a solution to the problem of in-

TABLE 18.2 Explanations and Interventions for Intergroup Problems

Explanatory model	*Central causes of conflict*	*Access to solutions*	*Mediating process(es)*
Realistic-conflict theory	Conflicting material interests; competition for scarce resources	Cooperative intergroup interaction	Common goal; joint efforts; positive perception of interdependence
Reinforcement approach	Social approval from in-group/disapproval from outgroup	Positive reward interdependence of ingroup and outgroup	Intergroup success
Similarity-attraction link	Perceived dissimilarity	Interaction	Increase of (perceived) similarity
Contact hypothesis	Lack of personal contacts; "ethnic encapsulation"	Prepared contacts (i.e., under conditions of readiness and equal status	Disconfirmation of stereotypes
Ignorance model	Lack of knowledge and familiarity	Information; increase of familiarity	Reduction of anxiety
Expectation-states theory	Negative expectations	Expectation training for ingroup and outgroup	Reversal of expectations
Social identity theory/situational identity theory	Social categorization (lack of differentiation and depersonalization of outgroup); competitive social comparison	Decategorization (differentiation of outgroup, personalization of its members); differentiation of self from ingroup; personalization of self in contact with outgroup member(s)	Low situational salience of categorical perceptions and category boundaries

Note. Adapted from Miller and Harrington (1990, p. 45). Copyright 1990 by Praeger Publishers, Inc. Adapted by permission.

tergroup bias; however, none of these approaches seems to be sufficient. The first approach on Miller and Harrington's (1990) list is "realistic-conflict theory," which states that competition between groups for scarce resources (not only supplies for survival, but also social needs) will increase ingroup cooperation on the one hand, but will increase intergroup competition on the other hand. As an adequate mediator of creating a general cooperative intergroup situation, Miller and Harrington (1990) cite introduction of a superordinate goal in order to create cooperative interdependence. That is, the members of both groups *have* to work together if they want to reach their common goal.

Although realistic-conflict theory has been a "major impetus behind many of the interethnic classroom techniques developed to promote acceptance and harmony among members of different ethnic groups" (Miller & Harrington, 1990, p. 46), some concerns should be mentioned. First, educational efforts to promote intercultural relations should not be focused on realistic conflicts, such as a scarcity of resources. Such problems are beyond the domain of the classroom. If there are no conflicts, however, introduction of common goals could instigate awareness of an underlying potential for conflict; this would be most difficult to manage. Finally, if there are already realistic conflicts (e.g., one subgroup of a society dominates the job market), interpersonal education must not be conceived of as a sort of repair job. Educational activities are at their best in preventing conflicts—in Caplan's (1964) terms, in primary prevention of conflicts—but they often fail as a means of crisis intervention at the classroom level. As Kounin (1970) has shown, both good and less qualified educators seem to have equally poor success in effectively managing problems once these are manifested in their classrooms.

In addition to these problems, the research reported above suggests that beyond cooperation to gain access to the common goal, the realistic-conflict approach will produce mutual acceptance and harmony at best for uncertainty-oriented members of the originally competing groups. From all our research on cooperative learning and social interaction (Huber et al., 1992; Huber & Scholz, 1995), it seems likely that only uncertainty-oriented students will actually benefit from these situations. Indeed, it is our belief that those students whom Axhausen and Feil (1984) described as coming "prepared" and bringing "a readiness to learn more about each other"—that is, those who benefited from superordinate goals—were uncertainty-oriented. Those who left the situation were probably certainty-oriented.

The "reinforcement approach" applied to the domain of intercultural relations (see Table 18.2) describes a basic linkage of reward and liking. Social situations in which members of majority and minority groups are brought to strive together toward a common goal, and in which each step to goal achievement is equally rewarding for both groups (positive interdependence), should be helpful in overcoming prejudices. "The positive affect associated with reward can then be generalized to members of the outgroup, who were presumably instrumental in obtaining the goal" (Miller & Harrington, 1990, p. 46). However, according to the social (or situational) identity approach (see below), the perception of others and presumptions of their instrumentality may be modified by a number of additional conditions.

We would also question the reinforcement approach for certainty-oriented persons. For example, in the Sorrentino et al. (1995) study reported earlier in this chapter, it was found that whereas uncertainty-oriented persons tended to be accurate and unbiased in their recall of past positive or negative events with their partners, certainty-oriented persons were significantly more likely to distort their judgments on the basis of heuristic devices (e.g., the trust they had in their partners). Given this and recent findings on reconstruction of past memory (see Ross & Conway, 1986; Johnson & Sherman, 1990), it should not be very surprising to discover that certainty-oriented persons distort their judgments of reward in the direction of their stereotypes of the outgroup.

Moreover, we do know that certainty-oriented persons are more likely to think in terms of categories or stereotypes, and to see greater differentiation between categories, than uncertainty-oriented persons (see Roney & Sorrentino, 1987). This predisposition to think categorically, combined with reliance on heuristic devices in making important judgments (see also Sorrentino et al., 1988), may serve further to dispel any attempts at changing attitudes through mutual reinforcement and many other approaches shown in Table 18.2. For example, the "ignorance model" and the "contact hypothesis" (Allport, 1954) have already been discussed as more or less explicit bases of the Munich projects to reduce prejudice in children. Both approaches presume a lack of familiarity, and recommend attacking prejudices either by supplying information apt to disconfirm stereotypes (especially about characteristics, customs, and conditions of life of the members of the other group) or by initiating concrete social interaction between differing groups. We suspect that this will work fine for uncertainty-oriented people, but that it will not work or may even backfire for certainty-oriented people. From the studies on personal orientations toward uncertainty versus certainty, we may conclude that the most widespread intervention—that is, informing groups more thoroughly about each other and bringing them into personal contact—may facilitate personal change and interpersonal improvement for uncertainty-oriented people. However, this approach should offer a serious challenge to certainty-oriented people. They should have little desire to be forced to face facts and to go through personal experiences that may destabilize their cognitive structures and confront them with the relativity of their value system. Most probably, they will take from such an ambivalent situation just those aspects that help them to maintain or even stabilize their prevailing structures.

In an Israeli study, the Nachloat project (Sharan & Rich, 1984), Middle Eastern children and Western children were brought together in "activity-oriented classrooms" where peer tutoring and mutual help were encouraged. The interventions resulted in better academic achievement than in conventional classrooms; however, there was no "change in sociometric selections of Middle Eastern children by their Western peers in the activity-oriented classrooms" (Sharan & Rich, 1984, p. 195). A study in integration and attitudes in desegregated Israeli classrooms by Ambar (1976), reported in Bizman and Amir (1984), showed that Middle Eastern students changed positively in their evaluation of their Western peers, in their sociometric preferences for them, and in their willingness for joint activities. However, Western students "merely assert[ed] their willingness to participate in joint activities (in other words, they reconcile[d] themselves to the situation of mutual contact)" (Bizman & Amir, 1984, p. 166), but no other changes could be found. If we assume that the Middle Eastern students were more uncertainty-oriented than their Western peers in this sample, the results would agree with our findings about sociometric choices in class-rooms (see above) as well as the hypothetical effects of group-specific expectations related to differing social status (see below).

According to the similarity–attraction link described in Table 18.2, the proportion of similar attitudes shared by people generally elicits a specific degree of attraction (Byrne, 1971; Byrne & Griffith, 1966). Dissimilarity, however, is supposed to lead to rejection (Rosenbaum, 1986). Interventions promoting intergroup relations should therefore try to decrease the degree of perceived dissimilarity between groups. However, the linkages between perceived similarity and attraction seem to be more complex in the real world than in the limited and controlled laboratory environment. Because of the polarizing effects of evaluation (see below), the perception of similarity to members of another group may not make that group's members more attractive; on the contrary, it may make them quite unpleasant. For example, according to Lerner's just-world theory (Lerner, 1980), the more similar an innocent victim is to us, the more we will derogate that person in order to preserve our belief in a just world.

Differences in uncertainty orientation should also moderate the expected similarity–attraction linkage. As a testable hypothesis, we propose that despite a general correlation of similarity and attraction, uncertainty-oriented people are more likely to experience a sort of attraction of opposite poles than certainty-oriented people; this attraction may contribute to increased contacts with differing people, simply because of their differences. On the other hand, if attempts are made to get certainty-oriented persons to perceive the outgroup as "birds of a feather," certainty-oriented people may show reactance (Brehm, 1993) and "flock together" even more with the ingroup, polarizing their perceptions and evaluations even further (see below).

The same problem arises when interventions are based on conclusions from "expectation-states theory" (Berger, Cohen, & Zelditch, 1972; see Table 18.2). According to this theory, influences of cultural or group-specific expectations correlated with social status must be controlled for. Otherwise, interpersonal contacts and interaction will probably reinforce existing prejudices favoring high-status participants and putting down low-status participants, instead of correcting participants' unrealistic expectations about themselves and others (Cohen, 1992). Therefore, biased expectations should be corrected for both high-and low-status groups before they enter social interaction. Reversed expectations should then mediate the reduction of prejudices. However, there are a number of problems with this. We have to find ways to alter both high-status and low-status people's expectations toward others and themselves. Even if we master this task successfully, we doubt that all members of a high-status group interacting with members of a low-status group whose behavior no longer conforms to general expectancies will readily appreciate this new experience and integrate it into more egalitarian points of view. Again, the challenge to reorganize expectation states as a result of controversial experiences should be greater for uncertainty-oriented people than for certainty-oriented people.

Miller and Harrington (1990) then introduce "social identity theory"

(Tajfel, 1978; Tajfel & Turner, 1979, 1986)—or, as they call it, "situational identity theory"—as a more adequate base to explain bias in interpersonal relations and to derive strategies for educational interventions. As can be seen in Table 18.2, this theory is a cognitive–motivational one, in which cognitive processes (i.e., classification of people according to social categories) and motivational processes supporting self-esteem interact (cf. Billig, 1985). The theory's emphasis is predominantly on motivation—on people's need to feel good about themselves. Self-esteem is fueled from two sources: personal identity (including beliefs about individual traits, skills, abilities, etc.) and social identity (derived from belonging to a particular social group). Depending on situational factors, attention and information processing are focused more on personal or more on social determinants of identity. The self-esteem quality or affective valence of personal and social characteristics of identity stems from the evaluations and emotional significance assigned to them. Although seen as stable in many conditions, "self-esteem is a labile state that modulates with situations and during interactions" (Miller & Harrington, 1990, p. 52).

Our impression is that researchers have cared more about situational variations (e.g., conditions threatening self-esteem by unfavorable comparisons with members of other groups) than about interindividual differences. Recommendations for interventions in interpersonal relations thus aim above all at balancing the influence of social categorization and competitive social comparison. In general, Miller and Harrington (1990) suggest:

> To eliminate categorical responding, the basis of the social comparison process for the perceiver needs to shift from social characteristics to personal characteristics. Simultaneously, there needs to be a shift away from the competitive nature of the comparison, in which all characteristics must be better or worse than others . . . and toward the valuing of diversity, differences, and uniqueness. This latter orientation regards differences as [a] valuable resource for whatever task must be confronted, rather than as a potential challenge to one's self-esteem. (p. 56)

The "latter orientation" seems to describe exactly how uncertainty-oriented people regard interpersonal situations, and the problematic orientation that leads (according to this theory) to biased perceptions of others for the sake of one's own self-esteem seems to apply primarily to certainty-oriented people. Intervention strategies founded on this approach therefore promise to reduce uncertainty-oriented people's prejudices, but will probably harden those of certainty-oriented people. Remember that participants in successful interventions were described as experiencing difference as "mutual enrichment," and they were motivated to gain or learn from each other (Axhausen & Feil, 1984).

Interactive relations of persons and situations are of particular interest in the light of other findings contradictory to social identity theory. Hinkle and Brown (1990) summarized three topics in their review: (1) There are persons who do *not* favor their ingroup, but show outgroup favoritism; (2) with multiple dimensions for comparison, there is ingroup favoritism on some dimensions and outgroup favoritism on others (these are average results, of course, and it should be revealing to study for which persons which dimensions contribute to feeling good about themselves); and (3) there is no consistent positive relation between ingroup identification and intergroup differentiation.

Because of these contradictions, Miller and Harrington (1990) prefer the label of "situational identity theory" to "social identity theory." For them, which of the available categories will become salient, and which meaning is attributed to belonging to this category or not belonging to it, depend on the conditions of a specific social situation. If situational conditions accentuate membership in a particular social group, then people tend to react to others in terms of group-relevant categorizations. That is, first, they tend to assimilate perceptions of persons with whom together they feel as "we"; thus, similarity is seen not only with regard to the critical category (e.g., gender), but also with regard to many other personal characteristics. Second, they tend to have contrasting appraisals of outgroup members, who thus are seen in more characteristics than only the critical category as quite different from "us." Third, they tend to have polarizing views, differentiating among members of the ingroup despite their similarity, but perceiving outgroup members as all alike—as typical representatives of their group-defining category.

From Miller and Harrington's (1990) perspective, these mechanisms provide the key for educational interventions. The authors contrast social categorization, and its consequences of undifferentiated and depersonalizing perceptions of outgroup members, with interventions that support decategorization and differentiated perception of the "others." However, decategorization will be insufficient in most situations to transform automatic reactions to members of another category into balanced, differentiated, and finally personalized interactions. Decategorization aims at cognitive change, but motivation for change and the accompanying emotions are not taken into account in this concept.

From a motivational point of view, it is necessary that the members of a "we" group become involved in interactions with "others" as *persons*, as Miller and Harrington (1990) explain:

> When an ingroup member takes an active, personal role in an interaction with an outgroup member, the ingroup member's attention differentiates the self from the ingroup and identification with the ingroup is diminished. This latter effect is as important as the differentiation of the particular outgroup member from other members of the outgroup. Likewise, personalization of the self in the interaction, or self-disclosure, is as important as personalization of the other. These are parallel and reciprocal processes. (p. 56)

Miller and Harrington (1990) suggest a number of appropriate classroom interventions supporting personalized encounters, and they discuss possible problems as well as possible solutions. The importance of personalized contacts and the accentuation of mutual self-disclosure in interventions based on social (or situational) identity theory should warn us not to conceive of this approach as a general recipe for resolving interpersonal and intergroup conflicts. May we assume that personalized contacts will cause similar effects for all people? Will all people, regardless of their cultural background, experience differences of world views and the relativity of their own position as challenges for reflection and topics for constructive debates leading to mutual enrichment? From the point of view of the theory of uncertainty orientation, the answer is no. Once again, we would expect the predicted effects of these interventions for uncertainty-oriented people, but certainty-oriented people would not be expected to profit as much (if at all) from such interventions.

FUTURE DIRECTIONS

Clearly, in a broader sense, the concept of uncertainty is a major force to be reckoned with. Our analysis of the literature suggests, however, that those who wish to improve interpersonal communication and intergroup relations have considered uncertainty primarily from the perspective of uncertainty-oriented persons. This is most unfortunate, because we suspect that once one goes beyond the "halls of ivy" or academic settings, the rest of the population is primarily certainty-oriented (see Sorrentino, Raynor, Zubek, & Short, 1990). Hence, uncertainty-oriented people have been making recommendations for solving problems among people who see the world quite differently.

Our concept of uncertainty orientation can also be seen as part of two of the major dimensions Hofstede (1991) uses to distinguish one culture from another: (1) avoidance of uncertainty, and (2) individualism (vs. collectivism). High avoidance of uncertainty and collectivism are associated with certainty-oriented persons, and low avoidance of uncertainty and individualism (i.e., self-orientation) are features of uncertainty-oriented persons (see Sorrentino & Roney, 1990). Finally, it is important to note that we have obtained the within-culture differences we expect. Sorrentino et al. (1990) found that university populations were indeed higher in uncertainty orientation than lay populations (e.g., factory workers), and these findings have been replicated by Sorrentino et al. (1995).

Answers to the question of how to cope with the uncertainty bias in interpersonal and intergroup relations are most important in educational settings. As we have shown, there are many suggestions on how to improve communicative skills or promote better intergroup relations. As a result of our analysis, however, we have concluded that uncertainty-oriented participants will benefit more from such strategies than certainty-oriented participants will. This problem is even worse in cases where the recipients of an educational endeavor are educators themselves, who are expected to expand their own interpersonal competencies in order to help their students to do so later.

Kempas (1994) found that certainty-oriented docents (teachers of adult education courses) arranged significantly less stimulating, open learning situations, and that they tried more to limit degrees of freedom for their leaders and stay in control, than did uncertainty-oriented docents. In order to change this situation, Kempas (1994) tried to develop training procedures offering differen-

TABLE 18.3   Characteristics of Educational Settings for Uncertainty-Oriented and for Certainty-Oriented Persons

Training situation for uncertainty-oriented participants	*Training situation for certainty–oriented participants*
Opportunities to find out autonomously about the topic	Orientation by well-structured information
Opportunities to discuss the topic and reflect on its personal relevance	Maintenance of clarity about the topic through well-structured learning assignments
Opportunities for exchange with and feedback from other participants	Avoidance of controversies and contradictory opinions
Opportunities for experiments and firsthand experiences	Introduction of routines based on clear principles or rules
High degree of social interaction among participants	Reduction of threats to the participants' self-esteem by careful dosage of possible criticism

Note. Adapted from Kempas (1994). Copyright 1994 by G. Kempas. Adapted by permission of the author.

tiated challenges for uncertainty-oriented and certainty-oriented docents. Her goal was to meet the first subgroup of participants' preferences for flexible, open learning situations, while not frightening the members of the second subgroup. The key method was to modify traditional approaches—for instance, methods for team learning—in such a way that a variety of more or less structured learning situations could be offered, among which the participants could choose. Gradually, certainty-oriented participants were encouraged and guided to expose themselves to more open learning situations in the course, and these docents were encouraged to apply less structured methods in their own teaching assignments. The most important principles of this approach are summarized in Table 18.3.

These principles were also realized in a training course for leaders of communication training, by offering the same task with varied degrees of freedom for the participants (Kempas, 1994). By solving this task, they could learn about interview techniques. Maximal structure was provided in an arrangement where the participants could analyze a videotaped interview assisted by a set of categories. In a minimally structured situation, the participants could role-play a roughly outlined interview situation, discuss their roles and their experiences with them, and develop general interview guidelines, which were afterwards compared with the categories given to the high-structure group.

The rationale of this approach corresponds with the principles of the aptitude–treatment–interaction approach, which has been suggested repeatedly to resolve the problems of teaching methods tuned to the needs of an abstract "average" learner only (Corno & Snow, 1986; Cronbach & Snow, 1977; Peterson, 1988). There is ample evidence for strong relations between aptitude and achievement in relation to various educational treatments. We may expect comparable interactions between learners' uncertainty or certainty orientation and learning effects of educational treatments designed to promote interpersonal communication and intercultural relations. However, there is a danger of serious misunderstanding of the principles of aptitude-treatment-interaction when they are applied to concrete classroom practices. On the classroom level, the possibilities of differential treatment may be filtered by the teachers' "bounded rationality" (Lee & Porter, 1990). In Kempas's research, boundaries could be seen in some docents' certainty orientation.

Thus adapting instruction to student characteristics may lead to restricting instead of promoting their development—even if restriction is not intended at all. The criterion of individual orientation toward uncertainty versus certainty may be conceived of by some teachers as representing a stable trait of students. Consequently, curricular accommodation to student diversity may result in offering different educational goals for differing students; this will set into action a dynamic of cumulating divergency. However, if we want to improve interpersonal relations, we want to promote the same instructional goals for all students. If some students' orientations seem to be barriers to their approaching the common goals, these differences should be seen as a challenge for educational reactions. Concrete, step-by-step instructional conditions should be provided that are appropriate to help certainty-oriented learners become more open to varying, finally even controversial points of views in social interactions. There are many opportunities in this strategy for adapting the curriculum to interindividual differences, as well as for adapting the students to curricular demands.

The strategy of adapting interpersonal situations to personal characteristics of learners proved to be successful in the cases cited above, in which the goal was to promote interpersonal skills. The problems are much more complex, as we have already seen, if we want to arrange group situations in order to promote intergroup relations. Clearly, the classrooms of the future will be ethnically mixed, and we must increase the mutual acceptance of students of different ethnic backgrounds. The major principles suggested from the point of view of social psychology, however, appear to apply only to students who are uncertainty-oriented. Reducing the salience of social categories in group processes, reducing threats to identity, and providing opportunities for increasing interpersonal skills and for personalized interaction—all of which are suggested by Miller and Harrington (1993)—will not work for certainty-oriented persons. Similarly, from the point of view of intercultural pedagogy, Pagé (1992) has discussed the principles of pointing to overlapping category memberships, thematizing shared membership in a superordinate category, facilitating personalized encounters, and promoting intergroup cooperation as means of promoting intergroup relations. These also do not appear to be promising means for certainty-oriented persons.

So what do we do with certainty-oriented people? Although we feel that laboratory research must precede any recommendations we could make at this point, we are encouraged by some of the implications from our earlier research.

For example, we know that certainty-oriented persons do rely on heuristics when important (and even life-threatening) information is presented to them (Brouwers & Sorrentino, 1993; Sorrentino et al., 1988). So perhaps we should spend more time presenting them with such heuristics, such as leaders they respect, attractive role models, and people they deem experts, to endorse positive intergroup relations. We also know that they will in fact systematically process information when it is *not* important to them personally. So perhaps we can present them with positive information about outgroups in contexts that are not personally relevant. Our guess is that if certainty-oriented students were asked to read about why intergroup relations should be positive, they would analyze the arguments much more carefully if they anticipated no interaction with the other group than if they did. Finally, there is the possibility of returning to noncognitive, non-self-oriented means of changing behavior—yes, behavior modification. Rewarding positive interaction, rather than espousing self-enrichment, might go much further in establishing positive interactions for these students. But, again, this is *only* speculation at this point.

CONCLUSIONS

In this chapter, we have tried to elaborate on how the topics of interpersonal communication and intergroup relations are approached predominantly from an uncertainty-oriented point of view. Hence, suggestions for intervening in interpersonal relations are usually focused on uncertainty-oriented persons' preferences and habits in social situations. We have briefly described the dimension of uncertainty versus certainty orientation and have discussed the consequences of individuals' differing locations on this dimension for varying ways of coping with uncertain situations. This has shed new light on the criticized uncertainty bias in the fields of interpersonal communication and of intercultural relations, and on recommendations for educational interventions in these fields. Recent research has shown that the approach of adapting learning situations to learners' personal characteristics can be effective in the case where uncertainty versus certainty orientation is the critical characteristics. However, the strategy of minimizing the situational uncertainty load for certainty-oriented learners has been applied until now only to group situations arranged to promote interpersonal skills. The available recommendations for promoting better intergroup relations, when groups experience problems because of differing race, ethnical background, gender, religious orientation, and so forth, are of course all based on creating intergroup contacts. However, the measures suggested for dealing with ingroup preference and outgroup rejection seem to be designed only for uncertainty-oriented group members. Unfortunately, there are no empirical data as to differential effects of these interventions on uncertainty-oriented and certainty-oriented members of suboptimally interacting groups. Studies in this field are urgently needed to clarify the uncertainty bias of recommendations for promoting intergroup relations, and above all to develop nonbiased approaches to intercultural education.

Uncertainty has indeed colored the 20th century. Given the economic, social, and political turbulence evident at present, we suspect that concerns with uncertainty will continue to increase well into the 21st century. We hope that more people will realize that whereas uncertainty may be a charismatic concept for some, it is a terribly frightening concept for others. This must be taken into account if social psychologists and other helping professionals are to promote and produce harmony in interpersonal and intergroup relations.

Acknowledgments

Our thanks to Susan Beaufort, Julie Carswell, Victoria Esses, Tory Higgins, Gordon Hodson, James Olson, Kimberly Quinn, Robert Renaud, Angela Rosati, and Marie Walker for their helpful comments regarding this chapter. The research reported here was done with support from the Social Sciences and Humanities Research Council of Canada, and from the North Atlantic Treaty Organization: Scientific Affairs Division.

Notes

1. See Volumes 1 and 2 of this *Handbook* for detailed descriptions of the theory of uncertainty orientation and earlier findings (i.e., Sorrentino & Short, 1986; Sorrentino, Raynor, Zubek, & Short, 1990).

2. Tory Higgins points out that these criticisms are true mainly for "information transmission" and "social relationship" models of communication. They do not apply to models such as the "communication game" (Higgins, 1981), in which other goals, especially interpersonal goals, are emphasized. Although this may be true, we do feel that models such as the communication game and related notions of shared reality found in the present volume of this *Handbook* (see Hardin & Higgins, Chapter 2) are also amenable to examination in light of individual differences in uncertainty orientation.

3. As empirical findings (e.g., Worthy, Gary, & Kahn, 1969; Sermat & Smyth, 1973) have shown, communication tends to follow a reciprocity norm; partners try to adapt to each other's variations in speaking (e.g., reciprocation of amount and intimacy of information exchanged). As uncertainty is reduced by ongoing communication, the need for symmetric exchanges is also reduced. Now talking and listening may be distributed unevenly, without causing experiences of dominance and submission, which can threaten further interactions.

References

Allport, G. W. (1954). *The nature of prejudice*. Reading, MA: Addison-Wesley.

Altman, I., & Taylor, D. A. (1973). *Social penetration: The development of interpersonal relationships*. New York: Holt, Rinehart & Winston.

Ambar, B. (1976). *The influence of integration in junior high school on changes of parents and children*. Unpublished master's thesis, Bar-Ilan University, Ramat Gan, Israel.

Atkinson, J. W. (1964). *An introduction to motivation.* Princeton, NJ: Van Nostrand.

Atkinson, J. W., & Raynor, J. O. (Eds.). (1974). *Motivation and achievement.* New York: Holt, Rinehart & Winston.

Aronson, E. (1978). *The jigsaw classroom.* Beverly Hills, CA: Sage.

Axhausen, S., & Feil, C. (1984). *Zum Abbau von Vorurteilen bei Kindern und Jugendlichen: Praktische Erfahrungen, theoretische Erklärungsansätze und pädagogische Modellvorstellungen* [*About the reduction of prejudices in children and youth: Practical experiences, approaches to theoretical explanations, and suggestions of pedagogical models*]. München: Deutsches Jugendinstitut.

Batelaan, P., & Gundara, J. S. (1993). Cultural diversity and the promotion of values through education. *European Journal of Intercultural Studies, 3*(2-3), 61-80.

Berger, C. R. (1979). Beyond initial interactions. In H. Giles & R. S. Clair (Eds.), *Language and social psychology* (pp. 122-144). Oxford: Blackwell.

Berger, C. R., & Bradac, J. J. (1982). *Language and social knowledge: Uncertainty in interpersonal relations.* London: Arnold.

Berger, C. R., & Calabrese, R. (1975). Some explorations in initial interactions and beyond: Toward a developmental theory of interpersonal communication. *Human Communication Research, 1,* 99-112.

Berger, C. R., & Kellerman, K. A. (1983). To ask or not to ask: Is that a question? In R. Bostrom (Ed.), *Communication yearbook* (Vol. 7, pp. 342-368). Beverly Hills, CA: Sage.

Berger, J., Cohen, B. P., & Zelditch, M., Jr. (1972). Status characteristics and social interaction. *American Sociological Review, 37,* 241-255.

Billig, M. (1985). Prejudice, categorization, and particularization: From a perceptual to a rhetorical approach. *European Journal of Social Psychology, 15,* 79-103.

Bizman, A., & Amir, Y. (1984). Integration and attitudes. In Y. Amir, S. Sharan, & R. Ben-Ari (Eds.), *School desegregation: Cross-cultural perspectives* (pp. 155-188). Hillsdale: Erlbaum.

Brehm, J. W. (1993). Control, its loss, and psychological reactance. In G. Weary, F. Gleicher, & K. L. Marsh (Eds.), *Control motivation and social cognition* (pp. 3-30). New York: Springer-Verlag.

Brouwers, M. C., & Sorrentino, R. M. (1993). Uncertainty orientation and protection motivation theory: The role of individual differences in health compliance. *Journal of Personality and Social Psychology, 65,* 102-112.

Byrne, D. (1971). *The attraction paradigm.* New York: Academic Press.

Byrne, D., & Griffith, D. (1966). A development investigation of the law of attraction. *Journal of Personality and Social Psychology, 4,* 699-702.

Campani, G., & Gundara, J. S. (1994). Overview of intercultural policies within the European Union. *European Journal of Intercultural Studies, 5*(1), 3-8.

Campbell, D. T. (1965). Ethnocentric and other altruistic motives. In D. Levine (Ed.), *Nebraska Symposium on Motivation* (Vol. 13, pp. 281-310). Lincoln: University of Nebraska Press.

Caplan, G. (1964). *Principles of preventive psychiatry.* New York: Basic Books.

Chaiken, S. (1980). Heuristic versus systematic information processing and the use of source versus message cues in persuasion. *Journal of Personality and Social Psychology, 39,* 752-756.

Cohen, E. G. (1992). *Designing groupwork: Strategies for heterogenous classrooms* (2nd ed.). New York: Teachers College Press.

Condor, S., & Brown, R. (1988). Psychological processes in intergroup conflict. In W. Stroebe, A. W. Kruglanski, D. Bar-Tal, & M. Hewstone (Eds.), *The social psychology of intergroup conflict* (pp. 3-26). Berlin: Springer-Verlag.

Corno, R., & Snow, R. E. (1986). Adapting teaching to individual differences among learners. In M. C. Wittrock (Ed.), *Handbook of research on teaching* (3rd ed., pp. 605-629). New York: Macmillan.

Coulby, D. (1993). Cultural and epistemological relativism and European curricula. *European Journal of Intercultural Studies, 3*(2-3), 7-18.

Cronbach, L. J., & Snow, R. E. (1977). *Aptitudes and instructional methods: A handbook for research on interactions.* New York: Irvington.

Driscoll, D. M., Hamilton, D. L., & Sorrentino, R. M. (1991). Uncertainty orientation and recall of person-descriptive information. *Journal of Personality and Social Psychology, 17,* 494–500.

Dyer, M. G. (1983). The role of affect in narratives. *Cognitive Science, 7,* 211–242.

Fiddle, S. (Ed.). (1980). *Uncertainty: Behavioral and social dimensions.* New York: Praeger.

Gundara, J. S. (1993). Leitlinien for interkulturelles kooperatives Lernen [Guidelines for intercultural cooperative learning]. In G. L. Huber (Ed.), *Neue Perspektiven der Kooperation* [*New perspectives of cooperation*] (pp. 33–37). Baltmannsweiler, Germany: Schneider-Verlag Hohengehren.

Hastie, R. (1980). Memory for behavioral information that confirms or contradicts a personality impression. In R. Hastie, T. M. Ostrom, E. B. Ebbesen, R. S. Wyer, D. L. Hamilton, & D. E. Carlston (Eds.), *Person memory: The cognitive basis of social perception* (pp. 155–177). Hillsdale, NJ: Erlbaum.

Higgins, E. T. (1981). The "communication game": Implications for social cognition and persuasion. In E. T. Higgins, C. P. Herman, & M. P. Zanna (Eds.), Social cognition: The Ontario Symposium (pp. 343–392). Hillsdale, NJ: Erlbaum.

Hinkle, S., & Brown, R. (1990). Intergroup comparison and social identity: Some links and lacunae. In D. Abrams & M. A. Hogg (Eds.), *Social identity theory: Constructive and critical advances* (pp. 48–70). New York: Harvester/Wheatsheaf.

Hofstede, G. (1991). Empirical models of cultural differences. In N. Bleichrodt & P. J. D. Drenth (Eds.), *Contemporary issues in cross-cultural psychology* (pp. 4–20). Amsterdam: Swets & Zeitlinger.

Huber, G. L., & Roth, J. W. H. (1994). *Pädagogische Ansätze zur Prävention von Konflikten zwischen Gruppen* [*Pedagogical approaches to prevention of intergroup conflicts*] (Arbeitsbericht Nr. 33). Tübingen, Germany: Abteilung Pädagogische Psychologie des Instituts für Erziehungswissenschaft I der Universität Tübingen.

Huber, G. L., & Scholz, G. (1995). *Entscheidungsprozesse von Schülern in Lernsituationen* [*Students' processes of decision making in learning situations*] (Report in preparation on the project Hu 348/8-1 & Scho484-1/1 to the Deutsche Forschungssgemeinschaft). Tübingen, Germany: Abteilung Pädagogische Psychologie am Institut für Erziehungswissenschaft I der Universität Tübingen.

Huber, G. L., Sorrentino, R. M., Davidson, M. A., Eppler, R., & Roth, J. W. H. (1992). Uncertainty orientation and cooperative learning: Individual differences within and across cultures. *Learning and Individual Differences, 4,* 1–24.

Johnson, M. K., & Sherman, S. J. (1990). Constructing and reconstructing the past and the future in the present. In E. T. Higgins & R. M. Sorrentino (Eds.), *Handbook of motivation and social cognition: Foundations of social behavior* (Vol. 2, pp. 482–526). New York: Guilford Press.

Kempas, G. (1994). *Lehren lernen: Auswirkungen interpersoneller Differenzen auf die Lernprozesse Lehrender* [*Learning to teach: Effects of interpersonal differences on learning processes of teachers*]. Unpublished doctoral dissertation, Fakultät für Sozial- und Verhaltenswissenschaften der Universität Tübingen.

Kounin, J. S. (1970). *Discipline and group management in classrooms.* New York: Holt, Rinehart & Winston.

Lachman, R., Lachman, J. L., & Butterfield, E. C. (1979). *Cognitive psychology and information processing.* Hillsdale, NJ: Erlbaum.

Lee, O., & Porter, A. C. (1990). Bounded rationality in classroom teaching. *Educational Psychologist, 25,* 159–171.

Lerner, M. J. (1980). *The belief in a just world: A fundamental delusion.* New York: Plenum Press.

Miller, N., & Harrington, H. J. (1990). A situational identity perspective on cultural diversity and teamwork in the classroom. In S. Sharan (Ed.), *Cooperative learning: Theory and research* (pp. 39–75). New York: Praeger.

Miller, N., & Harrington, H. J. (1993). Social categorization and intergroup acceptance: Principles for the design and development of cooperative learning teams. In R. Hertz-Lazarowitz & N. Miller (Eds.), *Interaction in cooperative groups: The theoretical anatomy of group learning* (pp. 203–227). New York: Cambridge University Press.

Mishler, E. G. (1975). Studies in dialogue and discourse: II. Types of discourse initiated and sustained through questioning. *Journal of Psycholinguistic Research, 4*, 99–121.

Müller, R. (1980). *Diagnostisches Soziogramm* [*Diagnostic sociogram*]. Braunschweig, Germany: Westermann.

Pagé, M. (1992). Kooperatives Lernen und sozialer Pluralismus [Cooperative learning and social pluralism]. In G. L. Huber (Ed.), *Neue Perspektiven der Kooperation* [*New perspectives of cooperation*] (pp. 11–21). Baltmannsweiler, Germany: Schneider-Verlag Hohengehren.

Perotti, A. (1994). The impact of the Council of Europe's recommendations on intercultural education in European school systems. *European Journal of Intercultural Studies, 5*(1), 9–17.

Peterson, P. L. (1988). Selecting students and services for compensatory education: Lessons from aptitude–treatment interaction research. *Educational Psychologist, 23*, 313–352.

Pettigrew, T. F. (1986). The intergroup contact hypothesis reconsidered. In M. Hewstone & R. Brown (Eds.), *Contact and conflict in intergroup encounters* (pp. 169–195). Oxford: Blackwell.

Petty, R. E., & Cacioppo, J. T. (1981). *Attitudes and persuasion: Classic and contemporary approaches*. Dubuque, IA: W. C. Brown.

Planalp, S., & Honeycutt, J. M. (1985). Events that increase uncertainty in personal relationships. *Human Communication Research, 11*, 593–604.

Reich, H. H. (1994). Intercultural education in Germany. *European Journal of Intercultural Studies, 4*(3), 14–24.

Robinson, E. (1993, July 7). Flood of migrants may be "crisis of the age." *International Herald Tribune* (Frankfurt), pp. 1–2.

Rogers, M., Miller, N., & Hennigan, K. (1981). Cooperative games as an intervention to promote cross-racial acceptance. *American Educational Research Journal, 18*, 513–518.

Roney, C. J. R., & Sorrentino, R. M. (1987). Uncertainty orientation and person perception: Individual differences in categorization. *Social Cognition, 5*, 369–382.

Rosenbaum, M. E. (1986). The repulsion hypothesis: On the non-development of relationships. *Journal of Personality and Social Psychology, 51*, 1156–1166.

Ross, M., & Conway, M. (1986). Remembering one's own past: The construction of personal histories. In R. M. Sorrentino & E. T. Higgins (Eds.), *Handbook of motivation and cognition: Foundations of social behavior* (Vol. 1, pp. 122–144). New York: Guilford Press.

Sermat, V., & Smyth, M. (1973). Content analysis of verbal communication in the development of a relationship: Conditions influencing self-disclosure. *Journal of Personality and Social Psychology, 26*, 332–346.

Shannon, C. E., & Weaver, W. (1949). *The mathematical theory of communication*. Urbana: University of Illinois Press.

Sharan, S., & Rich, Y. (1984). Field experiments on ethnic integration in Israeli schools. In Y. Amir & S. Sharan (Eds.), *School desegregation: Cross-cultural perspectives* (pp. 189–217). Hillsdale, NJ: Erlbaum.

Sorrentino, R. M., Bobocel, D. R., Gitta, M. Z., Olson, J. M., & Hewitt, E. C. (1988). Uncertainty orientation and persuasion: Individual differences in the effects of personal relevance on social judgements. *Journal of Personality and Social Psychology, 55*, 357–371.

Sorrentino, R. M., & Hewitt, E. C. (1984). The uncertainty-reducing properties of achievement tasks revisited. *Journal of Personality and Social Psychology, 47*, 884–899.

Sorrentino, R. M., Hewitt, E. C., & Raso, P. A. (1992). Risk-taking in games of chance and skill: Informational and affective influences on choice behavior. *Journal of Personality and Social Psychology, 62*, 522–533.

Sorrentino, R. M., Holmes, J. G., Hanna, S. E., & Sharp, A. (1995). Uncertainty orientation and trust: Individual differences in close relationships. *Journal of Personality and Social Psychology, 68*(2), 314–327.

Sorrentino, R. M., Raynor, J. O., Zubek, J. M., & Short, J. C. (1990). Personality functioning and change: Informational and affective influences on cognitive, moral, and social development. In E. T. Higgins & R. M. Sorrentino (Eds.), *Handbook of motivation and cognition: Foundations of social behavior* (Vol. 2, pp. 193–228). New York: Guilford Press.

Sorrentino, R. M., & Roney, C. J. R. (1990). Uncertainty orientation: Individual differences in the self-inference process. In J. M. Olson & M. P. Zanna (Eds.), *The Ontario Symposium: Vol. 6. Self-influence processes* (pp. 239–257). Hillsdale, NJ: Erlbaum.

Sorrentino, R. M., Roney, C. J. R., & Hanna, S. E. (1992). Uncertainty orientation. In C. P. Smith (Ed.), *Motivation and personality: Handbook of thematic analysis* (pp. 428–439). Cambridge, England: Cambridge University Press.

Sorrentino, R. M., & Short, J. C. (1986). Uncertainty orientation, motivation, and cognition. In R. M. Sorrentino & E. T. Higgins (Eds.), *Handbook of motivation and cognition: Foundations of social behavior* (Vol. 1, pp. 379–403). New York: Guilford Press.

Srull, T. K., Lichtenstein, M., & Rothbart, M. (1985). Associative storage and retrieval processes in person memory. *Journal of Experimental Psychology: Learning, Memory, and Cognition, 11*, 316–345.

Stephan, W. G. (1987). The contact hypothesis in intergroup relations. In C. Hendrick (Ed.), *Review of personality and social psychology* (Vol. 9, pp. 13–40). Newbury Park, CA: Sage.

Stephan, W. G., & Stephan, C. W. (1984). The role of ignorance in intergroup relations. In N. Miller & M. B. Brewer (Eds.), *Groups in contact: The psychology of desegregation* (pp. 229–257). New York: Academic Press.

Tajfel, H. (1978). The psychological structure of intergroup relations. In H. Tajfel (Ed.), *Differentiation between social groups: Studies in the social psychology of intergroup relations* (pp. 65–93). London: Academic Press.

Tajfel, H., & Turner, J. C. (1979). An integrative theory of social conflict. In W. G. Austin & S. Worchel (Eds.), *The social psychology of intergroup relations* (pp. 33–47). Monterey, CA: Brooks/Cole.

Tajfel, H., & Turner, J. C. (1986). An integrative theory of intergroup relations. In S. Worchel & W. G. Austin (Eds.), *Psychology of intergroup relations* (2nd ed., pp. 7–24). Chicago: Nelson-Hall.

Wittek, F., Nijdam, M., & Kroeger, P. (1993). Cultural and linguistic diversity in the education systems of the European Community. *European Journal of Intercultural Studies, 4*(2), 7–18.

Worthy, M., Gary, A. L., & Kahn, G. M. (1969). Self-disclosure as an exchange process. *Journal of Personality and Social Psychology, 13*, 59–64.

Author Index

Subject Index